Paul's Letters to His Kinsfolk

PAUL'S LETTERS

TO

HIS KINSFOLK.

HOUGOUMONT.

ROBERT CADELL, EDINBURGH.

MDCCCXLI.

CONTENTS.

Paul's Letters

to

His Kinsfolk.

ADVERTISEMENT. [1834.]

This Part contains "Paul's Letters to His Kinsfolk," written mostly during Sir Walter Scott's tour on the Continent in the summer of 1815,—and being indeed, to a considerable extent, the substance of his private letters to his own family.

LETTER I.

PAUL TO HIS SISTER MARGARET.

Introductory—Sea-Sickness—The Flemings—Houses—Women—Dress—Cottages.

It is three long weeks since I left the old mansion-house, which, for years before, has not found me absent for three days, and yet no letter has assured its quiet inmates and neighbours whether my curiosity has met its punishment. Methinks I see the evening circle assembled, and anxiously expressing their doubts and fears on account of the adventurous traveller. The Major will talk of the dangers of outposts and free corps, and lament that I could not have marched under the escort of his old messmates of the * * * * regiment. The Laird will speak scholarly and wisely of the dangers of highway robbery and overturns, in a country where there are neither justices of peace nor turnpikes. The Minister, again, will set up his old bugbears of the Inquisition, and of the Lady who sitteth upon the Seven Hills. Peter, the politician, will have his anxious thoughts on the state of the public spirit in France,—the prevalence of Jacobinical opinions,—the reign of mobs, and of domiciliary visits,—the horrors of the lantern, and of the guillotine. And thou, my dear sister, whose life has been one unwearied course of affectionate interest in the health and happiness of a cross old bachelor brother, what woful anticipations must thy imagination have added to this accumulation of dangers! Broken sleep, bad diet, hard lodging, and damp sheets, have, in your apprehension, already laid me up a patient in the cabaret of some miserable French village, which neither affords James's Powders, nor Daffy's Elixir, nor any of those infallible nostrums which your charity distributes among our village patients, undiscouraged by the obstinacy of those who occasionally die, in despite both of the medicine and physician. It well becomes the object of so much and such varied solicitude, to remove it as speedily as the posts of this distracted country will permit. I anticipate the joy in every countenance when my packet arrives; the pleasure with which each will seize the epistle addressed to himself, and the delight of old James, when, returned from the post-office at * * *, he delivers with an air of triumph the long-expected despatches; and then, smoothing his grey hairs with one hand, and holding with the other, the handle of the door, lingers in the parlour, till he, too, has the reward of his diligence, in learning his master's welfare.

Till these news arrive, I cannot flatter myself that things will go perfectly right at the old chateau; or rather my vanity suggests, that the absence of so principal a person among its inmates and intimates, has been a chilling damp upon the harmless pleasures and pursuits of those who have remained behind. I shall be somewhat disappointed, if the Major has displayed alacrity in putting his double-barrel in order for the moors; or if the Laird has shown his usual solicitude for a seasonable sprinkling of rain to refresh the turnip-field. Peter's speculations on politics, and his walks to the bowling-green, have been darkened, doubtless, and saddened, by the uncertainty of my fate; and I even suspect the Parson has spared his flock one *Seventhly* of his text in his anxiety upon my account.

For you, my dear Margaret, can I doubt the interest you have given me in your affections, from the earliest period of recollection, when we pulled *gowans* together upon the green, until the moment when my travelling-trunk, packed by your indefatigable exertions, stood ready to be locked, but, ere the key could be turned, reversing the frolics of the enchanted chest of the Merchant Abudah, sprung once more open, as if in derision of your labours? To you, therefore, in all justice, belong the first fruits of my correspondence; and while I dwell upon topics personal to myself, and therefore most interesting to you, do not let our kind friends believe that I have forgotten my promise, to send each of them, from foreign parts, that species of information with which each is most gratified. No! the Major shall hear of more and bloodier battles than ever were detailed to Young Norval by his tutor the Hermit. The Laird shall know all I can tell him on the general state of the country. Peter shall be refreshed with politics, and the Minister with polemics; that is, if I can find any thing of the latter description worth sending; for if ever there existed a country without a sense of religion of any kind, it is that of France. The churches indeed remain, but the worship to which they are dedicated has as little effect upon the minds of the people, as that of the heathen Pantheon on the inhabitants of modern Rome. I must take Ovid's maxim, " *Tamen exoute nullum;* " and endeavour to describe the effects which the absence of this salutary restraint upon our corrupt and selfish passions, of this light, which extends our views beyond the bounds of a transitory world, has produced upon this unhappy country. More of this, however, hereafter. My first letter is addressed to you, my dear sister, and must therefore be personal.

Even your partiality would be little interested in my journey through England, or the circumstances attending my embarkation. And of my passage, it is enough to say, that sea-sick I was even unto the uttermost. All your fifteen infallible recipes proved unavailing. I could not brook the sight of lavender-drops; gingerbread nuts were detestable to my eyes, and are so to my recollection even at this moment. I could as soon have swallowed the horns of the Arch-fiend himself as the dose of hartshorn; and for the great goblet of sea-water, " too much of water had I, poor Ophelia." In short, he that would see as much misery, and as much selfishness, as can well be concentrated, without any permanent evil being either done or suffered, I invite him to hire a berth aboard a packet. Delicacy is lost; sympathy is no more; the bands of love and friendship are broken; one class of passengers eat and drink joyously, though intermingled with another who are expressing their inward grievances in a manner, which, in any other situation, seldom fails to excite irresistible sympathy. The captain and the mate, comforters by profession, indeed exhort you from time to time, to be of good cheer, and recommend a glass of grog, or possibly a pipe of tobacco, or it may be a morsel of fat bacon, to allay the internal commotion; but it is unnecessary to say how ill the remedies apply to the disorder. In short, if you are sick, sick you must be; and can have little better comfort than in reflecting that the evil must be of short duration, though, were you to judge from your immediate feelings, you might conceive your life was likely to end first. As I neither met with a storm nor sea-fight, I do not know what effect they might produce upon a sea-sick patient; but such is the complete annihilation of energy; such the headache, the nausea, and depression of spirits, that I think any stimulus, short of the risk of being shot or drowned, would fail of rousing him to any exertion. The best is, that arrival on the land proves a certain remedy for the sorrows of the sea; and I do not think that even your *materia medica* could supply any other.

Suppose your brother, then, landed among the mynheers and yafrows of Holland and Belgium, as it is now the fashion to call what, before our portentous times, was usually named Flanders. Strange sights meet his eyes; strange voices sound in his ears; and yet, by a number of whimsical associations, he is eternally brought back to the land of his nativity. The Flemings, in particular, resemble the Scotch in the cast of their features, the sound of their language, and, apparently, in their habits of living, and of patient industry. They are, to be sure, a century at least behind in *costume* and manners; but the old chateau, consisting of two or three narrow houses, joined together by the gables, with a slender round turret ascending in the centre of the building, for the purpose of containing the staircase, is completely in the old style of Scottish dwelling-houses. Then the avenue, and the acre or two of ground, planted with fruit-trees in straight lines; the garden, with high hedges, clipped by the gardener's art into verdant walls; the intermixture of statues and vases; the fountains and artificial pieces of water, may still be seen in some of our ancient mansions; and, to my indifferent taste, are no unnatural decorations in the immediate vicinity of a dwelling-place, and infinitely superior to the meagreness of bare turf and gravel. At least they seem peculiarly appropriate to so flat a country as Belgium, which, boasting no objects of natural beauty or grandeur, and being deprived, in a great measure, even of the grace of living streams of water, must necessarily supply these deficiencies by the exertions of art. Nor does their taste appear to have changed since the days of William III. There seem to be few new houses built; and the old chateaux, and grounds around them, are maintained in the original style in which they were constructed. Indeed, an appearance of antiquity is one of the most distinguishing features which strike the traveller in the Low Countries. Dates, as far back as the fifteenth, and even fourteenth centuries, are inscribed upon the front of many of the houses, both in the country and in the towns and villages. And although I offended your national pride, my dear sister, when I happened to observe, that the Scotch, who are supposed to boast more than other nations of their ancient descent, in reality know less of their early history than any other people in Europe, yet, I think, you will allow, that our borough towns afford few visible monuments of the high claims we set up to early civilisation.

Our neighbours, the English, are not much more fortunate in this respect, unless we take into the account the fortresses built for the purpose of defence on the frontiers of Wales and Scotland, or their ancient and beautiful churches. But we look in vain for antiquity in the houses of the middling ranks; for the mansions of the country gentlemen, and the opulent burghers of the fifteenth and sixteenth centuries, have, generally speaking, long since given place to the architecture of the earlier part of the last age, or the more fantastic structures of our own day. It is in the streets of Antwerp and Brussels, that the eye still rests upon the forms of architecture which appear in the pictures of the Flemish school; those fronts, richly decorated with various ornaments, and terminating in roofs, the slope of which is concealed from the eye by windows and gables still more highly ornamented; the whole comprising a general effect, which, from its grandeur and intricacy, amuses at once, and delights the spectator. In fact, this rich intermixture of towers, and battlements, and projecting windows, highly sculptured, joined to the height of the houses, and the variety of ornament upon their fronts, produces an effect as superior to those of the tame uniformity of a modern street, as the casque of the warrior exhibits over the slouched broad-brimmed beaver of a Quaker. I insist the more on this, for the benefit of the fireside at * * * *, who are accustomed to take their ideas of a fine street from Portland Place, or from the George Street of Edinburgh, where a long and uniform breadth of causeway extends between two rows of ordinary houses of three stories, whose appearance is rendered mean, by the disproportioned space which divides them, and tame, from their unadorned uniformity.

If you talk, indeed, of comforts, I have no doubt that the internal arrangement of the last-named ranges of dwellings is infinitely superior to those of the ancient Flemings, where the windows are frequently high, narrow, and dark; where the rooms open into each other in such a manner as seems to render privacy impossible; where you sometimes pass into magnificent saloons, through the meanest and darkest of all possible entrances; and where a splendid corridor conducts you, upon other occasions, to a room scarce worthy of being occupied as a pig-sty,—by such pigs at least, whose limbs are bred in England. It is for the exterior alone that I claim the praise of dignity and romantic character; and I cannot but think, that, without in the least neglecting the interior division necessary for domestic comfort, some of these beauties might, with great advantage, be adopted from the earlier school of architecture. That of the present day seems to me too much to resemble the pinched and pared foot of the ambitious Princess, who submitted to such severe discipline, in order to force her toes into the memorable glass slipper.

These marks of ancient wealth, and burgher-like opulence, do indeed greatly excel what could be expected from the architecture of Scotland at the same period. But yet, to return to the point from which I set out, there is something in the height of the houses, and the mode of turning their gables toward the street, which involuntarily reminds me of what the principal street of our northern capital was when I first recollect it.

If you enter one of these mansions, the likeness is far from disappearing. The owner, if a man of family, will meet you with his scraggy neck rising in shrivelled longitude out of the folds of a thinly-plaited stock. The cut of his coat, of his waistcoat, his well-preserved cocked-hat, his periwig, and camblet riding-coat, his mode of salutation, the kiss bestowed on each side of the face, all remind you of the dress and manners of the old Scotch laird. The women are not, I think, so handsome as my fair countrywomen, or my walks and visits were

unfortunate in the specimens they presented of female beauty; but, then, you have the old dress, with the screen, or mantle, hanging over the head, and falling down upon each shoulder, which was formerly peculiar to Scotland. The colour of this mantle is indeed different—in Scotland it was usually tartan, and in Flanders it is uniformly black. The inhabitants say they derive the use of it from the Spaniards, of whose dominions their country was so long a principal part. The dress and features of the lower class bear also a close resemblance to those of Scotland, and favour the idea held by most antiquaries, that the Lowlanders, at least, are a kindred tribe. The constant intercourse our ancestors maintained with Flanders, from which, according to contemporary accounts, they derived almost every article which required the least skill in manufacture, must have added greatly to those points of original similarity.

The Flemings are said to be inferior to their neighbours of Holland in the article of scrupulous attention to cleanliness. But their cottages are neat and comfortable, compared to those of our country; and the garden and orchard, which usually surround them, give them an air of ease and snugness, far preferable to the raw and uninviting appearance of a Scotch cottage, with its fractured windows, stuffed with old hats and pieces of tattered garments, and its door beset on one side by a dunghill, on the other by a heap of coals, or peats.

These statistics, by dear Margaret, rather fall in the Laird's province than yours. But your departments border closely upon each other; for those facts, in which he is interested as a Seigneur de Village, affect you as a Lady Bountiful, and so the state of the cottages is a common topic, upon which either may be addressed with propriety.

Adieu! I say nothing of the pad nag and poor old Shock, because I am certain that whatever belongs peculiarly to Paul will be the object of special care during his absence. But I recommend to you to take some of the good advice which you lavish upon others; to remember that there are damps in Scotland as well as in Holland, and that colds and slow fevers may be caught by late evening walks in our own favoured climate, as well as in France or Belgium. Paul ever remains your affectionate Brother.

LETTER II.

PAUL TO HIS COUSIN THE MAJOR.

Bergen-op-Zoom—British Attack—General Skerret —Night Scene.

AFTER all the high ideas, my dear Major, which your frequent and minute and reiterated details had given me, concerning the celebrated fortress of Bergen-op-Zoom, in former years the scene of your martial exploits, I must own its exterior has sadly disappointed me. I am well enough accustomed, as you know, to read the terms of modern fortification in the Gazette, and to hear them in the interesting narratives of your military experience; and I must own, that bastions and ravelins, half-moons, curtains, and palisades, have hitherto sounded in my ears every whit as grand and poetical as donjons and barbicans and portcullises, and other terms of ancient warfare. But I question much if I shall hereafter be able to think of them with exactly the same degree of respect.

A short reflection upon the principles of modern defence, and upon the means which it employs, might, no doubt, have saved me from the disappointment which I experienced. But I was not, as it happened, prepared to expect, that the strongest fortress in the Netherlands, or, for aught I know, in the world, the masterpiece of Cohorn, that prince of engineers, should, upon the first approach of a stranger, prove so utterly devoid of any thing striking or imposing in its aspect. Campbell is, I think, the only English poet who has ventured upon the appropriate terms of modern fortification, and you will not be surprised that I recollect the lines of a favourite author,—

> "the tower
> That, like a giant standard-bearer, frown'd
> Defiance on the roving Indian power.
> Beneath, each bold and promontory mound,
> With embrazure emboss'd and armour crown'd,
> And arrowy frize, and wedged ravelin,
> Wove like a diadem its tracery round
> The lofty summit of that mountain green." [1]

But, in order to give dignity to his arrowy frize and ravelin, the Bard has placed his works on the edge of a steepy ascent. Bergen-op-Zoom is nothing less. Through a country as level as the surface of a lake, you jolt onward in your cabriolet, passing along a paved causeway, which, as if an inundation were apprehended, is raised upon a mound considerably higher than the champaign district which it traverses. At length, you spy the top of a poor-looking spire or two, not rising proudly pre-eminent from a group of buildings, but exhibiting their slender and mean pinnacles above the surrounding glacis, as if they belonged to a subterranean city, or indicated the former situation of one which had been levelled with the ground. The truth is, that the buildings of the town, being sunk to a considerable depth beneath the sloping ramparts by which it is surrounded and protected, are completely hidden, and the defences themselves, to an inexperienced eye, present nothing but huge sloping banks of earth, cut into fanciful shapes and angles, and carefully faced with green turf. Yet the arrangement of these simple barriers, with reference to the command of each other, as well as of the neighbouring country, has been held, and I doubt not justly, the very perfection of military science. And, upon a nearer approach, even the picturesque traveller finds some gratification. This is chiefly experienced upon his entrance into the town. Here, turning at a short angle into a deep and narrow avenue, running through these mounds, which at a distance seemed so pacific and unimportant, he finds himself still excluded by drawbridges and ditches, while guns, placed upon the adjoining batteries, seem ready to sweep the ground which he traverses. Still moving forward, he rolls over drawbridges, whose planks clatter under the feet of his horses, and through vaulted arches, which resound to the eternal smack of his driver's whip. He is questioned by whiskered sentinels, his passports carefully examined, and his name recorded in the orderly-book; and it is only after these precautions that a stranger, though as unwarlike as myself, is permitted to enter the town. The impression is a childish one; yet a Briton feels some degree of unpleasant restraint, not only at undergoing a scrutiny, to which he is so little accustomed, but even from the consciousness of entering a place guarded with such scrupulous minuteness. It is needless to tell you, my dear Major, how much this is a matter of general routine in fortified places on the continent, and how soon the traveller becomes used to it as a matter of course. But I conclude you would desire to have some account of my first impressions upon such an occasion. To you, who speak as familiarly of roaring cannon

> "As maids of fifteen do of puppy-dogs,"

my expectations, my disappointment, and my further sensations, will probably appear ridiculous enough.

These formidable fortifications will soon be of little consequence, and may probably be permitted to go to decay. Bergen-op-Zoom, a frontier town of the last importance, while the Princes of Orange were only Stadtholders of the Seven United Provinces, is a central part of their dominions, since the Netherlands have been united into a single kingdom. Meantime, the town is garrisoned by a body of Land-poliz, which corresponds nearly to our local militia in the mode in which it is levied. All the disposable forces of the Netherlands have been sent forward into France, and more are still organizing to be despatched in the same direction.

In the evening, by permission of the commandant, I walked round the scene of your former exploits. But you must forgive me if my attention was chiefly occupied by the more recent assault under our brave countryman, Lord Lynedoch,[2] which was so boldly undertaken, and so strangely disappointed, when success seemed almost certain. I was accompanied in my walk by a sensible native of the place, a man of Scotch descent, who spoke good English. He pretended to point out with accuracy the points on which the various assaults were made, and the spots where several of the gallant leaders fell. I cannot rest implicit faith in his narrative, because I know, and you know still better, how difficult it is to procure a just and minute account of such an enterprise, even from those who have been personally engaged in it, and how imperfect, consequently, must be the information derived from one who himself had it at secondhand. Some circumstances, however, may be safely taken upon my guide's averment, because they are such as must have consisted with his own knowledge. But, first, it may be observed in general, that the history of war contains no example of a bolder attempt; and, if it failed of success, that failure only occurred after almost all the difficulties which could have been foreseen had been encountered and surmounted. In fact, the assailants, successful upon various points, were already in possession of by far the greater number of the bastions; and had they fortunately been in communication with each other, so as to have taken uniform measures for attacking the French in the town, they must have become

---

[1] Gertrude of Wyoming, p. iii., st. 25.
[2] General Sir Thomas Grahame of Balgowan in Perthshire, created Baron Lynedoch in 1814. See the Vision of Don Roderick (Sir W. Scott's Poetical Works, vol. ix.,) and notes.

masters of the place. It is even confidently said, that the French commandant sent his aid-de-camp to propose a capitulation; but the officer being killed in the confusion, other and more favourable intelligence induced the Frenchman to alter his purpose. It has been generally alleged, that some disorder was caused by the soldiers, who had entered the town, finding access to the wine-houses. My conductor obstinately denied this breach of discipline. He said, that one of the attacking columns destined to cross the stream which forms the harbour, had unhappily attempted it before the tide had ebbed, and were obliged to wade through when it was of considerable depth; and he allowed, that the severity of the cold, joined to the wetting, might give them the appearance of intoxication. But when the prisoners were put under his charge in the church, of which he was sexton, he declared solemnly, that he did not see among them one individual who seemed affected by liquor. Perhaps his own predilections, or a natural desire to please his auditors, may have influenced his opinion. To resist such temptations to excess is not among the numerous excellences of the British soldier.

The fate of a Dutch officer in our service, who led the attack upon one of the bastions, was particularly interesting. He was a native of the town, and it was supposed had been useful in furnishing hints for the attack. He led on his party with the utmost gallantry; and although the greater number of them fled, or fell, under a heavy fire—for the enemy were by this time upon the alert—he descended into the main ditch, crossed it upon the ice, and forced his way, followed by a handful of men, as far as the internal defences of the place. He had already mounted the inner glacis, when he was wounded in many places, and precipitated into the ditch; and, as his followers were unable to bring him off, he remained on the ice until next morning, when, being still alive, he became a prisoner to the French. Their first purpose was to execute him as a traitor, from which they were with difficulty diverted by a letter from the British general, accompanied by documents to establish how long he had been in the English service. The unfortunate gentleman was then permitted to retire from the hospital to his own house in the town, where he did not long survive the wounds he had received.[1]

I did not, you may believe, fail to visit the unfortunate spot, where Skerret, so celebrated for his gallantry in the Peninsula, Gore, Mercer, Carleton, Macdonald, and other officers of rank and distinction, fell upon this unfortunate occasion.[2] I was assured that General Skerret, after receiving a severe wound by which he was disabled, gave his watch and purse to a French soldier, requesting to be carried to the hospital; and that the ruffian dragged him down from the banquette only to pierce him with his bayonet. But I have since learned, from better authority, that this gallant officer fell on the spot.

While I listened to the details of this unhappy affair, and walked slowly and sadly with my conductor from one bastion to another, admiring the

strength of the defences which British valour had so nearly surmounted, and mourning over the evil fate which rendered that valour fruitless, the hour of the evening, gradually sinking from twilight into darkness, suited well with the melancholy subject of my inquiries. Broad flashes of lambent lightning illuminated, from time to time, the bastions which we traversed; and the figure of my companion, a tall, thin, elderly man, of a grave and interesting appearance, and who seemed, from his voice and manner, deeply impressed by recollections of the melancholy events which he detailed, was such as might appear to characterise their historian. A few broad and heavy drops of rain occasionally fell and ceased. And to aid the general effect, we heard from below the hollow roll of the drums announcing the setting of the watch, and the deep and sullen WER DA of the sentinels, as they challenged those who passed their station. I assure you this is no piece of imaginary scenery got up to adorn my letter, but the literal circumstances of my perambulation around the ramparts of Bergen-op-Zoom.

I presume you are now in active preparation for the moors, where I wish you much sport. Do not fail to preserve for me my due share in your friendship, notwithstanding that, on the subject of Bergen-op-Zoom, I am now qualified to give you story for story. Such are the advantages which travellers gain over their friends. My next letter to you shall contain more interesting, as well as more recent and more triumphant, military details.

I must not omit to mention that, in the Church of Bergen-op-Zoom, a tablet of marble, erected by their brother officers, records the names of the brave men who fell in the valorous, but ill-fated attack upon this famous fortress. For them, as for their predecessors who fell at Fontenoy, the imagination of the Briton will long body forth the emblematic forms of Honour and Freedom weeping by their monuments. Once more, farewell, and remember me.

LETTER III.

PAUL TO HIS COUSIN PETER.

Retrospect—Surrender of Paris—Bourbons Restored—Emigrants—Noblesse—Clergy—Liberalists.

THY politics, my dear Peter, are of the right Scottish cast. Thou knowest our old proverbial character of being *wise behind the hand*. After all, the wisdom which is rather deduced from events than formed upon predictions, is best calculated for a country politician, and smacks of the prudence as well as of the aforesaid proverbial attribute of our national character. Yet, believe me, that though a more strict seclusion of the dethroned Emperor of France might have prevented his debarkation at Cannes, and although we and our allies might have spared the perilous farce of leaving him a globe and sceptre to play withal, there were, within France itself, elements sufficiently jarring to produce, sooner or later, a dreadful explosion. You

---

[1] I have since been informed, from unquestionable authority, that this officer was not ill-treated by the French. It is remarkable, that he had personally ventured into the town to ascertain the possibility of success, the day before the attack was made.—S.

[2] See Gazette of General Sir Thomas Grahame's despatches, dated Calmhout, 10th March, 1814, &c., in the *Edinburgh Annual Register* of that year, Appendix, p. ccliii., &c.

daily politicians are so little in the practice of re-collecting last year's news, that I may be excused recalling some leading facts to your recollection, which will serve as a text to my future lucubrations.

The first surrender of Paris had been preceded by so much doubt, and by so many difficulties, that the final victory seems to have been a matter not only of exultation, but even of surprise, to the victors themselves. This great event was regarded, rather as a gratification of the most romantic and extravagant expectations, than as a natural consequence of that course of reaction, the ebb of which brought the allies to the gates of Paris, as its tide had carried Bonaparte to those of Berlin and Vienna. Pleased and happy with themselves, and dazzled with the glory of their own exploit, the victors were in no humour to impose harsh conditions upon the vanquished ; and the French, on their part, were delighted at their easy escape from the horrors of war, internal and external, of siege, pillage, and contribution. Bonaparte's government had of late become odious to the bulk of the people, by the pressure of taxation, by the recurring terrors of the proscription, but, above all, by the repeated disasters which the nation had latterly sustained. The constitutional charter, under which the Bourbon family were restored, was not only a valuable gift to those who really desired to be ensured against the re-establishment of despotism, but operated as a salvo to the wounded feelings of the still more numerous class, who wished that the crimes and calamities of the Revolution should not appear to be altogether thrown away, and who could now appeal to this Bill of Rights, as a proof that the French nation had not sinned and suffered in vain. The laboratory and chemical apparatus which were to have produced universal equality of rights, had indeed exploded about the ears of the philosophical experimentalists, yet they consoled themselves with the privileges which had been assured to them by the King upon his restoration.—

> " So though the Chemist his great secret miss,
> For neither it in art or nature is,
> Yet things well worth his toil he gains,
> And doth his charge and labour pay,
> With good unsought, experiments by the way."

All parties being thus disposed to be pleased with themselves, and with each other, the occupation of the capital was considered as the close of the disasters which France had sustained, and converted into a subject of general jubilee, in which the Parisians themselves rejoiced, or affected to rejoice, as loudly as their unbidden guests. But this desirable state of the public mind was soon overcast, and the French, left to their own reflections, began speedily to exhibit symptoms both of division and dissatisfaction.

The first, but not the most formidable of their causes of discontent, arose from the pretensions of the emigrant noblesse and clergy.

At the restoration of Charles II., (to which we almost involuntarily resort as a parallel case,) the nobility and gentry of England, who had espoused the cause of his father, were in a very different condition from the emigrant nobles of France. Many had indeed fallen in battle, and some few by the arbitrary sentence of the usurper's courts of justice ; but the majority, although impoverished by fines and sequestrations, still resided upon their

patrimonial estates, and exercised over their tenantry and cottagers the rights of proprietors. Their influence, though circumscribed, was therefore still considerable ; and had they been disposed to unite themselves into a party, separate from the other orders of the state, they had power to support the pretensions which they might form. But here the steady sense and candour, not alone of Ormond and Clarendon, but of all the leading Cavaliers, induced them to avoid a line of conduct so tempting yet so perilous. The dangers of reaction, according to the modern phrase, were no sooner sounded into the public ear by the pamphlets and speeches of those who yet clung to a republic, than every purpose, whether of revenge, or of a selfish and separate policy, was disowned in a manifesto, subscribed by the principal Royalists, in which they professed to ascribe their past misfortunes not to any particular class of their fellow-citizens, but to the displeasure of the Almighty, deservedly visiting upon them their own sins and those of the community. Such was the declaration of the Cavaliers at that important crisis ; and though there were not wanting *royalistes purs et par excellence*, who, like Swift's correspondent, Sir Charles Wogan,[1] censured the conduct of Clarendon for suffering to escape so admirable an opportunity to establish despotic authority in the crown, and vest feudal power in the nobility, I need not waste words in vindicating his moderate and accommodating measures to my discerning friend Peter.

The scattered remnants of the French noblesse, who survived to hail the restoration of the Bourbons, while they possessed no efficient power, held much more lofty pretensions than had been preferred by the aristocracy of Britain at the Restoration. It would be unjust to subscribe to the severe allegation, that they had forgot nothing, and learned nothing, during their long exile ; yet it can hardly be either doubted or wondered at, that they retained their prejudices and claims as a separate and privileged class, distinguished alike by loyalty and sufferings in the cause of the exiled family, to a point inconsistent with the more liberal ideas of a community of rights, which, in despite both of the frenzy of the Revolution and the tyranny of Bonaparte, had gradually gained ground among the people at large. And, while the once-privileged classes maintained such pretensions, they were utterly devoid of the means of effectually asserting them. Long years of banishment had broken off their connexion with the soil of France, and their influence over those by whom it is cultivated. They were even divided among themselves into various classes ; and the original emigrants, whose object it was to restore the royal authority by the sword, looked with dislike and aversion upon the various classes of exiles of a later date, whom each successive wave of the Revolution had swept from their native land. Their own list did not appear to exhibit any remarkable degree of talent ; those among them whose exile was contemporary with their manhood, were now too old for public business, and those who were younger, had become, during their long residence abroad, strangers, in a manner, to the customs and habits of their country ; while neither the aged nor the young had the benefit of practical experience in public affairs. It

---

[1] See Sir Walter Scott's edition of *Swift's Works*, vol. xvii.

was not among such a party, however distinguished by birth, by loyalty, by devotion in the royal cause, that Louis XVIII. could find, or hope to find, the members of a useful, active, and popular administration. Their ranks contained many well qualified to be the grace and ornament of a court; but few, it would seem, fitted for the support and defence of a throne. Yet who can wonder, that the men who had shared the misfortunes of their sovereign, and shown in his cause such proofs of the most devoted zeal, were called around him in his first glimpse of prosperity; and that, while ascending the throne, he entertained towards this class of his subjects, bound to him, as they were,

" By well-tried faith, and friendship's holy ties,"

the affections of a kind and grateful master? One distinguished emigrant, observing the suspicion and odium which so excusable a partiality awakened against the monarch, had the courage to urge, that, to ensure the stability of the throne, their sentence of banishment should have continued by the royal edict for ten years at least after the restoration of the house of Bourbon. It was in vain that the advocates of Louis called upon the people to observe, that no open steps had been taken in favour of the emigrants. Their claims were made and pleaded upon every hand; and, if little was expressly done in their favour, suspicion whispered, that the time was only waited for when ALL could be granted with safety. These suspicions, which naturally occurred even to the candid, were carefully fostered and enlarged upon by the designing; and the distant clank of the feudal fetters was sounded into the ears of the peasants and burghers, while the uncertainty of property alarmed the numerous and powerful proprietors of forfeited domains.

The dislike to the clergy, and the fear of their reviving claims upon the confiscated church-lands, excited yet greater discontent than the king's apprehended partiality to the emigrants. The system of the Gallic Church had been thoroughly undermined before its fall. Its constitution had been long irretrievably shattered; the whole head was sick, and the whole heart was faint. Doctrines of infidelity, everywhere general among the higher ranks, were professed by none with more publicity than by the superior orders of the clergy; and, respecting moral profligacy, it might be said of the church of France as of Ilion,

" Intra muros peccatur, et extra."

It is no wonder, that, in a system so perverted, neither the real worth of many of the clergy, nor the enthusiastic zeal of others, was able to make a stand against the tide of popular odium, skilfully directed towards the Church and its ministers by the reigning demagogues. Our Catholic Highland neighbour must also pardon us, if we account the superstitious doctrines of his Church among the chief causes of her downfall. The necessity of manning outworks, which are incapable of being effectually defended, adds not a little to the perplexities of a besieged garrison. Thus the sarcasms and sneers, justified, at least in our heretical eyes, by some part of the Catholic doctrines, opened the way for universal contempt of the Christian system. At any rate, nothing is more certain, than that a general prejudice was, during the Revolu-

447

tion, successfully excited against the clergy, and that, among the lower Parisians in particular, it still exists with all its violence. Even on the day when the rabble of the Fauxbourgs hailed the triumphal return of Bonaparte to his throne, their respect for the hero of the hour did not prevent them from uttering the most marked expressions of dislike and contempt when Cardinal Fesch appeared in the procession. The cry was general, A bas la calotte! and the uncle of the restored emperor was obliged to dismount from his palfrey, and hide himself in a carriage.

The King and the Comte D'Artois are, in their distresses, understood to have sought and found consolation in the exercise of religious duties. They continued, in gratitude, those devotions which they had commenced in humble submission, and their regard was naturally extended to the ministers of that religion which they professed and practised. Conduct in itself so estimable, was, in the unhappy state of the public mind, misrepresented to their subjects. The landholders were alarmed by fear of the re-establishment of tithes; the labouring poor, and the petty shopkeeper, regarding the enforcing tho long-neglected repose of the Sabbath, as a tax upon their industry and time, amounting to the hire of one day's labour out of the seven. The proprietors of church-lands were alarmed, more especially when the rash zeal of some of the priesthood refused the offices of the Church to those who had acquired its property. The Protestants in the south of France remembered the former severities exercised against them by the sovereigns of the house of Bourbon, and trembled for their repetition under a dynasty of monarchs, who professed the Catholic faith with sincerity and zeal. Add to these the profligate, who hate the restraints of religion, and the unthinking, who ridicule its abstracted doctrines, and you will have some idea how deeply this cause operated in rendering the Bourbons unpopular.

Those who dreaded, or pretended to dread, the innovations which might be effected by the influence of the clergy and the nobles,—a class which included, of course, all the old partisans of democratical principles,—assumed the name of Constitutionalists, and afterwards of Liberalists. The one was derived from their great zeal for the constitutional charter; the other from their affected superiority to the prejudices of ancient standing. Their ranks afforded a convenient and decent place of refuge for all those, who, having spent their lives in opposing the Bourbon interest, were now compelled to submit to a monarch of that family. They boasted, that it was not the person of the king to which they submitted, but the constitution which he had brought in his hand. Their party contained many partisans, especially among men distinguished by talent. Democracy, according to Burke, is the foodful nurse of ambition; and men, who propose to rise by the mere force of their genius, naturally favour that form of government which offers fewest restraints to their career. This party was also united and strengthened by possessing many of those characters who had played the chief parts in the revolution, and who were fitted, both by talents and experience, to understand and conduct the complicated ramifications of political intrigue.

Among those best qualified to "ride on the whirlwind and direct the storm," was the celebrated Fouché, Duke of Otranto, whose intimate acquaintance with every intrigue in France had been acquired when he exercised the office of minister of the police under the emperor. There is every reason to think that this person had no intention of pushing opposition into rebellion; and that it was only his purpose to storm the cabinet, not to expel the monarch. It cannot be denied, that there were among the Liberalists the materials for forming, what is called, in England, a constitutional opposition, who, by assailing the ministry in the two Chambers, might have compelled them to respect the charter of the Constitution; and to those amongst them, who were actuated by either the love of rational liberty, or by a modified and regulated spirit of ambition, the reign of the Bourbons afforded much greater facilities than the restoration of the military despotism of Bonaparte. Even to the very last moment, Fouché is said to have looked round for some *mezzo termine*, some means of compromise, which might render unnecessary the desperate experiment of the emperor's restoration. When Napoleon had landed, and was advancing towards Lyons, Fouché demanded an audience of the king upon important business. The interview was declined, but two noblemen were appointed by Louis to receive his communication. He adverted to the perilous situation of the king; and offered even yet, provided his terms were granted, to arrest Napoleon's progress towards the capital. The ministers required to know the means which he meant to employ. He declined to state them, but professed himself confident of success. On his terms he was less reserved. He announced them to be, that the Duke of Orleans should be proclaimed lieutenant-general of the kingdom; and that Fouché himself and his party should immediately be called to offices of trust and power. These terms were of course rejected; but it was the opinion of the well-informed person from whom I had this remarkable anecdote, that Fouché would have been able to keep his word.

His recipe was not, however, put to the test; and he and his party immediately acceded to the conspiracy, and were forced onward by those formidable agents, of whom it may be observed, that, like fire and water, they are excellent servants, but dreadful masters,—I mean the army, whose state, under the Bourbons, deserves the consideration of a separate epistle.—Ever, my dear friend, I remain sincerely yours, PAUL.

LETTER IV.

TO THE SAME.

Retrospect—the Army—Unpopularity of Louis—the Army dissatisfied—Irritation of the French—Departure of Allied Troops—Insults offered to Foreigners—Hostile Feelings of Government—Conspiracy in the Army—Bonaparte's Return—the Army join him—his Arrival at Paris—all hopes of Peace removed—Liberals join Bonaparte—the Royalists.

I LEFT off in my last with some account of the Constitutionalists, Liberalists, or whatsoever they are called, who opposed, from various causes, the measures of Louis XVIII., without having originally any purpose of throwing themselves into the arms of Bonaparte. To this desperate step they

were probably induced by the frank and universal adhesion of the army to the commander under whom they had so often conquered. No man ever better understood both how to gain and how to maintain himself in the hearts of his soldiers than Bonaparte. Brief and abrupt in his speech, austere and inaccessible in his manners to the rest of his subjects, he was always ready to play the *bon camarade* with his soldiers; to listen to their complaints, to redress their grievances, and even to receive their suggestions. This accessibility was limited to the privates and inferior officers. To the mareschals and generals he was even more distant and haughty than to his other subjects. Thus he connected himself intimately and personally with the main body of the army itself, but countenanced no intermediate favourite, whose popularity among the troops might interfere with his own.

To the motives of personal attachment, so deeply rooted, and so industriously fostered, must be added the confidence of the soldiers in military talents so brilliantly displayed, and in the long course of victory which had identified the authority of Napoleon with the glory of the French arms. To a train of the most uniform and splendid success, they might indeed have opposed the reverses of the Peninsular war, or the disastrous retreat from Moscow, and the battle of Leipsic, with all the subsequent reverses; but, as soldiers and as Frenchmen, they were little inclined to dwell upon the darker shades of the retrospect. Besides, partiality and national vanity found excuses for these misfortunes. In the Peninsula, Bonaparte did not command; in Russia, the elements fought against him; at Leipsic, he was deserted by the Saxons; and in France, betrayed, as they pretended, by Marmont. Besides, a great part of the soldiers who, in 1814-15, filled the French ranks, had been prisoners of war during Bonaparte's last unfortunate campaigns, and he was only experimentally known to them as the victor of Marengo, Ulm, Austerlitz, Jena, Friedland, and Wagram. You cannot have forgotten the enthusiasm with which the prisoners on parole at —— used to speak of the military renown of the emperor; nor their frank declaration at leaving us, that they might fight with their hands for the Bourbons, but would fight with hand and heart for Napoleon. Even the joy of their return seemed balanced, if not overpowered, by the reflection, that it originated in the dethronement of the emperor. To recollect the sentiments of these officers, unsuppressed even in circumstances most unfavourable for avowing them, will give you some idea of the ardour with which they glowed when they found themselves again in arms, and forming part of a large and formidable military force, actuated by the same feelings.

It was the obvious policy of the Bourbons to eradicate, if possible, this dangerous attachment, or to give it a direction towards the reigning family. For this purpose, every attention was paid to the army; they were indulged, praised, and flattered; but flattery, praise, and indulgence, were only received as the surly mastiff accepts, with growling sullenness, the food presented to him by a new master. There was no common tone of feeling to which the Bourbons could successfully appeal. It was in vain they attempted to conjure up the antiquated fame of *Henri Quatre* to men who, if ever they had heard of that monarch, must have known that his martial exploits were as much beneath those of Bonaparte, as his moral character was superior to the Corsican's. In the reigning family there was no individual who possessed so decided a military character as to fill, even in appearance, the loss which the army had sustained in their formidable commander, and the moment of national difficulty was unfortunately arrived, in which the personal activity of the monarch, a circumstance which, in peaceful times, is of little consequence, was almost indispensably essential to the permanence of his authority.

Burke says somewhere, that the King of France, when restored, ought to spend six hours of the day on horseback. "I speak," he adds, "according to the letter." The personal infirmities of the good old man, who has been called to wear this crown of thorns, put the required activity out of the question. But the justice of the maxim has not been the less evident. Not only the soldiers, but the idle and gaping population of Paris, despised the peaceful and meritorious tranquillity of Louis XVIII., and recalled with regret the bustling and feverish movements of Bonaparte, which alternately gave them terror, and surprise, and amusement. Indeed, such was the restless activity of the ex-emperor's disposition, that he contrived, as it were, to multiply himself in the eyes of the Parisians. In an incredibly short space of time, he might be seen in the most distant quarters of the city, and engaged in the most different occupations. Now he was galloping along a line of troops,—now alone, or with a single aid-de-camp, inspecting some public building,—in another quarter you beheld him in his carriage,—and again found him sauntering among the objects of the fine arts in the Louvre. With a people so bustling, so active, and so vainglorious as the French, this talent of ubiquity went a great way to compensate the want of those virtues which the emperor did not pretend to, and which the legitimate monarch possesses in such perfection. "The King," said an Englishman to a Frenchman, "is a man of most excellent dispositions."—"Sans doute."—"Well read and well informed."—"Mais, oui."—"A gentleman in his feelings and manners."—"Assurément, Monsieur, il est né François."—"Placable, merciful, moral, religious."—"Ah, d'accord—mais après tout," (a mode in which a Frenchman always winds up his argument,) "il faut avouer, qu'un Roi qui ne peut monter à cheval est un bien chétif animal."—This opinion, in which the possession of the equestrian art was balanced against all mental qualities, is not peculiar to the person by whom it was delivered; and it is certain that the King's affairs suffered greatly by his being unable to show himself, even in the exterior appearance, as a military commander. Ney, who was probably for the time sincere in his professions of zeal to the sovereign whom he so soon afterwards deserted, recommended that he should review the regiments as they passed through Paris, even if it were in a litter. But the affecting apology of the King is best pleaded in the words of his own manifesto. "Enfeebled by age and twenty-five years of misfortune, I cannot say, like my ancestor, Rally around my white plume; but I am willing to follow to the dangers to which I cannot lead."

None of the royal family, unfortunately, possessed the temper and talents necessary for supplying the King's deficiencies. The Duke d'Angoulême, like his father Monsieur, was retired, and understood to be bigoted to the Catholic observances, and much ruled by the clergy. The Duke de Berri, with more activity, had a fierce and ungovernable temper, which often burst out upon improper and unseemly occasions. Under their auspices, the attempts to new-model the army, by gradually introducing officers attached to the royal family, gave much offence, without producing any sensible advantage. In some instances the new officers were not received by the corps to whom they were sent; in some they were deprived of the influence which should attend their rank, by the combination of the soldiers and officers; in other cases, they were perverted by the universal principles of the corps whom they were appointed to command; and, finally, there were instances, as in the case of Labedoyère, in which the court were imposed upon by specious professions, and induced to promote persons the most inimical to the royal interests. The re-establishment of the household troops, in which a comparatively small body of gardes de corps were, at a great expense, and with peculiar privileges, established as the immediate guardians of the King's person, was resented by the army in general, but more especially by the ci-devant imperial, now royal, guards.

In a word, matters had gone so far, that the army, as in Cromwell's time, existed as an isolated and distinct body, not under the government of the Legislature, but claiming exclusive rights and privileges, and enjoying a separate and independent political existence of its own. Whenever this separation between the civil and military orders takes place, revolution and civil war cannot be far distant.

But there was one powerful cause of irritation common to the French nation in general, though particularly affecting the army. That very people of Europe, the most ambitious of fame in arms, who so lately and so fully stood possessed of the palm of conquest, which for centuries had been the object of their national ambition, had at once lost that pre-eminence, and with it

> "The earthquake-voice of victory,
> To 'them' the breath of life." [1]

The height to which their military reputation had been raised, the enormous sacrifices which had been made to attain it, the rapid extension of their empire, and the suddenness of their fall in power and in esteem, were subjects of the most embittered reflection. We in Britain vainly imagined, that the real losses which France sustained in extending her influence and her triumphs, must have disgusted her with the empty fame for which she paid so dearly. But however the French might feel under the immediate pressure of each new conscription, nothing is more certain than that their griefs, like the irritation of men impressed into our naval service, were forgotten in the eclat of the next victory, and that all the waste of blood and treasure by which it was obtained, was accounted a cheap expenditure for the glory of France. [2]

When a people, with minds so constituted, beheld within the walls of their capital the troops of

---

[1] Byron's Ode to Napoleon.
[2] "A more tremendous system certainly never appeared for

the desolation and subjection of the world. Every country was to be compelled in succession to furnish men for the plan the nations whom they had so often, subdued, their first effort was to disguise, even from themselves, the humiliation to which they were subjected. When they had looked so long upon a stranger as to be certain he was not laughing at them, which seemed to be their first apprehension, their usual opening was a begging of the general question:— " You know we were not conquered—our reception of the King was a voluntary act—our general and unanimous joy bears witness that this is the triumph of peace over war, not of Europe over France." With such emollients did they endeavour to dress the surface of a wound which internally was inflamed and rankled.

These harmless subterfuges of vanity held good, until they had forgotten the late alarming and precarious state in which their country had been placed, and particularly until the departure of the allied troops (a measure most impolitically precipitate) had removed the wholesome awe which the presence of a superior force necessarily imposed. Then instantly operated the principle of Tacitus— *qui timeri desierint, odisse incipient.* A thousand hostile indications, trifling perhaps individually, but important from their number and reiteration, pointed out the altered state of the public mind towards the allies. The former complaisance of the French nation, founded perhaps as much upon their good opinion of themselves as on their natural disposition to oblige others, was at once overclouded, and the sight of a foreigner became odious, as reminding them of the aspect of a conqueror. Caricatures, farces, lampoons, all the *petite guerre* by which individual malice has occasionally sought gratification, were resorted to, as the only expressions of wounded feeling now competent to the Great Nation. The equanimity with which the English in particular gave the losers leave to laugh, as loudly as losers and beaten men could, rather exasperated than appeased the resentment of the French. The most unoffending foreigners were exposed to insult, and embroiled in personal quarrels with gratuitous antagonists in the public places of Paris, where, in former times, the name of a stranger was a sufficient protection, even when an aggressor. All these circumstances indicated a tone of feeling, ulcerated by the sense of degradation, and which burned to regain self-opinion, by wreaking vengeance on their conquerors. The nation was in the situation of losing gamblers, who reflect indeed upon their losses with mortification and regret, but without repenting the folly which caused them; and like them also, the French only waited some favourable conjuncture again to peril the remains of their fortune upon the same precarious hazard.

The language of the Government of France was gradually and insensibly tinged by the hostile passions of her population. The impatient and irri-

tated state of the army dictated to her representative, even at the Congress, a language different from what the European republic had a right to expect from the counsellors of the monarch whom their arms had restored. It is probable the Government felt that their army resembled an evoked fiend pressing for employment, and ready to tear to pieces even the wizard whom he serves, unless instantly supplied with other means of venting his malevolence. But if it was a part of the Bourbon policy, rather to encounter the risk and loss of an external war, than to leave their army in peace, and at leisure to brood over their discontents 'and disgraces, they had no time allowed them to make the ungracious experiment. A plot was already on foot and far advanced, to ensure, as it was supposed, the recovery of the national glory, by again placing on the throne him, under whose auspices, and by whose unparalleled military successes, it had been formerly raised to the highest pitch of military splendour.

Such was the influence of the various causes which I have endeavoured to detail, that the reception of the insinuations of the conspirators, particularly in the army, exceeded their wishes, and that their plot nearly broke out before the time proposed. It is at least pretty certain that their zeal outwent the discretion of their principal, and that Napoleon more than once declined the invitations which he received to return from Elba. The co-operation of Murat was a point of extreme moment; and until a Neapolitan army could approach the north of Italy, Bonaparte's situation must have been desperate, supposing him to have received a check in the south of France at the outset of his expedition. A series of dark intrigues, therefore, commenced between the principal conspirators and King Joachim, which ended in his winding up his courage to the perilous achievement which they recommended. In the north of Italy were many officers and soldiers who had formerly served under Eugene Beauharnois. And it was reasonably believed, considering the weak state of the Austrians, that Murat's army, Neapolitans as they were, might have at least made their way so far as to have recruited their ranks by the union of these veterans.

Internally the conspiracy proceeded with the most surprising secrecy and success. The meetings of the chief leaders were held under the auspices of Madame Maret, Duchess of Bassano. But subordinate agents were to be found everywhere, and more especially among the coffeehouses and brothels of the Palais Royal, those assemblages of every thing that is desperate and profligate. " Bonaparte," said a Royalist to me the other day, "had with him all the *rouge-men* and all the *rouge-women,* and, in our country, their numbers are nineteen out of twenty." One of these places of nocturnal

---

der and conquest of others. If any one nation presumed to be dissatisfied, the population of another was to be driven in arms to oppress it. The application of this dreadful organization was obvious. If any portion of this compulsory army exhibited signs of discontent, it was only necessary to march it to the most wasteful point of service, and it would be destroyed before it had become dangerous, and yet not till it had performed a certain quantity of needful work for its fell employer. His vast designs have been hitherto executed with the most lavish profusion of human blood ; he cares neither for distance, seasons, country, famine, nor disease. To overpower a certain part of an enemy's army, it is necessary to surprise, out-number, and surround it. Frequently he can

450

only do this by making his men perform marches that are beyond the ordinary powers of human nature, and through countries scarcely passable. It is indifferent to him how many thousands drop from mere fatigue and want. It is sufficient that enough reach the point of action to accomplish his purposes. If he disperses the enemy, he gains a new extent of human population to drive into his ranks, and to make the instruments, however unwilling, of new depredations. Being consumed so fast, there is no time for mutiny, and little demand for pay. *For a certain time, therefore, this terrible engine of war acts in his favour with dreadful energy ; though it is one which may ultimately recoil upon himself.*—*Quarterly Review,* May, 1809, p. 446.

rendezvous, called the Café Montaussier, was distinguished for the audacity with which its frequenters discussed national politics, and the vociferous violence with which they espoused the cause of the dethroned emperor. That the police, whose surveillance, in Bonaparte's reign, extended to the fireside and bedchamber of every citizen, should have either overlooked, or observed with supine indifference, those indications of treason in places open for public rendezvous, argues the incapacity of the superior directors, and the treachery of those who were employed under them. Even the partial discovery of Excelman's correspondence with Murat served but to show the imbecility of a government, who could not, or durst not, bring him to punishment. The well-known symbol of the Violet, by which Bonaparte's friends intimated his return to France with the reappearance of that flower in spring, was generally known and adopted, at least two months before the period of his landing, yet attracted no attention on the part of the police. Indeed, so gross was their negligence, that a Frenchman, finding his friend ignorant of some well-known piece of news, observed, in reply, *Vous êtes apparemment de la police?* as if to belong to that body inferred a necessary ignorance of every thing of importance that was going forward in the kingdom.

With so much activity on the one side, and such supine negligence on the other, joined to a state of public feeling so favourable to his enterprise, one is scarcely surprised at Napoleon's wonderful success. The mass of the army went over to him as one man ; and the superior officers, who found their influence too feeble to check the progress of the invader, took, with a few distinguished exceptions, the resolution to swim along with the stream which they could not oppose. But, however discontented with the government of the Bourbons, the middling ranks in civil life were alarmed as with a clap of thunder by this momentous event. They beheld themselves once more engaged in a war with all Europe, and heard once more the Prussian trumpets at the gates of the metropolis. To dispel these alarms, Napoleon, with a versatile address, which could hardly have succeeded anywhere save in France, endeavoured to put such a colour upon his own views as best suited those whom he was immediately addressing. To the army, his proclamation, issued at Lyons, held forth immediate war, conquest, and the re-establishment of the military fame of France. But, when he reached Paris, he seemed anxious to modify this declaration. He appealed to the Treaty of Paris, by which he pretended to abide, and he expressed himself contented that the rights and boundaries of France should be limited according to the wishes of the allied powers as there expressed. He did more ; he even alleged that his enterprise was executed with their connivance. With the assurance of a shameless charlatan, as one author expressed it, he asserted, that his escape was countenanced by England, otherwise, as he reasoned with apparent force, how was he permitted to leave Elba! and that his restoration had the approbation of Austria would be made manifest, he pretended, by the immediate return of Maria Louisa and her son to the French territory. He even carried the farce so far as to prepare and send away state carriages to meet those valued pledges of his father-in-law's

451

amity, conscious that the success of this gross imposition would serve his cause during the moments of general doubt and indecision, though certain to be discovered in a very few days. Meanwhile, an attempt was actually made to carry off his son from the city of Vienna, and defeated only by the want of presence of mind in one of the conspirators, who being arrested by the police, imprudently offered a handful of gold to obtain his escape, which excited the attention and suspicion of the officer who had seized him. No doubt, had the attempt succeeded, the restoration of the child would have been represented as the effects of the favour of Austria towards the father.

The declarations of the allied powers soon removed the hopes of peace, by which those who were pacifically disposed had been, for a short time, flattered. A war, of a kind altogether new, with respect to the extent of the military preparations, was now approaching and imminent, and the address of Chatterton's Sir Charles Baldwin to the English might have been well applied to the people of France,—

> " Say, were ye tired of godly peace,
>   And godly Henry's reign,
> That you would change your easy days
>   For those of blood and pain?
>
> " Ah! fickle people, ruin'd land,
>   Thou will know peace no moe,
> When Richard's sons exalt themselves,
>   Thy streets with blood shall flow."

But there remained comfort to the more peaceable part of the community in the confidence of assured victory, so warmly expressed by the soldiers ; and then they hoped that the short and successful war would conclude so soon as France should be restored to, what they were pleased to term, her natural boundaries. *Paix au dela du Rhin* was the general wish—the soldiers affected to aim at no more remote conquest—the citizen was willing to face the burdens of a war for an object so limited, and for the re-establishment of *la gloire nationale*. And thus were the versatile people of Paris induced to look with an eye of hope, instead of terror, upon the approaching storm.

Those who were attached to the parties of the Liberalists and Royalists saw Bonaparte's successful progress with other eyes. But the Liberalists, severed from the family of Bourbon by the opinions and incidents which I have already detailed to you, were, in a manner, forced into the service of the new emperor, although, doubtless, their wishes were to substitute a government of a more popular construction for that of the restored monarch. Their chiefs, too, the philosophical Carnot, and the patriotic Fouché, did not disdain to accept, from the hand of the restored heir of the Revolution, the power, dignities, and emoluments which he artfully held out to them. And, in becoming a part of his administration, they were supposed to warrant to him the attachment of their followers ; while Napoleon, by professing to embrace the constitution, with some stipulations in favour of general freedom, was presumed to give a sufficient pledge that henceforth he was to regard himself only as the head of a limited monarchy. How far this good understanding would have survived his return to Paris with victory, it is scarce necessary to inquire ; for not even the adhesion of Carnot and Fouché prevented symptoms of open feud between their party and the Imperialists, evinced in many tart debates in the

Lower Chamber of Representatives, from which it is evident that they regarded each other with aversion and suspicion, and that their union was not likely to survive the circumstances which occasioned it.

In the meanwhile, they were embarked in a common cause; and it does not appear that the Liberalists were slack in affording assistance to Bonaparte in his preparations for external war. Like the factions in Jerusalem, during her final siege, they suspended their mutual discussions until they should have repulsed the common enemy. There is, nevertheless, a rumour, which is at least countenanced by the favour which Fouché for some time held at the court of Louis XVIII., that even while the king was at Ghent, the wily chief of the Liberalists maintained a correspondence with his ex-monarch. But, in general, that party, comprehending the various classes of Liberalists, from the Constitutionalist to the Jacobin, may be considered as having identified themselves with the Imperialists, and undertaken the same chance of battle to which the adherents of Bonaparte had made their solemn appeal.

There was a third party in France, and a powerful one, if its real force could have been mustered and called into action. For, notwithstanding all that I have said of the various causes which divided the opinions of the nation, it must necessarily be supposed that the Bourbon family had, in many provinces, an equal, and in some a predominating interest. Unfortunately, the Royalists, being taken at unawares, remained altogether stupified and paralyzed by the sudden and unanimous defection of the army. The premature, or ill-conducted attempts of resistance at Marseilles and Bourdeaux, were so easily subdued, as to discredit and discountenance all farther opposition. In La Vendée only there was an open military resistance to Bonaparte under the banners of the King, and there it was speedily brought to an end by the exertions of the Imperial General, who has since received just credit for employing more mild means for that purpose than were authorized by his instructions.

The Royalists, in the other provinces, contented themselves with opposing a sort of *vis inertiæ* to the efforts which Napoleon made for calling forth the national force, and awaited with anxiety, but without any active exertion, the expected progress of the allies. This passive resistance was particularly remarkable in the departments of the North, several of which would render Napoleon no assistance, either in recruits or money, and where entreaties, threats, and even attempts at force, could not put in motion a single battalion of the National Guard.

On the other hand, the Eastern departments, which bordered on Germany, met the wishes of Bonaparte in their utmost extent. They remembered the invasion of the preceding year with all the feelings of irritation which such recollections naturally produce. Accordingly, they formed free corps of volunteers—laboured at fortifying towns and passes—constructed *têtes-du-pont*—and multiplied all means of defence which the face of the country afforded. Thus it happened, fortunately for Bonaparte, that the part of the kingdom whose inhabitants were most disposed to consider the war as a national quarrel, was that of which the

territory was most immediately open to invasion.

I shall continue this statement, my dear Peter, in a letter to the Major, to whose department the military details properly belong; and, in the meanwhile, am ever yours,

PAUL.

LETTER V.

PAUL TO THE MAJOR.

Promptitude of Napoleon—Military Preparations —Defeat of Murat—Disposition of the French Army—Artillery—Cavalry—Cuirassiers—Infantry—Bonaparte's Plan for Opening the Campaign—Proposed Advance into Belgium—Self-importance of the Soldiery—their Feuds—the Army Assembled—Bonaparte's Address.

I PRESUME, my dear Major, that our political friend has communicated to you my last epistle. My next enters upon high matters, which I have some scruple to treat of to you; for who would willingly read lectures upon the art of war before Alexander the Great! But, after all, as Waterloo was a battle very different from that of Bunker's-hill, and from two or three other later actions, with the details of which you often regale us, I conceive that even a bungling account of it from a tactician so wretched as I am, may afford some matter for your military commentaries. At any rate, active investigation has not been wanting; as I have surveyed the fields of action, and conversed familiarly with many of the distinguished officers, who there laid a claim to the eternal gratitude of their country. Your kindness will excuse my blunders, and your ingenuity will be applied to detect and supply my deficiencies.

No part of Napoleon's political life, marked as it has always been by the most rapid and extraordinary promptitude in military preparation, affords such a display of activity, as the brief interval which occurred between his resuming the imperial sceptre, and resigning it, it is to be presumed, for ever. Although the conciliating the Liberalists, and paralyzing the Royalists, occupied some time; and although it was necessary to sacrifice several days to show, and to the national love of fanfaronade, he was never an instant diverted from his purpose. While he seemed to be fully occupied with the political discussions of the various parties, —with shows, and processions, and reviews of corps of children under twelve years old, his more serious preparations for the death-struggle which he expected to encounter, were as gigantic in their character as incessant in their progress. Every effort was used to excite the population to assume arms, and to move forward corps of national guards to relieve in garrison the troops of the line now called into more active service. And while Bonaparte was convoking in the Champ de Mai, as his mock assembly of the people was fantastically entitled, a number of persons to whom the revolution had given dangerous celebrity, together with his own military adherents,—a class of men of all others most unfit for being members of a deliberative assembly,—while, I say, this political farce was rehearsing and acting, the real tragedy was in active preparation. Cannon, muskets, arms of every description, were forged and issued from the manufactories and arsenals with incredible celerity. The old corps were recruited from the conscripts of 1814; retired veterans were again called forth to their banners; new levies were instituted, under the various names of free-corps, federés, and volunteers; the martial spirit of France was again roused to hope and energy; and the whole kingdom seemed transformed at once into an immense camp, of which Napoleon was the leader and soul. One large army defiled towards Belgium, where the neighbourhood of the English and Prussian troops excited alarm; other armies were assembled in Alsace, in Lorraine, in Franche Comté, at the foot of the Alps, and on the verge of the Pyrenees. It only remained to be discovered on which side the storm was to burst.

There is little doubt, that Bonaparte, reckoning upon the success of Murat, or hoping at least on his making a permanent diversion, had destined the north of Italy for the first scene of active and personal warfare. A threat in that quarter would have been sufficient to divert from the main struggle the whole force of Austria, already sensible, from sad experience, how vulnerable she was through her Italian frontier. Many of the Russian troops would probably have been detached to her assistance, and while a triple barrier of fortresses and garrisons of the first order, with a strong covering army, was opposed on the frontier of Flanders to the English and Prussian armies, Bonaparte himself might have taken the field on the theatre of his original triumphs, and have removed the war from the French territory, with the certainty, in case of success, that his army would be recruited among the Cisalpine veterans of Eugene Beauharnois. But Austria, on this pressing alarm, exerted herself with an activity unknown to her annals; and the troops which she rapidly hurried forward to meet Murat, exhibited, in the very first conflicts, the military superiority of the northern warriors.— "These barbarians," said the Neapolitans, after the skirmish at Rimini, "fight as if they had two lives; what chance have we against them, who pretend only to one?" And to save that single title to existence, Murat's army fled with such celerity, and so little resistance, that the campaign was ended almost as soon as begun, and with it terminated the reign of King Joachim over the delicious kingdom of Naples. No King, in a fairy tale, ever obtained a crown so easily, or lost it in a manner so simple, and at the same time so speedy. His discomfiture was attended with the most disadvantageous consequences to Bonaparte, who thus appeared hermetically sealed within the realm of France, by hostile armies advancing on all hands, and compelled to await the conflict upon his own ground.

But he neither lost courage, nor slackened his preparations, on account of his relative's disaster. The French grand army, already in the highest order, was still farther augmented in number and equipments. It became now obvious, that Flanders, or the adjoining French frontier, must be the scene of action. The general headquarters were fixed at Laon; a very strong position, where some preparations were made for forming an army of reserve, in case of a disaster. The first corps occupied Valenciennes, and the second Maubeuge, communicating by their right wing with the armies

assembled in the Ardennes and on the Moselle, and resting their left upon the strong fortifications of Lisle. Here they waited the numerous reinforcements of every kind which Bonaparte poured towards their position.

The deficiency of artillery was chiefly apprehended. The allies had, in 1814, carried off most of the French field-trains. But, by incredible exertions, the loss was more than supplied; for, besides the usual train attached to separate corps, each division of the army had a park of reserve, and the imperial guard, in particular, had a superb train of guns, consisting almost entirely of new pieces. It is remarkable, that in casting these fine engines of war, the old republican moulds had, in general, been employed; for I observed, that most of the guns taken at Waterloo have engraved upon them the emphatic inscriptions, Liberté, Egalité, Fraternité, and so forth; not to mention others, which, in honour of philosophy, bore the names of Voltaire, Rousseau, and other writers of deistical eminence. The army in all possessed more than three hundred guns; a quantity of artillery which has been thought rather beyond the proportion of its numbers.

Cavalry was another species of force in which Bonaparte was supposed to be peculiarly weak. But the very reverse proved to be the case. The care of Louis XVIII. had remounted several of the regiments which had suffered in the campaigns of 1813 and 1814; and the exertions of Napoleon and his officers completed their equipment, as well as the levy of others; so that a finer body of cavalry never took the field. They were upwards of twenty thousand in number; of whom the lancers were distinguished by their address, activity, and ferocity; and the cuirassiers, of whom there are said to have been nine regiments, by the excellence of their appointments, and the superior power of their horses. This last corps was composed of soldiers selected for their bravery and experience, and gave the most decisive proofs of both in the dreadful battle of Waterloo. Their cuirasses consisted of a breastplate and back, joined together by clasps, like the ancient plate-armour. Those of the soldiers were of iron, those of the officers of brass, inlaid with steel. They are proof against a musket-ball, unless it comes in a perfectly straight direction. To these arms was added a helmet, with cheek-pieces, and their weapons of offence were a long broadsword and pistols. They carried no carabines. The horses of the cuirassiers, although, upon trial, they proved inferior to those of our heavy cavalry, were probably better than those of any other corps in Europe. They were selected with great care, and many of the carriage and saddle-horses, which Bonaparte had pressed for the equipment of the army, were assigned to mount these terrible regiments. Yet, however formidable the aspect and onset of cuirassiers may be, emboldened as they are by a sense of comparative security, and affecting the imagination of those whom they assail by the flash and display of their panoply, it may be doubted whether the use of defensive arms for the body is, upon the whole, to be recommended. The weight of the cuirass becomes, in the course of a campaign, burdensome both to man and horse; and, after a few hours' active exertion in action, the horse of course is blown, and the rider, rendered less active as a swordsman by the unpliable armour in which he is sheathed, is outstripped, out-manœuvred, and cut down, by his more agile opponent.

Of the infantry of the French, it was impossible to speak too highly, in point of bravery and discipline in the field. The *élite* of the army consisted of the imperial guards, who were at least 20,000 strong. These chosen cohorts had submitted with the most sullen reluctance to the change of sovereigns in 1814; and no indulgence nor flattery, which the members of the Bourbon family could bestow upon them, had availed to eradicate their affection to their former master, which often displayed itself at times, and in a manner, particularly offensive to those who were their temporary and nominal commanders. The imperial guards were pledged, therefore, as deeply as men could be, to maintain the new revolution which their partiality had accomplished, and to make good the boast, which had caused France to rely " upon their stars, their fortune, and their strength." The other corps of infantry, all of whom participated in the same confidence in themselves and their general, might amount, including the artillery, to 110,000 men, which, with the guards and cavalry, formed a gross total of 150,000 soldiers, completely armed and equipped, and supplied, even to profusion, with every kind of ammunition. So fascinated was this brilliant army with recollection of former victories, and confidence in their present strength, that they not only heard with composure the report of the collected armies which marched against them from every quarter of Europe, but complained of the delay which did not lead them into instant battle. They were under a general who knew well how to avail himself of those feelings of confidence and ardour.

It had been supposed, as well in France and in the army, as in other parts of Europe, that Bonaparte meant to suffer the allies to commit the first hostile act, by entering the French territory. And although the reputation of being the actual aggressor was of little consequence, where both parties had so fully announced their hostile intentions, it was still supposed that a defensive war, in which he could avail himself of the natural and artificial strength of French Flanders, might have worn out, as in the early war of the revolution, the armies and spirits of the allies, and exposed them to all those privations and calamities peculiar to an invading army, in a country which is resolutely defended.

But the temper of Bonaparte, ardent, furious, and impetuous, always aiming rather at attack than defence, combined with the circumstances in which he found himself, to dictate a more daring system of operations.

His power was not yet so fully established as to ensure him the national support during a protracted war of various chances, and he needed now, more than ever, the dazzling blaze of decisive victory to renew the charm, or *prestige*, as he himself was wont to call it, once attached to his name and fortunes. Considerations peculiar to the nature of the approaching campaign, probably united with those which were personal to himself. The forces now approaching France greatly exceeded in numbers those which that exhausted kingdom could levy to oppose them, and it seemed almost impossible to protect her frontiers at every vulnerable point. If

the emperor had attempted to make head against the British and Prussians in French Flanders, he must have left open to the armies of Russia and Austria the very road by which they had last year advanced to Paris. On the other hand, if, trusting to the strength of the garrison towns and fortresses on the Flanders frontiers, Napoleon had conducted his principal army against those of the Emperors of Russia and Austria, the numerous forces of the Duke of Wellington and Blucher might have enabled them to mask these strong places by a covering army, and either operate upon the flank of Napoleon's troops, or strike directly at the root of his power by a rapid march upon the capital. Such were the obvious disadvantages of a defensive system.

A sudden irruption into Belgium, as it was more suited to the daring genius of Napoleon, and better calculated to encourage the ardour of his troops, afforded him also a more reasonable prospect of success. He might, by a rapid movement, direct his whole force against the army either of England or of Prussia, before its strength could be concentrated and united to that of its ally. He might thus defeat his foes in detail, as he had done upon similar occasions, with the important certainty, that one great and splendid victory would enable him to accomplish a levy *en masse*, and thus bring to the field almost every man in France capable of bearing arms; an advantage which would infinitely more than compensate any loss of lives which might be sustained in effecting it. Such an advantage, and the imposing attitude which he would be thereby entitled to assume towards the allies, might have affected the very elements upon which the coalition was founded, and afforded to Bonaparte time, means, and opportunity, of intimidating the weak and seducing the stronger members of the confederacy. In Belgium, also, if successful, he might hope to recruit and extend his army by new levies, drawn from a country which had so lately been a part of his own kingdom, and which had not yet had time to attach itself to the new dynasty to which it had been assigned. For this purpose, he carried muskets with him to equip an insurrectionary army, and officers of their own nation to command them; and although the loyal Belgians were much shocked and scandalized at the hopes expressed by those preparations, it may be presumed they would not have been so confidently entertained without some degree of foundation.

The proposed advance into Belgium had the additional advantage of relieving the people of France from the presence of an army, which, even upon its native soil, was a scourge of no ordinary severity. The superiority which long war and a train of successes had given to the military profession in France, over every other class of society, had totally reversed in that country the wholesome and pacific maxim, *Cedant arma togæ*. In the public walks, in the coffeehouses and theatres of Paris, the conduct of the officers towards a *pekin*, (a cant word by which, in their arrogance, they distinguished any citizen of a peaceful profession,) was, in the highest degree, insolent and overbearing. The late events had greatly contributed to inflame the self-importance of the soldiery. Like the prætorian bands of Rome, the janizaries of Constantinople, or the strelitzes of Moscow, the army of France possessed all the real power of the state.

They had altered the government of their country, deposed one monarch, and re-elevated another to the throne which he had abdicated. This gave them a consciousness of power and importance, neither favourable to moderation of conduct nor to military discipline. Even while yet in France, they did not hesitate to inflict upon their fellow-subjects many of those severities, which soldiery in general confine to the country of an enemy; and, to judge from the accounts of the peasantry, the subsequent march of the allies inflicted upon them fewer, or at least less wilful evils, than those which they had experienced at the hands of their own countrymen. These excesses were rarely checked by the officers; some of whom indulged their own rapacity under cover of that of the troops, while the recent events which invited soldiers to judge and act for themselves, had deprived others, who, doubtless, viewed this license with grief and resentment, of the authority necessary to enforce a wholesome restraint upon their followers.

This looseness of discipline was naturally and necessarily followed by dissensions and quarrels among the troops themselves. The guards, proud of their fame in arms, and of their title and privileges, were objects of the jealousy of the other corps of the army, and this they repaid by contumely and arrogance, which led, in many cases, to bloody affrays. The cavalry and infantry had dissensions of old standing, which occasioned much mutiny and confusion. Above all, the license of pillage led to perpetual quarrels, where one regiment or body of troops, who were employed in plundering a village or district, were interrupted by others who desired to share with them in the gainful task of oppression.

These feuds, and the laxity of discipline in which chiefly they originated, may be traced to Bonaparte's total disuse in this, as in his more fortunate campaigns, of the ordinary precautions for maintaining an army by the previous institution of magazines. By neglecting to make such provision, he no doubt greatly simplified his own task as a general, and accelerated, in the same degree, his preparations for a campaign, and the march of an army unencumbered with forage-carts. But he injured, in a much greater proportion, the discipline and moral qualities of his soldiery, thus turned loose upon the country to shift for their own subsistence; and,—had such a motive weighed with him,—he aggravated, in a tenfold degree, the horrors of warfare.

The evils arising from the presence of his army were now to be removed into the territories of an enemy. The marches and combination of the various corps d'armée were marked in a distinguished manner by that high military talent which planned Bonaparte's most fortunate campaigns. In the same day, and almost at the same hour, three large armies; that from Laon, headed by the emperor himself; that of the Ardennes, commanded by the notorious Vandamme; and that of the Moselle, under the orders of General Girard, having broken up from their different cantonments, attained, by a simultaneous movement, a united alignement upon the extreme frontiers of Belgium. The good order and combination with which the grand and complicated movements of these large armies were executed, was much admired among the French officers, and received as the happy augury of future success.

455

To his army thus assembled, Bonaparte, upon the 14th of June, 1815, made one of those inflated and bombastic addresses, half riddle, half prophecy, which he had taught the French armies to admire as masterpieces of eloquence. He had not neglected his system of fortunate days; for that upon which he issued his last proclamation was the anniversary of the Marengo and Friedland victories; on which, as well as after those of Austerlitz and Wagram, he assured his troops he had fallen into the generous error of using his conquests with too much lenity. He reminded his soldiers of his victory over Prussia at Jena; and having no such advantage to boast over the English, he could only appeal to those among his ranks who had been prisoners in Britain, whether their situation had not been very uncomfortable. He assured them they had the private good wishes of the Belgians, Hanoverians, and soldiers of the Confederation of the Rhine, although for the present forced into the enemy's ranks; and concluded by asserting, that the moment was arrived for every courageous Frenchman to conquer or die.

This speech was received with infinite applause (comme de raison,) and on the morning of the subsequent day (15th June) his army was in motion to enter Belgium.

But my exhausted paper reminds me that this must be the boundary of my present epistle.—
Yours, affectionately,

PAUL.

LETTER VI.

PAUL TO THE MAJOR—IN CONTINUATION.

Campaign opens—British and Prussian Positions —Treachery of Fouché—Bonaparte's advance— Occupation of Charleroi—Crossing of the Sambre —Ney commands the Left Wing—Bonaparte the Centre and the Right—Advance of the Allied Troops—Cameron's Gathering—Black Brunswickers—Brussels—Action at Quatre Bras— French occupy Le Bois de Bossu—Are repulsed by General Maitland—Post at Quatre Bras— Charge by French Cavalry—Gallant defence of the 42d—Loss of the British—Confidence inspired by their success.

I GAVE you, in my last, some account of the auspices under which Bonaparte opened the last of his fields. The bloody game was now begun; but, to understand its progress, it is necessary to mark the position of the opposite party.

Notwithstanding the fertility of Belgium, the maintenance of the numerous troops which were marched into that kingdom from Prussia, and transported thither from England, was attended with great burdens to the inhabitants. They were therefore considerably dispersed, in order to secure their being properly supplied with provisions. The British cavalry, in particular, were cantoned upon the Dender, for the convenience of forage. The Prussians held the line upon the Sambre, which might be considered as the advanced posts of the united armies.

Another obvious motive contributed to the dislocation of the allied force. The enemy having to choose his point of attack along an extended frontier, it was impossible to concentrate their army upon any one point, leaving the other parts of the boundary exposed to the inroads of the foe; and this is an advantage which the assailant must, in war, always possess over his antagonist, who holds a defensive position. Yet the British and Prussian divisions were so posted, with reference to each other, as to afford the means of sudden combination and mutual support; and, indeed, without such an arrangement, they could not have ultimately sustained the attack of the French, and Bonaparte's scheme of invasion must have been successful on all points.

But though these precautions were taken, it was generally thought they would not be necessary. A strong belief prevailed among the British officers, that the campaign was to be conducted defensively on the part of the French; and when the certain tidings of the concentration of the enemy's forces, upon the extreme frontier of Belgium, threatened an immediate irruption into that kingdom, it was generally supposed, that, as upon former occasions, the road adopted by the invaders would be that of Namur, which, celebrated for the sieges it had formerly undergone, had been dismantled, like the other fortified places in Flanders, by the impolicy of Joseph II., and is now an open town. And I have heard it warmly maintained by officers of great judgment and experience, that Bonaparte would have had considerable advantages by adopting that line of march in preference to crossing at Charleroi. Probably, however, these were compensated by the superior advantage of appearing on the point where he was least expected. In fact, his first movements seem to have partaken of a surprise.

It is not to be supposed that the Duke of Wellington had neglected, upon this important occasion, the necessary means to procure intelligence, —for skill in obtaining which, as well as for talent in availing himself of the information when gained, he was pre-eminently distinguished on the Peninsula. But it has been supposed, either that the persons whom he employed as his sources of intelligence, were, upon this occasion, seduced by Bonaparte, or that false information was conveyed to the English general, leading him to believe that such had been the case, and of course inducing him to doubt the reports of his own spies. The story is told both ways; and I need hardly add, that very possibly neither may be true. But I have understood from good authority, that a person, bearing, for Lord Wellington's information, a detailed and authentic account of Bonaparte's plan for the campaign, was actually despatched from Paris in time to have reached Brussels before the commencement of hostilities. This communication was intrusted to a female, who was furnished with a pass from Fouché himself, and who travelled with all despatch in order to accomplish her mission; but, being stopped for two days on the frontiers of France, did not arrive till after the battle of the 16th. This fact, for such I believe it to be, seems to countenance the opinion, that Fouché maintained a correspondence with the allies, and may lead, on the

other hand, to suspicion, that though he despatched the intelligence in question, he contrived so to manage, that its arrival should be too late for the purpose which it was calculated to serve. At all events, the appearance of the French upon the Sambre was at Brussels an unexpected piece of intelligence.

The advance of Bonaparte was as bold as it was sudden. The second corps of the French attacked the outposts of the Prussians, drove them in, and continued the pursuit to Marchienne-du-pont, carried that village, secured the bridge, and there crossing the Sambre, advanced towards a large village, called Gosselies, in order to intercept the Prussian garrison of Charleroi, should it retreat in that direction. The light cavalry of the French, following the movement of the second corps as far as Marchienne, turned to their right after crossing that river, swept its left bank as far as Charleroi, which they occupied without giving the Prussians time to destroy the bridge. The third corps d'armée occupied the road to Namur, and the rest of the troops were quartered between Charleroi and Gosselies, in the numerous villages which everywhere occur in that rich and populous country. The Prussian garrison of Charleroi, with the other troops which had sustained this sudden attack, retired in good order upon Fleurus, on which point the army of Blucher was now concentrating itself.

The advantages which the French reaped by this first success, were some magazines taken at Charleroi, and a few prisoners; but, above all, it contributed to raise the spirits and confirm the confidence of their armies.

Upon the 16th, at three in the morning, the troops which had hitherto remained on the right of the Sambre, crossed that river; and now Bonaparte began to develope the daring plan which he had formed, of attacking, upon one and the same day, two such opponents as Wellington and Blucher.

The left wing of the French army, consisting of the 1st and 2d corps, and of four divisions of cavalry, was intrusted to Ney, who had been suddenly called from a sort of disgraceful retirement to receive this mark of the emperor's confidence. He was commanded to march upon Brussels by Gosselies and Frasnes, overpowering such opposition as might be offered to him in his progress by the Belgian troops, and by the British who might advance to their support.

The centre and right wing of the army, with the imperial guards (who were kept in reserve,) marched to the right towards Fleurus against Blucher and the Prussians. · They were under the immediate command of Bonaparte himself.

The news of Napoleon's movements in advance, and of the preliminary actions between the French and Prussians, reached Brussels upon the evening of the 15th. The Duke of Wellington, the Prince of Orange, and most other officers of distinction, were attending a ball given on that evening by the Duchess of Richmond. This festivity was soon overclouded.[1] Instant orders were issued that the garrison of Brussels, the nearest disposable force,

---

[1] The popular error of the Duke of Wellington having been *surprised*, on the eve of the battle of Waterloo, at a ball given by the Duchess of Richmond at Brussels, was first corrected, on authority, in the "History of Napoleon Bonaparte," which forms a portion of the "Family Library." The Duke had, before one o'clock of that day, received intelligence of Napoleon's decisive operations, and it was intended to put off the

ball; but, on reflection, it seemed highly important that the people of Brussels should be kept in ignorance as to the course of events, and the Duke not only desired that the ball should proceed, but the general officers received his commands to appear at it, each taking care to quit the apartment as quietly as possible at ten o'clock, and proceed to join his respective division *en route*.

should move out to meet the approaching enemy; similar orders were issued to the cavalry, artillery, and the guards, who were quartered at Enghien; other troops, cantoned at greater distances, received orders to move to their support.

Our two distinguished Highland corps, the 42d and 92d, were among the first to muster. They had lain in garrison in Brussels during the winter and spring, and their good behaviour had attracted the affection of the inhabitants in an unusual degree. Even while I was there, *Les petits Ecossois*, as they called them, were still the theme of affectionate praise among the Flemings. They were so domesticated in the houses where they were quartered, that it was no uncommon thing to see the Highland soldier taking care of the children, or keeping the shop, of his host. They were now to exhibit themselves in a different character. They assembled with the utmost alacrity to the sound of the Cameron's Gathering, a well-known pibroch, the corresponding words of which are, " *Come to me, and I will give you flesh,*" an invitation to the wolf and the raven, for which the next day did, in fact, spread an ample banquet, at the expense of our brave countrymen as well as of their enemies. They composed part of Sir Thomas Picton's division, and early in the morning of the 16th marched out together with the other troops, under the command of that distinguished and lamented officer. The Duke of Brunswick, also, marched out at the head of his " black Brunswickers," so termed from the mourning which they wore for his father, and which they continue to wear for the gallant prince who then led them.[1] Those whose fate it was to see so many brave men take their departure on this eventful day, " gay in the morning as for summer sport," will not easily forget the sensations which the spectacle excited at the moment, and which were rendered permanent by the slaughter that awaited them.[2] Fears for their own safety mingled with anxiety for their brave defenders, and the agony of suspense sustained by those who remained in Brussels to await the issue of the day, was related to me in the most lively manner by those whose lot it was to sustain such varied emotions. It has been excellently described in a small work, entitled " Circumstantial Details of the Battle of Waterloo,"[3] which equals, in interest and authenticity, the " Account of the Battle of Leipsic by an Eyewitness," which we perused last year with such eager avidity.

The anxiety of the inhabitants of Brussels was increased by the frightful reports of the intended vengeance of Napoleon. It was firmly believed that he had promised to his soldiers the unlimited plunder of this beautiful city, if they should be able to force their way to it. Yet, even under such apprehensions, the bulk of the population showed no inclination to purchase mercy by submitting to the invader, and there is every reason to believe,

that the friends whom he had in the city were few and of little influence. Reports, however, of treachery were in circulation, and tended to augment the horrors of this agonizing period. It is said there was afterwards found, in Bonaparte's portfolio, a list, containing the names of twenty citizens, who, as friends of France, were to be exempted from the general pillage. I saw also a superb house in the Place Royale of Brussels, employed as a military hospital, which I was told belonged to a man of rank, who, during the battle of the 18th, believing the victory must rest with Bonaparte, had taken the ill-advised step of joining the French army. But whatever might be the case with some individuals, by far the majority of the inhabitants of every class regarded the success of the French as the most dreadful misfortune which could befall their city, and listened to the distant cannonade, as to sounds upon which the crisis of their fate depended. They were doomed to remain long in uncertainty; for a struggle, on which the fate of Europe hung, was not to be decided in a single day.

Upon the 16th, as I have already mentioned, the left wing of the French, under General Ney, commenced its march for Brussels by the road of Gosselies. At Frasnes they encountered and drove before them some Belgian troops who were stationed in that village. But the gallant Prince of Orange, worthy of his name, of his education under Wellington, and of the rank which he is likely to hold in Europe, was now advancing to the support of his advanced posts, and reinforced them so as to keep the enemy in check.

It was of the utmost importance to maintain the position which was now occupied by the Belgians, being an alignement between the villages of Sart à Mouline and Quatre Bras. The latter farm-house, or village, derives its name from being the point where the highway from Charleroi to Brussels is intersected by another road at nearly right angles. These roads were both essential to the allies; by the high-road they communicated with Brussels, and by that which intersected it with the right of the Prussian army stationed at St. Amand. A large and thick wood, called Le Bois de Bossu, skirted the road to Brussels on the right hand of the English position; along the edge of that wood was a hollow way, which might almost be called a ravine; and between the wood and the French position were several fields of rye, which grows in Flanders to an unusual and gigantic height.

In this situation, it became the principal object of the French to secure the wood, from which they might debouche upon the Brussels road. The Prince of Orange made every effort to defend it; but, in spite of his exertions, the Belgians gave way, and the French occupied the disputed post. At this critical moment, the division of Picton, the corps of the Duke of Brunswick, and shortly after the

---

[1] The father of the Duke of Brunswick who fell at Quatre Bras, was commander-in-chief of the Prussian forces at Jena, where he received his mortal wound, 14th October, 1806.

[2] " The unreturning brave—alas!
Ere evening to be trodden like the grass
Which now beneath them, but above shall grow
In its next verdure, when this fiery mass
Of living valour, rolling on the foe,
And burning with high hope, shall moulder cold and low.

" Last noon beheld them full of lusty life,
Last eve in Beauty's circle proudly gay,

The midnight brought the signal-sound of strife,
The morn the marshalling in arms,—the day
Battle's magnificently-stern array!

Thunder-clouds close o'er it, which when rent,
The earth is cover'd thick with other clay,
Which her own clay shall cover, heap'd and pent,
Rider and horse,—friend, foe,—in one red burial blent."
Childe Harold, Canto iii.

[3] Published by Booth and Egerton, London.

division of the guards from Enghien came up, and entered into action. "What soldiers are those in the wood?" said the Duke of Wellington to the Prince of Orange. "Belgians," answered the Prince, who had not yet learned the retreat of his troops from this important point. "Belgians!" said the Duke, whose eagle eye instantly discerned what had happened, "they are French, and about to debouche on the road; they must instantly be driven out of the wood." This task was committed to General Maitland, with the grenadiers of the Guards, who, after sustaining a destructive fire from an invisible enemy, rushed into the wood with the most determined resolution. The French, who were hitherto supposed unrivalled in this species of warfare, made every tree, every bush, every ditch, but more especially a small rivulet which ran through the wood, posts of determined and deadly defence, but were pushed from one point to another until they were fairly driven out of the position. Then followed a struggle of a new and singular kind, and which was maintained for a length of time. As often as the British endeavoured to advance from the skirts of the wood, in order to form in front of it, they were charged by the cavalry of the enemy, and compelled to retire. The French then advanced their columns again to force their way into the wood, but were in their turn forced to desist by the heavy fire and threatened charge of the British. And thus there was an alternation of advance and retreat, with very great slaughter on both sides, until, after a conflict of three hours, General Maitland retained undisputed possession of this important post, which commanded the road to Brussels.

Meantime the battle was equally fierce on every other point. Picton's brigade, comprehending the Scotch Royals, 92d, 42d, and 44th regiments, was stationed near the farm-house of Quatre Bras, and was the object of a most destructive fire, rendered more murderous by the French having the advantage of the rising ground; while our soldiers, sunk to the shoulders among the tall rye, could not return the volleys with the same precision of aim. They were next exposed to a desperate charge of the French heavy cavalry, which was resisted by each regiment throwing itself separately into a solid square. But the approach of the enemy being partly concealed from the British by the nature of the ground, and the height of the rye, the 42d regiment was unable to form a square in the necessary time. Two companies, which were left out of the formation, were swept off and cut to pieces by the cavalry. Their veteran colonel, Macara, was amongst those who fell. The adjutant of the regiment, the last (as was his duty) to retreat within the square, was involved in the charge of the lancers, and only escaped by throwing himself from his horse, and thus rejoining the regiment, which had for some minutes seen him in the utmost peril of death, without the possibility of assisting him.

Some of the men stood back to back, and maintained an unyielding and desperate conflict with the horsemen who surrounded them, until they were at length cut down. Nothing could be more galling for their comrades than to witness their slaughter, without having the power of giving them assistance. But they adopted the old Highland maxim, "To-day for revenge, and to-morrow for mourning," and received the cuirassiers with so dreadful and murderous a fire, as compelled them to wheel about. These horsemen, however, displayed the most undaunted resolution. After being beaten off in one point, they made a desperate charge down the causeway leading to Brussels, with the purpose of carrying two guns, by which it was defended. But at the moment they approached the guns, a fire of grape-shot was opened upon them; and, at the same time, a body of Highlanders, posted behind the farm-house, flanking their advance, threw in so heavy a discharge of musketry, that the regiment was in an instant nearly annihilated.

The result of these various attacks was, that the French retreated with great loss, and in great confusion; and many of the fugitives fled as far as Charleroi, spreading the news that the British were in close pursuit. But pursuit was impracticable, for the English cavalry had so far to march, that when they arrived upon the ground night was approaching, and it was impossible for them to be of service. Ney therefore re-established himself in his original position at Frasnes, and the combat died away with night-fall. The British had then leisure to contemplate the results of the day. Several regiments were reduced to skeletons by the number of killed and wounded. Many valuable officers had fallen. Among these were distinguished the gallant Duke of Brunswick,[1] who in degenerate times had remained an unshaken model of ancient German valour and constancy. Colonel Cameron, so often distinguished in Lord Wellington's despatches from Spain, fell while leading the 92d to charge a body of cavalry, supported by infantry.[2] Many other regretted names were read on the bloody list. But if it was a day of sorrow, it was one of triumph also.

It is true, that no immediate and decisive advantage resulted from this engagement, farther than as for the present it defeated Napoleon's plan of advancing on Brussels. But it did not fail to inspire the troops engaged with confidence and hope. If, when collected from different quarters, after a toilsome march, and in numbers one half inferior to those of the enemy, they had been able to resist his utmost efforts, what had they not to hope when their forces were concentrated, and when their artillery and cavalry, the want of which had been so severely felt during the whole of that bloody day, should be brought up into line! Meanwhile they enjoyed the most decided proof of victory, for the British army bivouacked upon the ground which

---

[1] "The Duke of Brunswick received the mortal when in the act of lighting a fresh cigar at the pipe of his dragoons! In how unheroic an attitude may one a heroic death!"—*MS. Journal.*

[2]   "Through battle's rout and reel,
Storm of shot and hedge of steel,
Led the grandson of Lochiel,
        Valiant Fassiefern.
Through steel and shot he leads no more,
Low laid 'mid friends' and foemen's gore;

But long his native lake's wild shore,
And Sunart rough, and high Ardgower,
        And Morven, long shall tell,
And proud Bennevis hear with awe,
How, upon bloody Quatre Bras,
Brave Cameron heard the wild hurra
        Of conquest as he fell!"
Sir WALTER SCOTT's *Poetical Works,* [royal 8vo, 1841.] p. 642.

had been occupied by the French during the battle, with the strongest hopes that the conflict would be renewed in the morning with the most decisive success. This, however, depended upon the news they should hear from Fleurus, where a furious cannonade had been heard during the whole day, announcing a general action between Napoleon and Prince Marshal Blucher. Even the Duke of Wellington was long ere he learned the result of this engagement, by which his own ulterior measures necessarily must be regulated. The Prussian officer sent to acquaint him with the intelligence had been made prisoner by the French light troops; and when the news arrived, they bore such a cloudy aspect as altogether destroyed the agreeable hopes which the success at Quatre Bras had induced the army to entertain.

But pledged as I am to give you a detailed account of this brief campaign, I must reserve the battle of Ligny to another occasion. Meanwhile, I am ever sincerely yours,

PAUL.

LETTER VII.

PAUL TO THE MAJOR—IN CONTINUATION.

BATTLE OF LIGNY.

Bonaparte's Plan for Attacking Blucher—Blucher's Position—Number of Troops on both Sides—Mutual hostility of the Prussians and the French—The two Armies join Battle—Vicissitudes of the Contest—Storming of St. Amand—Taking of Ligny—Charge of the Imperial Guards—Charge of the French Cavalry—Blucher's Horse shot—Repulse of the French Cavalry—Prussians Retreat—Concentration of the Prussian Army at Wavre—Loss of the Prussians—British Army Retreats—Bonaparte resolves to turn his whole Force against the British—Retreat of the British—Pursuit of the French—Bad state of the roads—French Cavalry checked in two attacks—British Army retire upon Waterloo—Headquarters of the Duke of Wellington—Headquarters of Bonaparte—Storminess of the Night—Melancholy Reflections of the British—Triumphant Confidence of the French—Remarks on Bonaparte's Plan of Attack.

WHEN Bonaparte moved with his centre and right wing against Blucher, he certainly conceived that he left to Ney a more easy task than his own; and that the Maréchal would find no difficulty in pushing his way to Brussels, or near it, before the English army could be concentrated in sufficient force to oppose him. To himself he reserved the task of coping with Blucher, and by his overthrow cutting off all communication between the Prussian and British armies, and compelling each to seek safety in isolated and unconnected movements. The Prussian veteran was strongly posted to receive the enemy, whom upon earth he hated most. His army occupied a line where three villages, built upon broken and unequal ground, served each as a separate redoubt, defended by infantry, and well furnished with artillery. The village of St. Amand was occupied by his right wing, his centre was posted at Ligny, and his left at Sombref. All these hamlets are strongly built, and contain several

459

ral houses, with large court-yards and orchards, each of which is capable of being converted into a station of defence. The ground behind these villages forms an amphitheatre of some elevation, before which runs a deep ravine, edged by straggling thickets of trees. The villages were in front of the ravine; and masses of infantry were stationed behind each, destined to reinforce the defenders as occasion required.

In this strong position Blucher had assembled three corps of his army, amounting to 80,000 men. But the fourth corps, commanded by Bulow, (a general distinguished in the campaign of 1814,) being in distant cantonments between Liege and Hannut, had not yet arrived at the point of concentration. The force of the assailants is stated in the Prussian despatches at 130,000 men. But as Ney had at least 30,000 soldiers under him at Quatre Bras, it would appear that the troops under Bonaparte's immediate command at the battle of Ligny, even including a strong reserve, which consisted of the first entire division, could not exceed 100,000 men. The forces, therefore, actually engaged on both sides, might be nearly equal. They were equal also in courage and in mutual animosity.

The Prussians of our time will never forget, or forgive, the series of dreadful injuries inflicted by the French upon their country after the defeat of Jena. The plunder of their peaceful hamlets, with every inventive circumstance which the evil passions of lust, rapine, and cruelty could suggest; the murder of the father, or the husband, because " the pekin looked dangerous," when he beheld his property abandoned to rapine, his wife, or daughters, to violation, and his children to wanton slaughter; such were the tales which the Prussian Landwehr told over their watch-fires to whet each other's appetite to revenge. The officers and men of rank thought of the period when Prussia had been blotted out of the book of nations, her queen martyred by studied and reiterated insult, until she carried her sorrows to the grave, and her king only permitted to retain the name of a sovereign to increase his disgrace as a bondsman. The successful campaign of 1814 was too stinted a draught for their thirst of vengeance, and the hour was now come when they hoped for its amplest gratification.

The French had, also, their grounds of personal animosity, not less stimulating. Those very Prussians, to whom (such was their mode of stating the account) the emperor's generosity had left the name of independence, when a single word could have pronounced them a conquered province; those Prussians, admitted to be companions in arms to the victors, had been the first to lift the standard of rebellion against them, when the rage of the elements had annihilated the army with which Napoleon invaded Russia. They had done more: they had invaded the sacred territory of France; defeated her armies upon her own soil; and contributed chiefly to the hostile occupation of her capital. They were commanded by Blucher, the inveterate foe of the French name and empire, whom no defeat could ever humble, and no success could mitigate. Even when the Treaty of Paris was received by the other distinguished statesmen and commanders of the allies as a composition advantageous for all sides, it was known that this veteran had expressed his displeasure at the easy terms on which

France was suffered to escape from the conflict. Amid the general joy and congratulation, he retained the manner (in the eyes of the Parisians) of a gloomy malecontent. A Frenchman, somewhat acquainted with our literature, described to me the Prussian general, as bearing upon that occasion the mien and manner of Dryden's spectre-knight:—

" Stern look'd the fiend, and frustrate of his will,
    Not half sufficed, and greedy yet to kill."

And now this inveterate enemy was before them, leading troops, animated by his own sentiments, and forming the vanguard of the immense armies, which unless checked by decisive defeat, were about to overwhelm France, and realize those scenes of vengeance which had been in the preceding year so singularly averted.

Fired by these sentiments of national hostility, the ordinary rules of war, those courtesies and acts of lenity which on other occasions afford some mitigation of its horrors, were renounced upon both sides. The Prussians declared their purpose to give and receive no quarter. Two of the French divisions hoisted the black flag, as an intimation of the same intention ; and it is strongly affirmed that they gave a more sanguinary proof of their mortal hatred by mutilating and cutting off the ears of the prisoners who fell into their hands at crossing the Sambre. With such feelings towards each other, the two armies joined battle.

The engagement commenced at three in the afternoon, by a furious cannonade, under cover of which the third corps of the French army, commanded by Vandamme, attacked the village of St. Amand. They were received by the Prussians with the most determined resistance, in despite of which they succeeded in carrying the village at the point of the bayonet, and established themselves in the church and churchyard. The Prussians made the most desperate efforts to recover possession of this village, which was the key of their right wing Blucher put himself at the head of a battalion in person, and impelled them on the French with such success, that one end of the village was again occupied ; and the Prussians regained possession of that part of the heights behind it, which, in consequence of Vandamme's success, they had been obliged to abandon. The village of Ligny, attacked and defended with the same fury and inveteracy, was repeatedly lost and regained, either party being alternately reinforced from masses of infantry, disposed behind that part of the village which they respectively occupied. Several houses enclosed with courtyards, according to the Flemish fashion, formed each a separate redoubt, which was furiously assailed by the one party, and obstinately made good by the other. It is impossible to conceive the fury with which the troops on both sides were animated. Each soldier appeared to be avenging his own personal quarrel ; and the slaughter was in proportion to the length and obstinacy of a five hours' combat, fought hand to hand within the crowded and narrow streets of a village. There was also a sustained cannonade on both sides, through the whole of the afternoon. But in this species of warfare the Prussians sustained much heavier loss than their antagonists, their masses being drawn up in an exposed situation upon the ridge and sides of the heights behind the villages, while those of the French were sheltered by the winding hollows of the lower grounds.

While this desperate contest continued, Bonaparte apparently began to doubt of its ultimate success. To ensure the storming of St. Amand, he ordered the first corps of infantry, which was stationed near Frasnes, with a division of the second corps commanded by Girard, and designed to be a reserve either to his own army or to that of Marshal Ney, to move to the right to assist in the attack. Of this movement Ney complained heavily afterwards in a letter to Fouché, as depriving him of the means of ensuring a victory at Quatre Bras.

The reinforcement, as it happened, was unnecessary, so far as the first corps was concerned ; for about seven o'clock Vandamme had, after reiterated efforts, surmounted the resistance of the Prussians at St. Amand ; and Girard had obtained possession of Ligny. Sombref, upon the left of the Prussian line, was still successfully defended by the Saxon general, Thielman, against Maréchal Grouchy ; and the Prussians, though driven from the villages in front of the amphitheatre of hills, still maintained their alignement upon the heights themselves, impatiently expecting to be succoured, either by the English, or by their own fourth division under Bulow. But the Duke of Wellington was himself actively engaged at Quatre Bras ; and Bulow had found it impossible to surmount the difficulties attending a long march through bad roads and a difficult country. In the meanwhile, Bonaparte brought this dreadful engagement to a decision by one of those skilful and daring manœuvres which characterised his tactics.

Being now possessed of the village of Ligny, which fronted the centre of the Prussian line, he concentrated upon that point the imperial guards, whom he had hitherto kept in reserve. Eight battalions of this veteran and distinguished infantry, thrown into one formidable column, supported by four squadrons of cavalry, two regiments of cuirassiers, and the horse-grenadiers of the guard, traversed the village of Ligny, now in flames, at the *pas de charge*, threw themselves into the ravine which separates the village from the heights, and began to ascend them, under a dreadful fire of grape and musketry from the Prussians. They sustained this murderous discharge with great gallantry, and, advancing against the Prussian line, made such an impression upon the masses of which it consisted, as threatened to break through the centre of their army, and thus cut off the communication between the two wings ; while the French cavalry, at the same time, charged and drove back that of the Prussians.

In this moment of consternation, the cause of Europe had nearly suffered a momentous loss in the death or captivity of the indomitable Blucher. The gallant veteran had himself headed an unsuccessful charge against the French cavalry ; and his horse being shot under him in the retreat, both the fliers and pursuers passed over him as he lay on the ground ; an adjutant threw himself down beside his general, to share his fate ; and the first use which the Prince-Marshal made of his recovered recollection was, to conjure his faithful attendant rather to shoot him than to permit him to fall alive into the hands of the French. Meantime, the Prussian cavalry had rallied, charged, and in their turn repulsed the French, who again galloped past the Prussian general, as he lay on the ground covered with the cloak of the adjutant, with the same precipitation as in their advance. The general was then disengaged and remounted, and proceeded to organize the retreat, which was now become a measure of indispensable necessity. .

The Prussian artillery, being disposed along the front of an extended line, could not be easily withdrawn, and several pieces fell into the hands of the French. Blucher's official despatch limits the number of guns thus lost to fifteen, which Bonaparte extends to fifty. But the infantry, retiring regularly, and in masses impenetrable to the cavalry of the pursuers, amply preserved that high character of courage and discipline, which, in the campaigns of the preceding year, had repeatedly enabled them to convert retreat and disorder of one day into advance and victory upon the next. In their retreat, which they continued during the night, they took the direction of Tilly; and in the next morning were followed by General Thielman, with the left wing, who, after evacuating the village of Sombref, which he had maintained during the whole preceding day, formed the rear-guard of the Prince-Marshal's army. Being now at length joined by the fourth corps, under General Bulow, the Prussian army was once more concentrated in the neighbourhood of the village of Wavre, ten miles behind the scene of their former defeat; and the utmost exertions were used by Blucher, and the officers under him, to place it in a condition for renewing the conflict.

The carnage of the Prussians in this unsuccessful battle was very great. I have heard it estimated at twenty thousand men, killed, wounded, and prisoners, being one-fourth part of their whole army. Bonaparte, however, only rates it at fifteen thousand *hors de combat*; an enormous loss, especially considering that, owing to the inveteracy of the combat, and the steady valour displayed by the vanquished in their retreat, there were hardly any prisoners taken.

The events of the 16th had a material influence on the plans of the generals on either side. While the Duke of Wellington was proposing to follow up his advantage at Quatre Bras, by attacking Ney at Frasnes, he received, on the morning of the 17th, the news that Blucher had been defeated on the preceding day, and was in full retreat. This left the Duke no option but to fall back to such a corresponding position as might maintain his lateral communication with the Prussian right wing; since, to have remained in advance, would have given Bonaparte an opportunity either to have placed his army betwixt those of England and Prussia, or, at his choice, to have turned his whole force against the Duke's army, which was inferior in numbers. The English general accordingly resolved upon retreating towards Brussels; a movement which he accomplished in the most perfect order, the rear being protected by the cavalry under the gallant Earl of Uxbridge.[1]

Meantime, Bonaparte had also taken his resolution. The defeat of the Prussians had placed it in his option to pursue them with his whole army, excepting those troops under Ney, who were in front of the Duke of Wellington. But this would have been to abandon Ney to almost certain destruction; since, if that general had been unable, on the preceding day, to make any impression on the

van of the British army alone, it was scarce possible he could withstand them, when supported by their main body, and joined by reinforcements of every kind. In the supposed event of Ney's defeat, Bonaparte's rear would have been exposed to a victorious English army, while he knew, by repeated experience, how speedily and effectually Blucher could rally his Prussians, even after a severe defeat. He made it his choice, therefore, to turn his whole force against the English, leaving only Grouchy and Vandamme, with about twenty-five thousand men, to hang upon the rear of Blucher; and by pursuing his retreat from Sombref to Wavre, to occupy his attention, and prevent his attempting to take a share in the unexpected action with the British.

Napoleon probably expected to find the English army upon the ground which it had occupied during the 16th. But the movement of his own forces from St. Amand and Ligny to Frasnes, had occupied a space of time which was not left unemployed by the Duke of Wellington. The retreat had already commenced, and the position at Quatre Bras was, about eleven in the forenoon, only occupied by a strong rear-guard, destined to protect the retrograde movement of the British general. Bonaparte put his troops in motion to pursue his retiring enemy. The day was stormy and rainy in the extreme; and the roads, already broken up by the English artillery in their advance and retreat, were very nearly impassable. The cavalry, whose duty it became to press upon the rear of the English, were obliged to march through fields of standing corn, which being reduced to swamps by the wetness of the season, rendered rapid movement impossible. This state of the weather and roads was of no small advantage to the British army, who had to defile through the narrow streets of the village of Genappe, and over the bridge which there crosses a small river, in the very face of the pursuing enemy. Their cavalry once or twice attacked the rear-guard, but received so severe a check from the Life Guards and Oxford Blues, that they afterwards left the march undisturbed. I am assured, that the Duke of Wellington, in passing Genappe, expressed his surprise that he had been allowed to pass through that narrow defile, unharrassed by attack and interruption, and asserted his belief, founded upon that circumstance, that Napoleon did not command in person the pursuing divisions of the French army. A French officer, to whom I mentioned this circumstance, accounted for this apparent want of activity, by alleging the heavy loss sustained upon the 16th, in the battles of Quatre Bras and Ligny; the necessary disorganization of the French cavalry after two such severe actions; the stormy state of the weather upon the 17th, and the impracticability of the roads for the movements of the cavalry. You, as a military critic, will be best judge how far this defence is available. I notice the same observation in an Account of the Battle of Waterloo, by a British Officer on the Staff.[2]

With little further interruption on the part of the enemy, the British army retired upon the ever-memorable field of Waterloo, and there took up a position upon the road to Brussels, which I shall endeavour to describe more fully in my next Letter.

---

[1] Created, in 1815, Marquis of Anglesea.

[2] Published by Ridgway, Piccadilly.

The Duke had caused a plan of this, and other military positions in the neighbourhood of Brussels, to be made some time before by Colonel Carmichael Smith, the chief engineer. He now called for that sketch, and, with the assistance of the regretted Sir William de Lancy and Colonel Smith, made his dispositions for the momentous events of next day. The plan itself, a relic so precious, was rendered yet more so, by being found in the breast of Sir William de Lancy's coat, when he fell, and stained with the blood of that gallant officer. It is now in the careful preservation of Colonel Carmichael Smith, by whom it was originally sketched.

When the Duke of Wellington had made his arrangements for the night, he established his headquarters at a petty inn in the small village of Waterloo, about a mile in the rear of the position. The army slept upon their arms upon the summit of a gentle declivity, chiefly covered with standing corn.

The French, whose forces were gradually coming up during the evening, occupied a ridge nearly opposite to the position of the English army. The villages in the rear of that rising ground were also filled with the soldiers of their numerous army. Bonaparte established his headquarters at Planchenoit, a small village in the rear of the position.

Thus arranged, both generals and their respective armies waited the arrival of morning, and the events it was to bring. The night, as if the elements meant to match their fury with that which was preparing for the morning, was stormy in the extreme, accompanied by furious gusts of wind, heavy bursts of rain, continued and vivid flashes of lightning, and the loudest thunder our officers had ever heard. Both armies had to sustain this tempest in the exposed situation of an open bivouac, without means either of protection or refreshment. But though these hardships were common to both armies, yet, (as was the case previous to the battle of Agincourt,) the moral feelings of the English army were depressed below their ordinary tone, and those of the French exalted to a degree of confidence and presumption unusual even to the soldiers of that nation.

The British could not help reflecting, that the dear-bought success at Quatre Bras, while it had cost so many valuable lives, had produced, in appearance at least, no corresponding result: a toilsome advance and bloody action had been followed by a retreat equally laborious to the soldier; and the defeat of the Prussians, which was now rumoured with the usual allowance of exaggeration, had left Bonaparte at liberty to assail them separately, and with his whole force, excepting such small proportion as might be necessary to continue the pursuit of their defeated and dispirited allies. If to this it was added, that their ranks contained many thousand foreigners, on whose faith the British could not implicitly depend, it must be owned there was sufficient scope for melancholy reflections. To balance these, remained their confidence in their commander, their native undaunted courage, and a stern resolution to discharge their duty, and leave the result to Providence.

The French, on the other hand, had forgotten in their success at Ligny, their failure at Quatre Bras, or, if they remembered it, their miscarriage was ascribed to treachery; and it was said that Bourmont and other officers had been tried by a

462

military commission and shot, for having, by their misconduct, occasioned the disaster. This rumour, which had no foundation but in the address with which Bonaparte could apply a salve to the wounded vanity of his soldiers, was joined to other exulting considerations. Admitting the partial success of Wellington, the English Duke, they said, commanded but the right wing of the Prussian army, and had, in fact, shared in Blucher's defeat, as he himself virtually acknowledged, by imitating his retreat. All, therefore, was glow and triumph. The Prussians were annihilated, the British defeated, "the Great Lord"[1] astounded. Such were literally the reports transmitted to Paris, and given to the French public. There is no reason in the present instance to suspect, that the writers of these gasconades were guilty of intentional exaggeration. No one supposed the English would halt, or make head, until they reached their vessels; no one doubted that the Belgian troops would join the Emperor in a mass; it would have been disaffection to have supposed there lay any impediment in their next morning's march to Brussels; and all affected chiefly to regret the tempestuous night, as it afforded to the despairing English the means of retiring unmolested. Bonaparte himself shared, or affected to share, these sentiments; and when the slow and gloomy dawning of the morning of the 18th of June showed him his enemies, still in possession of the heights which they occupied overnight, and apparently determined to maintain them, he could not suppress his satisfaction, but exclaimed, while he stretched his arm towards their position with a motion as if to grasp his prey, *Je les tiens donc, ces Anglois!*

The exultation of the French was mixed, according to their custom, with many a scurril jest at the expense of their enemies. The death of the Duke of Brunswick was the subject of much pleasantry among such of the French officers as sought to make their court to Jerome, the ex-king of Westphalia. To please this phantom Monarch, they ridiculed the fatality which always, they said, placed these unlucky Dukes of Brunswick in concurrence with the conqueror of their States, and condemned them successively to perish as it were by his hand. The national dress of our poor Highlanders, whose bodies were found lying in the lines which they had occupied in the field of Quatre Bras, furnished more good jests than I care to record. But, as I heard a Frenchman just now observe, "*Il rit bien, qui rit le dernier.*"

Before entering upon such particulars as I can collect of the battle of Waterloo, let me notice your criticism upon the affairs of the 16th. You say, first, that Bonaparte ought not to have attacked both the English and Prussian armies on the same day, and you call my attention to the argument detailed in Maréchal Ney's letter to Fouché. And, secondly, you are of opinion, that, having defeated the Prussians at Ligny, Napoleon should have pursued the routed army of Blucher with his whole cavalry at least, and rendered it impossible for him to rally sooner than under the walls of Maestricht. Such, you say, is the opinion of all military judges in our neighbourhood, by which I know you mean all our friends with blue coats and red collars, whe-

---

[1] This was the common appellation of Lord Wellington among the Spaniards during the Peninsular War.

ther half-pay captains, ex-officers of volunteers, commanders of local militia, or deputy-lieutenants. " Never a man's thought in the world keeps the road-way better than thine," my dear Major ; but in despite of this unanimous verdict against the ex-Emperor, I will venture to move for a writ of error.

Upon the first count of the indictment, be pleased to reflect, that Bonaparte's game was at best a difficult one, and that he could embrace no course which was not exposed to many hazards. It is not the ultimate success, or miscarriage, of his plan, by which we ought to judge of its propriety, but the rational prospects which it held out before being carried into execution. Now be it remembered, that, upon the 16th, Blucher's army was already concentrated at Ligny, while that of Lord Wellington was only moving up in detail to Quatre Bras. Maréchal Ney would scarcely have recommended to Napoleon to move straight towards Brussels by Quatre Bras and Genappe, leaving upon his right, and eventually in his rear, an army of 80,000 Prussians, expecting hourly to be joined by Bulow with 20,000 more, altogether disengaged and unoccupied. The consequence of such a movement must necessarily have been, that, menaced by the enemy's whole force, the Duke of Wellington might have relinquished thoughts of collecting his army in a post so much in advance as Quatre Bras ; but a concentration upon Waterloo would have been the obvious alternative ; and if the Emperor had advanced to that point and attacked the English without their receiving any assistance from the untouched army of the Prussians, we must suppose Blucher less active in behalf of his allies when at the head of an entire army, than he proved himself to be when commanding one which had sustained a recent defeat. In a word, if left unattacked, or masked only by a force inferior to their own, the Prussians were in a situation instantly to have become the assailants ; and, therefore, it seems that Bonaparte acted wisely in sending, in the first instance, the greater part of his army against that body of his enemies which had already combined its forces, while he might reasonably hope, that the divisions under Ney's command could dispose of the British troops as they came up to the field of battle wearied and in detail. In fact, his scheme had, in its material points, complete success, for Napoleon did defeat the Prussians ; and, by his success against them, compelled the English to retreat, and gained an opportunity of attacking them with his whole force in a battle, where the scale more than once inclined to his side. If, in the conjoined assault of the 16th, Ney failed in success over an enemy far inferior in numbers, it can only be accounted for by the superior talents of the English general, and the greater bravery of the soldiers whom he commanded. Something like a conscious feeling of this kind seems to lurk at the bottom of the maréchal's statement, who scarce pardons the Emperor for being successful upon a day on which he was himself defeated.

The manner in which Ney complains of being deprived of the assistance of the first brigade, held hitherto in reserve, between his right and the left wing of Napoleon, and withdrawn, as he alleges, to the assistance of the latter just when, on his side, " victory was not doubtful," savours of the same peevish criticism. Napoleon sent for these troops when their aid appeared essential to carry

the village of St. Amand, and thereby to turn the right flank of the Prussians, and he restored them to their original position the instant he perceived a possibility of carrying his point without them. Surely more could not have been expected in the circumstances. Of the tone the maréchal assumes to his fallen master, and the reproaches which he permits himself to cast upon him, I will only say, in the words of Wolsey,

" Within these forty hours Surrey had better
Have burned his tongue than said so."

Upon the other point of censure it is more difficult to give a satisfactory explanation. The French seem to have considered the Battle of Ligny as being of a character less decisive than complete victory, and a consciousness of the unbroken force of the retiring enemy certainly checked the vivacity of the pursuit. The French carried the positions of the Prussians with great slaughter ; but the precipitate retreat, and the numerous prisoners announced in Bonaparte's bulletin, are now universally allowed to be apocryphal. Blucher, whose open and frank avowal of the defeat he sustained claims credit for the rest of his narrative, assures us, that the Prussian army was again formed within a quarter of a league from the field of battle, and presented such a front to the enemy as deterred him from attempting a pursuit. We ought therefore to conclude, (paying always the necessary deference to Bonaparte's military skill,) that although the Prussians had been driven from their positions, yet their retreat must have been conducted with such order that no advantage would have resulted from pursuing them with a small force, while the necessity of making a movement with his main body to the left, in order to repair the disaster sustained by Ney, rendered it impossible for Napoleon to press upon their retreat with an overwhelming superiority of numbers.

These reflections, which I hazard in profound submission to your experience, close what occurs upon the important events of the 16th and 17th days of June last. Ever, my dear Major, &c.

PAUL.

LETTER VIII.

TO THE SAME.

BATTLE OF WATERLOO.

Field of Waterloo Described—Disposition of the British Forces—Valley between the Armies—Hougoumont—Position of the French Army—Dawn of the 18th—Preparations of the French—Communication between the British and Prussians—Commencement of the Battle—Spot where Bonaparte was posted—Advance of French Cavalry—Determination of the British Troops—First Attack of the French—Their partial Success—Defence of Hougoumont—Renewed attack upon it—Resistance of the Black Brunswickers—Formation of the Regiment into Squares—Attack upon Mount St. John—Inefficiency of Light Cavalry—Temporary Superiority of the French—Charge of the Heavy Brigade—Instance of Military Indifference—Feats of Personal Valour—Corporal Shaw—Sir John Elley—French Cavalry beaten off—Alarm at Brussels on the arrival of French Prisoners—Contest renewed on the Right Wing—Charges of French Cavalry—Courage of Indi-

THE field of battle at Waterloo is easily described. The forest of Soignies, a wood composed of
beech-trees, growing uncommonly close together, is
traversed by the road from Brussels, a long broad
causeway, which, upon issuing from the wood,
reaches the small village of Waterloo. Beyond
this point the wood assumes a more straggling
and dispersed appearance, until about a mile farther, where at an extended ridge, called the heights
of Mount St. John, from a farm-house situated
upon the Brussels road, the trees almost entirely
disappear, and the country becomes quite open.[1]
Along this eminence the British forces were disposed in two lines. The second, which lay behind
the brow of the hill, was, in some degree, sheltered from the enemy's fire. The first line, consisting
of the élite of the infantry, occupied the crest of
the ridge, and were on the left partly defended by
a long hedge and ditch, which, running in a straight
line from the hamlet of Mount St. John towards
the village of Ohain, gives name to two farm-
houses. The first, which is situated in advance of
the hedge, and at the bottom of the declivity, is
called La Haye Sainte (the holy hedge); the other,
placed at the extremity of the fence, is called Ter
la Haye. The ground at Ter la Haye becomes
woody and broken, so that it afforded a strong
point at which to terminate the British line upon
the left. A road runs from Ter la Haye to Ohain
and the woody passes of St. Lambert, through
which the Duke of Wellington kept up a communication by his left with the Prussian army. The
centre of the English army occupied the village of

Mount St. John, on the middle of the ridge, just
where the great causeway from Brussels divides
into two roads, one of which branches off to Nivelles, and the other continues the straight line to
Charleroi. A strong advanced post of Hanoverian
sharp-shooters occupied the house and farm-yard
of La Haye Sainte, situated in advance upon the
Charleroi road, and just at the bottom of the hill.
The right of the British army, extending along the
same eminence, occupied and protected the Nivelles
road as far as the enclosures of Hougoumont, and,
turning rather backwards, rested its extreme right
upon a deep ravine. Advanced posts from thence
occupied the village called Braine la Leude,[2] on
which point there was no engagement. The ground
in front of the British point sloped easily down into
lower ground, forming a sort of valley, not a level
plain, but a declivity varied by many gentle sweeps
and hollows, which, though quite dry, seem as if
formed by the course of a river. The ground then
ascends in the same manner to a ridge opposite to
that of Mount St. John, and running parallel to it
at the distance of twelve or fourteen hundred yards.
This was the position of the enemy. It is in some
points nearer, and in others more distant from the
heights, or ridge, of Mount St. John, according as
the valley between them is of greater or less breadth.
The valley between the two ridges is entirely
open and unenclosed, and on that memorable day
bore a tall and strong crop of corn. But in the
centre of the valley, about half way betwixt the
two ridges, and situated considerably to the right
of the English centre, was the Chateau de Gou-
mont, or Hougoumont. This is (or rather was) a
gentleman's house of the old Flemish architecture,
having a tower, and, as far as I can judge from its
ruins, a species of battlement. It was surrounded
on one side by a large farm-yard, and on the other
opened to a garden divided by alleys in the Dutch
taste, and fenced by a brick wall, and an exterior
hedge and ditch. The whole was encircled by an
open grove of tall trees, covering a space of about
three or four acres, without any underwood. This
chateau, with the advantages afforded by its wood
and gardens, formed a strong point d'appui to the
British right wing. In fact, while this point was
maintained, it must have been difficult for the
French to have made a serious attack upon the extremity of our right wing. On the other hand, had
they succeeded in carrying Hougoumont, our line
must have been confined to the heights, extending
towards Merke Braine, which rather recede from
the field, and would have been in consequence
much limited, and crowded in its movements. As
far as I understand the order of battle, the British
line upon this right wing at the commencement of
the action, rather presented the convex segment of
a circle to the enemy; but as repeated repulses
obliged the French to give ground, the extreme
right was thereby enabled to come gradually round,
and the curve being reversed, became concave, en-
filading the field of battle and the high-road from
Brussels to Charleroi, which intersects it.[3]

---

[1] "The wood of Soignies is supposed to be a remnant of
the forest of Ardennes, famous in Boiardo's 'Orlando,' and
immortal in Shakspeare's 'As You Like It.' It is also celebrated in Tacitus as being the spot of successful defence by
the Germans against the Roman encroachments."—BYRON.
[2] Or Braine the Free, to distinguish it from Braine le Compte,
or Braine belonging to the count.—S.
[3] "As a plain, Waterloo seems marked out for the scene

of some great action, though this may be mere imagination.
I have viewed with attention those of Platæa, Troy, Mantinea,
Leuctra, Chæronea, and Marathon; and the field around
Mont St. Jean and Hougoumont appears to want little but a
better cause, and that undefinable but impressive halo which
the lapse of ages throws around a consecrated spot, to vie in
interest with any or all of these, except, perhaps, the last mentioned."—BYRON.

Such was the position of the British army on this memorable morning. That of the French is less capable of distinct description. Their troops had bivouacked on the field, or occupied the villages behind the ridge of La Belle Alliance. Their general had the choice of his mode of attack upon the English position, a word which, in this case, can only be used in a general sense, as a situation for an order of battle, but not in any respect as denoting ground which was naturally strong, or easily defended.

The imperfect dawn of the 18th was attended by the same broken and tempestuous weather, by which the night had been distinguished. But the interval of rest, such as it was, had not been neglected by the British, who had gained time to clean their arms, distribute ammunition, and prepare every thing for the final shock of battle. Provisions had also been distributed to the troops, most of whom had thus the means of breakfasting with some comfort.

Early in the morning numerous bodies of French cavalry began to occupy all the ridge of La Belle Alliance, opposite to that of Mount St. John, and as our horse were held in readiness to encounter them, an engagement was expected between the cavalry of both armies, which our infantry supposed they would only view in the capacity of spectators. The desertion of a French officer of cuirassiers, attached to the party of Louis XVIII., conveyed other information; he assured Lord Hill, and subsequently the Duke of Wellington, that a general attack was intended, which would commence on our right by a combined force of infantry and cavalry.

In the meanwhile, the communication between our army and the Prussians by our left flank had been uninterrupted. An officer of engineers, who was despatched so early as four in the morning, accompanied Bulow's division, already on march to our assistance, struggling with the defiles of St. Lambert, through roads which were rendered worse and worse by every succeeding regiment and brigade of artillery. One sentiment, this gentleman assured me, seemed unanimous among the Prussians—an eager and enthusiastic desire to press forward to obtain their share of the glories and dangers of the day, and to revenge their losses upon the 16th. The common soldiers cheered him and his companion as they passed. "Keep your ground, brave English!" was the universal exclamation, in German, and in such broken English or French as they found to express themselves— "Only keep your ground till we come up!"—and they used every effort accordingly to get into the field. But the movement was a lateral one, made across a country naturally deep and broken, rendered more so by the late heavy rains; and, on the whole, so unfit for the passage of a large body of troops, with their cavalry, artillery, &c., that even these officers, well mounted as they were, and eager to make their report to the department from which they had been despatched, did not reach the field of battle till after eleven o'clock.

The engagement had already commenced. It is said Bonaparte fired the first gun with his own hand, which is at least doubtful. But it is certain that he was in full view of the field when the battle began, and remained upon it till no choice was left him but that of death or rapid flight. His first post

465

was a high wooden observatory, which had been constructed when a trigonometrical survey of the country was made by order of the King of the Netherlands some weeks before. But he afterwards removed to the high grounds in front of La Belle Alliance, and finally to the foot of the slope upon the road to Brussels. He was attended by his staff, and squadrons of service destined to protect his person. Soult, Ney, and other officers of distinction, commanded under him, but he issued all orders and received all reports in person.

The clouds of cavalry, which had mustered thicker and thicker upon the skirts of the horizon in the line of La Belle Alliance, began now to advance forward. One of our best and bravest officers confessed to me a momentary sinking of the heart when he looked round him, considered how small was the part of our force properly belonging to Britain, and recollected the disadvantageous and discouraging circumstances under which even our own soldiers laboured. A slight incident reassured him. An aid-de-camp galloped up, and, after delivering his instructions, cautioned the battalion of the Guards, along whom he rode, to reserve their fire till the enemy were within a short distance. "Never mind us," answered a veteran guards-man from the ranks,—"never mind us, sir; we know our duty." From that moment my gallant friend said, that he knew the hearts of the men were in the right trim, and that though they might leave their bodies on the spot, they would never forfeit their honour. A few minutes afterwards the unparalleled conflict began.

The first attack of the French, as had been announced by the royalist officer, was directed towards our right wing, embracing the post of Hougoumont and the high road to Nivelles. A glance at any plan of this ground will show, that occupying the latter with artillery, would have enabled the French to have pushed forward to the very centre of our line, especially if Hougoumont could have been carried about the same time.

Under the eye of Bonaparte himself, who was then stationed on the ridge to the left of La Belle Alliance, the combinations for the attack were made with great skill and rapidity, and so completely concealed from our troops by the nature of the ground, that just before it took place, the cavalry on our extreme right expected orders to advance against some squadrons which showed themselves, as in the act of deploying towards Braine la Leude. But the enemy's motions were directed towards a more vital point.

About half-past eleven o'clock, the whole of the French second corps d'armée, amounting to three divisions, each consisting of 10,000 men, commenced a most desperate attack upon the post of Hougoumont. It was defended by the light companies of the Guards, who were stationed in the chateau and the garden, partly in the wood, in conjunction with a corps of sharpshooters, chiefly Nassau troops. The defence was supported by the whole second brigade of Guards under Major-General Byng, placed on a rising ground in the rear, so as to preserve the power of reinforcing the garrison.

The first division of the French, commanded by Jerome Bonaparte, commenced the assault, which, after a short but violent struggle, terminated in their retreating with great loss. But the attack was almost instantly renewed with incredible fury by the second division, commanded by General Foy. The fury of their onset was such, that the sharpshooters of Nassau Ussingen, to whom the grove of Hougoumont had been confided, abandoned that part of the post, and the chateau itself must have been carried, but for the stubborn and desperate courage of that detachment of the Guards to whom the defence was intrusted. A French officer, followed by a few men, actually forced his way into the courtyard of the chateau, but all were there bayoneted. Colonel Macdonnell, the brother of our Highland Chief Glengarry, was obliged to fight hand to hand among the assailants, and was indebted to personal strength no less than courage for his success in the perilous duty of shutting the gates of the courtyard against the enemy. The Spanish general, Don Miguel Alava, and his aides-de-camp, exerted themselves to rally the scattered sharpshooters of Nassau, and Don Nicholas de Mennuisir was particularly distinguished by his activity. But they passed the right of our troops in great disorder, their faces and hands blackened with smoke and powder, and showing yet sterner signs of the conflict in which they had been engaged, and to the furies of which they seemed unwilling again to commit themselves. "What would the Spaniards have done," said a prince distinguished for his own personal spirit and courage, as well as for his experience in the Peninsular war,— "What would the Spaniards have done, Don Miguel, in a fire like that of Waterloo!"—"At least, sir," retorted the Castilian, "they would not, like some of your father's subjects, have fled without seeing their enemy!"—By the rout of these light troops, and the consequent occupation of the wood by the French, Hougoumont was, for great part of the action, completely an invested and besieged post, indebted for its security to the walls and deep and strong ditches with which the garden and orchard were surrounded, but much more to the valiant and indomitable spirits of those by whom these defences were maintained. The French have since asserted, that their ill success was in great measure owing to their ignorance that the exterior hedge of the orchard masked a strong and thick garden wall, so that those who surmounted the one obstacle were suddenly overwhelmed by the fire from this second defence. When, however, it is remembered that Bonaparte, who himself superintended the attack, had by his side a person born and bred within half a mile of the chateau, it seems very unlikely that he should have omitted to make himself acquainted with the local means of defence. It was currently reported, that, during the attack, the bailiff or steward of the proprietor fired more than once from the summit of the tower upon the British, by whom the court and garden were defended, and that he was at length discovered and shot. At any rate, the place was most furiously assailed from without, and as resolutely defended, the garrison firing through the holes which they knocked out in the garden walls, and through the hedge of the orchard; and the assailants making the most desperate attempts to carry the post, but in vain. About one o'clock the wood was regained by six companies of the Guards under Colonel Hepburn, superseding Lord Saltoun, who had hitherto commanded in the wood, while Colonels Woodford and Macdonnell directed the defence of

the buildings and garden. The attack of the Guards under Colonel Hepburn drove back Foy's division with immense loss, again occupied the wood, and reinforced the little garrison in the chateau.

Still, however, Hougoumont being in some degree insulated, and its defenders no longer in direct or undisturbed communication with the rest of the British army, the French cavalry were enabled to pour round it in great strength to the attack of the British right wing. The light troops, who were in advance of the British line, were driven in by the fury of this general charge, and the foreign cavalry, who ought to have supported them, gave way on all sides. The first forces who offered a steady resistance were the Black Brunswick infantry. They were drawn up in squares, as most of the British forces were, during this memorable action, each regiment forming a square by itself, not quite solid, but nearly so, the men being drawn up several files deep. The distance between these masses afforded space enough to draw up the battalions in line when they should be ordered to deploy, and the regiments were posted with reference to each other much like the alternate squares upon a chess-board. It was therefore impossible for a squadron of cavalry to push between two of these squares, without finding themselves at once assailed by a fire in front from that which was to the rear, and on both flanks from those betwixt which it had moved forward. Often and often during that day was the murderous experiment resorted to, and almost always with the same bad success.

Yet, although this order of battle possesses every efficient power of combination for defence against cavalry, its exterior is far from imposing. The men thus drawn up occupy the least possible space of ground, and a distinguished officer, who was destined to support the Brunswickers, informed me, that when he saw the furious onset of the French cavalry, with a noise and clamour that seemed to unsettle the firm earth over which they galloped, and beheld the small detached black masses which, separated from each other, stood each individually exposed to be overwhelmed by the torrent, he almost trembled for the event. But when the Brunswick troops opened their fire with coolness, readiness, and rapidity, the event seemed no longer doubtful. The artillery also, which was never in higher order, or more distinguished for excellent practice, made dreadful gaps in the squadrons of cavalry, and strewed the ground with men and horses, who were advancing to the charge. Still this was far from damping the courage of the French, who pressed on in defiance of every obstacle, and of the continued and immense slaughter which was made among their ranks. Or if the attack of the cavalry was suspended for a space, it was but to give room for the operation of their artillery, which, within the distance of one hundred and fifty yards, played upon so obvious a mark as our solid squares afforded with the most destructive effect. "One fire," said a general officer, whom I have already quoted, "struck down seven men of the square with whom I was for the moment; the next was less deadly—it only killed three." Yet under such a fire, and in full view of these clouds of cavalry, waiting like birds of prey to dash upon them where the slaughter should afford the slightest opening, did these gallant troops close their files over their dead and dying comrades, and resume with stern composure that compact array of battle which their discipline and experience taught them afforded the surest means of defence. After the most desperate efforts on the part of the French to push back our right wing, and particularly to establish themselves on the road to Nivelles, and after a defence on the part of the British which rendered these efforts totally unavailing, the battle slackened in some degree in this quarter, to rage with greater fury, if possible, towards the left and centre of the British line.

It was now upon the village of Mount St. John, and making use of the causeway or high-road between that hamlet and La Belle Alliance, that Bonaparte precipitated his columns, both of infantry and cavalry, under a tremendous fire of artillery, that was calculated to sweep every obstacle from their course. The ridge of the hill was upon this occasion very serviceable to the British, whose second line was posted behind it, and thus protected in some degree from the direct fire, though not from the showers of shells which were thrown on purpose to annoy the troops, whom the enemy with reason supposed to be thus sheltered. The first line derived some advantage from a straggling hedge, (the same which, as already mentioned, gives the name of La Haye Sainte to the farm,) extending along their centre and left, and partly masking it, though, so far from being strong enough to serve as an intrenchment or breastwork, it could be penetrated by cavalry in almost every direction. Such as it was, however, its line of defence, or rather the troops by whom it was occupied, struck awe into the assailants; and while they hesitated to advance to charge it, they were themselves in their turn charged and overwhelmed by the British cavalry, who, dashing through the fence at the intervals which admitted of it, formed, charged, and broke the battalions which were advancing upon their line. The French cavalry came up to support their infantry, and where the British were in the least dispersed, which, from the impetuosity of the men and horses, was frequently unavoidable, our troops suffered severely. This was particularly experienced by some distinguished regiments, whom the military fashion of the times has converted into hussars, from that excellent old English establishment formerly called Light-Dragoons, which combined with much activity a degree of weight that cannot belong to troopers more slightly mounted. You, who remember one or two of the picked regiments of 1795, cannot but recollect at once the sort of corps which is now in some degree superseded by those mounted on light blood horses. It is at least certain, that after the most undaunted exertions on the part of the officers, seconding those of the Earl of Uxbridge, our light cavalry were found to suffer cruelly in their unequal encounter with the ponderous and sword-proof cuirassiers, and with the lancers. In every instance (and there were but too many) in which our cavalry pushed temporary success too far, they were overpowered by the weight and numbers of the enemy, and driven back with great loss. Many were killed,

and several made prisoners, some of whom the French afterwards massacred in cold blood. Even the German Legion, so distinguished for discipline and courage during the Peninsular conflicts, were unequal, on this occasion, to sustain the shock of the French cavalry. And thus, such had been Bonaparte's dexterity in finding resources, and in applying them, the French seemed to have a temporary superiority in that very description of force, with which it was supposed altogether impossible he could be adequately provided. It was upon this occasion that Sir John Elley, now quarter-master-general, requested and obtained permission to bring up the heavy brigade, consisting of the Life Guards, the Oxford Blues, and Scotch Greys, and made a charge, the effect of which was tremendous. Notwithstanding the weight and armour of the cuirassiers, and the power of their horses, they proved altogether unable to withstand the shock of the heavy brigade, being literally rode down, both horse and man, while the strength of the British soldiers was no less pre-eminent when they mingled and fought hand to hand. Several hundreds of French were forced headlong over a sort of quarry or gravel pit, where they rolled a confused and undistinguishable mass of men and horses, exposed to a fire which, being poured closely into them, soon put a period to their struggles. Amidst the fury of the conflict, some traces occurred of military indifference which merit being recorded. The Life Guards, coming up in the rear of the 95th, which distinguished regiment acted as sharpshooters in front of the line, sustaining and repelling a most formidable onset of the French, called out to them, as if it had been on the parade in the Park, " Bravo, ninety-fifth! do you *lather* them and we'll *shave* them !" The Scottish *amor patriæ* also displayed itself on this occasion. The Scotch Greys coming up to the support of a Highland regiment, all joined in the triumphal shout of " Scotland for ever !"—Amid the confusion presented by the fiercest and closest cavalry fight which had ever been seen, many individuals distinguished themselves by feats of personal strength and valour. Among these should not be forgotten Shaw, a corporal of the Life Guards, well known as a pugilistic champion, and equally formidable as a swordsman. He is supposed to have slain or disabled ten Frenchmen with his own hand, before he was killed by a musket or pistol-shot.[1] But officers, also, of rank and distinction, whom the usual habits of modern war render rather the directors than the actual agents of slaughter, were in this desperate action seen fighting hand to hand like common soldiers. " You are uncommonly savage to-day," said an officer to his friend, a young man of rank, who was arming himself with a third sabre, after two had been broken in his grasp: " What would you have me do ?" answered the other, by nature one of the most gentle and humane men breathing; " we are here to kill the French, and he is the best man to-day who can kill most of them ;"—and he again threw himself into the midst of the combat. Sir John Elley, who led the charge of the heavy brigade, was himself distinguished for personal prowess.

[1] This brave man is said to have carried death to every one against whom he rode. His own was occasioned rather by the loss of blood from many cuts, than the magnitude of any one. He had been riding about fighting the whole of the day with his body streaming. At evening he stretched himself on the ground, close by a wounded comrade, and soon fell asleep. In the morning he was found dead, with his face leaning on his hand, as if life had been extinguished while he was in a state of insensibility.

He was at one time surrounded by several of the cuirassiers ; but, being a tall and uncommonly powerful man, completely master of his sword and horse, he cut his way out, leaving several of his assailants on the ground, marked with wounds, indicating the unusual strength of the arm which inflicted them. Indeed, had not the ghastly evidences remained on the field, many of the blows dealt upon this occasion would have seemed borrowed from the annals of knight-errantry, for several of the corpses exhibited heads cloven to the chine, or severed from the shoulders. The issue of this conflict was, that the French cavalry were completely beaten off, and a great proportion of their attacking columns of infantry, amounting to about 3000 men, threw down their arms, and were sent off to Brussels as prisoners. Their arrival there added to the terrors of that distracted city ; for a vague rumour having preceded their march, announcing the arrival of a column of French, they were for a long time expected as conquerors, not as prisoners. Even when they entered as captives, the sight of the procession did not relieve the terrors of the citizens ; the continued thunder of the cannon still announced that the battle was undecided, and the manner of the prisoners themselves was that of men who expected speedy freedom and vengeance. One officer of cuirassiers was particularly remarked for his fine martial appearance, and the smile of stern contempt with which he heard the shouts of the exulting populace. " The emperor," he said, " the *emperor* will shortly be here ;" and the menace of his frowning brow and clenched hand indicated the fatal consequences which would attend his arrival.

The contest was indeed so far from being decided, that it raged with the most uninterrupted fury ; it had paused in some degree upon the centre and left, but only to be renewed with double ferocity in the right wing. The attack was commenced by successive columns of cavalry, rolling after each other like waves of the sea. The Belgian horse, who were destined to oppose them, again gave way, and galloped from the field in great disorder. Our advanced line of guns was stormed by the French, the artillery-men receiving orders to leave them, and retire within the squares of the infantry. Thus, at least, thirty pieces of artillery were for the time abandoned ; but to an enemy who could not either use them or carry them off. The scene now assumed the most extraordinary and unparalleled appearance. The large bodies of French cavalry rode furiously up and down amongst our small squares of infantry, seeking with desperate courage some point where they might break in upon them, but in vain, though many in the attempt fell at the very point of the bayonets.

In the meantime, a brigade of horse-artillery, commanded by the lamented Major Norman Ramsay, opened its fire upon the columns. They retreated repeatedly, but it was only to advance with new fury, and to renew attempts which it seemed impossible for human strength and courage ultimately to withstand. As frequently as the cavalry retreated, our artillery-men, rushing out of the squares in which they had found shelter, began again to work their pieces, and made a destructive fire on the retiring squadrons. Two officers of artillery were particularly noticed, who, being in a square which was repeatedly charged, rushed out

of it the instant the cavalry retreated, loaded one of the deserted guns which stood near, and fired it upon the horsemen. A French officer observed that this manœuvre was repeated more than once, and cost his troop many lives. At the next retreat of his squadron, he stationed himself by the gun, waving his sword, as if defying the British officers again to approach it. He was instantly shot by a grenadier, but prevented, by his self-devotion, a considerable loss to his countrymen. Other French officers and men evinced the same desperate and devoted zeal in the cause which they had so rashly and unhappily espoused. One officer of rank, after leading his men as far as they would follow him towards one of the squares of infantry, found himself deserted by them, when the British fire opened, and instantly rode upon the bayonets, throwing open his arms as if to welcome the bullet which should bring him down. He was immediately shot, for the moment admitted of no alternative. On our part, the coolness of the soldiers was so striking as almost to appear miraculous. . Amid the infernal noise, hurry, and clamour of the bloodiest action ever fought, the officers were obeyed as if on the parade ; and such was the precision with which the men gave their fire, that the aid-de-camp could ride round each square with perfect safety, being sure that the discharge would be reserved till the precise moment when it ought regularly to be made. The fire was rolling or alternate, keeping up that constant and uninterrupted blaze, upon which, I presume, it is impossible to force a concentrated and effective charge of cavalry. Thus, each little phalanx stood by itself, like an impregnable fortress, while their crossing fires supported each other, and dealt destruction among the enemy, who frequently attempted to penetrate through the intervals, and to gain the flank, and even the rear of these detached masses. The Dutch, Hanoverian, and Brunswick troops, preserved the same solid order, and the same ready, sustained, and destructive fire, as the British regiments with whom they were intermingled.

Notwithstanding this well-supported and undaunted defence, the situation of our army became critical. The Duke of Wellington had placed his best troops in the first line ; they had already suffered severely, and the quality of those who were brought up to support them was in some instances found unequal to the task. He himself saw a Belgian regiment give way at the instant it crossed the ridge of the hill, in the act of advancing from the second into the first line. The Duke rode up to them in person, halted the regiment, and again formed it, intending to bring them into the fire himself. They accordingly shouted *En avant! en avant!* and, with much of the manner which they had acquired by serving with the French, marched up, dressing their ranks with great accuracy, and holding up their heads with military precision. But as soon as they crossed the ridge of the hill, and again encountered the storm of balls and shells, from which they had formerly retreated, they went to the right-about once more, and fairly left the Duke to seek more resolved followers where he could find them. He accordingly brought up a Brunswick regiment, which advanced with less apparent enthusiasm than *les Braves Belges*, but kept their ground with more steadiness, and behaved very well. In another part of the field, the Hanoverian hussars of Cumberland, as they were called, a corps distinguished for their handsome appearance and complete equipments, were ordered to support a charge made by the British. Their gallant commanding-officer showed no alacrity in obeying this order, and indeed observed so much ceremony, that, after having been once and again ordered to advance, an aid-de-camp of the Duke of Wellington informed him of his Grace's command, that he should either advance or draw off his men entirely, and not remain there to show a bad example and discourage others. The gallant officer of hussars, considering this as a serious option, submitted to his own decision, was not long in making his choice, and having expressed to the aid-de-camp his sense of the Duke's kindness, and of the consideration which he had for raw troops, under a fire of such unexampled severity, he said he would embrace the alternative of drawing his men off, and posting them behind the hamlet of Saint John. This he accordingly did, in spite of the reproaches of the aid-de-camp, who loaded him with every epithet that is most disgraceful to a soldier. The incident, although sufficiently mortifying in itself, and attended, as may be supposed, with no little inconvenience at such a moment, had something in it so comic, that neither the General nor any of his attendants were able to resist laughing when it was communicated by the incensed aid-de-camp. I have been told many of the officers and soldiers of this unlucky regiment left it in shame, joined themselves to other bodies of cavalry, and behaved well in the action. But the valiant commander, not finding himself comfortable in the place of refuge which he had himself chosen, fled to Brussels, and alarmed the town with a report that the French were at his heels. His regiment was afterwards in a manner disbanded, or attached to the service of the commissariat.

These circumstances I communicate to you, not in the least as reflecting upon the national character, either of the Hanoverians or Belgians, both of whom had troops in the field, by whom it was gloriously sustained ; but as an answer to those who have remarked, that the armies not being greatly disproportioned in point of numbers, the contest ought to have been sooner decided in favour of the Duke of Wellington. The truth is, that the Duke's first line *alone*, with occasional reinforcements from the second, sustained the whole brunt of the action ; and it would have been in the highest degree imprudent to have made any movement in advance even to secure advantages which were frequently gained, since implicit reliance could not be placed upon the raw troops and militia, of whom the support was chiefly composed. With 80,000 British troops, it is probable the battle would not have lasted two hours, though it is impossible it could in that event have been so entirely decisive, since the French, less completely exhausted, would probably have been able to take better measures for covering their retreat.

Meanwhile the battle raged in every point. The centre and left were again assaulted, and, if possible, more furiously than before. The farm-house of La Haye Sainte, lying under the centre of the British line, was at last stormed by the French troops, who put the gallant defenders to the sword.

They were Hanoverian sharpshooters, who had made good the post with the most undaunted courage, whilst they had a cartridge remaining, and afterwards maintained an unequal contest with their bayonets through the windows and embrazures. As the entrance of the farm fronted the high-road, and was in the very focus of the enemy's fire, it was impossible to send supplies of ammunition by that way ; and the commanding officer unfortunately had not presence of mind to make a breach through the back part of the wall, for the purpose of introducing them. "*I* ought to have thought of it," said the Duke of Wellington, who seems to have considered it as his duty to superintend and direct even the most minute details of that complicated action ; " but," as he added, with a very unnecessary apology, " my mind could not embrace every thing at once." The post meanwhile, though long maintained by the enemy, was of little use to them, as our artillery on the ridge were brought to plunge into it, and the attempt to defend it as a point of support for his future attacks, cost Bonaparte more men than he had lost in carrying it. On the right Hougoumont continued to be as fiercely assailed, but more successfully defended. The carnage in that point was dreadful ; the French at length had recourse to shells, by which they set on fire, first, a large stack of hay in the farm-yard, and then the chateau itself. Both continued to blaze high in the air, spreading a thick black smoke, which ascended far over that of the cannonade, and seemed to announce that some dreadful catastrophe had befallen the little garrison. Many of the wounded had been indeed carried into the chateau for shelter, and, horrible to relate, could not be withdrawn from it when it took fire. But the Guards continued to make good the garden and the courtyard, and the enemy's utmost efforts proved unable to dispossess them. The various repulses which the French had met with in this part of the field, seemed by degrees to render their efforts less furious, and the right wing re-established its complete communication with this *point d'appui*, or key of the position, and reinforced its defenders as occasion demanded.

During this scene of tumult and carnage, the Duke of Wellington exposed his person with a freedom which, while the position of the armies, and the nature of the ground, rendered it inevitably necessary, made all around him tremble for that life on which it was obvious that the fate of the battle depended. There was scarcely a square but he visited in person, encouraging the men by his presence, and the officers by his directions. Many of his short phrases are repeated by them, as if they were possessed of talismanic effect. While he stood on the centre of the high-road in front of Mount St. John, several guns were levelled against him, distinguished as he was by his suite, and the movements of the officers who came and went with orders. The balls repeatedly grazed a tree on the right-hand of the road, which tree now bears his name. " That's good practice," observed the Duke to one of his suite ; " I think they fire better than in Spain." Riding up to the 95th, when in front of the line, and even then expecting a formidable charge of cavalry, he said, " Stand fast, 95th—we must not be beat—what will they say in England ?"[1] On another occasion, when many of the

---

. " In action prompt, in sentence brief,—
' Soldiers, stand firm.' exclaim'd the Chief,
469

' England shall tell the fight !'
On came the whirlwind—like the last

best and bravest men had fallen, and the event of the action seemed doubtful even to those who remained, he said, with the coolness of a spectator, who was beholding some well-contested sport—" Never mind, we'll win this battle yet." To another regiment, then closely engaged, he used a common sporting expression ; " Hard pounding this, gentlemen ; let's see who will pound longest." All who heard him issue orders took confidence from his quick and decisive intellect; all who saw him caught mettle from his undaunted composure. His staff, who had shared so many glories and dangers by his side, fell man by man around him, yet seemed in their own agony only to regard his safety. Sir William De Lancey, struck by a spent ball, fell from his horse—"Leave me to die," he said to those who came to assist him, "attend to the Duke."[1] The lamented Sir Alexander Gordon,[2] whose early experience and high talents had already rendered him the object of so much hope and expectation, received his mortal wound while expostulating with the General on the personal danger to which he was exposing himself. Lieutenant-Colonel Canning, and many of our lost heroes, died with the Duke's name on their expiring lips. Amid the havoc which had been made among his immediate attendants, his Grace sent off a young gentleman, acting as aid-de-camp, to a general of brigade in another part of the field, with a message of importance. In returning he was shot through the lungs, but, as if supported by the resolution to do his duty, he rode up to the Duke of Wellington, delivered the answer to his message, and then dropped from his horse, to all appearance a dying man. In a word, if the most devoted attachment on the part of all who approached him, can add to the honours of a hero, never did a general receive so many and such affecting proofs of it; and their devotion was repaid by his sense of its value, and sorrow for their loss. "Believe me," he afterwards said, "that nothing, excepting a battle lost, can be half so melancholy as a battle won. The bravery of my troops has hitherto saved me from that greater evil; but, to win even such a battle as this of Waterloo, at the expense of the lives of so many gallant friends, could only be termed a heavy misfortune, were it not for its important results to the public benefit."[3]

In the meanwhile it seemed still doubtful whether these sacrifices had not been made in vain ; for the French, though repulsed in every point, continued their incessant attacks with a perseve-rance of which they were formerly deemed incapable ; and the line of chequered squares, hitherto successfully opposed to them, was gradually, from the great reduction of numbers, presenting a diminished and less formidable appearance. One general officer was under the necessity of stating, that his brigade was reduced to one-third of its numbers, that those who remained were exhausted with fatigue, and that a temporary relief, of however short duration, seemed a measure of peremptory necessity. "Tell him," said the Duke, "what he proposes is impossible. He, and I, and every Englishman in the field, must die on the spot which we now occupy."—"It is enough," returned the general ; "I, and every man under my command, are determined to share his fate." A friend of ours had the courage to ask the Duke of Wellington, whether in that conjuncture he looked often to the woods from which the Prussians were expected to issue?—"No," was the answer ; "I looked oftener at my watch than at any thing else. I knew if my troops could keep their position till night, that I must be joined by Blucher before morning, and we would not have left Bonaparte an army next day. But," continued he, "I own I was glad as one hour of daylight slipped away after another, and our position was still maintained."—"And if," continued the querist, "by misfortune the position had been carried?"—"We had the wood behind to retreat into."—"And if the wood also was forced?"—"No, no ; they could never have so beaten us but we could have made good the wood against them."— From this brief conversation it is evident, that in his opinion, whose judgment is least competent to challenge, even the retreat of the English on this awful day would have afforded but temporary success to Bonaparte.

While this furious conflict lasted, the Prussian general, with the faith and intrepidity which characterise him, was pressing forward to the assistance of his allies. So early as between three and four o'clock, the division of Bulow appeared menacing the right flank of the French, chiefly with light troops and cavalry. But this movement was foreseen and provided against by Bonaparte. Besides the immense force with which he sustained the main conflict, he had kept in reserve a large body of troops, under Count Lobau, who were opposed to those of Bulow with a promptitude which appeared like magic ; our officers being at a loss almost to conjecture whence the forces came, which

---

But fiercest sweep of tempest-blast—
On came the whirlwind—steel-gleams broke
Like lightning through the rolling smoke;
  The war was waked anew,
Three hundred cannon-mouths roar'd loud,
And from their throats, with flash and cloud,
  Their showers of iron threw.
Beneath their fire, in full career,
Rush'd on the ponderous cuirassier,
The lancer couch'd his ruthless spear,
And hurrying as to havoc near,
  The cohorts' eagles flew.
In one dark torrent, broad and strong,
The advancing onset roll'd along,
Forth harbinger'd by fierce acclaim,
That, from the shroud of smoke and flame,
Peal'd wildly the imperial name."
    SIR WALTER SCOTT'S *Poetical Works*, p. 502.

[1] This accomplished officer had been married in the April preceding, to the beautiful daughter of Sir James Hall of Dunglass, Bart. ; and the young lady reached the Netherlands in time to witness his death.

[2] Brother to the Earl of Aberdeen, who has erected a monument on the spot where he received his wound.
[3] " Period of honour as of woes,
  What bright careers 'twas thine to close ;—
  Mark'd on thy roll of blood what names
  To Britain's memory, and to Fame's,
  Laid there their last immortal claims !
  Thou saw'st in seas of gore expire
  Redoubted PICTON's soul of fire—
  Saw'st in the mingled carnage lie
  All that of PONSONBY could die—
  DE LANCEY change Love's bridal-wreath,
  For laurels from the hand of Death—
  Saw'st gallant MILLER's failing eye
  Still bent where Albion's banners fly,
  And CAMERON, in the shock of steel,
  Die like the offspring of Lochiel ;
  And generous GORDON, 'mid the strife,
  Fall while he watch'd his leader's life.—
  Ah! though her guardian angel's shield
  Fenced Britain's hero through the field,
  Fate not the less her power made known,
  Through his friends' hearts to pierce his own !"
    SIR WALTER SCOTT's *Poetical Works*, p. 505.

appeared as it were to rise out of the earth to oppose this new adversary. The engagement (which consisted chiefly in sharpshooting) continued in this quarter, but with no great energy, as the Prussian general waited the coming up of the main body of Blucher's army. This was retarded by many circumstances. We have already noticed the state of the cross-roads, or rather tracks, through which a numerous army had to accomplish their passage. But besides, the effects of the battle of Ligny were still felt, and it was not only natural but proper that Blucher, before involving himself in defiles from which retreat became impossible, should take some time to ascertain whether the English were able to maintain their ground until he should come up to their assistance. For, in the event of their being routed, with the usual circumstances of defeat, before the Prussians arrived, Blucher must have found himself in a most critical situation, engaged in the defiles of St. Lambert, with one victorious French army in front, and another pressing upon his rear at Wavre. Such at least is the opinion of our best and most judicious officers. But the loyalty of the Prince-Marshal's character did not permit him long to hesitate upon advancing to the support of his illustrious ally.

Grouchy and Vandamme, with their combined forces, amounting to upwards of thirty thousand men, had followed the Prussian rear (commanded by Tauenzein) as far as Wavre, less, it would seem with the purpose of actual fight, than of precipitating the retreat, which they supposed Blucher to have commenced with his whole army. At length Tauenzein halted upon the villages of Wavre and Bielge, on the river Dyle, and there prepared to defend himself. It is probable that, about this time, the appearance of Bulow's corps on Bonaparte's right flank made the French general desirous the Prussians should be attacked in a different and distant point, in such a serious manner as might effectually engage their attention, and prevent their detaching more forces to the support of Wellington. Accordingly orders were despatched to Grouchy to make a serious attack upon that part of the Prussian army which was opposed to him. But Bonaparte was not aware, nor does Grouchy seem to have discovered, that the forces he was thus to engage only consisted of a strong rear-guard, which occupied the villages and position upon the Dyle to mask the march of the main army under the Prince-Marshal himself, which was already defiling to the right through the passes of St. Lambert, and in full march to unite itself with Wellington and Bulow. The resistance of Tauenzein, however, was so obstinate as to confirm Grouchy in the belief that he was engaged with a great proportion of the Prussian army. The bridge at Wavre, particularly, was repeatedly lost and gained before the French were able to make their footing good beyond it. At length a French colonel snatched the eagle of his regiment, and rushing forward, crossed the bridge, and struck it into the ground on the other side. His corps followed with a unanimous shout of *Vive l'Empereur!* and although the gallant officer who thus led them on was himself slain on the spot, his followers succeeded in carrying the village. That of Bielge at the same time fell into their hands, and Grouchy anxiously expected from his Emperor orders to improve his success. But no such orders arrived; the sound of the cannon in

that direction slackened, and at length died away; and it was next morning before Grouchy heard the portentous news that awaited him, announcing the fate of Napoleon and his army.

The French have since pretended, that their defeat was, in a great measure, owing to Grouchy's neglecting to make a lateral movement to his own left to the support of Napoleon. They ascribe this to the rapacity of Vandamme, who is said to have urged Grouchy to continue his movement upon Brussels, rather than to unite himself with Bonaparte, in order that their division might have the first share of the pillage of the city. If, however, this division of the French army had not fought at Wavre, where, with difficulty, they defeated the Prussian rear-guard, it seems clear, that Tauenzein, who showed great generalship, would have become the assailant, upon their manifesting a purpose of closing up towards the army of Napoleon. In either case they would have had the same number of enemies to dispose of, and consequently would have had the same difficulty in rendering effectual assistance to Bonaparte in his last exigency. There is no doubt, however, that their remaining inactive on the other side of the Dyle annihilated Napoleon's last chance of succour.

Meantime Blucher pressed the march of his forces through the defiles which separated him and Wellington. Notwithstanding the consequences of his fall upon the 16th, the veteran insisted upon leaving his carriage and being placed on horseback, that he might expedite the march by precept and example. The sun was, however, near setting before his forces appeared in strength issuing from the woods upon the flank of the contending armies. It seems to have been one of Bonaparte's leading errors to miscalculate the moral force of the Prussian character, and especially that of Blucher. Though it was now obvious that the army of the Prince-Marshall was appearing on the field, Napoleon deluded himself to the last by a belief that they were followed by Grouchy, and either retreating, or moving laterally in the same line with him; a circumstance which countenances the report of those French officers who allege orders to this purpose had been sent to Grouchy, although that Marshal denied having ever received them. In this mistake Bonaparte obstinately persisted until the consequences proved fatal to the very last chance which he had of covering his own retreat. It was for some time supposed, that he mistook the Prussians for his own forces under Grouchy. This was not the case, nor was it possible it could be so. His real error was sufficient for his destruction, without exaggerating it into one that would indicate insanity. But, as appears from Maréchal Ney's letter, Bonaparte spread among the soldiers, by means of the unfortunate Labedoyere, his own belief that Grouchy was advancing to their support. He imagined, in short, that at the very worst, his own general had made a lateral movement corresponding to that of Blucher, and was as near to support as the other was to attack him. In this belief, all the slaughter and all the repulses of that bloody day did not prevent his risking a desperate and final effort.

Notwithstanding the perseverance with which Bonaparte had renewed his attacks upon the English position, and the vast number of his best cavalry and infantry who had fallen in the struggle, he had still in reserve nearly 15,000 men of his own guard, who, remaining on the ridge of La Belle Alliance, or behind it, had scarcely drawn a trigger during the action. But about seven o'clock at night their Emperor determined to devote' this proved and faithful reserve, as his last stake, to the chance of one of those desperate games in which he had been frequently successful. For this purpose he left the more distant point of observation, which he had for some time occupied upon the heights in the rear of the line, and descending from the hill, placed himself in the midst of the highway fronting Mount St. John, and within about a quarter of a mile of the English line. The banks, which rise high on each side, protected him from such balls as did not come in a direct line. In attaining this place of security, he incurred the only personal risk which he ran in the action. As they galloped towards the hollow way, a bullet struck off the pommel of an officer's saddle who was near him. Bonaparte coolly observed, " You must keep in the ravine." Here he caused his guards to defile before him, and acquainting them that the English cavalry and infantry were entirely destroyed, and that to carry their position they had only to sustain with bravery a heavy fire of their artillery, he concluded by pointing to the causeway, and exclaiming, " There, gentlemen, is the road to Brussels !" The prodigious shouts of _Vive l' Empereur,_ with which the Guard answered this appeal, led our troops, and the Duke of Wellington himself, to expect an instant renewal of the attack, with Napoleon as the leader. Many an eye was eagerly bent to the quarter from whence the clamour proceeded ; but the mist, as well as the clouds of smoke, rendered it impossible to see any object distinctly. None listened to the shout with more eager hope than our own Great General, who probably thought, like the Avenger in Shakspeare,

" There thou should'st be :
By this great clatter one of the greatest note
Seems bruited."——

All, indeed, expected an attack headed by Bonaparte in person ; and in failing upon this instant and final crisis to take the command of his Guards, whom he destined to try the last cast of his fortune, he disappointed both his friends and enemies.

The imperial Guard, however, rallying in their progress such of the broken cavalry and infantry of the line as yet maintained the combat, advanced dauntlessly. But the repeated repulses of the French had not been left unimproved by the British. The extreme right of the line, commanded by General Frederick Adam, under Lord Hill, had gradually, and almost imperceptibly gained ground after each unsuccessful charge, until the space between Hougoumont and Braine la Leude being completely cleared of the enemy, the British right wing, with its artillery and sharpshooters, was brought round from a convex to a concave position, so that our guns raked the French columns as soon as they debouched 'upon the causeway for their final attack. Our artillery had orders during the whole action to fire only upon the infantry and cavalry of the French, and not to waste their ammunition and energy in the less decisive exchange of shot with the French guns. The service of the artillery was upon this occasion so accurate, and at the same time so destructive, that the heads of the French attacking columns were enfiladed, and

in a manner annihilated, before they could advance upon the high-road. Those who witnessed the fire and its effects, describe it to me as if the enemy's columns kept perpetually advancing from the hollow way without ever gaining ground on the plain, so speedily were the files annihilated as they came into the line of the fire. Enthusiasm, however, joined to the impulse of those in the rear, who forced forward the front into the scene of danger, at length carried the whole attacking force into the plain. But their courage was obviously damped. They advanced, indeed, against every obstacle till they attained the ridge, where the British soldiers lay on the ground to avoid the destructive fire of artillery, by which the assault was covered : but this was their final effort. " Up, Guards, and at them," cried the Duke of Wellington, who was then with a brigade of the Guards. In an instant they sprung up, and, assuming the offensive, rushed upon the attacking columns with the bayonet. This body of the Guards had been previously disposed in line, instead of the squares which they had hitherto occupied. But the line was of unusual depth, consisting of four ranks instead of two. " You have stood cavalry in this order," said the General, " and can therefore find no difficulty in charging infantry." The effect of their three fatal cheers, and of the rapid advance which followed, was decisive. The Guards of Napoleon were within twenty yards of those of our Sovereign, but not one staid to cross bayonets with a British soldier. The consciousness that no support or reserve remained to them, added confusion to their retreat. This was observed by both generals with suitable emotion. The Duke of Wellington perceived the disorder of the French retreat, and the advance of the Prussians on their right flank, where they were already driving in all that was opposed to them. It was remarked that the sharpness and precision of the Duke's sight enabled him to mention both these circumstances two or three minutes before they could be discovered by the able officers around him. He immediately commanded the British troops to form line, and assume the offensive. The whole line formed four deep, and, supported by the cavalry and artillery, rushed down the slopes and up the corresponding bank, driving before them the flying French, whose confusion became each moment more irretrievable. The tirailleurs and cavalry, amounting to several regiments of the Imperial Guard, gallantly attempted to cover the retreat. They were charged by the British cavalry, and literally cut to pieces.

Bonaparte saw the issue of the fight with the same accuracy as the English General, but with far different feelings. He had shown the utmost coolness and indifference during the whole day, and while he praised the discipline and conduct of particular corps of the British army, whose gallantry he witnessed, he affected to lament their necessary and inevitable destruction. Even to reports which were incessantly brought to him of the increasing strength and progress of the Prussians upon his right flank, he turned an indifferent ear, bending his whole attention, and apparently resting his final hope, upon the success of the ultimate attack by the Imperial Guards. When he observed them recoil in disorder, the cavalry intermixed with the foot and trampling them down, he said to his aid-de-camp, " _Ils sont mêlés ensemble !_" then looked down, shook his head, and became, according to the expression of his guide, pale as a corpse. Immediately afterwards two large bodies of British cavalry appeared in rapid advance on each flank; and as the operations of the Prussians had extended along his right flank, and were rapidly gaining his rear, Bonaparte was in great danger of being made prisoner. He then pronounced to Bertrand, who was always by his side, the fatal words, " All is over, it is time to save ourselves,"[1] and left to their fate the army which that day had shed their blood for him with such profusion. His immediate attendants, about ten or twelve in number, scrambled along with him out of the hollow way, and gaining the open plain, all fled as fast as their horses could carry them, or the general confusion would admit, without a single attempt, on Bonaparte's part, to rally his army or cover their retreat. In one instance alone he displayed some spirit of the *fanfaronade* by which his conduct was frequently distinguished. In passing a battery of fourteen guns near to the observatory, he ordered that before they were deserted fourteen rounds should be fired from each;—as if in such a moment the precision of a review would be required from an army, to which he was himself setting the example of precipitate flight. Whatever may be thought of Bonaparte's behaviour on former occasions, it would appear, either that prosperity had clouded his energy of mind, or that he was in some degree wanting to himself on the conclusion of this memorable day. For, after having shown, during the progress of the battle, great judgment, composure, and presence of mind, the mode of his retreat was much less than honourable to a soldier, who had risen by personal courage and conduct to the greatest pitch of power that was ever enjoyed by an individual.

At half-past nine the fugitive arrived at Genappe, and experienced great difficulty in getting through the narrow street and over the bridge at that village, which was so encumbered with cannon and baggage-carts, that it was more than an hour ere he could obtain a free passage. From thence he pursued his flight, still upon the spur, to Quatre Bras, and from Quatre Bras to Gosselies, where he dismounted, and walked on foot to Charleroi. He stopped for the first time in a meadow beyond that town, and, for the first time that day, took some refreshment. In the course of his flight, he received from time to time the reports brought him by different officers, of the disastrous fate of the army which he had abandoned. From the neighbourhood of Charleroi he again resumed his rapid flight towards Paris.

Meanwhile the front attack of the English, and that of the Prussians upon the flank, met with slight opposition. Just as the English army had deployed into line for the general charge, the sun streamed out, as if to shed his setting glories upon the conquerors of that dreadful day. Fatigue and diminution of numbers, even wounds, were forgotten, when the animating command was given to assume the offensive. Headed by the Duke of Wellington himself, with his hat in his hand, the line advanced with the utmost spirit and rapidity. The fire of the enemy from one hundred and fifty pieces of artillery did not stop them for a single moment, and in a short time the French artillerymen deserted their guns, cut loose their traces, and mingled in the flight, now altogether confused and universal, the fugitives trampling down those who yet endeavoured to keep their ranks. The first line had hardly the vestige of military order when it was flung back on the second, and both became then united in one tide of general and undistinguished flight. Baggage-waggons, artillery-carts, guns overthrown, and all the impediments of a hurried flight, cumbered the open field as well as the causeway, without mentioning the thick-strewn corpses of the slain, and the bodies of the still more miserable wounded, who in vain shrieked and implored compassion, as fliers and pursuers drove headlong over them in the agony of fear or the ecstasy of triumph. All the guns which were in line along the French position, to the number of one hundred and fifty, fell into the immediate possession of the British. The last gun fired was a howitzer, which the French had left upon the road. It was turned upon their retreat, and discharged by Captain Campbell, aid-de-camp to General Adam, with his own hand, who had thus the honour of concluding the battle of Waterloo, which, it has been said, Bonaparte himself commenced.

There remained, however, for the unhappy fugitives, a flight and pursuit of no ordinary description. And here the timely junction of the Prussians was of the last consequence to the common cause of Europe. The British cavalry were completely wearied with the exertions of the day, and utterly incapable of following the chase. Even the horses of the officers were altogether unable to strike a trot for any length of way, so that the arrival of the Prussians, with all their cavalry fit for instant and rapid operation, and organized by so active a quarter-master-general as Gneisenau, was essential to gathering in the harvest, which was already dearly won and fairly reaped.

The march and advance of the Prussians crossed the van of the British army, after they had attacked the French position, about the farm-house of La Belle Alliance; and there, or near to that spot, the Duke of Wellington and Prince-Marshal Blucher met to congratulate each other upon their joint success, and its important consequences. The hamlet, which is said to have taken its name from a little circumstance of village scandal,[2] came to bear an unexpected and extraordinary coincidence with the situation of the combined armies, which inclines many foreigners even now to give the fight the name of the Battle of La Belle Alliance. Here, too, the victorious allies of both countries exchanged military greeting,—the Prussians halting their regimental bands to play " God save the King," while the British returned the compliment with three cheers to the honour of Prussia. The Prince-Marshal immediately gave orders that every man and horse in his army capable of action should press upon the rear of the fugitives, without giving them a moment's time to rally. The night was

---

1 " A présent c'est fini . . . Sauvons nous."—S.
2 A woman who resided here, after marrying two husbands in her own station of creditable yeomanry, chose to unite herself, upon her becoming a second time a widow, to her own hind or ploughman; and the name of La Belle Alliance was bestowed on her place of residence in ridicule of this match. —S.

illuminated by a bright moon, so that the fliers found no refuge, and experienced as little mercy.

To the last, indeed, the French had forfeited all claim ; for their cruelty towards the Prussians taken upon the 16th, and towards the British wounded and prisoners made during the battle of the 18th, was such as to exclude them from the benefit of the ordinary rules of war. Their lancers, in particular, rode over the field during the action, despatching with their weapons the wounded British, with the most inveterate rancour ; and many of the officers who have recovered from the wounds they received on that glorious day, sustained the greatest danger and most lasting inconvenience from such as were inflicted by those savages, when they were in no condition either to offend others or to defend themselves. The *Quoi ! tu n'es pas mort ?* of the spearman, was usually accompanied with a thrust of his lance, dealt with an inveteracy which gives great countenance to the general opinion, that their orders were to give no quarter. Even the British officers who were carried before Bonaparte, although civilly treated while he spoke to them, and dismissed with assurances that they should have surgical assistance and proper attendance, were no sooner out of his presence than they were stripped, beaten, and abused. Most of the prisoners whom the French took from our light cavalry were put to death in cold blood, or owed their safety to concealment or a speedy escape. In short, it seemed as if the French army, when they commenced this desperate game, had, like Bucaniers setting forth upon a cruise, renounced the common rules of war, and bonds of social amity, and become ambitious of distinguishing themselves as enemies to the human species. This unnatural hatred, rashly announced and cruelly acted upon, was as fearfully avenged. The Prussians listened not, and they had no reason to listen, to cries for mercy from those who had thus abused their momentary advantages over themselves and their allies ; and their light horse, always formidable on such occasions, made a fearful and indiscriminate slaughter, scarce interrupted even by the temptation of plundering the baggage with which the roads were choked, and unchecked by an attempt at résistance. Those soldiers who had begun the morning with such hopes, and whose conduct during the battle vindicated their having done so, were now so broken in heart and spirits, that scores of them fled at sight of a single Prussian hussar.

Yet it is remarkable that, amid the countless number who fell, both of privates and officers, we do not notice many of those names distinguished in the bulletins of Bonaparte's former campaigns. Whether the marshals, doubting the success of their old master, hazarded themselves less frankly in his cause, or did so with better fortune than belonged to our distinguished and undaunted Picton, Ponsonby, and other officers of high rank, whose loss we lament, it is not for me to conjecture. But, except Duhesme and Friant, neither of whose names was very much distinguished, we hear of no general officers among the French list of the slain. The latter was killed by a ball close to the turncoat Ney, who commanded the imperial guards in the last attack. The death of Duhesme had something in it which was Homeric. He was overtaken in the village of Genappe by one of the Duke of Brunswick's black hussars, of whom he

474

begged quarter. The soldier regarded him sternly, with his sabre uplifted, and then briefly saying, " The Duke of Brunswick died yesterday," bestowed on him his death's wound.

Κάτθαν καὶ Πάτροκλος, ὅπερ σίο πολλὸν ἀμείνων.

General Cambrone was said also to have fallen after refusing quarter, and announcing to the British, by whom it was offered, " The Imperial Guard can die, but never surrender." The speech and the devotion of the general received honourable mention in the Minutes of the Chamber of Representatives. But the passage was ordered to be erased next day, it being discovered that General Cambrone was a prisoner in Lord Wellington's camp.

The French retreat was utter rout and confusion, the men deserting their officers, the officers the men, all discipline neglected, and every thing thrown away which could for a moment impede the rapidity of their panic flight. A slight attempt was made to halt at the village of Genappe, but there, and at Charleroi, and wherever else the terrified fugitives attempted to pause, a cannon-shot or two, or the mere sound of a Prussian drum or trumpet, was sufficient to put them again to the rout.

The English remained on the field of battle and the villages adjacent. Be it not forgotten, that, after such attention to their wounded companions, as the moment permitted, they carried their succours to the disabled French, without deigning to remember that the defenceless and groaning wretches who encumbered the field of battle in heaps, were the same men who had displayed the most relentless cruelty on every temporary advantage which they obtained during this brief campaign. They erected huts over them to protect them from the weather, brought them water, and shared with them their refreshments—showing in this the upright nobleness of their own dispositions, and giving the most vivid testimony of their deserving that victory with which Providence had crowned them —a victory as unparalleled in its consequences, as the battle itself was in its length, obstinacy, and importance. Adieu ! my dear Major. Excuse a long letter, which contains much which you may have heard better told, mixed with some things with which you are probably not yet acquainted. The details which I have ventured to put into writing, are most of them from the authority of officers high in command upon that memorable day, and I may therefore be allowed to hope that even repetitions will be pardoned, for the sake of giving more authenticity to the facts which I have narrated. Yours, &c.

PAUL.

LETTER IX.

PAUL TO HIS SISTER MARGARET.

English Visitors to Waterloo—De Coster, Bonaparte's Guide—Appearance of the Field of Battle —Livrets of the French Soldiers—German Prayerbooks—Letters—Gentle Shepherd—Quack Advertisements—Crops trampled down—Houses and Hamlets ruinous—Claim of Damages—Hougoumont—Relics taken by Visitors—Number Slain in the Battle—Plunder obtained by the Peasants —Sale of Relics of the Battle—MS. of French

Songs—Romance of Dunois—The Troubadour—
Cupid's Choice—Reflections suggested by these
Poems—Chanson—Romance de Troubadour—
Chanson de la Folie.

I SHOULD now, my dear sister, give you some description of the celebrated field of Waterloo. But although I visited it with unusual advantages, it is necessary that I should recollect how many descriptions have already appeared of this celebrated scene of the greatest event of modern times, and that I must not weary your patience with a twice-told tale. Such and so numerous have been the visits of English families and tourists, as to enrich the peasants of the vicinity by the consequences of an event which menaced them with total ruin. The good old Flemish housewife, who keeps the principal cabaret at Waterloo, even when I was there, had learnt the value of her situation, and charged three prices for our coffee, because she could gratify us by showing the very bed in which the *Grand Lord* slept the night preceding the action.[1] To what extremities she may have since proceeded in taxing English curiosity, it is difficult to conjecture. To say truth, the honest Flemings were at first altogether at a loss to comprehend the eagerness and enthusiasm by which their English visitors were influenced in their pilgrimages to this classic spot. Their country has been long the scene of military operations, in which the inhabitants themselves have seldom felt much personal interest. With them a battle fought and won is a battle forgotten, and the peasant resumes his ordinary labours after the armies have left his district, with as little interest in recollecting the conflict, as if it had been a thunder-storm which had passed away. You may conceive, therefore, the great surprise with which these honest pococurantes viewed the number of British travellers of every possible description who hastened to visit the field of Waterloo.

I was early in making my pilgrimage, yet there were half a dozen of parties upon the ground at the same time with that to which I belonged. Honest John de Coster, the Flemish peasant, whom Bonaparte has made immortal by pressing into his service as a guide, was the person in most general request, and he repeated with great accuracy the same simple tale to all who desired to hear him. I questioned him long and particularly, but I cannot pretend to have extracted any information in addition to what has been long ago very accurately published in the newspapers. For I presume you would be little interested in knowing, that, upon this memorable occasion, the ex-emperor rode a dappled horse, and wore a grey surtout with a green uniform coat; and, in memory of his party's badge, as I suppose, a violet-coloured waistcoat, and pantaloons of the same. It was, however, with no little emotion that I walked with De Coster from one place to another, making him show me, as nearly as possible, the precise stations which had been successively occupied by the fallen Monarch on

that eventful day. The first was at the farm of Rossum, near to that of La Belle Alliance, from which he had witnessed the unsuccessful attack upon Hougoumont. He remained there till about four o'clock, and then removed into the cottage of De Coster, where he continued until he descended into the ravine or hollow way. There was a deep and inexpressible feeling of awe in the reflection, that the last of these positions was the identical place from which he, who had so long held the highest place in Europe, beheld his hopes crushed and his power destroyed. To recollect, that within a short month, the man whose name had been the terror of Europe, stood on the very ground which I now occupied—that right opposite was placed that commander whom the event of the day hailed *Vainqueur du Vainqueur de la terre*—that the landscape, now solitary and peaceful around me, presented so lately a scene of such horrid magnificence—that the very individual who was now at my side, had then stood by that of Napoleon, and witnessed every change in his countenance, from hope to anxiety, from anxiety to fear and to despair,—to recollect all this, oppressed me with sensations which I find it impossible to describe. The scene seemed to have shifted so rapidly, that even while I stood on the very stage where it was exhibited, I felt an inclination to doubt the reality of what had passed.

De Coster himself seems a sensible, shrewd peasant. He complained that the curiosity of the visitors who came to hear his tale, interfered a good deal with his ordinary and necessary occupations: I advised him to make each party, who insisted upon seeing and questioning him, a regular charge of five francs, and assured him that if he did so, he would find that Bonaparte had kept his promise of making his fortune, though in a way he neither wished nor intended. Père de Coster said he was obliged to me for the hint, and I dare say has not failed to profit by it.[2]

The field of battle plainly told the history of the fight, as soon as the positions of the hostile armies were pointed out. The extent was so limited, and the interval between them so easily seen and commanded, that the various manœuvres could be traced with the eye upon the field itself, as upon a military plan of a foot square. All ghastly remains of the carnage had been either burned or buried, and the relics of the fray which yet remained were not in themselves of a very imposing kind. Bones of horses, quantities of old hats, rags of clothes, scraps of leather, and fragments of books and papers, strewed the ground in great profusion, especially where the action had been most bloody. Among the last, those of most frequent occurrence were the military *lirrets*, or memorandum-books of the French soldiers. I picked up one of these, which shows, by its order and arrangement, the strict discipline which at one time was maintained in the French army, when the soldier was obliged to enter in such an account-book, not only the state of

---

[1] The Duke of Wellington's cook, a Frenchman, who had been with him during most of the Peninsular campaigns, exhibited, on the 18th of June, a confidence in his Grace's fortune, which ought to be recorded. While the battle was raging, successive fugitives, in passing the little *auberge* in the village of Waterloo, where this man was busy in his vocation, gave him impatient warning that he had better pack up and secure his retreat, for that assuredly his master would want no dinner at Waterloo that day. The cook's answer
475

was always, "*Monseigneur n'a rien dit.*" He continued to work among his pots and pans as usual, and the Duke found an excellent dinner, of thirty covers, ready when he reached, late in the evening, the humble roof where he had fixed his headquarters.

[2] A very minute narrative of Bonaparte's conduct during the whole day, taken down from the mouth of this peasant, forms a curious article in the Appendix.—S.

his pay and equipments, but the occasions on which he served and distinguished himself, and the punishments, if any, which he had incurred. At the conclusion is a list of the duties of the private soldier, amongst which is that of knowing how to dress his victuals, and particularly to make good soup. The *livret* in my possession appears to have belonged to the Sieur Mallet, of the 2d battalion of the 8th regiment of the line: he had been in the service since the year 1791, until the 18th of June, 1815, which day probably closed his account, and with it all his earthly hopes and prospects. The fragments of German prayer-books were so numerous, that I have little doubt a large edition had been pressed into the military service of one or other party, to be used as cartridge-paper. Letters, and other papers, memorandums of business, or pledges of friendship and affection, lay scattered about on the field—few of them were now legible. A friend picked up a copy of *The Gentle Shepherd*, where the Scotch regiments had been stationed; a circumstance which appeals strongly to our national feeling, from the contrast between the rustic scenes of the pastoral and that in which the owner of the volume had probably fallen. Quack advertisements were also to be found where English soldiers had fallen. Among the universal remedies announced by these empirics, there was none against the dangers of such a field.

Besides these fragments, the surface of the field showed evident marks of the battle. The tall crops of maize and rye[1] were trampled into a thick black paste, under the feet of men and horses—the ground was torn in many places by the explosion of shells, and in others strangely broken up and rutted by the wheels of the artillery. Such signs of violent and rapid motion recorded, that

Rank rush'd on rank, with squadron squadron closed,
The thunder ceased not, nor the fire reposed.

Yet, abstracting from our actual knowledge of the dreadful cause of such appearances, they reminded me not a little of those which are seen upon a common a few days after a great fair has been held there. These transitory memorials were in a rapid course of disappearing, for the plough was already at work in several parts of the field. There is, perhaps, more feeling than wisdom in the wish, yet I own I should have been better pleased, if, for one season at least, the field where, in imagination, the ploughshare was coming in frequent contact with the corpses of the gallant dead, had been suffered to remain fallow. But the corn which must soon wave there will be itself a temporary protection to their humble graves, while it will speedily remove from the face of nature the melancholy traces of the strife of man.

The houses and hamlets which were exposed to the line of fire have of course suffered very much, being perforated by cannon-balls in every direction. This was particularly the case at La Haye Sainte. The inhabitants of these peaceful cottages might then exclaim, in the words of our admired friend,—

" Around them, in them, the loud battle clangs:
  Within our very walls fierce spearmen push,
  And weapon'd warriors cross their clashing blades.
  Ah, woe is me! our warm and cheerful hearths,
  And rushed floors, whereon our children play'd,
  Are now the bloody lair of dying men!"[2]

There was not, indeed, a cottage in the vicinity but what, ere the eve of the fight, was crowded with the wounded, many of whom had only strength to creep to the next place of cover, that they might lay them down to die.

The village of Saint John, and others within the English position, had escaped with the demolition of the windows, and the breaches of the walls from without. The hamlets lying on the opposite heights, within the French line of bivouac, having been plundered to the bare walls, had sustained internal as well as external damage. Among other claims upon English generosity, and which may serve to illustrate the idea which foreigners have formed of its illimitable extent, one was made by a proprietor of this district for a considerable sum, stated to be the damage which his property had sustained in and through the battle of Waterloo. He was asked, why he thought a claim so unprecedented in the usual course of warfare would be listened to. He replied, that he understood the British had made compensation in Spain to sufferers under similar circumstances. It was next pointed out to him that no English soldier had or could have been accessary to the damage which he had sustained, since the hamlets and houses plundered lay within Bonaparte's position. The Fleming, without having studied at Leyden, understood the doctrine of consequential damages. He could not see that the circumstance alleged made much difference, since he argued, if the English had not obstinately placed themselves in the way, the French would have marched quietly on to Brussels, without doing him any material damage; and it was not until he was positively informed that his demand would not be granted that he remained silenced, but not satisfied.

Hougoumont (a name bestowed, I believe, by a mistake of our great commander, but which will certainly supersede the more proper one of Chateau-Goumont) is the only place of consideration which was totally destroyed. The shattered and blackened ruins of this little chateau remain among the wreck of its garden, while the fruit-trees, half torn

---

1   " But other harvest here,
Than that which peasant's scythe demands,
Was gather'd in by sterner hands,
     With bayonet, blade, and spear.
No vulgar crop was theirs to reap,
No stunted harvest thin and cheap!
Heroes before each fatal sweep
     Fell thick as ripen'd grain:
And ere the darkening of the day,
Piled high as autumn shocks, there lay
The ghastly harvest of the fray,
     The corpses of the slain.

" Ay, look again—that line so black
And trampled, marks the bivouack,
Yon deep-graved ruts the artillery's track,
     So often lost and won;

And close beside, the harden'd mud
Still shows where, fetlock-deep in blood,
The fierce dragoon, through battle's flood,
     Dash'd the hot war-horse on.
These spots of excavation tell
The ravage of the bursting shell—
And feel'st thou not the tainted steam
That reeks against the sultry beam,
     From yonder trenched mound?
The pestilential fumes declare
That Carnage has replenish'd there
     Her garner-house profound."
          Sir WALTER SCOTT'S *Poetical Works*, p. 501.

2 Joanna Baillie's *Ethwald*, a Tragedy, *Part Second*

down, half fastened to the walls, give some idea of the Dutch neatness with which it had been kept ere the storm of war approached it. The garden wall being secured by a strong high hedge, it is supposed the French continued the attack for some time before they were aware of the great strength of their defences. Yet it is strange that Bonaparte, who witnessed the assault, never asked De Coster, who stood at his elbow, in what manner the garden was enclosed.

The wall was all loop-holed for the use of musketry, and the defenders also maintained a fire from scaffolds, which enabled them to level their guns. Most visitors bought peaches, and gathered hazelnuts and filberts in the garden, with the pious purpose of planting, when they returned to England, trees, which might remind them and their posterity of this remarkable spot. The grove of trees around Hougoumont was shattered by grape-shot and musketry in a most extraordinary manner. I counted the marks upon one which had been struck in twenty different places, and I think there was scarce any one which had totally escaped. I understand the gentleman to whom this ravaged domain belongs is to receive full compensation from the government of the Netherlands.

I must not omit to mention, that, notwithstanding the care which had been bestowed in burying or burning the dead, the stench in several places of the field, and particularly at La Haye Sainte and Hougoumont, was such as to indicate that the former operation had been but hastily and imperfectly performed. It was impossible, of course, to attempt to ascertain the numbers of the slain; but, including those who fell on both sides before the retreat commenced, the sum of forty thousand will probably be found considerably within the mark, and I have seen officers of experience who compute it much higher. When it is considered, therefore, that so many human corpses, besides those of many thousand horses, were piled upon a field scarcely two miles long, and not above half a mile in breadth, it is wonderful that a pestilential disease has not broken out, to sum up the horrors of the campaign.

If the peasants in the neighbourhood of Waterloo suffered great alarm and considerable damage in the course of this tremendous conflict, it must be acknowledged they had peculiar and ample means of indemnification. They had, in the first place, the greatest share of the spoils of the field of battle, for our soldiers were too much exhausted to anticipate them in this particular. Many country people were at once enriched by the plunder of the French baggage, and not a few by that of the British, which, having been ordered to retreat during the action, became embarrassed on the narrow causeway leading through the great forest of Soignies, and was there fairly sacked and pillaged by the runaway Belgians and the peasantry; a disgraceful scene, which nothing but the brilliancy of the great victory, and the consequent enthusiasm of joy, could have allowed to be passed over without strict inquiry. Many of our officers, and some but ill able to afford such a loss, were in this manner deprived of all their clothes and baggage at the moment of their advance into the territories of France. The servants of the officers themselves were sometimes accessary to this pillage; and it is said, that one of these fugitive domestics, with the address of one of

Molière's servants, or Terence's slaves, had the art to extract from his master's parents a sum of money, which he pretended to have laid out upon his funeral, before they had received tidings that the pretended defunct had escaped the slaughter.

A more innocent source of profit has opened to many of the poor people about Waterloo, by the sale of such trinkets and arms as they collect daily from the field of battle; things of no intrinsic value, but upon which curiosity sets a daily increasing estimate. These memorials, like the books of the Sibyls, rise in value as they decrease in number. Almost every hamlet opens a mart of them as soon as English visitors appear. Men, women, and children rushed out upon us, holding up swords, pistols, carabines, and holsters, all of which were sold when I was there à prix juste, at least to those who knew how to drive a bargain. I saw a tolerably good carabine bought for five francs; to be sure there went many words to the bargain, for the old woman to whom it belonged had the conscience at first to ask a gold Napoleon for it, being about the value it would have borne in Birmingham. Crosses of the Legion of Honour were in great request, and already stood high in the market. I bought one of the ordinary sort for forty francs. The eagles which the French soldiers wore in front of their caps, especially the more solid ornament of that description which belonged to the Imperial Guards, were sought after, but might be had for a few sous. But the great object of ambition was to possess the armour of a cuirassier, which at first might have been bought in great quantity, almost all the wearers having fallen in that bloody battle. The victors had, indeed, carried off some of these cuirasses to serve as culinary utensils, and I myself have seen the Highlanders frying their rations of beef or mutton upon the breast-plates and back-pieces of their discomfited adversaries. But enough remained to make the fortunes of the people of St. John, Waterloo, Planchenoit, &c. When I was at La Belle Alliance I bought the cuirass of a common soldier for about six francs; but a very handsome inlaid one, once the property of a French officer of distinction, which was for sale in Brussels, cost me four times the sum. As for the casques or head-pieces, which, by the way, are remarkably handsome, they are almost introuvable, for the peasants immediately sold them to be beat out for old copper, and the purchasers, needlessly afraid of their being reclaimed, destroyed them as fast as possible.

The eagerness with which we entered into these negotiations, and still more the zeal with which we picked up every trifle we could find upon the field, rather scandalized one of the heroes of the day, who did me the favour to guide me over the field of battle, and who considered the interest I took in things which he was accustomed to see scattered as mere trumpery upon many a field of victory, with a feeling that I believe made him for the moment heartily ashamed of his company. I was obliged to remind him that as he had himself gathered laurels on the same spot, he should have sympathy, or patience at least, with our more humble harvest of peach-stones, filberts and trinkets. Fortunately the enthusiasm of a visitor, who went a bow-shot beyond us, by carrying off a brick from the house of La Belle Alliance, with that of a more wholesale amateur, who actually purchased the door of the said mansion for two gold Napoleons, a little mitigated my military friend's censure of our folly, by showing it was possible to exceed it. I own I was myself somewhat curious respecting the use which could be made of the door of La Belle Alliance, unless upon a speculation of cutting it up into trinkets, like Shakspeare's mulberry-tree.

A relic of greater moral interest was given me by a lady, whose father had found it upon the field of battle. It is a manuscript collection of French songs, bearing stains of clay and blood, which probably indicate the fate of the proprietor. One or two of these romances I thought pretty, and have since had an opportunity of having them translated into English, by meeting at Paris with one of our Scottish men of rhyme.

ROMANCE OF DUNOIS.

It was Dunois, the young and brave, was bound for Palestine,
But first he made his orisons before Saint Mary's shrine:
' And grant, immortal Queen of Heaven," was still the sol-
   dier's prayer,
' That I may prove the bravest knight, and love the fairest
   fair."

His oath of honour on the shrine he graved it with his sword,
And follow'd to the Holy Land the banner of his Lord;
Where, faithful to his noble vow, his war-cry fill'd the air,—
' Be honour'd aye the bravest knight, beloved the fairest fair."

They owed the conquest to his arm, and then his liege-lord said,
" The heart that has for honour beat by bliss must be repaid,—
My daughter Isabel and thou shall be a wedded pair,
For thou art bravest of the brave, she fairest of the fair."

And then they bound the holy knot before Saint Mary's shrine,
That makes a paradise on earth if hearts and hands combine;
And every lord and lady bright that were in chapel there,
Cried, " Honour'd be the bravest knight, beloved the fairest
   fair!"

THE TROUBADOUR.

Glowing with love, on fire for fame,
A Troubadour that hated sorrow,
Beneath his lady's window came,
   And thus he sung his last good-morrow:
" My arm it is my country's right,
   My heart is in my true love's bower;
Gaily for love and fame to fight
   Befits the gallant Troubadour."

And while he march'd with helm on head
   And harp in hand, the descant rung,
As, faithful to his favourite maid,
   The minstrel-burden still he sung ·
" My arm it is my country's right,
   My heart is in my lady's bower;
Resolved for love and fame to fight,
   I come, a gallant Troubadour."

Even when the battle-roar was deep,
   With dauntless heart he hew'd his way,
'Mid splintering lance and falchion-sweep,
   And still was heard his warrior-lay:
" My life it is my country's right,
   My heart is in my lady's bower;
For love to die, for fame to fight,
   Becomes the valiant Troubadour."

Alas! upon the bloody field
   He fell beneath the foeman's glaive,
But still, reclining on his shield,
   Expiring sung the exulting stave:—
" My life it is my country's right,
   My heart is in my lady's bower;
For love and fame to fall in fight
   Becomes the valiant Troubadour."

The tone of these two romances chimes in not unhappily with the circumstances in which the manuscript was found, although I do not pretend to have discovered the real effusions of a military bard, since the first of them, to my certain knowledge, and I have no doubt the other also, is a common and popular song in France.[1] The following Anacreontic is somewhat of a different kind, and less connected with the tone of feeling excited by the recollection, that the manuscript in which it occurs was the relic of a field of battle:—

It chanced that Cupid on a season,
   By Fancy urged, resolved to wed,
But could not settle whether Reason
   Or Folly should partake his bed.

What does he then?—Upon my life,
   'Twas bad example for a deity—
He takes me Reason for his wife,
   And Folly for his hours of gaiety.

Though thus he dealt in petty treason,
   He loved them both in equal measure;
Fidelity was born of Reason,
   And Folly brought to bed of Pleasure.

There is another verse of this last song, but so much defaced by stains, and disfigured by indifferent orthography, as to be unintelligible. The little collection contains several other ditties, but rather partaking too much of the freedom of the corps de garde, to be worthy the trouble of transcription or translation.

I have taken more pains respecting these poems than their intrinsic poetical merit can be supposed to deserve, either in the original or the English version; but I cannot divide them from the interest which they have acquired by the place and manner in which they were obtained, and therefore account them more precious than any other of the remains of Waterloo which have fallen into my possession.

Had these relics of minstrelsy, or any thing corresponding to them in tone and spirit, been preserved as actual trophies of the fields of Cressy and Agincourt, how many gay visions of knights and squires and troubadours, and *sirventes* and *lais*, and courts of Love and usages of antique chivalry, would the perusal have excited! Now, and brought close to our own times, they can only be considered as the stock in trade of the master of a regimental band; or at best, we may suppose the compilation to have been the pastime of some young and gay French officer, who, little caring about the real merits of the quarrel in which he was engaged, considered the war, by which the fate of Europe was to be decided, only as a natural and animating exchange for the pleasures of Paris. Still the gallantry and levity of the poetry compels us to contrast its destined purpose, to cheer hours of mirth or of leisure, with the place in which the manuscript was found, trampled down in the blood of the writer, and flung away by the hands of the spoilers, who had stripped him on the field of battle. I will not, however, trouble you with any further translations at present; only, to do justice to my gallant Troubadour, I will subjoin the original French in the postscript to this letter. It is a task of some difficulty; for accurate orthography was not a quality of the original writer, and I am myself far from possessing a critical know-

---

Paul has since learned that these two romances were written by no less a personage than the Duchesse de St. Leu, Hortense Beauharnois, Ex-Queen of Holland.]—See Sir Wal-

ter Scott's *Poetical Works*, where these translations also appear, pp. 650, 651.

ledge of the French language, though I have endeavoured to correct his most obvious errors. I am, dear sister, affectionately yours,

PAUL.

POSTSCRIPT.

CHANSON.

Partant pour la Syrie le jeune et beau Dunois,
Alla prier Marie de bénir ses exploits,
" Faites, O Reine immortelle," lui dit-il en partant,
" Que j'aime la plus belle, et sois le plus vaillant."

Il grave sur la pierre le serment de l'honneur,
Et va suivre en guerre le Comte et son Seigneur ;
Au noble vœu fidèle il crie en combattant,
" Amour à la plus belle, gloire au plus vaillant."

On lui doit la victoire—" Dunois," dit son Seigneur
" Puisque tu fais ma gloire, je ferai ton bonheur,
De ma fille Isabelle sois l'époux à l'instant,
Car elle est la plus belle, et toi le plus vaillant."

A l'autel de Marie ils contractent tous les deux ;
Cette union chérie qui seule les rend heureux,
Chacune Dame à la Chapelle s'écrie en les voyant,
" Amour à la plus belle, honneur au plus vaillant !"

ROMANCE DE TROUBADOUR.

Brûlant d'amour, en partant pour la guerre,
Le Troubadour, ennemi de chagrin,
Pensoit ainsi à sa jeune bergère,
Tous les matins en chantant ce refrain :
   " Mon bras à ma patrie,
   Mon cœur pour mon amie,
   Mourir gaiment pour la Gloire et l'Amour,
   C'est le devoir d'un vaillant Troubadour."

Dans le bivouac le Troubadour fidèle ;
Le casque au front, la guitare à la main,
Dans son delire, à sa jeune bergère,
Chantoit ainsi le joyeux refrain :
   " Mon bras à ma patrie,
   Mon cœur pour mon amie,
   Mourir gaiment pour la Gloire et l'Amour,
   C'est le devoir d'un vaillant Troubadour."

Dans les combats déployant son courage,
Le courage au cœur, la glaive à la main,
Etoit le même au milieu du carnage,
Chaque matin, en chantant le refrain :
   " Mon bras à ma patrie,
   Mon cœur à mon amie,
   Mourir gaiment pour l'honneur et l'amour,
   C'est le devoir d'un vrai Troubadour."

Ce brave, hélas ! déployant son courage,
Aux ennemis en bravant le destin,
Il respiroit sur la fin son ame,
Nommant sa belle, et chantant le refrain :
   " Mon bras à ma patrie,
   Mon cœur à mon amie,
   Mourir gaiment pour l'honneur et l'amour,
   C'est le devoir d'un vrai Troubadour."

CHANSON DE LA FOLIE.

De prendre femme un jour, dit-on,
L'Amour conduit la Fantaisie,
On lui proposa la Raison,
On lui proposa la Folie.—
Quel choix feroit le Dieu fripon,
Chacune d'eux est fort jolie—
Il prit pour femme la Raison,
Et pour maitresse la Folie.

Il les aimoit toutes les deux,
Avec une constance égale,
Mais l'époux vivant au mieux,
Avec la charmante rivale,
Naquit un double rejeton,
De la double galanterie,
L'amant [1] naquit de la Raison,
Et le Plaisir de la Folie.

* * * *

[1] Ita in MS.
479

LETTER X.

PAUL TO —— , ESQ. OF —— .

Flemish Farms—Brussels—Face of the Country—Forests—Antwerp Dock-yards—Bombardment of Antwerp—Carnot the Governor—Union of Flanders and the Netherlands—Difference of Religion—Antwerp Cathedral—Pictures carried off by the French—Rubens' Descent from the Cross—Painting in the Chapel where he is buried—Wax Figures—Effect of the Union on Dutch Commerce—King of the Netherlands—Belgian troops—Flemish Ballad-singers—Kindness to the British of the People of Brussels—of Antwerp—Reaping-Scythe—Clumsiness of Flemish Furniture and Implements—Apparatus for Shoeing a Horse.

THE obligation which I contracted to write to you, my dear friend, upon subjects in some degree connected with your statistical pursuits, hangs round the neck of my conscience, and encumbers me more than any of the others which I have rashly entered into. But you will forgive the deficiencies of one, who, though fifteen years doomed to be a farmer, has hitherto looked upon his sheep and cows rather as picturesque objects in the pasture, than subjects of profit in the market, and who, by some unaccountable obtuseness of intellect, never could interest himself about his turnips or potatoes, unless they were placed upon the dinner-table. Could I have got an intelligent Flemish farmer to assist me, I have little doubt that I might have sent you some interesting information from that land of Goshen, where the hand of the labourer is never for an instant folded in inactivity upon his bosom, and where the rich soil repays with ready gratitude the pains bestowed in cultivation. Promptitude and regularity, the soul of all agricultural operations, are here in such active exertion, that before the corn is driven out of the field in which it has been reaped, the plough is at work upon the stubble, leaving only the ridges occupied by the shocks. The fertility of the soil is something unequalled, even in our best carse lands, being generally a deep and inexhaustible mould, as favourable for forest-trees as for cultivation. Cheapness is the natural companion of plenty ; and I should suppose that Brussels, considered as a capital, where every luxury can be commanded, is at present one of the economical places of residence in Europe. I began a brief computation, from which it appeared, that I might support myself with those comforts or luxuries which habit has rendered necessary to me, maintaining at the same time decent hospitality, and a respectable appearance, for about the sum of direct taxes which I pay to the public in Scotland. But ere I had time to grumble at my lot, came the comfortable recollection, that my humble home in the north is belted in by the broad sea, and divided from all the convulsions that have threatened the continent, that no contending armies have decided the fate of the world within ten miles of my dwelling, and that the sound of cannon never broke my rest, unless as an early *feu-de-joie.* These, with the various circumstances of safety and freedom connected with them, and arising out of them, are reasons more than sufficient for determining my preference in favour of my own homely home.

But for such as have better reasons than mere

economy for choosing a short residence abroad, Brussels possesses great attractions. The English society there, so far as I saw it, is of the very first order, and I understand that of the principal families of the Netherlands is accessible and pleasant. This, however, is wandering from the promised topics— *revenons à nos moutons.*

The farm-houses and cottages in the Netherlands have an air of ease and comfort corresponding with the healthy and contented air of their inhabitants. That active industry, which eradicates every weed, prevents the appearance of waste and disorder, and turns every little patch of garden or orchard-ground to active profit, is nowhere seen to more advantage than in the Netherlands; and the Flemish painters copied from nature when they represented the groups of trees and thickets in which their cottages are usually embosomed. These thickets, and the woods of a larger scale, which are numerous and extensive, supply the inhabitants with fuel, though there are also coal-mines wrought to considerable extent near Charleroi. The woods are chiefly of beech, but varied with birches, oaks, and other trees. The oaks, in particular, seem to find this a favourite soil, and are to be seen sprouting freely in situations where the surface appears a light and loose sand. In the lower strata, no doubt, they find a clay soil better adapted to their nourishment.

The forests of Flanders were formerly of a more valuable description than at present, for the trees fit for ship-timber have been in a great measure cut down by Bonaparte's orders, in his eager desire to create a navy at Antwerp. Nothing could better mark the immensity of his projects, and the extensive means which he had combined for their execution, than the magnificent dock-yards which he created in that city. The huge blocks of hewn stone, of the most beautiful grey colour, and closest grain, each weighing from two to four tons, which were employed in facing the large and deep basins which he constructed, were brought by water from the quarries of Charleroi, at the distance of sixty miles and upwards. The fortifications also which Bonaparte added to those of the city, were of the most formidable description. Nevertheless the British thunders reached his vessels even in their well-defended dock-yards, as was testified by several of them having been sunk during the bombardment by Sir Thomas Graham, of which the masts yet remain visible above water. The people of Antwerp did not speak with much respect of the talents of Carnot, (their governor during the siege,) considered as an engineer, although we have often heard them mentioned with applause in England. They pointed out the remains of a small fascine battery, which was said to be misplaced, and never to have done any execution, as the only offensive preparation made by order of this celebrated mathematician. In other respects the citizens were agreeably deceived in Carnot, whose appointment to the government of the city was regarded with the greatest apprehensions by the inhabitants, who remembered that he had been the minister and instrument of Robespierre. He gave them, however, no reason to complain of him, and the necessary measures which he adopted of destroying such parts of the suburbs as interfered with the fire of the batteries, and the defence of the place, were carried into execution with as much gentleness and

moderation as the inhabitants could have expected. The town itself, being studiously spared by the clemency of the besieging general, suffered but little from the British fire, though some houses were ruined by the bombs, and particularly the *Douane,* or French custom-house, whose occupants had so long vexed the Flemings by their extortion, that its destruction was regarded by them with great joy.

Belgium, or Flanders, has of late acquired a new political existence, as a principal part of the kingdom of the Netherlands. I am no friend, in general, to the modern political legerdemain, which transfers cities and districts from one state to another, substituting the "natural boundaries," (a phrase invented by the French to justify their own usurpations,) by assuming a river or a chain of mountains, or some other geographical line of demarcation, instead of the moral limits which have been drawn, by habits of faith and loyalty to a particular sovereign or form of government, by agreement in political and religious opinions, and by resemblance of language and manners; limits traced at first perhaps by the influence of chance, but which have been rendered sacred and indelible by long course of time, and the habits which it has gradually fostered. *Arrondissements,* therefore, Indemnities, and all the other terms of modern date, under sanction of which cities and districts, and even kingdoms, have been passed from one government to another, as the property of lands and stock is transferred by a bargain between private parties, have been generally found to fail in their principal object. Either a general indifference to the form of government and its purposes, has been engendered in those whom superior force has thus rendered the sport of circumstances; or, where the minds of the population are of a higher and more vigorous order, the forced transference has only served to increase their affection to the country from which they have been torn, and their hatred against that to which they are subjected. The alienation of the Tyrol from Austria may be quoted as an example of the latter effect; and it is certain, that this iniquitous habit of transferring allegiance in the gross from one state to another, without consulting either the wishes or the prejudices of those from whom it is claimed, has had the former consequences of promoting a declension of public spirit among the smaller districts of Germany. Upon the map, indeed, the new acquisitions are traced with the same colour which distinguishes the original dominions of the state to which they are attached, and in the accompanying gazetteer, we read that such a city with its liberties, containing so many thousand souls, forms now a part of the population of such a kingdom: But can this be seriously supposed (at least until the lapse of centuries) to convey to the subjects, thus transferred, that love and affection to their new dynasty of rulers, that reverence for the institutions in Church and State, those wholesome and honest prejudices in favour of the political society to which we belong, which go so far in forming the love of our native country? "Care I for the limbs, the thewes, the sinews of a man—Give me the spirit!" —and when the stipulations of a treaty, or the decrees of a conqueror, can transfer, with the lands and houses, the love, faith, and attachment of the inhabitants, I will believe that such *arrondissements* make a wholesome and useful part of the state to which they are assigned. Until then the attempt seems much like that of a charlatan who should essay to ingraft, as a useful and serviceable limb, upon the person of one patient, the arm or leg which he has just amputated from another.

But though it seems in general sound and good doctrine, to beware of removing ancient land-marks, and although the great misfortunes of Europe may be perhaps traced to the partition of Poland, in which this attempt was first made upon the footing of open violence, yet the union between the Low Countries and the States of Holland must be admitted to form a grand exception to the general rule. It is, indeed, rather a restoration of the natural union which subsisted before the time of Philip the Second, than a new modelled arrangement of territory; the unsettled situation of Flanders, in particular, having long been such as to make it the common and ordinary stage, upon which all the prize-fighters of Europe decided their quarrels. To a people too often abandoned to the subaltern oppression of governors sent from their foreign masters, it is no small boon to be placed under a mild and mitigated monarchy, and united with a nation whose customs, habits, and language, are so similar to their own. Still, however, such is the influence of the separate feelings and opinions acquired during the lapse of two centuries, that many prejudices remain to be smoothed away, and much jealousy to be allayed, and soothed, before the good influence of the union can be completely felt.

The first and most irritating cause of apprehension is the difference of religion. The Flemings are very zealous, and very ignorant Catholics, over whom their clergy have a proportional power. The King's declared purpose of toleration has greatly alarmed this powerful body, and the nerve which has thus been touched has not failed to vibrate through the whole body politic. The Bishop of Ghent, formerly a great adherent and ally of Bonaparte, has found his conscience alarmingly twinged by so ominous a declaration on the part of a Calvinistic monarch, and has already made his remonstrance against this part of the proposed constitution in a pastoral letter, which is couched in very determined language.[1] But the present royal family are too surely seated, and the times, it may be hoped, too liberal, for such fulminations to interfere with the progress of toleration. Meanwhile the King neglects nothing that fairly can be done to conciliate his new Catholic subjects. He has recently pledged himself to use his utmost exertions

to recover from the possession of the French the pictures which they carried away from various churches in the Netherlands, and particularly from Brussels and Antwerp. Among the last, was the chef-d'œuvre of Rubens, the Descent from the Cross, which, with two corresponding pictures relative to the same subject, once hung above the high altar in the magnificent church at Antwerp, where the compartments, which they once filled, remain still vacant to remind the citizens of their loss. All the other ornaments of that church, as well as of the cathedral, shared the fate of this masterpiece, excepting only a painting which Rubens executed to decorate the chapel in which he himself lies buried; and which an unusual feeling of respect and propriety prevented the spoilers from tearing away from his tomb. The composition of the picture is something curious; for, under the representation of a Holy Family, and various characters of the New Testament, the artist has painted his grandfather, his father, his three wives, and his mistress,—the *last* in the character of the Virgin Mary, to whom the others are rendering homage. He has also introduced his own portrait, a noble martial figure, dressed in armour, and in the act of unfurling a banner. Whatever may be thought of the decorum of such a picture, painted for such a place, the beauty of the execution cannot be sufficiently admired. While the English traveller is called upon for once to acknowledge the moderation of the French, who have left at least one monument of art in the place to which it was most appropriate, he will probably wish they had carried off with them the trash of wax figures, which, to the disgrace of good taste and common sense, are still the objects of popular adoration. Abstracted from all polemics, one can easily conceive that the sight of an interesting painting, representing to our material organs the portrait of a saint, or an affecting scene of Scripture, may not only be an appropriate ornament in the temple of worship, but, like church-music, may have its effect in fixing the attention, and aiding the devotion of the congregation. It may be also easily understood, and readily forgiven, that when kneeling before the very altar to which our ancestors in trouble resorted for comfort, we may be gradually led to annex a superstitious reverence to the place itself: But when, in the midst of such a cathedral as that of Antwerp, one of the grandest pieces of Gothic architecture which Europe can show,—when among the long-drawn aisles, and lofty arches, which seem almost the work of demi-gods, so much does the art and toil bestowed surpass what modern

[1] I take this opportunity to announce the correction of a very gross error in the first edition of these Letters, where the name of the Bishop of Liege had, through misinformation, been inserted for that of the Bishop of Ghent. The extent of this mistake, which I deeply regret, will be best understood by the following extract from a letter, in which it is pointed out and corrected. The authority of the writer is beyond dispute, and Paul readily admits the inaccuracy of his notes, though taken upon the spot.

"The Bishop of Liege was never an adherent or ally of Bonaparte. On the contrary, driven from his principality or bishopric, (for the See of Liege was formerly both,) he took refuge at Ratisbone, where his residence has, I believe, ever been, and where he has never ceased to enjoy the respect of those who were most opposed to the views of the usurper. So far from his conscience having been alarmingly twinged by the king's proposed toleration, that, recommended by his majesty to the Archbishopric of Malines in the room of the Abbé de Pradt, he repaired to Brussels when the constitution

was proposed, and acted there, at a very critical moment, as the most strenuous supporter of that very toleration which he is accused so erroneously as having opposed. You, who were present with me at Brussels when the constitution of the Low Countries was proposed and adopted, were a personal witness of the laudable conduct of this worthy prelate, and can speak of it as it deserves. It would have been impossible for the Bishop of Liege to have issued a pastoral letter, not only of the nature in question, but of any kind whatever; because, though still styled Bishop, he has in effect no diocese, that of Liege having been abolished during the French occupancy. I should conceive the prelate whose name ought to have been cited in this part of the work, to be the Bishop of Ghent, to whom all that has thus been erroneously attributed to the Prince-Bishop of Liege, will exactly apply, except that I am not aware of his having, as stated in the 33d page, had *brethren* in his intolerance, at least episcopal brethren, the Bishop of Tournay having been the only bishop of the Netherlands who adopted a similar course of opposition."—S.

times can present,—when, in the midst of such a scene, we find a wax figure of the Virgin, painted, patched, frizzled, and powdered ; with a tarnished satin gown, (the skirt held up by two cherubs,) paste ear-rings and necklace, differing in no respect, but in size, from the most paltry doll that ever was sold in a toy-shop ; and observe this incongruous and ridiculous *swamy* the object of fervid and zealous adoration from the votaries who are kneeling before it, we see the idolatry of the Romish Church in a point of view disgusting and humiliating as that of ancient Egypt, and cease to wonder at the obstinacy of the prelate aforesaid, and that part of the priesthood, who fear the light which universal toleration would doubtless throw upon the benighted worship of their great Diana. In the meanwhile, the promise of the King to procure restoration of the pictures, is received by most of the Flemings as a pledge, that the religion which he himself professes, will not prevent his interesting himself in that of the Catholics ; and I think there can be little doubt that, under the gradual influence of time and example, the grosser points of superstition will be tacitly abandoned here, as in other Catholic countries.

The Dutch have a more worldly subject of jealousy in the state of their commerce, which cannot but be materially affected by the opening of the Scheldt, whenever that desirable event shall have taken place, and also by the principal residence of the government being changed from the Hague to Brussels. But they are a reflecting people, and are already aware that the operation of both these changes will be slow and gradual ; for commerce is not at once transferred from the channels in which it has long flowed ; and for some time, at least, family recollections and attachments will make the royal family frequent residents in Holland, notwithstanding the charms of the palace of Lacken. In the meanwhile the Dutch gain the inestimable advantage of having the battle turned from their gates, and of enjoying the protection of a strong barrier placed at a distance from their own frontier,—blessings of themselves sufficient to compensate the inconvenience which they may for a time sustain, until they transfer their capital and industry to the new channels offered for them by the union.

Nothing could have happened so fortunate for the popularity of the house of Orange as the active and energetic character of the hereditary prince. His whole behaviour during the actions of Quatre Bras and Waterloo, and the wound which (it may be almost said fortunately) he received upon the latter occasion, have already formed the strongest bond of union between his family and their new subjects, long unaccustomed to have sovereigns who could lead them to battle, and shed their blood in the national defence. The military force, which he is at this moment perpetually increasing, is of a respectable description ; for, though some of the Belgian troops behaved ill during the late brief campaign, there were other corps, and particularly infantry and artillery, both Dutch and Flemings, whose firmness and discipline equalled those of any regiments in the field. The *braves Belges* are naturally proud of the military glory they have acquired, as well as of the prince who led them on. In every corner of Brussels there were balladsingers bellowing out songs in praise of the prince

and his followers. I, who am a collector of popular effusions, did not fail to purchase specimens of the Flemish minstrelsy, in which, by the way, there is no more mention of the Duke of Wellington, or of John Bull, than if John Bull and his illustrious general had had nothing to do with the battle of Waterloo.

This little omission of the Flemish bards proceeds, however, from no disinclination to the Duke or to England. On the contrary, our wounded received during their illness, and are yet experiencing during their convalescence, the most affecting marks of kindness and attention from the inhabitants of Brussels. These acts of friendship towards their allies were not suspended (as will sometimes happen in this world) until the chance of war had decided in favour of the English. Even on the 17th, when the defeat of Blucher, and the retreat of the Duke of Wellington, authorized them to entertain the most gloomy apprehensions for their own safety, as well as to fear the vengeance of the French for any partiality they might show towards their enemies, the kind citizens of Brussels were not deterred from the exercise of kindness and hospitality. They were seen meeting the wounded with refreshments ; some seeking for those soldiers who had been quartered in their houses, others bestowing their care on the first disabled sufferer they met with, carrying him to their home, and nursing him like a child of the family, at all the cost, trouble, and risk, with which their hospitality might be attended. The people of Antwerp, to which city were transferred upon the 17th and 18th most of those who had been wounded at Quatre Bras, were equally zealous in the task of the good Samaritan. Many of our poor fellows told me, that they must have perished but for the attention of those kind Flemings, whose

" Entire affection scorned nicer hands,"

since many of the highest and most respectable classes threw pride and delicacy aside to minister to the wants of the sufferers. On their part, the Flemings were often compelled to admire the endurance and hardihood of their patients. " Your countrymen," said a lady to me, who spoke our language well, " are made of iron, and not of flesh and blood. I saw a wounded Highlander stagger along the street, supporting himself by the rails, and said to him, I am afraid you are severely hurt. ' I was born in Lochaber,' answered the poor fellow, ' and I do not care for a wound ;' but ere I could complete my offer of shelter and assistance, he sunk down at my feet a dying man." In one house in Brussels, occupied by a respectable manufacturer and his two sisters, thirty wounded soldiers were received, nursed, fed, and watched, the only labour of the medical attendants being to prevent their hosts from giving the patients wine, and more nourishing food than suited their situation. We may hope the reciprocal benefits of defence and of hospitality will be long remembered, forming a kindly connexion between England and a country, which, of all others, may be most properly termed her natural ally.

I have again wandered from agriculture into politics and military affairs, but I have little to add which properly belongs to your department, since I have no doubt that you have already sate in judgment upon the Flemish plough, rake, and hayfork, presented to the Highland Society by one of its most active members. The most remarkable implement of agriculture which fell under my observation was a sort of hooked stick, which the reaper holds in his left hand, and uses to collect and lay the corn as he cuts it with a short scythe. The operation is very speedy, for one person engaged in it can keep two or three constantly employed in binding the sheafs. But I suppose it would only answer where the ground is level and free from stones.

The furniture of the Flemings, and, generally speaking, their implements of labour, &c., have a curious correspondence with what we have been accustomed to consider as their national character; being strong and solid, but clumsy and inelegant, and having a great deal more substance employed in constructing them than seems at all necessary. Thus the lever of an ordinary draw-well is generally one long tree; and their waggons and barges are as huge and heavy as the horses which draw them. The same cumbrous solidity which distinguishes the female figures of Rubens, may be traced in the domestic implements and contrivances of his countrymen. None would have entertained you more than the apparatus provided for securing a horse while in the act of being shod, a case in which our Vulcans trust to an ordinary halter and their own address. But a Flemish horse is immured within a wooden erection of about his own size, having a solid roof supported by four massive posts, such as a British carpenter would use to erect a harbour-crane. The animal's head is fastened between two of these huge columns with as many chains and cords as might have served to bind Baron Trenck; and the foot which is to be shod is secured in a pair of stocks, which extend between two of the upright beams. This is hardly worth writing, though ridiculous to look at; but there is something, as Anstey says, "so clumsy and clunch" in the massive strength of the apparatus, in the very unnecessary extent of the precaution, and in the waste of time, labour, and materials, that it may be selected as an indication of a national character, displaying itself in the most ordinary and trifling particulars.

Adieu, my dear friend; I am sorry I can send you no more curious information on your favourite subject. But it would be unnecessary to one who is skilled in all the modern arts of burning without fire, and feeding without pasture; and who requires no receipts from Holland to teach him how to lay on so much fat upon a bullock or a pig, as will make the flesh totally unfit for eating. Yours affectionately,

PAUL.

LETTER XI.

TO THE SAME.

183

I HAVE now, my dear friend, reached Paris, after traversing the road from Brussels to this conquered capital through sights and sounds of war, and yet more terrible marks of its recent ravages. The time was interesting, for although our route presented no real danger, yet it was not, upon some occasions, without such an appearance of it as naturally to impress a civilian with a corresponding degree of alarm. All was indeed new to me, and the scenes which I beheld were such as press most deeply on the feelings.

We were following the route of the victorious English army, to which succours of every sort, and reinforcements of troops recently landed in Flanders, were pressing eagerly forward, so that the towns and roads were filled with British and foreign troops. For the war, although ended to all useful and essential purposes, could not in some places be said to be actually finished. Condé had surrendered but a few days before, and Valenciennes still held out, and, as report informed us, was to undergo a renewal of the bombardment. Another and contrary rumour assured us that an armistice had taken place, and that, as *non-combatants*, the garrison would permit a party, even as alarming as our own, to pass through the town without interruption. I felt certainly a degree of curiosity to see the most formidable operation of modern war, but, as I was far from wishing the city of Valenciennes to have been burnt for my amusement, we were happy to find that the latter report was accurate. Accordingly, we passed the works and batteries of the besiegers, unquestioned by the Dutch and Prussian videttes, who were stalking to and fro upon their posts, and proceeded to the gate of the place, where we underwent a brief examination from the non-commissioned officer on duty, who looked at our passports, requested to know if we were military men, and being answered in the negative, permitted us to enter a dark, ill-built, and dirty town. "And these are the men," I thought, as I eyed the ill-dressed and ragged soldiers upon duty at the gates of Valenciennes, "these are the men who have turned the world upside down, and whose name has been the nightmare of Europe, since most of this generation have written man!" They looked ugly and dirty and savage enough certainly, but seemed to have little superiority in strength or appearance to the Dutch or Belgians. There was, indeed, in the air and eye of the soldiers of Bonaparte, (for such these military men still called themselves,) something of pride and self-elation, that indicated undaunted confidence in their own skill and valour; but they appeared disunited and disorganized. Some wore the white cockade, others still displayed the tri-colour,

...nd one prudent fellow had, for his own amusement and that of his comrades, stuck both in his hat at once, so as to make a *cocarde de contenance*, which might suit either party that should get uppermost. We were not permitted to go upon the ramparts, and I did not think it necessary to walk about a town in possession of a hostile soldiery, left to the freedom of their own will. The inhabitants looked dejected and unhappy, and our landlady, far from displaying the liveliness of a Frenchwoman, was weeping-ripe, and seemed ready to burst into tears at every question which we put to her. Their apprehensions had been considerably relieved by General Rey having himself assumed the white cockade; but as he still refused to admit any of the allied troops within the city, there remained a great doubt whether the allies would content themselves with the blockade, to which they had hitherto restricted their operations against Valenciennes. The inhabitants were partial, the landlady said, to the English, with whom they were well acquainted, as Valenciennes had been a principal depôt for the prisoners of war; but they deprecated their town being occupied by the Prussians or Belgians, in whose lenity they seemed to place but little reliance.

On the road next day we met with very undesirable company, being the disbanded garrison of Condé, whom the allies had dismissed after occupying that town. There is, you may have remarked, something sinister in the appearance of a common soldier of any country when he is divested of his uniform. The martial gait, look, and manner, and the remaining articles of military dress which he has retained, being no longer combined with that neatness which argues that the individual makes part of a civilized army, seem menacing and ominous from the want of that assurance. If this is the case even with the familiar faces of our own soldiery, the wild and swarthy features, mustaches, and singular dress of foreigners, added much, as may well be supposed, of the look of banditti to the garrison of Condé. They were, indeed, a true sample of the desperate school to which they belonged, for it was not many days since they had arrested and put to death a French loyalist officer, named Gordon, solely for summoning them to surrender the town to the king. For this crime the brother of the murdered individual is now invoking vengeance, but as yet fruitlessly, at the court of the Tuileries. These desperadoes, strolling in bands of eight or ten or twenty, as happened, occupied the road for two or three miles, and sullen resentment and discontent might easily be traced in their looks. They offered us no rudeness, however, but contented themselves with staring hard at us, as a truculent-looking fellow would now and then call out *Vive le Roi!* and subjoin an epithet or two to show that it was uttered in no mood of loyal respect. At every cross-road two or three dropped off from the main body, after going, with becoming grace, through the ceremony of embracing and kissing their greasy companions. The thought involuntarily pressed itself upon our mind, what will become of these men, and what of the thousands who, in similar circumstances, are now restored to civil life, with all the wild habits and ungoverned passions which war and license have so long fostered! Will the lion lie down with the kid, or the trained freebooter return to the peaceable and la-

borious pursuits of civil industry! Or are they not more likely to beg, borrow, starve, and steal, until some unhappy opportunity shall again give them a standard and a chieftain!

We were glad when we got free of our military fellow-travellers, with whom I should not have chosen to meet by night, or in solitude, being exactly of their appearance who would willingly say "*Stand*" to a true man. But we had no depredations to complain of, excepting the licensed extortions of the innkeepers,—a matter of which you are the less entitled to complain, because every prudent traveller makes his bargain for his refreshments and lodging before he suffers the baggage to be taken from his carriage. Each reckoning is, therefore, a formal treaty between you and mine host or hostess, in which you have your own negligence or indifference to blame, if you are very much overreached. It is scarce necessary to add, that the worst and poorest inns are the most expensive in proportion. But I ought not to omit informing you, that notwithstanding a mode of conducting their ordinary business, so much savouring of imposition, there is no just room to charge the French with more direct habits of dishonesty. Your baggage and money are always safe from theft or depredation; and when I happened to forget a small writing-box, in which there was actually some money, and which had the appearance of being intended for securing valuable articles, an ostler upon horseback overtook our carriage with it before I had discovered my mistake. Yet it would have cost these people only a lie to say they knew nothing of it, especially as their house was full of soldiers of different nations, whose presence certainly afforded a sufficient apology for the disappearance of such an article. This incident gave me a favourable opinion of this class of society in France, as possessed at least of that sort of limited honesty which admits of no peculation excepting in the regular way of business.

The road from Brussels to Paris is, in its ordinary state, destitute of objects to interest the traveller. The highways, planned by Sully, and completed by his followers in office, have a magnificence elsewhere unknown. Their great breadth argues the little value of ground at the time they were laid out; but the perfect state in which the central causeway is maintained, renders the passage excellent even in the worst weather, while the large track of ground on each side gives an ample facility to use a softer road during the more favourable season. They are usually shadowed by triple rows of elms, and frequently of fruit-trees, which have a rich and pleasant effect. But much of the picturesque delights of travelling are lost in France, owing to the very circumstances which have rendered the roads so excellent. For as they were all made by the authority of a government, which possessed and exercised the power of going as directly from one point to another as the face of the country admitted, they preserve commonly that long and inflexible straight line, of all others least promising to the traveller, who longs for the gradual openings of landscape afforded by a road, which, in sweet and varied modulation, "winds round the cornfield and the hill of vines," being turned as it were from its forward and straight direction by respect for ancient property and possession, some feeling for the domestic privacy and convenience, some sympathy even for the prejudices and partialities, of a proprietor. I love not the stoical virtue of a Brutus, even in laying out a turnpike-road, and should augur more happily of a country (were there nothing else to judge by) where the public appears to have given occasionally a little way to spare private property and domestic seclusion, than of one where the high-road goes right to its mark without respect to either. In the latter case it only proves the authority of those who administer the government; in the former, it indicates respect for private rights, for the protection of which government itself is instituted.

But the traveller in France, upon my late route, has less occasion than elsewhere to regret the rectilinear direction of the road on which he journeys, for the country offers no picturesque beauty. The rivers are sluggish, and have flat uninteresting banks. In the towns there sometimes occurs a church worth visiting, but no other remarkable building of any kind; and the sameness of the architecture of the 15th century, to which period most of them may be referred, is apt to weary the attention, when you have visited four or five churches in the course of two days. The fortifications of the towns are of the modern kind, and consequently more formidable than picturesque. Of those feudal castles which add such a venerable grace to the landscape in many places of England and Scotland, I have not seen one, either ruinous or entire. It would seem that the policy of Louis XI., to call up his nobility from their estates to the court, and to render them as far as possible dependent upon the crown,—a policy indirectly seconded by the destruction of the noble families which took place in the civil wars of the League, and more systematically by the arts observed during the reign of Louis XIV.,—had succeeded so entirely, as to root out almost all traces of the country having ever been possessed by a *noblesse campagnarde*, who found their importance, their power, and their respectability, dependent on the attachment of the peasants among whom they lived, and over whom their interest extended. There are no ruins of their ancient and defensible habitations; and the few, the very few country houses which the traveller sees, resemble those built in our own country about the reign of Queen Anne; while the grounds about them seem in general neglected, the fences broken, and the whole displaying that appearance of waste, which deforms a property after the absence of a proprietor for some years.

The furious patriots of the Revolution denounced war against castles, and proclaimed peace to the cottage. Of the former they found comparatively few to destroy, and of the latter, in the English sense of the word, there were as few to be protected. The cultivator of the fields in France, whether farmer or peasant, does not usually live in a detached farm-house or cottage, but in one of the villages with which the country abounds. This circumstance, which is not altogether indifferent, so far as it concerns rural economics, blemishes greatly the beauty of the landscape. The solitary farm-house, with its little dependences of cottages, is in itself a beautiful object, while it seldom fails to excite in the mind, the idea of the natural and systematic dependence of a few virtuous cottagers upon an opulent and industrious farmer, who exercises over them a sort of natural and patriarchal authority, which has not the less influence because the subjection of the hinds, and their submission to their superior, is in some degree voluntary. A large village, composed of many farmers and small proprietors, who hire their labourers at large, and without distinction, from amongst the poorer class of the same town, is more open to the feuds and disputes which disturb human society, always least virtuous and orderly when banded in crowds together, and when uninfluenced by the restraints of example and of authority, approaching, as closely as may be, to their own station in society.

Another uncomfortable appearance in French landscape, is the total want of enclosure. The ground is sedulously and industriously cultivated, and apparently no portion of it is left without a crop. But the want of hedges and hedge-row trees gives, to an eye accustomed to the richness of England, a strange appearance of waste and neglect, even where you are convinced, on a closer examination, that there exists in reality neither the one nor the other. Besides, there is necessarily an absence of all those domestic animals which add so much in reality, as well as in painting and descriptive poetry, to the beauty of a country. Where there are no enclosures, and where, at the same time, the land is under crop, it is plain that the painter must look in vain for his groups of cattle, sheep, and horses, as the poet must miss his lowing herd and bleating flock. The cattle of France are accordingly fed in the large straw-yards which belong to each *métairie*, or farm-house, and the sheep are chiefly grazed in distant tracts of open pasture. The former practice, as a mode of keeping not only the stall-fed bullock, but the cows destined for the dairy, has been hailed with acclamation in our own country by many great agriculturists, and by you among others. But until I shall be quite assured that the rustic economics profit by this edict of perpetual imprisonment against the milky mothers of the herd, in proportion to the discomfort of the peaceful and useful animal thus sequestered from its natural habits, and to the loss of natural beauty in the rural landscape, thus deprived of its most pleasing objects, I would willingly move for a writ of Habeas Corpus in favour of poor Crummie,[1] made a bond-slave in a free country. At any rate, the total absence of cattle from the fields, gives a dull and unanimated air to a French landscape.

In travelling also through such parts of France as I have seen, the eye more particularly longs for that succession of country-seats, with their accompaniments of parks, gardens, and paddocks, which not only furnish the highest ornaments of an English landscape, but afford the best and most pleasing signs of the existence of a mild and beneficent aristocracy of landholders, giving a tone to the opinions of those around them, not by the despotism of feudal authority and direct power, but, as we have already said of the farmer, by the gradual and imperceptible influence which property, joined with education, naturally acquires over the more humble cultivator of the soil. It is the least evil consequence of the absence of the proprietor, that with him vanish those improvements upon the soil, and upon the face of nature, which are produced by opulence under the guidance of taste. The eye in this country seldom dwells with delight upon

<hr>

[1] *Crummie*—a cow, *Scottice.*

trees growing, single or in groups, at large and unconfined, for the sole purpose of ornament, and contrasting their unrestrained vegetation and profusion of shade with such as, being trained solely for the axe, have experienced constant restraint from the closeness of the masses in which they are planted, and from the knife of the pruner. The French forests themselves, when considered in their general effect, though necessarily both numerous and extensive, as furnishing the principal fuel used by the inhabitants, are not generally so disposed as to make an interesting part of the scenery. The trees are seldom scattered into broken groups, and never arranged in hedge-rows, unless by the sides of the highways. Large woods, or rather masses of plantations, cannot and do not supply the variety of landscape afforded by detached groves, or the rich and clothed appearance formed by a variety of intersecting lines composed of single trees.

The absence of enclosures gives also, at least to our eyes, an unimproved and neglected air to this country. But, upon close inspection, the traveller is satisfied that the impression is inaccurate. The soil is rich, generally speaking, and every part of the land is carefully cropped and cultivated. Although, therefore, the ground being undivided, except by the colour of the various crops by which it is occupied, has, at first sight, that waste and impoverished appearance to which the inhabitant of an enclosed country is particularly sensible, yet the returns which it makes to the cultivator amply contradict the false impression. It is truly a rich and fertile land, affording in profusion all that can render subsistence easy, and abounding with corn, wine, and oil. When we consider France in this light, it is impossible to suppress our feelings of resentment at their regular ambition, which carried the inhabitants of so rich a country to lay yet more waste the barren sands of Prussia, and encumber with their corpses the pathless wilderness of Moscow and Kalouga.

But the hour of retaliation is now come, and with whatever feelings of resentment we regard the provocation, it is impossible to view the distress of the country without deep emotions of compassion. From one hill to another our eye descried the road before us occupied by armed bands of every description, horse, foot, artillery, and baggage, with their guards and attendants. Here was seen a long file of cavalry moving on at a slow pace, and collecting their forage as they advanced. There a park of artillery was formed in a corn-field, of which the crop was trampled down and destroyed. In one place we passed a regiment of soldiers pressing forward to occupy some village for their night-quarters, where the peasant must lay his account with finding his military guests whatever accommodation they are pleased to demand from him; in another we might see, what was still more ominous to the country through which the march was made, small parties of infantry or of cavalry, detached upon duty, or straggling for the purpose of plunder. The harvest stood ripened upon the fields, but it was only in a few places that the farmer, amid the confusion of the country, had ventured upon the operation of reaping it, unless where he was compelled by the constraint of a military requisition, or the commands of a commissary. It would have been a new sort

of harvest-home for you and your faithful *Grieve*,[1] to have seen the labour of leading in the crop performed by an armed force, and your sheaves moving to headquarters instead of the farm-yard, under the escort of an armed and whiskered Prussian, smoking his pipe with great composure on the top of each cart. Sometimes odd enough rencontres took place during this operation. A Prussian commissary, with his waggons, met some French peasants driving their carts, which occasioned a temporary stop to both parties. While some of the Frenchmen seemed zealously engaged in clearing way for the military men, others approached the waggons, and having previously contrived to ascertain that none of the Prussians understood French, they loaded them with all the abusive epithets which that language affords; taking care, however, amid the vivacity of their vituperation, to preserve such an exterior of respect in their manner and gestures, as induced the honest Prussians to suppose the Frenchmen were making apologies for the temporary obstruction which they had given to their betters. Thus the one party were showering *coquins*, and *voleurs*, and *brigands* upon the other, who ever and anon with great gravity withdrew their pipes from their mouths to answer these douceurs with *Das ist gut —sehr wohl*,[2] and similar expressions of acquiescence. It would have been cruel to have deprived the poor Frenchmen of this ingenious mode of expectorating their resentment, but I could not help giving them a hint, that the commissary who was coming up understood their language, which had the instant effect of sending the whole party to their horses' heads.

The inhabitants had hastened to propitiate the invaders, as far as possible, by assuming the badges of loyalty to the house of Bourbon. Nothing marked to my mind more strongly the distracted state of the country, than the apparent necessity which every, even the humblest individual, thought himself under, of wearing a white cockade, and displaying from the thatch of his cottage a white rag, to represent the *pavillon blanc*. There was a degree of suspicion, arising from this very uniformity, concerning the motives for which these emblems were assumed; and I dare say the poor inhabitants might many of them have expressed their feelings in the words of Fletcher,—

> " Who is here that did not wish thee chosen,
> Now thou art chosen ? Ask them—all will say so,
> Nay swear't—'tis for the king; but let that pass."

With equal zeal the inhabitants of the towns were laying aside each symbol that had reference to Bonaparte, and emulously substituting a loyal equivalent. The sign-painter was the cleverest at his profession who could best convert the word *Imperial* into *Royal*; but there were many bunglers, whose attempts produced only a complicated union of the two contradictory adjectives. Some prudent housekeepers, tired apparently of the late repeated changes, left a blank for the epithet, to be inserted when the government should show some permanency.

These numerous testimonies of acquiescence in the purpose of their march, were in some measure lost upon the allied troops. The British, indeed, preserved the strictest propriety and discipline, in obedience to the orders issued and enforced by the

---

[1] *Grieve*—A land-steward or bailiff, *Scottice*.

[2] " *That is good* "—" *very well*."

commander-in-chief. But as the army was necessarily to be maintained at the expense of the country through which they passed, heavy requisitions were issued by the commissaries, which the French authorities themselves were under the necessity of enforcing. Still as pillage and free-booting, under pretext of free quarters and maintenance, was strictly prohibited and punished, the presence of the English troops was ardently desired, as a protection against those of other nations.

Our allies the Prussians, as they had greater wrongs to revenge, were far less scrupulous in their treatment of the invaded country. When our road lay along their line of march, we found as many deserted villages as would have jointured all Sultan Mahmoud's owls. In some places the inhabitants had fled to the woods, and only a few miserable old creatures, rendered fearless by age and poverty, came around us, begging, or offering fruit for sale. As the peasants had left their cottages locked up, the soldiers as regularly broke them open, by discharging a musket through the key-hole, and shattering all the wards at once by the explosion. He who obtains admission by such violent preliminaries is not likely to be a peaceful or orderly guest; and accordingly furniture broken and destroyed, windows dashed in, doors torn down, and now and then a burnt cottage, joined with the state of the hamlets, deserted by such of the terrified inhabitants as were able to fly, and tenanted only by the aged and disabled, reminded me of the beautiful lines describing the march of a conqueror,—

"Amazement in his van with Flight combined,
And Sorrow's faded form and Solitude behind."

A friend of mine met with an interesting adventure at one of these deserted villages. He had entered the garden of a cottage of somewhat a superior appearance, but which had shared the fate of the rest of the hamlet. As he looked around him, he perceived that he was watched from behind the bushes by two or three children, who ran away as soon as they perceived themselves observed. He called after them, but to no purpose. The sound of the English accent, however, emboldened the mother of the family to show herself from a neighbouring thicket, and at length she took courage to approach him. My friend found to his surprise that she understood English well, owing to some accident of her life or education, which I have forgotten. She told him her family were just venturing back from their refuge in the woods, where they had remained two days without shelter, and almost without food, to see what havoc the spoilers had made in their cottage, when they were again alarmed by the appearance of troops. Being assured that they were English soldiers, she readily agreed to remain, under the confidence which the national character inspired; and having accepted what assistance her visitor had to offer her, as the only acknowledgment in her power, she sent one of the children to pull and present to her guest the only rose which her now ruined garden afforded. " It was the last," she said, " she had, and she was happy to bestow it on an Englishman." It is upon occasions such as these that the French women, even of the lowest class, display a sort of sentimental delicacy unknown to those of other countries. Equal distress, but of a very different kind, I witnessed in the perturbation of a Flemish peasant,

487

whose team of horses had been put in requisition to transport the baggage of an English officer of distinction. As they had not been returned to the owner, whose livelihood and that of his family depended on their safety, he had set out in quest of them, in an agony of doubt and apprehension that actually had the appearance of insanity. Our attention was called to him from his having seated himself behind our carriage, and an expostulation on our part produced his explanation. I never saw such a sudden transition from despair to hope, as in the poor fellow's rugged features, when he saw, in the descent between two hills, a party of English dragoons with led horses. He made no doubt they could only be his own, and I hoped to see such a meeting as that of Sancho with Dapple, after their doleful separation. But we were both disappointed; the led horses proved to be those of my friend General A——,[1] who probably would not have been much flattered by their being mistaken, at whatever distance, for Flemish beasts of burden. I believe, however, my ruined peasant obtained some clew for recovering his lost property, for he suddenly went off in a direction different from that which we had hitherto afforded him the means of pursuing. It is only by selecting such individual instances that I can make you comprehend the state of the country between Mons and Paris.

The Prussians having used this military license, the march of such of our troops as pursued the same route became proportionally uncomfortable. A good bluff quarter-master of dragoons complained to me of the discomforts which they experienced from the condition to which the country had been reduced, but in a tone and manner which led me to conjecture, that my honest friend did not sympathize with the peasant, who had been plundered of his wine and brandy, so much as he censured the Prussians for leaving none for their faithful allies:

" O noble thirst!—yet greedy to drink all."

In the meanwhile, it is no great derogation from the discipline of the English army to remark, that some old school-boy practices were not forgotten; and that, where there occurred a halt, and fruit-trees chanced to be in the vicinity, they instantly were loaded like the emblematic tree in the frontis-piece of Lilly's Grammar, only with soldiers instead of scholars; and surrounded by their wives who held their aprons to receive the fruit, instead of satchels, as in the emblem chosen by that learned grammarian. There were no signs of license of a graver character.

In the midst of these scenes of war and invasion, the regulations of the post establishment, which, as is well known, is in France entirely in the charge of the Government and their commissaries or lessees, were supported and respected. A proclamation in four different languages, French, German, English, and Prussian, and signed by four generals of the different countries, was stuck up in every post-house. This polyglot forbade all officers and soldiers, whether belonging to the King of France, or to the allies, from pressing the horses, or otherwise interfering with the usual communication of Paris with the provinces. The post-houses were accordingly inhabited and protected amid the general desolation of the country, and we experienced no interruption on our journey.

---

[1] Sir Frederick Adam.

While the villages and hamlets exhibited such scenes as I have described, the towns appeared to have suffered less upon this awful crisis, because the soldiers were there under the eye of their officers, and in each garrison-town a military commandant had been named for the maintenance of discipline. Some were indeed reeking from recent storm, or showed half-burnt ruins which had been made by bombardment within a week or two preceding our arrival. Cambray had been carried by escalade by a bold coup-de-main, of which we saw the vestiges. The citizens, who were chiefly royalists, favoured the attack; and a part of the storming party entered by means of a staircase contained in an old turret, which terminated in a sally-port opening to the ditch, and above in a wicket communicating with the rampart. This pass was pointed out to them by the towns-people. The defenders were a part of the National Guard, whom Bonaparte had removed from the district to which they belonged, and stationed as a garrison in Cambray. The garrison of Peronne, formerly called *Peronne la Pucelle*, or the Virgin Fortress, because it had never been taken, were military of the same amphibious description with those of Cambray. The town is strongly situated in the Somme, surrounded by flat ground and marshes, and presents a formidable exterior.[1] But this, as well as the other fortresses on the iron-bound frontier of Flanders, was indifferently provided with means of resistance. Bonaparte in this particular, as in others, had shown a determination to venture his fortunes upon a single chance of war, since he had made no adequate provision for a protracted defence of the country when invaded. It was one instance of the inexperience of the garrison of Peronne, that they omitted to blindfold the British officer who came to summon them to surrender. An officer of engineers, of high rank and experience, had been called to this mission, and doubtless did not leave unemployed the eyes which the besieged, contrary to custom in such cases, left at liberty. Upon his return, he reported the possibility of carrying a horn-work which covers a suburb on the left side of the river. The attempt was instantly made, and being in all respects successful, was followed by the surrender of the garrison, upon the easy conditions of laying down their arms, and returning to the ordinary civil occupations from which Bonaparte's mandate had withdrawn them. So easy had been these achievements that the officers concerned in them would hardly be prevailed upon to condescend to explain such trifling particulars. Yet to me, who looked upon ramparts a little injured indeed by time, but still strong, upon ditches containing twelve feet deep of water, and a high glacis surmounting them, upon palisades constructed out of the trees which had been felled to clear the esplanade around the fortifications, the task of surmounting such obstacles, even though not defended at all, seemed a grave and serious undertaking. In all these towns, so far as I could discover, the feeling of the people was decidedly in favour of the legitimate Monarch; and I cannot doubt that this impression is correct, because elsewhere, and in similar circumstances, those who favoured Bonaparte were at no pains to suppress their inclinations. In one or two towns they were preparing little *fêtes*

to celebrate the King's restoration. The accompaniments did not appear to us very splendid; but when a town has been so lately taken by storm, and is still garrisoned by foreign troops and subjected to military requisitions, we could not expect that the rejoicings of its inhabitants should be attended with any superfluity of splendour.

Meanwhile we advanced through this new and bewildering scene of war and waste, with the comfortable consciousness that we belonged to the stronger party. The British drums and bugle-horns sung us to bed every night, and played our reveillée in the morning; for in all the fortified towns through which we passed, there were British troops and a British commandant, from more than one of whom we experienced attention and civility.

When we reached Pont de St. Maxence, which had been recently the scene of an engagement between the Prussians and French, we found more marked signs of hostile devastation than in any place through which we had yet travelled. It is a good large market-town, with a very fine bridge over the Oise, an arch of which had been recently destroyed, and repaired in a temporary manner. The purpose had probably been to defend the passage; and as the river is deep, and the opposite bank is high and covered with wood, besides having several buildings approaching to the bridge, I presume it might have been made a very strong position. It had been forced, however, by the Prussians, in what manner we found no one to tell us. Several houses in this town had been burnt, and most of them seemed to have been pillaged. The cause was evident, from the number of embrasures and loop-holes for musketry which were struck out in the houses and garden-walls. The attempt to turn a village into a place of defence is almost always fatal to the household gods, since it is likely to be burnt by one or other of the parties, and certain to be plundered by both. Military gentlemen look upon this with a very different eye; for I have been diverted to hear some of them, who have given me the honour of their company in my little excursions from Paris, censure a gentleman or farmer with great gravity for having built his house and stationed his court of offices in a hollow, where they were overlooked and commanded; whereas, by placing the buildings a little higher on the ridge, or more towards right or left, they might, in case of need, have acquired the dignity of being the *key* of a strong position, and, in all probability, have paid for their importance by sharing the fate of Hougoumont.

We were informed at St. Maxence that the hand of war had been laid yet more heavily upon the neighbouring town of Senlis, through which lay our direct route to Paris, and near which an action had taken place betwixt a part of Blucher's army and that of Grouchy and Vandamme, which, falling back to cover the French capital after the battle of Waterloo, had accomplished a retreat that placed those who commanded it very high in public estimation. We felt no curiosity to see any more of the woes of war, and readily complied with a proposal of our postilions to exchange the route of Senlis for that of Chantilly, to which they undertook to carry us by a cross road through the forest. *Le beau chemin par terre,* or fine greensward road, which they had urged as so superior to the public causeway, had unfortunately not possessed the same power of re-

---

[1] See Quentin Durward, chap. xxv. *Waverley Novels.*

sisting the tear and wear of cavalry, artillery, and baggage-waggons. It was reduced to a sort of continued wet ditch, varying in depth in a most irregular manner, and through which the four stallions that drew us kicked, plunged, snorted, and screamed, in full concert with the eternal smack of the whips, as well as shrieks, whoops, and oaths of the jack-booted postilions, lugging about our little barouche in a manner that threatened its demolition at every instant. The French postilions, however, who, with the most miserable appliances and means, usually drive very well, contrived, by dint of quartering and tugging, to drag us safe through roads where a Yorkshire post-boy would have been reduced to despair, even though his horses had not been harnessed with ropes, fastened together by running nooses.

The forest of Chantilly was probably magnificent when it was the chase of the princely family of Condé; but all the valuable timber-trees have been felled, and those which now remain appear, generally speaking, to be about twenty years old only, consist chiefly of birch, and other inferior timber used for firewood. Those who acquired the domains of the emigrants after the Revolution, were generally speculating adventurers, who were eager to secure what they could make of the subject in the way of ready money, by cutting timber and selling materials of houses, partly in order to secure the means of paying the price, and partly because prudence exacted that they should lose no time in drawing profit from a bargain, of which the security seem rather precarious.

The town and palace of Chantilly, rendered classical by the name of the great Prince of Condé, afforded us ample room for interesting reflection. The town itself is pleasant, and has some good houses agreeably situated. But in the present state of internal convulsion, almost all the windows of the houses of the better class were closed, and secured by outer shutters. We were told that this was to protect them against the Prussians, with whom the town was crowded. These soldiers were very young lads, chiefly *landwehr*, or militia, and seemed all frolicksome, and no doubt mischievous youths. But, so far as I could see, there was no ill-nature, much less atrocity, in their behaviour, which was rather that of riotous school-boys of the higher form. They possessed themselves of the jack-boots of our postilions, and seemed to find great entertainment in stumping up and down the inn-yard in these formidable accoutrements, the size and solidity of which have been in no degree diminished since the days of Yorick and La Fleur. But our Prussian hussars were seen to still greater advantage in the superb stables of Chantilly, which have escaped the fury that levelled its palace. The huge and stately vault, which pride, rather than an attention to utility, had constructed for the stud of the Prince of Condé, is forty feet high, two hundred yards in length, and upwards of thirty-six feet in width. This magnificent apartment, the enormity of whose proportions seemed better calculated for the steeds of the King of Brobdingnag than for Houyhnhnms of the ordinary size, had once been divided into suitable ranges of stalls, but these have been long demolished. In the centre arises a magnificent dome, sixty feet in diameter, and ninety feet in height; and in a sort of recess beneath the dome, and fronting the principal entrance, is a superb foun-

tain, falling into a huge shell, and dashing over its sides into a large reservoir, highly ornamented with architectural decorations. This fountain, which might grace the court of a palace, was designed for the ordinary supply of the stable. The scale of imposing magnificence upon which this building was calculated, although at war with common sense and the fitness of things, must, in its original state of exact order and repair, have impressed the mind with high ideas of the power and consequence of the prince by whom it was planned and executed, and whose name (Louis Henry de Bourbon, seventh Prince of Condé) stands yet recorded in an inscription, which, supported by two mutilated genii, is displayed above the fountain. But what would have been the mortification of that founder, could he have witnessed, as we did, the spacious range with all its ornaments broken down and defaced, as if in studied insult; while its high and echoing vault rung to the shouts, screams, and gambols of a hundred or two of the dirtiest hussars and lancers that ever came off a march, to whose clamours the shrill cries of their half-starved and miserable horses added a wild but appropriate accompaniment. Yet, whatever his feelings might have been to witness such pollution, they would have been inferior to those with which his ancestor, the Great Condé, would have heard that the Sarmatian partisans who occupied Chantilly formed part of an invading army, which had marched, almost without opposition, from the frontiers to the capital, and now held in their disposal the fates of the house of Bourbon and of the kingdom of France.

The old domestic of the family who guided me through these remains of decayed magnificence, cast many a grieved and mortified glance upon the irreverent and mischievous soldiers as they aimed the butts of their lances at the remaining pieces of sculpture, or amused themselves by mimicking his own formal address and manner. " *Ah les barbares! les barbares!*"—I could not refuse assent to this epithet, which he confided to my ear in a cautious whisper, accompanied with a suitable shrug of the shoulders; but I endeavoured to qualify it with another train of reflections:—" *Et pourtant, mon ami, si ce n'étoit pas ces gens-là!*"—" *Ah oui, Monsieur, sans eux nous n'aurions peut-être jamais revû notre bon Duc—Assurément c'est un bon revenant—mais aussi, il faut avouer qu'il est revenu en assez mauvaise compagnie.*"

At some distance from these magnificent stables, of which (as frequently happens) the exterior does more honour to the architect's taste than the inside to his judgment, are the melancholy remains of the palace of the Prince of Condé, where the spectator can no longer obey the exhortation of the poet,—

" *Dans sa pompe élégante, admires Chantilly,*
  De héros en héros, d'âge en âge embelli."

The splendid chateau once corresponded in magnificence with the superb offices which we had visited, but now its vestiges alone remain, a mass of neglected ruins amid the broad lake and canals which had been constructed for its ornament and defence. This beautiful palace was destroyed by the revolutionary mob of Paris early in the civil commotions. The materials, with the lead, iron, carpenter work, &c., were piled up, by those who appropriated them, in what was called Le Petit Chateau, a smaller edifice annexed to the principal palace, and communicating with it by a causeway. Thus the small chateau was saved from demolition, though not from pillage. Chantilly and its demesnes were sold as national property, but the purchasers having failed to pay the price, it reverted to the public; so that the King, upon his restoration, had no difficulty in reinstating the Duke of Bourbon. The lesser chateau has been lately refitted in a hasty and simple style, for the reception of the legitimate proprietor ; but the style of the repairs makes an unavoidable and mortifying contrast with the splendour of the original decorations. Rich embossed ceilings and carved wainscot are coarsely daubed over with white-wash and size-paint, with which the remains of the original gilding and sculpture form a melancholy association. The frames alone remained of those numerous and huge mirrors,

> "In which he of Gath,
> Goliath, might have seen his giant bulk
> Whole without stooping, towering crest and all "
> MILTON.

But the French artisans, with that lack of all feeling of *contenance*, or propriety, which has well been described as a principal deficiency in their national character, have endeavoured to make fine things out of the frames themselves, by occupying the room of the superb plates of glass with paltry sheets of blue paper, patched over with gilded *fleur-de-lis*, an expedient the pitiful effect of which may be easily conceived. If I understood my guide rightly, however, this work ought not to be severely criticized, being the free-will offering of the inhabitants of Chantilly, who had struggled, in the best manner their funds and taste would admit, to restore the chateau to something like an habitable condition when it was again to be possessed by its legitimate owner. This is the more likely, as the furniture of the duke's own apartment is plain, simple, and in good taste. He seems popular among the inhabitants, who, the day preceding our arrival, had, under all the unfavourable circumstances of their situation, made a little *fête* to congratulate him upon his restoration, and to hail the white flag, which now once more floated from the dome of the offices, announcing the second restoration of the Bourbons.

Beside the Petit Chateau are the vestiges of what was once the principal palace, and which, as such, might well have accommodated the proudest monarch in the world. It was situated on a rock, and surrounded by profound and broad ditches of the purest water, built in a style of the richest Gothic architecture, and containing within its precincts every accommodation which pomp or luxury could desire. The demolition has been so complete, that little remains excepting the vaults from which the castle arose, and a ruinous flight of double steps, by which visitors formerly gained the principal entrance. The extent, number, and intricacy of the subterranean vaults, were such as to afford a retreat for robbers and banditti, for which reason the entrances have been built up by order of the police. The chateau, when in its splendour, communicated with a magnificent theatre, with an orangery and greenhouse of the first order, and was surrounded by a number of separate parterres, or islands, decorated with statuary, with *jets d'eau*, with columns, and with vases, forming a perspective of the richest architectural magnificence. All is now

destroyed, and the stranger only learns, from the sorrowful tale of his guide, that the wasted and desolate patches of ground intersected by the canals, once bore, and deserved, the names of the Gallery of Vases, the Parterre of the Orangerie, and the Island of Love. Such and so sudden is the downfall of the proudest efforts of human magnificence. Let us console ourselves, my dear friend, while we look from the bartizan of the old mansion upon the lake, and its corresponding barrier of mountains, that the beauties with which Nature herself has graced our country are more imperishable than those with which the wealth and power of the house of Bourbon once decorated the abode of Chantilly.

I may add, that the neighbourhood of Chantilly exhibits more picturesque beauty than I had yet remarked in France.

PAUL.

LETTER XII.

PAUL TO HIS SISTER.

Paris—Tuileries—Reflections—Tuileries—Parisian Punning—Statue of Bonaparte—Public Works by Bonaparte—Want of Pavement—Courts before the Houses—No Smoke over Paris—The Seine—Church of St. Genevieve—Tombs in the Pantheon—Mirabeau and Marat—Voltaire and Rousseau—Anecdote.

YOUR question, my dear sister, What do I think of Paris? corresponds in comprehensive extent with your desire that I would send you a full and perfect description of that celebrated capital; but were I to reside here all my life, instead of a few weeks, I am uncertain whether I could distinctly comply with either request. There is so much in Paris to admire, and so much to dislike, such a mixture of real taste and genius, with so much frippery and affectation,—the sublime is so oddly mingled with the ridiculous, and the pleasing with the fantastic and whimsical, that I shall probably leave the capital of France without being able to determine which train of ideas it has most frequently excited in my mind. One point is, however, certain :—that, of all capitals, that of France affords most numerous objects of curiosity, accessible in the easiest manner ; and it may be therefore safely pronounced one of the most entertaining places of residence which can be chosen by an idle man. As for attempting a description of it, that, you know, is far beyond the limits of our compact, which you must have quite forgotten when you hinted at such a proposal. The following sketch may not, however, be uninteresting.

If we confine our observation to one quarter of Paris only, that, namely, which is adjacent to the Royal Palace, I presume there is no capital which can show so many and such magnificent public edifices within the same space of ground. The Tuileries, whose immense extent makes amends for the deficiencies of the architecture, communicate with the royal gardens, which are used as public walks, and these again open into the Place de Louis Quinze, a large octagon, guarded by a handsome balustrade, richly ornamented at the angles, having, on the one hand, the royal gardens with the range of the palace, on the other the Champs Elysées, a large space of ground, planted and laid out in regular walks like those of Hyde-Park. Behind is the extensive colonnade of a palace, called by Bonaparte the Temple of Victory, and since the Restoration the Temple of Concord. Another large and half-finished temple was rising in the front by the command of Bonaparte, which was dedicated to the honour of soldiers who had died in battle. The building was to have been consolidated solely by the weight of the massive stones made use of, and neither wood, iron, or lime, was to be employed in its construction; but schemes of ambition as ill cemented interrupted its progress. A line of buildings extend on either hand, forming a magnificent street, called La Rue Rivoli, which runs parallel with the iron palisade of the garden of the Tuileries.

It was on the second night after my arrival in Paris, that, finding myself rather too early for an evening party to which I was invited, I strolled out, enjoying the pure and delicious air of a summer night in France, until I found myself in the centre of the Place de Louis Quinze, surrounded, as I have described it, by objects so noble in themselves, and so powerfully associated with deep historic and moral interest. "And here I am at length in Paris," was the natural reflection, "and under circumstances how different from what I dared to have anticipated! That is the palace of Louis le Grand, but how long have his descendants been banished from its halls, and under what auspices do they now again possess them! This superb esplanade takes its name from his luxurious and feeble descendant; and here, upon the very spot where I now stand, the most virtuous of the Bourbon race expiated, by a violent death inflicted by his own subjects, and in view of his own palace, the ambition and follies of his predecessors. There is an awful solemnity in the reflection, how few of those who contributed to this deed of injustice and atrocity now look upon the day, and behold the progress of retribution. The glimmering lights that shine among the alleys and parterres of the Champs Elysées, indicate none of the usual vigils common in a metropolis. They are the watch-fires of a camp, of an English camp, and in the capital of France, where an English drum has not been heard since 1436, when the troops of Henry the Sixth were expelled from Paris. During that space, of nearly four centuries, there has scarce occurred a single crisis which rendered it probable for a moment that Paris should be again entered by the English as conquerors; but least of all could such a consummation have been expected at the conclusion of a war, in which France so long predominated as arbitress of the continent, and which had periods when Britain seemed to continue the conflict only in honourable despair."

There were other subjects of deep interest around me. The lights which proceeded from the windows and from the gardens of the large hotel occupied by the Duke of Wellington, at the corner of the Rue des Champs Elysées, and which chanced that evening to be illuminated in honour of a visit from the allied sovereigns, mingled with the twinkle of the camp-fires, and the glimmer of the tents; and the music, which played a variety of English and Scottish airs, harmonized with the distant roll of the drums, and the notes of that beautiful point of war which is performed by our bugles at the

setting of the watch. In these sounds there was pride, and victory, and honour, some portion of which descended (in imagination at least) to each, the most retired and humblest fellow-subject of the hero who led, and the soldiers who obeyed, in the achievements which had borne the colours of Britain into the capital of France. But there was enough around me to temper the natural feelings of elation, which, as a Briton, I could not but experience. Monuments rose on every side, designed to commemorate mighty actions which may well claim the highest praise that military achievement alone, abstracted from the cause in which it was accomplished, could be entitled to. From the centre of the Place Vendôme, and above the houses of the Rue Rivoli, arose the summit of the celebrated column which Bonaparte had constructed upon the plan of that of Trajan; the cannon taken at Ulm and Austerlitz affording the materials of its exterior, and which is embossed with a detailed representation of the calamities and subjection of Austria. At no great distance lay the Bridge of Jena, an epithet which recalls the almost total annihilation of the kingdom of Prussia. In the front of the Tuileries are placed, on a triumphal arch, the Venetian Horses, the trophies of the subjugation of Italy, and in the neighbouring Louvre are deposited the precious spoils of victories gained and abused in every country of Europe, forming the most resistless evidence, that the hand which placed them there had once at its arbitrary disposal the fortunes of the greater part of the civilized world. No building among the splendid monuments of Paris, but is marked with the name, or device, or insignia of an emperor, whose power seemed as deeply founded as it was widely extended. Yet the gourd of the prophet, which came up in a night and perished in a night, has proved the type of authority so absolute, and of fame so diffused; and the possessor of this mighty power is now the inhabitant of a distant and sequestered islet, with hardly so much free-will as entitles him to claim from his warders an hour of solitude, even in the most solitary spot in the civilized world. The moral question presses on every bosom, Was it worth while for him to have climbed so high to render his fall the deeper, or would the meanest of us purchase the feverish feelings of gratified ambition, at the expense of his reflections, who appeared to hold Fortune chained to his footstool! Could the fable of the Seven Sleepers have been realized in Paris, what a scene of astonishment would have been prepared for those, who, falling asleep in 1813, awakened from their torpor at the present moment! He who had seen the Pope place the crown upon the head of Napoleon, and the proud house of Austria compelled to embrace his alliance, Prussia bent to the dust beneath his footstool, England excluded from each continental connexion of commerce or alliance, Russia overawed and submissive, while Italy, Germany, and the greater part of Spain, were divided as appanages among his brothers and allies,—what would have been the surprise of the waking moment, which should have shown him the Prussian cannon turned upon the bridges of Paris, and the sovereigns of Austria, Russia, and Prussia, with the representatives of almost all the other nations of Europe, feasting in the capital of France with the general and minister of England, supported by a force which made resistance equally frantic and hopeless! The revolution of ages must have appeared to him to have been accomplished within the space of little more than twenty-four months.[1]

From this slight sketch, you may have some general idea of the magnificence of that quarter of Paris which adjoins to the Tuileries, crowded as it is with palaces, public monuments, and public buildings, and comprehending in its circuit ornamented gardens and extended walks, open to the inhabitants for exercise or pleasure. I ought also to describe to you the front of the palace itself, a magnificent range of buildings, corresponding with the Louvre, another immense royal mansion, from which the Tuileries is only divided by the superb square, called La Place du Carousel. The only screen betwixt this square and the court of the Tuileries, is a magnificent railing of wrought iron, which gives freedom to the eye, not only to survey the extended front of the chateau, but to penetrate through the central vestibule of the palace into the gardens beyond, and as far as the Champs Elysées. In the centre of this screen the public have admittance to the courtyard of the palace, beneath a triumphal arch, which Bonaparte erected in imitation of that of Septimus Severus. The effect of this monument seems diminutive when compared to the buildings around; the columns, made of a mixed red and white marble, are rather gaudy; and the four celebrated Venetian horses, formed of Corinthian brass, which occupy the top of the arch, have been injudiciously harnessed with gilded trappings to a gilded car, driven by a gilded Victory. It is said Bonaparte intended to have placed his own figure in the car; but it came to his ears, (for he was self-tormentor enough to inquire after such matters,) that the disaffected had hailed it, as likely to afford a good opportunity for calling him mountebank with impunity, since, while they should point to the chariot, the epithet *Le Charlatan* might easily be substituted for *Le Char le tient.*[2] Thus a threatened pun saved Napoleon's image one descent at least, by preventing its temporary elevation; and it also saved the French taste the disgrace of adding another incongruity to the gilded car, harness, and driver. This monument is now undergoing considerable alterations. The Austrians are busy in exchanging for plain slabs of marble, the tablatures placed around the arch: The sculptures almost all relate to the humiliation of the Emperor of Austria, there represented cap-in-hand before Bonaparte, who appears covered, and in an authoritative posture. The French rebelled against the mutilation of this monument at

its commencement, and attempted something like a riot, but were instantly called to order by a strong Prussian guard. The work now goes on quietly, and not without some respect to the feelings of the Parisians; for there are blinds of wood put up before the scaffolding, to save their eyes the mortification of seeing its progress. It is not doubted that the horses themselves will be removed in due time.[3]

In the meanwhile, the statue of Bonaparte, which was last year taken down from the pillar in the Place Vendôme, is said to have experienced an odd transition. It had been exchanged for a certain number of busts and small figures of Louis XVIII., just as a large piece of coin of one reign is given for an equivalent in the small money of another. The figure of the abdicated emperor for some time found refuge in the yard of an artist, by whom it has since been sold to an Englishman. The purchase is believed to be made in behalf of the Duke of Wellington, in which case the statue will be a striking ornament to the palace destined by national gratitude as an acknowledgment at least of the debt, which even the wealth and generosity of Britain cannot pay in full.[4]

To return to the works of Bonaparte. It cannot be denied that he showed great ability and dexterity in availing himself of that taste for national display, which is a leading feature of the French character. Yet this was, at least, as much evinced in the address with which he adopted and carried through the half-accomplished plans of Louis XIV. and his successors, as in any work of original genius which can be decidedly traced to his own design. The triumphal arch, and the pillar in the Place Vendôme, are literal, almost servile, imitations of the column of Trajan and the arch of Severus. But the splendid extension of the Louvre, by the combination of that striking pile with the Tuileries, upon the side which had been left unfinished, although the work of Bonaparte, and bearing his name, is, in fact, only a completion of the original design of Louis XIV. One original plan Napoleon may indeed claim as his own—the project, namely, of erecting a stupendous bronze figure of an elephant upon the site of the Bastile. The sort of castle, or Howdar, with which this monstrous statue was to have been accoutred, was designed for a reservoir, the water of which, being discharged through the trunk into a large cistern, or fountain, surrounding the pedestal on which the animal was placed, was to supply with water all that quarter of Paris. The model of this gigantic grotesque is exhibited in stucco near the place which it was designed to have occu-

[1] " 'Tis done—but yesterday a King!
And arm'd with kings to strive—
And now thou art a nameless thing:
So abject—yet alive!
Is this the man of thousand thrones
Who strew'd our earth with hostile bones,
And can he thus survive?
Since he, miscall'd the Morning Star,
Nor man nor fiend hath fallen so far.

" Ill-minded man! why scourge thy kind,
Who bow'd so low the knee?
By gazing on thyself grown blind,
Thou taught'st the rest to see.
With might unquestion'd,—power to save,—
Thine only gift hath been the grave
To those that worshipp'd thee;
Nor till thy fall could mortals guess
Ambition's less than littleness!
492

" Thanks for that lesson—it will teach
To after-warriors more
Than high Philosophy can preach,
And vainly preach'd before.
That spell upon the minds of men
Breaks never to unite again,
That led them to adore
Those Pagod things of sabre sway
With fronts of brass and feet of clay."
BYRON'S *Ode to Napoleon.*

[2] The common edition of the story is, that a punster, pointing to the *empty* car, said, *Le Char l'attend.*

[3] This removal has since taken place.—See a very lively account of the circumstances, and its effect upon the feelings of the Parisians, in Mr. John Scott's " Paris Revisited."—S.

[4] The statue of Napoleon was replaced on the pillar of the Place Vendôme soon after the Revolution of July, 1830.

pied, and such is the deference of the present government for the feelings of *la gloire nationale*, that they have not yet ventured to avow, that, in a time of national poverty and distress, they mean to dispense with erecting a monument, which, after being accomplished at immense expense, must appear *bizarre* and fanciful, rather than grand and impressive. In the meanwhile they are, in justice to the ancestors of the present king, reclaiming for the Bourbons those public buildings, which, by inscriptions and emblems, Napoleon had consecrated to his own dynasty. N.'s are everywhere disappearing, or undergoing a conversion into H.'s and B.'s, an operation in which the royal stone-cutters are as much called upon to exert their dexterity as the poor sign-painters in Roye, Peronne, and Cambray. They have, indeed, the same benefit of experience, having, not very long ago, accomplished the counterpart of the metamorphosis. Such are the minute and ridiculous consequences which indicate a change of government, as much as the motion of straws, twigs, and withered leaves upon the surface, indicates the progress and subsiding of a torrent.

On the whole, it must be acknowledged, that Bonaparte, though unscrupulous in appropriating the merit of his predecessors, bent an earnest and active attention to perfecting whatever grand or magnificent plans they had left uncompleted, thus establishing his own reputation as heir of the monarchy, as well as of the revolution. His ambition to distinguish himself sometimes soared beyond popular prejudice, and hurried him into extravagances of expense, which the Parisians seem in general to deem unnecessary. Such is the plan of his Rue de l'Empereur, now Rue de la Paix, a fine street, running from the Place Vendôme to the Boulevards des Capucines, which not only boasts a breadth corresponding to the magnificence of the buildings, but is actually accommodated with *two gutters*, one on each side, instead of that single kennel in the centre, where the filth floats or stagnates in all the other streets in Paris. But even the Emperor Napoleon, in the height of his dignity, dared not introduce the farther novelty of a pavement on each side. This would be, indeed, to have destroyed that equality between horse and foot, walkers, drivers, and driven, which appears to give such delight to a Parisian, that if you extol to him the safe pavements and footpaths of an English street or road, he will answer with polite composure— "*C'est tres bien pour Messieurs les Anglois—pour moi, j'aime la totalité de la rue.*" Good phrases, saith Justice Shallow, are and ever must be commended ; and this, of *la totalité de la rue*, reconciles a Parisian walker to all the inconveniences of being ridden down or driven over. But the privilege of *totality* by no means compensates to the aged, the timid, the infirm, not to mention females and children, for the accidents to which they are exposed. At present these are multiplied by the numerous accession of strangers, all of whom drive in their own way, and give their own mode of warning, which the pedestrian must construe rightly upon his own peril. Here he hears the *Hey! hey!* of a member of the English Four-in-hand Club ; there he is called to attention by the *Gare! gare!* of a Parisian petit maitre, or a German Freyherr ; and having escaped all these hair-breadth risks, he may be ridden down at the next turning by a

drosky, the driver of which, a venerable Russian charioteer, with a long beard flowing down to his girdle, pushes right on to his destined course with the most unperturbed apathy, without giving passengers warning of any kind to shift for themselves.

The risk, however, to pedestrians, does not form my only objection to the French metropolis, abstracted always from those splendid streets which belong to the quarter of the Tuileries. The rest of Paris, excepting the *Boulevards*, a peculiar sort of open suburb by which it is surrounded, is traversed by narrow streets, which divide buildings dark, high, and gloomy, the lower windows grated with projecting iron-rails of the most massive description, and the houses belonging to persons of importance opening by what is called a *porte-cochère*, or carriage-entrance, into courts which intervene between them and the street. By thus sequestering their mansions, the great do indeed deprive the shopkeeper, or roturier, who lives opposite, of the power of looking upon the windows of his neighbour, the duke, count, or marquis. Nevertheless, mansions constructed upon this unsocial and aristocratic plan, by which the splendour of the habitations of the noble and wealthy is reserved and veiled, as too dazzling and precious to form a part of the public street, cannot contribute to the general beauty of the city in which they are placed. I do not, however, mean to say, that the other quarters of Paris, though gloomy, dark, and traversed chiefly by these narrow and perilous passes, are devoid of a strong and peculiar interest. On the contrary, the constant appearance of public edifices, distinguished in history, of Gothic churches and halls, of squares and *places*, surrounded by stately buildings, perpetually, even in the most disagreeable quarters of Paris, reminds us that we are in a capital early distinguished for arts and arms, and where even the rudeness and inconvenience of many streets, joined to the solid, massive, and antique structures to which they give access, argue at once early importance and ancient dignity.

It appears a remarkable peculiarity to a British eye, when Paris is viewed from a distance, that over buildings so closely piled together, there arises not that thick and dense cloud of smoke which sometimes graces and dignifies, but more frequently deforms, a view of London, or any other large town in our island. This is owing to the Parisians using wood for fuel, and that frequently in the shape of charcoal, but always sparingly, and in stoves, instead of our sea-coal burnt in open chimneys. Seen from the heights of Montmartre, or the dome of St. Genevieve, Paris exhibits a distinct mass of houses, steeples, and towers, unclouded, but also unsoftened, by the dusky canopy which hangs over a British city. My Parisian friends laughed heartily, and, on the whole, deservedly, at my regretting the absence of this dusky accompaniment, which does nevertheless add a shadowy importance, and even a softness to the landscape, or, admitting associations, and pleading on those to which we are accustomed, gives an assurance of business and life to what, without such an indication of living bustle, seems not unlike the appearance of the town in the Arabian tale, whose inhabitants had been all petrified. I own this is a prejudiced feeling, and do not contest the right which a Frenchman has to associate with the cloud which overhangs our metropolis, all that is disgusting, and perhaps unhealthy, in the gross evaporation of our coarser fuel.[1]

The Seine is usually appealed to by the Parisians as the principal beauty of their city, and it is at least one of its greatest conveniences. But Lord Chesterfield furnished an answer to the proud question, whether England could show the like—" Yes —and we call it Fleet-ditch." This gasconade is like that of the French veteran lecturing upon invasion, who spits upon the ground, and says to his audience, " Voila la Tamise,"—a hyperbole which may be excused from ignorance, as no French soldier has happened to see the Thames for many a century, excepting as a guest or a prisoner in England. But, laying jests aside, the Seine is far from having the majestic appearance of the Thames, being diminutive both in depth and breadth, and strait-waistcoated by a range of ungraceful quays, a greater deformity than those of London, because rendered conspicuous by the narrowness of the stream. The river being divided also at two intervals by small islands, completely occupied by buildings, we are induced to entertain a contemptuous opinion of the Seine, as completely subjugated and tyrannized over by the despotic authority of human art. Several of the walks along its side are nevertheless most interesting, particularly the Quai de Voltaire, from which the passenger views the superb and long extent of colonnade belonging to the Louvre, while farther down the river are seen the gardens of the Tuileries and the trees of Les Champs Elysées.

The finest views of Paris are to be seen from the heights of Montmartre, which rise as close behind the city as the Calton-hill in respect to Edinburgh, and from some of the steeples, particularly that of St. Genevieve, a magnificent new church of Grecian architecture originally dedicated to the titular saint of Paris; next polluted by the appellation of the Temple of Reason; then solemnly entitled the Pantheon, because it was to be the place for depositing the bodies of departed sages and patriots; and lastly restored by Bonaparte to the character of a Christian church, without taking away its destination as a general mausoleum for departed worth. The honours, however, of those who received this distinction, were not always permanent. There was "no snug lying in the abbey." Several of those revolutionary chiefs whose remains the faction of the day had installed in this sanctuary, were torn from thence shortly afterwards, and thrown, like the corpse of Sejanus, into the common-sewer of the city. The bodies of other heroes of the day have been withdrawn in secret, lest they should suffer the same fate. In some instances the temporary tenant of the tomb was dispossessed, and made to give way to a popular character of more recent celebrity. Thus the corpse of Mirabeau was removed from the Pantheon to make room for that of Marat; on which occasion one of the family of the former returned thanks to Heaven for an expulsion, which, as he expressed himself, "re-established the honour of his house." The corpse of the villain Marat, after having had at least the honour of one bloody sacrifice, in the

trial and execution of a man who had offered an insult to his temporary monument, was soon after, 28th July, 1793, dragged from the church, and thrown into the common-sewer of the Rue de Montmartre. At length, weary or ashamed of their own versatility, the National Convention, in the year 1795, decreed that no citizen should receive the honours of the Pantheon until ten years after his death; a decree which amounted almost to a universal sentence of exclusion, in a country where the present occupies solely the attention of the public. Of all those to whom the various legislative bodies of France decreed this posthumous distinction, there have only remained in the Pantheon the tombs of two authors, Voltaire and Rousseau. The remains of those distinguished literary characters were deposited here, during the early fervour of the Revolution, with shouts and with hymns, and with tears, and with transports of that universal philanthropy, which shortly afterwards made its real character evident to the world. A painted wooden sarcophagus, much like a deal packing-box in form and materials, is laid above the grave of each, with a mouldering inscription expressive of what the Legislative Assembly intended to do for the honour of the philosophers whose talents illumined the 18th century. But the rotten board on which their decrees are registered, frail as it is, has proved a record more permanent than the power that placed it there. The monuments of despotism are more durable than those of anarchy; and accordingly some of Bonaparte's generals and senators are buried in the Pantheon, and, though men of inferior note, have been suffered to enjoy in quiet that repose, which even the tomb could not secure for the Republican demagogues.

In visiting this church, or temple, I was entertained by the dry answer of an Englishman, who had followed us up to the dome without the observation of the sexton. Our guide seemed a little hurt at the stranger's presumption, and from time to time addressed to him a few words of reprehension, stating the risk he ran of being bewildered in the vaults, and perhaps shut up there. As I perceived my countryman did not understand in what he had given offence, I explained to him the sexton's remonstrance. " Tell him," answered the stranger, with great gravity, " that if the misfortune he threatens had really befallen me, I would have had only to call out Sixpence, and all Paris would have come to my rescue." With deference, however, to this honest specimen of John Bull, the access of the public to what is worthy of notice in Paris is much less frequently impeded by a functionary stretching forth his hand for a fee, than is the case in London; and when we recollect the mode in which the various departments of St. Paul's and Westminster Abbey are secured by a dozen of petty turnpikes and tax-gatherers, we may judge more fairly of the sexton of St. Genevieve.

The liberality of the French nation, in affording every possible means to the public of enjoying the collections of curiosities, or of scientific objects, made for their behalf, instead of rendering them sources of profit to some obscure pensioner, per-

---

[1] " A mighty mass of brick, and smoke, and shipping,
Dirty and dusky, but as wide as eye
Could reach, with here and there a sail just skipping
In sight, then lost amidst the forestry

Of masts; a wilderness of steeples peeping
On tiptoe through their sea-coal canopy;
A huge, dun cupola, like a foolscap crown
On a fool's head—and there is London town!"
Don Juan, canto x., st. 82

vades all their establishments; and strangers, for whose use and convenience even greater facilities are afforded than are given to the natives, are called upon to acknowledge it with gratitude. If there be in this open display of the treasures which they possess some traces of national pride, it is in this case an honest and fair pride, and those who derive so much benefit from its effects ought to be the last to question its motive. One or two of these objects of curiosity I shall briefly notice in my next letter, not with the purpose of giving a regular description of them, but to mark, if I can, by a few characteristic strokes, the peculiarities which attracted my own attention.

Adieu; I rest ever your affectionate

Paul.

LETTER XIII.

THE SAME TO THE SAME.

Garden of Plants—Museum of French Monuments—Central Museum—Hall of Sculptures—Malmaison.

I HAVE already said, my dear sister, that of all capitals in the world, Paris must afford the most delightful residence to a mere literary lounger; and if we add, that his fortune is limited, (as is usually the case with such a character,) it will suit him, after a little experience, as well in point of economy as of taste. The *Jardin des Plantes*, the National Library, the Collection of French Monuments, the National Institute, above all, the Grand Museum in the Louvre, are gratuitously opened to his inspection and use, while theatres, and public amusements of various kinds, in the evening, may be frequented for little expense.

I know that nothing in Paris would delight you more than the *Jardin des Plantes.* This grand botanical garden, of several acres extent, richly stocked with the most varied and curious productions of the vegetable world, is equally interesting to the scientific student, and to the idler, who seeks only for shaded walks and interesting and beautiful points of view. The variety of the ground, the disposition of the trees, and the neighbourhood of the Seine, afford the last in considerable variety; while the shade, so grateful in this warm climate, is secured by many a long alley and avenue. The establishment is maintained entirely at the expense of the public. The learned in physics may here have the advantage of a chemical laboratory, of lectures upon botany and natural history by men of approved science, of an anatomical collection, and a valuable library, composed of works relative to natural history. There is also a menagerie upon a great scale of splendour, as well as of comfort to the animals with which it is tenanted. Those which are of a dangerous description are properly secured, but still with due attention to their habits and convenience. The bears, for example, inhabit subterranean residences, each of which opens into a sunk area, of depth enough to prevent escape, but of such extent that Bruin may repose himself, or take exercise, at his pleasure, I seldom pass this place without seeing some of the Prussian or Russian soldiers engaged in talking to and feeding the bears, whom, in this southern clime, they probably regard as a kind of countrymen. The elephant,

485

a most magnificent animal of the kind, has, as befits his good sense and civilized behaviour, a small paddock around his cabin, secured from the public by a strong palisade. He had a mate some years ago, but is now a widower; very good-humoured, however, and familiar with the passengers. Gentler animals, such as the varieties of the deer species, are allowed space in proportion to their size; and it is only the fiercer tribes of Africa and Asia, lions, tigers, and leopards, which are committed to strict confinement. These also are kept clean, and made as comfortable as circumstances will permit; and, on the whole, it is impossible to conceive an institution of the kind managed with more respect to the feelings and convenience of the creatures contained in it. If a stranger is curious to know the names of the various animals, there is always some Frenchman near, who, either merely to do the honours to Monsieur l'Etranger, or at most for *quelque chose pour boire*, walks with you through the collection, and displays at once his eloquence, and that sort of information which is frequently found among the Parisians, even of the lower orders. To me, who am no naturalist, such a guide seems often as interesting a specimen as any in the collection. The contrast of his meagre looks and tattered dress, with the air of patronage which he assumes towards the stranger under his charge; his pompous encomiums on the objects he exhibits; his grave injunctions not to approach too near the grates of the more dangerous quadrupeds; the importance with which he gives the scientific appellation of each animal, condescendingly adding that which is in more vulgar use; and the polite gratitude of his *"Monsieur est tres honnête,"* when he pockets his little gratuity, and puts on the *schakos*, which he has hitherto held in his hand for the sake of aiding his eloquence,—all these points brought together give a character of the lower rank not to be met with out of France, and rarely out of Paris.

The antiquary who visits Paris, must be deeply interested by a visit to the Museum *des Monumens Français*, assembled by Mons. Le Noir, in the church, convent, and gardens of Les petits Augustins. This collection proved a sort of asylum for such monuments of art as could be saved from popular fury during the first revolutionary fever, comprehending the tombs of princes, legislators, and heroes. When the churches were sacked and pillaged, and the property of the clergy was confiscated to the use of the nation, Mons. Le Noir had the courage to attempt to save from impending ruin objects invaluable for the history of the arts and for that of the nation, and he had the address to devise a probable mode of succeeding in a plan, which, in those furious days, might have been represented as savouring of aristocracy and *insevisme*. He obtained from the National Assembly a recommendation to their Committee of Alienation, to watch over and protect the monuments of art in the churches and domains which they had confiscated to national use. This was followed by a warrant, authorising a Committee of Savants, of whom Le Noir was most active, to select and transport to Paris those relics of antiquity, and there to arrange them in one general collection, so as to afford a view of the progress of the arts during the several periods of French history. Much exertion accordingly has been made, and upon the whole with considerable success, to dispose this various and miscellaneous collection according to centuries, and at the same time to place the productions of each era in the best and fittest order. You accompany, therefore, in the progress of the arts and that of history, as you wander from hall to hall, and compare the rude images of Clovis and Pharamond with what the Italian chisel produced to commemorate departed greatness, in that happy epoch which the French artists call *Le Siècle de la Renaissance.* Several monuments, the size of which rendered them unfit for a cloister, are erected in the gardens; and particularly the tomb of Abelard and Heloise, with those of Des Cartes, Molière, La Fontaine, Boileau, and others dear to French literature.

Yet such is the caprice of the human mind, that even from this rich mental feast we return with some degree of dissatisfaction. The inspection of the Museum inspired me at least with a feeling greater in degree, but similar in origin, to that with which I have regarded a collection of engraved English portraits—

" Torn from their destined page—unworthy meed
Of knightly counsel or heroic deed,"—

and compiled to illustrate a Grainger, at the expense of many a volume defaced and rendered imperfect. Far deeper is that sensation rooted, when we consider that the stones accumulated around us have been torn from the graves which they were designed to mark out and to protect, and divided from all those associations arising from the neighbourhood of the mighty dead. It is also impossible, with the utmost care and ingenuity, that the monuments should be all displayed to advantage; and even the number of striking objects, huddled together, diminishes the effect which each, separately, is calculated to produce upon the mind. These wayward reflections will arise, and can only be checked by the recollection, that without prosecution of the plan wisely adopted and boldly followed out, the relics around us would have ceased to exist; and that the ingenious collector, far from being the plunderer of a wreck, has saved and protected its scattered fragments, which must have otherwise perished for ever.

If, in the Museum of *Monumens Français,* we contrast with advantage the principle and mode by which the collection is formed, with the effect produced by the present arrangement, and pardon, for the sake of the former, the necessary imperfections attached to the latter, no such favourable result can be drawn by the reflecting traveller, who visits the inimitable collection of paintings and statues in the Louvre, called the Central Museum of the Arts. It is indeed, abstractedly, a subject of just pride to a nation, that she can exhibit to strangers this surprisingly magnificent display of the works of human genius when in its most powerful and active mood, awakened as it were from the sleep of ages, and at once bringing to the service of art such varied talent as never was nor will be equalled. But if, with these exulting considerations, it were possible for the French to weigh the sum of evil which they have suffered and inflicted to obtain this grand object of national vanity, they might well view the most magnificent saloon in Europe as a charnel-vault, and the works of Raphael, Titian, and Salvator, as no better than the sable and tattered scutcheons which cover its mouldering walls. Each picture, indeed, has its 496

own separate history of murder, rapine, and sacrilege. It was, perhaps, the worst point in Bonaparte's character, that, with a firm and unremitting attention to his own plans and his own interest, he proceeded from battle to plunder, less like a soldier than a brigand or common highwayman, whose immediate object is to rifle the passenger whom he has subdued by violence or intimidation. But Napoleon knew well the people over whom he was called to rule, and was aware that his power was secure, despite of annihilated commerce and exhausted finances, despite of his waste of the lives of Frenchmen and treasure of France, despite of the general execration of the human race, echoed from the Baltic to the Mediterranean, providing he could prove to the Parisians that he was still the Emperor of the World, and Paris its capital. *Savants,* therefore, *amateurs,* and artists, whose skill and taste might supply the deficiency of his own, regularly attended upon his military expeditions; and when a city had surrendered, or had otherwise fallen into his power, whatever it possessed in public or private property evincing excellence in the arts, was destined to augment the Central Museum, and furnish a topic of consolation to those Parisians whose sons, perhaps, had fallen in battle under its walls. For this purpose every town in Italy was ransacked, and compelled by open violence, or a still more odious influence exercised under pretext of treaties, to surrender those specimens of sculpture and painting, whose very names had become associated with the classical situations, from which a true admirer of the arts would have deemed it sacrilege to have torn them. The Low Countries were compelled to yield up those masterpieces of the Flemish school, which are prized by amateurs as almost equal to those of Italy. Dresden, long famous for its collection of paintings, which Frederick the Great contented himself with admiring, was plundered, and only saved in part by the submission of the Elector.[1] Berlin and Potzdam underwent a similar fate; and while Bonaparte affected to restore to the subdued Monarch of Prussia his crown and kingdom, he actually pillaged his palaces of their most precious and domestic ornaments. Vienna was severely ransacked, with every inferior town in the Emperor's dominions, and that even at the period of an alliance cemented by the conqueror's union with a daughter of the house of Austria. The ancient capital of the Czars was destined to consign its old magnificence to the same accumulated heap of spoil. But there the robber's arm was shortened, and the plunder of the Kremlin was retaken ere it had crossed the Beresina. The very ornaments of the apartments were acquired by the same iniquitous means which had filled them with paintings and statues. The twelve granite pillars which supported the Hall of Sculpture were plundered from Aix la Chapelle, and the beautifully wrought bronze folding-doors at the upper end of the Grand Saloon were the spoils of a church at Rome. *Omnis Thaida Thais olet.* The collection in all its parts, magnificent and unmatched as it is, savours of the cruelty, perfidy, and rapine, by which it was accumulated.

[1] It is believed that this is a mistake—that in fact no picture was ever carried to Paris from the gallery at Dresden. —ED.

Many have therefore been tempted to think, that there was less wisdom or justice than magnanimity in the conduct of the allies during the preceding year, who, to save the feelings of the French, which in this case had no title to a moment's consideration, sacrificed the justice due to their own despoiled countries, and let pass the opportunity of giving a great moral lesson, without inflicting on France a single hardship, excepting what might flow from her wounded vanity. But Prussia, it seems, was satisfied with a promise (ill kept by the restored family) that her property should be redelivered when affairs were settled in France; and for the other nations no stipulation seems to have been made. If the allies on this occasion neglected to reclaim by force their own property when in their power, it would, nevertheless, have been just, and perhaps prudent, in the Bourbon family, to have, of their own accord, relinquished spoils which could only remind them of their own misfortunes. But they were too anxious to establish themselves in the opinion of their new subjects as good Frenchmen, to recollect that justice, open and even-handed, is the first duty of a Monarch. They were afraid to face the clamour which would have stigmatized an act of honest restitution as the concession of cowardice. As Bonaparte had been the heir of the Revolution, they were willing to be the heirs of Bonaparte, and appear to have been as little disposed to the doctrine of restitution as the worthy corregidor of Leon, who succeeded to the treasures of Captain Rolando's subterranean mansion. At least they were not unwilling, like the sons of a usurer, to possess treasures of such value, without sharing the guilt of the original acquisition. They did not reflect, that every token which carried back the Frenchman's recollection to the Emperor, must excite comparisons, among the thoughtless and unprincipled, highly unfavourable to the legitimate possessor of the crown.

The day of reckoning is at length arrived. The Museum, when I first arrived in Paris, was still entire. But Blucher, who was not, it seems, to be foiled a second time, has since made several visits, attended by a German artist, for the purpose of ascertaining and removing the pictures which belong to Prussia, or to the German States now united with her. The French guardians of the Museum also attended, no longer to decide upon the point of view in which the spoils of nations should be disposed, but to plead, occasionally and timidly, that such a picture formed no part of the cabinet of Potzdam, but had been stolen from some other collections. These demurrers were generally silenced by a " Tais toi," or " Halt Maul,"[1] from the veteran of Leon and Waterloo, who is no friend to prolonged discussions. If you ask, whether Prussia has recovered all the pictures which had been carried off at different times, I fancy I may return the same emphatic answer given by an old Scotch serving-man, when his master asked him if he had been careful to pack up all his wardrobe at leaving a friend's house,—" At least, your honour." Not that I suppose the Prince-Marshal has got a single article to which the French had any just title, but the late enlargement of the dominions of Prussia has greatly extended her claims of restitution in right of states and cities newly annexed to her

dominions; and I fancy she did not permit them to be over minutely scrutinized. Still, however, though nearly a hundred pictures have in this manner gradually disappeared, I have not missed one of those masterpieces to which the attention of the visitor is earliest directed and longest riveted. It is when the claims of Italy and the Netherlands shall be enforced that the principal disgorging of spoil will take place; and when that day comes, I believe it will drive some of the French amateurs to actual distraction. Their attachment to these paintings and statues, or rather to the national glory which they conceive them to illustrate, is as excessive as if the Apollo and Venus were still objects of actual adoration; and on the day of their departure I anticipate them exclaiming with Micah, " Ye have taken away my gods, and ye are gone away, and what have I more ! How then say ye unto me, what aileth me !"

It is, however, understood to be definitively settled by the allied sovereigns, that the French must undergo this mortification; as is evident by the generals, at the capitulation of Paris, having refused to sanction an article of the treaty proposed by the French, for securing the possession of these monuments. It is a severe mortification, doubtless; but, independent of the undeniable justice of the measure, it is wholesome that the French should have in future no trophies to appeal to as memorials that they had exercised a power over other states which their victors never had courage to retaliate; or to exhibit as emblems of past conquest, and as the incentive to new wars. The contents of the Museum have been found by bitter experience to perpetuate recollections, which, for the peace of France and of Europe, ought to be effaced as speedily and absolutely as possible. Such associations render the removal of the objects which excite them as necessary a precaution, as the burning of Don Quixote's library to prevent the recurrence of his frenzy.

With respect to the arts, you know I pretend to no skill in the province of the amateur; but the best judges seem to allow, that the dispersion of this immense collection is by no means unfavourable to their progress and improvement. We readily admit, and each spectator has felt, that nothing can be more magnificent, more august, more deeply impressive, taken as a whole, than that noble gallery, prolonged to an extent which the eye can hardly distinctly trace, and crowded on every side with the noblest productions of the most inspired artists. Fourteen hundred paintings, each claiming rank as a masterpiece, disposed upon walls which extend for more than twelve hundred feet in length, form, united, a collection unparalleled in extent and splendour. But a part of this charm vanishes when we have become familiar with the coup d'œil; and the emotions of surprise and pleasure which the transient visitor receives, are gained in some degree at the expense of the student, or studious amateur. In a saloon of such length and height, lighted too from both sides, it is impossible that all the pictures can be seen to advantage; and, in truth, many cannot be seen at all. In a selection where all is excellent, and worthy of studious and heedful attention, this is a disadvantage of no common kind. But it is not the only one. Each of these paintings, almost without exception, has in it something excellent; but, independent of the loss which they sustain in common, by being so much crowded together, and by making part rather of one grand and brilliant whole, than subjects important enough for detached and separate consideration, the merit of some of these *chefs d'œuvre* so far exceeds that of others, as altogether to divert the attention from objects of inferior, though still of exquisite skill. Few possessing even the most eager love for the art, though they have consumed hours, days, weeks, and months, in the Museum, have been able to escape that fascination which draws them to the Transfiguration of Raphæl, the Communion by Domenichino, the Martyrdom of the Inquisitor, and some other masterpieces. About fifty pictures at most, therefore, are copied, studied, examined, and worshipped, while more than twenty times that number are neglected and unseen, and, with all their admitted excellence, draw as little attention as the Nymphs and Graces in the suite of Venus. This shows that the appetite of taste, as well as of epicurism, may be satiated and rendered capricious by the exhibition of too rich and sumptuous a banquet, and that, our capacity of enjoyment being limited, there is no wisdom in an injudicious accumulation of means for its gratification. To the young student in particular, the feelings of satiety are peculiarly hazardous ; for either he becomes accustomed to indulge a capricious and presumptuous contempt of works which he has slightly studied, or he is deterred from boldly and vigorously venturing upon a laborious and difficult art, when he sees that excellence, of a pitch to which he dare not aspire, may, in company with the ultimate efforts of genius, be insufficient to secure respect and attention.

It might be added, that there are particular points, in which even those distinguished and selected patterns of supereminence, which throw every inferior degree of merit into shadow, lose, in some measure, the full impression of their own merit, by being disjoined from the local associations with a view to which they were painted. This is especially the case with the religious subjects executed for altar-pieces, and for the ornaments of chapels, where the artist had laboured to suit not only his size of figures and disposition of light to the place which the painting was to occupy, but had also given them a tone of colouring and a general character, harmonizing with the solemnity, not only of the subject, but of the scene around. To many a thorough-paced and hackneyed connoisseur, who considers the finest painting merely as a subject for his technical criticism, the divesting it of these exterior accompaniments will seem of little consequence. But those who love the art for the noble and enthusiastic feelings by the excitement of which it is best applauded, will feel some difference in considering a scripture-piece over the altar of a Gothic church, and in viewing the same painting where it forms part of an incongruous assemblage of landscapes and flower-pieces, with a group of drinking boors placed on one side, and an amour of Jupiter upon the other.

These observations apply only to the ostentatious assemblage of so many and such various specimens of the art in one extensive gallery. But had this objection not existed—had these paintings been so disposed in various apartments as to give each its appropriate situation, and secure for each that portion of attention which it merits, still objections would remain to the whole system. There is no wisdom in venturing as it were the fortunes of the world of art in one single collection, exposed to total and irredeemable destruction either from accidental fire, or the havoc of war, or popular frenzy. Had the Museum existed during the first years of the Revolution, its danger must have been most imminent, and twice during the space of a very few months has it narrowly escaped the risks which must have attended it had Paris been stormed.

Independent even of these considerations, and admitting this general accumulation of the treasures of art to be as desirable as it is certainly august and impressive, I should still hesitate to say that Paris is the city where they ought to be reposited. The French school, though it has produced many good artists, has been as remarkable for wanting, as the Italians for possessing, that dignity and simplicity of feeling which leads to the sublime. Poussin alone excepted, there is a flutter and affectation, a constraint of attitude to create point, and a studied contrast of colour and light to bring out effect, which marks the national taste ; and from the charms of such Dalilahs, as Dryden calls similar flourishes in poetry, they never have weaned themselves, nor ever will. Their want of real taste and feeling may be estimated by the unawed audacity with which they have in several notorious instances undertaken to repair, and even to alter, the masterpieces which conquest and rapine had put within their power. The same deficiency of real taste is evinced by the rash comparisons which they make between their schools of music and painting and those of Italy, in which Gay's lines still describe the present Parisian as well as him of his own day :—

> " Mention the force of learn'd Correlli's notes,
> Some squeaking fiddler of their ball he quotes ;
> Talk of the spirit Raphael's pencil gives,
> Yet warm with life, whose speaking picture lives,
> ' Yes, sir,' says he, ' in colour and design,
> Rigaut and Raphael are extremely fine.' "

Where the taste of those with whom he must naturally associate is systematically deficient, the young artist may lose as much through the influence of a French preceptor, as he could gain by studying in the Museum. I might also hint how little a capital like Paris, containing so many temptations to idleness and dissipation, is a safe abode for the young artist. But enough has been said to justify the sacrifice now exacted from France, however it may lower her pride, and mortify her vanity. First, it is a demand of justice, and therefore must be enforced ; and next, the artist, though he must in future extend his travels, and visit various cities in search of those excellences which are now to be seen collected in the Louvre, will have greater benefit from the experience which has cost him some toil ; and if he must traverse Switzerland and Italy, to view the sculptures of ancient Greece, and the paintings of modern Rome, he will have the double advantage of taking lessons on his route from Nature herself, in the solitary grandeur of the one, and the profuse luxuriance of the other. He will judge of the scenery which trained these great artists, as well from his own experience, as from their representation, and may perhaps be enabled to guess how they composed as well as how they executed.

The taste of the French seems to be turned more towards the Hall of Sculptures than the Gallery of Paintings. I think I can trace something of a corresponding partiality in the works of David, their greatest living artist, whose figures, though often nobly conceived and disposed, have a hardness of outline, resembling statuary. My own taste, formed probably on habit, (for we see few good statues in Britain,) would have inclined otherwise; and, I grieve to say, I was rather disappointed with some of those statues of antiquity from which I expected most pleasure. One monument can disappoint nobody—I mean the Apollo Belvidere, the sublime simplicity of whose attitude, and the celestial expression of his countenance, seem really more than mortal. It is said there is a chance of his visiting England; while I looked upon so exquisite a specimen of ancient art, I could not muster virtue enough to wish the report false; but writing in my solitary closet, and in mature consideration, I do hope sincerely that neither by purchase, nor gift, or otherwise, however fairly, will Britain possess herself of that or any other the least part of those spoils, since the French would eagerly grasp at such a pretext for alleging that we sought the gratification of our own selfish ends, while we affected to render justice to others. Indeed, unless I am much mistaken, the personage whose taste might be most gratified by such an acquisition, would not enter into a transaction calculated to throw the slightest shade of suspicion on the pure faith of Britain, to acquire all that Phidias ever carved, or Raphael painted. This fine statue, and the other specimens of art, seem to rise in value with the French as the hour of parting with them approaches. They talk to them, weep to them, kneel to them, and bid adieu to them, as if they were indeed restored to the rank of idols. But Baal boweth down, Nebo stoopeth—the hammer and wedge have given awful note of preparation; the Venus, the Dying Gladiator, and many other statues, have been loosened from their pedestals, and stand prompt for returning to their native and appropriate places of abode. Many a lowering eye and frowning brow marks the progress of these preparations; and such is the grotesque distress in the countenances of others, that, as Poins says of Falstaff, if it were not for laughing I could pity them.

After all, however, the French are not objects of compassion, even in the despoiled state, as they express themselves, to which they are likely to be reduced. France possesses, as public property, besides the paintings of her own school, a noble collection formed by the Bourbon race, and the Borghese pictures, honestly bought and paid for by Bonaparte. She has also to boast the gallery of the Luxembourg palace, containing that splendid series of historical pictures by Rubens, commemorating the principal actions in the life of Mary de Medicis, to the brilliancy of which there can only be objected the incongruous mixture of mythological and allegorical personages, with characters of historical reality. But this mixture of truth and fiction, and men and genii, and heathen gods and Christian emblems, seems to me so inconsistent, that, could I entertain the ambitious hope of possessing a picture of Rubens, I would prefer one of his boar-hunts, or groups of peasants going to market, to the most splendid picture in the Luxembourg gallery.

At Malmaison there are also some fine paintings, besides a number of good copies from the pictures of the Museum. This was the abode of Josephine, of whom all speak with regret and affection. I was particularly struck with the figure of a dancing Nymph, in marble, which, to my poor judgment, might have been placed beside any of the Grecian monuments in the Hall of Sculptures, without suffering much disparagement. It was cut by Canova, that eminent artist, who, as he remonstrated formerly against the transference of the works of art from Italy, has now the satisfaction of superintending their restoration to that classical land.

This ample subject has exhausted my paper. I remain, my dear sister, affectionately yours,

PAUL.

LETTER XIV.

PAUL TO THE MAJOR.

Bonaparte's Flight to Paris—Debates in the Chambers—Deputation to the Soldiers—Anxiety of the Chambers—Indifference of Bonaparte—He leaves the Capital—Preparations for defending Paris—Allies advance upon the South—Capitulation of Paris — Reflections — Rumoured Conspiracies—National Guard — Gardes de Corps — Gens d'Armes—Maréchal M'Donald—Number of Foreign Troops—Austrians—Russians—Prussians—Chateau de Montmorency—Prussian Officers—Strict Discipline among the British—Prussian Order of Faith and Honour—Its influence in the Army—Highlanders—Good Conduct of the Allied Forces—Affray with the Mob—Guards of the Allied Monarchs—Castle of Vincennes—Motley assemblages in the Museum—Reviews—Anecdote of Colonel Hepburn.

YOUR appetite for military details, my dear Major, is worthy of one who assisted at the defence of Bergen-op-Zoom, in the year 1747, since it cannot be sated with the ample feast which I sent you from Waterloo. Here, indeed, I see little around me but military of all nations; but how to describe the gay, glittering, and at the same time formidable scene, a scene too so new to all my habits, is a point of no little difficulty. Paris is one great camp, consisting of soldiers of almost all nations, and is under the military authority of the Prussian Baron Muffling, as commandant for the allies. You are not ignorant of the proceedings which led to this extraordinary crisis, but I shall briefly recall them to your memory.

The only division of the French army which remained entire after the rout of Waterloo, was that of Grouchy and Vandamme, which, by a retreat that did these generals the highest honour, was not only conducted unbroken under the walls of Paris, but gained some accession of strength from the wrecks of the main army. Upon their arrival they found matters in a most singular state of crisis. Bonaparte had anticipated the tidings of the field of Waterloo, and brought, like a certain general renowned in song, the news of his own defeat to the good city of Paris. It would seem that he expected the Liberalists would now, in this last and critical danger, have made common cause with him, strengthened his hands with all the power that unanimity could bestow upon a dictator, called upon the nation to rally around his standard, and tried yet one desperate chance for conquest. But he had measured his importance according to former, not according to existing circumstances. The Rump of the old Conventionalists saw no more to overawe them in Bonaparte defeated, than their predecessors of the Long Parliament had seen in Richard Cromwell. They instantly made known to him, and with no friendly voice, that the times demanded his resignation ; they called his ministers before them authoritatively, and intimated by every movement their intention to take the reins of government into their own hands. Napoleon had no alternative left him but that of defiance or of abdication. In the former case, he might indeed have dissolved the refractory Chambers, for the troops, and the lower class of the Parisian populace, who were armed under the name of Federés, were resolute in his behalf. But he was not resolute in his own determination. It was in vain that his brother Lucien, who, having resumed the thorny paths of politics, was disposed to tread it with his former audacity, urged him to march a body of troops to the Chambers, dissolve them at once, and take the full power into his own hands. Success over the Chambers was indeed certain, but its consequences would have called upon Napoleon to live or die with the troops who should achieve it : of the first he had little hope, and for the last slender inclination. He therefore attempted by a compromise to transfer his crown, now entwined with thorns, to the head of his infant son. The proposition was for some time evaded by the Assembly, and Bonaparte's adherents could only procure an indirect and dubious assent to this condition. Lucien pleaded, and Labedoyere bullied in vain ; and the Chambers having possessed themselves of this brief and precarious authority, began such a course of debate as Swift ascribes to his Legion Club,—

"While they sit and pick their straws,
Let them dream of making laws."

Instead of active preparations to oppose or avert the progress of foreign invaders, the Parisians saw with astonishment their senators engaged in discussions of abstract theory, or frivolous points of form. A matter-of-fact man, who wished to know the distance betwixt Saint Quentin (then Lord Wellington's headquarters) and Paris, was called to order, as going into matter irrelevant to the subject of debate. The question, however, was not mal-apropos. Grouchy's army arrived, and the allies were not long behind him. The Chambers, who had by this time assumed all the old-fashioned mummery and jargon of the Convention, sent forth a deputation of its members, decorated with three-coloured scarfs, to harangue the soldiers and the Federés ; and they were conjured by the members who proposed the deputation to apprize the soldiers, that the representatives were ready to mix with them in their ranks, since, to those who fell, the day of their death would be that of their resurrection. It was supposed that Mons. Garnier, not much accustomed to such terms, had meant to say immortality, but this impropriety of expression greatly maimed the energy of his eloquence.

The representatives went forth with their fine scarfs. They harangued the soldiers, and the armed banditti called Federés, upon the original principles of liberty and the unprescriptible rights of man, and recommended to them, as a rallying word, Vive la Nation, Vive la Liberté! But

the charm was as ineffectual as that used by the Abbess of Andouillets. The soldiers and fede : only answered with shouts of Vive l'Empereur. The representatives affected to consider these acclamations as referring to Napoleon II., and having, like the Duke of Buckingham, thanked their loving friends and countrymen for sentiments which they had never expressed, they returned to make their report to the Chambers. There was, in truth, only one point of union between these assemblies of soi-disant legislators and the French troops, which was an obstinate determination, founded upon a combined sense of crime and fear of punishment, to resist to the uttermost the restoration of the legitimate sovereign, although every wise man in France had long seen it was the sole measure which promised to avert the impending ruin of the country. Upon this topic the most furious speeches were made, the most violent resolutions entered into ; and the Lower Chamber, in particular, showed that it wanted only time and power to renew the anarchy, as it had adopted the language, of the early Revolution. But there were cold fits to allay this fever, and the perturbation of mind by which individuals began to find themselves agitated, broke out amid their bullying ridiculously enough. Merlin of Douai (an old hack'd engine of Philip Egalité, and Robespierre, under the last of whom he promulgated the bloody edict against suspected persons) announced to the Chamber of Representatives his having received an untimely visit of two persons in a fiacre, demanding to speak to him on the part of the president of the provisional government ; that the hour being one in the morning, he had refused them admittance—happily so refused them—since, in the unanimous opinion of Merlin himself, of his wife, and honest Regnault de St. Jean d'Angely, these untimely visitors could mean nothing good to his person. On this annunciation, vigorous measures were proposed for the protection of Monsieur Merlin, when Boulay de la Meurthe stopped farther proceeding, by informing the assembly that the supposed emissaries of royalty were in fact what they called themselves, messengers from the president upon a matter of emergency, which they had communicated to himself upon being refused access to Merlin. One member's terrors were excited by seeing in the street a wounded officer, those of another broke out upon spying—not a peer, as used to be the cause of alarm in St. Stephen's—but, sight more appalling, a royal Garde de Corps in full uniform under the gallery ! These alarms were faithfully reported to the Chambers, and though the wiser representatives suppressed their own fears, there were many indications that they did not less deeply entertain them.

The anxiety of the Government and of the Chambers was singularly contrasted by the extreme indifference of him who had been the origin of all the turmoil and bloodshed, and who continued for some time to travel from the palace of Bourbon Elysées to Malmaison and back again, to give fêtes there, and to prepare for a journey no one could say whither, with as much composure as if the general distraction concerned him as little, or less, than any other temporary sojourner in France. To complete this scene of characteristic affectation, he sent a message to the Chambers to request copies of two books which he desired might be placed at his disposal. But the near approach of the allies at length accelerated his departure ; and on the 29th June, when they were within three leagues of the city, he finally left the capital, which he had lately called his own, to make the best defence or capitulation they could. At first the Chambers resolved upon defence. But the means were very imperfect.

When Bonaparte, before leaving Paris for Aves- nes, consulted Carnot on the means necessary for the defence of the metropolis, the latter is said to have estimated them at two hundred millions, and the labour of three years. " And when that sum of treasure and labour has been expended, sixty thousand good troops," continued the ex-director, " and a sustained assault of twenty-four hours may render it all in vain." Nevertheless Bonaparte undertook preparations for this gigantic and hope- less task. The heights of Montmartre were forti- fied with extreme care, and amply supplied with artillery. The village of St. Denis was also strongly garrisoned ; and a partial inundation being accom- plished by means of stopping two brooks, the water was introduced into the half-completed canal De l'Ourcq, the bank of which being formed into a parapet, completed a formidable line of defence on the northern side of the city, resting both flanks upon the Seine. The populace of Paris had la- boured at these lines with an enthusiasm not sur- passed in the most exalted frenzy of the Revolu- tion ; nor were their spirits or courage at all low- ered by the approach of the conquering armies of England and Prussia, in the act of being support- ed, if need were, by the whole force of Russia and Austria. They confided in what had repeatedly and carefully been impressed upon their minds— that Paris could only fall by treachery ; and boast- ed that they had now Massena, and Soult, and Da- voust, (as much celebrated for the military talent as for the atrocity which he displayed in the de- fence of Hamburgh,) to direct the defence of the capital, instead of Marmont, by whom, in the pre- ceding year, they were taught to believe it had been basely betrayed.

But although the line of defence to the north was such as to justify temporary confidence, the city on the opposite side was entirely open, ex- cepting the occupation of the villages of Issy, and the heights of St. Cloud and Meudon. These two points, if they could have been maintained, would have protected for a time that large and level plain which stands on the south side of Paris, and which now presented no advantages for defence, except- ing an imperfect attempt at a trench, and a few houses and garden-walls accommodated with loop- holes for the use of musketry. On this defenceless side, therefore, the allied generals resolved to make the attack, and the Prince-Marshal, on the 30th June, crossed the Seine at St. Germains, and oc- cupying Versailles, threatened the French position at Meudon, Issy, and the heights of St. Cloud, while the Duke of Wellington, holding Gonesse, opened a communication with the Prussians by a bridge at Argenteuil. The French, though their situation was desperate, did not lose courage, and one gleam of success shone on their arms. General Excelmans, by a well-conducted assault, surprised the Prussians who occupied Versailles, and made prisoners some cavalry. But the French were as- saulted in their turn driven from the heights of St. Cloud, from Issy, and from Meudon, and forced

close under the city itself. This happened on the 2d July, and Blucher had already sent to the Bri- tish general to request the assistance of a battery of Congreve's rockets,—a most ominous prepara- tion for the assault which he meditated. Mean- while, the wealthy and respectable Parisians were equally apprehensive of danger from their defen- ders and from the assailants. The temper of the French soldiers had risen to frenzy, and the mob of the Fauxbourgs, animated by the same feelings of rage, vomited threats and execrations both against the allies, and against the citizens of Paris who favoured the cause of peace and legitimacy. Such was the temper of this motley garrison, as formidable to the capital as the presence of an in- censed enemy, when, upon the 3d July, the terms of capitulation between the allies and Massena, who acted as commander-in-chief of the French, were arranged and signed, Paris once more sub- jected to the mercy of Europe, and the Queen of Provinces a second time made a bondswoman.

A brief but fearful period of anarchy passed ere the French army, now men without a cause and without a leader, evacuated Paris and its vicinity, and ere their yet more savage associates, the fede- rés, could be prevailed upon to lay down their arms, with which they still threatened death and devastation to each royalist, or rather to property and all its possessors. The firmness of the Na- tional Guards is universally acknowledged to have saved Paris in that awful moment, when, in all human probability, the first example of plunder would have been followed both by the populace and by the foreigners, and a scene of universal blood, rapine, and conflagration, must have become the necessary consequence.

There are indeed fervent politicians, whom now and then of an evening we have heard breathe an ardent wish that Paris had been burnt to the ground. These are words soon spoken in the energy of pa- triotic hatred, or a desire of vengeance for out- raged morality ; but if we can picture to ourselves without shrinking those horrid scenes which ensue,

" Where the flesh'd soldier, rough and hard of heart,
  In liberty of bloody hand shall range,
  With conscience wide as hell,"

we ought yet to remember upon how many thou- sands such dreadful vengeance must have fallen, who can only be justly considered as common suf- ferers by the very acts of aggression of which Eu- rope has such strong reason to complain, and how many thousands more age and incapacity exempted even from the possibility of having been sharers in the offence. It is impossible to look around upon this splendid capital without remembering the af- fecting plea which the Deity himself condescended to use with his vindictive prophet : " Should not I spare Nineveh, that great city, wherein are more than six score thousand persons that cannot discern between their right hand and their left hand, and also much cattle !" Least of all ought we to wish that any part of the British forces had been parta- kers in the horrid license that must have followed on such a catastrophe, during which the restraints of discipline and the precepts of religion are alike forgotten in the headlong course of privileged fury. It was observed of the veteran army of Tilly, that the sack of Magdeburg gave a death- blow to their discipline ; and we know how the troops of France herself were ruined by that of

Moscow. In every point of view, therefore, as well with regard to the agents as the sufferers, the averting the destruction of Paris, when it appeared almost inevitable, has added to the glories which the Duke of Wellington has acquired in this immortal campaign. For it is not to be denied, that to his wise and powerful interference, restraining the vindictive ardour of Blucher, yet accelerating, by his tone of decision, the reluctant surrender of Davoust, was chiefly owing the timely arrangement of the articles of capitulation, in consequence of which the King of France again obtained possession of his capital, and the allied armies became the peaceful garrison of Paris.

By the time I reached the capital the political convulsions had entirely subsided, and the royal government, to all external appearance, was in as quiet an exercise of authority as if Louis XVIII. had never been dispossessed of the throne. But the public mind was not as yet accustomed to consider the change as permanent, being influenced and agitated by a thousand gloomy reports of plots and conspiracies, as the sea, after the storm has subsided, continues still to heave and swell with the impulse it has received. It was said, in particular, that Labedoyere, who had been found concealed in Paris, and there arrested, was agent of a conspiracy, in which the federés of the Fauxbourgs, with the disbanded soldiers of the army of the north, were to be enlisted. One party of the conspirators were to wear the dress and arms of the Parisian National Guard, and so accoutred were to assault simultaneously the hotels of the Emperors of Austria and of Russia, of the King of Prussia, of Lord Castlereagh, of the Duke of Wellington, and of Blucher; while other bands, disguised in the uniforms of the allied troops, should storm the posts of the National Guard, and particularly those maintained at the palace of the Tuileries. That a project so wild and impracticable should have been seriously attempted, I can hardly credit; but that so many reckless and desperate men as were now in Paris were meditating something of peril and violence, is extremely probable, for at this very time all the guards maintained on the illustrious personages I have mentioned were on a sudden strongly reinforced, and unusual strictness was exercised by the sentinels in challenging those who approached their posts. In going home to my hotel upon this night, I was stopped and interrogated more than six times, and in a new language at each post. The word *English* was a sufficient answer upon every occasion. Indeed, the great and combined military force would have rendered any such conspiracy an effort of fruitless, though perhaps not bloodless, frenzy.

The internal duty of Paris is chiefly performed by the National Guard, who, in dress and appearance, remind me very much of the original or blue regiment of Edinburgh Volunteers. They furnish picquets for the various guards upon public places, and around the Tuileries; a severe duty for the respectable class of citizens of whom these regiments are composed, since I suppose at least five hundred men are required for the daily discharge of it. But the corps is very numerous, and a consciousness that the peace of the city and security of property depend upon its being regularly and punctually performed, reconciles these citizen-soldiers to their task.

The guards upon the King's person and palace are intrusted to the Gardes de Corps, or household troops, fine-looking men, very handsomely, though not gaudily, dressed. They are said, with few exceptions, to have behaved with great loyalty in the late trying crisis; but as they are an expensive corps, holding the rank of gentlemen, and being paid accordingly, it is supposed their numbers will be much limited in future. They are very civil in their deportment, and in the discharge of their duty, particularly to English strangers. My infirmities perhaps claimed a little compassion, and it is no discredit to them that I have seen Messrs. les Gardes de Corps feel the claim, and make a little way, by the influence of voice and authority, for one who was not so able to make it for himself. And indeed there was a kind of chivalrous feeling in most of these gentlemen, a modesty of demeanour, a gentleness of conduct towards the crowd, and a deference to the claims of hospitality, a sense, in short, that he who has the momentary power should use it with tenderness and forbearance, which might be mere urbanity, but which a professed aristocrat is apt to consider as mixed with a higher feeling. This corps, I have been informed, suffered much in attending the King to the frontiers; a few, who had been selected from Bonaparte's followers in a spirit of conciliation, returned to their first vocation; but the rest followed their master as far as they were permitted, and experienced much hardship and distress in consequence, besides the actual slaughter of many of their companions. A stranger is an indifferent judge of such matters, but I am so old-fashioned as to think that a body of real men-at-arms, chosen from the younger sons of the nobility and gentry, is not only a graceful institution as a defence and ornament to the throne, but may in France be the means of retrieving the real military character, so dishonoured and disgraced of late years.

There is another armed force, of a very different description, frequently seen in Paris,—the patroles of the modern gens d'armes, or military police; men picked out for the office, and who, in files of two or four, upon foot or horseback, constantly parade every part not only of Paris, but of France. Their dress and arms are those of heavy dragoons, and therefore they may be at first thought less adapted for discharging their peculiar duty, which is that of police-officers. But there is a very perfect system, of which these are the agents, and when, as in the case of the late effort of Bonaparte, the police seems to have proved ineffectual, it is not the fault of the inferior and operative agents, but of those superintendents from whom they received their signals. These gens d'armes were the agents so dreaded under the imperial government, whose appearance made every knee tremble, and every cheek grow pale. If they are less formidable under a legitimate sway, it is because even the enemies of the constitution may shelter their crimes beneath the laws instituted for the protection of innocence. Throughout all France, however, the ubiquity of the police is something striking and singular. In the most retired scene which you can choose, if you see a solitary horseman, or still more, if you see two riding together, it is five to one that they belong to the gens d'armerie. At this moment they have full employment for their address and omnipresence; and I believe it is exercised in no common degree, unless we should give credit to the scandal of the *royalistes purs*, who pretend that Fouché under the Bourbons is a much more tractable person than Fouché under the Republic and under Bonaparte.

The National Guards, Gardes de Corps, or household troops, and the Gens d'Armes, compose the only French military force to be at present seen in Paris. Maréchal M'Donald, Duke of Tarentum, is intrusted with the difficult task of disbanding and reorganizing the army beyond the Loire, the remnants, namely, of the old Imperial army. M'-Donald is equally remarkable for military skill and loyalty; his march from the extremity of Italy to unite himself with Moreau, previous to the battle of Novi, and the successful retreat which he made even after losing that dreadful and well-fought action, against the redoubted Suwarrow, prove his military talent, as his behaviour during Bonaparte's last invasion has established his military faith. Your question is ready, I know, my dear Major, *Which* of the M'Donalds is he? for of true blood you unquestionably have already deemed him. To satisfy a wish so laudable, I can inform you from the best authority, that the Maréchal is descended of that tribe or family of the M'Donalds of Clanronald who are called M'Eachen, or Sons of Hector, as claiming their descent from a cadet of the house of Clanronald, so named. The father of the Duke of Tarentum was engaged in our affair (I love a delicate expression) of 1745, and was very useful to Prince Charles Edward during his rash enterprise. He was a Highlander, bred to the Church, and educated in France. He spoke, therefore, Gaelic, English, French, and Latin, and was besides, intelligent, bold, and faithful. He was one of the seven who embarked with the unfortunate Chevalier when his expedition of knight-errantry had utterly failed. On his return to France, M'-Eachen took the more general name of his tribe, and appears to have preferred the military service to resuming his studies for the Church. His son is now one of the most respectable characters whom the French army list presents to us. I had letters to him from his friends in Skye, but had not the good fortune to meet him at Paris. He was more usefully engaged; and, by all accounts, the King could not have reposed confidence in a more loyal and gallant character. How should it be otherwise! Is he not a Scotchman, and a M'Donald!—eh, Major!

Of foreign troops, all included, there are generally said to be in France to the number of a million; but I am informed from the best authority, that they do certainly amount to EIGHT HUNDRED THOUSAND MEN, an assembly of troops scarce paralleled save in the annals of romance.[1] Of these the British, Prussians, and Russians, are nearest to Paris, so stationed as to have an army of one hundred and fifty thousand men within a day's march of the city.

The Austrians are chiefly in the south of France. The French complain more of the severity of the usage which the inhabitants receive from them, than of the rest of the allies. Those whom we see here are part of the Emperor's Hungarian guards, selected men, of fine and tall figure, which is set off by their white dress. They are unquestionably,

in point of exterior appearance, the handsomest of the allied troops; but, though tall and bulky men, want the hardy and athletic look of the British, Russians, and Prussians. Tell the ladies also, that this same white uniform looks better upon a line of troops in the field, than worn by an individual officer in a ball-room, whose appearance involuntarily, and rather unfairly, reminds me of the master of a regimental band. The hussar uniforms of Austria are very handsome, particularly those of the Hungarians, to whose country the dress properly belongs.

The Russians are in the neighbourhood in very considerable force. I was present at a splendid review which was made of these northern warriors by the Allied Sovereigns, the Duke of Wellington, &c. The principal avenue of the Champs Elysées was crowded with troops of all sorts; and the reflection of the sun appeared almost intolerably bright. The monarchs, generals, and their suite, occupied the centre of the Place Louis Quinze, almost the very spot in which Louis XVI. was beheaded, and for more than two hours the troops defiled before them without a pause, in a close column, whose front occupied the whole space afforded by the breadth of the avenue. The infantry were fine, firm, steady-looking men, clean, handsome, but by no means remarkable for stature. From the green uniform, and the short and sturdy make of the Russians, the French nicknamed them *Cornichons*, as if they resembled the green cucumbers, so called when pickled. They had a formidable train of artillery, in the highest possible order, and were attended by several regiments both of dragoons and cuirassiers. The cuirassiers of the guard had burnished steel breastplates, which glanced to the sun, and made a noble display. The cuirasses of the other regiments seemed to be of hammered iron. The cavaliers were remarkably fine men; the horses, excepting those of the officers, seemed to be of an inferior description, and rather weak for that sort of service; but the general effect was indescribably grand. The troops swept on, wave rolling as it were after wave, to the number of at least twenty thousand men, the sound of one band of martial music advancing as the other died away, and the interminable column moving on as if the procession would stretch out to the crack of doom. During this grand display of the powers of the North, the ground was kept by the regular Cossacks of the Russian guard, very fine men, and under good discipline. The irregular Cossacks, and light troops of a similar description, are only occasionally seen in Paris; but their Hettman, Prince Platow, is a constant resident in the capital, and to him these children of the desert are occasionally summoned. The appearance of the proper Cossack is prepossessing. He has high features, keeps his long blue coat strictly clean, and displays some taste for splendour in his arms and accoutrements, which are often richly decorated with silver. But the Tartar tribes, whom the French unite under the same general appellation, have frequently a most uncouth and savage appearance. Cloaks of sheepskin, bows, arrows, shields made of dried hides, and other appointments savouring of the earliest state of society, were seen among them; from which the French, whom even invasion, with all its ills, cannot deprive of their jest, call them *Les Cupidons de Nord.* I saw one man who had come with his tribe from near to the Great Wall of China, to fight against the French under the walls of Paris! The poor fellow was in the hospital from a very natural cause, the injury which his feet had sustained in so long a march. But these wilder light troops were judiciously kept at a distance from Paris, where the splendour and wealth of the shops formed rather too strong temptations for Tartar morality.

The Prussian troops have gradually assumed a more respectable exterior, as the new clothing, at the expense of France, has been completed and delivered. They are a handsome fair-haired race of men; their uniforms almost exclusively blue and red. Both they and the Russians seem to think, that the beauty of the male form consists in resembling as much as possible a triangle, or rather a lady in an old-fashioned pair of high stays. So they draw their waists tight by means of a broad belt, or some similar contrivance, and stuff out and pad the breast and shoulders till the desired figure is attained. Almost all of them are young men, summoned to arms by the situation of Europe, and their own country in particular,—a call which was obeyed with such ardent enthusiasm, that I suppose no civilized kingdom ever had under arms, as a disposable force, so large a proportion of its population. Many regiments are composed of *landwehr*, or militia, and some of volunteers. It necessarily follows, from this intermixture of various descriptions of force, that they cannot be all under the same degree of strict military discipline; and to this must be attributed the irregularities they committed upon their march, and which were sometimes imputed to them in their quarters. They have never been accused, however, of gross violence, of assailing life or honour, or of wantonly injuring the churches or public buildings, crimes which were objected to the French armies in Prussia. Their resentment, indeed, was stirred at the name of the Bridge of Jena, and they had made preparations for the destruction of that useful and beautiful edifice. But the intercession of the Duke of Wellington procured a delay, until the King of Prussia upon his arrival repealed this hasty and vindictive order.

I saw a large body of these troops quartered in the celebrated Chateau de Montmorency. The owner of this fine seat, and the beautiful domain annexed, was attached to Bonaparte, had fled upon Napoleon's first exile, and had returned to share his triumph. The brief interval before the battle of Waterloo, which compelled him to a second retreat, had been employed in refitting the chateau with painting, panelling, and sculpture, in the most expensive style. The Prussians were now busily undoing all that he had commenced, and the contrast between recent repair and the work of instant destruction was very striking. The rich furniture was stripped by the female followers of the camp, and the soldiers were boiling their camp-kettles with the gilded frames of pictures, the plate-glass windows were smashed to pieces, and the breaches repaired by old jackets and pantaloons. One of my friends, who had been long in the Spanish war, observed with composure, that the chateau was in a way of being handsomely *ramped*, a technical word for what was going on, which you may insert at my peril in your collection of military phrases. When quartered upon inhabited houses, the French

chiefly complained of the extent of the Prussians' appetite, as a craving gulf, which they found it very difficult to fill. They were, they allowed, not otherwise cruel or ill-natured; but, like the devouring cannibal in the voyages of Aboulfouaris, their hunger could not be lulled to sleep longer than three hours at a time. Much of this was undoubtedly greatly exaggerated.

It is certain, however, that means have been put into the power of the Prussian officers to indulge themselves in the pleasures of Paris to an extent which their pay and allowances, if limited to those drawn in their own country, could not possibly have afforded. They are the principal customers to the expensive *restaurateurs*, the principal frequenters of coffee-houses, of theatres, and of the Palais Royal, at regular and irregular hours—all indications of an expense not within the ordinary reach of subaltern officers. It is said, that some of our German subsidiary troops made application to the Duke of Wellington to be put upon the same footing with the Prussians in these extra advantages. His Grace, we are assured, expressed to them (with the fullest acknowledgment of their meriting every indulgence which could be wisely bestowed) his decided opinion, that all expedients which tended to place the soldier upon a different footing of expense and luxury in France, from that which he held in his native country, were injurious to discipline, detrimental to the character of the army, and to the interest of the sovereign. His practice expresses the same doctrine. The British troops receive regularly the allowances and rations to which they would be entitled in England, and which are here raised at the expense of France; but neither directly nor indirectly do they obtain further indulgence. The strong sense and firmness for which the Duke is as much distinguished as for skill in arms and bravery in the field of battle, easily saw that the high and paramount part which Britain now holds in Europe, that pre-eminence, which, in so many instances, has made her and her delegates the chosen mediators when disputes occurred amongst the allied powers, depends entirely on our maintaining pure and sacred the national character for good faith and disinterested honour. The slightest complaint, therefore, of want of discipline or oppression, perpetrated by a British officer or soldier, has instantly met with reprehension and punishment, and the result has been the reducing the French to the cruel situation of hating us without having any complaint to justify themselves for doing so, even in their own eyes. Our officers of rank have, in many instances, declined the quarters appointed them in private houses; and, where they were accepted, have arranged themselves in the mode least likely to derange the family, and have declined uniformly the offers to accommodate them with wine, or provisions, which were made as a matter of course. They receive the reward of this moderation in the public respect, which, however the French may dislike us as a nation, they are compelled to pay to individual merit and courtesy.

On the other hand, strange and alarming whispers are thrown abroad respecting the situation of the Prussian army. It is hinted, that they are somewhat out of control, and look up less to the King than to their generals as their paramount superiors. Blucher holds the first rank ostensibly;

but it is pretended, that General Gneisenau, so celebrated for his talents as a quarter-master-general, possesses most real influence. Much of this is supposed to be exerted by means of secret societies, particularly that called The Order of Faith and Honour. This association, which derived its first institution from the laudable and patriotic desire of associating against French tyranny, has retained the secret character with which it was necessarily invested when the foreign enemy possessed the fortresses of Prussia, but which now seems useless at least, if not capable of being rendered hazardous. Almost all the officers of this army belong to this secret society, which is a sort of institution that has peculiar charms for Germans; and it is said to be an object of jealousy to the Government, though it cannot be supposed dangerous while headed by the loyal Blucher.

Our forces, in general, are admired for their appearance under arms, although, like their countrymen under Henry V.,

" They are but warriors for the working day,
Their gayness and their gilt are all besmirch'd
With rainy marching in the painful field."

The serviceable state of the men, horses, and equipments, fully compensates, to the experienced eye, every deficiency in mere show.

The singular dress of our Highlanders makes them particular objects of attention to the French. In what class of society they rank them, may be judged from part of a speech which I heard a French lady make to her companion, after she had passed two of these mountaineers:—" Aussi j'ai vu les sauvages Américains." It was very entertaining to see our Highlanders making their bargains upon the Boulevards, the soldier holding his piece of six sous between his finger and thumb, with the gripe of a smith's vice, and pointing out the quantity of the commodity which he expected for it, while the Frenchman, with many shrugs and much chattering, diminished the equivalent as more than he could afford. Then Donald began to shrug and jabber in his turn, and to scrape back again what the other had subtracted; and so they would stand for half an hour discussing the point, though neither understood a word which the other said, until they could agree upon le prix juste.

The soldiers, without exception, both British and foreigners, conduct themselves in public with civility, are very rarely to be seen intoxicated, though the means are so much within their reach, and, considering all the irritating circumstances that exist, few quarrels occur between them and the populace. Very strong precautions are, however, taken in case of any accidental or premeditated commotion. A powerful guard of Prussians always attends at the Pont Neuf and Pont Royal, with two pieces of artillery turned upon each bridge, loaded with canister shot, horses saddled, matches burning, and all ready to act on the shortest warning. The other day an unpleasant accident took place. Some of the Parisian populace, while the Prussian officer of the day was visiting a post, quarrelled with the orderly soldier who held his horse; the animal took fright, and escaped the man's hold; the officer came out, and was hustled and insulted by the mob. In the meanwhile, the orderly-man galloped off, and returned with about thirty of his companions, who charged with their lances couched, as if they threatened death and destruction; but, with much

dexterity, tilted up the point of the spear when near a Frenchman's body, and, reversing the weapon, only struck with the butt. They made five or six of the most tumultuous prisoners, who were carried before Baron Muffling, reclaiming loudly the safe-guard of the police, and demanding to be carried before a French judge. But, in the present situation of this capital, the commandant preferred subjecting them to military chastisement; and a truss of straw being laid down for each culprit, they were stretched out, and received a drubbing à la militaire with the reins and girths of the hussars' horses. The appearance of the sufferers acted as a sedative upon the temper of the mob, none of whom chose to seek further personal specimens of the Prussian discipline. It seemed a strong measure to the English spectators; but the question is, whether a good many lives were not saved at the expense of the shoulders of those sufferers; for where combustibles are so plenty, the least spark of fire must be trodden out with as much haste as may be. In other frays, it has happened that Prussian soldiers have been killed; in which case, the district where the accident happened is subjected to severe contributions, unless they can arrest the perpetrator. The Palais Royal, where such scenes are chiefly to be apprehended, is trebly guarded every night by a company of the National Guard, one of British, and one of Prussians.

As a matter of courtesy between the allied powers, the duty of mounting guard upon the person of the monarchs is performed by the troops of each nation in succession: So that our guardsmen mount guard on the Emperor of Russia, the Russians on the Emperor of Austria, and the Highlanders, perhaps, on the King of Prussia, in rotation;—a judicious arrangement, which tends to show both the French and the allied troops the close and intimate union of the sovereigns in the common cause of Europe. The important post of Montmartre, which, in its present state of strong fortification, may be called the citadel of Paris, is confided to the care of the British, who keep guard with great and unusual strictness. Even foreign officers are not admitted within these works, unless accompanied by an Englishman. The hill is bristled with two hundred pieces of cannon; and they make frequent discovery of military stores and ammunition buried or concealed. All these will fall to our share; and, I trust, the two hundred guns will be sent to keep company with the hundred and fifty taken at the battle of Waterloo.

In the meanwhile, it is a strange and most inconsistent circumstance, that the Castle of Vincennes, within three miles of Paris, lying in the midst of these armies, and of no more strength than the White Tower of London, or any other Gothic keep, affects to hold out against the allied army. The commandant, although he has hoisted the white flag, will neither receive a Royalist nor an allied soldier within the castle, and gives himself great airs of defiance, as if encouraged by an impunity which he only owes to contempt, and to the reluctance of the allied sovereigns to increase the King of France's difficulties and unpopularity by punishing the gasconade as it deserves.

I do not observe that the soldiers of the allied nations intermix much in company with each other, although they seem on kind and civil terms when occasionally thrown together. The Museum, which

2 L

is open to all ranks and conditions, frequently, besides its other striking beauties, exhibits a moving picture of all the nations of Europe in their military dresses. You see the tall Hungarian, the swarthy Italian, the fair-haired Prussian, the flat-faced Tartar, English, Irish, Guardsmen, and Highlanders, in little bands of two or three, strolling up and down a hall as immense as that of the Caliph Vathek, and indulging their curiosity with its wonders. The wildest of them appeared softened and respectful, while forming a part of this singular assemblage, which looks as if all the nations of Europe had formed a rendezvous at Paris by military representation. Some of their remarks must of course be very entertaining. One or two I caught. " By ——, Jack," said an English dragoon to his comrade, pointing to a battle-piece by Salvator, " look at the cuirasses—they have got the battle of Waterloo here already."—" Pooh, you blockhead," said the other, " that an't the battle of Waterloo ; don't you see all the horses have got long tails ?" I asked a Highland sergeant, who was gazing earnestly on the Venus de Medicis, " How do you like her, countryman ?"—" God bless us—is your honour from Inverness ?" was the first exclamation ; and then, " I am told she is very much admired—but I'll show your honour a much better proportioned woman,"—and the ambitious sergeant, himself a remarkably little man, conducted me to a colossal female figure, eight feet high. There is no disputing the judgment of artists, but I am afraid the beauties of this statue are not of a kind most obvious to the uninitiated.

Where there are monarchs at the head of conquering armies, the pomp of war must of course be displayed in its full glories. We have reviews of many thousands every morning, from seven o'clock until ten or eleven. That of the British cavalry was very much admired, notwithstanding the dust which enveloped their movements. The Russians and Prussians exhibited, upon another occasion, the manœuvres of a mock engagement, the Emperor commanding the Prussian army, and the King of Prussia, in the dress of a colonel of the Russian guards, enacting the general of the Muscovites. After the battle, the two potentates met, and greeted each other very handsomely. On another occasion, the Prussians entertained us with a rehearsal of the battle of Issy, or the movements of the French army and their own in the attack and defence of that village, upon the 2d of June. At one of these reviews the Russians were commanded by the Emperor to charge in line, expressly for the gratification of the English general. You know it is surmised, that the British claim pre-eminence over all other nations, because the steadiness and bottom of the individual soldiers permit them to hazard a general charge in line, whereas the column is adopted for the purpose of attack by the French and all other foreigners. Perhaps this was designed as a rebuke to our national vanity. However, the Russians went through the manœuvre admirably well, dressing a line of very great length with the utmost accuracy, during an advance of half a mile.

It must be owned that a politician more gloomy than myself, might draw evil augury from the habits, which the reigning sovereigns of Europe may possibly acquire by being for years the inmates of camps, and compelled by the pressure of the immi-

nent crisis to postpone the duties of the sovereign to those of the general. War has been described as " the game of princes ;" and we know how easily the habit of gambling is acquired, and how irresistible it soon becomes. If it should happen that these powerful monarchs, influenced by the military ideas and habits which have been so long uppermost, should find a state of peace a tedious and dull exchange for the animating perils of war, it will be one instance, among many, of the lasting evils which French aggression, and the necessary means of counteracting it, have entailed on the kingdoms of Europe. I confide, however, something in the wisdom of these princes, and a great deal in the pacific influence of a deity whose presence we all deprecate, notwithstanding the lessons of wisdom which she is supposed to teach—I mean the Goddess of Poverty.

Two circumstances struck me in the grand military spectacle which I have mentioned,—the great number of actors, and, comparatively speaking, the total absence of spectators. The scale of the exhibition cannot indeed be wondered at, considering the importance of the actors :

> " Ha ! Majesty, how high thy glory towers,
> When the rich blood of kings is set on fire !"

But, in the neighbourhood of so populous a city as Paris, the inhabitants of which have been so long famous for their attachment to public spectacles, one might have thought spectators enough would have been found besides the military amateurs not immediately engaged, and a few strangers. But I never saw above a hundred Frenchmen, and those of the very lowest order, looking on at these exhibitions, not even at that made in the Place Louis Quinze, under their very eyes. This is the strongest sign of their deeply feeling their present state of humiliation, and proves, more than a thousand others, that they taste the gall in all its bitterness, and that the iron has entered into their soul. In my next letter to my friend Peter, I will communicate what else I have observed on the state of the public mind in France. But I must first acquit myself of my promise to our ghostly father, the parson. Yours entirely,

PAUL.

Postscript.[1]—By the by, you must allow me to add to my Waterloo anecdotes, one which relates to a gallant countryman of ours, in whose family you well know that we feel the interest of old and sincere friendship : I mean Colonel Francis Hepburn, of the 3d regiment of Guards, who had the distinguished honour of commanding the detachment sent to the relief of Hougoumont, when it was attacked by the whole French division of Jerome Bonaparte. He had the charge of maintaining, with his own single battalion, this important post, when the communication was entirely cut off by the French cavalry, and it was not until they were repulsed, that he was reinforced by two battalions of Hanoverians and one of Brunswickers. Colonel Woodforde of the Coldstream Guards, who in the morning reinforced Lieutenant-Colonel Macdonell, commanded in the house and garden, and Colonel Hepburn in the orchard and wood. I am particular in mentioning this, because the name of Lieu-

---

[1] This postscript is retained, although, in the present edition of these Letters, the name of the gallant officer alluded to appears in its proper place, p. 465.—S.

tenant-Colonel Home, who acted under Colonel Hepburn, appeared in the Gazette instead of his, by a mistake incidental to the confusion of the day, which rendered it impossible accurately to distinguish individual merit. The error has been admitted, but there is a difficulty in correcting it publicly, though there can be none in making our friends in Scotland acquainted with the real share which the relative of our deceased friend, the best and kindliest of veterans, had in the most memorable battle that ever was fought, and which in no degree takes away from the admitted gallantry of his countryman, Lieutenant-Colonel Home. Colonel Hepburn, as you will remember, was engaged in the Spanish war, and severely wounded at the battle of Barossa.

LETTER XV.

PAUL TO THE REV. MR. ———, MINISTER OF THE GOSPEL AT ———.

Solemnities of the Catholic Church—Little regard paid to the Authority of the Pope—Churches not attended—Disregard of Religion—Bonaparte's Church Establishment—Imperial Catechism—Efforts of Louis to restore Reverence for Religion—Alarm of the French Protestants—Toleration Recommended—Decay of Religion and Morality in France—French and British contrasted—Gambling—Palais Royal—Superstition of the French—l'Homme Rouge—Bonaparte's Faith in Destiny.

Do not blame me, my dear friend, if I have been long in fulfilling my promise to you. Religion, so ample a field in most countries, has for some time been in France an absolute blank. From my former letters you must have learned, that in Flanders the Catholic system still maintains itself in great vigour. The churches are full of people, most of them on their knees, and their devotion, if not enlightened, seems fervent and sincere. One instance I saw with peculiar pleasure, at Malines—Two *Religieuses*, sisters of charity, I believe, entered the church at the head of a small school of about twenty poor children, neatly, though coarsely dressed, and knelt down with them to their devotions. I was informed, that the poor nuns had dedicated their little income and their whole time, struggling occasionally with all the difficulties incident to a country convulsed by war and political revolutions, to educate these children in the fear of God, and in useful knowledge. Call them nuns, or call them what you will, I think we will neither of us quarrel with an order who thus employ their hours of retirement from the world.

I was less edified by the frequent appearance of a small chapel and an altar, on the side of the road, where the carman will sometimes snatch a flying prayer, while his huge waggon wanders on at the will of the horses. But your own parishioners sometimes leave their horses' heads for less praiseworthy purposes, and therefore much cannot be said on that score. The rites and solemnities of the Catholic Church made less impression on me than I expected; even the administration of high mass, though performed by a cardinal, fell far short of what I had anticipated. There is a fidgeting about the whole ceremony, a perpetual dressing and

507

undressing, which seems intended to make it more elaborate and complex, but which destroys the grandeur and simplicity so appropriate to an act of solemn devotion. Much of the imposing exterior may now indeed be impaired—the church was the first object of plunder wherever the French came, and they have left traces of a rapacity which will not soon be erased. The vestments look antiquated and tawdry, the music is but indifferent, the plate and jewels have all vanished. The priests themselves are chiefly old men, on whom the gaudy dresses with which they are decorated, sit awkwardly, and who seem, in many instances, bowed down by painful recollections, as much as by infirmity. In a word, the old dame of Babylon, against whom our fathers testified so loudly, seems now hardly worth a passing attack, even in the *Nineteenthly* of an afternoon's sermon, and is in some measure reduced to the *pavé*. Old John Bunyan himself could hardly have wished to see her stand lower in influence and estimation, than she does in the popular mind in France; and yet a few years, and the Giant Pope will be, in all probability, as innoxious as the Giant Pagan. Indeed, since his having shared the fate of other giants, in being transported, like a show, from place to place, by the renowned charlatan Bonaparte, his former subjects have got familiar with his terrors, and excommunication scarcely strikes more horror than the *fee fa fum* of a nursery tale.

It is remarkable, that this indifference seems to have extended to the enemies, as well as the subjects, of the Catholic Church. When Rome was stormed in 1527, the chief amusement of the reformed German soldiers was insulting the rites of the Roman religion, and ridiculing the persons of their clergy. But in 1815, when the conquering armies of two Protestant kingdoms marched from Brussels to Paris, the idea of showing scorn or hatred to the Catholic religion never occurred to any individual soldier. I would gladly ascribe this to punctuality of discipline; but enough was done, by the Prussians at least, to show, that that consideration alone would not have held back their hands, had they felt any temptation to insult the French through the medium of their religion. But this does not seem to have appeared to them a vulnerable point, and not a crucifix or image was touched, or a pane of painted glass broken, that we could see or hear of, upon the route.

In the churches which we visited, very few persons seemed to attend the service, and these were aged men and women. In Paris this was still more remarkable; for, notwithstanding the zeal of the Court, and the example which they exhibit of strict attention to the forms of the Church,—an example even too marked for good policy,—those of the city of Paris are, with a few exceptions, empty and neglected. It is melancholy to think that, with the external forms and observances of religion, its vital principles also have fallen into complete disuse and oblivion. But those under whose auspices the French Revolution commenced, and by whom its terrors were for a time conducted, found their own interest intimately and strictly connected with the dissolution of the powerful checks of religious faith and moral practice. And although the Directory afterwards promulgated, by a formal edict, that France acknowledged the existence of a Supreme Being, and, with impious mockery, appointed a fête in his honour, all opportunity of instruction in religious duties was broken off by the early destination of the youth of France to the trade of arms. A much-esteemed friend at Paris happened to have a domestic of sense, information, and general intelligence above his station. His master upon some occasion used to him the expression, " It is doing as we would be done by,—the Christian maxim." The young man looked rather surprised: " Yes," repeated my friend, " I say it is the doctrine of the Christian religion, which teaches us not only to do as we would be done by, but also to return good for evil."—" It may be so, sir," answered the valet; " but I had the misfortune to be born during the heat of the Revolution, when it would have been death to have spoken on the subject of religion, and so soon as I was fifteen years old, I was put into the hands of the drill sergeant, whose first lesson to me was, that, as a French soldier, I was to fear neither God nor devil." My friend, himself a soldier, and a brave one, but of a very different cast of mind from that which was thought necessary for the service of France, was both shocked and astonished at this strong proof of the manner in which the present generation had been qualified, from their childhood, to be the plagues of society. This bent of the youth cannot be more strongly illustrated than by the behaviour of the lads who were educated at the College of Navarre, who, immediately on learning Bonaparte's landing and first success, rebelled against their teachers, and, taking possession of one of the towers of the college, declared for war and for the Emperor. The consideration that they were thus perverted in their early youth, and rendered unfit for all purposes but those of mischief, is the best consolation for such French patriots as mourn over the devastation which has overwhelmed the youth of their country.

Bonaparte, who, when not diverted from his purpose by his insatiable ambition, had strong views of policy, resolved upon the re-establishment of the Church as a sort of outwork to the Throne. He created, accordingly, archbishops, bishops, and all the appendages of a hierarchy. This was not only intended that they might surround the imperial throne with the solemn splendours of a hierarchy, and occasionally feed their master's ears with flattery in their pastoral charges,—an office which, by most of them, was performed with the most humiliating baseness,—but also in order to form an alliance between the religious creed which they were enjoined to inculcate, and the sentiments of the people towards the imperial dignity. The imperial catechism, promulgated under authority, proclaimed the duties of the catechumen to the Emperor, to be love, obedience, fidelity, and military services; the causes assigned were Napoleon's high and miraculous gifts, his immediate mission from the Deity, and the consecration by the Pope; and the menace to disloyalty was no less than eternal condemnation—here and hereafter. I am sorry to say, that this summary of *jus divinum* was not entirely of Bonaparte's invention; for, in a Prussian catechism for the use of the soldiers, entitled, " *Pflichten der Unterthanen*," (the Duties of Subjects,) and printed at Breslau, in 1800, I find the same doctrines expressed, though with less daring extravagance. Bonaparte reaped but little advantage from his system of church government, partly owing to the materials of which his monarchy was

constructed, (for the best and most conscientious of the clergy kept aloof from such promotion,) partly from the shortness of his reign, but principally from the stern impatience of his own temper, which could not long persist in apparent veneration for a power of his own creating, but soon led the way in exposing the new prelates to neglect and contempt.

We must learn to look with better hope upon the more conscientious efforts for re-establishing the altar, which have been made by the King. Yet we cannot but fear, that the order of the necessary reformation has been, to a certain extent at least, the reverse of what would really have attained the important purposes designed by the Sovereign. The rites, forms, and ceremonies of a Church, all its external observances, derive, from the public sense of religion itself, the respect which is paid to them. It is true, that, as the shell of a nut will subsist long after the kernel is decayed, so regard for ceremonies and forms may often remain when true devotion is no more, and when ignorant zeal has transferred her blind attachment from the essence of religion to its mere forms. But if that zeal is quenched, and that attachment is eradicated, and the whole system is destroyed both in show and in substance, it is not by again enforcing the formal observances which men have learned to contemn and make jest of, that the vivifying principle of religion can be rekindled. Indeed, far from supposing that the foundation of the altar should be laid upon the ritual of the Romish Church, with all the revived superstitions of the twelfth century, it would be more prudent to abandon to oblivion, a part at least of what is shocking to common sense and reason ; which, although a Most Christian King might have found himself under some difficulty of abrogating, when it was yet in formal observance, he certainly cannot be called upon to renew, when it has fallen into desuetude. The Catholics of this age are not excluded from the lights which it has afforded ; and the attempt to re-establish processions, in which the officiating persons hardly know their places, tales of miraculous images, masses for the souls of State criminals, and all the mummery of barbarous ages, is far from meeting the enlarged ideas which the best and most learned of them have expressed. The peculiar doctrines of their Church prohibit, indeed, the formal rejection of any doctrine or observance which she has once received ; but I repeat, that the time is favourable in France for rebuilding the Gallican Church on a more solid basis than ever, by leaving room for the gradual and slow reformation introduced by the lapse of time, instead of forcing back the nineteenth century into the rude and degrading darkness of the ages of excommunications and crusades. It is with the hearts of the French, and not with the garments of their clergy, that the reformation, or rather the restoration, of religion ought to commence ; and I conceive the primary object should be securing the instruction of the rising generation in religious and moral duties, as well as in general education, by carefully filling up the ranks of the parochial clergy, on whose patient and quiet attention to the morals of their flocks the state of the nation must depend, and not upon the colour of the cap, the tinkle of a bell, or the music of high mass.

The truth is, that the King's most natural and justifiable zeal for the establishments of religion, which were his chief consolation in adversity, has already given alarm to several classes of his subjects. Bigoted or interested priests have been already heard misrepresenting the intentions of their sovereign, so far as to affirm, he means to restore to the Church all her rights, and impose anew upon the subject the burdens of tithes, and the confusion which must arise from the reclamation of the church lands. How these reports, malignantly echoed by the enemies of the royal family, sound in the ears of men of property, I leave to your own judgment; and can only regret that it is as difficult as it is desirable, for the King to oppose them by a public contradiction.

It is chiefly in the southern districts, where the French Protestants still maintain themselves, that this alarm is excited, cherished, and fostered, by those who care for neither one religion nor the other, farther than as the jealousies and contentions of both may be engines of bloodshed, depression, and revolution. In the province of Languedoc, especially, the angry passions of both parties are understood to be at full tide; and it unfortunately happens that the contending parties are there envenomed by political hatred. Bonaparte, whose system of national religion included universal toleration, extended his special protection to the professors of the reformed doctrines, and by an organic law concerning worship, published in the year X., guaranteed to them the free exercise of their religion, being the first public indulgence which had been extended to them since the revocation of the Edict of Nantes. A system of consistories was established for their internal church-government; and so highly were they favoured, that the public exercise of the Catholic religion, by processions, or other ritual observances, performed without the walls of the church, was positively prohibited in such towns as had consistorial churches belonging to the Protestants. This distinction in favour of a body of subjects, amounting, it has been computed, to two millions of souls, attended by the triumph conferred by the interdiction of the Catholic rites where their eyes could be offended by them, raised the spirits of the Protestants as much as it exasperated and depressed those of the Catholics. The sects took their ranks in political contest accordingly; and although interests of various kinds prevented the rule from being absolute, yet it was observed, during the last convulsions of state, that the Catholics of the South were in general royalists, whereas many of the Protestants, in gratitude for past favours conferred on their Church, in jealousy of the family of Bourbon, by the bigotry of whose ancestors their fathers had suffered, and confiding in the tolerant spirit of Bonaparte, lent too ready and willing aid to his usurpation. During that event, and those which followed, much and mutual subject of exasperation has unfortunately taken place between these contending parties. Ancient enmities have been awakened, and, amid contradictory reports and statements, we can easily discover that both parties, or individuals at least of both, have been loud in their appeal to principles of moderation when undermost, and very ready, when they obtained the upper hand, to abuse the advantages which the changes of the state had alternately given to them. This is a deep and rankling wound, which will require to be treated with no common skill. The Protestants of the South

509

are descendants of the ardent men who used to assemble by thousands in the wilderness—I will not say with the scoffer, to hear the psalms of Clement Marot sung to the tune of *Reveillez vous, belle endormie*—but rather, as your Calvinistic heroes of moor and moss, in the days of the last Stuarts, are described by a far different bard, dear in remembrance to us both, for the affectionate sympathy and purity of his thoughts and feelings; when in the wilderness

> " arose the song, the loud
> Acclaim of praise : The wheeling plover ceased
> Her plaint ; the solitary place was glad,
> And on the distant cairns the watcher's ear
> Caught doubtfully at times the breeze-borne note." [1]

On the other hand, the Catholics are numerous, powerful in the hope of protection and preference from the crown, and eager to avenge insults, which, in their apprehension, have been aimed alike at the throne and the altar. If we claim for the Protestants, whose nearer approach to our own doctrines recommends them to our hearts as objects of interest, the sympathy which is due to their perilous situation, let us not, in candour, deny at least the credit of mistaken zeal to those whom different rites divide from us. In the name of that Heaven, to whose laws both forms of religion appeal, who has disclaimed enforcing the purest doctrines by compulsion, and who never can be worshipped duly or acceptably by bloody sacrifices, let us deprecate a renewal of those savage and fatal wars, which, founded upon difference of religious opinion, seem to convert even the bread of life itself into the most deadly poison. British interference, not surely so proposed as to affront France's feelings of national independence, (a point on which late incidents have made her peculiarly irritable,) but with the earnest and anxious assurances of that good-will, for which our exertions in behalf of the royal family, and our interest in the tranquillity of France, may justly claim credit,—might, perhaps, have some influence with the Government. But in what degree, or how far it may be prudent to hazard it, can only be known to those upon whom the momentous charge of public affairs has devolved at this trying crisis. We need not now take up the parable of Lord Shaftesbury, when he compared the Reformed churches of France and Savoy to the sister of the spouse in the Canticles, and asked the astonished peers of Charles the Second, " What shall be done for our sister in the day when she shall be spoken for ?" But it is certain, that the security of the Protestant religion abroad is now, as in the days of that statesman, a wall and defence unto that which we profess at home ; and at all times, when England has been well administered, she has claimed and exercised the rights of intercession in behalf of the Reformed Churches. I trust, however, that our mediation will be, in the present case, unnecessary, and that the King himself, with the sound judgment and humane disposition which all parties allow him to possess, will show himself the protector of both parties, by restricting the aggressions of either. In the meanwhile, admire the singularity of human affairs. In Ireland discontents exist, because the Catholics are not possessed of all the capacities and privileges of their Protestant fellow-subjects ;—in the Netherlands, the Catholic

[1] Grahame's *Sabbath*.

clergy murmur at the union, because the King has expressed his determination to permit the free exercise of the Protestant religion amid his Catholic dominions ;—and in the south of France the sword is nearly drawn, upon the footing of doubts, jealousies, and apprehensions of mutual violence, for which neither party can allege any feasible ground, except mutual dislike and hatred. We may, without offence, wish that all of them would qualify their zeal for the doctrinal part of their religion with some part of that meekness of spirit, which would be the best proof of its purity.

To return to the religious and moral state of France.—It is remarkable that the dissolution of religious principle, the confusion of the Sabbath with the ordinary days of the week, the reduction of marriage to a state of decent and legal concubinage, from which parties can free themselves at pleasure, have, while thus sapping the foundations of the social affections, as well as of religious faith, introduced more vices than crimes ; much profligacy, but less atrocity than might have been expected. A Frenchman, to whom you talk of the general decay of morality in his country, will readily and with truth reply to you, that if every species of turpitude be more common in France, delicts of that sort against which the law directs its thunders, are much more frequent in Britain. Murders, robberies, daring thefts, such as frequently occur in the English papers, are little known in those of Paris. The amusements and habits of the lower orders are, on all occasions of ordinary occurrence, more quiet, peaceable, and orderly, than those of the lower English. There are no quarrels on the street, intoxication is rarely practised even by the lowest of the people, and when assembled for the purpose of public amusement, they observe a good-humoured politeness to each other and to strangers, for which certainly our countrymen are not remarkable. To look at the thousands of rabble whom I have seen streaming through the magnificent apartments at Versailles, without laying a finger upon a painting or an article of furniture, and afterwards crowding the gardens, without encroaching upon any spot where they could do damage ; to observe this, and recollect what would be the conduct of an English mob in similar circumstances, compels one to acknowledge, that the French appear, upon such occasions, beyond comparison the more polished, sensible, and civilized people. But release both parties from the restraints imposed by the usual state of society, and suppose them influenced by some powerful incentive to passion and violence, and remark how much the contrast will be altered. The English populace will huzza, swear, threaten, break windows, and throw stones at the Life Guards engaged in dispersing them ; but if a soldier should fall from his horse, the rabble, after enjoying a laugh at his expense, would lend a hand to lift him to his saddle again. A French mob would tear him limb from limb, and parade the fragments in triumph upon their pikes. In the same manner, the Englishman under arms retains the same frank, rough loyalty of character, without the alert intelligence and appearance of polished gallantry, which a French soldier often exhibits to strangers. But it would be an outrage to our countrymen to compare the conduct of the two armies when pursuing a defeated enemy, or entering a country as invaders,

when every evil passion is awake, and full license is granted to satiate them.

The cause of so extraordinary a contrast may, I think, be expressed in very few words. The French act from feeling, and the British from principle. In moments, therefore, when the passions are at rest, the Frenchman will often appear, and be in reality, the more amiable of the two. He is generally possessed of intelligence and the power of reflection, both of which are great promoters of that limited sort of honesty which keeps the windy side of the law. He piques himself upon some understanding and perception of the fine arts, by which he is told his country is distinguished, and he avoids the rudeness and violence which constitute a barbarian. He is, besides, habitually an observer of the forms and decencies of society, and has ample means of indulging licentious passions, without transgressing them. The Frenchman is further, by nature and constitution, a happy and contented mortal, satisfied with little, and attached to luxuries of the more simple kind ; and a mind so constituted is usually disposed to extend its cheerfulness to others. The Englishman of low rank is, in some degree, the reverse of all this. His intelligence seldom goes beyond the art to which he is trained, and which he most frequently practises with mechanical dexterity only ; and therefore he is not by habit, unless when nature has been especially bountiful, much of a reasoning animal. As for pretending to admire or criticize the fine arts, or their productions, he would consider such an effort of taste as the most ridiculous affectation, and therefore readily treats with contempt and disrespect what he would upon system be ashamed to understand. Vice and crime are equally forbidden by the Englishman's system of religious morals ; if he becomes stained with gross immorality, he is generally ready to rush into legal delict, since, being divested of the curb of conscience, and destroyed in his own esteem, he becomes, like a horse without a bridle, ready to run upon any course which chance or the frenzy of the moment may dictate. And this may show why, though the number of vicious persons is greater in France than in England in an enormous ratio, yet the proportion of legal criminals is certainly smaller. As to general temper and habits, the Englishman, less favoured in climate, and less gay by constitution, accustomed to be a grumbler by his birthright, very often disdains to be pleased himself, and is not very anxious to please others. His freedom, too, gives him a right, when casually mixed with his betters, to push, to crowd, to be a little riotous and very noisy, and to insult his neighbours on slight provocation, merely to keep his privileges in exercise. But then he is also taught to respect the law, which he invokes as his own protection ; to weigh and decide upon what is just and unjust, foul and fair ; to respect the religion in which he has been trained, and to remember its restraints, even in the moment of general license. It might indeed be wished that some of the lighter and more amiable qualities of the French could be infused into our populace. But what an infinitely greater service would the sovereign render to France, who should give new sensibility to those moral principles which have too long lain torpid in the breasts of her inhabitants !

This great end can only be reached by prudent

and prospective regulations; for neither religion nor morality can be enforced upon a nation by positive law. The influence of parochial clergy, and of parochial schools, committed to persons worthy of the important trust, are, as I before hinted, the most obvious remedies. But there are others of a prohibitory and preventive nature. It is in the power of government to stop some grand sources of corruption of morals, and to withdraw their protection and license at least, from those assemblies which have for their direct object the practice of immoralities of every sort. The Palais Royal, in whose saloons and porticos Vice has established a public and open school for gambling and licentiousness, far from affording, as at present, an impure and scandalous source of revenue to the state, should be levelled to the ground, with all its accursed brothels and gambling-houses,—rendezvouses the more seductive to youth, as being free from some of those dangers which might alarm timidity in places of avowedly scandalous resort. Gaming is indeed reduced to all the gravity of a science, and, at the same time, is conducted upon the scale of the most extensive manufacture. In the *Salon des Etrangers*, the most celebrated haunt of this Dom-Daniel, which I had the curiosity to visit, the scene was decent and silent to a degree of solemnity. An immense hall was filled with gamesters and spectators; those who kept the bank, and managed the affairs of the establishment, were distinguished by the green shades which they wore to preserve their eyes—by their silent and grave demeanour—and by the paleness of their countenances, exhausted by constant vigils. There was no distinction of persons, nor any passport required for entrance, save that of a decent exterior; and on the long tables, which were covered with gold, an artisan was at liberty to hazard his week's wages, or a noble his whole estate. Youth and age were alike welcome; and any one who chose to play within the limits of a trifling sum, had only to accuse his own weakness if he was drawn into deeper or more dangerous hazard. Every thing seemed to be conducted with perfect fairness; and indeed the mechanical construction of the E O tables, or whatever they are called, appears calculated to prevent the possibility of fraud. The only advantage possessed by the bank (which is, however, enormous) is the extent of its funds, by which it is enabled to sustain any train of reverse of fortune; whereas most of the individuals who play against the bank are in circumstances to be ruined by the first succession of ill luck; so that ultimately the smaller ventures merge in the stock of the principal adventurers, as rivers run into the sea. The profits of the establishment must indeed be very large to support its expenses. Besides a variety of attendants who distribute refreshments to the players gratis, there is an elegant entertainment, with expensive wines, regularly prepared about three o'clock in the morning, for those who choose to partake of it. With such temptations around him, and where the hazarding an insignificant sum seems at first venial or innocent, it is no wonder if thousands feel themselves gradually involved in the whirlpool whose verge is so little distinguishable, until they are swallowed up, with their time, talents, and fortune, and often also both body and soul.

This is Vice with her fairest vizard; but the same unhallowed precincts contain many a secret cell for the most hideous and unheard-of debaucheries, many an open rendezvous of infamy, and many a den of usury and of treason; the whole mixed with a Vanity-fair of shops for jewels, trinkets, and baubles, that bashfulness may not lack a decent pretext for adventuring into the haunts of infamy. It was here where the preachers of the Revolution first found, amidst gamblers, money-jobbers, desperadoes, and prostitutes, ready auditors of their doctrines, and active hands to labour in their vineyard. In more recent times, it was here that the plots of the Bonapartists were adjusted, and the number of their partisans recruited and instructed concerning the progress of the conspiracy; and from hence the seduced soldiers, inflamed with many a bumper to the health of the Exile of Elba, under the mystic names of *Jean de l' Epée*, and *Caporal Violet*, were dismissed to spread the news of his approaching return, and prepare their comrades to desert their lawful sovereign. In short, from this central pit of Acheron—in which are openly assembled and mingled those characters and occupations which, in all other capitals, are driven to shroud themselves in separate and retired recesses—from this focus of vice and treason, have flowed forth those waters of bitterness of which France has drunk so deeply. Why, after having occasioned so much individual and public misery, this source of iniquity is not now stopped, the tenants expelled, and the buildings levelled to the ground, or converted to some far different purpose, is a question which the consciences of the French ministers can best answer. Thus far at least is certain, that, with the richest soil, and the most cultivated understandings, a people brave even to a fault, kind-tempered, gay, and formed for happiness, have been for twenty years the plague of each other and of Europe; and if their disorders can be plainly traced to want of moral character and principle, it cannot be well to maintain amongst them, for the sake of sharing its polluted profits, such a hot-bed of avowed depravity.

If the French have no strong sense of religion or its precepts, they are not without a share of superstition; and an impostor is at present practising among them, who, by all accounts, is as successful as Joanna Southcote herself. This lady, a woman, I am assured, of rank and information,[1] pretends, like Baron Swedenborg, to an immediate intercourse with the spiritual world, and takes her ecstatic trances for the astonishment of parties of good fashion, to whom, on her return to her senses, she recounts the particulars of her visit to the spiritual world, and whom she treats with explanations of their past lives, and predictions of the future. It is said her art has attracted the attention of some men of high rank in the armies of our allies.

If you disbelieve the powers of this lady, you may also distrust the apparition of *l'Homme Rouge*, or

---

[1] This lady, Madame Krudener, was said to have acquired subsequently a powerful influence over the mind of the Emperor Alexander; and it is very generally believed. that her conversations with him in Paris were mainly instrumental in suggesting the idea of the Holy Alliance: It is certain, that, in her later sermons, she held it up almost as a new covenant.

After many wanderings from place to place, in what she believed her heaven-ordained mission, she was at length transported by the police to the Russian frontier, in 1824, and died at Karafubasar, in the Crimea, on the 13th December of the same year.

the Red Man, said to have haunted Napoleon as the demon did Ras Michael,[1] and advised him in matters of importance. He was, saith the legend, a little muffled figure, to whom, whenever he appeared, access was instantly given, for the spectre was courteous enough to request to be announced. At Wilna, before advancing into Russia, while Bonaparte was engaged in tracing the plan of his march, he was told this person requested to speak with him.' He desired the attendant to inform his summoner that the Emperor was engaged. When this reply was communicated to the unknown, he assumed an authoritative voice and accent, and, throwing open his cloak, discovered his dress under it, which was red, without mixture of any other colour, " Tell the Emperor," said he, " that *l'Homme Rouge* MUST speak with him." He was then admitted, and they were heard to talk loud together. As he left the apartment, he said publicly, " You have rejected my advice ! you will not again see me till you have bitterly repented your error." The visits of *l'Homme Rouge* were renewed on Bonaparte's return from Elba ; but before he set out on his last campaign, Napoleon again offended his familiar, who took leave of him for ever, giving him up to the red men of England, who became the real arbiters of his destiny. If you have not faith enough for this marvellous story, pray respect the prophecy which was made to Josephine, by one of the negro soothsayers in the West Indies, that she should rise to the highest pinnacle of modern greatness, but without ever being a *queen;* that she should fall from thence before her death, and die in an hospital. I can myself vouch for the existence of this prophecy before the events which it was supposed to predict, for it was told me many years ago, when Bonaparte was only general of the army of Italy, by a lady of rank, who lived in the same convent with Josephine. The coincidence of the fortune-teller's presages with the fact, would have been marred by the circumstances of the ex-empress's death, had not somebody's ingenuity discovered that her house, as the name *Mal-maison* implies, had once been an hospital. Bonaparte, it is well known, had strange and visionary ideas about his own fated destiny, and could think of fortune like the Wallenstein of the stage. The following lines from that drama, more grand in the translation of Coleridge than in the original of Schiller, seem almost to trace the career of Napoleon :—

" Even in his youth he had a daring soul:
His frame of mind was serious and severe
Beyond his years ; his dreams were of great objects.
He walk'd amid, as if a silent spirit,
Communing with himself : Yet have 1 known him
Transported on a sudden into utterance
Of strange conceptions ; kindling into splendour.
His soul reveal'd itself, and he spoke so
That we look'd round perplex'd upon each other,
Not knowing whether it were craziness,
Or whether 'twere a God that spoke in him.

Thenceforth he held himself for an exempted
And privileged being, and, as if he were
Incapable of dizziness or fall,
He ran along the unsteady rope of life,
And paced with rapid step the way to greatness;
Was Count and Prince, Duke, Regent, and Dictator,
And is all, all this too little for him ;
He stretches forth his hand for a King's crown,
And plunges in unfathomable ruin." [2]

Farewell, my dear friend ; light and leisure are

exhausted in this long detail, concerning the religion of which the French have so little, and the superstition of which they have a considerable portion.

You will groan over many parts of this epistle, but the picture is not without its lights. France has afforded many examples, in the most trying crisis, of firmness, of piety, of patience under affliction ; many, too, of generosity and courtesy and charity. The present Royal Family have been bred in the school of adversity, and it is generally allowed that they have the inclination, though perhaps they may mistake the means, of ameliorating the character of the nation, to the government of which they have been so providentially restored.

LETTER XVI.

PAUL TO HIS COUSIN PETER.

Louis' first Ministry—Fouché—Execution of Labedoyere—Fouché—Prejudices in France against England—State of Parties—Royalists—Imperialists—Liberalists—The Army—General good-will of the People—French Nationality—Champ de Mai—Love of Show—Representation of France—Want of Political Information — Factions — French Manners — Lord Castlereagh—Duke of Wellington—Lord Cathcart—Conclusion.

I AM in the centre, you say, of political intelligence, upon the very arena where the fate of nations is determined, and send you no intelligence. This seems a severe reproach ; for, in England, with a friend in the Foreign-office, or the advantage of mixing in a certain circle of society, one can always fill up a letter with political events and speculations some days sooner, and somewhat more accurately, than they appear in the newspapers. But they manage matters otherwise in France. The conferences between the ministers of the allied powers and those of Louis XVIII., are conducted with great and praiseworthy secrecy. They are said to be nearly concluded ; but a final arrangement will probably be postponed by an unexpected change of ministry in the Tuileries.

All politicians were surprised (none more than thou, Peter,) at the choice which the King made of his first ministry. That Fouché, who voted for the death of his brother, Louis XVI., who had been an agent of Robespierre and a minister of Bonaparte —who, in the late Revolution, was regarded as a chief promoter of the unexpected and unnatural union between the discontented patriots, or Liberalists, and the followers of the ex-emperor—that he should have been named minister of police under the restored heir of the Bourbons, seemed wonderful to the Royalists. His companions in the provisional government saw themselves with equal astonishment put under the *surveillance* of their late associate, in his new character ; and the letters between him and Carnot, when the latter applied to Fouché, agreeably to the royal proclamation, that a place of residence might be assigned to him, fully, though briefly, express their characteristic feelings. " *Où veux tu que je m'en aille, Traitre?*" signed

---

CARNOT, was a brief question, to which the minister of police as briefly replied, " *Où tu veux, Imbécille.*" FOUCHÉ.

There are two ways of considering the matter ; —with reference to the minister who accepted the office, and with regard to the sovereign who nominated him.

On the former point little need be said. Times of frequent and hasty changes, when a people are hurried from one government to another, necessarily introduce among the leading statesmen a versatility of character, at which those who are remote from the pressure of temptation hold up their hands and wonder. In looking over our own history, we discover the names of Shaftesbury and Sunderland, and of many other statesmen eminent for talent, who changed their political creed with the change of times, and yet contrived to be employed and trusted by successive governments who confided in their fidelity, at least while they could make that fidelity their interest. Independent and steady as the English boast themselves, there were, during the great Civil War, very many persons who made it an avowed principle to adhere to the faction that was uppermost, and support the administration of the day, and these prudential politicians existed in numbers enough to form a separate sect, who, in the hypocritical cant of the times, assumed the name of *Waiters upon Providence.* This accommodating line of conduct has been rendered so general in France, during the late frequent changes of government, as to give matter for a catalogue of statesmen and remarkable persons, extending to about four hundred and fifty pages, which has been recently published, under the name of the *Dictionnaire des Girouettes,* in which we find the names of almost all the men distinguished for talents or influence, now alive in France, with a brief account of the changes of their political lives. The list grew so scandalously comprehensive, that the editor announces his intention of suppressing, in a second edition, all those who had changed only *once,* considering them, comparatively, as men of steady political faith and conscience. They must know little of human nature, who can suppose the result would be otherwise with the mass of mankind, in times when universal example sanctioned changes of principle, which were besides pressed upon each individual by ambition, by avarice, by fear, by want, in short, by their interest under the most powerful and seductive forms. The conduct of Fouché, therefore, is by no means singular ; although, if it be true, that, in assuming power under Bonaparte, his real wish was to serve the King, his case merits a particular distinction,—whether favourable or no, may be reasonably doubted.

That Fouché should have accepted power was, therefore, in the order of things, as they have lately gone in France. But, that the King should have trusted, or at least employed him, and that his appointment should have given acknowledged satisfaction to the Duke of Wellington and to Lord Castlereagh, thou, Peter, wilt think more difficult to account for. Consider, however, that Fouché was at the head of a numerous faction, comprehending the greater part of that third party in the state, which, as uniting all shades of those who use the word Liberty as their war-cry, are generally called Liberalists. If these were divided from the King in the moment of his return, what remained to him

save the swords of a few nobles and men of honour, the scattered and subdued bands of La Vendée, which had been put down by a convention with General Lamarque, and the inert wishes of the mass of the population, who might indeed cry *Vive le Roi,* but had plainly showed they loved their own barns better than the house of Bourbon ? The bayonets of the allies, indeed, surrounded Paris, but Bonaparte was still in France and at large, the army of the Loire continued independent and unbroken, many garrisons held out, many provinces were still agitated ; and the services of Fouché, who held in his hand the various threads of correspondence through the distracted kingdom, who knew the character and principles of each agitator, and the nature of the materials he had to work with ; who possessed, in short, that extent of local and personal knowledge peculiar to one who had been long the head of the French police, were essentially necessary to the establishment of the royal authority, and to preventing a scene of blood and total confusion. That Fouché served the King with great address, cannot be doubted, and his admission into the high office of trust, which he has for some time enjoyed, was a great means of calming the public mind, and restoring to confidence those, who, feeling themselves involved in the general defection, might otherwise have been rendered desperate by the fear of punishment. Talleyrand, also, whose loyalty to the house of Bourbon, during the last usurpation, was never doubted, is understood to have expressed his strong sense of the peremptory necessity of receiving Fouché and his party into power at least, if not into confidence. So much, therefore, for the propriety, or rather necessity, of a measure, which looked strange enough when viewed from a distance, which could not be agreeable to the King personally, and which had its political inconveniences ; but, nevertheless, was at the time essential to the royal interest. The first benefit which resulted from this appointment was the close and vigilant pursuit that compelled Napoleon to surrender to the English. The same activity exercised by this experienced politician and his agents, decided and secured a bloodless counter-revolution in most of the towns in France. Upon the general interests of Europe, Fouché is well understood to have entertained such just and moderate views, as were acceptable to the ministers of the allied powers, and particularly to those of Britain.

Notwithstanding these advantages, it is not supposed that Fouché will keep his ground in the ministry, and it is believed the change will occasion the resignation of Talleyrand.[1] As the King's party appears better consolidated, and his power becomes more permanent, the faction of the *Royalistes purs et par excellence* acquires numbers and courage, and becomes daily more shocked with the incongruity of Fouché's high place in the administration. His influence is supposed to have one effect, which, if true, is a very bad one—that, namely, of delaying the selecting and bringing to punishment the more notorious agents of the last usurpation. All who know this nation must be aware of what importance it is that their ruler should not seem to fear

---

[1] This anticipation was verified shortly after the writer left Paris.

them; and the King ought to know that his authority will seem little more than an idle pageant till he shall show he is possessed of the power of vindicating and maintaining it. On the other hand, nothing can be more impolitic than to keep up the memory of this brief usurpation, and the insecure and jealous feelings of all connected with it, by long hesitation on the choice of victims to the offended laws. The sooner that two or three principal criminals can be executed, some dangerous agitators banished, and a general amnesty extended to all the rest, without exception, the sooner and the firmer will the royal authority be established. We have as yet had only one example of severity, in the fate of Labedoyere, although no good reason can be given why others of superior consequence, such as Ney and Massena, should not share his fate. But the death of this comparatively subordinate agent has acted as a sedative upon the spirit of faction. Last week nothing was heard but threats and defiance, and bold declarations, that the government would not, and dared not, execute the sentence. The rights of the Bourbons seemed to have been so long in *abeyance* that it was thought scarce possible to be guilty of treason against them, or that they should dare to regard and punish it as such. This is a popular feeling which the King must remove by a display of firmness, or it will most assuredly once more remove his throne. Accordingly, the execution of this criminal has had some effect, and the tone of mutiny and defiance is greatly lowered. The execution took place in the evening, and there was no remarkable concourse of people. Labedoyere died with great firmness, but his fate apparently made little impression on the bystanders. I met parties of them returning from the fatal scene, which had not a whit abated the usual vivacity of their prattle. One of the gens d'armes alone testified some sympathy with the sufferer: "*Quelle dommage!*" said he to an English gentleman, "*il n'avoit que vingt-huit ans.*" The handsome sufferer, however, finds the usual degree of favour in the eyes of the fair. One lady talked of his execution as *an horreur*, an atrocity unequalled in the annals of France. "Did Bonaparte never order such executions?"—"Who! the Emperor!—never."—"But the Duc D'Enghien, madam!" continued the persevering querist.— "*Ah! parlez moi d'Adam et d'Eve,*" was the reply. A retrospective of three or four years was like looking back to the fall of man; and the exclamation affords no bad key to the French character, to whom the past is nothing, and the present every thing.

The attacks upon Fouché in our English newspapers are said to have no small share in unsettling his power, as they are supposed to express the opinion of our nation against him. I have great reason to doubt whether his successor may not be appointed out of a class to whom we are, as a nation, less acceptable. For, with a few exceptions, I do not think that the English are so much disliked even by the military men and Imperialists, as they are by the nobility and pure royalists. This class of politicians, whatever may be thought of their bias to despotism, number among them so much of high honourable feeling and sincere principle, that I willingly look for some apology for their entertaining sentiments towards England and Englishmen, which, to say the least, are an indif-

ferent requital for our former hospitality and our late effective assistance. I will, therefore, make every allowance for the natural prejudice which they entertain against us for having, as they may conceive, stopped short in the services which it was in our power to have rendered them, and declined to back their pretensions to complete restoration of the rights and property which they have forfeited in the King's cause. I will permit them to feel as Frenchmen as well as royalists, and to view with a mingled sensation, the victory of Waterloo and the capture of Paris, although their own interest and that of the King was immediately dependent on the success of the allies. I can suppose, that it is painful for them to see foreigners residing at Paris as lords of the ascendant; and it may be a laudable sensibility to the misfortunes of their country, which makes them at this moment retreat from the duties of hospitality, and shun mixing in society with those whose best blood has been so recently shed in the King's service. I can even forgive them that, being conscious of their weakness in point of numbers and influence (unless through that of the sovereign,) they are glad to snatch opportunities of making common cause with the bulk of their countrymen at the expense of foreigners, and are therefore fain to lead the cry against the allies, and especially against our country, in order to show, that whatever may be their interests, their hearts have always been French. But while we pardon the motives, we must be allowed to smile at the expressions of this animosity. One would almost suppose, while hearing them, that our interference in the affairs of France was altogether gratuitous and unnecessary, and had only prevented a grand *re-action*, by which Napoleon would have been walked out of the kingdom as he had walked into it, and a counter-revolution accomplished, as nearly resembling that which concludes the Rehearsal, as the last usurpation seemed in ease and celerity to rival that of King Phys. and King Ush. in the same drama. They even extol the conduct of those commandants upon the frontier, who, in defiance of their sovereign's mandate, and with a brutal indifference to human life, maintain, without motive, or means, or hope, a senseless opposition to the allied troops. Some of these have been honourably acquitted when brought to trial; all are praised and caressed, as having maintained the frontiers of France against foreigners, instead of being shot or degraded for the bloodshed occasioned by their resistance both to their country and to the King's allies. Upon the same principle, I suppose, the governor of Vincennes, who still holds out his old Donjon, is to be considered as a true patriot, although he, and those who think like him, have no object in view but to show a reckless and unavailing resistance to their victors. In one of the King's proclamations to his subjects on his restoration, he has been made to take credit, that not one of his own followers had been permitted to draw a sword in defence of his rights, &c. If the state of the royal army was indeed justly rated at twenty-four thousand men and forty pieces of cannon, as given in an order of the day, signed by the Duke of Feltre, on 7th April, 1815, we may with right complain of the mistaken tenderness which withheld such a force from the conflict, and demand from the King of France a reckoning for the lives of forty thousand brave men killed in his quarrel, many of whom might have been saved by such a reinforcement. But if the attendants of the King consisted chiefly of a few hundred officers and gardes de corps, to whom the arrival of *cinq Cent Suisses* (that is, not five hundred Swiss, as a sanguine Englishman was led to interpret the phrase, from the pleasure with which he heard the incident detailed, but five individuals of the corps called *les Cent Suisses,*) was hailed as a timely reinforcement, it should be considered, that, since the days of chivalry are ended, and since no single knight can now rout a legion of cuirassiers with his own good sword, the King must have owed his restoration to Wellington and Blucher; and those who only walked forward in the path which our swords hewed out for them, ought to bear with some patience the measures to which their own proved weakness, and the experienced art and strength of their powerful adversaries, compel us to have recourse. It was, I think, Edward I., who replied with scorn to a competitor for the Scottish crown, in whose cause he had invaded Scotland, when, after the victory at Dunbar, he ventured to remind him of his pretensions, *Ne avons nous autre chose a faire que avons reaumeys gagner?* [1] Such an answer we might have returned to Louis XVIII. had we inclined to support any other competitor among the ample choice which the provisional government held out to us; and although we claim no merit for following the open path of faith and loyalty to an unfortunate ally, we ought at least to escape the censure of those who have been most benefited by our exertions, and who confessedly were unable or unwilling to assist themselves.

In the meanwhile, if it is meant to confine the King's choice of ministers to the faction of *royalistes purs*, we are afraid his choice will be limited; for, excepting a few individuals who have been employed in Russia, where strangers are more readily promoted to offices of confidence than elsewhere, we know few who have had the means of acquiring experience in state business. Brave, loyal, and gallant, the French noblesse are by their charter; but the heat of temper which confounds friends and foes; the presumption which pushes direct to its object without calculation of obstacles; a sense of wrongs received, and a desire of vengeance, make them dangerous counsellors at such a crisis as the present.

From the more violent portion of the opposite faction, (inclusive of the Imperialists, who are now hastily melting into the ranks of the general opposition,) the King can, I fear, look for little cordiality, and only for that degree of support which he can make it their interest to afford him. Still, however, there are many cases where ability without principle may be successfully employed, when it would be unsafe to trust to principle unguided by experience and prudence; just as a proprietor will sometimes find it his interest to employ, in the management of his affairs, a skilful knave rather than an honest fool. This is taking an extreme case: there are many degrees between a *jacobin saragé* and a *royaliste pur*, and some of the wisest and best of each party will perhaps at length see the necessity of joining in an administration exclusive of neither, which should have at once for its object the just rights of the throne, and the constitutional liberties of the subject. To such a coalition, the King's name would be indeed a tower of strength; but founded upon a narrower basis, must run the risk of falling itself, and bearing to ground all who adhere to it.

It must be owned, nevertheless, that the general rallying point of the *Liberalists* is an avowed dislike to the present Monarch and his immediate connexions. They will sacrifice, they pretend, so much to the general inclinations of Europe, as to select a King from the Bourbon race; but he must be one of their own choosing, and the Duke of Orleans[2] is most familiar to their mouths. And thus these politicians, who assume the title of *Constitutional Royalists*, propose to begin their career by destroying hereditary succession, the fundamental principle of a limited monarchy. In Britain, we know that the hereditary right of succession is no longer indeed accounted divine and indefeasible, as was the principle of *our* ancient *royalistes purs et par excellence*; but the most sturdy Whig never contended that it could be defeated otherwise than by abdication or forfeiture, or proposed the tremendous measure of changing the succession purely by way of prevention or experiment. In the most violent times, and under the most peculiar circumstances, the Exclusion Bill, although founded upon an acknowledged and plausible ground of incapability, and levelled against the person of a successor, not of an existing monarch, was rejected as a dangerous innovation on the Constitution. It is in order to prevent, as far as possible, such violent and hazardous experiments, that we impute the faults of monarchs not to themselves but to their ministers, and receive, in a political sense, the well-known maxim, that the king can do no wrong. For the same reason, in the height of popular indignation against James II., the word *abdication* was selected in preference to *desertion* or *forfeiture*, to express the manner in which the throne became vacant at the Revolution. But the doctrine now held in France strikes at the very foundation of hereditary right, being founded on no overt act of the Sovereign tending to affect the liberties of his subjects, but upon jealousies and fears that he has, or may call, evil counsellors around him, to attempt the re-establishment of the feudal rights of the nobility and the domination of the Church. In this grand counterpart to our constitutional maxim, it is not even alleged that the King *has* done wrong, but it is assumed that he *will* do wrong, and proceedings are to be grounded on this prediction as if the evil foreseen already existed. The fact seems to be, that the objections of this faction to the present line is much more a matter of taste or caprice than they are willing to acknowledge. The vanity of the nation, and especially of this class of statesmen, who have not the least share of it, is affronted at being compelled to receive back from the conquering hand of the allies the legitimate monarch, in whose causeless expulsion they had assisted. They would willingly have had a bit of sugar with the wholesome physic which was forced upon them by English and Prussian bayonets, and they still long for something which may give them an ostensible pretext to say, that their own conduct had

---

[1] *I. e.* "Have we nothing to do but to conquer kingdoms for you?"—S.

[2] Called to the throne in August, 1830, as *Louis-Philippe Roi des Français!*

not been entirely inconsistent, nor their rebellion altogether fruitless. Hence the obstinacy of Bonaparte's two Chambers to the very last, in rejecting Louis XVIII. Hence the nicknames of *Le Préfet de l'Angleterre*, and Louis *l'Inevitable*, which their wit attached to the restored monarch; and to this feeling of mortified vanity, less than to any real fears of aggression upon their liberties, may be traced their wish to have a king whose title should be connected with the Revolution, and who might owe his crown more to their courtesy than to his own right. But who will warrant those that set such a dangerous stone rolling, where its course will stop? The body now united in one mass of opposition to the *royalistes purs*, comprehend among themselves a hundred various shades of difference, from the Constitutionalist of 1814 to the Republican of 1793, or the Imperialists of Bonaparte's time. It happened regularly in the French Revolution, that so soon as one point was gained or yielded, which the popular party represented as an ultimatum, new demands were set up by demagogues, who affected to plead still higher doctrines of freedom than those with which their predecessors had remained satisfied; the force of those who had been satisfied with the concessions being uniformly found insufficient to defend the breach they themselves had stormed, until all merged in anarchy, and anarchy itself in military tyranny. We have seen already the progress of an Orleans faction, as well as its fatal termination. We have no desire to give another whirl to the revolutionary E O table, or once more to shuffle the cards for the chance of turning up such trumps as will best suit the political gamblers of the Palais Royal.

Besides these two violent parties, one of which aims to restore the abrogated tyranny of priests and seigneurs, and the other to render a hereditary monarchy an elective one at a sweep, there are two classes of great importance, namely, the army and the mass of the people. Much must undoubtedly depend on the disposition of the former, which has been for some time accustomed to act as a deliberative body, and which, however mutilated and disjoined, will, like the several portions of a snake, continue long to writhe under the same impulses by which it was agitated when entire. Every effort is now making to place this formidable engine in the hands of the Crown, by the dissolution and new-formation of the regiments, by recruits, and by the addition of separate corps, levied in the places most attached to the royal interest. But this is, in a great measure, counteracted by the insane policy which, as we have already noticed, applauds in military men the very conduct that indicates, as in the case of Huningen, and other places defended after the King's restoration, an opposition to his mandates; and if bravery alone be accounted a sufficient apology for rebellion, the French Government will certainly have enough of both. Were a breach, therefore, to take place at this moment between the King and the Constitutionalists, I have little doubt that great part of the army would take part with the latter, though perhaps more out of pique than principle. The Royalists, with all their vehemence in words, have already shown how infinitely inferior they are to the opposite party in intrigue, as well as in audacity; and discontented soldiers may be seduced to declare for a change of dynasty, or for a republic, as readily as for a Bona-

516

parte. Besides, distant and secure as is Napoleon's present place of exile, we have but scotched the snake, not killed him; but while life lasts, especially after his extraordinary return from Elba, there will not be wanting many to rely upon a third *aratar* of this singular emanation of the Evil Principle. This is an additional and powerful reason for the King to avoid, in thought, act, and deed, the slightest innovation on the liberties of his subjects as ascertained by the constitutional charter, as a certain means to provoke a contest in which he would prove inferior.[1]

If you ask me, then, what are the legitimate resources of this unfortunate monarch, placed between the extremes of two violent factions? I would answer, that, under God, I conceive them to rest upon the good-will of the mass of the people of France. The agitators and intriguers of both parties bear an exceedingly small proportion to the numbers of those who only desire peace, tranquillity, and the enjoyment of the fruits of their industry, under a mild and steady government. With this class of people Louis XVIII. is deservedly popular; their tears attended his expulsion, and their rejoicings his return. It is true, that this general feeling of good-will and affection was not strong enough to bring armies to the field, though it threw great obstacles in the way of the usurper. But it is also true, that this class of Loyalists were taken totally at unawares, and became only apprized of their danger when it was too late to take measures for encountering a veteran army, masters of all the fortresses in the kingdom. The general class of proprietors are also (for the present) disheartened, drained of the young and active spirits whom Bonaparte sacrificed in his wars, rendered callous by habit to the various changes of government, and more passive under each than it is possible for Englishmen to comprehend. But there is very generally among the middling orders in France, and among all, indeed, who are above the lowest vulgar, a kind and affectionate feeling towards the King, well deserved by his mild and paternal character, and which further experience of the blessings of peace, and of a settled government, will kindle into zealous attachment. The best policy of the monarch is, to repress the ardent tempers of the clergy and nobles; to teach them that their real interest depends upon the crown; and that they will themselves be the first sufferers, if they give pretext for a new attack upon the Bourbons, by setting up pretensions equally antiquated and ill adapted with a free government. At the same time it may be necessary for the King, by exhibiting vigour and decision in his measures, to convince the more violent of the opposite faction, that they cannot renew their attempts against the throne with the facility and impunity which heretofore have attended them. The very violence with which these parties oppose each other affords the King the means of mediating betwixt both. Let the people at length see clearly that the King desires no more than his own share in the constitution, but that he stands prepared to defend his own rights, as well as theirs. It may, perhaps, take some time to awaken the indifferent from that palsy of the mind which we have alluded to, and to put to rest the jealous fears of the proprietors of national pro-

[1] Witness July, 1830!

perty. But good faith and persevering steadiness on the part of the Crown may accomplish both, and with these fears will subdue the hopes entertained by those who delight in change; revolution will become difficult in proportion as its chance of success shall disappear; the ardent spirits who have frequented its dangerous paths will seek more pacific avenues to wealth and distinction; and from being her own plague and the terror of her neighbours, France may again be happy in herself, and the most graceful ornament in the European commonwealth.

Upon the subject of awakening France to her true interests, use might surely be made of the principle uppermost in the heart of every Frenchman, and which is capable of guiding him to much good or evil, the interest, namely, which high and low take in the glory of their country. Through the abuse of this sentiment, (noble in itself, because disinterested,) Napoleon was enabled to consolidate his usurped government in such a manner that it required all his own rashness to undermine it. Did the people ask for bread!—he showed them a temple. Did they require of him the blood of their children!—he detailed to them a victory,—and they retired, satisfied that, if they suffered or wept, France had been rendered illustrious and victorious. It cannot be, that so strong and disinterested a sentiment should be applicable to evil purposes alone; nor do I believe the French so void of reflection or common sense, as not to be made capable, by experience, of valuing themselves as much upon personal freedom, an equal system of laws, a flourishing state of finance, good faith to other nations, and those moral qualities which equally adorn a people and individuals, as they now esteem their country decorated by an unnecessary palace, or by a bloody and fruitless victory. It is true, that the reformation must begin where the corruption was first infused, and that, although converts may be gained gradually to the cause of sound reason, yet we must necessarily be obliged to wait the effects of a better education upon the rising race, before real and genuine patriotism can be generally substituted for what is at present merely national vanity.

This appetite for glory has of late been fed with such unsubstantial food, as has apparently rendered the French indifferent to the distinction betwixt what is unreal and what is solid. Any thing connected with show and splendour,—any thing, as Bayes says, calculated to elevate and surprise, is what they expect from their governors, as regularly as the children of London expect a new pantomime at Christmas. Bonaparte contrived to drown the murmurs which attended his return to Paris, in the universal speculation which he excited by announcing his purpose of holding a *Champ de Mai*, which is much the same as if William III. had paved the way to the throne by summoning a *Wittenagemot*. In England, some would have thought the Prince of Orange had lost his senses, and some, that he was speaking Dutch. But all in England knew the meaning of a National Convention, the denomination by which William distinguished the assembly which he convoked. In Paris, it was exactly the contrary—the people did not want to see a national convention, or a national assembly either—they knew, like Costard, "whereuntil that did amount;" but the Champ de Mai

517

was something new, something not easily comprehended; and it would have been a motive with many against expelling Bonaparte prematurely, that they would have lost the sight of the Champ de Mai. And thus they sacrificed their good sense to their curiosity, and showed their minds were more bent on the form of the assembly than on its end and purposes. After all, the *fête* was indifferently got up, and gave little satisfaction, notwithstanding the plumes and trains of the principal actors. But still it had its use. The Bourbons have been compelled also to sacrifice to this idol; and the King is himself obliged, contrary to his own good sense and taste, to conform to this passion for theatrical effect. A man, for example, was condemned to death, to whom it had been resolved to extend the royal pardon, and the King imagined, *tout bonnement*, that he had nothing to do but issue one from his chancery. But no—that would have been to defraud the public of their share in the scene. So he was advised to go, (by pure accident,) in the course of his evening drive, into some remote corner of the city, where he was to meet (also accidentally) with the municipality, who were to fall on their knees, and beg mercy for this delinquent, which the King was then to grant with characteristic grace and bounty, and all the bystanders were to shout *Vive le Roi*. It must not be supposed that a nation, so shrewd and ingenious as the French, are really blinded by these exhibitions *got up* for their amusement. But they are entertained for the time, and are no more disgusted with the want of reality in the drama, than with the trees upon the stage for being made of pasteboard. They consider the accompaniments as of more importance than the real object of the representation, and fall under the censure due to Prior's

> " Idle dreamer,
> Who leaves the pie to gnaw the streamer."

To reclaim hawks which have been accustomed to so wild a flight, requires all the address of a falconer. Yet there is at the bottom a strong fund of disinterested patriotism to work upon; for who will deny its existence to a people, the bulk of whom have, on all occasions, thought always of the nation, and never of themselves individually! Should, therefore, the present King meet with a minister calculated like Fabius to arrest immediate dangers, and protract or evade angry discussions, until such a long train of quiet shall have elapsed, that men's minds have become estranged from all ideas of force and violence, he may, even in his own time, lay such a foundation of a better system, as will lead future Frenchmen to place their pride less in vain parade or military glory, than in the freedom, arts, and happiness of France.

The approaching meeting of the National Representatives, if they meet, as the time so peremptorily demands, in the spirit, not of partisans, but of conciliators, may do much to accelerate so desirable an issue. But it is too much to be feared, that it will be found very difficult to assemble such a body of representatives, as may be justly considered as the organ of the nation. Could such a senate be convoked, we should hear on every side the language of peace and moderation, nor would the debates be warmer or more obstinate, than is necessary for elucidation of the measure proposed. Such an assembly, in the name of the proprietors of France, would deprecate the senseless agitation of theoretical questions, would recommend brief sentence on a limited and narrow selection of the principal agents of the last usurpation, whose fate seems essential to the vindication of justice, and the intimidation of the disaffected; and when that painful duty was executed, would proceed with joy to the more agreeable task of promulgating such a general amnesty as would throw a perpetual veil over the crimes and errors of that unhappy period. I might add, that such a senate would proceed by secret committees to tent the wounds of the country, to turn their attention towards the state of religion and morals, and to ensure the means of bringing up the rising generation, at least, free from the errors of their fathers. In their adjustment of foreign relations, such a council of state would recollect, that if the country had suffered reiterated humiliation, it was in consequence of reiterated aggression; and, avoiding painful and irritating discussions concerning the past, they would offer by such moderation the surest guarantee for peace and amity in future. Such would be the language of the representatives of the people, did they really speak the sense of the proprietors of France—not that those proprietors are sufficiently enlightened to recommend the special measures for attaining peace and tranquillity, but because they are sighing for that state of good order to which the measures of an enlightened representation ought to conduct them. But I have doubts whether this calm and wise course can be expected from the senators to be shortly assembled, since we hear of nothing on all sides but the exertions made by the two political factions of Royalists and Liberalists, to procure returns of their own partisans. We must, therefore, prepare to witness a warm, and, perhaps, a deadly war waged between two contending parties, of which one proposes a complete reaction and restoration of things, as they stood in the reign of Louis XV., with the advantages perhaps of new confiscations to avenge those by which they were themselves ruined, and the other proposing a gratuitous and uncalled-for alteration of the laws of succession, while each is content to hazard in the attempt a renewal of the horrors of the Revolution.

You may wonder that a spirit should be expected to prevail among the representatives, so different from that of the mass of the people by whom they are chosen. The cause seems to be, that those gradations, not of rank only, but of education, intelligence, and habits of thinking upon political men and measures, which enable Englishmen both to choose representatives, and to watch their conduct when chosen, cannot at present be said to exist in France. Those who propose themselves as candidates are men altogether distinct in their habits of thinking from the voters whom they are to represent. They are considered as politicians by profession, as men belonging to a class entitled exclusively to be chosen, and who, when chosen, relieve their electors from all further trouble in watching or directing their political conduct. The electors may assemble in their organic colleges, and may give their suffrages to a candidate for the Chamber of Representatives; but it will be in the same manner as they might choose a person to repair the town-clock, when almost all the voters are ignorant of the means which the artist is to adopt for its

regulation, and probably some of them cannot tell the hour by the dial-plate when the machine is put in order. On the contrary, the class in England upon whom the election of Parliament devolves, are trained to their task by long habit, by being freeholders, members of common councils, vestries, and other public bodies, or by hearing affairs of a public nature discussed upon all occasions, whether of business or pleasure, and are thereby habituated to consider themselves as members of the body politic. Though, therefore, many may be seduced by interest, biassed by influence, or deluded by prejudice, there will be found among the mass of the British electors, taken generally over the kingdom, a capacity of judging of the fitness of their representatives, a distinct power of observing with attention their conduct in their high office; and they possess means also, collectively speaking, of making their own opinion heard and respected, when there is pressing occasion for it.

I do not mention this difference between the inhabitants of the two countries, as a reason for refusing to France the benefits of a free representation, but to show, that, for some time at least, it cannot have the salutary effect upon the political horizon of that country which arises from the like institution in our own, where there exists an intimate and graduated connexion between the representative and electors, a general diffusion of political knowledge, and a systematic gradation from the member of parliament to the lowest freeholder;—where, in short, there is a common feeling between the representative and his constituent, the one knowing the nature of the power delegated, as well as the other does that which he receives, and both, though differing in extent of information, having something like common views upon the same subject. It may be long ere this general diffusion of political information takes place in France. It will, however, follow, if time is allowed for it by years of peace, and of that good order which promotes quiet and general discussion of political rights. A freeholder, who, suffered free-quarters from pandours and cossacks twice in one year, has scarce tranquillity of mind sufficient to attend to theoretical privileges and maxims of state. But if called upon repeatedly to exercise his right of suffrage, he will gradually begin to comprehend the meaning of it, and to interest himself in the conduct of the representative to whom he gives his voice. Thus, as freemen make a constitution, so a free constitution, if not innovated upon, and rendered ineffectual, will in time create a general and wholesome freedom of spirit amongst those who have to exercise the privileges which it bestows. Did such a general feeling now exist in France, we should not have to apprehend the desperate results which may attend the struggle of two parties only intent upon their own factious interests—a nobility and clergy, on the one hand, eager to resume privileges inconsistent with general freedom, and on the other, a turbulent oligarchy, of considerable talent and little principle, prepared to run the race of the Brissotins in 1792, and to encounter all the risks with which it was proved to be attended.

To the dangers of this collision of steel and flint is to be added that which arises from the quantity of tinder and touch-wood, which lies scattered around to catch and foster every spark of fire;—an army dishonoured and discontented, bands of royalists, half-organized soldiers, half-voluntary partisans, thousands whom Bonaparte had employed in his extended system of espionage and commercial regulation ; hundreds, also of a higher class, selected generally for talent, activity, and lack of principle, who have now lost their various posts, as Mauris, Prefets, Sous-prefets, Commis, and so forth—all of whom would find their interest in a civil war. And what will restrain the factious from pushing the crisis to this extremity ! Only a jealous fear of the allies, whose occupation of the fortresses in the north of France will, in that case, prove her best security ; or perhaps the slender chance, that the members of the representation may be wise enough to sacrifice their mutual feuds to the general weal, and remember that they are summoned to wage their contest with the arms of courtesy, and not to push political debate into revolutionary frenzy. I leave them, therefore, with a sincere wish that they may not forget, in the vehemence of their internal dissensions, the duty which they owe to a distracted public, which they may at pleasure involve in a civil war by their mutual violence, or save from that dreadful crisis by their temper and moderation.

You must not expect from me any general view of French manners, or habits of society ; and it is the less necessary, as you will find ample means of forming your judgment in the very spirited and acute work of Mr. John Scott, published during the preceding year. I am inclined to think, that while he has touched the French vices and follies with enough of severity, he may not in some instances have done full justice to the gallant, amiable, and lively disposition, by which, in spite of an execrable education, and worse government, that people are still widely distinguished from other nations on the continent. But the ingenious author had prescience enough to discover the latent danger of the royal government of 1814, when it was disguised and disowned by the members of that government themselves ; nor has he in these affairs omitted an opportunity to plead the cause of freedom, religion, and morality, against that of tyranny, infidelity, and licentiousness. I ought also to mention the Travels in France in the years 1814-15, the joint production of two young gentlemen [1] whose taste for literature is hereditary ; and I am informed, that another ingenious friend (Mr. S——n of Edinburgh,) whose extreme assiduity in collecting information cannot fail to render his Journal interesting, intends to give it to the public. [2] To such works I may safely refer you for an ample description of Paris, its environs, public places, and state of manners.

I should willingly have endeavoured to form my own views of the state of French society, as well as of their politics ; but the time has been altogether unfavourable, as the persons of fashion in Paris have either retired to the country, or live in strict seclusion from foreigners, upon principles which it is impossible not to respect. The strangers, therefore, who now occupy this capital, form a class altogether distinct from the native inhabitants, and seek for society among each other. It was very different, I am told, upon the former entry of the allied troops, which, for some time, the Parisians regarded more as a pacification than a conquest. The Russian and Prussian officers were then eagerly sought after, and caressed by the French nobility ; and the allied monarchs, on entering the Parisian theatres, were received with the same honours as in their own. But this is all over. The last cast was too absolute for victory or ruin, and the die has turned up against France. One class of Frenchmen lament the event of the war as a national misfortune ; and even those who have the advantage of it, feel, that, in its cause, progress, and conclusion, it will be recorded as a national disgrace. " You own yourself," said I to a lively French friend, a great anti-imperialist, as he writhed his face and shrugged when he passed a foreign officer, —" you own yourself, that they only treated your countrymen as they have merited."—" Very true— and the man that is hanged has no more than his deserts—but I don't like to look at the hangman."

Amid this dereliction, you must not suppose that we sojourners in Paris suffer solitude for want of good society. The extended hospitality of the Duke of Wellington, and of Lord and Lady Castlereagh, has afforded rallying points to the numerous English strangers, who have an opportunity of meeting, in their parties, with almost all the owners of those distinguished names, which for three years past have filled the trumpet of fame. Our minister, whose name will be read with distinction in this proud page of our annals, and to whose determined steadiness in council much of the success of 1814 is unquestionably due, occupies the palace of Pauline Borghese, now that of the British embassy. The Duke of Wellington lives in a large hotel at the corner of the Rue des Champs Elysées, furnished most elaborately by some wealthy courtier of Napoleon. Among its chief ornaments, is a very fine picture of the ex-emperor, and a most excellent bust of the same personage. It is a thing to remember, that I have seen in that hotel, so ornamented, the greatest and the bravest whom Europe can send forth, from Petersburg to Cadiz, assembled upon the invitation of the British General, and yielding to him, by general assent, the palm of military pre-eminence. In mentioning those whose attentions rendered the residence of the British at Paris pleasant and interesting, I ought not to forget Lord Cathcart, whose situation as ambassador to the Russian court gave him opportunities of gratifying the curiosity of his countrymen, by presenting them to the Emperor, who has of late played such a distinguished part in European history, and by making them known to such men as Barclay de Tolli, Platow, Czernicheff, and other heroes of Kalouga and Beresina, where the spear of the mighty was first broken. [4] Besides the notice of these public characters, my stay in Paris was made happy by the society of many friends, both in the civil and military departments. You know my inherent partiality for the latter class, when they add gentle manners and good information to the character of their profession ; and I can assure you, that as there never was a period when our soldiers were more respected for discipline and bra-

---

[1] Travels in France during the years 1814-15, comprising a Residence at Paris during the stay of the Allied armies, and at Aix at the period of the landing of Bonaparte, 2 vols. 8vo.

—the joint production of Archibald Alison, and Patrick Fraser Tytler, Esqs., Advocates.
[2] This pledge has been amply redeemed by Mr. James Simpson's lively and interesting " Visit to Flanders."—S.

very, so the character of the British officers for gallantry and humanity, for general information, and for the breeding of gentlemen, never stood higher than at the capture of Paris. In such society, whatever secret discontents might in reality exist, Paris was to us like a frozen lake, over whose secret and fathomless gulfs we could glide without danger or apprehension; and I shall always number the weeks I have spent here among the happiest of my life.

In a short time, it is imagined, the greater part of the foreign troops will be withdrawn towards their own countries, or to the occupation of the fortresses they are to hold in guarantee. It will then be seen whether the good intentions of the King, and the general desire of the country for peace, will be sufficient to maintain the public tranquillity of France amid the collision of so many angry passions; and there will, at the worst, remain this consolation, that if this restless people should draw the sword upon each other, effectual precautions have been taken by the allies to prevent them from again disturbing the peace of Europe.

With the hope of speedily rejoining the beloved circle round the fire-side, and acting, in virtue of my travelled experience, the referee in all political disputes, I am ever your affectionate friend,

PAUL.

APPENDIX.

No. I.

RELATION

Of what was done and said by Napoleon Bonaparte in the course of the 18th of June, 1815, during and after the Battle of Waterloo:—Drawn up from the Depositions of Jean Baptiste De Coster, who served him as Guide on that Day.[1]

JEAN BAPTISTE DE COSTER, aged about 53, born in the village of Corbeek-loo, near Louvain, has resided in the Walloon country for 33 years. He is five feet ten inches high, and of robust appearance. He is intelligent, and answers the questions put to him with an air of great sincerity. He expresses himself with facility, and understands French very well.

Before the invasion of Bonaparte, De Coster occupied a little inn, with about six acres of ground. On the approach of the French army on the 17th, he retired with his family, composed of his wife and seven children, into the wood of the abbey of Awyiers, where he spent the night between the Saturday and Sunday. At six in the morning, he left the wood to go to church, and from thence to the house of his brother, situated at Planchenoit. He found there three French generals, who asked him if he had lived long in the country, and if he was well acquainted with the neighbourhood. On his answering in the affirmative, one of them sent him to Napoleon, accompanied by a domestic, and with a letter.

Napoleon had passed the night in the farm-house of Caillou, and had left it at six o'clock. De Coster found him in the farm-house called Rossum, where he arrived at eight o'clock, and was immediately presented to Bonaparte, who was standing in a room about twenty feet long and sixteen broad, in the middle of a great many officers of his staff. Bonaparte asked him if he was well acquainted with the *localities* of the country, and if he was willing to act as his guide. De Coster having given a satisfactory answer, Napoleon told him that he should accompany him, adding, "Speak to me, my friend, with frankness, and as if you were among your children."

The farm of Rossum is situated near that called La Belle Alliance. The Emperor stopped there till almost noon. During this time, De Coster was kept in view, in the courtyard of the farm, by a soldier of the guard, who, while walking with him, informed him of the strength of the army, telling him that it consisted, on passing the frontiers, of 150,000 men, of whom 40,000 were cavalry, among which latter troops were 9000 cuirassiers, 7000 of the young guard, and 8 to 9000 of the old guard. This soldier bestowed great praise on the bravery which the English had displayed at Quatre Bras. He particularly admired the intrepid *sang-froid* of the Scotch Highlanders, "who would not budge," said he, in his military phrase, "but when the bayonet was put to their posteriors."

While De Coster thus remained in the courtyard of the farm-house, Bonaparte made him be called three different times, to ask him information as to the maps of the country, which he was incessantly consulting. He questioned him chiefly on the distance of the different towns of Brabant from the field of battle, and made him say what were the towns he had seen in his youth. De Coster named fourteen, which seemed to please Bonaparte. He expressed also much satisfaction on hearing that De Coster was a Fleming, and that he spoke the Flemish and Walloon languages equally well. He recommended to him above all, to give nothing but certain information, and to answer to things of which he was not assured, merely by shrugging his shoulders. He frequently repeated these intimations, adding, that if he succeeded, his (De Coster's) reward should be a hundred times greater than he could imagine. He freed him also from any particular mark of respect, telling him, that, without taking off the night-cap which he wore, he had only to salute by putting his hand to his forehead.

At noon, Bonaparte went out with his staff, and placed himself on an eminence by the side of the causeway, at a very little distance in rear of the farm, from whence he had a view of the whole field of battle. Persons very soon came to tell him, that the attack on the farm and chateau of Hougoumont, which he had ordered to commence at eleven o'clock, had not succeeded.[2]

At one o'clock the battle became general. Bonaparte remained in his first station, with all his staff, till five o'clock. He was on foot, and walked constantly backwards and forwards, sometimes with his arms crossed, but more frequently with his hands behind his back, and with his thumbs in the pockets of his slate-coloured great-coat. He had his eyes fixed on the battle, and took out alternately his watch and snuff-box. De Coster, who was on horseback near him, frequently remarked his watch. Bonaparte, perceiving that he also took snuff, and that he had no more, frequently gave him some.

When he saw that his attempts to carry the position of the chateau of Hougoumont had been vainly reiterated, he took a horse, quitted the farm of Rossum at five o'clock, and, moving forward, placed himself opposite to the house of De Coster, at the distance of a gun-shot from La Belle Alliance. He remained in the second station till seven o'clock. It was at that moment that he first perceived, by means of his glass, the arrival of the Prussians; he mentioned it to his aid-de-camp, who, having directed his glass towards them, saw them also. Some minutes afterwards, an officer came to inform him that the corps of Bulow was approaching; Bonaparte answered, that he knew it, and gave orders that his guards should make a movement on the centre of the English army. He himself, again moving forward at the gallop, went and placed himself, with his staff, in a ravine formed by the causeway, half way between La Belle Alliance and La Haye Sainte. This was his third and last position.

Bonaparte and his suite had been in great danger before arriving at this ravine; a ball even carried away the pommel of the saddle of one of his officers, without either touching him or his horse. Bonaparte merely told him coldly, that he ought to keep within the ravine.

There were at this place batteries on both sides of the road. Perceiving that one of the guns of the battery on the left was not making a good fire, he alighted from his horse, mounted on the height at the side of the road, and advanced to the third gun, the firing of which he rectified, while cannon and musket-

---

[1] The original French of this Relation was appended to the earlier editions of Paul's Letters, but it has not been thought necessary to preserve it in this collection.

[2] De Coster thinks, that what hindered this attempt from succeeding, was a wall which surrounds the chateau in the inside, and which was concealed from the French by a hedge which surrounds it on the outside. Four thousand men found shelter behind this wall, while it was struck by the French balls.—S.

balls were whistling round him. He returned with tranquillity, with his hands in the pockets of his great coat, and took
his place among the officers.

In this position, he saw the eight battalions of the old guard,
to whom he had given orders to penetrate the centre of the
English army, advance upon La Haye Sainte. Three of these
battalions were destroyed before his eyes, while crossing the
causeway, by the fire from the farm-house and batteries; nevertheless the French made themselves masters of them, and
the Hanoverians who occupied them were obliged to surrender for want of ammunition.

To support his foot-guards, Bonaparte brought forward his
horse-guards, composed of eight or nine regiments. He was
waiting with the utmost anxiety the result of this charge,
when he saw this *élite* of his army annihilated in an instant,
while ascending the bank on which La Haye Sainte is situated.
This was the last attempt: when he saw the old guard destroyed, he lost all hope; and, turning to Bertrand, said, "All
is now over—let us save ourselves."

It was half an hour past eight. Without taking any measure,—without giving any orders,—and thinking only of escaping the Prussians, Bonaparte, accompanied by his staff, set
off at full speed for Genappe, following the line of the causeway at a certain distance in the fields. Once only, in passing
a battery of fourteen guns, he ordered, before abandoning it,
fourteen shots to be fired from each gun.

It was half past nine o'clock when he arrived at Genappe.
The single street which forms this village was so choked up
with caissons and cannon, that it took a whole hour for him
and his staff to get through it, passing along the houses, which
now were void of inhabitants. There was, however, no other
road to take, because the left was occupied by the Prussians,
and there was no other bridge but that of Genappe for crossing the river.

From Genappe he directed his course towards Les Quatre
Bras, pressing on with renewed haste, and always in the apprehension of being prevented by the Prussians. When he had
passed this last place he was more tranquil; and when he arrived at Gossely, he even lighted from his horse, and went the rest
of the way to Charleroi (that is to say, nearly a league) on foot.
He passed through Charleroi on horseback, at about half-past
two in the morning, and went into a meadow called Marcenelle, beyond the town. There a large fire was made for him,
and two glasses and two bottles of wine were brought, which
he drank with his officers; he took no other refreshment. A
sack of oats was scattered on the ground, which the horses
ate, bridled as they were. At a quarter before five, after having taken another guide, (who received the horse which De
Coster had used,) Bonaparte again mounted his horse, made
an inclination of his head to De Coster, and went away. Bertrand gave De Coster a single Napoleon, which was all he received, and disappeared likewise, as did the whole staff, leaving De Coster alone, who was obliged to return home on
foot.

During the time that he had passed with Bonaparte, De Coster was not in any respect ill treated: only when, in their
flight, they had arrived at Les Quatre Bras, one of the officers,
who perceived that a second guide whom they had with them
had made off, tied, by way of precaution, the bridle of De Coster's horse to the saddle of his own.

Bonaparte, from the moment he began his retreat till he arrived in the meadow of Marcenelle, did not stop anywhere,
and did not speak to anybody. He had taken no nourishment
since leaving the farm of Rossum, and, as De Coster thinks, he
had not even taken any thing since six o'clock in the morning.

He did not appear at all moved by the events of the battle.
De Coster, who was much afraid, often stooped on his horse's
neck to shun the balls which he heard whistling over his head.
Bonaparte repeatedly expressed his dissatisfaction at this, telling him, that these movements made the officers believe he
was hit; —and added, that he would not draw the balls any
better by stooping down than by keeping upright.

During the battle, he had frequent occasion to do justice to
the bravery of the army which was opposed to him. He chiefly
praised the Scotch Greys, and expressed regret at seeing them
suffer so much, while they manœuvred so well, and handled
the sabre so dexterously.

Till half-past five he retained good hopes, and repeated every
instant that all went well.—His generals partook of these
hopes.—It may be added, that during the whole action he displayed the same calmness and *sang-froid*, that he never manifested any ill-humour, and spoke always with great gentleness to his officers.

He never was at any time in danger of being taken; having
had, even at the third station where he was nearest the enemy, twelve pieces of cannon and three thousand grenadiers of
his guard around him.

He made no use of the observatory constructed six weeks
before the battle by the Dutch engineers.

During the flight, he received pretty frequently news of the
army, from officers who had succeeded in escaping from the
pursuit of the allies.

De Coster's house having been used by the French in their
bivouac, the doors and windows, and all the wood it contained,
were burnt. The rent which he paid for it was 100 francs; the
proprietor, after having repaired it, has let it to another person for 125 francs. De Coster resides at present at the hamlet

of Joli-Bois, on the high-road between Waterloo and Mount
St. Jean.

This relation was drawn up at Waterloo on the 8th of January 1816, in the Inn of Jean De Nivelles, from De Coster's answers to the questions put to him. It was read to him next
day, and corrected from his observations.

Brussels, 12th January, 1816.

No. II.

ACCOUNT OF THE DEFENCE OF HOUGOUMONT, DURING THE BATTLE OF WATERLOO, ON THE 18TH OF JUNE, 1815.

BY THE
RIGHT HON. SIR JOHN SINCLAIR, BART.

It appears to me, that the battle of Waterloo is the greatest event recorded in history. We all know the important
results which have already taken place, owing to the victory
we there obtained. Had it been the reverse, it is impossible
to calculate the mischief that would have followed. It is not
easy keeping together an unsuccessful alliance; and the expenses of a protracted war might have proved ruinous to the
financial system of Great Britain, which at present experiences
such difficulties, notwithstanding the immense savings which
were effected, in consequence of the successful termination of
that dreadful conflict.

The battle of Zama is the only event in history that can be
put in comparison with that of Waterloo. There, two disci-
plined armies, under two great generals, were opposed to each
other, and the conflict, it may be said, terminated the rival-
ship between Rome and Carthage. But the results of even
that great battle were greatly inferior to those of Waterloo,
on which depended, not only the fate of two rival nations,
but of Europe, and of the world at large. It is singular that
the modern, like the ancient Hannibal, should have laid the
foundation of his military fame in Italy, and the modern
Scipio in Spain.

Having visited the field of battle, I became anxious to collect detailed information regarding the transactions which had
taken place there. The defence of Hougoumont, in particular, struck me as being of peculiar importance; and having
applied to some distinguished officers who were employed in
that service, by their aid, and from a personal inspection of
the place, I have been enabled to draw up the following short
account of the circumstances connected with its defence. I
am happy in this opportunity of contributing to do justice to
the British Guards who there so gallantly maintained the
character they have long enjoyed, for firmness, intrepidity,
and valour.

THE ACCOUNT.

When the Duke of Wellington had fixed on the ground
where he resolved to await the attack of the French army,
he found, on the right of his position, an old Flemish mansion called Gomont, or Hougoumont, by defending which, it
appeared to him that much advantage might be derived. The
buildings consisted of an old tower and chapel, and a number
of offices, partly surrounded by a farm-yard. There was also
a garden, enclosed by a high and strong wall, and round the
garden a wood, or orchard, and a hedge, by which the wall
was concealed. The necessary steps were taken to strengthen
these means of defence, by loop-holing, or perforating the
walls, for the fire of musketry, and erecting scaffolding to
give the troops within an opportunity of firing from the top of
the wall. These judicious measures greatly assisted the successful defence that was afterwards made against such reiterated and desperate attacks.

On the evening of the 17th, the following troops were allotted
for the defence:—1. The second brigade of Guards, commanded
by Major-General Sir John Byng; and, 2. The light companies
of the first brigade. The force was disposed of as follows:—
The light companies of the Coldstream and Third Guards, under Lieutenant-Colonel Macdonnell, occupied the house and
garden; those of the first regiment occupied the wood to the
left; these were under the command of Lieutenant-Colonel
Lord Saltoun; the rest of the brigade was placed about 300
yards in the rear, in a commanding situation, and in readiness
to support the garrison, if necessary. The whole amounted to
from 1400 to 1500 men. To this force was added, immediately
previous to the action, about 300 of the Nassau troops, some
of whom, however, did not remain long, owing, it is said, to
their not having been sufficiently supplied with ammunition.

The action commenced at thirty-five minutes past eleven
o'clock, as appears from the information of an officer who
looked at his watch (which he was satisfied was correct as to
time) as soon as the first gun was fired.

The force of the enemy employed in making the attack was
very great. It consisted of the whole of the second corps,
under the command of the Count de Reille. This corps, which
amounted to 30,000 men, was formed into three divisions. The
division commanded by Jerome Bonaparte commenced the
attack, but was soon driven back (about half-past twelve)
with great loss. A most desperate attack was next made by
the division of General Foy, who succeeded in gaining great
part of the wood, and had nearly surrounded the house; but

four companies of the Coldstream, and two of the Third regiment, moving promptly down and attacking them, they were driven back with immense slaughter, and some prisoners were taken from them. Several other attempts were made by the enemy against this post during the course of the day, until their general retreat,[1] but they did not obtain any advantage. In a most determined and gallant attack, made between twelve and one o'clock, an officer and a few men got inside of the gate of the farm-yard, but they were all killed; and at no period of the day was the communication cut off. Reinforcements of men and ammunition were sent in whenever they were requisite. The attack against the position of Hougoumont lasted, on the whole, from twenty-five minutes before twelve, until a little past eight at night.

At several periods during the day, reinforcements from the Coldstream and the Third regiment of Guards, were sent down to the support of the light companies, employed in the defence of the house, garden, and wood.[2] The latter was repeatedly occupied by the enemy, who were as often driven from it again, until, at last, these posts were occupied by the whole brigade, with the exception of two companies. About six in the evening, when the second line was brought forward, some Hanoverian battalions occupied the ground where the second brigade of Guards had been placed at the commencement; and a Brunswick regiment was sent down to the wood more to the left than when the Guards held it.

The loss of the Guards, in killed and wounded, in the defence of Hougoumont, amounted to twenty-eight officers, and about 800 sergeants and rank and file. The foreign troops (Nassau and Brunswickers) might lose about 100.

The loss of the enemy was enormous. The division of General Foy alone lost about 3000 men; and the total loss of the enemy in the attack of this position is estimated at above 10,000 men in killed and wounded.

It is said that the enemy were ignorant of the strength of the position, the garden wall being concealed by the wood and hedge; but the wall was so protected by trees, that it would not have been easy to have brought cannon to play against it,

and besides, it was of great thickness. The enemy brought guns to a height on the right of the position, which enfiladed it, and caused great loss; and they succeeded in setting fire to a hay-stack, and a part of the buildings, by means of shells,[3] but that did not prevent the garrison from occupying the remaining part.

It has been said that the inhabitants of the place were not friendly to the English; but this is quite a mistake. They left it with much trepidation when the cavalry of the enemy appeared in the evening of the 17th. They returned, however, for a short time, early on the 18th, to take some things away. Their conduct on the whole rather implied "friendship for the English, and terror of the French."

Such are the most interesting particulars regarding the defence of Hougoumont, which does such infinite credit to the determined courage of the troops employed in that service, and which certainly most essentially contributed to the ultimate success at the battle of Waterloo.[4]

It was very satisfactory to find, that nothing could surpass the high ideas entertained on the Continent of the steadiness, valour, energy, and discipline of the British army.[5] It was remarked to me, that scarcely any other troops possessed that firmness and discipline, joined to what we would call bottom, or a happy union of strength of body and resolution, or firmness of mind, sufficient to have resisted for so many hours the violent, desperate, and reiterated attacks of the French at the battle of Waterloo,[6] where the force of an immense artillery,[7] of numerous bodies of cavalry, variously armed, and many of them protected by defensive armour, and from 80,000 to 90,000 infantry, the élite of the French army, were all combined for the destruction of an enemy numerically much inferior.[8] It was observed, however, that the discipline of the French had become too loose, whilst that of the Germans remained too mechanical; but that the discipline of the British army was distinguished by a happy medium, which, when joined to that military skill and coolness by which the hero of Waterloo is so eminently distinguished, almost ensured a victory.[9]

London, March 18, 1816.

---

[1] Late in the evening, when the second corps had been as completely beaten as the first corps had been on the left, Bonaparte ordered forward the Imperial Guards, and part of that fine body of men was directed against Hougoumont.—S.

[2] When part of the Third regiment of Guards was sent into the wood before one o'clock, Colonel Hepburn of that corps superseded Lord Saltoun, who, having but few men left, obtained permission to join his battalion, where he again distinguished himself. Colonel Woodford, of the Coldstream, who went with the reinforcement into the house, was senior to Colonel Macdonnell, but, in consideration of that officer's gallant conduct, Colonel Woodford refused taking the command, and each undertook the defence of a particular portion of the post they occupied.—S.

[3] It was the tower that was burnt, and the fire penetrated to the chapel. The guide pointed out to me a crucifix of wood which the fire had attacked, and, as it was damaged only in a part of the foot, it was supposed to have been saved by a miraculous interposition of Providence.—S.

[4] It has been observed that Ossian peculiarly excels in the description of battles; and in no poet, whether ancient or modern, can passages be found more applicable to the battle of Waterloo, than the following from the poem of Fingal, as translated by the Rev. Dr. Ross:—

"As roll a thousand waves to the shore, the troops of Swaran advanced: as meets the shore a thousand waves, so the sons of Erin stood firm. There were the groans of death! The hard crash of contending arms: shields and mails in shivers on the ground: swords like lightning gleaming in the air: the cry of battle from wing to wing: the loud, bloody, but encounter: chief mixing his strokes with chief, and man with man.

"As the lightning of night on the hill: as the loud roar of the sea when roll the waves on high: as thunder behind the rocks, were the noise and fury of the battle. Though Cormack's hundred bards had been there to describe the scene in song, feeble had been their voice to relate the countless number of the slain, so many were the deaths of heroes, whose blood was poured upon the plain."

It was his description of battles that made Ossian so great a favourite with Bonaparte.—S.

[5] I found that the Scotch corps were great favourites on the Continent, and a respectable friend of mine, the Viscount Vanderfosse, at Brussels, having expressed himself with much feeling and eloquence on the subject, I requested him to send me in writing what he had stated in conversation, and the following is a literal translation of the letter he sent me:—

"Brussels, January 5, 1816.

"SIR,—You desire to have in writing the eulogium which I made you yesterday, on the Scotch regiments, which have so valiantly defended our country and our laws at the battle of Waterloo. I shall endeavour to make use of the same words as formerly, since a Scotchman, enlightened and patriotic as you are, has thought them worthy of remembrance.

"Since the arrival of the English troops on the Continent, their discipline was remarked by all those who had any communication with them, and in particular by those who, like

myself, had had an opportunity of seeing them in this country during the campaigns of 1793 and 1794. At that epoch, your warriors displayed the greatest bravery; but England had not yet accumulated those numerous laurels acquired under the command of the great and immortal WELLINGTON.

"Among these respectable warriors, the Scotch deserve to be particularly commemorated; and this honourable mention is due to their discipline, their mildness, their patience, their humanity, and their bravery, almost without example.

"On the 16th and 18th of June, 1815, their valour was displayed in a manner the most heroic. Multiplied, constant, and almost unheard-of proofs were given, I do not say merely of courage, but of a devotion to their country, quite extraordinary and sublime.

"Nor must we forget that these men, so terrible in the field of battle, were mild and tranquil out of it. The Scotch Greys, in escorting the French prisoners on the evening of the 18th, showed compassion to those unfortunate victims of war, while as yet the result of that decisive day was unknown, and perhaps uncertain.

"I am not afraid of giving myself up to those feelings of gratitude, which all the Belgians will ever retain towards those, without whom they would no longer have had a country; but even gratitude shall never carry me beyond truth. All that I have now said in praise of your excellent countrymen, would, I am sure, be confirmed, if necessary, by all the inhabitants of this kingdom; and the more you enquire into details and facts respecting their virtue and their glory, the more would the reality of what I have now repeated, at your desire, be established.

"Receive, sir, the renewed assurance of my esteem and gratitude towards your loyal nation; and permit me to join in the cry, at the sound of which your excellent countrymen have braved the most imminent dangers, and have triumphed over them,—' Scotland for ever!'

"I have the honour to be, SIR,
"Your very humble and obedient servant,
(Signed) "VISCOUNT VANDERFOSSE,
"First Advocate at the Superior Court of Justice at Brussels."—S.

[6] In the Austrian account it is said, "That no infantry less practised, and less cool than the English, could have resisted such attacks."—S.

[7] The French were greatly superior in the number of cannon in the action. They had above 300; the English only about 66.—S.

[8] The French, in all, had about 75,000 men, and the British about 55,000 (including all the foreign troops,) at the battle of Waterloo.—S.

[9] The Duke of Wellington retained the same presence of mind during the dreadful conflict, as it had been a common field-day; and a foreign officer, of great experience and merit, assured me "that he had served with all the most distinguished generals on the Continent, but that none of them possessed so many of the qualities essential for a great commander, as the Duke of Wellington."—S.

PARTICULARS REGARDING MARSHAL GROUCHY'S ARMY.

I was fortunate enough to meet at Brussels with some of the most distinguished officers who had served in Grouchy's army; and with great readiness they answered several questions I put to them, regarding that part of the French force. I shall here give a translation of the questions sent, and the answers they returned, which contain some interesting particulars.

1. At what time was the corps of Marshal Grouchy separated from the grand army?—*Answer.* On the morning of the 17th of June.

2. What was its force, and the generals by whom it was commanded?—*Answer.* The force consisted in all of 45,000 men; of whom 39,000 were infantry, and 6000 cavalry. The principal officers were Generals Vandamme, Gerard, and Excelmans.

3. What were the orders given to the Marshal, and what progress did he make in their execution?—*Answer.* The orders of the Marshal were, to march upon the army of the enemy, so as to prevent the junction between Wellington and Blucher. He arrived, to carry that object into effect, at Gembloux on the 17th, which the Prussian army had quitted about twelve at noon, for Wavre. The Marshal left Gembloux with his army on the morning of the 18th, to find out the Prussians, and to fight them. The second corps of cavalry, consisting of 4000 men, commanded by General Excelmans, discovered the rear-guard of the Prussians near a place called Baraque, about ten o'clock in the morning. General Excelmans brought his cavalry to the Dyle, ready to pass that river, when about twelve the Marshal arrived, with General Vandamme's corps, and gave orders to march upon Wavre; this he did, after we had defeated the rear-guard of the Prussian army, which were from 8000 to 10,000 men.

4. Did you hear at Wavre the firing at the battle of Waterloo, or Mount St. Jean?—*Answer.* About mid-day the cannonade was heard, and it was then that General Gerard, and several other officers, insisted strongly with the Marshal to cross the Dyle, and to approach nearer to the Emperor, leaving a small corps of observation before the Prussians, who had been beat, and had retired to Wavre. But the Marshal constantly refused, and continued his route on Wavre. General Excelmans commanded the advanced guard, and would not have quitted the Dyle, had it not been in consequence of express orders given by the Marshal in person, which he was compelled to obey.

5. To what circumstance was it owing that the army of Marshal Grouchy was of no use at the battle of Waterloo or Mount St. Jean?—*Answer.* Because the Marshal committed the fault of employing his whole army, whereas, at the utmost, 10,000 men would have been sufficient to have kept the rear-guard of the Prussians in check.

6. Did Napoleon send any orders to Marshal Grouchy during the battle?—*Answer.* Several officers were sent before mid-day by the Emperor to search for Marshal Grouchy, but only one of them (Col. Zenowitz) arrived at Wavre, and not till about six o'clock in the evening. The Marshal then resolved to pass the Dyle at Limale with a part of his army, but it was too late.

7. What became afterwards of Marshal Grouchy's army?—*Answer.* It was about eleven o'clock in the morning of the 19th that the Marshal learnt that the Emperor had been beaten. The attack which he intended to make on the road from Brussels to Louvain was, therefore, given up; and the army passed the Dyle at four points—Wavre, Limale, Limilet, and Ottigny. General Excelmans with his corps pushed on to Namur, where he arrived in the evening, and where the Marshal arrived next day. The allies attacked the rearguard, commanded by Vandamme. The conflict was very obstinate, but the allies suffered so much, that our retreat afterwards was unmolested.

These officers added, that, in their opinion, "Si les ordres de l'Empereur eussent été exécutés par le Maréchal Grouchy, les armées Anglaise et Prussienne étoient perdues sans ressource." This cannot be admitted. It is said that Grouchy was over-persuaded by Vandamme to push on to Wavre, in the hopes of getting first to Brussels, and securing the plunder of that town to themselves.

523

END OF PAUL'S LETTERS TO HIS KINSFOLK.

HOME.

BY MISS SEDGWICK.

FRIENDLY TO THOUGHT, TO VIRTUE, AND TO PEACE,
O, FRIENDLY TO THE BEST PURSUITS OF MAN,
DOMESTIC LIFE.

COWPER.

PREFATORY NOTICE.

———

WHEN first the "Standard Library" was offered to public notice, the reproduction of the best works of our trans-atlantic brethren, an object kept in view from the commencement of the series, was announced as a part of the scheme then projected. The present work, which is already favourably known in England, is offered as a guarantee that the pledge already given shall in due time be amply redeemed. Miss Sedgwick has for some years been well known as an authoress of no common powers, and she is peculiarly distinguished by the superior excellence of her later productions, in comparison with those of earlier date, in which she has too much trammelled herself with the threadbare plot and characters of the common-place novel. "HOME," the first in which she completely emancipated herself from imaginary chains, and has wholly relied on her own native power and *national* material, has been there-fore chosen as the most fitting for presentation to the English reader. In this work, to use the words of a very com-petent judge (Miss Harriet Martineau*), "Miss Sedgwick makes her final escape from the atmosphere of conven-tionalism, and breathes freely amidst nature and truth, as they surround her in her own happy land. She was made for a higher destiny than to tell tales to morbid minds in candle-light retreats; and she has come forth to shed sunshine and kindle sympathy in the homes of New England first, and then in kindred retirements of the Old World. The English will no longer have to turn away from her pages, disappointed to find there faint reflections of a worn-out human life and character. They may learn of her now: she gives them what is fresh, and tells them much that is new. She gives them what no traveller who sees with European eyes can impart; and what not even a personal survey can communicate; she gives them American manners, informed and actuated by American life; by thoughts and feelings growing up from birth, with which no stranger can intermeddle. The benefit is communi-cated unconsciously, and therefore all the more efficaciously. She relies on fact, and on her own American heart and eyes. She gives us perhaps the first true insight into American life; and for this we should owe her hearty thanks, if her writings had far less of other kind of merit than they exhibit."

* In a review of Miss Sedgwick's works in the Westminster Review, for October 1837.

HOME.

CHAPTER I.

GOING TO HOUSE-KEEPING.

My house a cottage more
Than palace; and should fitting be
For all my use, no luxury.—COWLEY.

IN a picturesque district of New England,—it matters not in which of the Eastern States, for in them all there is such unity of character and similarity of condition, that what is true of one may be probable of all,—in one of them there is a sequestered village called Greenbrook. The place derives its name from a stream of water which bears this descriptive appellation,

" As if the bright fringe of herbs on its brink,
Had given their stain to the wave they drink,
And they, whose meadows it murmurs through,
Have named the stream from its own fair hue."

There is one particularly beautiful spot, where this little river, or rather brook (for it is not wider than the *Tiber* at Washington), winds through a lovely meadow, and then stretches round a rocky peninsula,—curving in and out, and lingering as if it had a human heart and loved that which it enriched. On a gentle slope, rising from the meadow and catching the first rays of the morning sun, stood an old-fashioned parsonage, about half a mile from the village and at right angles with it, so that its road and shaded side-walks, and the goings-out and comings-in of his flock, could be overlooked by the good pastor. Parson Draper's were not the days of agricultural and horticultural societies, and just as he received the place, he was content to hold and leave it. He cut the hay from the meadow, and pastured a few sheep in the beautiful wood of maples, oaks, and beeches, that sheltered him from the north-west wind,—where, if they did not find the sweetest pasture in the world, they looked prettily, cropping their scanty food from the rocky knolls, or grouped together in the shaded dells.

The good man, according to his views of them, performed his duties faithfully. He read diligently large books of divinity, preached two sermons (never an old one) every Sabbath, was punctual at weddings and funerals, and abstracted no time from these sacerdotal offices to improve his rugged garden, or till his little farm. He had but two children, the one a worthless son, and the other a girl, a most dutiful and gentle creature, who married a merchant, lived prosperously in a city for two or three years, and then returned a widow, penniless, and with an only son, to her father's house. She bore her reverses meekly, and directed all her energies to one object,—the *sine quâ non* of a New-England mother,—a good education for her son. The boy, William Barclay, found only happiness in the change. He was released from what seemed to him a prison, a nursery in a narrow City street, and permitted to feed grandfather's sheep, to harness his horse, sometimes to ride and drive him; in short, to employ those faculties that employed are blessings, and unemployed, tormentors.

The parsonage, as we have said, was apart from the village. Either because of his early solitude, or through the leading of his mother, who turned back from the world, loved to commune with God in his works, or from an innate love of natural beauty, William Barclay knit his heart to this home of his childhood; and when his grandfather died, and the place was sold, and he was compelled to leave it, he felt much as might our first parents, when from Paradise they "took their solitary way."

His mother had a pittance, and this, with straining every nerve, and now and then a lift from a friend, enabled her to go on with her favourite project. She and her son were received in the families of her friends, and changed their abode according to the liberality or convenience of their patrons. But William was kept at his books, and this repaid her for every sacrifice and every exertion. William, however, was not of a temper to brook this strain on his mother, and partial dependance on others. As soon as he was of an age to comprehend it, he renounced the idea of what is technically called an education, the four years at college,—threw himself on his own exertions, and by *hook and by crook*, that is, by infinite ingenuity and diligence, and by the most severe self-denial and frugality, he supported himself, obtained the rudiments of an excellent education, and learned the art of printing. At the age of twenty-two he was the conductor of a valuable printing-press in the city of New York, in partnership with Norton, its proprietor, and with a reasonable prospect of a joint property in the concern. In the mean time, his earnings were sufficient to enable him to maintain a family and *go a-head*. Thankful ought we to be, that in our favoured land a working man need not wait till he be bald or grey before he may, with prudence, avail himself of the blessed institution of marriage;—that if, like William Barclay, he be capable, diligent, frugal, and willing to dispense with superfluities, he may, while hope is unblighted, resolution vigorous, and love in its early freshness, assume the responsibilities of a married man. In Europe, — ay, in what *was* "merry England," it is not so ; the kind order of nature and Providence is baffled, and the working man, be he "capable, diligent, and frugal," has an alms-house in his perspective, or the joyless alternative, a life of safe and pining singleness.

"And this is our *home*," said Mrs. Barclay to her husband, as they entered a small, newly-built, two-story house in Greenwich Street.

"Yes, dear Anne ; and if it were but in Greenbrook, and a little stream before it, and an oak wood on one side, and a green lane to the road on the other, we should stand a good chance at love in a cottage."

"I see how it is, William ; I have yet to cure you of your home-sickness for the old parsonage. Who knows but we may go there some time or other ? In the mean time, let us try if we cannot be happy with love in a small house, instead of a cottage."

"You could make the happiness of any home to me, Anne. Shifted about as I have been from pillar to post, I scarcely know what home is, from experience ; but it is a word that to my mind expresses every motive and aid to virtue, and indicates almost every source of happiness. I am sure of content ; but will not you, Anne, contrast this little dwelling with your father's spacious house, and when you look into the dirty street, or into our poor, cramped, ten-feet yard, will you not pine to see the golden harvests we left waving on the sunny slopes of Greenbrook, or for the beautiful view, from your window, of meadow and mountain ? Will you not miss the pleasant voices of home ?—the footsteps of sisters and brothers ?"

"Yes," replied the wife, smiling through the tears that gushed from nature's fount at the picture of her father's house—"Yes, I shall miss all this, —for who ever did, or ever can, forget a happy home ? I may even shed many tears, William ; but they will be like the rain that falls when the sun shines,—there will be no cloud over the heart. I am sure I shall never repent the promise made this night three weeks, forsaking all others to cleave to you alone."

"I trust you will not, Anne. But I cannot help wishing I was not obliged at once to put you to such a test. This house seems to me smaller than when I hired it ; this parlour is scarcely big enough to turn in."

"Now it struck me as just of the right size. I always had a fancy for a snug parlour. Nothing looks so forlorn as a large, desolate, cold, half-furnished, shabby parlour."

Mr. Barclay smiled.—"You have certainly contrived, Anne, to make the large parlour look disagreeable."

"And I will try my best to make the small one agreeable."

A look from her husband indicated his belief that she could not fail. "And can you say any thing for this little bed-room ?" he asked, opening the door into an adjoining apartment.

After an instant's survey she replied, "It suits me exactly."

"But that is an ugly jut."

"It's not pretty, but how neatly the bureau fits in,—and this nice little closet, what a blessing !

—a grate too ! I did not expect this. It suits me exactly," she repeated with hearty emphasis. "But perhaps you did not mean this for our apartment."

"You must decide that. There is a room above this precisely like it."

"Then this shall be for mother, — she minds stairs and we do not. And here she shall have her rocking-chair and Bible, and I trust she will have a happy home after all."

This "after all" meant years of miserable shifting and changing, which old Mrs. Barclay had endured with the patience of a martyr. No wonder William Barclay felt grateful to his wife when he perceived his mother's happiness was her first care. He told her so.

"Wait," she said, "till I deserve your thanks. But now tell me where this little passage leads to ?—to the kitchen ?—this is nice ! I could not bear to think of thrusting Martha down into one of these New York cellar kitchens ; they are so dark and dismal, after being used to our light, airy, sociable country kitchens. Martha will be delighted."

Mr. Barclay confessed he had made a sacrifice to secure a pleasant apartment for Martha, a young girl whom his wife (in country phrase) had "taken to bring up." "I had to decide," he said "between two houses of equal rent, — the apartments in the other were larger than these, but the kitchen was under ground, and would have seemed dismal to Martha, and I knew you would wish to begin housekeeping with as much happiness as possible beneath your roof."

"At your old tricks, William, doing kind acts and giving the credit to another. However, I have generosity enough to approve this sacrifice of a little for us, to a great deal for Martha. Mother says there would not be half so much complaining of help, if the master and mistress had a religious sense of their duties to them, and took proper pains to promote their happiness. Home should be the sweetest of all words even to the humblest member of a family."

This sentiment was echoed from William Barclay's heart and tongue, and then the young pair proceeded to examine together their furniture, which had been purchased by the husband according to a few general directions from the wife, the funds being furnished by her father. We shall not give an inventory, but merely note that there were no superfluities,—no gewgaws of any description,—no mantel-glass, ornamented lamp, vase of Paris flowers, tawdry pictures ;—such are sometimes seen where there is a lamentable deficiency of substantial comforts. But there was, what in these *dressed-up* houses is sacrificed to show ;—ample stores of household linen, fine mattresses, as nice an apparatus for ablutions as a disciple of Combe could wish ; jugs, basins, and tubs large enough, if not to silence, to drown a travelling Englishman ; and finally one luxury, which long habit and well cultivated taste had rendered essential to happiness, — a book-case filled with well selected and well bound volumes. They paused before it, while Mrs. Barclay ran over the titles of some of the books ; " 'History of England,'—'Universal History,'—Marshall's Washington,'—'American Revolution,'—'Shakspeare,'—'Milton,'—'Pope,'—'Addison,'—'Goldsmith,'—' Fenelon,'—' Taylor,'—' Law,'—' Johnson's Dictionary,'—' Calmet's Dictionary,'—' Lempriere,'—' Biographical Dictionary.' — O what a capital Atlas! How in the world, William, did you contrive to afford so many books! When father made an estimate of the cost of our furniture, he allowed twenty-five dollars for books! That, he said, would buy a Bible, the histories of England and America, a cookery book, and dictionary, — quite enough, he said, for a nest egg." *

"Your father is frugal, Anne, and so must we be; but we have a right to select the department in which we prefer sparing, and that is not books. Since I have earned more than I was obliged to spend, I have made a yearly investment in books, as the stock which would yield the best income. I had thus accumulated those heavy volumes on the lower shelves; and as ladies sometimes think heavy books heavy reading, I filled up the case with such as I hoped would suit your taste, and profit us both. All these were bought with your money."

"All these! how was that possible!"

"I will tell you. In purchasing your furniture, my dear wife, whenever two articles were offered of equal intrinsic value, the one ornamental and the other plain, I bought the plain one, and passed over the saving made to the book fund. For instance, I was offered a remarkably pretty Geneva clock, which cost fifty dollars in Paris, for thirty dollars. A clock I thought essential to the punctual arrangement of house affairs; and to convince myself of the propriety of buying this particular clock, this *bargain*, I reasoned as people do when they would persuade themselves to that, which in their secret souls they know is not quite right. 'I have bought nothing ornamental; surely we have a right to one indulgence of this sort,—I may never meet with such a bargain again,—it will just suit Anne's taste.' This last thought turned the scale, and I was on the point of concluding the purchase when the master of the shop said, 'If you really want the clock for a time-piece merely, here is an article of excellent mechanism, which costs only five dollars.' I shut my eyes against the pretty Geneva clock, bought the five-dollar article, hung it up in the kitchen, and with the money saved I purchased that row of books. Instead of twenty-five dollars' worth of glass and gilding, we have some of the best productions of the best minds. Instead of a poor gratification of our vanity, or at best of our eyes, we have a productive capital, from which we may derive exhaustless pleasure, which hundreds may share, and which those who come after us may enjoy. O, who can estimate the value of a book!"

"Books are your *penates*, William."

"If so, Anne, I have greatly the advantage of the ancients. Their household gods were dumb idols,—mine have living and immortal souls."

Mr. Barclay was a printer and might magnify his art; but what honour is not due to that art, which makes the spirits of the departed our familiar companions and instructors,—which realises the doctrine of metempsychosis, and transfuses the souls of the departed into the living!

* The father-in-law's allowance exceeded that which Byron allows to the intellectual wants of women, by the two histories and the dictionary.

"Anne, you do not tell me whether you are satisfied with my selection."

"I see but one deficiency."

"O, a Bible! You do not think I have omitted that. No, that I consider as essential to a home as the foundation-stone to an edifice. But the Family Bible is for daily use, and has its proper station in the parlour. Neither have I omitted the other item on your father's list; the cookery book is on a shelf in the kitchen, with a few other instructive and entertaining volumes for Martha's use. I believe that whatever tends to improve the minds and hearts of domestics will, to say the worst of it, not injure their service; and that every wise provision for their happiness, multiplies the chances of their attachment and fidelity. We are novices, Anne, and may be wrong; but at any rate we will try it."

Mrs. Barclay was a loving and, with good reason, a trustful wife, and ready to co-operate with her husband in all his benevolent purposes. They looked at the neat *spare room*, which according to the fashion of their fathers, they had consecrated to hospitality; and after pleasing themselves with the expectation, that this and that relative or friend would occasionally occupy it, they returned to the parlour, and naturally fell to the retrospect of the long and checkered track by which Providence had led them to this happy beginning of their married life. Perhaps this review was for the hundredth time; but it mattered not. Such subjects never lose their interest for the parties concerned. To others there was nothing striking in the history of their quiet lives; but circumstances, to the individuals they affect, take the hue of their feelings; and glowing hopes and deep emotions produce an effect on ordinary events resembling the alternations of shadows and sun-beams on a familiar landscape.

Mrs. Barclay was one of the ten children of a rich farmer; but there is nothing appalling to the most modest aspirant in the riches of a New England farmer, and the little, sweet-tempered, bright Anne Hyde was very early (so early that it seemed to him as a morning dream) the tenant and joint proprietor of all William Barclay's castles in the air. And he seemed to her, in the memory of her childhood, to run, like a golden thread, through all its web. She fondly recalled the time when, one bitter cold day, he left a skating party to drag her home on his sled; and that unlucky day when she fell in climbing over the fence, tore her frock, and spilled her strawberries, and he re-filled her basket from his, and took her home to his gentle mother to mend the rent; thus saving her from disgrace with her own mother, whose temper, poor woman, was a little the worse for the wear and tear of ten children. And well she remembered the time when, in choosing sides for spelling, he chose her before her pretty competitor, Fanny Smith, who was certainly the best speller; and their standing together at poor Lucy Grey's funeral, and crying so bitterly; and the next day their tying up a wreath of apple-blossoms and laying it on her grave; and their first singing-school; and though at meeting he sat with the bass and she with the treble, she never heard any voice but his. All she could not remember was the time when she did not love him. But it mattered not when or where the starting point was, in the snows of winter or the pleasant summer field,—in the school or church-yard,—when the heart was merry or sad; certain it was, their affection had grown with their growth, and the stream that was now to flow in one deep, inseparable current, was as pure and fresh as when it first gushed forth from its separate founts.

The Barclays closed their first evening at home by reading together in that holy book whose truths and precepts were to inform and govern their lives. They then knelt at the domestic altar, while William Barclay, in a tone of cheerful, manly devotion, dedicated his home to Him "who setteth the solitary in families," and from that day it was hallowed by domestic worship.

Few persons, probably, have thought so much as William Barclay of the economy of domestic happiness. He had lived in various families, and had seen much waste and neglect of the means of virtue and happiness which Providence supplies through the social relations. He had made a chart for his future conduct, by which he hoped to escape at least some of the shoals and quicksands on which others make shipwreck. He believed that a household, governed in obedience to the Christian social law, would present as perfect an image of heaven, as the infirmity of human nature, and the imperfections in the constitution of human affairs would admit. That he purposed well is certain; how far he succeeded, will be imperfectly disclosed in the following pages.

CHAPTER II.

A GLIMPSE AT FAMILY GOVERNMENT.

Pour forth thy fervors to a healthful mind,
Obedient passions and a will resigned.—JOHNSON.

THE skilful cultivator discerns in the germination of the bud the perfection or the disease, that a superficial observer would first perceive in the ripening or the blighted fruit. And the moral observer, if equally skilled, might predict the manhood from the promise of the youth. Few are so skilled, and we seldom turn over ten years of life without surprise at the development of qualities we had not perceived. The happy accidents, —they could not be called virtues, but rather the result of circumstances,—have vanished like the dews of morning. The good-natured, light-hearted, generous youth, as his cares increased, and his health abated, has become petulant, gloomy, and selfish; the gay, agreeable girl, moping and censorious. There were many who wondered that persons who seemed nothing extraordinary in their youth, should turn out as the Barclays had; and they wondered too, how in the world it was that everything went right with the Barclays; and then the puzzle was solved in the common way,—" It was their luck." They did not see that the Barclays had begun right, that they had proposed to themselves rational objects, and had pursued them with all the power of conscience and of an unslacking energy.

That happy, if not happiest portion of married life, when the thousand clustering joys of parents are first felt, when toil is hope without weariness, passed brightly away with them. Twelve years

had thus passed; their cares were multiplied, and their enjoyments, a hundred fold. Mr. Barclay's accumulating responsibilities sometimes weighed heavily upon him. He was, like most persons of great sensibility, of an apprehensive temper. The little ailments of his children were apt to disturb his serenity, and, for the time being, it was destroyed by the moral diseases that break out in the healthiest subjects. His wife was of a happier temperament. Her equal, sunny temper soon rectified the disturbed balance of his. She knew that the constitution of weak and susceptible childhood was liable to moral and physical maladies, and that, if well got through, it became the more robust and resisting for having suffered them. Her husband knew this too, and was consoled by it,—after the danger was past.

Our friends were now in a convenient house, adapted to their very much improved fortune and increased family. The family were assembled in a back parlour. Mrs. Barclay was at some domestic employment, to facilitate which Martha had just brought in a tub of scalding water. Charles, the eldest boy, with a patience most unboyish, was holding a skein of yarn for grandmama to wind; Alice, the eldest girl, was arranging the dinner-table in the adjoining room; Mary, the second, was amusing the baby at the window; Willie was saying his letters to aunt Betsey;—all were busy, but the busiest was little Haddy, a sweet child of four years, who was sitting in the middle of the room on a low chair and who, unobserved by the rest, and herself unconscious of wrong, was doing deadly mischief. She had taken a new, unfinished, and very precious kite belonging to her brother Wallace, cut a hole in the centre, thrust into it the head of her pet Maltese kitten, and was holding it by its fore paws and making it dance on her lap; the little animal looking as demure and formal as one of Queen Elizabeth's maids of honour in her ruff. At this critical juncture Wallace entered in search of his kite. One word of prefatory palliation for Wallace. The kite was the finest he had ever possessed; it had been given him by a friend, and that friend was waiting at the door, to string and fly it for him. At once the ruin of the kite, and the indignity to which it was subjected, flashed on him, and perhaps little Haddy's very satisfied air exasperated him. In a breath he seized the kitten, and dashed it into the tub of scalding water. His father had come in to dinner, and paused at the open door of the next room. Haddy shrieked, —the children all screamed,—Charles dropped grandmama's yarn, and, at the risk of his own hand, rescued the kitten; but seeing its agony, with most characteristic consideration, he gently dropped it in again, and thus put the speediest termination to its sufferings.

The children were all sobbing. Wallace stood pale and trembling. His eye turned to his father, then to his mother, then was riveted on the floor. The children saw the frown on their father's face, more dreaded by them than ever was flogging, or dark closet with all its hobgoblins.

" I guess you did not mean to, did you, Wally?" said little Haddy, whose tender heart was so touched by the utter misery depicted on her brother's face, that her pity for him overcame her sense of her own and pussy's wrongs. Wallace sighed deeply, but spoke no word of apology or justification. The children looked at Wallace, at their father, and their mother, and still the portentous silence was unbroken. The dinner-bell rang. "Go to your own room, Wallace," said his father. "You have forfeited your right to a place among us. Creatures who are the slaves of their passions, are, like beasts of prey, fit only for solitude."

"How long must Wallace stay up stairs?" asked Haddy, affectionately holding back her brother who was hastening away.

"Till he feels assured," replied Mr. Barclay, fixing his eye sternly on Wallace, "that he can control his hasty temper; at least so far as not to be guilty of violence towards such a dear good little girl as you are, and murderous cruelty to an innocent animal;—till, sir, you can give me some proof that you dread the sin and danger of yielding to your passions so much that you can govern them. The boy is hopeless," he added in a low voice to his wife, as Wallace left the room.

"My dear husband! hopeless at ten years old, and with such a good, affectionate heart as his! We must have patience."

A happy combination for children is there in an uncompromising father and an all-hoping mother. The family sat down to table. The parents were silent, serious, unhappy. The children caught the infection, and scarcely a word was said above a whisper. There was a favourite dish on the table, followed by a nice pudding. They were eaten, not enjoyed. The children realised that it was not the good things they had to eat, but the kind looks, the innocent laugh, and cheerful voice, that made the pleasure of the social meal.

"My dear children," said their father, as he took his hat to leave them, "we have lost all our comfort to-day, have not we?"

"Yes, sir,—yes, sir," they answered in a breath.

"Then learn one lesson from your poor brother. Learn to dread doing wrong. If you commit sin, you must suffer, and all that love you must suffer with you; for every sin is a violation of the laws of your Heavenly Father, and he will not suffer it to go unpunished."

If Mr. and Mrs. Barclay had affected their concern, to overawe and impose on their children, they would not have been long deceived; for children, being themselves sincere, are clear-sighted. But they knew that the sadness was real; they felt that it was in accordance with their parents' characters and general conduct. They never saw them ruffled by trifles. Many a glass had been broken, many a greasy knife dropped, many a disappointment and inconvenience incurred, without calling forth more than a gentle rebuke. These were not the things that moved them, or disturbed the domestic tranquillity; but the ill temper, selfishness, unkindness, or any moral fault of the children, was received as an affliction.

The days passed on. Wallace went to school as usual, and returned to his solitude, without speaking or being spoken to. His meals were sent to his room, and whatever the family ate, he ate. For the Barclays took care not to make rewards and punishments out of eating and drinking, and thus associate the duties and pleasures of a moral being with a mere animal gratification. "But ah!" he thought, as he walked up and down

his apartment, while eating his pie or pudding, "how different it tastes from what it does at table!" and though he did not put it precisely in that form, he felt what it was that "sanctified the food." The children began to venture to say to their father, whose justice they dared not question, "How long Wally has stayed up, stairs!" and Charles, each day, eagerly told how well Wallace behaved at school. His grandmother could not resist her desire to comfort him, she would look into his room to see "if he were well," "if he were warm enough," or "if he did not want something." The little fellow's moistening eye and tremulous voice evinced his sensibility to her kindness, but he resolutely abstained from asking any mitigation of his punishment. He overheard his aunt Betsey (Mrs. Barclay's maiden sister) say, "It is a sin, and ridiculous besides, to keep Wallace mewed up so, just for a little flash of temper. I am sure he had enough to provoke a saint."

"We do not keep him mewed up, Betsey," replied Mrs. Barclay, "nor does he continued mewed up, for a single flash of temper; but because, with all his good resolutions, his passionate temper is constantly getting the better of him. There is no easy cure for such a fault. If Wallace had the seeds of consumption, you would think it the extreme of folly not to submit to a few weeks' confinement, if it afforded a means of ridding him of them; and how much worse than a consumption is a moral disease!"

"Well," answered the sister, "you must do as you like, but I am sure we never had any such fuss at home;—we grew up, and there was an end on't."

"But may be," thought Wallace, "if there had been a little more fuss when you were younger, it would have been pleasanter living with you now, aunt Betsey."

Poor aunt Betsey, with many virtues, had a temper that made her a nuisance wherever she was. The Barclays alone got on tolerably with her. There was a disinfecting principle in the moral atmosphere of their house.

Two weeks had passed when Mr. Barclay heard Wallace's door open, and heard him say, "Can I speak with you one minute before dinner, sir?"

"Certainly, my son." His father entered and closed the door.

"Father," said Wallace, with a tremulous voice, but an open cheerful face, "I feel as if I had a right now to ask you to forgive me, and take me back into the family."

Mr. Barclay felt so too, and kissing him, he said, "I have only been waiting for you, Wallace; and, from the time you have taken to consider your besetting sin, I trust you have gained strength to resist it."

"It is not consideration only, sir, that I depend on; for you told me I must wait till I could give you *proof*; so I had to wait till something happened to try me. I could not possibly tell else, for I always do resolve, when I get over my passion, that I never will get angry again. Luckily for me,—for I began to be horribly tired of staying alone,—Tom Allen snatched off my new cap and threw it in the gutter. I had a book in my hand, and I raised it to send it at him; but I thought just in time, and I was so glad I had governed my passion, that I did not care about my cap, or Tom, or anything else. ' But one swallow doesn't make a summer,' as aunt Betsey says ; so I waited till I should get angry again. It seemed as if I never should ; there were provoking things happened, but somehow or other they did not provoke me,—why do you smile, father ?"

" I smile with pleasure, my dear boy, to find that one fortnight's resolute watchfulness has enabled you so to curb your temper that you are not easily provoked."

" But stay, father, you have not yet heard all ; yesterday, just as I was putting up my arithmetic, which I had written almost to the end without a single blot, Tom Allen came along and gave my inkstand a jostle, and over it went on my open book ; I thought he did it purposely,—I think so still, but I don't feel so sure. I did not reflect then,—I doubled my fist to strike him."

" O, Wallace !"

" But I did not, father, I did not,—I thought just in time. There was a horrid choking feeling in my throat, and angry words seemed crowding out ; but I did not even say, ' Blame you.' I had to bite my lips, though, so that the blood ran."

" God bless you, my son."

" And the best of it all was, father, that Tom Allen, who never before seemed to care how much harm he did you, or how much he hurt your feelings, was really sorry; and this morning he brought me a new blank book nicely ruled, and offered to help me copy my sums into it ; so I hope I did *him* some good as well as myself, by governing my temper."

" There is no telling, Wallace, how much good may be done by a single right action, nor how much harm by a single wrong one."

" I know it, sir ; I have been thinking a great deal since I have been up stairs, and I do wonder why God did not make Adam and Eve so that they could not do wrong."

" This subject has puzzled older and wiser heads than yours, my son, and puzzled them more than I think it should. If we had been created incapable of sin, there could have been no virtue. Did you not feel happier yesterday after your trial, than if it had not happened ?"

" O yes, father ; and the strangest of all was, that after the first flash, I had not any bad feelings towards Tom."

" Then you can see, in your own case, good resulting from being free to do good or evil. You certainly were the better for your victory, and, you say, happier. It is far better to be virtuous than sinless,—I mean, incapable of sin. If you subdue your temper, the exercise of the power to do this will give you a pleasure that you could not have had without it."

" But if I fail, father !" Wallace looked in his father's face with an expression which showed he felt that he had more than a kingdom to gain or lose.

" You cannot fail, my dear son, while you continue to feel the worth of the object for which you are striving ; while you feel that the eye of God is upon you ; and that not only your own happiness, but the happiness of your father, and mother, and brothers, and sisters,—of our *home* depends on your success."

" But, father, did you ever know anybody that

had such a passionate temper, that learned to govern it always ?"

" Yes, my child, but not all at once. You are placed in the happiest circumstances to obtain this rule over your own spirit. The Americans are said to be distinguished for their good temper. I believe this is true, not from any natural superiority in them to French, English, or Irish, but because they are brought up among their equals, and compelled from childhood to govern their tempers ; one cannot encroach on the rights of another."

" But is it not so with all Americans, father ?"

" No; those in the Southern States, unfortunately, have not these restraints,—this equal pressure on all sides, and they are esteemed more irascible and passionate than the people of the North. This is one of the thousand misfortunes that result from slavery. But we must always remember, my son, that the virtue or vice produced by circumstances is not to be counted to the individual. It is the noble struggle and resistance against them, that makes virtue. It was this that constituted the merit of Washington's subjugation of his temper."

" Was he,—was General Washington passionate, father ?"

" Yes ; quite as irascible and passionate, naturally, as you are ; and yet you know it was his equanimity, his calmness, in the most irritating circumstances, that made him so superior to other men."

" Was he pious, sir ?"

" He had always a strong sense of his responsibility and duty to his Creator."

" And I guess, too, he had good parents, and a pleasant home, and he hated to make them all unhappy."

" I guess he had, Wallace," replied his father, smiling ; " but I can give you another example for your encouragement. Which among the Apostles appears to you to have been the gentlest,—what we should call the sweetest tempered ?"

" O, St. John, sir."

" And yet he appears at one time to have been very impetuous,—what you and I call hasty tempered. He was for calling down fire on the offenders' heads. So you see that even a grown-up person, if he has the love of Christ in him, and lays his precepts to heart, so that he will really strive to be perfect as his Father in heaven is perfect, may, at any age, subdue his temper ; though the work is far easier if he begins when a child, as you have, in earnest, my dear boy. You have manifested a virtuous resolution ; and you not only have my forgiveness, and my entire sympathy, but I trust you have the approbation of your Heavenly Father. Come, come along to your mother ; take her happy kiss, and then to dinner. We have not had one right pleasant dinner since you have been up stairs."

" Stop one moment, father." Wallace lowered his voice as he modestly added, " I don't think I should have got through it alone, but every day I have prayed to God to help me."

" You have not been alone, my dear son," replied his father, much moved, " nor will you ever be left alone in your efforts to obey God ; for, you remember, Jesus has said, ' If a man keep my words, my Father will love him, and we will come unto him and make our abode with him.' God, my son, is present in every dictate of your conscience, in every pure affection and holy emotion of your soul."

A farmer who has seen a beautiful crop bend under the storm, and after it rise stronger and more promising than ever, can have some feeble conception of Mr. Barclay's satisfaction, while, leaving Wallace with their mother, he assembled the children in the dining-room, and recounted to them as much as he deemed proper of his conversation with their brother.

The dinner-bell sounded, and Wallace was heard running down stairs before his mother, his heels as light as his heart. The children, jumping up behind and before him, shouted out his welcome. Grandmama wiped her eyes, and cleared her voice to say, " Dear me, Wally, how glad we all are to see you !" Even aunt Betsey looked smiling, and satisfied, and unprovokable for an hour to come.

Others may think, with aunt Betsey, that Wallace's punishment was out of proportion to his offence ; but it must be remembered, that it was not the penalty for a single offence, but for a habit of irascibility that could not be cured without serious and repeated efforts. Mr. Barclay held whipping, and all such summary modes of punishment, on a par with such nostrums in medicine as peppermint and lavender, which suspend the manifestation of the disease, without conducing to its cure. He believed the only effectual and lasting government,—the only one that touches the springs of action, and in all circumstances controls them, is *self*-government. It was this he laboured to teach his children. The process was slow but sure. It required judgment, and gentleness, and, above all, patience on the part of the parents ; but every inch of ground gained was kept. The children might not appear so orderly as they whose parents are like drill-sergeants, and who, while their eyes are on the fugel-man, appear like little prodigies ; but, deprived of external aid or restraint, the self-regulating machine shows its superiority.

CHAPTER III.

A FAMILY DINNER.

The fault, dear Brutus, is not in our stars,
But in ourselves, that we are underlings.—SHAKSPEARE.

As we have entered Mr. Barclay's dining-room, we are tempted to linger there, and permit our readers to observe the details of the dinner. The right ministration of the table is an important item, in *home* education. Mr. Barclay had a just horror of hurrying through meals. He regarded them as something more than means of sustaining physical wants,—as opportunities of improvement and social happiness. Are they not so ? and is there any danger of affixing an undue importance to that, which may teach, at the rate of *three lessons a day*, punctuality, order, neatness, temperance, self-denial, kindness, generosity, and hospitality ! The conventional manners of high-bred people are meant to express these virtues ; but alas ! with them the sign often exists without the thing signified. In middling life, the form cannot exist without the spirit. The working men and working women of our country need not remain for twelve hours

chained to the oar like galley-slaves ; and if they will give up a little money for what the wealth of "the Rothschilds and the Barings" cannot purchase, *time*, and devote that time to such a ministration of their meals, as shall secure " Earth's best angel, health," as a guest at the family board,—as shall develop the mind by conversation, and cultivate refined manners,—they will find the amount of good resulting to the home circle incalculable.

Alice and Mary Barclay took their " weeks about," as they called it, to arrange and wait on the table. The table was set with scrupulous neatness. " Mother sees everything," was their maxim ; and sure she was to see it, if the salt was not freshly stamped, the castors in order, and every napkin, glass, spoon, knife, and dish put on, as the girls said, by plummet and line. These are trifles in detail, but their effect on the comfort and habits of a large family of children can scarcely be magnified. Few tables in the land were more frugal than the Barclays', and few better served. They did not, however, sacrifice the greater to the less, and there were occasions when their customary forms gave place to higher matters.

" Here is our dinner," said Mr. Barclay, turning his eye that had been riveted on the happy, noisy children, to the table where Martha (still the only domestic) was placing the last dish.

" The dinner here, and I have not changed my cap !" said Mrs. Barclay.

" And I have not brushed my hair !"—" Nor I,"—" Nor I," exclaimed, in a breath, half a dozen treble voices.

" It's all my fault, — forgetting to ring the warning bell," said Martha, turning her eye from Wallace to his mother, in explanation of her lapse of memory.

" Never mind, Martha. Better to forget rules for once, than forget your part in the family joy."

" That's good, mother ! let us break all rules to-day,—let Wally sit by me."

" O no ! mother ; by me ! by me !" exclaimed other voices.

" No. Take your usual place, Wallace, by Haddy."

" O, where is dear little Haddy !" asked Wallace, and was answered by her bouncing into the room. She had been left up stairs to finish a task. She took her seat beside Wallace. There was some whispering between them, and it was plain by her glad eye and her putting her chubby arm around her brother and hugging him close to her, that pussy and the kite were drowned in Lethe.

" I guess, Miss Haddy," said aunt Betsey, " you got some help about your task."

" Aunt Betsey !" replied the little girl, with a quivering lip, " indeed I did not,—*that would be doing a lie*." How forcibly the " oracles of nature" come from the unperverted mind of a child ! She who made this reply was but four years old.

The blessing was asked, a usage observed at Mr. Barclay's table. Whatever objection may be urged against it from its abuse, he considered the example of the Saviour a definitive precedent for him. His distinct and touching manner of acknowledging the bounties of Providence fixed the attention. It was feeling, not form.

" You have forgotten the napkins to-day, Alice," said her mother.

Alice smiled, and replied in a low voice, " It was Wallace's fault ; just as I was going for them I heard him call father, and I forgot them."

It was Alice's turn to serve the table,—a task always assigned to one, in order to avoid the confusion of the alternate jumping up and down of half a dozen little bodies, the dropping of knives and forks, the oversetting of glasses, and the din and clatter of a disorderly table.

" There is a nice crust for you, Wallace," said Alice, as she passed round the bread ; " you love crust."

" Aunt Betsey," called out little Haddy, who unluckily observed her aunt trespassing against one of the ordinances of the table, " it is not proper not to use the butter-knife !"

" Hush, Haddy," breathed her brother, but not in time. The antagonist principle was strong in aunt Betsey's mind. She cherished with equal fervour dislikes and partialities ; and poor little Haddy was no favourite.

" I wonder which is worst," she replied, " to use my own knife as I was brought up to, or for a little saucebox like you to set me right."

Willie, aunt Betsey's pet, dropped his spoon, put up his lips, and kissed the angry spot away.

" I guess, Alice," said Mary, " you mean to brush Wally's place clean enough." Alice smiled. She had unconsciously bestowed double pains in brushing away her brother's crumbs. How naturally affection makes the most ordinary services its medium.

" O, Mary !" said Mrs. Barclay, " I forgot when I gave you the pudding, that you complained of a head-ach this morning."

" It is gone now, mother."

" It may come back, my dear."

Mary put down her spoon, and gently pushed away her plate, saying, without the slightest shade of dissatisfaction, " It looks very good."

Alice placed a dish of strawberries on the table, the first of the season,—saying as she did so, " Rather a scant pattern, mother."

" Yes, barely a taste for each."

" Give mine to Wally, then," said Mary.

" And mine too,—and mine too," echoed and re-echoed from both sides the table.

" And mine too !" repeated little Willie, the urchin next his mother, who had been contentedly eating his potatoe without asking for, or even looking at, the more inviting food on the table.

The children laughed at his parrotry, and Alice, kissing his head as she passed, said, " Thank you for nothing, Willie."

" Why for nothing ! why not thank him as well as the rest !" asked aunt Betsey.

" Because I suppose mother won't give him any strawberries."

" Why, Anne, you are not going to be so ridiculous as not to give him strawberries ! You may as well starve him to death at once and done with it. There is nothing in the world so wholesome as strawberries."

" No fruit is wholesome for him, just now," said Mrs. Barclay ; and she continued to dispense the strawberries, without manifesting the slightest irritation at her sister's interference. She had often explained to her the reason of the very strict regimen of her younger children ; but aunt

Betsey was one of those who forget the reason, and feel the fact.

As the Barclays had no nursery maid, they were obliged to bring their children to the table, when, with ordinary habits, they would have been nuisances. To prevent this, as well as early to implant self-denial, they were not tantalized with " a very little of this," and " just a taste of that." They saw delicacies come on and go off without snatching, reaching, asking for them, or even craving them. Many a time has a guest, on seeing the youngling of the flock eating his potatoes or dry bread, remonstrated like aunt Betsey on the superfluous hardship. But the Barclays knew it was not so. The monster appetite was thus early tamed. Its pleasures were felt to be inferior pleasures,—to be enjoyed socially and gratefully, but forbearingly. The children were spared the visitations that proceed from overloaded stomachs. They rarely had occasion for a physician. " How lucky Mrs. Barclay is with her children," would her wondering neighbours exclaim ; " they never have any sudden attacks, never any fevers, and when half the children in the city are dying with measles and hooping-cough, these horrible diseases pass lightly over them ; what can it be !"

This is no fiction, but truth (though feebly set down) from life.

We left Mrs. Barclay distributing the strawberries. The front door opened ; " There comes Harry Norton, just in time for some strawberries," exclaimed Alice. " O dear ! no, it's Mr. Anthon ; it won't be quite so pleasant to give them up to him."

Charles rose to vacate his seat, saying, " Give him my share, mother."

" O no, mine," said Alice.

" He shall have both. Thank you, my children ; one would be hardly enough to offer him."

Charles and Alice retired to a window, while Mr. Anthon seated himself in the vacated chair, and fell to devouring the berries. " Bless my heart," he exclaimed after he had finished them, " I believe you have given me your place, children, and your strawberries too ; and you look just as contented as if you had eaten them yourselves. It's lucky it was not my young ones,—the house would not have held them. There's a great difference in children ; yours, Barclay, seem gentlemen and ladies, ready made to your hand." Mr. Barclay knew they were not " ready made," but he abstained from disturbing the self-complacent belief that all differences were made by nature. " Speaking of gentlemen and ladies," resumed Mr. Anthon, " I called to consult you about the propriety of people of our condition sending their children to a dancing-school. Wife is for their going, but women folks,—your pardon, ma'am," (to Mrs. Barclay,) " are always for outside show ; so I told her I would not say yes or no, till I had heard the pros and cons from you. The first thing to be settled is, whether dancing is desirable."

" Do you mean whether we desire it, Mr. Anthon ! I guess we do !"

" I dare say, Miss, but that is nothing to the purpose."

" I beg your pardon, my friend, that is very much to the purpose. If the children relish dancing, it is an argument in its favour. Youth must have amusement. Active amusements are best.

If we lived in the country, where our children could have free exercise in the open air, dancing would be unimportant; but while they are condemned to the unnatural life of a city, we should supply them with every artificial means of developing and improving their persons. I hope never to see my girls dance to display fine dancing,—this would mortify me; nor would I have them waste their time and health in dancing in crowded rooms, at unseasonable hours; but when you and I, Anthon, and half a dozen friends are talking over news and politics, and what not, it is enlivening to our children to dance away for an hour or two after the piano or the flute, or whatever instrument they may happen to have."

"Good lack! do you mean your children shall learn music too?"

"If they fancy it. Alice already plays tolerably, and Charles plays a very good accompaniment on the flute. I wish them to learn whatever will increase the attractions of their home, and tend to raise them above coarse pleasures."

"O, this is all very well for rich people."

"But far more important for us, Anthon. Dancing, certainly; as I think, there is nothing that conduces more to ease and grace, than learning to dance,—learning *to make legs*, as Locke says."

"What a funny expression!" exclaimed Mary, who, as well as the rest, was an attentive listener to the conversation.

"Yes, my dear, odd enough; but Mr. Locke probably meant learning to use them gracefully. The legs and arms of boys who are never taught to dance, are apt to be in their own and every one else's way. I do not wish my boys to suffer as I have from blundering into a room, and feeling when I had to bow to half a dozen gentlemen and ladies, as if I had to run a muck. I said I consider dancing far more important to our children than to what are called fashionable people, and for the reason that *they* have other opportunities of cultivating graceful and easy manners."

"They have more occasion for them."

"I am not sure of that. We do not yet realise that we live in a new state of things, and that the equality, which is the basis of our institutions, should also, as far as possible, be the basis of education. There is no sort of inferiority about which young people suffer more than that of manners. There are other things certainly far more important, but this is for ever before their eyes, pressing on their observation,—is seen and felt at every turn. The morals of manners we try to teach our children at home; arbitrary rules and external graces they must take the usual means of acquiring."

"Well, you certainly are odd, Barclay."

"What do you mean by that?"

"I suppose I may speak out, for neither you nor your wife are touchy."

"Yes, pray speak out, my friend: my wife and I both approve the speaking-out principle."

Mr. Anthon fidgeted on his chair. He felt a good-natured reluctance to criticising his friend, and perhaps a secret consciousness that it was bold in him to do so. After a little hesitation he sheltered himself under that broad, common, and cowardly shield, "they say," and proceeded: "The say, Barclay, that you are very inconsistent; that your family is the plainest dressed family, for peo-

ple of your property, that enter the church-doors; that your furniture,—now I don't mean to be impertinent; I know that everything is as neat and as comfortable here as can be;—but they say you might afford to have things a little smarter—more like other folks, who don't think of sending their children to expensive schools, and to this, and that, and the other; three of them, I heard a person say, attended Griscom's course of lectures on natural philosophy, with you and your wife. That of itself runs up to a sum that would buy some pretty articles."

"It does so, Anthon, and therefore I cannot buy 'pretty articles.' I am a prosperous man in my business, but my income is limited, and I must select those objects of expenditure that appear to me wisest. Now I had rather Alice should learn to draw, than that she should wear the prettiest ear-rings in New York, or any *hard-ware* of that description. I would rather my boys should learn from Professor Griscom, something of the nature and riches of the world they live in, than to have a mirror the whole length of my mantel-piece. No, Anthon, I can spare money elsewhere, but, till I am compelled, I'll not spare it in the education of my children."

"Well, I never thought you was such an ambitious man."

"What do you mean by that?"

"Why, that you are calculating to make all your children gentlemen and ladies."

"May I ask you what you mean by making them gentlemen and ladies?"

"It is plain enough what I mean,—lawyers, doctors, and ministers, and wives for such gentlefolks."

"I shall be governed by circumstances; I do not intend, nor wish, Anthon, to crowd my boys into the learned professions. If any among them have a particular talent or taste for them, they may follow them. They must decide for themselves in a matter more important to them than to any one else. But my boys know that I should be mortified if they selected these professions, from the vulgar notion that they were more genteel,—a vulgar word that, that ought to be banished from an American's vocabulary—more genteel than agriculture and the mechanic arts. I have laboured to convince my boys, that there is nothing vulgar in the mechanic professions,—no particular reason for envying the lawyer or the doctor. They, as much as the farmer and the mechanic, are working men. And I should like to know what there is particularly elevating in sitting over a table and writing prescribed forms, or in inquiring into the particulars of diseases, and doling out physic for them. It is certainly a false notion in a democratic republic, that a lawyer has any higher claim to respectability,—gentility, if you please,—than a tanner, a goldsmith, a printer, or a builder. It is the fault of the mechanic, if he takes a place not assigned to him by the government and institutions of his country. He is of the *lower orders*, only when he is self-degraded by the ignorance and coarse manners, which are associated with manual labour in countries where society is divided into *castes*, and have therefore come to be considered inseparable from it. Rely upon it, it is not so. The old barriers are down. The time has come when 'being mechanical' we may appear on labouring days' as well as holidays, without the 'sign of our profession.' Talent and worth are the only eternal grounds of distinction. To these the Almighty has affixed his everlasting patent of nobility, and these it is which make the bright, 'the immortal names,' to which our children may aspire, as well as others. It will be our own fault, Anthon, if, in our land, society as well as government is not organized upon a new foundation. But we must secure, by our own efforts, the elevations that are now accessible to all. There is nothing that tends more to the separation into classes than difference of manners. This is a badge that all can see. I cannot blame a gentleman for not asking a clown to his table, who will spit over his carpet, and mortify himself and annoy everybody else with his awkwardness."

Mr. Anthon's head was rather oppressed by the matter for reflection that Barclay had put into it. After a thoughtful pause he said, " Well, seeing is believing."

" Yes, and I fear it will be some time yet before this new form of society which I anticipate, will be seen ; before men will seek to consort with men because they are intelligent, accomplished, and exemplary, and not because they live in fine houses, associate with *genteel* people, get masses of fashionable persons together to pass evenings in inanity, and exhaust their resources in extravagant and poisonous eating and drinking. Let me tell you, Anthon, there is too much struggling after all this; too much envy ; too much imitation of it among those who are called, and still call themselves, the middling classes,—my poor old friend Norton, for instance. But I see tokens of better times."

" Of your millennium, I suppose ; when farmers and mechanics are to range with the highest in the land ?"

" Yes, and I can point you to some heralds of this millennium. There is in this city, ———, whom we both know, strictly a working man. Did he not make a speech at a political meeting the other night, that would have done honour to any professional man in the state, not only full of good common sense, but expressed in choice language, and with enough of historical allusion to show that he was a well-read man ! His manner too was easy and unembarrassed ; such as becomes a man addressing his equals. I know a young man in Greenbrook, my native place, also a working man, a laborious and successful farmer, whose general attainments and *manners* qualify him for polished society ; who has some acquaintance with science, draws beautifully, and writes graceful verses."

" Do you mean that such a man as that in fact works ?"

" Yes, digs, plants, sows, and reaps ; and is contented to do so. His home is one of the most attractive and happy I have ever seen."

Mr. Anthon shook his head. " There may be two such men in the nation, but eagles do not fly in flocks. Your doctrine is quite captivating to you and me, who do not stand on the top round of the ladder, but it's quite contrary to the nature of things. ' One star differeth from another star in glory,' and there are angels and archangels in heaven."

" Yes, undoubtedly there must be angels and archangels. But what is it that constitutes their distinction ? Knowledge and goodness ;—these

make degrees in heaven, and they must be the graduating scale of a true democracy. I believe that the Christian law (of course seconding the law of nature) ordains equality,—democracy if you please, —and therefore that its progress and final stability are certain. The ladder is knocked down, my friend, and we stand on nature's level."

" That's what I call a pretty up and down level. You can't even off everybody. Now just look at the difference between your children and mine. Here are yours listening to our talk, and taking pleasure in it. Bless your heart, man, mine would have been out of the doors and windows before this time."

It would have been a delicate matter for Mr. Barclay to have admitted this difference, even if he had imputed it to the true cause, his habit of always associating with his children, and of making conversation, which he considered one of the most effective means of education, attractive and instructive to them. " We cannot," he said, " judge of the merits of a subject which we make personal. I am sorry we have come to this point, for I should like, right well, to make a convert of you. I shall comfort myself, as other people do, with the faith that my doctrine will prevail. It certainly will, if we *make* the equality, instead of merely claiming it."

" Ah, there's the rub ; how the deuce are we to make it ?"

" By the careful use of all the means we possess to train these young creatures ; by giving them sound minds in sound bodies ; by making them feel the dignity of well-informed minds, pure hearts, and refined manners. And for this we need not college education and foreign masters. Home is the best school,—the parent the best teacher. It is the opinion of some wise people, that the habits are fixed at twelve."

" The Lord have mercy on my children, then," interrupted Mr. Anthon.

" It is not my opinion," resumed Mr. Barclay ; " but I do think that what is done after that is hard work, both for parents and children. However, as our children are, for the most part, at home till the age of twelve, we see how much we have in our power, and how wisely Providence has confided the most important period of life to the care of the parent, by far the most interested teacher."

" Well, well," said Mr. Anthon, who had too much reason for feeling uncomfortably under these remarks, " it can't be expected of a business man to do so much with what you call home education. The wife must see to that. · My wife is a good soul, but she has not got Mrs. Barclay's knack. Come, is it not time for you to go to your office ?"

" Yes, past my usual time by a half hour. I always allow myself an hour with my family at dinner."

" An hour ! bless my heart ! We get through at our house in about ten minutes,—never exceed fifteen. My father made it a rule to choose the quickest eaters for his workmen. If they did not bolt in ten minutes, he concluded they were lazy or shiftless."

" Your father's bolting system would not suit me. I cannot judge for others, but I know that I am more diligent and active in business for having such an object ahead as a happy hour at home,— (an hour I must say, in praise of my good wife, never abridged by a want of punctuality on her part;) and I return to my office with more strength and spirits, for the little rest I give myself after I have swallowed my food. This is my experience, and it should be so according to the best medical theories."

"O dear!" said Mr. Anthon, with something between a sigh and a groan, "I wish I had thought of all these matters when I was a younger man; but it's too late now."

We would humbly recommend it to those for whom it is not too late, to think of "these matters."

CHAPTER IV.

THE REVERSE OF THE PICTURE.

"For who can eat, or who else can hasten hereunto, more than I?"

We shift the scene to Mr. Anthon's dinner-table. Enter Mr. Anthon, shouting to a little girl, who was scampering through the entry; "Laury, call the folks to dinner."

Laura screamed at the top of her voice, "Mother, father has come to dinner.—John,—Tom,—Anne,—Julia,—Dick,—where are you all? Dinner is ready."

"Sure to be away at dinner-time," said the father, "if they are under your feet all the rest of the day."

Tom and John, and they only, responded to the muster-call, and both entering the dining-room, seized the same chair: "It's my chair," cried Tom.

"No, it an't," says John; "I got it first."

"Be done disputing, boys," interposed the father; "is not there more than one chair in the room? Take another, Tom."

"It an't half fair," muttered Tom, obeying, however.

"Laury," said the mother, entering in the act of smoothing her hair with a side comb, "you an't surely going to sit down to dinner in your new frock, without an apron."

"I can't find my apron, mother."

"Look in the entry."

"I have looked there."

"Look in the bed-room."

"I have looked all over the bed-room."

"Well then, look in the pantry; hunt till you find it."

By this time the fumes of dinner had reached the olfactories of Anne and Julia, and they came racing down stairs, and entered, slamming the door after them.

"Leave open that door," said the father; "you always shut the doors in June, and leave them open in January."

"Mother, shan't John give me my place?" asked Anne, too intent on her invaded rights to listen to her father.

"It an't her place, mother; I sat here yesterday."

"But I sat here the day before."

"What consequence is it what place you have? Crowd in your chair there, next to John. We shall be through dinner, before you all get seated. Why don't you open the door, as I told you, Anne?"

"Julia came in last, sir."

"I told you to open it."

"I did not know you meant me more than Julia."

"If you don't hear, and mind too next time, you shall go without your dinner."

This threat made little impression on Anne, for she was occupied in forcing her chair in between her brothers, who were seated askew, or rather, as the French would say, en échelon. A natural consequence ensued; John's glass of cider was jostled out of his hand, and Tom's shin was pretty roughly hit (if one might judge from his outcries) by the leg of the chair. "All that cider over my clean cloth!" exclaimed the unhappy mother. "What are you crying for, Anne?"

"Tom struck me."

"I don't care if I did, she 'most murdered me."

"Laury, just hand me a piece of bread, too," said John to his sister, who had risen, at her father's request, to give him the bread.

"You may help yourself, Mr. John."

"Mother, can't Laury hand me the bread?"

"How can you be so disobliging, Laury? hand him the bread."

Laura, without budging an inch, stretched out her arm to its utmost length; John snatched at the bread-tray, and between them it went to the floor.

"Oh!" cried the mother, "you are the worst behaved children I ever saw. Sit down in your places, both of you. Julia, do you get up, and pick up the bread."

While Julia obeyed, Tom screamed out, "Mother, shan't Anne use the salt-spoon? She puts her fingers in the salt-cellar."

"Well, Tom put in his knife, mother, all drizzling with gravy; see here!" and she pointed to the salt-cellar, which afforded demonstration of the truth of her charge.

Before this controversy could be settled, Dick enters, his face daubed with ink from ear to ear. The children shouted, his mother bade him go and wash, and his father ordered him to sit down as he was and eat his dinner, saying, "He would be just as dirty afterwards, and he might wash then, and kill two birds with one stone." Dick eagerly obeyed, for he saw a pudding in perspective, and he gulped down his unchewed food, to be in readiness for it, in his haste upsetting a mustard-pot on one side, and making a trail of gravy from the gravy-boat to his plate on the other.

Two of the girls briskly cleared the table, piling the plates together and dropping the knives and forks all the way from parlour to kitchen; while the other children impatiently awaited the process, one thrumming on the table, another rocking back on the hind-legs of his chair; one picking his teeth with a dropped fork, and another moulding the crumbs of bread into balls, and all in turn chidden by the much-enduring mother. Finally appeared a huge blackberry pudding, hailed by smacking lips, and set down amid the still standing paraphernalia of the first course, and the wreck of mustard, cider, &c. A mammoth bit was scarcely passed to the father, when Laura cried out, "Help me first to-day, mother; 'cause Anne was helped first yesterday."

"I don't think you had best eat any to-day, Laury; you know you had a burning fever all night."

"O, mother! I know blackberry pudding won't hurt me."

"Stop whining, Laury," interrupted the father. "Do give her a bit, my dear; I never heard of blackberry pudding hurting any body."

A cry was heard from the adjoining bed-room. "The baby has waked," said the mother; "take her up, Julia, and hand her here." The baby, a poor, pale, teething thing, of a year old, but, like all babies in large families, an object of general fondness, was brought in. One fed her with pudding, another gave her a crumb of cheese, and a taste of cider. The mother ordered back a mutton-chop bone for her to suck; the father poured into her little blue lips the last drop of his bumper of wine, and then calling out, "Start your teams, boys," he sallied forth, the fifteen minutes, the longest allowed space for dinner, having been completely used up.

It would not be wonderful if John, Tom, and Dick, afterwards, as members of Congress, or, perchance, as higher officers, should elicit the strictures of foreign observers of our manners, and call down a sentence of inevitable and hopeless vulgarity upon democratic institutions. This might be borne; for, however much delicacy and refinement of manners may embellish life, it might be difficult to prove them essential to its most substantial objects. But would there not be some danger, that young persons, bred in such utter disregard of what the French call *les petites morales* (the lesser morals), would prove, as men and women, sadly deficient in the social virtues!

The Barclays might, when grown up, chance to pour an egg into a glass, instead of taking it from the shell, or they might convey their food to their mouths with a knife instead of a fork, in the presence of a carping Englishman; for these matters are merely conventional, and they might live and die in ignorance of them. But they would never dispense with the use of a tooth-brush,—never pick their teeth at table, sit on two legs of a chair, hawk, (we have come to delicate ground,) spit on the carpet or grate, or, in any other of the usual modes, betray the coarseness of early associations. They would not be among those who should elicit from foreigners such graphic descriptions as the following: "If you pass coffee-houses, taverns, or such like places, the street is full of chairs on which loll human bodies, while the legs belonging to them are supported against the wall or the pillars that support the awning. At such places the tobacco-juice is squirted about like a fire of rockets."

But this, after all, is but the mint and cummin. They would not be found wanting in the weightier matters—in the gentle courtesies of the social man,—in that politeness which comes from the heart, like rays from the sun,—nor in the very soul of good breeding, Christian grace and gentleness.

He who should embody and manifest the virtues taught in Christ's sermon on the mount, would, though he had never seen a drawing-room nor ever heard of the artificial usages of society, commend himself to all nations, the most refined as well as the most simple.

CHAPTER V.

A DEDICATION SERVICE.

Ye little flock, with pleasure hear;
Ye children, seek his face;
And fly with transports to receive
The blessings of his grace.—DODDRIDGE.

THANKS to the smiles of Heaven on our widespread land, the dissocial principles of the political economist of the old world do not apply here, and a large family of children is the blessing to an American, which it was to a patriarchal father. The Barclays had now been married fourteen years, and their seventh child was now six weeks old. The manner in which a new-born child is welcomed into the family group, shows, in a most touching aspect, the beauty and worth of the affections which spring from the family compact. The Sunday morning had come, when the baby (of course there was always a baby in the family) was to be *carried out* to be christened. If there is a sanctifying influence from the simple ordinances of our religion, they should not be omitted or carelessly performed. In the institution of these external rites, a wise reference seems to have been made to the mixed nature of man, partly spiritual and partly corporeal. Those are over bold, who would separate what God has joined together.

Mrs. Barclay came from her room with the baby in her arms, in its christening-dress; the children gathering round her, and exclaiming, "O, how sweet she looks!" "O mother, do let me kiss her!" "I won't tumble her cap,—just let me kiss the tips of her fingers." "See her, see her smile!" "How pretty she breathes!" "What a cunning little fist she makes." "Is not she a beauty, mother!"

They assembled in the parlour for a sort of private dedication service. "Now," said Mr. Barclay, looking at the little group about the baby with delight. "All take one kiss, and then go to your seats.—But where is grandmama!" The good old lady, dressed in her Sunday-best, and with spectacles and handkerchief in hand, answered the inquiry by entering and taking her seat in the rocking-chair.

"Now, father, tell us the secret," said Mary; "what have you decided to name her."

"O, say Emily Norton," cried Wallace.

"O, I hope you will not name her Emily Norton, sir," said Alice.

"Why not, Alice!" asked Charles; "I am sure Emily Norton is a sweet name."

Alice well knew the *why not* existing in her mind, but there was no time to explain.

"Please call her Hepsy Anne," asked one of the little ones, naming a favourite schoolmate.

"I speak to have it Aunt Betsey," said aunt Betsey's pet.

Mr. Barclay shook his head. "Mother says she must be named for grandmama."

"Ganmama!" cried little Willie, "what a funny name!"

"Euphemia is grandmama's name, my dear." The children looked grave. Euphemia sounded very strange and old-fashioned to their ears. "Or Effie," added Mr. Barclay, "if you like that better."

Effie, that prettiest of diminutives, gained all suffrages. Grandmama, who had one of the tenderest as well as kindest hearts in the world, looked, but could not speak, her pleasure. There is something that addresses itself to the passion for immortality, in the transmission of that which is even so extraneous as a name, to one, who in the order of nature will survive us. But it was not this that brought the tears to old Mrs. Barclay's eyes. The name recalled long silent voices, which in far-gone years, had rung it in her ears in tones of happiness and love. She said nothing, but took the baby in her arms and pressed it to her bosom. It was a pretty picture of infancy and age. As she replaced the infant in its mother's arms, " How kind it was of you," she said, " to give her my name. I thought everybody had forgotten it."

Children are most easily impressed through the medium of their senses, and the presence of their baby-sister served to enforce the simple exhortation which followed from their father. He was particularly careful, in talking to his children on religious subjects, to avoid an artificial solemn tone. He spoke as if the subject were (as it was), cheerful, dear, and familiar to him.

On this occasion he first called the attention of his children to the physical powers which God bestows on man,—the marvellous contrivance of the eye,—the uses and blessings of all the senses, —the construction of the little hand they so fondly kissed, so impotent now, but formed to be so nice and wonderful an instrument. He made their hearts beat quicker as he showed them the benevolence and wisdom manifest in the arrangement of the little frame on which their curious eyes were fixed. He then endeavoured to enable them to form some conception of what was meant by man being made in the image of God,—of the sublime intellectual and moral faculties ; and when their faces beamed with a comprehension of the worth of the spirit, he spoke of the temptations and trials to which it must be exposed,—of the happiness or misery that awaited it. And the destiny of this precious little creature, they were told, was in some measure confided to them. They were to lead her by their good example, to shelter her from temptation, to feed her affections from their own loving hearts, so that this new member of their family might be one of the family of heaven.

He spoke to them of the tenderness of the Saviour in bidding little children to come to him ; and of the certainty, that if they loved him, and kept his commandments, they would be loved by him,—of all which this beneficent being had done to secure the lambs in the fold, and to bring back the wanderers. His simple eloquence made them realise that there was a glorious nature embodied in the little form before them, capable, if rightly developed and cherished, of becoming the disciple of Jesus, and child of God. Before he had wearied them, and while, as he saw by their moistened eyes and glowing cheeks, their hearts burned within them, he asked them to kneel with their parents and dedicate their little sister to their heavenly Father, and ask of Him, who was more ready to give than they to ask, grace to perform their duty to her.

When, a few hours after, the rite of baptism was administered in church, the children did not look upon it as an empty or incomprehensible form, but they understood its meaning and felt its value.

How easy it is to interweave the religious with the domestic affections, and how sadly do those sin against the lights of nature, who neglect to form this natural union !

CHAPTER VI.

SUNDAY AT MR. BARCLAY'S.

" The Sabbath was made for man, not man for the Sabbath."

WE hope not to bring down the charge of Sabbath-breaking on Mr. Barclay, if we venture to inform our readers, that his mode of passing Sunday differed, in some important particulars, from that which generally obtains in the religious world. His whole family, whatever the weather might be, attended public worship in the morning. He was anxious early to inspire his children with a love of going to the house of God, and with a deep reverence for public worship, which (with one of our best uninspired teachers) he believed to be " agreeable to our nature, sanctioned by universal practice, countenanced by revealed religion, and that its tendencies are favourable to the morals and manners of mankind."

Happily his pastor was beloved by his children, and Mr. Barclay therefore had none of the frivolous pretexts and evasions of duty to contend with, which are as often the fault of the shepherd as of the flock. Mr. Barclay loved to associate in the minds of his children the word and works of God, and after the morning service was closed, the father, or mother, or both, as their convenience served, accompanied the young troop to the Battery, the only place accessible to them where the works of God are not walled out by the works of man. There, looking out on the magnificent bay, and the islands and shores it embraces, they might feel the presence of the Deity in a temple not made with hands, they might see the fruits of his creative energy, and, with sea and land outspread before them, feel that

" When this orb of sea and land
    Was moulded by His forming hand,
    His smile a beam of heav'n imprest
    In beauty on its ample breast."

Mr. Barclay certainly would have preferred a more retired walk. On Sunday, more than any other day, he regretted the sequestered haunts of Greenbrook, where he might have interpreted the religious language of nature, without encountering observation or criticism. But he would not sacrifice the greater to the less, and he was willing to meet some curious eyes and perhaps uncharitable judgments, for the sake of cultivating in his children that deep and ineffaceable love of nature, which can only be implanted or rather cherished in childhood. He was careful in these Sunday walks to avoid the temptations to frivolity in the way of his children, and he never encouraged remarks upon the looks, dress, and gait of those they met.

Restricted as they were by their residence to a single walk where the view of nature was unobstructed, their topics were limited ; but children will bear repetition, if the teacher has a gift for varied and happy illustration. A walk on the Battery suggests many subjects to a thinking mind. A few of these would occur to a careless observer. The position of the city at the mouth of a noble navigable river,—a position held sacred by the orientals ; Long Island, with its inviting retreats for the citizen, and its ample garden-grounds seemingly designed by Providence to supply the wants of a great metropolis ; Governor's Island, with its fortifications and military establishment, —a picture to illustrate the great topic of peace and war, on which a child's mind cannot be too soon, nor too religiously enlightened ; the little Island where the malefactor suffers his doom, an object to impress a lesson of his country's penal code ; Staten Island with its hospitals and quarantine ground, to elicit important instruction concerning these benevolent institutions, and their abuses in ill-governed countries ; the telegraph, the light-house, and the ship, the most striking illustration of man's intelligence, industry, skill, and courage ; the lovely shaded walks of Hoboken, over which the sisters Health and Cheerfulness preside ; and, finally, the Narrows, the outlet to that path on the great deep, which the Almighty has formed to maintain the social relations and mutual dependence of his creatures.

There may be some who think that these are not strictly religious topics, not perfectly suited to the Lord's day. But perhaps a little reflection will convince them, that all subjects involving the great interests of mankind may be viewed in a religious light ; and if they could have listened to Mr. Barclay, as leaning over the Battery railing, he talked to the cluster of children about him, they would have perceived that the religious light, like the sun shining on the natural world, shows every subject in its true colours and most impressive aspect.

At half-past one, the Barclays returned invigorated and animated by the fresh sea-breezes to a cold dinner prepared without encroaching on the rest of Martha's Sabbath. The dinner was only distinguished from that of other days by being rather simpler and more prolonged, for they dedicated a part of this day, in the emphatic words of Jesus, "made for man," to social intercourse. That, to be happy, must be spontaneous and free.

"I wonder," said a lady, on one occasion, to Mrs. Barclay, "that you don't take your children to church Sunday afternoons. It is the best way of keeping them still."

Mrs. Barclay smiled ; and Mary answered, " I am sure you would not think so, Mrs. Hart, if you were to see Willie ;—he fidgets all the time."

"No,—no, Miss Mary," spoke up Willie, "mother says I sit very still when they sing ; but I do get tired with the preaching part,—I wish they would leave that out."

"So do I," said Mary ; " I own, when I go in the afternoon I cannot help going to sleep."

"Then you never sleep in the morning. Mary?"

"O no,—never."

"I thought you never went in the afternoon."

"Sometimes," said Mrs. Barclay, "when I am not well, I send her with the little ones, as I suppose other mothers do, to get them out of the way, and into a safe place. I am sorry ever to do this, for the heart is apt to be hardened by an habitual

inattention to solemn truths, by hearing without listening to them."

"You must have a pretty long, tiresome afternoon."

"Tiresome !" exclaimed Mary, "I guess you would not think so, if you were here, Mrs. Hart. Sunday afternoon is the pleasantest of all the week. Is not it, Willie ?"

"Yes, indeed, 'cause mother stays with us all the time."

"And reads to us," added Mary.

"And shows us pictures," said Willie ; "and lets Patrick and Biddy come and see them too."

"They are Bible pictures, Mrs. Hart, and so mother reads something in the Bible that explains them."

"And sometimes she tells us Bible stories," said Willie ; "and sometimes stories of real live children,—real,—not book children, you know."

"And sometimes," continued Mary, still eager to prove to Mrs. Hart, that the Sunday afternoons were not tiresome, "mother writes a little sermon on purpose for us, not a grown-up sermon. Then she teaches us a hymn ; then she teaches us to sing it ; and when she wants to read to herself, she sets us all down, Willie and Biddy, and all, with our slates to copy off some animal. I wish you could see Willie's,—his horses look like flying dragons."

"O Mary !" interrupted Willie ; "well, you know mother said your cow's legs were broken, and her horns ram's horns."

"This is a singular occupation for Sunday," said Mrs. Hart.

Mary perceived the implied censure. "O but, ma'am," she said, " you don't know what we do it for. After we have finished, mother tells us all about the animal, how its frame is contrived for its own happiness, how God has prepared its food, for you know the Bible says the young ravens cry unto him and he feedeth them ;—and then she explains what she calls the relations between man and animals, and Pat Phealan says mother makes him feel as if the dumb creatures were his first cousins, Pat is so droll. He says he never throws a stone at a dog now, and he can't bear to see the men so cruelly whip their horses, —' he won't, plase God he ever owns one ;' you know Pat is Irish. No, Mrs. Hart, you would not think it was wicked for us to draw pictures on Sunday, if you were to hear mother teach us about them, or to see our little books of natural history, where we write down what she says."

"Wicked, my dear ! I did not say it was wicked."

"No, ma'am,—but——"

"If I did think so," added Mrs. Hart, rightly interpreting Mary's hesitation to speak, "I think so no longer. I too am learning of your dear mother, Mary. I should like to know how the rest of your family pass the Sunday afternoon. May I question Mary, Mrs. Barclay ?"

"Certainly ; we make no secret of our mode of passing Sunday, though we do not wish to proclaim it. We do not expect to reform the world, even if we should be satisfied with the result of our experiment. To tell you the truth, Mrs. Hart, we have long thought it would be better to have but one religious service on Sunday,—that people satisfy their consciences by just sitting down within the four walls of a church, no matter how languid their attention, how cold their hearts, when they get there,—that much most precious time is thus wasted, the only time that the great mass of the working world have to consecrate to spiritual subjects and active charities. We think clergymen would preach better and their people hear *more* if there was but one sermon. These being our opinions, our duty is plain, and we therefore quietly follow the course conscience dictates to us, hoping to be kindly judged by those from whom we differ with all humility, and being well aware that those, who depart from the received usages of the religious world, should be diffident of themselves. Do not, I beseech you, think that we underrate or distrust the value of public worship. We reverence it as one of the most important and dearest of all social institutions, and we are therefore most anxious that its effect on our children's minds should not be impaired. Now if you are not tired out with my long preface, ask Mary what questions you please; if she cannot answer them I will."

"Thank you. Well, Mary, what do Charles, and Wallace, and Alice, Sunday afternoon?"

Mary bridled up with the conscious dignity of a witness giving testimony in a matter of high concernment. "Father says, ma'am, that as Sunday is the *Lord's day*, we ought to be faithful servants and spend it in his service; and he thinks that those who have more knowledge than others, should give it to them, just as the rich give their money to the poor. So we have a little school here Sunday afternoons, ten children, sometimes more, from father's families "—

"'Father's families!' what means the child?"

"The families father takes care of,—sees to, you know,—that is, he visits them, knows all about their affairs, advises the parents and instructs the children, and the parents too I guess sometimes, and now and then helps them, and so on."

"And sometimes he goes a sailing with them," interposed Willie.

"Sailing!" Mrs. Hart rolled up her eyes with irrepressible astonishment.

"Yes," said Mrs. Barclay in explanation, "he has, upon some occasions, done this. When he has found the parents exhausted by their labours, people that could not read, and thus refresh their minds at home, or, as is often the case, the children pining for fresh air, he has taken a little party of them down to Whitehall, and gone over with them to some quiet spot on Long Island; and while they have been regaling on the fresh, sweet air, he has found opportunity to speak a word in season to them. And a word goes a great way with them, from those that show an interest in their little pleasures, and share them, as if they really felt that these poor creatures, in their low condition, were their brethren and sisters, and children of the same Father. It makes a great difference whether you do them a kindness to discharge your conscience of a duty that presses on it, or from an affectionate interest in them."

"This is a new view of the subject to me," said Mrs. Hart, "but I'll think on't. Well Mary, how do the children manage the school! they are rather young for such a business."

"O, they don't do the managing part. Father and mother do that; and grandmama or Martha sits in the room to see that all goes on smooth. Aunt Betsey tried it, but"—

"My dear Mary!"

"Mother, I am sure Mrs. Hart knows Aunt Betsey. Two of the children," continued Mary, "teach, and one goes with father to see his families, and they take turns; and father and mother come in and talk to them."

Mrs. Barclay helped out Mary's account with some explanations: "Some of the children," she said, "are Catholics, and of course would not attend church in the afternoon. The Catholics are shy of sending their children to the public schools, but they have not manifested any reluctance to trust them to us, probably from our intimate knowledge of them at their homes, and from having realized some advantage from our instruction there; for we have done what we could to improve their domestic economy. *Home* influences, even among the poor and ignorant, are all in all for good and for evil, for weal and for woe. We have some tough subjects, as you may imagine; but patience; 'Patience and hope' is our motto. Besides, we really get attached to them; and love, you know, lightens all labour."

"Yes mother," said Mary; "that is just like what father read us out of Shakspeare last evening.

'I do it
With much more ease, for my good will is to it.'"

"The children," continued Mrs. Barclay, "are quite competent to hear the lessons of their classes. We spend our time in talking of whatever the occasion may suggest. Sometimes we elucidate or impress a passage of Scripture,—sometimes we strive to deepen and fix a sentiment. As most of their parents are Irish, they are quite ignorant of the history, government, and laws of their adopted country. Mr. Barclay endeavours to enlighten them on these subjects. He tries to make them feel their privileges and duties as American citizens, and to instruct them in the happy, exalted, and improving condition of man at the present time, and in our country, compared with what it has been heretofore, or is elsewhere. I take upon myself the more humble, womanly task of directing their domestic affections, and instructing them, as well as I am able, in their every-day, home duties. We wish to make them feel the immense power and worth of their faculties, and their responsibility to God for the proper use of them."

"Truly," said Mrs. Hart, "your time is spent quite as profitably as it would be at church; but do you not get excessively wearied?"

"The weariness soon passes off."

"And the compensation remains?"

"Yes, it does; I say it not boastfully, but with thankfulness to Him who liberally rewards the humblest labourer in his field."

"And then, Mrs. Hart, our Sunday evenings are so pleasant," said Mary; "do, mother, let me tell about them."

"Very well, my dear, but remember what I told you to-day about the Pharisees."

"O yes, ma'am, that there might be Pharisees now-a-days as well as in old times; but I am sure it is not Pharisaical to tell Mrs. Hart how happy we all are on Sunday evenings."

"I am sure it is not, Mary. Go on; what is the order of Sunday evening?"

"O ma'am, there is not any order at all,—that is, I mean, we don't go by rules. I should hate

c

that, for it would seem just like learning a lesson over, and over, and over again. We do just what we happen to fancy. Sometimes father reads to us, and sometimes mother, and sometimes we read ourselves. Sometimes we write off all that we can remember of the sermon, and sometimes we take a text and write a little sermon ourselves,—father, and mother, and all,—pretty short mine are. But the shortest of all was Willie's. You remember, mother, that which he asked you to write for him. What was it, Willie?"

" 'My peoples, if you are good, you'll go to heaven; and if you an't, you won't.' You need not laugh, Mary; father said it was a *very* good sermon."

"Go on, Mary. I want to know all about these Sunday evenings."

"Well, ma'am; sometimes we write down what we did last week, what we wish we had done and what we wish we had not, and what we mean to do next week. Sometimes we form a class,—father, mother, and all, and we ask questions, in turn, from the Bible, 'what such a king did?'—'when such a prophet lived?'—'where such a river runs?'—'where such a city stood?' and so on; trying most of all to puzzle father and mother, and get them to the foot of the class. Sometimes father makes us all draw our own characters, and then he draws them for us; and—O dear! Mrs. Hart, when we come to put them together, as Wallace said, ours looked crooked enough, and out of joint. Once father gave us for a lesson, to write all we could remember of the history of our Saviour. We were not to look in the Bible. We thought it would be very easy, but it took us three Sunday nights. But the pleasantest of all, you know what the pleasantest of all is, mother,—a story from father. O, I forgot about your lists, mother."

"You have remembered quite enough, my child."

"Enough," said Mrs. Hart, "to make me envy your pleasant Sunday evenings *at home*, and to inspire me with the desire, as far as I can, to go and do likewise."

CHAPTER VII.

A TRUE STORY.

"The ants are a people not strong,
Yet they prepare their meat in summer.

AMONG "father's families," as Mary had called those who were the particular subjects of her father's bounty and supervisorship, was one by the name of Phealan. John Phealan was a laborious, honest Irishman, who, having lost his wife and being left with the care of three children, had recourse to the usual consolation, and, in the space of two or three months, took unto himself another help-meet, the widow O'Neil, who had worn her decent weeds for the canonical term of a year and a day. "It was quite natural it should plase God to bring them together at last," John said; "though it was by the hard manes of taking Judy, —bless her soul,—to himself; for he and Rosy were born within a stone's throw, and saw the same sun rise and set for the first twenty years of their lives at home, in Ireland, whereas Judy was

a stranger till he took her to be the mother of his children."

"It was quite natural, John," replied Mr. Barclay to this speech, which was meant as a sort of apology to his friend for a step that he feared would not meet with Mr. Barclay's approbation; "quite natural, but our natural inclinations sometimes make us lose sight of prudence; and I am afraid the widow O'Neil's children and yours together will be more than one house will hold, as they say, John. The widow,—I beg your pardon, John;—your wife has two children of her own?"

"Two! bless your eyes, sir; yes, two and two to that, and a stray into the bargain."

"A stray! what do you mean by that?"

"I mane Biddy McClure, sir, the child of her poor mother that's gone to rest. Ellen, the mother, poor thing, died on Rosy's bed; so Rosy, with a full heart in her, as she has, could do no less than take on the baby with her own, though she was bid turn it over to the orphan asylum;—the Lord help poor Biddy! never to know a home or a mother."

"But where was her father?"

"She never had any to spake of, sir."

"I suppose now, John, you would be glad to get her into the orphan asylum."

"Plase the Lord, no, sir; it would be an ill turn to do Rosy, to cast away the chicken she's brooded under her own wing. Besides, sir, my mother that's gone,—peace to her soul!—always said there was a blessing to the roof that sheltered an orphan child."

Mr. Barclay thought there could scarcely fail to be a blessing upon a roof that hung over such generous hearts, and for once he was persuaded out of his prepossessions against this clubbing together of families, that so commonly issues in unhappiness. He could not, however, forbear saying, "I trust, John, you will have no additions to this family."

"We lave that with the Lord; if they come they'll find a welcome."

"A large family is a heavy burden to a poor man, John."

John scratched his head, and admitted what was undeniable, but with a mouthful of blessings on the country, he said, "No honest working man in it need go to bed to dream of hungry children."

Time went on, and in due succession two more children appeared, and found the welcome John Phealan had promised. Mr. Barclay took an especial interest in seeing how far virtuous exertions and naturally happy tempers could triumph over unfavourable circumstances. He kept his eye on the family. He found Phealan ready to be guided by his advice, and Phealan's wife docile to the instructions of Mrs. Barclay; always replying to them, "I'll do my *endeavours*, madam." And so faithfully did she do them, that, contrary to common experience, and in the teeth of political economy, this little confederation lived on prosperously and happily, like the famous family of natural haters, the dog, cat, rat, bird, snake, and squirrel, proving that there are no natural discordances or antipathies that may not be overcome by moral force. There were now and then some little clashings among the children, but they passed over as harmless as light summer showers.

But alas! a storm did come, that threatened utter desolation. Both Phealan and his wife were carried off by an epidemic, after a week's illness. What was to be done! Of the last marriage there were two children living, one five and the younger less than a year old. Little Biddy Mac Clure was not yet quite seven. A friend of the Phealans adopted the child of five years, but no one could be found to take the baby, and poor Biddy was too young for service. Mr. Barclay consulted with the elder children, and realised a rich harvest in the fruits of his instructions to them. They were all earning something, and were able to estimate their resources and make rational calculations for the future. They could pay their room-rent, and support the baby and Biddy; and if old Miss Jones, who had lost the use of her legs, and rented a dark little room in the garret, would live in their room rent-free, and just look a little after Biddy nursing the baby, while they were out at their places, they could keep together yet, and need not send the baby and Biddy,—a jewel was Biddy,—to any orphan asylum but their own. This plan, calling forth such virtuous exertions from these young creatures, was approved by the Barclays. Never a week passed that the Phealans were not visited by one of them, and such counsel or aid given as the exigencies of these little worthies required. The family was actually kept comfortably afloat for eighteen months. Then Miss Jones took it into her head to retire to a relation's in the country; but fortunately Mary Phealan, the oldest of the family, married respectably just at this juncture, having stipulated that if the family did break up, she should take the baby for her own. The family, Mr. Barclay said, must break up; but what should be done with Biddy! Biddy was a general favourite, and the children, after a consultation, agreed that they would pay her board until she was old enough to go to service. Mr. Barclay did not quite like this plan. He thought Biddy would be living in idleness for two or three years, and forming bad habits, or no habits at all, when the foundation should be laying for future usefulness.

It may perhaps stimulate some reader's benevolence to know, that while Mr. Barclay was paying this minute attention to the concerns of the little orphan family, he was the principal manager of one of the most important printing establishments in New York.

"What is to be done with Biddy!" he asked his wife; "the little stray, as poor Phealan used to call her, must be provided for."

"Yes, she must. I have been thinking a great deal of her, and if I could only get Martha to consent, we might take her ourselves."

"My dear wife! the very plan I thought of, but I could not bear to propose anything which should increase your cares."

"O, that's nothing: you know I do not mind light burdens."

"I know you make all burdens light ; and I wish that your children may learn from you, that it is the light heart that makes the burden light, and not *vice versa*, as most people think."

"Thank you ; that's a compliment worth having, and I will see if it will make me eloquent to Martha ; but I dread the view she may take of the subject.

Mrs. Barclay had some reason for this dread. Martha had too long had her own way,—an excellent way it was,—to brook any interference with it. She was orderly to precision, and she had always said, (what she once said poor Martha was much given to always say,) this would be a terrible annoyance to her. She had before stoutly and successfully opposed a benevolent plan of Mrs. Barclay's, similar to the present, Mrs. Barclay having thought it wisest to yield her own wishes to her faithful servant's. Servant! we beg Martha's pardon, *help*. Serving most assiduously, she had an antipathy to the word *servant*. Was she not right! There must be new terms to express new relations. *Help* may have a ludicrous and perhaps an alarming sound to unaccustomed ears ; but is there a word in the English language more descriptive of the service rendered by a New-England domestic! truly a "republican independent dependent," and the very best servant, (this we say on the highest foreign, ay, *English* authority,) provided we are willing to dispense with obsequiousness and servility, for the capability and virtue of a self-regulating and self-respecting agent.

The Barclays' religion governed all their relations. They did not regard their servant as a hireling, but as a member of their family, who, from her humble position in it, was entitled to their protection and care. Martha was their friend ; the family joys and sorrows were part and parcel with hers, hers with theirs. As her qualifications increased with her years, and her labours with the growth of the family, they had augmented her wages ; never taking advantage of her preference of their house to withhold a just (others might have called it a generous) consideration for her labours, and quieting their consciences by a resolution to recompense her at some convenient season,—that future indefinite, so convenient to the debtor, so hopeless to the creditor.

Mrs. Barclay was certainly a most successful grower of the virtues ; but with the best moral cultivation, human infirmity is a weedy soil, and poor Martha sometimes, wearied with the unvaried routine of domestic service, became, like others, unreasonable and fretful. She was not fretted at in turn, and wondered at, as servants are (as if they alone should be exempt from human weakness), but sent to recreate herself in her native New England ; whence she returned, strong and cheerful, to her tasks.

But we are leaving too long unsettled the interests of our little friend Biddy.

"Martha," said Mrs. Barclay, "the Phealans are breaking up at last."

"Are they indeed, ma'am! I am sorry for it ; they have been a sight to behold, that family. I never could look at them without feelings."

"Courage!" thought Mrs. Barclay ; "if Martha once has what she calls feelings, all will go right."

"Poor Biddy," she continued, "is looking puny ; she has been too much shut up with the baby.— She is a nice, bright child."

"Yes, she is indeed, ma'am."

"I wish, Martha, she could get a good place."

"I wish she could, ma'am, but she is not fit for service yet."

"No, not exactly ; I suppose hardly anybody would be willing to take the trouble of her for two or three years yet, while she is going to school."

"I suppose not, but they would be well paid for it afterwards,—such a very good child."

"That they would, Martha; but there are so few persons that are willing to take trouble now, for a possible reward hereafter."

"I know it; there's few, even of those that aim to do right, that are willing to pay the cost. You and Mr. Barclay"—Martha stopped; it was not in her line to pay direct compliments.

"Mr. Barclay and I, you think, perhaps, might be willing to stretch out a helping hand to poor Biddy: and so we should, and would, but the trouble, Martha, would come upon you."

"O, ma'am, in such a case,—for a poor little orphan like Biddy, and so good too, I should not mind the trouble."

"If you really would not, Martha, I should take her joyfully into the family. But you must consider well; you will have her constantly with you. You know you don't like a child under your feet. If she is brought up in the family, you will have to teach her; for you know I do not choose to keep any one to wait on the children. It will be a task, and a long one, Martha; but then, if you should decide to undertake it, you will have the consolation of doing a great service to a fellow-creature. Think of it, Martha, and decide for yourself."

Martha took time for consideration, and then little Biddy was installed, a most happy and grateful member of the family; and Martha, who had been generously allowed to be a free agent in the good work, bore all the little trials it brought, with patience, and trained Biddy with a zeal that enters only into voluntary action.

> "The poorest poor
> Long for some moments in a weary life,
> When they can know and feel that they have been
> *   *   *   the dealers out
> Of some small blessings,—have been kind to such
> As needed kindness."

CHAPTER VIII.

A DARK DAY.

"A foolish son is the calamity of his father."

THERE are seldom allotted to humanity fourteen years of such success and happiness as had been experienced by the Barclays. In this time, Mr. Barclay had secured a competency. His competency did not merit the well-known satirical definition of being a "little more than a man has," but was enough to satisfy his well regulated desires, to provide for the education of his children, and to save his daughters from the temptation of securing a home, in that most wretched of all modes, by marrying for it. It was no part of his plan to provide property for his sons. Good characters, good education, and a *start* in the world, was all they were to expect. This they perfectly understood. As soon as they were capable of comprehending them, they were made acquainted with their father's affairs, minutely informed of the condition of his property, and his plans for the future. Mr. Barclay despised that mean jealousy with which some parents hide their pecuniary affairs from their children,—some husbands from their wives even, as if they were not joint and equal proprietors in the concern.

He had now nearly reached the period when he meditated a great change in his life. From the beginning of his career in the city, he had looked forward with a yearning heart to the time when he might retire to Greenbrook. His children often visited their relatives there. It was their Jerusalem, to which the heart made all its pilgrimages. The old parsonage had recently come into market: Mr. Barclay had purchased it; and it was a fixed matter, that in the ensuing spring, as soon as the house could be repaired, the family should remove thither. In the mean time, this long-hoped for event was the constant theme of father, mother, and children. Improvements and occupations were planned by day, and at night Mr. Barclay's dreams were of that home of his childhood. Again he was wading and swimming in that prettiest of all streams that circled the meadows, slaking his thirst from the moss-grown bucket, and making cups and saucers for little Anne Hyde from the acorns under the great oak tree at the end of the lane.

Alas! disappointment comes to the most prudent, when least expected and often when least deserved.

It was just before Christmas, about the annual period when business is investigated and its results ascertained. Mr. Barclay had been shut up all the morning in his counting-room with his elder partner, Norton. Their accounts stood fairly, and showed a prosperous business and great increase of profits. The old man did not seem at all animated by this happy state of things. He was absent and thoughtful, and nothing roused him till Mr. Barclay said, "I do not believe you will ever regret taking my advice and putting Harry into the printing-office."

"Never, never," repeated Norton emphatically.

"I should not be surprised," continued Mr. Barclay, "if he were in the end richer than his brother, and I am sure he will not be less happy, nor less respectable."

A half-suppressed groan escaped Norton.

"You are not well, sir?"

"No, I am not well,—I have not been well for a long time,—I never expect to be again."

"O, sir, you are needlessly alarmed."

"No, no; I am not alarmed, — not alarmed about my health."

"You have worked too hard this morning. You will feel better for the fresh air, I will walk home with you."

The fresh air did not minister to the mind diseased. Norton's depression continued during the walk. He said little, and that little in broken sentences, in praise of his son Harry. "He is an honest boy, Barclay,—good principles,—good habits,—owes them all to you, — he'll be able to shift for himself, if ———— he's a good boy, Barclay."

When they reached Norton's fine residence in Hudson Square, his daughter Emily, a child of eleven or twelve, met them at the door, exclaiming, "O, papa, the men have hung the lamps, and brought the flowers, and the rooms look beautifully!"

In her eagerness she did not at first give any heed to Mr. Barclay's presence; but when she did, she nodded to him, stammered through the last half of her sentence, turned on her heel, and briskly ran through the entry and up-stairs. Norton was roused, his energy was excited by what he deemed a necessary exertion, and he begged Mr. Barclay to enter, saying he had a word to say to him in private. Mr. Barclay followed him into one of his two fine drawing-rooms : the folding-doors were open, and both were furnished in a style that becomes the houses of our wealthiest merchants. The apartments were obviously in preparation for a party. The servants were going to and fro with the most bustling and important air. Norton looked round with a melancholy gaze, and then asked Mr. Barclay to follow him to a small breakfasting-room. He shut the door, and, after a little moving of the chairs and hemming, he said, "We are to have a great party this evening, Barclay."

"So I perceive, sir."

"It is a party that John's wife gives for Emily."

"Indeed !"

"It an't my fault, Barclay, nor Harry's—Heaven knows ; nor can it be called Em's—poor child ! these foolish notions are put in her head ; but it is John's wife's fault,—and John's too, I must own, that your folks are not asked."

"My dear sir, do not give yourself a moment's uneasiness about it. It would be no kindness to my family to invite them ; they know none of Mrs. John Norton's friends, and these fine parties are not at all in our way."

"It is the better for you, it is all cursed folly, —I see it too late."

Mr. Barclay responded mentally and most heartily, "Amen," and was going away, when Norton laid his hand on his arm, saying, "Don't blame Harry ; he is good and true,—he is your own boy, you've made him all he is ; don't blame him."

"I assure you I blame no one, my good friend," said Mr. Barclay, and hurried home, thinking a great deal of Norton's dejection, but not again of the party, till, in the evening, Harry Norton joined his family circle as usual, and stayed till bed-time ; but was not, as usual, cheerful and sociable.

The elder Norton was an uneducated man. He spent all his early life in toiling in a lean business, and accumulating, in consequence of his very frugal house-keeping, his small gains. When Mr. Barclay threw his talent into the concern, it at once became thriving ; and when John Norton, whose education his ignorant father had been quite incapable of directing, was of a marriageable age, he was reputed the son of a rich man. Being ambitious of a fashionable currency, he succeeded in marrying a poor stylish girl, who immediately introduced her notions of high life into her father-in-law's house, and easily induced the weak old man to fall into her plan of setting up a genteel establishment, and living fashionably ; "weakly imitating" (as has been pithily said) "what is weakest abroad." Old Norton had but three children ; two by a second marriage. Harry was in firm hands, and easily managed, but poor little Emily was removed from all her old associates, sent to a French school, and fairly inducted into a genteel circle.

The party was over, and a beautiful Christmas morning followed. Mrs. Barclay was in her nursery and Mr. Barclay still in his room, where he had already received the greetings of his children as they passed down stairs : "A merry Christmas, father !" and "The next at Greenbrook, and O how merry it will be !"

Another and hurried tap at the door, and "May I come in, Sir ?"

"Yes, Harry, come in. Mercy on us ! what is the matter, my boy ?"

Harry Norton was pale and breathless ; he burst into tears, and almost choking, exclaimed, "John has killed himself !"

"Your brother !—John !—God forbid !"

"Indeed he has, sir, and that is not the worst of it."

"What can there be worse ?"

"O, Mr. Barclay !" replied the poor lad covering his burning cheeks with both hands, "I cannot bear to tell."

What Harry in a broken voice, and tears poured out like rain for the shame of another, told, was briefly as follows. John, without education for business and without any capital of his own, had engaged largely in mercantile concerns, and had plunged deeply into that species of gaming called *speculation*. His affairs took a disastrous turn, and after his credit was exhausted, his paper was accepted by virtue of the endorsement of Norton and Co., which he obtained from his weak father without the concurrence or knowledge of Mr. Barclay. A crisis came. The old man refused any farther assistance. John committed a fraud, and, when soon after he perceived that detection and ruin were inevitable, he resolved on self-murder. He spent an hour or two at his wife's Christmas-eve party, talked and laughed louder than any body else, drank immeasurably of champagne, and retired to the City Hotel to finish the tragedy by the last horrid act. Thus, poor wretch ! did he shrink from the eye of man, to rush into His presence, with whom the great account of an outraged nature and a mis-spent life was to be settled.

His family were roused from their beds to hear the horrible news. The old man's health had long been undermined in consequence of his anxiety about his son's affairs, and the reproaches of his conscience for the secret wrong he had done his partner. The shock was too much for him. It brought on nervous convulsions. At the first interval of reason he sent for Mr. Barclay. Mr. Barclay hastened to him with poor Harry, who looked more like the guilty, than like the innocent victim of the guilt of another.

Reflections swarmed in Mr. Barclay's mind, as he passed to the dying man's room through the luxurious apartments where pleasure, so called, had, through the demands of waste and extravagance, led to the fatal issue. Some of the lamps were still burning, or smoking in their sockets. He passed the open door of the supper-room. There still stood the relics of the feast*,—fragments of Périgord pies, drooping flowers, broken pyramids,

* The writer was told by a lady, that after a party at her house where one of these mammoth punch-bowls had been nearly emptied, she offered a glass of the beverage to a servant; "No, I thank you, madam," he replied, "I belong to the Temperance Society." What a satire !

and piles—literally piles — of empty champagne bottles; an enormous whiskey-punch bowl, drained to the last drop, stood in a niche in the entry. The door of Mrs. Norton's apartments was open, —she in hysterics on the sofa, her attendants running in and out, their minds divided between the curiosity ever awake on such occasions and the wants of the weak sufferer. When at last Mr. Barclay reached the old man's apartment in the third story, he found him bolstered up in his bed, breathing painfully. When he saw Mr. Barclay, followed by Harry, a slight shivering passed over his frame. He stretched out his arm and closed his eyes; Mr. Barclay took his hand. Norton felt that there was no longer time for delay or concealment. He attempted to speak, but his organs were now weaker than his mind. After several futile efforts, his quivering lips uttered the words, "I have—much to tell you,—John—I —John—O, I cannot!"

"You need not, sir; Harry has told me."

Norton turned his eager eye to his son. The blood, that seemed to be congealed at his heart, once more flushed to his cheek. "All, Harry!" he asked in a husky voice.

"Yes, sir; Mr. Barclay knows all that we know."

Norton's eye again explored Mr. Barclay's face. No reproach was there,—not even a struggling and repressed displeasure,—nothing but forgiveness and pity. The poor man understood it, and felt it to his heart's core. He was past tears, but the veins of his forehead swelled, his features were convulsed, and he said in a broken voice, "O how kind! but I can't forgive myself;—poor John!— he's past it! I'm going, and I can't—I can't even ask God to—forgive me."

"My dear friend! do not say so, — God is infinitely more merciful than any of his creatures. He pitieth us, even as a father pitieth his children."

These words seemed to the poor man's spirit like water to parched lips. He looked at his son, and then at his little daughter, Emily, who was kneeling behind the bed with her face buried in the bed-clothes, and he realized in the gushing tenderness of his own parental feelings the full worth of that benignant assurance, which has raised up so many desponding hearts. "Can you —will you pray for me?" he asked.

"Most certainly I will."

"But now I mean,—aloud, so that I can hear you."

Mr. Barclay knelt at the bedside. Harry threw himself down by his sister, and put his arm around her. Her moanings ceased while their friend, in a low, calm voice, uttered his petitions for their dying father. It was no time for disguise or false colouring of any sort. Mr. Norton had lived, as many live, believing in the Bible and professing faith in Christ, but making a very imperfect and insufficient application of the precepts of Christianity to his life. In the main, he was a moral, kind-hearted, and well-intentioned man; but, misled by a silly ambition and an overweening fondness for a favourite son, he had destroyed him, deprived his younger children of their rights, and defrauded his best friend.

Mr. Barclay, in the name of the dying man, expressed his contrition for the evil he had done, and suffered to be done :—for the barrenness of his life compared to the fruits it should have produced. He acknowledged the equity of that law which deprived him of the peace of the righteous in his death. And then, even with tears, he besought the compassion that faileth not, the mercy promised by Jesus Christ and manifested to many who had backslidden and sinned grievously, but who, like the prodigal son, had returned and been received with outstretched arms. In conclusion, he alluded to himself. He fervently thanked God, that when he had come from the home of his fathers, a stranger to a strange city, he had been received, befriended, and generously aided by his departing servant; and he finished with a supplication that he might be heartily disposed, and enabled, to return to the children the favours received from the father.

Silence prevailed long after he ceased to speak. Harry and Emily were locked in one another's arms. Mr. Norton continued in fervent prayer. His eyes were raised and his hands folded. His spirit was at the foot of the cross, seeking peace in the forgiveness and infinite compassion there most manifest. When the old man's mental prayer was finished, there was comparatively peace on his countenance; but the spirit that struggles back over those self-erected barriers that have separated it from God, cannot have,—must not expect, —the tranquillity, the celestial joy, that is manifested in the death of those who have been faithful to life.

Mr. Norton murmured his thoughts in half-formed sentences: "He is merciful; — 'Come unto me'—I am heavy laden.—Harry is very good!—O—O, how good you are to me.—Poor Emy,—she won't have to go to the alms-house,— will she!"

Mr. Barclay turned his eye to the poor child, and for the first time noticed her dress. She had been wearied out with the party of the previous evening, and had fallen asleep without undressing; and now her ornamented pink silk frock, her rich necklace and ear-rings, were a painful comment on her father's words. "Such a dress on a poor child who has no certain refuge but the alms-house!" thought Mr. Barclay. He felt the deepest pity for her, but he was too honest to authorise false hopes. "No," he said in reply to Mr. Norton, "Emily shall not go to the alms-house,—she shall not be a dependant on any charity, public or private, if she is true to herself. I will see that she is qualified to earn her own living."

"O, that is best, far best,—you'll see to her,— that's enough, and poor Harry too!"

"Harry already earns his living. I will be his guardian. Shall I, Harry!"

"You always have been, sir," replied Harry, grasping his hand.

"Yes, yes,—he has;—God reward him,—he, not I."

"O, father, I did not mean that,—indeed I did not."

"Truth don't hurt me now," said the old man; "it's truth." And so it was.

CHAPTER IX.

A HOME FOR THE HOMELESS.

O bright occasions of dispensing good,
How seldom used, how little understood!—COWPER.

THE scene of life, not long after this, closed on Mr. Norton, and he was respectfully committed to the grave by those who regarded him as more sinned against, than sinning. Perhaps he was viewed in a different light by Mr. Barclay, whose estimate of a parent's power and responsibilities was different form, and much higher than most men's.

Mr. Barclay found John Norton's concerns, on investigation, not quite so bad as he feared. After settling the business and cancelling the endorsements of "Norton and Co.," the property vested in his printing-presses and that in the farm at Greenbrook remained. The press was a means of future accumulation, and the farm a polar star where he might still rest the eye of hope. It certainly was a severe disappointment to have the accumulations of years of vigorous labour swept away from him by the profligacy of others,—to have his dearest plans thwarted at the moment of their accomplishment; but he bore the evil patiently, as became a Christian who was forearmed against the uncertainties of life. "We must now," he said at the conclusion of a long conversation on their affairs with his wife, "we must now show our children, what we have often told them, that it is not the circumstances of life that make our happiness or virtue, but the temper in which we meet them."

The children were made acquainted with the unfortunate turn in their affairs, and the necessity of the indefinite postponement of their removal to Greenbrook. This they all took to heart; but no event can make children long unhappy. Some ten days after old Mr. Norton's interment, the Barclays were assembled round a well-lighted table. Mrs. Barclay, with a large work-basket before her, was putting in that stitch in time which absorbs so large a portion of the life of the mother of half a dozen children. Charles and Wallace were seated on each side of her, drawing, acquiring at a leisure hour some knowledge of an art for which a man in almost every pursuit has some occasion. Alice was basting hems and ruling copy-books for the little girls' next day's work. Mary was dressing a doll for her youngest sister. Grandmama knitting in the corner, and aunt Betsey making a very pretty dress for her pet; and finally Mr. Barclay was reading aloud the Life of Franklin, and making now and then such remarks as would tend to impress its valuable instruction on his children. He was interrupted by an involuntary exclamation from Alice of "O dear me!"

"What is the matter, Alice?"

"Nothing, only I can never make these red lines straight in my arithmetic book. I wish Harry Norton was here, he does them so neatly."

"I wish he was here too," echoed Mary; "this doll's arm torments me so,—I cannot make it stay on."

"I was just thinking," said Wallace, "I would give any thing to have him come in, to show me how to stump this foreground."

"O, that's easy enough, Wallace," said Charles; "but I never can do these arches without his help; I wonder he does not come."

"He cannot come, Charles, and leave Emily alone."

"Why cannot Emily come too?"

"Dear me! I am sure nobody wants her," said Mary.

"And why not? I wonder."

"Because she is so hateful."

"Mary, my dear child!—that's a hard word for you. Come here, and tell me what makes poor Emily so hateful."

"Because, sir, she is."

"Mary, dear," said grandmama, "your Bible tells you not to bring a 'railing accusation.'".

Grandmama's gentle admonitions were seldom disregarded by the children. Mary looked crestfallen, when aunt Betsey came to her aid.

"Mary is quite right," she said; "Emily Norton is the most disagreeable little upstart that ever I came across."

"But how is she disagreeable? Come, Mary, let us know. I suspect there is some prejudice in the case. It is very important to poor little Emily that you should have no prejudices against her."

"I don't think they are prejudices," murmured Alice in an under voice.

"I know they are!" exclaimed Wallace.

"I think they are too," said Charles.

"O, yes, boys, you think, because Miss Emily has such beautiful hair and eyes, and so forth, that she must be good."

"No, Alice," replied Charles, "it is not that; but I cannot believe that Harry Norton's own sister can be such a horrid creature."

"Dear me, Charles! I did not say she was a horrid creature, but I do say she is as different from Harry as night from day."

"My dear Alice, you speak very confidently, considering how little you know of Emily."

"Ah, father, that is the very thing. Miss Emily don't choose to know us. The first day we went to Smith's drawing-school, Sarah Scott asked her if she knew us. She said she knew our names. Sarah said something about our looking ladylike: Miss Emily drew up her little scornful mouth,—you need not smile, father, for those were Sarah's very words,—and said we might look so, but we were not so, for 'sister said nobody visited mother'—only think what a falsehood, sir!—and she advised Sarah not to get acquainted with us, for she said 'sister did not want her to.' Now, sir, do you think it is all prejudice?"

"Not all, my dear; but if we examine the matter, we may find that a part of it is. In the first place, I suspect the scornful mouth was an addition of Sarah Scott's; that young lady has a very lively imagination; and a sweeter-tempered mouth than Emily's, one farther removed from an expression of scorn, I never saw."

"So it is, sir, commonly, but you don't know how girls can twist and spoil their mouths when there are no grown people by. Besides, if Sarah did add that about the mouth, and I own she is apt to add and alter when she tells a story, I am sure she did not make the rest; for whenever

Emily meets Mary and me in Broadway, her eyes are suddenly staring every way; whatever else she sees, she never sees us."

"And," added Mary, "she is always dressed just like a grown-up lady.—O! she does look too proud!"

Mr. Barclay waited a moment as if expecting something more, and then asked, "Is this all, my children?"

"All in particular, sir," replied Alice.

"I am sure it is quite enough!" said aunt Betsey.

"Alice," said her father, "sit down on my knee,—here is another for you, Mary. Now let us see if we cannot find some apology for Emily."

"She will not care whether we do or not."

"O! my children, poor Emily has too much reason to care for your good opinion now."

"Why, sir, now I don't she go and live with Mrs. John Norton?"

"No. Poor Emily has no home now."

"No home, father!"

The thought touched all their young kind hearts, and Emily was at once placed in a new aspect. Mr. Barclay took advantage of the favourable moment to proceed. "What do you suppose, Alice, Mrs. Norton meant by telling Emily that nobody visited your mother?"

"I suppose she meant what she said, sir."

"Not at all, my dear. She meant that none of her visiting acquaintance visited us.—Mrs. Norton calls all the people out of her circle nobody."

"What a silly woman!"

"Very silly, my dear; and I am sure if you reflect on it, you will very soon think with me, that Emily was more to be pitied than blamed for the notions she got from this woman, into whose hands she fell when she was so very young. Her father, you all know, was not the wisest man in the world. She had no mother. Harry was too young to guide her. Mrs. John Norton flattered her vanity, removed her entirely from her early associates, indulged her in every idle wish, and would have probably ruined the poor child, had it not pleased Providence to remove her from her influence. Mrs. Norton has gone back to her uncle's, to live again in idle dependence upon him, and has shown how little real affection she had for Emily; for she has given herself no concern as to what is to become of her, though she knows she has not a penny, nor a relation to take care of her."

The children looked sad and pitiful.

"She is young enough, I believe," continued Mr. Barclay, "to be admitted either into the orphan's asylum or the alms-house."

"Both very good places for her," said aunt Betsey.

"Aunt Betsey!" exclaimed Charles; "Emily Norton go to the alms-house!"

"Harry's sister go to the alms-house,—awful!" cried Alice. "Do, father, let her come and live with us."

"Alice, are you beside yourself?" asked aunt Betsey. "After your father has been all but ruined by old Norton, to think of his taking upon himself the support of Emily!"

Mr. Barclay went on, without directly answering either Alice or her aunt. "I have seen a great deal of little Emily since her father's death, and

do not believe it will be difficult to give her right notions. Poor child, her heart is melted, and takes any impression you please to put upon it. She is anything but proud now, Mary; and the fine clothes that offended you so much, are all gone."

"Gone, father?"

"Yes. I told her the greatest honour that children in their case could do to a father's memory, was as far as possible to pay his debts; and I told her what exertions and sacrifices Harry had made. She immediately went up stairs, and packed up all her finery,—her little trinkets, and every ornamental thing she had in the world, and begged me to have them sold to pay the chambermaid, who had complained bitterly of the loss of the wages due to her."

"Did she, father?" said Mary; "her watch, her gold chain, and her real enamel buckle?"

"Yes, my dear, those, and every article but her necessary clothes."

"I always thought," said Wallace, "that Emily had something noble in her."

"I felt sure of it," said Charles.

"Most persons, my dear boys, have something noble in them, if you but touch the right spring to set it in motion. I think poor little Emily has fine qualities, but her character will depend much on the circumstances in which she is placed, fo she is easily influenced."

"I like persons who are easily influenced," said Wallace, as if thinking aloud. This was true, and a common disposition enough it is, with those who are strong-willed, and who seem born, like our friend Wallace, to influence others.

"I called in on Harry and Emily, as I came home to tea," continued Mr. Barclay. "Their house is in complete order for the auction which is to take place to-morrow. Harry has worked like a beaver, and with the help of one man and one woman, and little Emily, who has done all she could, everything is ready."

"O dear!" said Alice, heaving a deep sigh, "how sadly they must feel."

"No, Alice, they do not, and they ought not. It is family love and happy domestic intercourse that attaches us to the inanimate objects of our home. This table around which we have so many pleasant gatherings, — the sofa, — grandmama's rocking-chair,—the baby's cradle, are all so many signs, which, as often as you look upon them, call forth delightful feelings. No books or maps will ever look to you like those we have read and studied together. But suppose our parlour emptied of all it now contains, and costly furniture put in it, such as would make us appear genteel in other people's eyes; suppose we never entered it but to receive morning calls, or evening company; our vanity might be gratified, but do you think the furniture would excite any sensations worthy of the name of happiness?"

"No, sir—no," was the general verdict.

"The case I have supposed is just that of Harry and Emily,—the family moved into a new house when John Norton was married,—all the old furniture was sent to auction, and new was bought, Harry has passed most of his evenings with us, and poor little Emily, when they had not company at home, has been left alone with her father, who did not know how to amuse or instruct her, or with the servants, who were very unfit companions, for Mrs. John Norton was never nice in the selection of her servants, and was continually changing them. This evening, I found Harry and Emily in the little breakfast-room. There was a light on the table, and a book from which Harry had been reading to his sister; but they had drawn near the fire. They were sitting on the same chair. Emily's arm was round his neck, and she was listening to what he was saying with such a tender, confiding look—"

"I wonder what he was saying, father," said Alice.

"Something of their separation, I believe, my dear."

"But why need they be separated, father!—why can't they both come and live with us!"

It had been a settled matter, from the moment of Mr. Norton's death, that Harry was to come into the family.

"Are you crazy, Alice!" asked aunt Betsey.

"I am sure I don't think Alice crazy at all," said Mary. "There are two beds in our room, and Haddy sleeps with Alice, and I should like of all things to have Emily sleep with me."

"And it is exceedingly important," said Wallace, as wise as Socrates on the occasion, "that Emily should live in a good place, because, father says, her character depends so much on circumstances."

"And where can she go, if she don't come here!" asked the tender-hearted Charles.

The children had arrived at the very point Mr. Barclay desired.

"Your right dispositions, my dear children," he said, "gratify me; but you must remember that it is on your mother that the burden of an increased family must chiefly fall. Consult her. If she is willing to extend the blessing of a home to both these orphan children, at the cost, as must needs be, of much labour and self-denial to herself, she will set us an example of disinterestedness and benevolence that we will try to follow."

The children now all clustered round their mother. To Mrs. Barclay, sound in health, serene in temper, and of most benignant disposition, no exertion for others seemed difficult; and with one of her sweetest smiles she said, that, as far as she was concerned, she should be most happy that Harry and Emily should not be separated. The children clapped their hands, and returned to their father, shouting, "It's all settled."

"Not quite so fast; there is something yet to be considered. You all know that we allow ourselves a fixed sum for our annual expenses. If we indulge in the luxury of doing this kindness to Emily, we must all give up something. You and Mary, Alice, must give up the dancing-school that has been running in your heads for the last six weeks, and Charles and Wallace cannot have a drawing-master."

This suggestion seemed for a moment to abate the zeal of the young folks; but Alice, who was always the first to clear away obstructions, said, after a little reflection, "O! well, never mind the dancing-school. I have thought of a nice plan,—Emily is Mr. Chanaud's best scholar,—she can give us lessons in the garret. It is a good place for dancing, and we shall not disturb grandmama there."

"And as to the drawing, sir," said Charles,

"with a little of Harry's help we can teach ourselves; and when we have such a good motive for it, we shall take twice as much pains as if we had a master."

"Well, my good children, we will all take it into consideration, and if we are of the same mind to-morrow night, Emily shall come to us with Harry."

This conversation had not, as may well be supposed, occurred without much consultation between Mr. and Mrs. Barclay. They thought they could not do a more certain good, than by extending the advantages of their home to the young Nortons. They hoped this might be an acceptable expression of their gratitude to Providence for their domestic blessings. They knew their children had some prepossessions against Emily, and Mr. Barclay had undertaken to turn the current of their feelings in her favour. In this he had so far succeeded, that her entrance into the family was a favour accorded to them; and thus, instead of coming among them an object of their prejudice and distrust, they henceforth considered themselves as Emily's champions and protectors. Each one was anxious to shelter her infirmities, to set her in a favourable light, and to make her new home as happy as possible.

When all the family had retired excepting Mrs. Barclay and her sister, aunt Betsey jerked round her chair, put her feet on the fender, and gave vent to her pent-up feelings. By the way, it should be said in aunt Betsey's favour, that fretting was her safety-valve; she thus let off her petty irritations, and in conduct she was not less humane than most persons.

"You are the oddest people," she began, "that ever I came across; with seven children, and the Lord knows how many more you may have, the old lady and myself, and only Martha for help, to undertake these two children that have no claim on earth upon you. Claim! the children of your greatest enemy, the man that has all but ruined you, and in such an underhand way too,—a pretty reward for knavery! I hope you mean to put up a sign, William Barclay & Co.'s orphan asylum, or alms-house!"

Mrs. Barclay was too much accustomed to her sister's railing to be disturbed by it.

"If it were more the practice, Betsey," she mildly replied, "for those who have homes to extend the blessing to those who have them not, there would be little occasion for orphan asylums, and the charity now done by the public, would be more effectively done in private families."

"I see no advantage whatever in turning private houses into alms-houses and such sort of places. I always thought home was a sacred place, from which it was a duty to shut out everything disagreeable and unpleasant."

Fortunately aunt Betsey's self-love prevented her perceiving how hard this rule would bear upon herself. Her brother-in-law had given her a home, simply because her temper was so uncomfortable, that no other member of her family was willing to receive her,—none other could have borne and forborne with her,—none other would have made allowances for the trials of her single and solitary condition, and, by always opposing a smooth surface to her sharp corners, have gradually worn them down.

"It is a duty, as you say, Betsey," replied her sister, "to exclude everything permanently disagreeable from the family; for home should resemble heaven in happiness as well as love. But we cannot exclude from our earthly homes the infirmities of humanity. There are few persons, no *young* persons, who, if they are treated wisely and tenderly will not be found to have more good than evil in them. In the Nortons, I am sure, the good greatly preponderates. Our children, we think, will be benefited by having new excitements to kindness, generosity, and forbearance."

"Well, if your children must have these excitements, as you call them, why under the sun, don't you find some folks to take in, besides the children of the man that's robbed you of all you've been toiling for and saving, for this dozen years and more?"

"O, Betsey, it does seem to me that, seeing, you see not. I don't mean to hurt you,—but how can you help feeling Mr. Barclay's nobleness, his truly Christian spirit in this matter! how he has returned good for evil, and overcome evil with good!" Aunt Betsey said nothing, and Mrs. Barclay proceeded: "Our children, I am sure, cannot but profit by such an example."

"But they don't need it. You are both of you always teaching them."

"'Example is better than precept,' Betsey."

"Well, let that rest. But I should like to know how you can afford to set such examples?"

"As to that, the way is clear enough. Harry's earnings will pay his board and all his other expenses. He will only be indebted to us, for what, he says, he esteems above all other things, home in our house."

"But little Miss Emily cannot be boarded, clothed, and schooled for nothing."

"Certainly not; but the expense of feeding a little girl in a family where there are three abundant meals a day is really trifling. The cost of Alice's clothes has never exceeded thirty dollars a year; Emily's will not cost more."

"No, to be sure. You will not have to buy new for her. She is so much more slender than Alice, that I can easily manage to make Alice's old frocks over for her."

"Thank you, Betsey; but I would rather Alice should take hers. A person in the situation Emily will hold, should never be degraded in the eyes of others, or her own, by any such sign of dependence or inferiority. That is a very poor kindness done to the body, which results in injury to the mind."

Aunt Betsey was reduced to biting her nails, and her sister proceeded. "Emily's schooling, it is true, will be expensive. Pity it is, that it is so, in a country where, of all others, good teaching should be cheap and easily attained; but it is not so, at least in this city. However, Mr. Barclay is quite willing to meet the expense, whatever it may be."

"Oh, I dare say,—'Education the best investment of capital,'—you know he is always harping on that; but when you have precious little to invest, it is worth while to consider.—That's all I have to say."

"We have *considered*, Betsey. Mr. Barclay, whose noble nature it is, as you know, to impart of his abundance to others,—freely to give what he so freely receives,—says that his business was never more productive than at this moment. We cannot therefore go on fretting over our losses. We shall continue to live frugally, and to educate our girls and Emily to earn their own living, should it be necessary. Harry's highest ambition for Emily is, that she should be qualified for a teacher. He will be a great assistance to her."

"That he will. He is not like other boys,—Harry is not."

"I shall endeavour," continued Mrs. Barclay, "in my domestic school, to qualify Emily for the offices of wife and mother. These in all human probability she will fill,—she may never be a teacher. You will help us, Betsey, and we will not give grudgingly. If her faults trouble us, let us remember how sadly the poor child has been neglected. All children, the best of them, require patience."

"Patience!—yes, the patience of Job."

"Emily may prove better and more agreeable than we expect, and we may be thankful to Providence for enabling us to take the homeless young creatures into the family."

Aunt Betsey was softened by being put in the light of a participator in the boon to Emily, and, as she took up her lamp, to go to bed, she said in a tone of real kindness—"I'll try to do my part."

Ah, if all the individuals of the human family would "*do their part,*" there would be no wanderers, no outcasts. The chain of mutual dependence would be preserved unbroken, strong, and bright. All would be linked together in the bonds of natural affection and Christian love,—the bonds of unity and peace.

CHAPTER X.

A PEEP INTO THE HIVE.

"How doth the little busy bee
Improve each shining hour,
And gather honey all the day
From every opening flower."—WATTS.

MANY persons who act from generous impulses are soon checked and disheartened in a course of benevolence, merely from not having judiciously surveyed the ground before them and estimated the necessary amount of efforts, that is, *counted the cost*. Those who are true disciples of that devoted friend of man, whose whole life was a succession of painful efforts and self sacrifice, will not become wearied with a duty because it demands labour and self-denial. The Barclays knew that two additional members of their family must bring them additional anxiety and toil; and when it came, they endured it cheerfully, yes, thankfully, as faithful servants, who are zealous to perform well an extra task for a kind master.

Emily Norton, daintily bred and petted from her infancy, had the habits, though not the vicious dispositions, that sometimes grow out of indulgence. Her pride and little vanities had taken but slight root in her heart, and they were swept away by the storm that passed over her father's house. But never was a little fine lady more thoroughly helpless and good for nothing than Emily, when she entered the Barclay family; but, once in that hive, where every little busy bee did its appointed task, where labour was rendered cheerful by participation, and light by regularity and order, she gradually worked into the ways of the household, and enjoyed, through the whole of her after-life, the happy results of well-directed effort. But this was not achieved without much watchfulness and patience on the part of her benefactress, much good-natured forbearance on the part of the children, and many a struggle and heart-ache on the part of the poor child.

Many a scene resembling the following, occurred after she entered the family.

"You have promised to be one of my children, dear Emily," said Mrs. Barclay, at the close of a long conversation with her; "I intend to treat you precisely as I do them." She then went through with the enumeration of various household offices which she expected Emily to perform, and concluded with saying, "The girls take care of their apartment week and week about. I hold any want of neatness and order in a young lady's room to be an abomination, and I never excuse it. This is Alice's week; the next Mary's; the week after will be yours. In the mean time, observe how they manage, and when it comes to your turn, you will have learned their way. Remember, dear, there is a right and a wrong way to do everything."

Emily was sure, that before her turn came, she should know how to take care of the room as well as the other girls; but Emily was yet to learn that "practice alone makes perfect." Her week came. Alice entered her mother's room, and shutting the door after her, and lowering her voice, "Do mother," she said, "let Mary go and do our room, and let Emily come and 'tend the baby;—it's the only thing she is fit for."

"She certainly does that better than either you or Mary. She gives her undivided attention to it, while you and Mary must always be doing something else."

"I know that, mother, but then——"

"Then what?"

"'Tending baby is a lazy sort of business that just suits Emily."

"She is not lazy about it; on the contrary she is indefatigable in trying to please Effie and Effie's mother."

"So she is, ma'am, I own; and so I wish you would keep her at it, and let us do what she can't do, and we like best."

"That would hardly be just to either Emily or you, as there is a great deal besides 'tending baby that a woman ought to know how to do, and 'tending baby every woman must know how to do."

"Well I suppose she must learn, but I don't know when, nor how. To tell the truth, mother, she is a real cry-baby. It is almost school-time, and she has not touched the beds yet. They are just as we left them, this morning,—the bed-clothes stripped off, the pillows on the window-sill airing, and she sitting down and crying. I cannot get one word out of her."

"Perhaps she cannot turn over the mattresses, Alice."

"Mother!—those light mattresses!"

"Light to you, my dear, but you must remember that Emily probably never made a bed in her life, and that which is light to you, is an Herculean task to her. Suppose, Alice, you were to go to

live in another family, and were required to do something you had never done."

"I should try, mother; I should not sit down and cry." And so she would have done; for Alice, though by some months younger than Emily, had been in the habit of using all her faculties of mind and body. She was a Hebe in health, and the very spirit of cheerfulness, so that no task looked formidable in her eyes.

"Alice," said her mother, "if you were to see a poor child whose hands had been tied up from her birth, who by gross mismanagement had been robbed of the energy of her mind, and half the health and strength natural to her, would not you be grieved for her, and take pains to restore her to the use of her faculties?"

"To be sure I should, mother."

"Then go back to Emily. Do not ask her what troubles her. She will be ashamed to tell you, but offer to help her turn over the mattresses and assist her in whatever else seems to come awkwardly to her. Help her bear her burden at first, and after a while she will be able to bear it all herself. Be delicate and gentle with her, dear. Above all, do not laugh at her. Don't come to me again. Settle the matter yourself. It is best I should not interfere."

From the moment Alice felt that the responsibility of getting Emily on, rested on herself, she felt at once eager for success; and, more good-natured than the god in the fable, she hurried back to put her shoulder to the wheel.

"Emily, dear," she said kindly, "I don't think you feel very well this morning."

"Yes, I do, Alice, perfectly well," replied Emily in a voice that sounded as if it came from the tombs.

"Well, come then, Emily, you had better make haste,—it is past eight,—come, jump up,—I will give you a lift. These mattresses are too heavy for you, till you can get used to them, and then they will seem as light as a feather;" and, suiting the action to the word, she threw over the mattresses, while Emily crept languidly to the other side of the bed.

"Now let's beat it up, Emily, and then we will have the clothes on in an instant. There, smooth that sheet down, dear. Mother makes us as particular as old women about making up the beds,— lay the pillow straight, Emy,—plummet and line you know,—now, hem over the sheet this fashion, —there it is done! and I defy a Shaker to make a bed better."

Emily was inspired by Alice's cheerful kindness, and when they went to the other bed, she begged Alice to let her try to do it alone. She tried, as if she had a mountain to move, but all in vain. Alice looked the other way to hide her smiles.

"I can't possibly do it!" said Emily despairingly.

"Poor thing!" thought Alice, "her hands, as mother says, have indeed been tied; but we'll contrive to loosen them." "Take hold here, Emily," she said, "not with just the little tips of your fingers, but so,—with your whole hand,— there it goes!—O, you'll soon learn."

"Do you really think I ever shall, Alice?"

"Ever! Yes, indeed, very soon. I will show you a little every day, and you will edge on by degrees. The world was not made in a day, you know, as aunt Betsey says."

"But the sweeping, Alice! Do not, pray, tell anybody, but I never swept a room in my life."

A girl of her own age, who did not know how to sweep a room, seemed to Alice an object of equal wonder and commiseration. She, however, suppressed the exclamation that rose to her lips, and merely said, "Well, that is not your fault, Emily; take the broom and I will show you."

Emily took it. "O not so, Emily,—no, not so; just see me." Again Emily began, and looked so anxious and worked so desperately hard, that Alice could scarcely forbear laughing outright. She did, however, and very kindly and patiently continued to instruct Emily, till the mighty task was finished.

"O, you will learn after a while," she said as poor Emily set down the broom and sunk into a chair, out of breath and looking at her reddened palms. "I will teach you to sweep, and you shall teach me to dance, Emily."

"O, you are very, very kind, Alice. I am sure I think it is worth a great deal more to know how to sweep, than how to dance."

"And so do I," said Alice ; "and yet we take a great deal of pains for the one, and the other we learn, we don't know how."

Alice spoke truly. We learn *we don't know how* the arts of domestic life,—the manual of a woman's household duties.

Some among Mrs. Barclay's friends wondered she did not "get more out of Martha," and they never could exhaust their astonishment at what they called her *inconsistency* (a very convenient indefinite word) in giving her girls accomplishments, strictly so called, and putting them to the humblest domestic employments. The Barclays neither saw, nor had they ever occasion to feel, this incompatibility. They believed that there was no way so certain of giving their boys habits of order, regularity, and neatness, and of inspiring them with a grateful consideration for that sex whose lot it is to be the domestic ministers of boy and man, as the being early accustomed to receive household services from their mother and sisters, —from those they respected and loved. They believed too, that their girls, destined to play the parts of wives and mothers, in a country where it is difficult and sometimes impossible to obtain servants, would be made most independent and consequently most happy, by having their *getting along* faculties developed by use. These little operatives, by light labours which encroached neither upon their hours of study nor social pleasure, became industrious, efficient, and orderly, and were trained to be the dispensers of comfort in that true and best sphere of woman, *home*. Equal, too, would they be to either fortune ; if mistresses, capable, just and considerate towards those who served them ; and if, perchance, obliged to perform their own domestic labour, their practical acquaintance with the process would make it light and cheerful.

Never, we believe, was there a pleasanter domestic scene than the home of the Barclays ;— Martha, the queen bee, in her kitchen, as clean as any parlour, or as (to use the superlative degree of comparison) the kitchen of the pale, joyless Shakers ; her little handmaids in her school of mutual aid and instruction, with their sleeves rolled up from their fat, fair arms, their curls tucked under their caps, and their gingham aprons, learning the mysteries of cake and pastry manufacture, pickling, preserving, and other coarser arts ; while another little maiden, her eyes sparkling and her cheeks flushed with exercise, might be heard plying her broom "up stairs and down stairs and in the lady's chamber," and warbling songs that might soothe the savage breast, for they breathed the very soul of health and cheerfulness.

Nor were they in the least disqualified by these household duties for more refined employments ; and when they assembled in the evening, with their pretty work-boxes and fancy-work, their books and drawing, they formed a group to grace any drawing-room in the land.

Their labours and their pleasures were transitory, but the vivifying spirit of love and intelligence that informed them was abiding, and was carrying them on to higher and higher stages of improvement, and preparing them for that period to which their efforts and hopes pointed, when the terrestrial shall put on the celestial.

CHAPTER XI.

GOING HOME TO GREENBROOK.

"And yet, ere I descend to the grave,
May I a small house and large garden have,
And a few friends and many books, both true,
Both wise, and both delightful too."—COWLEY.

THE race, we well know, is not always to the swift, nor the battle always to the strong ; and the Barclays, like others, were sometimes thwarted in their plans and disappointed in their expectations. There were early indications in their eldest son of a fragile constitution, attended by the consequent preference of mental to corporeal labour. He had a fondness almost amounting to a passion for books, and his father, who sympathised in his tastes, and did not at first perceive the alarming influence of their gratification on his health, encouraged them. "Charles's destiny is certainly for one of the learned professions," he thought, and accordingly he stimulated him in the pursuits that would qualify him for them. But when, from thirteen to fifteen, he found that he was losing the little vigour he possessed, instead of gaining any,—that his eye was getting the sunken, and his cheek the pale and hollow appearance, that is so generally the effect of sedentary life in our country, (why, the physiologist must explain,)—he resolved to change his pursuits ; and he persuaded Charles (Charles was the most persuadable of mortals) to abandon his books and go and work on the farm at Greenbrook. "I had rather, my dear boy," he said, "see you a common healthful labourer in the country, than such a miserable dyspeptic as half our lawyers, doctors, and ministers ; when life is a burden to the possessor, it is not apt to be very profitable to anybody else."

So Charles henceforth passed nine months of every year with the skilful cultivator to whom Mr. Barclay rented his farm. At first this seemed very much like exile to the poor fellow ; but his character was too flexible and too well regulated, not to adapt itself to circumstances, and, instead of repining over defeated hopes, he set himself to work to see and increase the good of his new occupations. He found there was no occasion for his intellect to sleep on a farm, but that mother Earth had studies enough in her laboratory to employ all the faculties of her children; that there was a world of knowledge for the curious student of nature in the difference of soils, in the effect of temperatures, the nature of plants, the composition and application of manures, and the habitudes of animals. He felt an interest that never abated, in the improvement of the farm, and in beautifying it for the residence of the family. It was certainly to be their home at some future day; and in the meantime the mother and children came there to pass three months of every year, and always found some new charm, some new manifestation of Charles's taste, and affection for his family. The slope between the house and the river, with its natural terraces, was spread out to the morning sun, and Charles thought it was treason against nature not to improve it according to her suggestion. So the green turf gave place to a well spaded garden, where from year to year were planted shrubs, vines, and fruit trees. The strawberry beds were doubled, because strawberries were "mother's favourite fruit." Unwearied pains were taken to bring on the green-gages for father. A woody, *scrawny* lilac was permitted to remain, because grandmama had said, " It looked so natural that she loved to see it." But above all, an especial blessing seemed to fall on Emily's favourite plants and flowers; whatever she liked sprung up like the roses under the feet of the fairy's favourite, and grew and luxuriated as if the sunbeams and the dews of heaven were given to favouritism. The garden was overrun with violets of every species, and honeysuckles and white roses grew like weeds about the old porch, mounted over and even peeped into Emily's window, and ran round the pretty well-curb which Charles built over the old well, where " the old oaken bucket, the moss-covered bucket," of his grandfather's time, newly hooped, still swung. There is a magic that can direct and double the secret powers of nature; and Emily Norton, bright, sweet-tempered, and lovely, might call this magic into operation. The three summer months she passed at Greenbrook; the three winter months Charles was in New York; thus their intercourse was scarcely interrupted, and, for aught any one observed, it retained, from year to year, its frank, confiding, and fraternal character.

But Charles did not limit his interest to the family in New York. He was a prodigious favourite with the inhabitants of Greenbrook. The old people liked his " serious turn," and prophesied that he would make his grandfather's (the minister's) place good. The contemporaries of his parents pronounced him, some of them, " just like his father," and others " just like his mother," " but not quite equal to either." Every social pleasure was imperfect to the young, if Charles was not with them ; and even the poor labourers, black and white, said their work seemed light when Charles worked with them. Does the question of the transmission of the virtues belong to physiology, or to philosophy and religion !

We have now come to an important era in the history of the Barclays. Eight years, busy, fruit-ful years, have glided away,—their fortunes are repaired,—a partnership in the printing establishment is formed between Harry Norton and Wallace, and the family are now actually realising their long-cherished hopes, and removing to Greenbrook. The old parsonage, which had been built when there was a " glut " of timber and a scarcity of everything else, had still a firm foundation and sound rafters, and by dint of knocking away the old porch (without detriment, be it observed, to Emily's favourites), making a little addition here, and a little alteration there, it looked like a most comfortable dwelling to the passing stranger, and to Mr. Barclay, like an old friend in new apparel.

The Americans are sometimes reproached with being deficient in that love for the home of childhood, which is so general a feature of the human race, that it was supposed to be universal, till an exception was made to our discredit. If this be so, (we believe it is not, at least in New England, for which alone we can answer,) it should be remembered, in palliation of the unnatural sin, that our homes are comparatively recent, not consecrated by the memories of centuries, and that the Yankee boy, from the earliest period of forecast, dreams of seeking his fortune in the richer soil and kinder climate which his far-spread country provides for him. He goes, but his heart lingers at the *homestead*. Many a yeoman who has felled the trees of the western forest have we heard confess, that through weary months he pined with that bitterest of all maladies, home-sickness ; and that even after years had passed, no day went by that his thoughts did not return to his father's house, nor night that did not restore him to *the old place*. And when age and hardship have furrowed his cheek, and greyed and thinned his hair, and bent his sturdy frame, he may be seen travelling hundreds and hundreds of miles to revisit " *the old place*,"—to linger about the haunts of his childhood, and live over, for a few brief days, the sunny hours of youth. Then (as we have heard him) he says, " I have a richer farm at the West, than any in New England,—it is a wonderful *growing* country,—my house is bigger than Colonel R——'s or Doctor P——'s," (the palaces of his native village,) " but dear me ! it has not the look of *the old place*."

And if it be true that our hearts are dead to this love of " our own, our native land," why is it that so many, with the fire of enterprise burning in their young bosoms, and the *West* with mines of gold in its unbroken soil alluring them, still linger about *the old place*,—still patiently plough our stony hills, and subdue our cold morasses ! No ! God has not denied, to any of his creatures, from the time that the exiles of Judea hung their harps on the willows of a strange land, to the present moment, that strong love of birth-place which tempers, to the native, the fierce winds of the north, and the fiercer heats of the Equator,—which equalises every soil, and gives that inimitable, that " pleasant look " to *the old place*.

A few evenings after the family were quietly established at the old place, in a soft, fragrant June evening, they assembled on the piazza, just as the moon was rising above the hazy line of mountain that bounded the eastern horizon, and sending a flood of softened radiance through the valley. " O," exclaimed Effie, " how much bigger the moon looks, than it does in New York ! "

" That's because——" said William, eager to impart a little science which he had just acquired.

" Pshaw, Willie ! I don't always want to know the cause ; everything here is bigger, and brighter, and pleasanter, and sweeter than in New York, because it is, and that is enough."

William appealed to his father, whether it were not best always to find out the reason of the thing.

" Certainly, my dear boy, if you can ; unless like Effie, and Effie's father at this moment, you are so brimful of satisfaction that nothing can add to it."

" And do you think, sir," asked Harry Norton, who was sitting with Alice at one end of the piazza, under a closely-woven honeysuckle, " do you think you shall continue satisfied with your present tranquil enjoyments ! Will you not miss the occupation of the office ? "

" No, I shall substitute the occupations of my garden and farm, which are far more agreeable to me."

" But will you not miss the excitements of the city ? "

" I think not, Harry. The excitements of the country are underrated. Here nature is the kind and healthful minister to the keen appetite for sensation. The changes of the seasons, the rising and setting of the sun, droughts and floods, a good crop, a blight,—frosts and showers, are all excitements. In the country, the tie of human brotherhood is felt through the circle, the social electric chain is bound so closely that the vibration of every touch is felt. We not only sympathise with the great joys and sorrows of our neighbours, but in all the little circumstances that make up life. The whole village was alive this afternoon with the running away of Allen's horse ; and when they heard that the widow Ray's boy, Sam, had been thrown from the cart and injured, what sympathy was manifested ! what running to and from the windows ! what profferings of aid, advice, and consolation ! The wreck of an omnibus in Broadway would not have caused half so much commotion. The children were as much excited by their berrying frolic yesterday, as they would have been by a visit to Scudder's museum ; and they are as eager to see Deacon Bennett's twin lambs, as they would be to see a Chinese, or a mysterious or invisible lady."

" O, I do not doubt, sir, that children may find excitement anywhere ; but I speak of yourself and Mrs. Barclay."

" Ah, Harry, it is a sad mistake that some people, even at our time of life, make, to depend on *events* for excitement. How can we want for excitement in our brief lives, while there is so much knowledge to be gained and so much good to be done ? We have not here the abject poverty and brutish ignorance that exist among the foreigners in the city, but ' the poor we have always with us ;' the poor whose condition may be raised ; the sick whose sufferings may be alleviated ; the ignorant, who may be instructed ; the idle and vicious, who may be reclaimed. The *excitement* must be within ourselves, in a respect for our species, in a deep inexhaustible love for them."

" I ought to have known better," said Harry, " than to ask such an idle question, after living with you eight years. I see but one deficiency here ; you will miss the society of town."

" No, Harry, I think not. I confess that, in this matter of society, I have been somewhat disappointed. There has not been so rapid an improvement as I expected ; but we must have patience. It takes time to change the forms of society ; to give a new direction to a current that has been wearing into its channel for centuries. Distinctions in our city are favoured by great disparities of fortune, and cherished perhaps equally by the pride, arrogance, and little vanities of the exclusives, and the servile imitations, the eager striving, the want of real independence and self-respect in the second class. You know, Harry, that I have no fanciful expectations of a perfect equality, a dead level ; this can only exist among such savages as the Hottentots. But I believe the time will come,—not in my day, perhaps not in yours,—but it will come, as soon as the social spirit of the Christian religion is understood, when society will only be an extension of the intercourse of home, when we shall meet together for intellectual intercourse, for the generous exchange of knowledge and of all the charities of social life. Then the just and full influence of mind and heart will be felt on society, and then our religious emotions and affections will no longer be kept for the closet and the church. But to realise those social benefits which our religion has yet in store for us, we must first realise that we have a common nature and destiny.—I have made an harangue, instead of giving a plain answer to your question, whether I should not miss the society of town. You know that what is called society there, was inaccessible to me. While I was an actual printer with a moderate fortune, I was without the barriers. The mechanics in the city are unfortunately too much absorbed in their occupations to care for the pleasures of society, or to prepare their children for it. We had, you know, a few valuable friends with whom we lived on terms of intimacy ; but our intercourse was very limited, and we did not escape the reproach of being unsocial. Now, in Greenbrook, society,—you smile, Harry, but I do not mean society in the conventional sense,— approaches my standard. The intrinsic claims of each individual are known and admitted. Whether a man be lawyer, farmer, or mechanic, matters not, if he be intelligent and respectable. Mr. Barlow, one of the most eminent lawyers in the state, does not esteem my family one grade below his, and I esteem no man's below mine provided—"

" Ah, there is a *provided* then, sir ?"

" Stop, my dear fellow, hear me out,—provided my neighbour is a man of good morals, that he has knowledge and is willing to impart it, or, being ignorant, that he wishes to be enlightened ; and provided he does not offend against the usages of civilized society ?"

" But is there not a barrier in what you call the usages of civilized society, that will be effectual against some of your rough neighbours ?"

" I think not. They lack some refinements and graces, but these are not essential ; and if they never learn, their children will be very apt to do so, from a good example among their contemporaries. City families that remove into the country, so far from endeavouring to benefit their country neighbours by communicating any real refinements, alarm their pride by artificial manners, and by keeping up the modes of town life. We shall not be apt to do this. Mrs. Barclay arranges our domestic matters with such plainness and simplicity, that there is nothing appalling to our country neighbours ; and as to my girls, if they should give themselves any city airs, I will *dump* them in Greenwich Street again ; and let Miss Alice show off her *style* in the establishment offered by her rich lover."

"Father !—pray—"

"I beg your pardon, my dear girl. I thought Harry knew before this time to whom and to what you had preferred him."

"He knows," replied Alice, blushing, "that I prefer him to all the world."

"That is quite enough, Alice, and you shall tell or not tell particulars, as you like. But come, Harry, adjourn your whisperings to Alice, and hear me out. You know I have a notion, that, wherever we are placed in life, there we have a mission. I do not mean to assume the invidious character of a reformer in Greenbrook. No, but I mean to be a fellow-worker with my good friends and neighbours here. Many things they know better than I ; I some, better than they. All society should be a school of mutual instruction, and in this school much is effected by the silent and gentle force of example. I hope to do something in this way towards elevating the pursuits of my Greenbrook friends. We may perhaps teach them that more than they have thought of may be done in a well-regulated home."

"Yes, sir, and they might imitate you, if there were more Mr. and Mrs. Barclays in the world."

"Ah, Harry, it is not the superior capacity that accomplishes most, but setting out with a firm purpose to attain a certain object. Your mother, Alice, began life with a determination to make a happy home. As she is not present, I may say of her what she would not permit me to say, if she were here."

"O let me speak of her, sir," interrupted Harry Norton.

"Let me speak of her," said the modest Emily.

"O, I guess we all love to speak of mother, if speaking means praising," cried little Effie.

Grandmama's tremulous voice hushed all others. "'Her children arise up and call her blessed,'" she said ; "'her husband also, and he praiseth her.'"

"Yes, ma'am," said Harry ; "that and every other verse in Scripture that describes a virtuous woman, might be applied to her ; and those who have not the natural rights of children might rise up too and call her blessed,—those on whom she has bestowed a mother's care and tenderness. And what, that woman should do, has she left undone ! How faithfully she has performed all the duties of her lot ; how generously undertaken those that were not imposed on her. What sense she has manifested, what beautiful order and neatness in her domestic economy, and in a higher moral economy, how she excels all others. How she sees and foresees, and provides against all wants, avoids irritations and jealousies, economizes happiness, saving those little odds and ends that others waste. How she employs the faculties of

all, brings the virtue of each into operation, and if she cannot cure, shelters faults. She shows each in the best light, and is herself the light that shines on all,—the sun of her *home*."

"Do not flatter, Harry," said Mr. Barclay, in a voice, however, which proved that he felt this was no flattery.

"O, Mr. Barclay," said Emily, "we must sometimes speak out our hearts, or they would burst ?"

"It is testimony, not flattery," added Harry.

CHAPTER XII.

CROSS PURPOSES.

"The worst fault you have is to be in love."

A LETTER was one morning brought to Mrs. Barclay, while she was sitting amidst her family. She read it twice over, and then without speaking laid it on the table. "No bad news, I hope, mother !" said Alice inquiringly.

"It ought to be good news, Alice, and yet I am afraid we shall all feel as if it were very bad."

Mrs. Barclay took up the letter, and read it aloud. It proved to be an application from a Carolinian lady, to whom Emily had been recommended as a governess. There were three young children to be instructed, and very generous terms were offered. Mrs. Barclay made no comments.

"I am sure I ought to be very glad and thankful," said Emily, in a voice that indicated how far *I ought* was from *I am*.

"Glad and thankful," echoed Alice, "for an opportunity to leave us, just as we have all come to be so happy here ! No indeed, Emily, you shall not leave us now."

"Now nor ever," thought Wallace, "if I can prevent it." He looked eagerly towards his mother in the hope she would put in a discouraging word ; but she did not speak, and he ventured to say, "It is very little in the lady's favour, that she asks Emily to go to the South at this season."

"That is quite conclusive against the project, mother," said Charles.

"Neither you nor Charles, Wallace," replied their mother, "seems to have noticed that the lady states her residence to be a very healthy one, on a plantation."

The young men had received but one impression from the letter. The word plantation struck on Effie's ear ; "What, mother," she exclaimed, "let Emily go and live where there are slaves ! O no, that we will all vote against, won't you, Alice ! and you ! and you !" she continued, addressing each person in the room.

The vote was unanimous till she came to her mother, who said, "I am afraid we should always find some good reason against Emily's leaving us."

"And why need she ever leave us, mother ! Why not stay and teach us !"

"I have already taught you, dear Effie, all I know."

"Ah but, now we are at Greenbrook, you can have a new scholar."

"Who—Effie !" asked Emily, little aware of the toils into which she was falling.

"Charles."

"And what in the world can I teach Charles !"

"What you have taught all the rest of us,—

what you teach best,—and without seeming to try, too."

"And what can that be, Effie?"

The little girl threw her arms round Emily's neck, and looking fondly in her face, replied, "To love you."

Wallace was standing by the window, apparently absorbed in playing with a pet squirrel which Charles had tamed for Emily. His eye involuntarily turned towards her, and encountered hers. A blush suffused her cheek. Wallace flung the squirrel from him. "Did Bob bite you?" asked Effie, observing the sudden change of her brother's countenance.

"Yes,—no, no," he replied, and hurried out of the room in no very tranquil frame of mind. He went he knew not where, and did he knew not what, till Alice ran down the steps of the piazza, exclaiming, "Wallace! Wallace! don't break off those carnations; don't you see how nicely Emily has shaded them from the sun to preserve them as long as possible? O what a pity you have broken this off! Charles has taken such pains to have it as fine as possible for Emily."

"For *Emily*?"

There was a world of meaning in this concise inquiry, but Alice did not comprehend it. "Yes, for Emily. What is there strange in that? Emily is very fond of carnations."

The impetuosity which had appeared in outbreakings of temper in Wallace's childhood, was now manifest in decision, energy, and ardent affections. Natural qualities may be modified by moral education, not extirpated;—the stream will flow, its course may be directed. "Come with me down this walk, Alice," said her brother; "I have something to ask you, and you must answer me frankly." His voice became tremulous, but he proceeded; "Alice, you girls have a way of finding out one another's feelings:—I do not ask you to betray confidence, but you may have observed something,—there may have been some accidental betrayal,—tell me at once, Alice."

"Tell me what, Wallace?"

"You certainly understand me."

"Indeed I do not."

"Then in plain English, do you think Emily—" he stammered, but in plain English it must be spoken, and he proceeded, "has any partiality for Charles."

"Wallace!" exclaimed Alice, on whom the truth now for the first time glimmered.

"Answer me truly, my dear sister; all I want is, to know the truth."

"Why,—it is difficult to judge of Emy; she has a way of always laughing about such matters. She is not in the least sentimental, you know."

"Not foolishly sentimental, but she has strong feelings."

"Very strong."

"Then if she has a preference, I am sure she must at some time have betrayed it."

"Not of course, Wallace. I am sure your feelings are strong enough, and yet I never suspected—"

"There were reasons for that; but girls are always confidential.—Come, Alice, do put me out of misery."

"If I could, Wallace."

"Then you think she loves Charles?"

"Yes, I think she cares more for him than for any one else."

"I don't believe it!" The exclamation was involuntary. Wallace was ashamed; he tried to keep down his rising heart. "I beg your pardon, Alice," he said; "but—I may have been dreaming; what indications have you observed?"

"When we are together, she talks ten times as much of Charles, as of you."—"That is no proof," thought Wallace.—"When he was at Greenbrook and we in town," continued Alice, "we agreed to write to him alternately; her letter was always ready in time, filled and crossed, and often she wrote in my turn. Charles used to say it was like being at home to get one of her letters. To be sure there was nothing particular in them; they were such as a sister might write."

Wallace thought over the only two letters he had ever received from Emily. Snatches of letters they were, rambling and indefinite; but he thought they were not such as a sister would write, and he felt a painful sort of triumph in thinking they were not. "A little circumstance occurred not long ago," continued Alice, "that, as I thought, let me into the real state of Emily's feelings. The evening Harry and I made our engagement, we were walking on the Battery all the evening. The family believed I had been walking with Charles, and I did not feel to like undeceiving them; but when I went to our room with Emily, it seemed as if my heart would burst if I did not speak. I threw my arms around her neck, and called her my future sister. She misunderstood me; I felt her tears on my cheek, and she said something about my being too good, and Charles too good, and all that; so I was forced to relieve her embarrassment, and tell plainly my meaning. I believed she had only anticipated a little, for I was sure Charles loved her; are you not Wallace?"

"Yes, Alice, too sure; but I have been strangely blind,—it never occurred to me till within the last two hours. I am not equally sure that—" Emily loves him, he would have added; but he could not communicate the reasons of his long-cherished opinions, or rather hopes, on the subject of Emily's affections, and he abruptly turned away and left his sister to solitary and painful reflection. "Poor Wallace!" she thought, "it would have been far easier for Charles to have gotten over it; his feelings are so much more gentle and manageable."

Hour after hour passed away while Wallace unconsciously wandered along the river's bank, revolving the past, balancing every trifling circumstance to which love and hope and fear gave weight, and painfully meditating on the future, —on what he could do and what he ought to do; the *ought* soon becomes the *could* in a virtuous mind.

Circumstances had led the brothers very innocently into the indulgence of these jarring hopes. Nothing was more natural, than that an intimate intercourse with a girl very lovely in person and character, and attractive in manners, should excite their affections, and that affection in the boy should ripen into love in the man. It was not so natural that each should indulge his own hopes, form his own plans, and never suspect the sentiments of his brother. For the last half dozen years, Charles had been for nine months of every year at Green-brook, and when the brothers were together, they found the frank and affectionate intercourse of the family a safe and convenient shelter for their private feelings. Neither of them had for a long time had a distinct purpose, or been himself aware of the existence of an all-controlling sentiment. But, for a few months past, they had been waiting for the moment when their affairs should warrant the disclosure of their attachment, or any crisis (on the brink of which lovers always seem to themselves to be) should render it inevitable. In the meantime, Emily's entrance on her vocation of teacher had been, on some pretext, deferred from spring to fall, and from fall to spring. The truth was, none of the family could bear to part with her, and even Mr. and Mrs. Barclay were for once betrayed into the delay of a most excellent plan in favour of a present indulgence.

Wallace passed a sleepless night, the first in his healthy and happy life. It was not profitless; for, during the silent watches, he firmly resolved upon an immediate and frank disclosure to Charles. This he believed would prevent, as far as it was possible to prevent them, all future regrets and unhappiness. He could not bear to risk, for a moment, that the harmony and sweet affections, which had made their home a heaven, should give place to suspicion, secret jealousy, selfish competition, and possible hatred. "No," he said; "He who has commanded us to pluck out an eye if it offend us, will enable me or Charles to root out an affection which we have both innocently, though one of us blindly, cherished."

Wallace was (what all are not) true to the resolution formed in solitude; and early the next day he sought an interview with Charles. At first it was embarrassed and painful. Charles's delicate and somewhat reserved nature was shocked by having the secret he had so long cherished, known and canvassed. But by degrees the hearts of both were opened. Their mutual confidence called forth all the vigour of their mutual affections. The noblest powers of their nature were roused; and such was the glow of fraternal love, that each felt that success with Emily would be almost as hard to bear as failure. Emily's preference must of course decide the matter, and the sooner that decision was known, they felt to be the better. Charles proposed that the whole affair should be confided to their mother, and that she should ascertain for them which way Emily's heart leaned. Wallace was disinclined to this. He had always thought he would have no medium, not even his mother, in an affair of this sort. "If denial comes, it does not, Charles, matter how; but if acceptance, I would first know it from Emily's eye and lips."

The sensation that darted through Charles's bosom at this expression of Wallace, made him realise the precipice on which they stood, and stimulated his desire to have his fate decided at once. He again urged the mode he had suggested. "Let Emily," he said, "know the happiness she bestows, but never the pain she inflicts. If I am to.be her brother, Wallace, I would not for worlds that the frank affection she has shown me," ("ah, how misinterpreted!" he thought,) "should be withdrawn, or shackled with reserve,—a source of suffering to us both, to us all."

Wallace at length acquiesced, and felt and said that Charles was always more considerate, more generous than he. The brothers parted, and Charles hastened with his painful confidence to his mother. The mother, always ready to bear her part in the hopes and fears, success and disappointments, of her children, received his communication with tears of sympathy. But over every other feeling,—regret that the catastrophe had not been foreseen and avoided, anxiety for the future, and perplexity with the present,—the holy joy of the Christian mother triumphed; and from the depths of her heart arose a silent, fervent thanksgiving, that the religious principle of her sons had swayed their affections and been victorious over the temptations of the most subtile of the human passions.

The application of the southern lady was the theme on which Mrs. Barclay began her soundings of Emily; but how she discharged her delicate office, need not be told. A woman's management on such occasions is so marked by the adroitness and sagacity manifested by the lower orders of creation, that we might call it by the name we give to the inspiration of the bee and the bird, and say that one woman *instinctively* finds the clew that leads through the labyrinth of another's heart.

When Charles again met his mother, he read his fate in her face. "It is as I expected," she said; "Emily herself asks 'how it could be otherwise.'"

"Mother! you did not tell her that I—"

"No, no, my son, she does not suspect the nature of your feelings; but, as I was going to tell you, she said, amid the blushes and tears of her confession, that she feared it was very wrong, received as she had been into the family, to indulge such an affection for Wallace; but she could not help it. If he had gone away, as you did, she should have loved him as she does you and her brother Harry; but to be with him every day, and every day find him more and more—"

"You need not check yourself, mother; I can bear to hear why she loves Wallace."

Mrs. Barclay was proceeding;—Charles again interrupted her. "Never mind, dear mother; some other time I will hear the rest;" and he left her, to still in solitude the throbbings of his heart. Something must be allowed to human infirmity. Charles had fortunately a pretext of business, and in a few hours, without again seeing his brother or Emily, he was on his way to a distant part of the state.

Those hours which should have been the happiest of Wallace's life were clouded; but the clouds which are fraught with generous consideration for another are better than sunshine. It is good to have the joy of success tempered, the expectations of youth abated; and above all it is good, by personal and even bitter experience, to have our convictions strengthened, that the highest and only stable happiness results from an obedience to the sense of duty. Even in the first intoxicating moments of assured affection, the certainty of possessing Emily's love was less to Wallace than the certainty of having preserved his brother's unimpaired.

Charles's trial was the severest. His fondest hopes were suddenly annihilated. Emily, who unconsciously had shaped the plan of his life, and lit up his futurity, was lost to him for ever ; but even the possession of her pure and tender heart, lovely and beloved as she was, could not have inspired the holy emotions he felt, from the assurance that his love for Wallace was not abated one jot—that he could contemplate his happiness, not only without a pang of envy, but with gratitude to Heaven, that what was denied to him had fallen to his brother's lot.

Whence came this self-conquest : whence this power over the most selfish and exorbitant of the passions ! and at that period of life when passion is strongest and reason weakest ! It came from a *home* cultivation of the affections that spring from the natural and unchanging relations. It came from what the Apostle calls a " mystery," the knitting of hearts together in love ; and alas ! to a great portion of the world, the power of domestic love is still a mystery. The vital principle of the religion of Christ, the pervading element of the divine nature, *love*, was the informing spirit of the Barclays' home. This inspired their exertions, and their self-restraints, and that generous sympathy which enabled each to transfuse, as it were, his existence into a brother's,—to weep when he wept, and to rejoice when he rejoiced.

CHAPTER XIII.

FAMILY LETTERS.

" Yes let the rich deride, the proud disdain,
These simple blessings of the lowly train ;
To me more dear, congenial to my heart,
One native charm than all the gloss of art."
GOLDSMITH.

To the younger members of the Greenbrook family, the announcement of Wallace's and Emily's engagement was unmixed joy. " They had always," they said, " loved her like a sister," and now she was going to be their own sister. Horrid it would have been, to have had Emily go and live on a plantation among slaves. Mother had always said that Emily would make one of the best little housewives in the world, if she did not make a wonderful teacher, and they guessed mother knew all the while what was going to happen ; but that was nothing strange, mother knew everything ! And how nicely father fixed it to have Wallace and Harry Norton partners."—They wondered " if father meant that all should come out so like the end of a story-book when he took Harry and Emily home ! And what would Mr. Anthon say now ! O, he would say it was all father's *luck !* Poor Mr. Anthon ! To be sure he had bad luck enough, as he called it. John such a drunkard, and Dick acting so shockingly, and Anne quarreling with her mother-in-law." Thus the children dwelt on results ; older heads may speculate on causes.

Charles, in due time, returned to Greenbrook. His gentle and still affectionate manner (perhaps even more than usually so) betrayed no secret to Emily, but his increased thoughtfulness and occasional embarrassment did not escape his mother's vigilant eye. He was himself conscious of a weight on his spirits that he could not throw off, —an accustomed and delightful stimulus was withdrawn. It was the change from a day of sunshine

and ethereal atmosphere, to leaden skies and east winds. He fully realised that it was easy for a mind formed upon right principles to resolve upon a right course, but very hard to cure the same mind of long-indulged habits. There was not a walk, a view, a tree, or plant at Greenbrook, that did not tend by its associations to keep alive feelings which it was now his duty and most earnest endeavour to extinguish. Human virtues partake of the human constitution,—they are weak, and need external aid and support ; the true wisdom is to find this out and supply the remedy in time. After a conflict of weeks and months, Charles came to the conclusion that a change of climate is sometimes as essential to the mind, as the body ; and having frankly disclosed his reasons to his parents, he announced to them his determination, with their approbation, to remove to Ohio. The Greenbrook farm, he said, was no more than his father could manage without him at present, and the younger boys were coming on to take his place; for himself, he should find the excitement he wanted, in the activity and novelty of a new state ; and while he remembered his home, he should be stimulated to do some good, if he failed in getting all he hoped. He had communicated his plans to Wallace, and had received a letter from him filled with the most affectionate expostulations, but they had not changed his views. Charles was so important to the home circle, he filled so many places which nobody else could fill, that the whole family protested against his leaving them. His father and mother, after much anxious deliberation, were the first to acquiesce in his wishes. His removal was the greatest disappointment they had ever met with, but, once having made up their minds that it was best for him, they bore it cheerfully. Self-sacrifice is so common in good parents, that it strikes us no more than the falling of the rain, or the shining of the sun, or any other natural result of the beneficent arrangements of Providence.

Charles's departure was loudly lamented by the good people of Greenbrook. They liberally used the right which all social country gossips assume on such occasions, and " judged it a poor move for such a young man as Charles Barclay to leave his *privileges* in New England to rough it in the West. However, it was nothing strange ; all the boys caught the western fever now-a-days." But deeply as Charles regretted the " privileges" of a more advanced state of society, and above all the " privilege" of his blessed home, he had no reason to regret the vigorous resolution he had taken, when he found his mind recovering its cheerful tone, without which all the " privileges" that the happiest sons of New England ever toiled for and enjoyed, would have been unavailing to him. The healthful state of his mind, the " prosperity of his heart," is best exhibited in the following extract from a letter to his mother.

" I have profited by father's rule to drive out private and personal griefs by devotion to the well-being of others. Life is indeed too short to be wasted in brooding over disappointment, and I am convinced there is much more of selfishness than of sensibility in this brooding. The affections are given to us for activity and diffusion,—they are the fire to warm, not to consume us. I am a living witness, dear mother, against the corrupting eloquence we meet with in novels and poetry to persuade us that true love is an unconquerable passion ; I did love long and truly, as you know. My affections were worthily placed, and at first, I confess, I thought it impossible they should ever cease to be exclusively devoted to that one object. I remember the night before I left you, when I was expressing my dread of the solitariness that awaited me at my new residence, father said, 'O my son, you will soon have a family around you.' I replied querulously, 'I never shall have a family!' and I secretly wondered that father could so have forgotten the feelings of his youth, as to think that I could. Now I look forward to such an event as possible; my heart is free.

"I have much reason to rejoice that I came here; there is no time in these busy new settlements to look back. The 'go ahead' principle keeps hands and heads at work—and hearts too, dear mother. Do not imagine that in our eager devotion to physical wants, we forget what belongs to the lasting and nobler part of our nature. I have literally made a circulating library of the books father gave me; and if your household maxim holds good here, and 'the proof of the pudding is in the eating,' the eagerness with which they are devoured is a proof that they were well-selected. I have built a small log-house, with two apartments, at a short distance from the good family where I get my meals. One of the apartments is my bed-room, and I assure you it has quite a home look. A little pine table in the corner of the room is covered with the merino cloth which Mary and Haddy embroidered with braids for me; there is my flute, my portfolio, and the little pile of books that was always on my table at home,—then the quilt the girls made of bits of their pretty frocks is on my bed,—the curtains Emily hemmed and fringed before my windows. All these home-memorials, with your sweet picture hanging over the fire-place, do confoundedly blur my eyes sometimes.

"The other apartment is, at present, a reading-room. I have induced the young men to join me in a society which we call (you know we are fond of grand names in these parts) *Philomathian.* Our Philos subscribe for half a dozen newspapers, and three periodicals. They remain a week at the reading-room, where we meet on evenings and rainy days. These meetings keep alive a social spirit, and a barter-trade of our ideas, by which all gain, some more and some less. All gain, I say, and so it is; for the most humble has something peculiar in his observations and experience, by which those that are more highly endowed, and far better instructed, may profit. After a certain time our papers, &c. are put in circulation for the benefit of the womankind. My little reading-room serves another purpose that will particularly please you, mother. We meet in it every sabbath morning for religious service. I am reader to our little congregation. I find the sermons and other devotional books father selected, admirably adapted to our purpose. I began with reading prayers; but our settlers being chiefly from New England, prefer an extempore service. At first I felt *bashful* at being their organ, and, I confess it with shame, I thought more of those who were around me than of Him whom I addressed; but I soon learned to abstract myself, and to enter into the spirit of my petitions. We are but an extended family circle, perfectly acquainted with each other's condition, and feeling one another's wants; after our service we have a Sunday school. I adopt my father's mode of passing the afternoon, as far as practicable here. I visit the sick and the afflicted, and, where there are no such paramount claims, I impart what religious and moral instruction I can to the children, and to the ignorant who are but grown-up children.

"Tell father the slips of fruit-trees he gave me, are thriving on many a sunny patch,—growing while we are sleeping; and pray tell the girls, that their last package of flower seeds arrived safely, and they have come up famously. Eve had not a finer soil for her culture in Paradise than we have here. Flowers grow like weeds, and I know many a village in *old* Massachusetts, shame to them! that has not so many of these luxuries as there are in our little settlement, which has been opened to the sun but three years.

"I assisted two little bare-foot girls to-day to train a native clematis (a pretty species) over the logs of their hut. There is a honeysuckle and white rose clambering over my window, that came from slips I cut,—*you know where,* mother, the morning I left home. How soon may we plant a paradise in the wilds, if we will! The physical, moral, and intellectual soil is ready; it only wants the spirit of cultivation.

"That honeysuckle and white rose! They have recalled images of the past, but they are no longer spectres that trouble, but spirits that soothe me. How I wish I could be with you on the happy occasion at hand! I cannot, so there is an end of wishing; but pray tell Wallace, with my best love, that I rejoice in his joy, and have no feeling that may not exist when all marrying and giving in marriage is past, and we meet, as I humbly trust we shall, a family in heaven."

The happy occasion alluded to by Charles, was the double marriage of Alice and Harry Norton, Wallace and Emily.

"What a pity you were not here, dear Charles," wrote Mary Barclay to her brother, "we had such a delightful wedding. At first it was decided it should be quite private. Emily wished it so, and mother rather preferred it; but Alice, who, as father says, always goes for 'the greatest happiness to the greatest number,' said that she was to be married but once in her life, and that those who could get pleasure from looking at her, were quite welcome to it. The girls were dressed sweetly, but unexpensively; for father, you know, thinks a wedding a poor excuse for extravagance, or, to express it as he would, a woman is unfit to assume the most serious cares and responsibilities of life till she better estimates the use of money than to invest it in blond and pearls,—a common rigging now-a-days, even for portionless brides. Our brides looked pretty enough, in all conscience, in white muslins, and natural flowers. Father and mother had a long talk with us the evening before, and we did all our crying then, and one and all resolved we would have nothing but smiles at the wedding. Good old Mr. Marvin performed the ceremony. He was rather long and particular, and too *plain spoken*; but his age and right intentions were a warrant for his freedom, and his earnest feeling made amends for all. You remember his 'narrative style,' in prayer. He told our whole family history, and such a 'patriarch,' as he made of father! such a 'mother in Israel,' of mother! and such 'plants and polished corner stones' of their sons and daughters! There was an allusion that shocked us all to poor old Mr. Norton, and father's Christian conduct towards him, but happily it was so wrapped in Scripture phraseology, that I doubt if any understood it but such as were acquainted with the particulars. But when he spoke of the blessed issues of that painful business,—of the gentle Ruth and faithful Jacob (these were the names by which he designated Harry and Emily), who had been trained under our roof in the 'nurture and admonition of the Lord,' all hearts were touched. The only missing member of the family, dear Charles, was not forgotten, and we all joined in the earnest petition that the spirit of your father's house might rest on your new home; and that the waste places around you might blossom as the rose.

"After the ceremony, the crying, (alas, for our previous resolution!) the kissing, and the wishing were over, a tower of wedding-cake was set on the centre-table, wreathed, as Emily had requested, with roses and honeysuckles from those you planted for her. In spite of the searching and scrambling among the *ready* candidates for future weddings, little Effie got the ring. Fortune pets her as well as us. However, I suspected this was a contrivance of Biddy's, whose true Irish love of merry-making has been all called forth on this occasion. By the way, Biddy is an inexpressible comfort since we came to Greenbrook, where the family work is so much increased. She takes all the burden of it from Martha, and is as dutiful to her as a child could be. Martha says herself, she is paid a hundred fold for all the trouble she had with her.

"The brides leave us to-morrow, and I am so busy that I must finish my letter with half our wedding festivities untold,—how they danced while I played,—how Captain Fisher, who in his youth was drummer in a militia company, sent home for his old drum and played *en amateur* an accompaniment to the 'White Cockade,' and 'Haste to the Wedding!'—how the kind old people, who used to think dancing a sin, looked on complacently. They grow wiser, and we more rational.

"How lonesome we shall be to-morrow! O dear me! I wish, as Willie used to say, we had 'a big banging house where all my peoples as loves one another could live together and not make a noise.' Do you remember, Charles? .It seems but yesterday that we all laughed at this out-break of the loving little fellow's heart, and now he is getting a beard, and looking mannish. Well, the accomplishment of Willie's wish is reserved for a happier condition of existence, when we shall no more have to toil in cities, or go to the forests to make new abodes. Then, dear Charles, shall we dwell together in one home. Till then, *then*, yours, dear brother,

"Most affectionately,
"MARY BARCLAY."

CHAPTER XIV.

THE CONCLUSION.

"Thy mercy bids all nature bloom ;
The sun shines bright and man is gay ;
Thine equal mercy spreads the gloom,
That darkens o'er his little day."

"WHAT man is there that liveth and shall not see death?" The import of these words comes home at some time or other to every bosom. Some think of death at a moment of sudden alarm, in seasons of sickness, or in the silent watches of the night, when the ministry of the senses is suspended, and the consciousness of mortality presses on the spirit. But should not the thought of death be associated with the necessary pursuits and cheerful occupations of life? Not introduced, like the skeleton at the Egyptian feasts, to mingle gloom with gaiety, but to give a just colouring and weight to the affairs of life, by enabling us to estimate them in relation to this great circumstance of existence, habitually to associate life with immortality,—all action here with accountability and retribution hereafter.

"Of all the wonders that I yet have heard,
It seems to me most strange that men should fear
Seeing that death a necessary end,
Will come when it will come."

If a heathen, to whom the grave was still wrapped in silence and darkness, could from the mere consideration that death was inevitable, be supposed to await it with firmness, what ought we to expect from the Christian, for whom life and immortality have been brought to light,—who believes that there is a place prepared for him in his Father's house?

Does he believe that death is but a brief passage, a "circumstance" of life? that there is no *death* to those who believe in Jesus ; that the mortal shall put on immortality? that death shall be swallowed up in victory? if these are not words, but articles of faith, why does death bring such dismay and gloom into the home of the Christian? If Jesus were now to appear to his disciples, would he not have much reason to say to them, "O ye of little faith?"

Early in the autumn following the marriage of his children, Mr. Barclay returned from his usual daily walk to the village post-office with a letter in his hand. His face indicated anxiety and sorrow. Every eye was fixed on him for explanation. He gave the letter to Mrs. Barclay, and turning to the children said, "Your brother Charles is ill with a fever."

"Very ill, father?"

"Yes, Effie ; and he had been so for ten days when the letter was written."

"O father! and we have all been so happy when Charles perhaps was "——"dying," she would have said, but there are words hard to apply to those whose lives seem to be a portion of our own.

"Do you not think, Effie, it would have grieved Charles to have abated one particle of your happiness?"

"O yes, it would, father. Charles always loved to have us glad, and never sorry, and he always made us glad. But we shall never be glad again if he dies."

"Never, Effie!" Her father took her on his knee. "And what would Charles think, if we never could be happy because it had pleased our heavenly Father to take him a little before us to heaven?"

"I don't know sir, what people think in heaven, but I know what we feel on earth. Do you think he will die, father?" she added very softly, and laying her cheek to her father's.

"I fear he must, my child." The children, whose eyes were on their father, as if awaiting a sentence of life or death, could no longer restrain their tears. Mary and her mother were eagerly reading the letter. They too thought Charles must die, and when they had read through the physician's statement, and saw at the end of it, " *God's will be done*," written almost illegibly in Charles's hand, Mary hid her face on her mother's heaving bosom. Mr. Barclay took the letter and showed the line to the younger children, " Let us, too, my dear children, try honestly to say ' God's will be done.' Let us all bow down before our Father in heaven, and ask Him to give us the spirit of obedience and faith, that we may quietly submit to his holy will." They all gathered around him, and as they knelt with him they caught the spirit of his expressions of trust,—they felt what it was to be the children of light and not of darkness,— of the light from heaven which shines through the gospel of Christ.

Two days must pass before further intelligence could be received. In the meantime the sad news spread through Greenbrook, and a general sympathy pervaded the little community. Charles's gracious qualities had commended him to all hearts, and each family felt as if it were menaced with a calamity. When the stage-coach arrived, by which, as all knew, news must come from Charles, and Mr. Barclay was seen riding towards the post-office, many an eager and tearful eye followed him. "The mail is not opened, sir," said the post-master. By this time several persons had left their business, and were approaching to get the first intelligence. "O that I could get my letter and be away with it," thought Mr. Barclay, reluctant as every delicate person is, to betray emotion before observers. He was recalled to his better feelings.

"Shall I hold your horse for you, Mr. Barclay?" asked a voice almost for the first time low and gentle.

"Thank you, Dow," he replied; and giving him the bridle, he dismounted. Dow was a demi-outlaw, who lived on the outskirts of Greenbrook. Every man's face was set against him, and his against every man except Charles Barclay. And why was he an exception? "Charles," he said, "had treated him like a human creature, had done him many a good turn, and had many a laugh with him;" and now Dow had come from his mountain-hut, and stood with his rifle in his hand, and his shaggy cur at his side, awaiting the first breath of news from Charles.

"What are you standing there for?" said the post-master to a little girl on the door-step, "you are in my light, child."

"Mother wants to know, sir, what's in the letter." "Mother" was the widow Ely, to whom Charles had done many an unforgotten kindness.

"He's got a letter, has not he?" exclaimed old blind Palmer, whose quick ear caught the breaking of the seal. "Hush, Meddler!" he added, laying his hand on the head of the sagacious little terrier Charles had given him, and eagerly listening for the first word that should be uttered. Mr. Barclay devoured the contents of the letter at a glance, then threw it on the table, mounted his horse, and galloped homeward.

"He is dead!" exclaimed one.

"I do not believe it," said another.

"He has left the letter." "He has left it for us to read," was the natural conclusion. They did accordingly read the few lines announcing that the fever had reached its crisis and the patient was convalescing; and they were just about to say "how strangely Mr. Barclay had acted," when they felt their voices broken by their own emotions, and they realized how much more difficult it might be to control an unexpected joy, than a grief painfully prepared for.

After this came regular and encouraging accounts from Charles; but the first letter from himself, written with apparent effort, and at long intervals, checked their hopes. He expressed with manly piety his deep gratitude for the experience of his sickness. Over and over again, he thanked his parents for his religious education. He said that a tranquil reliance on the mercy of God, and faith in the immortality revealed by Christ and assured by his resurrection, had never, for a moment, forsaken him. He had but one inextinguishable earthly desire, and that was to see home. "Home and heaven blended together, in his thoughts by day and his dreams by night." The letter was filled with the most tender longings for a sight of his mother's face,—his father, and each brother and sister, were named in the most endearing language.

Soon after came a letter informing them that symptoms of a rapid consumption had appeared, which no longer admitted a doubt as to the termination of the disease, and that he had determined immediately to make an effort to reach home. He intended to embark the next day for New Orleans, whence he should go to New York, where he hoped to meet his parents. The letter indicated perfect firmness and tranquillity of mind. It contained his wishes as to the disposition of his effects. Some memorial was allotted to each member of the family, not forgetting Martha and Biddy; and some poor Greenbrook friends were remembered by bequests adapted to their necessities.

At the end of a few weeks he arrived at New York, where his parents were awaiting him, and whence they conveyed him by slow stages to Greenbrook. For the last few miles he was borne on a litter. His father, Wallace, and Harry Norton aiding to carry, or walking beside him, till his eyes rested on his beloved home, where, on every side, were traces of his tasteful and diligent hand.

Mary, with thoughtful care, had arranged his room precisely as he left it. When they laid him on his bed, no emotion was visible save a slight fluttering at his heart. His face was placid, and from his eye, which literally glowed, there came "holy revealings." He was alone with his brother. "O Wallace," he said, raising his eye gratefully to Him who had granted his last earthly prayer, "how pleasant it is to be here! How I longed for this! O *home, home!* Open wide those blinds, Wallace,"—he pointed to the east window opposite his bed. "Now raise my head and let it rest on your breast. I always loved to look on those hills when the sun was going down!"

It was one of those moments in the harmonies of nature, when the outward world seems to answer to the spirit. The valley was in deep shadow, while the summit of the hills, rich with the last softened, serious tints of autumn, was lighted,—kindled, with the rays of the sun. "The falling leaf! and the setting sun!" said Charles, without expressing in words, the relation to his own condition so manifest, "Is it not beautiful, Wallace?"

"Yes, very beautiful!" faintly echoed Wallace, his eye fixed on his brother's pale, serene brow, where it seemed to him there was a more beautiful light,—light from Heaven. As Wallace gently rested his cheek on that brow, what a contrast in the two faces, and yet what harmony! His was rich with health and untouched vitality. His eyes were suffused with tears, his brow contracted, and his lips compressed with the effort to subdue his struggling feelings. The beautiful colouring of health had long and for ever forsaken Charles. His cheeks were sunken, and there were dark shadows in their cavities; but there was an ineffable sweetness, a something like the repose of satisfied infancy on his lips, and such tranquillity on his smooth brow, that it seemed as if the seal of eternal peace were set there. A tear fell from Wallace's cheek on his. Charles faintly smiled, and looking up he said, "Why are you troubled, my dear brother! I am not,—kiss me, Wallace. Thank God, dear brother, our hearts have never been divided,—and yet we were tried."

"You were,—you were, Charles!" Wallace's voice in spite of his efforts was choked.

"Well, Wallace, if you have children, bring them up in that strict family love in which we were brought up. 'God is love,' and wherever love is, there cannot be strifes and envyings."

After a night of as much repose as could be obtained in Charles's circumstances, and made sweet to him by the sense of being under his father's roof, each member of the family was admitted to his apartment.

"This is too much happiness!" he said, as he welcomed one after another to his bedside.

He was too weak for sustained conversation; but some seasonable, and never-to-be-forgotten word, he uttered at intervals. And inquiries were to be made about the condition of the garden, and the grounds, and the affairs of the Greenbrook neighbourhood, all evincing that there was nothing in his past pursuits and interests discordant with his present circumstances. He wished his sisters to bring in their work-baskets, ("I cannot spare *your* hand, mother," he said, pressing his lips to it when he made the request,) that he might see them at their usual employments, and have more completely the feeling of being at home.

This was the first time that death had come into Mr. Barclay's habitation. He was received, not as an enemy, but as an expected friend,—as the messenger of God. The affections were not cooled nor abated, (was this ever the effect of religion?) and therefore their countenances were sad, and their hearts sorrowful; but it was sorrow without bitterness or repining. The visible domestic chain was for the first time to be broken,—a precious link for a time severed. The event was attended with peculiar disappointment to Mr. Barclay. Without favouritism there is often, perhaps always, a closer tie to one child than to another. There was a perfect sympathy between Charles and his father. Their minds seemed cast in the same mould. They had the same views and purposes in life,—the same resolute, steady application of their theories. Mr. Barclay had relied on Charles to be the guide and support of his younger children. But God had ordered it otherwise, and he submitted, as a Christian should submit, in the spirit of love and of a sound mind.

For two days Charles's disease seemed to be suspended, and the energies of nature to be called forth by moral causes; but on the third day he appeared to be rapidly sinking away. He could now only endure an upright position. His head rested on his mother's bosom. Little Effie, who read truly the fixed and intense looks of the family, but who could not imitate their calmness, shrunk behind her mother sobbing aloud.

"Come here, Effie," said her brother; "why do you cry?"

"Because Charles"—she could not speak the rest.

"Because I must die, Effie?"

"Yes," she faintly answered.

"It is not hard to die, dear Effie,—not if we love God, not if we believe the promises of Christ. Come closer, Effie, I cannot speak loud; I am going home, to a home like this, for love is there; to a better home than this, for there, there is neither sickness nor sorrow—"

"Rest now, my dear son," said the tender mother, as Charles paused from exhaustion, and closed his eyes.

"First, mother, let me tell Effie what is best of all in that home. There is no sin there, Effie."

"O, Charles, you never did anything wrong here."

"My dear little sister, I have done and felt much that was wrong, and it is because I know our God is a God of forgiveness and tender mercy, that I hope to be accepted of Him. Kiss me, Effie—be a good girl, and when you come to lie

on a sick bed you will have a great many pleasant thoughts. Mary, my dear sister, do not grieve so, —we shall very soon meet again. Alice, one last word, my sister,—do not give your heart too much to the world. Emily, my dear sister too, we shall be one family in heaven."

These and a few more short sentences (ever after treasured in faithful hearts) Charles uttered at long intervals; then, after a short pause, he said, "I am very weak,—father, lay your hand upon my breast, here,—what does this mean?"

His father perceived the tokens of dissolution; "It is death, my dear child," he replied.

Wallace offered to take his mother's place;— "No," said Charles, "my head is easiest on mother's bosom; mother, you are not afraid to see me die?"

"O, no, no, my son."

"Nor am I afraid to die, mother; God hath redeemed my soul from the power of the grave. Father, pray with us."

All felt their weakness, and the necessity for a stronger than a human arm to lean upon, and they bowed themselves in supplication to their Father in heaven, as children in trouble fly to the arms of their parents. The demands of the soul at such a moment are pressing and few. They were briefly expressed by the tender parent in the language of Scripture,—in words that in great exigencies are felt to convey the oracles of God.

"Thank you, dear father," said Charles, "I am better for this." He looked around on each one of the family and said, "It *is* hard parting,— but there is sweet peace here."

His voice had become more indistinct, and his spirit seemed to rise from the home where it lingered to that which awaited it. His lips still moved as if in prayer. Suddenly he raised both hands and said clearly, "Thanks be to God who giveth—" the bodily organs were too feeble for the parting soul. His father finished the sentence; "Thanks be to God, who giveth us the victory through our Lord Jesus Christ."

Charles bowed his head. A few moments longer they watched his ebbing life, and he was gone, gently as a child falls asleep on its mother's bosom. A deep, holy silence followed. It seemed as if all heard the voice of God, "It is I, be no afraid."

But then came the mortal feeling, the sense of separation, the poignant anguish of the parting stroke, and sighs and tears broke forth. They laid their cheeks to his, they kissed his forehead, his hands, sobbing, "Charles!—dear, blessed brother!"

The mother sat motionless, her son's head still resting on her bosom. She could not bear to change this last manifestation of his love to her. Mr. Barclay gently disengaged him from her arms, and laid him on the pillow, saying as he did so, "He was our *first-born!*"

What a world to the parent there is in these few words! They recall the hours of brightest, freshest hope, and deepest gratitude. They express what has been dearest and happiest in life, and when Mr. Barclay, after a moment's pause, added in a firmer voice, "The Lord gave, —the Lord hath taken away,—blessed be his name,"—it was the meek Christian triumphing over the man and father.

*"My children," he said, "it is finished. Now let us unite our hearts in thanksgiving to God for the life and death of your dear brother." They all knelt, while with a steady voice he poured out his heart. Memory, kindled by love, lighted up Charles's past life, and all, as it passed in review, was the subject, not of lamentation that it was gone, but of pious gratitude that it had been enjoyed. He blessed God for the healthful infancy of his son; for the obedience and docility of his childhood: for the progressive knowledge and virtue of his youth; and above all, for the faith in Jesus that had given effect to his life, and peace in the hour of death.

We have seen Mr. Barclay's home at its first consecration; we have seen it when the tender lights of blissful infancy fell upon it; when it was filled with the life, activity, and hope of joyous youth; when the poor and the orphan were gathered under the wing of its succouring charities; when pecuniary losses were met with tranquillity and dignity; when social pleasures clustered round its hearth-stone; when sons and daughters were given in happy marriage; but never have we seen an hour so blessed, as that which bore the assurance that death hath no sting, the grave no victory, in the home of the Christian.

LETTERS FROM ABROAD

TO

KINDRED AT HOME.

BY

MISS SEDGWICK,

AUTHOR OF " HOPE LESLIE," " POOR RICH MAN," ETC. ETC.

" Well, John, I think we must own that God Almighty had a hand in making other countries besides ours."
THE BROTHERS.

A NEW EDITION.

LONDON:
EDWARD MOXON, DOVER STREET.
MDCCCXLI.

LONDON :
BRADBURY AND EVANS, PRINTERS, WHITEFRIARS.

PREFACE.

An apology for a book implies that the public are obliged to read it; an obligation that would reverse the order of nature—transfer the power from the strong to the weak. But, unfortunately for them, there is a portion of the public who are, in a certain sense, obliged to read a book—the kind friends of the author; and among these, I say it gratefully, not boastfully, I have the happiness to number many of my countrymen personally unknown to me. Of *my friends*, then, I ask indulgence for the following pages. They are published rather with deference to the wishes of others than from any false estimate of their worth. Our tour was made under circumstances which forbade any divergence from the highway of all the travelling world, and, consequently, we passed over a field so thoroughly reaped, that not an ear, scarcely a kernel, remains for the gleaner. In addition to this, and to painful anxieties and responsibilities that accompanied us at every step, we were followed by intelligence of deep domestic calamity. On this subject I need not enlarge; the disqualifying influence of these circumstances will be comprehended without my opening the sanctuary of private griefs.

I was aware that our stayers-at-home had already something too much of churches, statues, and pictures, and yet that they cannot well imagine how much they make up the existence of Tourists in the Old World. I have sedulously avoided this rock, and must trust for any little interest my book may possess to the honesty with which I have recorded my impressions, and to the fresh aspect of familiar things to the eye of a denizen of the New World. The fragmentary state in which my letters appear, is owing to my fear of wearying readers less interested than my own family by prolonged details or prosing reflections, or disgusting them with the egotism of personal experience.

One word to my English reader, rather of explanation than apology, which I trust the case does not require. I have unscrupulously mentioned the names of such distinguished English people as it was my good fortune to see. I could have screened myself from reproach, by giving merely their initials; but, as they are too well known for this device to have afforded them any shelter, it seemed to me but a paltry affectation of delicacy. I might plead the authority of English travellers in the United States; but if wrong, no authority justifies it; and if right, it needs none. I have confined my notices strictly to public characters—to gallery portraits; for so such persons as Mr. Rogers, and even that most refined and delicate of gentlewomen Miss Joanna Baillie, may be strictly called, after the full exhibitions in Moore's Life of Byron, and Lockhart's Life of Scott.

I have violated no confidence, for none was reposed in me. My opportunities of social intercourse were few and brief, and I should have omitted these slight records of them, but for the wish to transmit to my friends at home my delightful impressions of those to whom we all owe many happy hours. Perhaps my anxiety is superfluous: the King of Ashantee was anxious to know what the English people said of him; but I never heard that the English people cared to know what the King of Ashantee said of them.

NEW YORK,
   June 25, 1841.

LETTERS, &c.

George Hotel, Portsmouth,
June 4, 1839.

MY DEAR C.—Captain S.'s cutter took us off the ship this morning at nine o'clock. It was at last a sad parting from our messmates, with whom we have been for a month separated from all the world, and involved in a common destiny; and from the ship, which seems like a bit of home, for the feet of the friends we have left there have trodden it.

When I touched English ground I could have fallen on my knees and kissed it; but a wharf is not quite the *locale* for such a demonstration, and spectators operate like strait jackets upon enthusiasm, so I contented myself with a mental salutation of the home of our fathers, the native land of one of our dearest friends, and the birth-place of "the bright, the immortal names" that we have venerated from our youth upward.

I forewarn you, my dear C., not to look for any statistics from me—any "valuable information." I shall try to tell you truly what I see and hear; to "chronicle," as our friend Mr. Dewey says, "while they are fresh, my sensations." Everything looks novel and foreign to us: the quaint forms of the old, sad-coloured houses; the arched, antique gateways; the royal busts niched in an old wall; the very dark colouring of the foliage, and the mossy stems of the trees. We seem to have passed from the fresh, bright youth to the old age of the world. The form and colouring of the people are different from those of ours. They are stouter, more erect, and more sanguine.

Our friends Dr. M. and his wife have decided to remain with us while we stay here, so we make eight in all; and as we stand in the bow-window of the George, staring, wondering, exclaiming, and laughing, we must make a group of "Home-spuns just come up to town" worthy Cruikshank's pencil. And, by-the-way, the passing equipages appear to us the originals of Cruikshank's illustrations, and the parties driving in them fac-similes of Pickwick (the modern Don Quixote) and his club.

Basil Hall is living here. We have had some discussion whether we should recal ourselves to his memory by sending to him Mr. A.'s letter and our cards. We have no individual claims on him, and, as Americans, there is no love lost between us. R. cited Scott's opinion that it is uncivil to both parties not to deliver promptly a letter of introduction; so, submitting to such sound authority, Dr. M. has gone off to leave ours at Captain Hall's door, and then he will leave his card at ours, and there the matter will end.

We have been walking over the town, over the ramparts, and through some fine gravelled avenues shaded with elms. Don't fancy our elms with their drooping embowering branches—no, nothing so beautiful—but what we call the English elm, with its upright stiff stem. As we straggled on down a green lane, we saw a notice "To let furnished," on the gate of a very attractive-looking cottage; so, being seized with a happy inspiration (a natural one, you may think it, for pushing Yankees), we determined, as applicants for the tenement, to see the inside of an English cottage; so, going up a narrow paved walk, we rang for admittance. I asked a pretty, neatly-dressed woman who appeared to show me the premises, and kept my countenance in spite of my tittering followers, while we were shown through a dining-room, drawing-room, two kitchens, and five bedrooms, all small, and furnished with extreme neatness and comfort. All this, with a very pretty little garden, we might have, without linen or plate, for four guineas a week. There was a lovely little court too in front, filled with shrubs and flowers; not a thimbleful of earth that did not do its duty. No wonder the woman took us at our word, for I am sure we looked as if we would fain set up our rest there.

I afterward followed R. into the garden, and encountered the deaf husband of our neat matron-guide. He showed me a filbert grafted upon an apple-tree by a bird having deposited a seed there. I asked, "Had the filbert borne fruit?" "Four guineas a week, ma'am," he answered, "and it's counted a very 'ealthy hair!" We felt it was quite time to retreat.

When we came home, we found that Captain Hall, Mrs. H., and some of their friends had left cards for us. "Very prompt," we thought; "and so this matter is done."

We ate with Dalgetty appetites our first English dinner: soup, salmon, mutton chops, and everything the best of its kind, and served as in a private gentleman's house, and, alas! with an elegance and accuracy found in few gentlemen's houses in our country. We have plenty of gentlemen, but gentlemen's servants are with us rare birds.

June 5.—We feel green and bewildered, as you may imagine ; and not knowing how to arrange our tour around the Isle of Wight, we were discussing it in some perplexity when Captain Hall and Mrs. H. were announced. They were just going off on a visit to the son of Wilberforce, who is rector at Brixton ; but Captain H. deciding at once that we must give the day to the Portsmouth lions, and that he would show them to us, deferred his departure till the evening ; and the half-hour before we set off was occupied in receiving a visit from Captain H.'s children, and instructions from a friend of Mrs. Hall, well acquainted with the localities, as to our progress around the island. Captain H. left us no time for dawdling. He has been a lion-hunter, and understands the art of lion-showing, and, what I think rather the nicest part of the art, what *not* to show. Off we set towards the sally-port. On the way we dropped into a Gothic church (a pretty episode enough) of the twelfth century. Captain H. pointed out a monument to Buckingham, Charles the First's favourite, who, as you may remember, was killed by Felton at Portsmouth.

We were to go first to the Victory, which is now kept here, "a kind of toy," as one of our seamen of the St. James said, but which, in fact, is something more than that—a receiving and drilling ship. We found a boat awaiting us, put (of course by Captain Hall's intervention) at our disposal by the commander of the Victory. It was manned with a dozen youngsters in the Victory's uniform, a white knit woollen blouse, with the word *Victory* in Marie-Louise blue on the breast. They were stout ruddy lads. The Victory, you know, is the ship in which Nelson won the battle of Trafalgar, and died in winning it. Captain H. led us to the quarter-deck, and showed us a brass plate inserted in the floor, inscribed with these words, "*Here Nelson fell !*" This was a thrilling sight to those of us who remembered when Nelson was held as the type of all gallantry, fighting for liberty against the world. R. was obliged to turn away till he could command his emotions, and I thought of the time when we were all children together at home, and I saw him running breathless up the lane, tossing his hat into the air and shouting, " Nelson ! Victory !" Truly, "the child is father to the man." We were received very courteously by the commander, Captain S., who invited us into an apartment which, saving the ceiling was a little lower, had the aspect of a shore drawing-room : there were sofas, show-books, flowers, piano, and a prettier garniture than these, a young bride, reminding us, with her pale delicate face and French millinery, of our fair young country-women—quite un-English. The Victory is Captain S.'s home, and the lady was his daughter.

We then went into the cockpit and groped our way to the dark, narrow state-room (a midshipman's) where Nelson was carried after he was shot down. Captain H. pointed to the beam where his head lay when he died. There a heroic spirit had passed away, and left a halo in this dark, dismal place. Place and circumstance are never less important to a man than when he is dying, and yet it was a striking contrast (and the world is full of such), the man dying in this wretched, dark, stifling hole, when his name was

resounding through all the palaces of Europe, and making our young hearts leap in the New World. Shall I tell you what remembrance touched me most as I stood there ! not his gallant deeds, for they are written in blood, and many a vulgar spirit has achieved such ; but the exquisite tenderness gleaming forth in his last words, " Kiss me, Hardy !" These touched the chord of universal humanity.

Our next step was from the poetic-romantic to the actual, from the Victory to the biscuit-bakery, a place where biscuits are made for naval stores by steam. A policeman started out upon us " like a spider," as Captain H. very descriptively said, and announced that all ingress to the art and mystery of steam-baking was forbidden to foreigners ; and we were turning away acquiescingly, for the most curious of our party had two or three years ago seen the process in full blast in one of our Western States, but Captain Hall would not be so easily baffled. He was vexed that an old rule, fallen into general discredit, should be applied to a biscuit-bakery and " such branches of learning ;" so he went to find the admiral, but he was not at his quarters ; and no dispensation being to be had, he declared the biscuits " all sour." Very sweet we thought them the next morning when we received an *amende* most honourable, in the shape of a note from Admiral Fleming, " regretting the disappointment Miss S. met with at the bakehouse, of which Captain Hall had informed him," (I can imagine in what animated terms,) " and which he would have prevented had he known her wishes," and concluding with saying, that having heard from Captain Hall of our intention of visiting the Isle of Wight, he had the pleasure of offering his yacht for our conveyance. Now this was surely the true spirit of courtesy ; and when this spirit is infused into international manners we may be called Christian nations, and not till then.

Well, the bakery being taboo, our conductor proposed we should next row off to the royal yacht by way of parenthesis in the day's doings. This yacht was built for George IV., and the fitting up, even to the pattern of the chintz, designed by his majesty : truly a fitting occupation for the monarch of the greatest nation in the world ! He had the ambition, I have known shared with him by some exquisite fine ladies, who cast away their gowns and burn their caps if they be imitated. The manufacturer gave a required pledge that the chintz of the royal yacht should never be copied. M. suggested it was not pretty enough, to make this a sacrifice on the part of the manufacturers. The yacht, however, is a bijou, the prettiest thing, I fancy, that has floated since Cleopatra's barge. The beds are wide and sumptuous, there are luxurious chairs and sofas, gilt pannellings, lamps with cable-chains and anchor-shaped ornaments, and a kitchen-range fit to serve an Apicius. There is a pretty library too ; but I suspect his majesty's proportion of mental and corporeal provision was much after Falstaff's fashion. R. remarked its incompleteness, and said to Captain H., " Our library in the St. James is superior to this ; it has your books."

If I could refresh you with the bottle of Madeira and plate of biscuits which Captain Hall contrived to conjure into the block manufactory, while a very clear-headed man was explaining to us its capital machinery, I might venture to drag you along with us through the rolling-mill and the Cyclops regions where the anchors are forged ; but here I let you off for this busily pleasant day, at the moment of our parting with Captain Hall, and the interchange of hearty wishes that we might meet again in the Isle of Wight. What a host of prejudices and false judgments had one day's frank and kind intercourse dispersed to the winds—for ever !

ISLE OF WIGHT.

Isle of Wight, June 6.

OUR transit from Portsmouth in the admiral's yacht was delightful. At the little town of Ryde we engaged two vehicles called flys, small covered carriages, each holding comfortably three persons, with two "intelligent lads" (as the proprietor of the equipages assured us) for drivers. François has a seat on the box, and we have sent our luggage to London, so that we are as unincumbered as if we were out for an afternoon's drive.

And here I am tempted to throw away my pen. It is in vain to attempt to convey to you our impressions of this lovely island, or to retain them myself by this poor record. Call it Eden ; call it Paradise ; and, after all, what conceptions have we of those Terræ Incognitæ? The Isle of Wight, they tell us, is a miniature of England. It has the exquisite delicacy and perfection of a miniature by a master-hand. I am resolved to be as virtuously abstemious as possible on the subject of scenery ; but you must be patient, and bethink yourself, my dear C., that it is not possible to be silent on what makes up so large a portion of a traveller's existence and happiness. When we had ascended the hill from Ryde and turned off into a green lane, we might have been mistaken for maniacs escaped from Bedlam, or rather, I think, for children going home for a holiday. We were thrusting our heads out of our little carriages, shouting from one to the other, and clapping our hands. And why these clamorous demonstrations ! We had just escaped from shipboard, remember ; were on the solid green earth, driving through narrow winding avenues, with sloping hills and lofty trees on each side of us, often interlacing over our heads (the trees I mean !), every inch of ground cultivated and divided by dark hedges filled with flowering shrubs, and sprinkled with thatched and mossy cottages—such as we have only seen in pictures— and the Solent Sea sparkling in the distance.

Our first halt was at Brading church. Blessed are those who make the scene of their labours fit shrines for the homage of the traveller's heart. So did Legh Richmond. A troop of children (twelve we counted) ran out to open the gate of the church-yard for us. One pointed out the "young cottager's" grave ; another was eager to prove she could repeat glibly the epitaphs "little Jane" had recited. They showed us Brading Church (built in the seventh century) and Richmond's house, and the trees under which he taught. We gathered some holly leaves from the tree that shades his court-yard, which we shall devoutly preserve to show you. We might have remained there till this time if our curiosity had

equalled the resources of our "train attendant." It is quite a new sight to us to see children getting their living in this way. We have little to show, and the traveller must grope his way as well as he can to that little. These children with us would have been at school or at the plough, looking to a college education in their perspective, or a "farm in the West :" something better than a few chance pennies from a traveller. But though there are few prizes for them in the lottery of life here, I was glad to see them looking comfortably clad, well fed, and healthy.

We diverged at the beautiful village of Shanklin, and walked to Shanklin Chine*, a curious fissure, worn, I believe, in the hills by a rivulet. The place is as wild as our ice-glen ; and the rocks, instead of being overgrown with palmy ferns, maiden's hair, and lichens, like ours, are fringed with sweet pease, wallflowers, stocks, hyacinths, and all growing at their own sweet will ; this betokens an old neighbourhood of civilisation.

A woman came forth from a cottage to unlock a gate through which we must pass to go up the Chine. K. says the beauties of Nature are as jealously locked up here as the beauties of a harem. It is the old truth, necessity teaches economy ; whatever can be made a source of revenue is so made, and the old women and children are tax-gatherers. At every step some new object or usage starts up before us ; and it strikes us the more because the people are speaking our own language, and are essentially like our own.

In the narrowest part of our pathway, where the rill had become a mere thread, we had the pleasure of encountering the Halls. They were walking to Bonchurch. We asked leave to join them. You may fancy what a delightful stroll we had with this very pleasant meeting, and such accidental accessories to the lovely scenery as a ship in the distance, a rainbow dropping into the sea, and the notes of a cuckoo, the first I had ever heard. History, painting, poetry, are at every moment becoming real, actual.

Bonchurch, at a short distance from the road, secluded from it by an interposing elevation, inclosed by a stone wall, and surrounded by fine old trees, their bark coated with moss, is, to a New-World eye, a picture "come to life." "Sixteen hundred and sixteen," said I to L., deciphering a date on a monument ; "four years before there were any white inhabitants in Massachusetts." "Then," she replied, "this is an Indian's grave." Her eyes were bent on the ground. She was in her own land ; she looked up and saw the old arched and ivied gateway, and smiled—the illusion had vanished.

VENTNOR.

WE have passed a *pleasant rainy day* at Ventnor. The Halls are here too, and we make frequent use of the Piazza by which our parlours communicate ; so our friendship ripens apace. We went, in spite of mist and rains, to pay another visit to Bonchurch, to "get it by heart," Captain H. says ; *into* our hearts we certainly have got it, and taken a drenching into the bar-

* Chine is a Hampshire word for a cleft in the rocks.

gain. But this was a cheap price to pay for the view we had, when, just at the summit of the hill, the mist rolled off like the furling of a sail, and we saw the village of Shanklin (the gem !), with its ivied walls, its roses, its everything that flowers, broad fields of corn, and the steep cliffs down to Shanklin Chine. Shall I ever forget the little in-and-out cottages jutted against the rocks, the narrow lanes that afford you glimpses, through green and flowery walls, of these picture-dwellings !

As we strolled down the road from Bonchurch I stopped at a cottage inhabited by *very* poor people. There were four distinct homes under one roof, and an inclosed strip of ground in front, four feet wide. This space was full of verbenas, stocks, roses, and geraniums ; and an old crone between eighty and ninety was tending them. I thought of the scrawny lilacs and woody rose-bushes in some of our court-yards, and blushed, or, rather, I shall blush if ever I see an English eye upon them ; for (shame to us !) it is the detection, and not the sin, that calls up the blush.

OUR first stop after leaving Ventnor was at St. Lawrence's Church, the smallest in England ; you shall have its dimensions from some poetry we bought of the beadle, his own manufacture.

> " This church has often drawn the curious eye
> To see its length and breadth—to see how high.
> At length to measure it was my intent,
> That I might verify its full extent.
> Its breadth from side to side above the bench
> Is just eleven feet and half an inch.
> The height from pavement to the ceiling mortar,
> Eleven feet, five inches and a quarter.
> And its length, from east to the west end,
> Twenty-five feet four inches, quarters three,
> Is just its measurement, as you may see."

The poet-bendle's brains, you may think, were graduated by the same scale as St. Lawrence's Church. However, I assure you, he was quite the beau-ideal of an old beadle, and he did his ciceroni work well, showing us where his lordship sat (Lord Yarborough, in whose gift is the rector-ship), and where sat the butler, and my lady's maid, and the parish officers. All these privileged people, who dwell in the atmosphere of nobility, had, to the old beadle's senses, something sweeter than the odour of sanctity. For the rest of St. Lawrence's audience, I fear they do not fare as well as the people in Doctor Franklin's dream, who, upon confessing to St. Peter at the gate of Heaven that they were neither Baptists nor Me-thodists, nor of any particular sect, were bidden come in and take the best seats they could find !

Among the epitaphs I read on the mouldering stones in St. Lawrence's churchyard, was one that pleased me for its quaint old ballad style. It was a husband's on his wife, beginning

> " Meek and gentle was her spirit,
> Prudence did her life adorn;
> Modest, she disclaimed all merit;
> Tell me, am not I forlorn ?"

I would not like to make too nice an inquisition as to how long he remained so ! *

---

* The following epitaph amused me: so like our own Puritan elegiac poetry :—

" *To the Memory of Charles Dixon*, SMITH AND FARRIER.
     " My sledge and hammer lie reclined,
     My bellows too have lost their wind,

WE went down to the beach for a good view of Black Gang Chine, a wild, grand-looking place, with masses of sandstone of different strata, vari-ously coloured, and rising to an elevation of some three hundred feet above the sea. Here Captain Hall, with his happy young people, again joined us, to part again immediately ; they to walk to Chale, and we to rejoin R. at the inn, where, for walking into the house and out of it, we paid a fee to a waiter of an aged and venerable aspect, accu-rately dressed in a full suit of black, and looking much like one of our ancient Puritan divines setting off for an " association." ·

As we approached Brixton, the girls and myself alighted to walk, that we might see this enchanting country more at leisure. I cannot give you an idea of the deliciousness of a walk here between the lovely hedges all fragrance, the air filled with the me-lody of birds, and the booming of the ocean waves for a bass. For one sweet singing-bird with us, I think there are twenty here ; and, included in this twenty, the nightingale, the blackbird, the lark, and the cuckoo ! The note of the English blackbird is electrifying, but yet I have heard none sweeter than our woodthrush, that little hermit of our solitudes. You would forgive me, dear C., for observing some contrasts that may perchance strike you as unpatriotic, if,

> " Borne, like Loretto's chapel, through the air,"

I could send over to you one of these picturesque cottages (any one of them), draped with ivy to the very top of the chimneys, and set it down beside our unsightly farmhouses.

At Brixton we again met Captain Hall. He had had the disappointment of finding that his friend, Mr. Wilberforce, was absent ; and intent on filling for us every little vacant niche with some pleasure, he had asked leave to show us a picture of the father in the son's library. H., in the effec-tiveness of his kindness, reminds me of L. M., and seems to me what our Shaker friends would call the "male manifestation" of her ever-watchful and all-accomplishing spirit.

We met two of the young Wilberforces, and begged the pleasure of shaking hands with them for their grandfather's sake. The boy bears a strong resemblance to him, and is, I hope, like his grandfather, sent into the world on an errand of mercy. Such a face is the superscription, by the finger of God, of a soul of benevolence.

The widow of Wilberforce was sitting in the library. She received us courteously. She has a dignified demeanour, and a very sweet counte-nance, on which I fancied I could see the record of a happy life and many a good deed done. If living in a healthy air produces the signs of health, why should not living one's whole life in an atmo-sphere of benevolence bring out into the expression the tokens of a healthy soul !

We walked over the grounds of the rectory. Have you a very definite idea of an English lawn ! The grass is shaven every week ; this, of course, produces a fresh bright tint, and to your tread it feels like the richest bed of moss you ever set your

> My fire's extinct, my forge decay'd,
> My vice all in the dust is laid ;
> My coal is spent, my iron gone,
> My last nail 's driven—my work is done ! "

foot upon. I fear we never can have the abundance and variety of flowers they have here. I see continually plants which remain in the open ground all winter, that we are obliged to house by the first of October. There was a myrtle reaching the second-story windows of Mr. Wilberforce's house.

In my strolls I avail myself of every opportunity of accosting the people, and when I can find any pretext I go into the cottages by the way-side. This, I suppose, is very *un-English*, and may seem to some persons very impertinent. But I have never found inquiries, softened with a certain tone of sympathy, repulsed. Your inferiors in condition are much like children, and they, you know, like dogs, are proverbially said to know who loves them. I stopped at a little cottage this morning, half smothered with roses, geraniums, &c., and, on the pretext of looking at a baby, made good my entrance. The little bit of an apartment, not more than six feet by ten, was as neat as possible. Not an article of its scanty furniture looked as if it had been bought by this generation ; everything appeared cared for, and well preserved ; so unlike corresponding dwellings with us. The woman had nine children ; six at home, and all tidily dressed. I have not seen in England a slovenly-looking person. Even the three or four beggars who stealthily asked charity of us at Portsmouth were *neatly* dressed.

I greeted, *en passant*, a woman sitting at her cottage window. She told me she paid for half of a little tenement and a bit of a garden ten pounds (fifty dollars) rent. And when I congratulated her on the pleasant country, " Ah," she said, "we can't live on a pleasant country !" I have not addressed one of these people who has not complained of poverty, said something of the difficulty of getting work, of the *struggling* for bread, which is the condition of existence among the lower classes here. Strange sounds these to our ears !

I was amused to-day, with something that marked the diversity of the condition from ours, in another way. I accosted a little girl who stood at a cottage-gate. She was as well dressed as S.'s girls, or any other of our well-to-do-in-the-world people. Among other impertinent questions I asked " Who lives here ?" " Mrs. So-and-so and Mrs. So-and-so." " Only two *ladies* !" I exclaimed, conforming my phrase to the taste of our cottage-dames. " They ben't ladies," she replied. " Indeed ! what are they ?" " They be's womans." Would such a disclaimer have been put in from one end of the United States to the other, unless in the shanty of *adopted* citizens ?

I will spare you all the particulars of my wayside acquaintance with a sturdy little woman whom I met coming out of a farm-yard, staggering under a load of dry furze, as much as could be piled on a wheelbarrow. A boy not more than five years old was awaiting her at the gate, with a compact little parcel in his arms snugly done up. " Now take *she*," he said, extending it to the mother, and I found the parcel was a baby not a month old ; so I offered to carry it, and did for a quarter of a mile, while the mother, in return, told me the whole story of her courtship, marriage, and maternity, with the last incident in her domestic annals, the acquisition of a baking of meal, some barm,

and the loan of her husband's mother's oven, and, lastly, of the gift of the furze to heat the oven. The woman seemed something more than contented—happy. I could not but congratulate her. " It does not signify," I said, " being poor, when one is so healthy and so merry as you appear." " Ah, that's natural to me," she replied ; " my mother had red cheeks in her coffin !" Happy are those who have that " *natural* to them," that princes, and fine ladies, and half the world are sighing for and running after.

The last part of our drive to Fresh-water Bay was through a highly-cultivated district, but the country had lost its romantic charm ; to the very sea-shore on both sides of us it was covered with barley, pease, and the finest of wheat. Save a glimpse of the sea in the distance, the bold headland of Black Gang Chine, and the downs before us, it was as tame as a cosset lamb. And, by-the-way, speaking of lambs and such fancy articles, immense flocks of sheep are grazing on these downs, and each is as big as three of our Merinos, and the mutton is delicious.

FRESH-WATER BAY.

We are at an inn within a few yards of the beach, with a shore of chalky cliffs, and a pretty arch in the rocks worn by the water ; and a jutting point before us called the Stag, from a fanciful resemblance, as I conjecture, to that animal boldly leaping into the waves. The Halls are here, and in a stroll with them last evening over the cliffs we encountered a man who lives, not " by gathering samphire " (which, by-the-way, we did gather), but by getting the eggs of sea-fowl that resort here in immense flocks, flattering themselves, no doubt, in their bliss of ignorance, that the cliffs are inaccessible[*]. Our egg-hunter had been successful, and had a sack of eggs hanging before him. He pays two guineas a-year to the lord of the manor, for the privilege of getting them, and sells them, he says, " to people in a decline." One lady, he told us, had paid him a shilling a-piece. " She," replied Captain H., with a lurking smile, " must have been far gone in a decline, I think." The man told us they had the art of emptying the egg-shell by perforating it with two pinholes, and blowing out the contents ; whereupon the captain, who leaves nothing unessayed, amid his children's merry shouts and ours, fairly rivalled the professor at his own art.

Sunday.—We have been to church for the first time in England. It was an old Gothic edifice. I thought of our forefathers with tenderness and with reverence. Brave men they were to leave these venerable sanctuaries, to go over the ocean —to " the depth of the desert's gloom."

---

[*] They are of very difficult access, as we were assured by seeing the process of letting the man down and sustaining him on the perpendicular cliff ; but nothing seems impossible to men who must die or struggle for their bread. The man was stout and very well-looking, but with an anxious and sad expression. I found he had a large family to feed, and among them four stalwart boys. I asked him what were their prospects. " None," he said, with an expression suited to the words, " but starvation."

It was a curious coincidence enough, that the first preacher we hear this side the water bears our own name. This it was, no doubt, that set my mind to running upon relationships and forefathers. Mr. S. is a poor curate, who, after twenty years' service, is compelled to leave his place here by the new order of things, which obliges his superior to do his own work. One feels a little distrustful of those reforms that destroy individual happiness and snap asunder old ties.

Monday.—We drove this morning to Carisbrooke Castle, an old ruin in the heart of the island. We were shown the window through which Charles I., when imprisoned here, attempted to escape. In spite of getting my first historical impressions from Hume, that lover of kings and supreme lover of the Stuarts, I never had much sympathy with this king of bad faith ; still it is not easy to stand at this window without a sorrowful sympathy with Charles. There he stood, looking on the land that seemed to him his inheritance by a Divine charter, longing for the wings of the birds that were singing round this window, to bear him to those friends who were awaiting him, and instead of him, had only the signal which he hung out of this window to give them notice of the defeat of his project.

Nothing, I know, is more tiresome than the description of old castles which you get from such raw tourists as we are, and may find in every guide-book ; but I wish I could do up my sensations and send them to you. As we passed the Elizabethan gate, and wound away up into the old keep, stopping, now and then, to look through the openings left for the exercise of the cross-bow, or as we wandered about the walls, and stood to hear the pebble descend into Carisbrooke well*, I felt as if old legends had become incorporate.

We expect nothing pleasanter than the week we have spent on the Isle of Wight. How much of our enthusiasm it may owe to our coming to it from shipboard, and to the fresh impressions of the Old World, of its thatched cottages, ivied walls, old churches and churchyards, and English cultivation, I cannot say. The English speak of it as all "*in little,*" a cockney affair, &c. ; but, if small, it has the delicacy and perfection of a cabinet picture.

SOUTHAMPTON.

MY DEAR C.,

Thursday, 13th.—The luxury of an English inn, after a day exhausting as our last on the Isle of Wight, has never been exaggerated, and cannot be overpraised. We have not been ten days in England, without having certain painful comparisons between our own inns and those of this country forced upon us. But I intend, after I have had more experience, to give you my observations on this subject in one plentiful shower, instead of annoying you with sprinkling them over all my letters.

Our intention was to have proceeded directly to London. Instead of this, we have loitered here two days, and why, I will tell you.

* The well is 200 feet in depth, 25 of masonry, and th rest cut through a solid rock.

Captain Hall's good taste was shocked at our leaving Southampton without seeing Netley Abbey ; and surely to leave this out, in seeing England, would be much like the omission of the Midsummer Night's Dream in reading Shakspeare. So yesterday morning, with a sky as clear and almost as deep as our own summer sky, we set off, accompanied by the Halls, for these beautiful ruins. They are much more entire than those of Carisbrooke. The walls are standing, and how long they have been so is touchingly impressed upon you by the tall trees that have grown up in the unroofed apartments. Shrubs four or five feet high fringe the tops of the walls, and flowers are rooted in the crevices. It seemed as if Nature, with a feeling of kindred for a beautiful work of art, would fain hide the wounds she could not heal—wounds of violence as well as time.

I shall spare you any description, for I should waste your time and mine. No description can convey as definite an idea as any of the hundred engravings you have seen of Netley Abbey ; and I am sorry to say to you, that even a Daguerreotype picture would give you no adequate impression of its beauty. There is nothing for you but to come and see these places ; their soul, their history, their associations, are untransfuseable. I have no extraordinary sensibility to such things, and I saw —— smiling at my tears ; and glad I should have been to have passed a day alone there, to have trodden the ground with undisturbed recollections of those who reared the beautiful temple, who were, in their time, the teachers of religion, the preservers of learning, the fountains of charity. It would not be easy to indulge this fancy, for, besides the guides that infested us, and a succession of hunters after the picturesque, R. detected some fellows stealing jackdaws' nests ; and Captain H. not only threatened them with the strong arm of the law, but, to secure these holy precincts from such marauders, he was at the pains to lodge information against them with the proper authority.

On our return from Netley we ascertained that the —— family are at their place, a short drive from Southampton. You know how much reason we have to wish to avail ourselves of our letters to them ; or, rather, you do not know how much, nor did we till we had seen them. So we sent off our letters, and went to Winchester with the Halls by the railroad. It was but the second day since this section of the road was opened, and it was lined with staring people, hurraing and clapping hands. The chief object of the excursion to us was the Cathedral, which is the largest in England. A part of it is of the Saxon order, and dates from the seventh century. What think you of our New-World eyes seeing the sarcophagi containing the bones of the old Saxon kings—the Ethelreds and Ethelwolfs, and of Canute the Dane ; the tombs of William Rufus, and of William of Wickham ; the chair in which bloody Mary sat at her nuptial ceremony ; besides unnumbered monuments and chapels built by kings and bishops ; to say nothing of some of the best art of our own time, sculpture by Flaxman and Chantrey ! Their details were lost upon us in the effect of the great whole ; the long-drawn aisles, the windows with their exquisite colouring, the lofty vault, the carved stones, the pillars and arches—those beautiful Gothic arches. We had some compensation for the unconsciousness of a lifetime of the power of architecture, in our overwhelming emotions. They cannot be repeated. We cannot see a cathedral twice for the first time, that is very clear!

I was not prepared for the sensations to be excited by visiting these old places of the Old World. There is nothing in our land to aid the imperfect lights of history. Here it seems suddenly verified. Its long-buried dead, or, rather, its dim spectres, appear with all the freshness of actual life. A miracle is wrought on poetry and painting. While they represented what we had never seen, they were but shadows to us; a kind of magic mirrors, showing false images; now they seem a Divine form, for the perpetual preservation of the beautiful creations of Nature and art.

It happened that while we were in Winchester Cathedral, service was performed there. I cannot tell how I might have been affected if it had been a more hearty service. There were the officials, the clergyman and clerk, a choir of boys, and, for the audience, half-a-dozen men, three or four women, octogenarians, or verging on the extreme of human life, and ourselves. I confess that the temple, and not He who sanctifies it, filled my mind. My eyes were wandering over the arches, the carvings, the Saxon *caskets*, &c., &c.*

When we arrived at the depôt at Southampton we found Mrs. ——, with her daughter, awaiting us with a welcome that made us forget we were strangers to them and strangers in a strange land—blessed forgetfulness! They transferred K. and myself to their carriage, and we drove home with them to B. Lodge; and, as the days here are eked out with a generous twilight till nearly ten o'clock, we had time to see their beautiful place, and to-day the pleasure has been repeated.

I cannot follow the rule I would fain have adopted, and compare what I see here to what is familiar to you at home. There is, for instance, in this place of Mrs. ——, a neatness, completeness, and perfection, of which we have but the beginning and faint shadowing. Our grounds are like our society, where you meet every degree of civilization. Here, every tree, shrub, and little flower is in its right place, and nothing present that should not be here. On one side of the house the garden is laid out in the fantastical French style, in the form of hearts and whimsical figures, but elsewhere it is completely English, with noble trees, that grow as nature bids them; hothouses, with grapes and pines; and a lawn that for hundreds of years, probably, has had its grass cropped every week through the growing months.

The house is, I fancy, rather a favourable specimen of the residences of the English gentry, spacious, and arranged with comfort and elegance; but not surpassing, in these respects, the first class of gentlemen's country-houses in America. But there are luxuries here that we have not, and shall not have for many a day.

* The prudence of not attempting a description of Winchester Cathedral, or an enumeration of its treasures, will be appreciated by those who know that a volume of 200 pages is devoted to this subject alone.

The walls are painted by the master of the house with views on the Rhine, from sketches of his own, and very beautiful they are. This is, to be sure, attainable to us; for a taste, and a certain facility in painting, is common enough among us; but when shall we see on our walls an unquestionable Titian, or a Carlo Dolce, or when, in a gentleman's country-house, an apartment filled with casts from the best antiques? Certainly not till our people cease to demand drapery for the chanting cherubs, and such like innocents!

Mrs. —— was a friend of Mrs. Siddons. She has a full-length picture of her by Lawrence, which represents a perfect woman in the maturity of her powers and charms, somewhat idealised, perhaps, as if the painter were infected by Mrs. ——'s enthusiasm, and to the fondness of a friend added the devotion of a worshipper. It is Mrs. Siddons; not a muse, queen, or goddess, though fit to be any or all of them. She is dressed in a very un-goddesslike short waist. Strange, that a woman who had her classic eye, and her passion for moulding forms after antique models, should submit to the tyranny of a French milliner's levelling fashion! Her beautiful arms are classically manifest—bare as Juno's. Lawrence employed thirty hours on each of them.

We all lunched with Mrs. ——. An English lunch is our country dinner, served at our country hour, and of much the same material. Different in the respect, that whatever is to be eaten is placed on the table at the same time, and very different, inasmuch as you are served by three or four men in livery, instead of a girl in a dress unquestionably of her own choosing. Mrs. ——'s vegetable-dishes are a precious relic of Mrs. Siddons. They are silver, and bear her initials and an inscription from the lawyers of Edinburgh, by whom they were presented to her.

After lunch, Miss —— took us in her carriage, stowing the girls in the rumble, through Lord Ashdown's and Mr. Fleming's parks. We drove a mile through the latter, with thick borderings and plantations of shrubbery on each side of us, so matted, and with such a profusion of rhododendron, as to remind me of passages in the wilds of western Virginia. This, you know, is a plant not native to this country, but brought with much pains and expense from ours. We have not English wealth to lavish on parks and gardens, but with taste and industry we might bring to our homes, and gratefully cherish, the beautiful plants that God has sown at broadcast in our forests. I declare to you, when I remember how seldom I have seen our azaleas, kalmias, &c., in cultivated grounds, while I meet them here in such abundance, it seems like finding a neglected child housed and gently entertained by strangers. Some of us returned to dine and pass the evening with Mrs. —— and her daughter; and we left B—— Lodge warmed to the heart's core with this realisation of our old poetic ideas of English hospitality*.

* I have abstained from transferring from my journal whatever was personal to our kind entertainers, certainly the paramount charm of their place. We owed the warmth of our reception to letters from their and our dear friend, Mrs. Butler. To her, too, we owed our admission to some of the best society in London, where her genius and character are held in the high estimation they deserve.

Friday, June 13.—We left Southampton this morning, feeling much, when we parted from Captain Hall and his family, as if we were launching alone on the wide world. He told us, at the last, if we got into any difficulty, if we were at Johnny Groat's even, to send for him. As far as the most thoughtful kindness and foresight can provide against difficulties, he has done so for us. Both he and Mrs. Hall have given us letters of introduction (unasked), and a score, at least, to their friends in London and Scotland, people of rank and distinction. To these they have added addresses to tradespeople of all descriptions, and all manner of instructions as to our goings on : a kind of mapping and charting inestimable to raw travellers like us. He has even had lodgings provided for us in London by his man of business, so that we shall find a home in that great, and, to us, unknown sea.

You will smile at all our letters running upon this theme of Captain H., and you may perchance fancy that our preconceived opinion of this gentleman is rather bribed by personal kindness than rectified. But remember that we had no claim upon his kindness. It is not our personal benefits (though, Heaven knows, we are most grateful for them) that I am anxious to impress upon you, but to give you the advantage of our point of sight of a character that some of our people have misunderstood, and some misrepresented. I have no such crusading notions as that I could set a whole nation's opinion right, but I should hope to affect yours, and perhaps half-a-dozen others. Captain H. has a mind wide awake, ever curious and active. These qualities have been of infinite service to him as a traveller, and to his charmed readers as well ; but it is easy to see how, among strangers, they might betray him into some little extravagances. Then he is a seaman and a Briton, and liable, on both scores, to unphilosophic judgments. With the faults that proceed from an excess of activity, we, of all people, should be most patient ; and certainly we might have forgiven some mistaken opinions in conformity to preconceived patterns, instead of imputing them to political prostitution. We might, indeed, had we been wise, have found many of his criticisms just and salutary, and thanked him for them, and have delighted in his frankness, his sagacity, and his vein of very pleasant humour ; but, alas ! our Saxon blood is always uppermost, and we go on cherishing our infallibility, and, like a snappish cook, had much rather spoil our own pie than have a foreign finger in it. It is an old trick of the English bull-dog to bark at his neighbour's door ; but let him do so, if he will caress you at his own.

I FEEL, my dear C., a disposition to self-glorification from one circumstance of our journey from Southampton. My girls and I took our seats on the top of the coach, paying for two inside seats, in case of rain, of which, I take it in England, there are always nine chances out of ten. You may well ask why I boast of this, when we gained the obvious advantage of using our eyes in this rich and new scene ; and when they are nearly as useless inside the coach as were Jonah's to him in his " extra exclusive." You know I am a coward on instinct, and to a novice a seat on the top of an English coach is startling; and it is somewhat perilous, the coach being topheavy with the number of passengers and mass of baggage, and we were not yet accustomed to the security of these smooth roads. And besides, you cannot expect us to be exempt from the general weakness of wishing to impress the grooms, porters, coachmen, innkeepers, &c., with our potentiality ! Many Americans give up the delight of travelling in England on account of its expensiveness, or come home with loud outcries against it, when, if they would forego the distinction of posting, and condescend to the humility of an outside seat, (infinitely the pleasantest,) they might travel here quite as cheaply as they can *by coach* at home*.

Did the sacrifices that a traveller makes to appearances never strike you as one of the ludicrous fatuities of human conduct, when you consider that his observers do not know whether he be " Giles Jolt," or any other member of the human family ?

We had good reason to be satisfied with our position. The coachman had driven twenty years on this same road, and was familiar with every inch of ground ; he exchanged salutations with the people by the way, and many professional jokes, and pointed out to us the wayside lions,—a seat of Lord Wellington, a hunting-box of George IV., &c. We came through Winchester and Basingstoke, passed many a field covered with the crimson blush of the cinquefoil, and bounded by hedges thick set with flowering shrubs. I trust your grandchildren may see such in our Berkshire. I had written to Miss Mitford my intention of passing the evening with her, and as we approached her residence, which is in a small village near Reading, I began to feel a little tremulous about meeting my " unknown friend." Captain Hall had made us all merry with anticipating the usual *dénouement* of a mere epistolary acquaintance.

Our coachman (who, after our telling him we were Americans, had complimented us on our speaking English, and " very good English too†") professed an acquaintance of some twenty years' standing with Miss M., and assured us that she was one of the " cleverest women in England," and " the doctor" (her father) a fine " old gentleman." And when he reined his horses up to her door, and she appeared to receive us, he said, " Now, you would not take that lady there for the great author, would you ?" and certainly we should have taken her for nothing but a kindly gentlewoman, who had never gone beyond the narrow sphere of the most refined social life. My foolish misgivings (H. must answer for them) were forgotten in her cordial welcome. K. and I descended from our airy seat ; and when Miss M. became aware who M. was, she said, " What ! the sister of —— pass my door ?—that must never be ; " so

* I should have said, as they could have done at home. The rates of travelling expenses are diminishing at such a rate, that you cannot predicate of this year what was true of the last. What is fixed in the United States ? A guide-book, written one season, would be in good part useless the next.

† We had a compliment of the same stamp the next day from a Londoner who was in the car with us. He assured us, with praiseworthy condescension, that we spoke English " uncommon correct."

M., nothing loath, joined us. Miss M. is truly "a pleasing person," and dressed a little quaintly, and as unlike as possible to the faces we have seen of her in the magazines, which all have a broad humour, bordering on coarseness. She has a pale grey, soul-lit eye, and hair as white as snow ; a wintry sign that has come prematurely upon her, as like signs come upon us, while the year is yet fresh and undecayed. Her voice has a sweet, low tone, and her manner a naturalness, frankness, and affectionateness, that we have been so long familiar with in their other modes of manifestation, that it would have been indeed a disappointment not to have found them.

She led us directly through her house into her garden, a perfect bouquet of flowers. "I must show you my geraniums while it is light," she said, "for I love them next to my father." And they were indeed treated like petted children, guarded by a very ingenious contrivance from the rough visitation of the elements. They are all, I believe, seedlings. She raises two crops in a year, and may well pride herself on the variety and beauty of her collection. Geraniums are her favourites ; but she does not love others less that she loves these more. The garden is filled, matted with flowering shrubs, and vines ; the trees are wreathed with honeysuckles and roses ; and the girls have brought away the most splendid specimens of heart's-ease to press in their journals. Oh, that I could give some of my countrywomen a vision of this little paradise of flowers, that they might learn how *taste and industry*, and an earnest love and study of the art of garden-culture, might triumph over small space and small means!

Miss Mitford's house is, with the exception of certainly not more than two or three, as small and humble as the smallest and humblest in our village of S—— ; and such is the difference, in some respects, in the modes of expense in this country from ours ; she keeps two men-servants (one a gardener), two or three maid-servants, and two horses. In this very humble home, which she illustrates as much by her unsparing filial devotion as by her genius, she receives on equal terms the best in the land. Her literary reputation might have gained for her this elevation, but she started on vantage-ground, being allied by blood to the Duke of Bedford's family. We passed a delightful evening, parting with the hope of meeting again, and with a most comfortable feeling that the ideal was converted into the real. So much for our misgivings. Faith is a safer principle than some people hold it to be*.

We finished our journey by the Great Western Railway. It is little short of desecration to cut up this garden country, where all rough ways were already made smooth, all crooked ones straight, with railroads. They seem to have been devised for our uncultivated lands and gigantic distances.

* I have not dared to draw aside the curtain of domestic life, and give the particulars of Miss M.'s touching devotion to her father. "He is all to me, and I am all to him," she said. God help them in this parting world!

London, 14th.—HERE we are, with a house to ourselves, in modest, comfortable, clean lodgings (but is not all England clean!) in Halfmoon-street. It is the London season, so called from Parliament being in session, and all the fashion and business of the kingdom congregating here at this time. We are told that we are fortunate in getting any lodgings at the West End, while the town is so filled ; and at the West End you must be if you would hope to live in the daylight of the known, that is, the fashionable world†.

Would you know what struck me as we drove from the depôt of the Western Railroad to our lodgings ? the familiar names of the streets, the neutral tint of the houses, the great superiority of the pavements to ours, and, having last seen New York, the superior cleanliness of the streets. I have all my life heard London spoken of as dismal and dark. It may be so in winter ; it is not now. The smoke colour of the houses is soft and healthy to the eye, so unlike our flame-coloured cities, that seem surely to typify their destiny, which is, you know, to be burned up, sooner or later—*sooner*, in most cases. And, having had nothing to do to-day but gaze from our windows, what think you has struck us as quite different from a relative position in our own city ?—the groups of ballad-singers, consisting usually of a man and woman, and one or two children. I have seen such in New York half-a-dozen times in my life, and they are always people from the Continent of Europe. Here, not half an hour passes without a procession of these licensed, musical, and, to us novices, irresistible beggars. Then there are the hawkers of flowers as irresistible, lovely bouquets of moss-rosebuds, geraniums, heliotropes, and what not. As we are in the neighbourhood of Piccadilly and the parks, our street is quite a thoroughfare, and we are every moment exclaiming at the superb equipages that pass our window. Nothing, I presume, of the kind in the world exceeds the luxury of an English carriage with all its appointments ; and yet, shall I confess to you that, after my admiration of their superb horses was somewhat abated, I have felt, in looking at them, much as I have at seeing a poor little child made a fool of by the useless and glittering trappings of his hobbyhorse. What would our labouring men, who work up the time and strength God

† As exact details of expenses are useful to inexperienced travellers, I may perhaps do a service to some one by giving the precise cost of our London lodging. We had a drawing and a dining-room, a bed-room and dressing-room on the second floor, and three bed-rooms on the third floor (all small), for seven guineas a week, and one guinea for firing and attendance. Under the term firing is included cooking. We lived simply, having regularly two dishes meat (or fish and meat), a pudding or tart, and the fruits in season, strawberries and cherries. Our breakfast was coffee and tea, bread, butter, rolls, muffins, and eggs. The cost to each person (one gentleman and five ladies) was a trifle more than two pounds twelve shillings (thirteen dollars) a week. Every article of food was perfect of its kind, and well served. The most fastidious could have found no ground of complaint. The high prices were raging when we left New York, and we found the common articles of food in London not higher, in some cases lower; for instance, for excellent cauliflowers we gave sixpence—twelve and a half cents.

gives them into independence, domestic happiness, and political existence—what would they, what should they say, at seeing three—four servants—strong, tall, well-made young men (for such are selected)—attached to a coach, one coachman and three footmen, two, of course, perfect supernumeraries! We "moralise the spectacle," too; observe the vacant countenance and flippant air of these men, chained to the circle of half-a-dozen ideas, and end with a laugh at their fantastical liveries; some in white turned with red, and some in red turned with white. Fancy a man driving, with a militia general's hat, feathers and all, with three footmen, one seated beside him and two behind, all with white coats, scarlet plush breeches, white silk stockings, rosettes on their shoes, and gold-headed batons in their white-gloved hands. There must be something "rotten in the state," when God's creatures, "possible angels," as our friend Doctor T. calls all human kind, look up to a station behind a lord's coach as a privileged place. "Possible angels" they may be; but, alas, their path is hedged about with huge improbabilities!

SINCE the first day of our arrival here, my dear C., we have been going on with the swiftness of railroad motion. I have made, *en passant*, a few notes in the hope of retaining impressions that were necessarily slight and imperfect; and now, at my first leisure, I am about to expand them for you. You shall have them honestly, without colouring or exaggeration. I can scarcely hope they will have any other merit; for, without any humble disclaimers which might be made as to the incompetency of the individual—that individual a woman, always more or less hampered—what is one month in London! one month among two millions of people!

Coming to the cities of the Old World, as we do, with our national vanities thick upon us, with our scale of measurement graduated by Broadway, the City-Hall, the Battery, and the Boston-Common, we are confounded by the extent of London, by its magnificent parks, its immense structures, by its docks and warehouses, and by all its details of convenience and comfort, and its aggregate of incalculable wealth. We begin with comforting ourselves with the thought "Why, these people have been at it these two thousand years, and Heaven knows how much longer." By degrees envy melts into self-complacency, and we say "they are our relations;" "our fathers had a hand in it;" we are of the same race, "as our new-planned cities and unfinished towers" shall hereafter prove. Mr. Webster said to me after we had both been two or three weeks here, "What is your impression now of London! my feeling is yet amazement."

I got my best idea of the source of the wealth and power of the country from visiting the docks and warehouses, which we did thoroughly, under the conduct of our very kind countryman, Mr. P. Vaughan, whose uncle, Mr. William Vaughan, had much to do with the suggesting and planning these great works. Do not fear I am about to give you a particular description of them, which you will get so much better from any statistics of London. Our "woman's sphere," the boundaries of which some of my sex are making rather inde-

finite, does not extend to such subjects. We yet have the child's pleasure of wonder, and we had it in perfection in passing through an apartment a hundred feet in length, appropriated to cinnamon, the next of equal extent to cloves, and so on and so on to a wine-vault under an acre of ground.

I never enter the London parks without regretting the folly (call it not cupidity) of our people, who, when they had a whole continent at their disposal, have left such narrow spaces for what has been so well called the lungs of a city; its breathing-places they certainly are*. I do not know the number of squares in London. I should think a hundred as large as our boasted St. John's Park, the Park, Washington and Union Squares. Their parks appear to me to cover as much ground as half our city of New York. The Regent's Park, the largest, contains 450 acres; Hyde Park, 395. Besides these, there are Green and St. James's Parks, which, however, are both much smaller than Hyde Park. I wonder if some of our speculating *lot*-mad people would not like to have the draining of their adorning-waters, and the laying-out of the ground into streets and building-lots, a passion as worthy as Scott's old Cummer's for streaking a corse. It would, indeed, be changing the living into the dead to drive the spirit of health and the healthiest pleasure from these beautiful grounds. The utilitarian principle, in its narrowest sense, has too much to do in our country. I can fancy a Western squatter coming into Regent's Park and casting his eye over its glades, gardens, and shrubberies, exclaim, "Why, this is the best of parara† land; I'll squat here!"

Yes, dear C., that surely is a narrow utilitarianism which would make everything convertible to the meat that perisheth; and to that would sacrifice God's rich provisions for the wants of man's spirit. The only chance a London tradesman has to feel that he has anything nobler in his nature than a craving stomach, is when he comes forth on Sunday from his smoky place of daily toil into these lovely green parks, where he and his young ones can lay themselves down on the greensward, under the shadow of majestic trees, amid the odour of flowers and the singing of birds: all God's witnesses even to their dulled senses. We have 300,000 souls now in New-York. We shall soon have our million; but, alas! we have no such paradise in preparation for them!

The Zoological Garden is in Regent's Park. As a garden merely, it is very beautiful; and I do not doubt its planner or planners had reference to the original type of all gardens. Its various and vast number of animals remind you at every turn of Milton's Paradise, though the women in blue and purple satin, and the men in the last fashion of Bond-street, bear little resemblance to

---

* A friend has suggested that this censure is unjust in regard to our largest cities, New York and Philadelphia; that, being built on a limited space inclosed by great bodies of water, our people could not afford to devote building-ground to other purposes. But, have they done what they could? What is the justification for the sacrifice of Hoboken? and has anything been done to secure the refinement of pleasure-grounds in our smaller towns and villages?

† The Western Anglicè for prairie.

the original specimens of those who, with their loyal subjects, were " to find pastime and bear rule."

" For contemplation he and valour form'd ;
For softness she, and sweet attractive grace."

All the representatives of the bird and animal creation that were housed in the ark appear to have their descendants here ; and, as if to guard them against dying of homesickness, they have their little surroundings made as far as possible to resemble their native places. They are accommodated, according to the national taste, with private lodgings, and space to roam and growl at will à l'Anglaise. There is sparkling water for aquatic birds, and ponds for the otter to dive in. There is space for the dainty giraffe, who seems hardly to touch the ground from very delicateness, to rove over, and trees, to whose topmost branches he stretches his flexile neck. The bear has his area, with poles to hug and climb, and the elephant his tank to swim in, and forest-like glades to lumber along ; and camels we saw in the distance grazing on fields of green grass ; and then there are " rows of goodliest trees " and " verdurous walls'; " " blossoms and fruits ; " all the luxuries of paradise, save authority, solitude, innocence, and a few such light matters. The garden has not been open more than twelve years. The price of admission is only one shilling English. This we should think liberal enough in our democratic country. The pleasure is made more exclusive on Sunday by the requisition of a member's ticket, but these are easily obtained. Several were sent us unasked. If you care for such shows, you may then, in addition to the birds and beasts, see the gentry and nobility !

I FANCY that most of our people, when they arrive in London, go to the Tower and Westminster Abbey, as the sights they have most and longest thirsted for. I have been told that Webster had not been half an hour in London when he took a cab and drove to the Tower ; and I liked the boyish feeling still fresh and perceptible, like the little rivulet whose hue marks it distinctly long after it has entered some great river. I have *not* seen the Tower ; not for lack of interest in it, for, ever since in my childhood my heart ached for the hapless state prisoner that passed its portals, I have longed to see it. We went there at an unfortunate hour ; the doors were closed ; and I was like a crossed child when I felt that I should never see the Black Prince's armour, nor the axe that dealt the death-blow to Anne Boleyn, nor the prison of Sir Walter Raleigh, nor any of the Tower's soul-moving treasures. We were admitted within the outer wall, which incloses an area where three thousand people live ; a fact that, as it is all I have to communicate, will, I hope, surprise you as much as it did me.

We went three times to Westminster Abbey, and spent many hours there ; hours that had more sensation in them than months, I might almost say years, of ordinary life. Why, my dear C., it is worth crossing the Atlantic to enter the little door by which we first went into the Abbey, and have your eyes light on that familiar legend, " O rare Ben Jonson !" And then to walk around and see the monuments of Shakspeare, Spenser, Milton,

and of other inspired teachers. You have strange and mixed feelings. You approach nearer to them than ever before, but it is in sympathy with their mortality. You *realise* for the first time that they are dead ; for who, of all your friends, have been so living to you as they ? We escaped from our automaton guide, and walked about as if in a trance.

There is much embodied history in the Abbey— facts recorded in stone. And there are startling curiosities of antiquity, such, for example, as a coronation-chair as old as Edward the Confessor's time, and the helmet of Henry V., and his saddle, the very saddle he rode on at Agincourt. I thought, as I looked at it, and felt the blood tingling in my veins, that his prophecy of being " freshly remembered," even " to the ending of the world," was in fair progress to fulfilment.

The Gothic architecture of parts of the Abbey is, I believe, quite unequalled ; but the effect of the whole is impaired by Protestant spoliations and alterations. Henry the Seventh's chapel, with its carved stone ceiling, is a proverb and miracle of beauty.

I was grievously disappointed in St. Paul's. I early got, from some school-book I believe, an impression that it was a model of architecture, that Sir Christopher Wren was a Divine light among artists, and sundry other false notions. It stands in the heart of the city of London, and is so defaced, and absolutely blackened by its coal-smoke, that you would scarcely suspect it to be of that beautiful material white Portland stone. A more heavy, inexpressive mass can hardly be found cumbering the ground. It takes time and infinite pains, depend on't, to educate the Saxon race out of their natural inaptitude in matters of taste. As you stand within and under the dome, the effect is very grand and beautiful. The statues here and at Westminster struck me as monstrous, and even curious, productions for an age when Grecian art was extant, or, indeed, for any age ; for there is always the original model, the human form. The artists have not taken man for their model, but the *English* man, of whom grace can scarcely be predicated, and the Englishman, too, in his national, and sometimes in his hideous military costume.

One of the sights that much pleased me was the Inns of Court. The entrance to it is from one of the thronged thoroughfares (Fleet-street, I believe), to which it seems a sort of episode, or rather, like a curious antique pendant to a chain of modern workmanship. The ground, now occupied by the lawyers, was formerly appropriated to the Knights Templars. Their chapel still remains ; a singular old structure it is. A part of it is in its original condition, as it was when the Du Bois Guilberts of the romantic days worshipped there. When I looked at their effigies in stone, I could almost hear their armour clanking and ringing on the pavement.

As you will perceive from my barren report to you, I have given very little time to sight-seeing, and less to public amusements. I went once to Covent Garden Theatre with Mrs. ———. She has a free ticket, which admits two persons ; one of the small fruits of her literary sowing, a species of labour which should produce to her a wide-spread and golden harvest. We went unattended —a new experience to me. Necessity has taught women here more independence than with us, and it has its advantages to both parties ; the men are saved much bother, and the women gain faculty and freedom. Mrs. —— proceeded with as much ease as if she were going to her own room at home, and we met with no difficulty or impertinence whatever, not even a stare. The play was Henry V., as it is restored by Macready, who, with a zeal that all true lovers of Shakspeare must venerate, is effacing the profane alterations of the poet's text ; such mangling, for instance, as Garrick made of the last scenes of Lear ; and, besides, is adding indescribably to the dramatic beauty of the representation by an elaborate conformity to the costume of the period which the play represents. Shakspeare himself would, I suspect, be somewhat startled by the perfection of scenic decoration and costume of Macready's presentation of Henry V. While the choruses are rehearsing by Time, there is a pictorial exhibition of the scenes he describes ; and this is managed with such art as to appear to the spectator, not a picture, but an actual scene. As he finishes, a curtain, which seems like a dissolving cloud, is withdrawn, and discloses the actors.

Covent Garden Theatre is much larger, more elegant, and more commodiously arranged than the best of ours. There is a certain indefinite pleasure proceeding from seeing a play of Shakspeare played in the land where he lived ; where he has seen them enacted, and himself enacted them. It is something like going to a friend's house for the first time after a long and close friendship with him. A few days since we were at Southampton, and passed through the arch under which Henry led his army when he embarked for the "fair and lucky war." This, and the recurrence of the names of localities that are now within our daily drives, gave me the *realising* sensation of which you may well be tired of hearing by this time. And, by-the-way, how could I describe this sensation without our expressive American (New England !) use of this word realise !

We went once to the Italian opera, and sat in the pit. The intermixture of gaily-dressed ladies with men in the pit gives it a civilised and lively aspect; it is something like turning a forest into a flower-garden. The pit of the opera is filled with people of respectable condition, as you may suppose from the cost of any box large enough for five or six people being seven or eight guineas. We paid two dollars for a seat. Mrs. —— was with us, expounding to us, and enjoying, as none but those who have the genius to the fingers' ends that makes the artist, can enjoy. The people who have the reputation of being the first singers in the world sang : Grisi, the young Garcia, Persiani, Lablache, Tamburini, and a very interesting young man, the son of an Italian marquis, whose *nom-de-guerre* is Mario. The little queen was in her box behind a curtain, as carefully hidden from her people as an oriental monarch ; not from any oriental ideas of the sacredness of her person, but that she may cast off her royal dignity, and have the privilege of enjoying unobserved, as we humble people do. No chariness of her countenance could make her "like the robe pontifical, ne'er seen but wondered at." She is a plain little body enough, as we saw when she protruded her head to bow to the high people in the box next to her : the queen-dowager, the Princess Esterhazy, and so on. Ordinary is the word for her ; you would not notice her among a hundred others in our village church. Just now she is suffering for the tragedy of Lady Flora, and fears are entertained, whenever she appears, that there will be voices to cry out " *Where is Lady Flora ?*" a sound that must pierce the poor young thing's heart. Ah ! she has come to the throne when royalty pays quite too dear for its whistle !

We had the ballet La Gitana after the singing— and Taglioni. No praise of her grace is exaggerated. There is music in every movement of her arms ; and if she would restrict herself within the limits of decency, there could not be a more exquisite spectacle of its kind than her dancing. I would give in to the ravings of her admirers, and allow that her grace is God's beautiful gift, and that fitting it is it should be so used. But could not this grace be equally demonstrated with a skirt a few inches longer and rather less transparent ! To my crude notions her positions are often disgusting ; and when she raised her leg to a right angle with her body, I could have exclaimed, as Carlyle did, " Merciful, Heaven ! where will it end !"

Familiarity must dull the sense to these bad parts of the exhibition ; for Mrs. —— quoted a Frenchwoman, who said, on seeing Taglioni, " Il faut être sage pour danser comme ça" (one must be virtuous to dance like that). I should rather have said " Il ne faut pas être *femme* pour danser comme ça." And I would divide the world, not as our witty friend —— does, into men, women, and Mary Wolstonecrafts, but into men, women, and balletdancers. For surely a woman must have forgotten the instincts of her sex before she can dance even as Taglioni does. I am not apt, as you know, my dear C., to run a tilt against public amusements ; but I hold this to be an execrable one ; and, if my voice could have any influence, I would pray every modest woman and modest *man*, for why should this virtue be graduated by a different scale for the different sexes ! every modest man and woman, then, in our land to discountenance its advancement there. If we have not yet the perfection of a matured civilisation, God save us from the corruptions that prelude and intimate its decline !

We spent a morning at the British Museum, and could have passed a month there profitably. It is on a magnificent scale, worthy this great nation. We have made a few excursions out of London. We took the fourth of July to drive to Hampton Court ; and so bright and warm it was, that, as far as the weather was concerned, we might have fancied ourselves at home, keeping our national festival. " Hampton's royal pile" was begun by Wolsey, who, " though of an humble stock," was born with a kingly ambition, and " fashioned to much honour from his cradle." His expenditure on this palace was most royal, and furnished, as you know, a convenient pretext for his master's displeasure. Henry put forth the lion's right—might—and took possession of it ; and the royal arms and badges of the Tudors are carved over the devices and arms of Wolsey. That part of the edifice which belongs to the age of the Tudors seemed to me alone to have any architectural interest or much beauty. It bears the marks of that era when feudal individual fortifications were giving place to the defences of a higher civilisation; when the country-house was superseding the castle. From the time of Henry VIII. to the first two Georges it has been at various times enlarged, and has been one of the regular establishments of the reigning family. It is now, with its extensive and beautifully-ornamented grounds, given up to the public, who are admitted within the gates without a fee! There is no picturesqueness, no natural beauty in the grounds, or, rather, to speak more accurately, in the face of the ground; for who shall presume to say that trees are not natural beauties, and such trees as the magnificent elms, chestnuts, and limes of Hampton, the most surpassingly beautiful of all natural beauties?

There is one walk of a mile to the Thames, and there is shrubbery, and fountains, and artificial bits of water, and aquatic birds, and plants, as we have good reason to remember; for one of our girls, fancying, with truly American naïveté, they were growing *wild*, and unchecked by the pithy admonition on sundry bits of board, "It is expected that the public will protect what is intended for public enjoyment," tempted our friend P. to pluck a lotus for her. He was forthwith pounced upon by a lad, one of the police curs, who seized for "the crown and country" the poor water-lily, and compelled P. to appear before one of the officials. The regular fine was ten shillings English; but the man was lenient; and, in consideration of our being Americans, (semi-barbarians!) P. was let off with paying a slight penalty for his good-natured gallantry. We left the gardens with reluctance for the duty of seeing the interior of the palace, and beginning with a princely hall one hundred feet in length, we circulated through more banqueting-rooms, drawing-rooms, "king's sleeping-apartments," "queen's bed-chambers," "king's presence-chambers," "king's and queen's dressing-rooms," "queen's galleries," tapestry galleries, and what not, than ever rose above the horizon of your plebeian imagination.

The apartments are nearly all hung with pictures. There is little furniture, strictly so called, remaining, and what there is, is faded and time-worn.

I give you the following opinion with all modesty, knowing that I am not a qualified judge; the collection of pictures struck me as proving that art is not native to the country. Of course the pictures are chiefly by foreign artists, but obtained by Englishmen who had an unlimited power of patronage and selection. In the immense number of pictures there are few to be remembered. The celebrated portrait of Charles the First on horseback, by Vandyke, rivets you before it by its most sad and prophetic expression. It is such a portrait as Shakspeare would have painted of Charles had he been an outside-painter.

Sir Peter Lely's flesh-and-blood beauties of Charles the Second's time fill one apartment. Hamilton* and Mrs. Jameson have given these fair dames an immortality they do not merit. They are mere mortal beauties, and not even the best specimens of their kind. They are the

* Mémoires de Grammont.

women of the coarsest English comedies; not such types of womanhood as Juliet, Desdemona, and Isabella. They have not the merit of individuality. They have all beautiful hands—probably because Sir Peter Lely could paint beautiful hands —and lovely necks and bosoms, most prodigally displayed. There is a mixture of finery and negligence in their dress that would seem to indicate the born slattern transformed into the fine lady. It would take a Mohammed's heaven of such beauties to work up into the spiritual loveliness of an exquisite head of St. Catherine, by Correggio, in another apartment of this gallery. What a text might be made of these counterfeit presentments of the sinner and the saint for an eloquent preacher in a Magdalen chapel!

Holbein's pictures were to me among the most interesting in the collection. Some one says that Holbein's pictures are " the prose of portrait-painting," the least poetic department of the art. If for " prose " you may substitute truth (and truth, to the apprehension of some people, is mighty prosaic), the remark is just. The truth is so self-evident, the individuality of his pictures so striking, that his portraits impress you as delineations of familiar faces; and there are the pictures of Wolsey, of Sir Thomas More, of Harry the Eighth at different epochs of his life, and of Francis the First. Think of seeing contemporaneous pictures of these men by an exact hand! " Oh, ye gentlemen who live at home at ease," ye may sometimes envy us; and this I say while every bone is aching with the fatigue of this sight-seeing day.

We wound up with the gallery of Raphael's cartoons, so named, as perhaps you do not know, from their being done on a thin pasteboard, called in Italian *cartone*. They were done by the order of Leo the Tenth, to serve as models for the tapestry of one of the halls of the Vatican, and sent to Brussels, where the tapestry was to be woven. After vicissitudes whose history would make a volume, William the Third had this gallery constructed for them, and they were taken from the boxes, in which they were found carelessly packed, and in slips, and put together, and placed in plain frames. These cartoons are the delight of the artistic world. Perhaps the sketches and unfinished paintings of great artists give the best indications of those revelations of beauty that are made to their minds, and to which they can never give material expression. Can ideal perfection be manifested by form and colour! My admiration of the cartoons was very earnest, albeit unlearned. Paul preaching at Athens struck me as the grandest among them.

We returned to London through Bushy Park, where the trees are the most magnificent I ever beheld, not excepting those of Western Virginia. We passed by Twickenham and Strawberry Hill, and came to Richmond Hill (Riche-mont) to dine. The view from this hill has been lauded in poetry and prose, and filled so many dull pages of dull journals, that I in much mercy spare you a repetition. If an Englishman were to select a single view in his country to give a stranger the best idea of the characteristics of English rural scenery, it would probably be that of Richmond Hill. It is a sea of cultivation, nothing omitted, imperfect, or unfinished. There are no words to exaggerate these characteristics. It is all strawberries and cream; satingly rich; *filled*

"With hills and dales, and woods, and lawns, and spires,
And glittering towers, and gilded streams, till all
The stretching landscape into smoke decays."

And yet, shall I confess it to you, I would have given all the pleasure I should get from it for a lifetime for one glance from S——'s hill at the valley with its wooden houses, straggling brown fences, and ragged husbandry! Yes, and apart from home associations, is there not more to kindle emotion in that valley, lying deep in her encircling hills, with their rich woodlands and rocky steeps, than in this monotonous beauty? The one is a drawing-room lady, the other a wood-nymph.

We sent away our carriage, and came home in a steamer, which was crowded when we got on board. At first we looked around in the most self-complacent manner, expecting, with our American notions, that seats would be offered on every side, as they would assuredly have been to all us womankind in one of our own steamers. Not a foot stirred. Some of us were positively unable to stand, and for those Mr. P. made an appeal to some men, who refused without hesitation, appearing to think our expectations were impertinent. We were too far gone to be fastidious, so we adopted the backwoods' expedient, and *squatted* upon what unoccupied territory we could find. If such personal selfishness and discourtesy is the result of a high civilisation, I am glad we have not yet attained it. The general indifference of our companions in the steamer to the scenery of the river reminded us of the strictures of English travellers in America in similar situations. Nothing can be more fallacious than the broad inferences drawn from such premises. They were probably people intent on errands of business, or, like us, tired parties of pleasure; and I am sure, at that moment, nothing less than Niagara or the Alps could have excited us to express an emotion. We landed at Hungerford stairs: R. said it reminded him of the landing-place at Chicago. It was rude enough for the Far West. You may imagine our wearied condition when I tell you that when we arrived at home, the girls voluntarily let me off from a promise to chaperone them to Mrs. B——'s concert, where Grisi and the other Italian stars were " choiring—to young-eyed cherubims," no doubt.

We have been to Windsor, with the great advantage of Mrs. —— for our companion and guide. She puts a soul and a voice into dumb things—and her soul! We failed to get a permission to see the private apartments, though Lady B. and some other potent friends stirred in our behalf. Only a certain number of tickets are issued during the week, and our application was too late; so we could not see the luxurious furnishings for royal domestic life, if royalty may have domestic life, or ever in

" Bed majestical
Can sleep so soundly as the wretched slave
Who, with a body fill'd and vacant mind,
Gets him to rest, cramm'd with distressful bread."

Windsor Castle, you know, is rich with the accumulated associations of ages, having been begun by Henry III., and enlarged and enriched from time to time down to George I., who put it in complete order. It stands on an eminence just above the little town of Windsor, which, built of brick and stone, is compact and clean, as is everything English, individual and congregate. It is said to be the best specimen of castellated architecture in England. Certainly it is very beautiful; and the most beautiful thing about it is the view from the terrace, which it would be little better than impertinent to describe in any other words than Gray's, in his invocation to those who stand on the terrace :

" And ye, that from the stately brow
Of Windsor's heights, the expanse below
Of grove, of lawn, of mead survey,
Whose turf, whose shade, whose flowers among,
Wanders the hoary Thames along,
His silver winding way."

But such a mead! such turf! such shade! " Father Thames " might be compared to an old king winding his way through his court; the very sheep that were lying on the grass under the majestic trees in the " Home Park," looked like princes of the blood. The most thought-awakening object in the view is undoubtedly the Gothic pile of Eton College, with its spires and antique towers. When the queen is at Windsor she walks every Sunday on this terrace, where she is liable to be jostled by the meanest of her subjects; and as the railway from London passes within a mile and a half of Windsor, she must often endure there collisions to which English blood has such repugnance.

We spent some hours in going through the magnificent apartments of the palace, looking at the pictures, the Gobelin tapestry, &c. &c. The quaint, curious banqueting-room of the knights of the Garter, with their insignia, pleased me best. Vacant places are left for future knights; but how much longer an institution will last that is a part of a worn-out machine, is a question which your children, dear C., may live to see solved.

We had enough of the enjoying spirit of children to be delighted, and felt much in the humour of the honest man who said to Prince Esterhazy, when he was blazing in diamonds, " Thank you for your diamonds." " Why do you thank me ? " naturally asked the prince. " You have the trouble of them, and I the pleasure of looking at them." Wise and happy man! He solved a puzzling problem. In truth, the monarch has not the pleasure of property in Windsor Castle that almost every American citizen has in the roof that shelters him. " I congratulate your majesty on the possession of so beautiful a palace," said some foreign prince to whom Victoria was showing it. " It is not mine, but the country's," she replied. And so it is, and all within it. She may not give away a picture, or even a footstool.

We went into St. George's chapel, which is included in the pile of buildings. We saw there the beautiful effect produced by the sun shining through the painted windows, throwing all the colours of the rainbow on the white marble pillars and pavement. The royal family are buried in the vaults of this chapel. There is an elaborate monument in wretched taste in one corner, to the Princess Charlotte. We trod on a tablet in the pavement that told us that beneath it were lying the remains of Henry VIII. and Jane Seymour!

It is such memorials as these that we are continually meeting, which, as honest uncle Stephen says, " give one feelings."

Lady B. had said to me in a note, " If you attend service in St. George's chapel, observe the waving of the banners to the music. It seems like a strange sympathy with the tones of the organ before one reflects on the cause." We did attend the service, and realised the poetic idea. The banner of every knight of the Garter, from the beginning of the institution, is hung in the choir.

This was the third time we had been present, since we came to England, at worship in the temples into which art has breathed its soul. First in Winchester Cathedral, then at Westminster Abbey, and now at this old royal chapel. The daily service appointed by the church was performing with the careless and heartless air of prescription. The clergyman and clerk hurried sing-songing through the form of prayers, that, perfect as they are, will only rise on the soul's wings. I felt the Puritan struggling at my heart, and could have broken out with old Mause's fervour, if not her eloquence. I thought of our summer Sunday service in dear J.'s " long parlour." Not a vacant place there. The door open into the garden, the children strewed round the door-step, their young faces touched with an expression of devotion and love—such as glows in the faces of the cherubs of the old pictures ; and for vaulted roof, columns, and storied glass, we had the blue sky, the everlasting hills, and lights and shadows playing over them, all suggestive of devotion, and in harmony with the pure and simple doctrine our friend Dr. Follen taught us. To me, there was more true worship in those all-embracing words, " Our Father !" as he uttered them, than in all the task-prayers I have heard in these mighty cathedrals. Here it is the temple that is greatest. Your mind is preoccupied, filled with the outward world. The monuments of past ages and the memorials of individual greatness are before you. Your existence is amplified ; your sympathies are carried far back ; the "inexorable past" does give up its dead. Wherever your eye falls you see the work of a power new to you—the creative power of art. You see forms of beauty which never entered into your " forge of thought." You are filled with new and delightful emotions ; but they spring from new impressions of the genius of man, of his destiny and history. No ; these cathedrals are not like the arches of our forests, the temples for inevitable worship ; but they are the fitting place for the apotheosis of genius *.

I promised to give you honestly my impressions, and I do so. I may have come too old and inflexible to these temples ; but, though I feel their beauty thrilling my heart and brimming my eyes, they do not strike me as in accord with the sim-

plicity, universality, and spirituality of the gospel of Jesus. Some modern unbelievers maintain that Christianity is a worn-out form of religion. Is it not rather true that the spirit escapes from the forms in which man, always running to the material, would embody it !

We took our lunch : and let me, en passant, bless the country where you can always command what is best suited " to restore the weak and 'caying nature," as —— pathetically called it in his before-dinner grace. For lunch they give you a cold round of beef, juicy and tender ; ham, perfectly cured, perfectly cooked, delicious bread and butter, or, indeed, what you will ; and all so neatly served !` Oh, my dear C., mortifying contrasts are forced on my ever-home-turning thoughts † !

We walked to Eton, and, most fortunately, came upon its classic play-ground at the moment the boys were let loose upon it. Of course, it was impossible not to recal Gray's doleful prophecy while looking at some former generation of Eton boys.—Mrs. —— repeated them :

> " These shall the fury passions tear,
> The vultures of the mind ;
> Disdainful anger, pallid fear,
> And shame that skulks behind ;
> Or pining love shall waste their youth,
> Or jealousy, with rankling tooth,
> That inly gnaws the secret heart,
> And envy wan, and faded care,
> Grim-visaged, comfortless despair,
> And sorrow's piercing dart."

This is undoubtedly powerful poetry, but is it the true sentiment ! I never liked it, and liked it less than ever when looking at these young creatures, among whom are the future teachers and benefactors of their land ; it may be a Collingwood, a Wilberforce, a Romilly, a Hallam. Should not the poet have seen within these bounding young frames immeasurable faculties, capacities for love and virtue, that eternity cannot exhaust !

The children here strike me as not having the bright, intellectual countenances of ours, which indicate their early development ; but, as a physical production, the English boy, with his brilliant complexion and sturdy frame, is far superior to ours.

We have nothing corresponding, my dear C., to the luxury of space and adornment of this playground of Eton. The eye does not perceive its boundaries ; the Thames passes through it, and the trees have been growing, and at a fair rate, for hundreds of years.

My DEAR C.—The London breakfast party is a species of entertainment quite unknown to us, and we should not find it easy to acclimate it. It is not suited to our condition of society. Suppose E. attempting such a thing at New York. She would naturally invite S. S. as the most agreeable woman of her acquaintance. The answer would probably be,

---

* If perchance there is one among my readers unacquainted with Bryant's Poems, he may thank me for referring to his Forest Hymn, beginning thus :—

> "The groves were God's first temples. Ere man learn'd
> To hew the shaft and lay the architrave,
> And spread the roof above them ; ere he framed
> The lofty vault, to gather and roll back
> The sound of anthems ; in the darkling wood,
> Amid the cool and silence, he knelt down,
> And offered to the Mightiest solemn thanks
> And supplication."

† What would probably be served for an extempore lunch at an American inn? Bread and butter, (probably fresh bread, and possibly not fresh butter,) pies, cakes, and sweetmeats. May not the superior muscle and colour of the English be ascribed in part to our different modes of feeding? Our inns improve from season to season, and will, in proportion as our modes of living become more wise and salutary.

—" The children are ailing, and she cannot come."
She, like most of our mothers, never leaves her
house, if there be a shadow in the nursery. Then
Mrs. B.—" No, she expects a few friends to dinner, and she must overlook her servants ;" and
so on, and so on.   But if the women, whose habits
are most flexible, could be managed, where would
you find half-a-dozen men at leisure ! D. must
be at the office of the " Life and Trust " at nine ;
and of our agreeable poets—our home-lions—
Bryant has his daily paper to get out, and Halleck,
like poor Charles Lamb, his (only) "heavy works,"
his ledger, for his morning task ; and, save some
half-dozen idlers, all the men in town are at their
counting-houses or offices, steeped to the lips in
business by nine o'clock in the morning. But
here the case is quite different : the women are
not so hampered with domestic life, and the men
are " rentiers," and masters of their time. The
breakfast party is not, however, I believe, of long
standing here. I have been told that it was
introduced by that Mr. Rogers whose household
designation among us is " Rogers the poet."
   The hour of the breakfast party is from ten to
eleven.   The number is, I believe, never allowed
to exceed twelve ; and only comes up to that when
the host is constrained, like a certain friend of
ours, by his diffusive benevolence, to extend his
invitation (his " ticket for six ") to a caravan of
travellers.
   The entertainment is little varied from our
eight-o'clock breakfasts.   There are coffee, tea
and chocolate, rolls, toast, grated beef and eggs,
and, in place of our solid beefsteaks and broiled
chickens, reindeers' tongues, sweetmeats, fruit,
and ices. These are not bad substitutes for
heavier viands, and for our variety of delicate
hot cakes. You see none of these, unless it be
the poorest of them all,—a muffin.
   On some occasions there were guests invited to
come after breakfast, to enjoy the social hour that
follows it.   Now that ideas travel so rapidly from
one quarter of the world to another, I trust some
steamer will bear to America that which is recently
received in England, and has, as long as other
cardinal points of philosophy, governed Continental
society, viz. that eating and drinking is not a necessary element in social intercourse.
   We had the pleasure of a breakfast at Rogers'.
Your long familiarity with his poetry tells you the
melancholy fact that he is no longer young ; a fact
kept out of your mind as far as possible on a personal acquaintance, by the freshness with which
he enjoys, and the generosity with which he imparts. I have heard him called cynical, and
perhaps a man of his keen wit may be sometimes
over-tempted to demonstrate it, as the magnani-
mous Saladin was to use the weapon with which
he adroitly severed a man's head from his body
at a single stroke. If so, these are the exceptions to the general current of his life, which, I
am sure, flows in a kindly channel. K. told me
he met him one winter in Paris, where he found
him enjoying art like a young enthusiast ; and
knowing every boy's name in the street he lived
in, and in friendship with them all. Does not this
speak volumes !
   He honoured our letters of introduction by
coming immediately to see us, and receiving us as
cordially as if we were old friends. He afterward

expressed a regret to me that he had not taken
that morning, before we plunged into engage-
ments, to show me Johnson's and Dryden's
haunts, the house where our Franklin lived, and
other classical localities. Ah ! this goes to swell
my pathetic reiteration of the general lament, " I
have had my losses ! "
   His manners are those of a man of the world (in
its best sense), simple, and natural, without any
apparent consciousness of name or fame to support. His house, as all the civilised world knows,
is a cabinet of art, selected and arranged with
consummate taste. The house itself is small—
not, I should think, more than twenty-five feet
front, and perhaps forty deep, in a most fortunate
location, overlooking the Green Park. The first
sight of it from the windows produces a sort of
coup-de-théâtre ; for you approach the house and
enter it by a narrow street. Every inch of it is
appropriated to some rare treasure or choice production of art. Besides the pictures (and " What,"
you might be tempted to ask, " can a man want
besides such pictures ! ") are Etruscan vases
(antiques), Egyptian antiquities, casts of the
Elgin marbles decorating the staircase wall, and
endless adornments of this nature. There are
curiosities of another species,—rare books, such as
a most beautifully-illuminated missal, exquisitely-
delicate paintings designed for marginal decorations, executed three hundred years ago, and
taken from the Vatican by the French—glorious
robbers ! In a catalogue of his books, in the
poet's own beautiful autograph, there were inserted
some whimsical titles of books, such as " Nebu-
chadnezzar on Grasses."
   But the most interesting thing in all the collection was the original document, with Milton's
name, by which he transferred to his publisher,
for ten pounds, the copyright of Paradise Lost*.
Next in interest to this was a portfolio, in which
were arranged autograph letters from Pope and
Dryden, Washington and Franklin, and several
from Fox, Sheridan, and Scott, addressed to the
poet himself. Among them was that written by
Sheridan, just before his death, describing the
extremity of his suffering, and praying Rogers to
come to him. But I must check myself. A catalogue raisonné of what our eyes but glanced over
would fill folios. I had the pleasure at breakfast
of sitting next Mr. Babbage, whose name is so
well known among us as the author of the self-
calculating machine. He has a most remarkable
eye, that looks as if it might penetrate science, or
anything else he chose to look into. He described
the iron steamer now building, which has a larger
tonnage than any merchant ship in the world, and
expressed an opinion that iron ships would supersede all others ; and another opinion that much
concerns us, and which, I trust, may soon be
verified—that in a few years these iron steamers
will go to America in seven days !
   Macaulay was of the party. His conversation

_____
* We were the next morning, after breakfasting with
Mr. R., in the presence of Carlyle, speaking of this deed of
sale and of Taglioni. He amused himself and us with calculating how many Paradise Losts she might pay for with
a single night's earnings ; and, after laughing at this picturesque juxtaposition of Milton and Taglioni, he added
seriously, " But there have been better things on earth
than Paradise Lost that have received worse payment ;
that have been paid with the scaffold and the cross !"

resembles his writings; it is rich and delightful, filled with anecdotes and illustrations from the abounding stores of his overflowing mind. Some may think he talks too much; but none, except from their own impatient vanity, could wish it were less.

It was either at Mr. Rogers', or at a breakfast a few days after at Mr. R.'s sister's (whose house, by-the-way, is a fair pendant for his), that we had much Monkbarns' humour, from worthy disciples of that king of old bachelors, on the subject of matrimony. H. said there had been many a time in his life when he should have married, if he could some fine day have walked quietly into a village-church, and met at the altar a lady having come as quietly into another door, and then, after the marriage service, each have departed their separate way, with no observation, no speculation upon the engagement, no congratulations before or after. Rogers, who seems resolved to win the crown of celibat martyrdom (is there a crown for it?) pronounced matrimony a folly at any period of life, and quoted a saying of some wicked Benedict, that, "no matter whom you married, you would find afterward you had married another person."

No doubt; but, except with the idealising lover, I believe the expectation is as often surpassed as disappointed. There is a generous opinion for a single woman of your married fortunes!

I BELIEVE, of all my pleasures here, dear J. will most envy me that of seeing Joanna Baillie, and of seeing her repeatedly at her own home; the best point of view for all best women. She lives on Hampstead Hill, a few miles from town, in a modest house, with Miss Agnes Baillie, her only sister, a most kindly and agreeable person. Miss Baillie—I write this for J., for we women always like to know how one another look and dress— Miss Baillie has a well-preserved appearance; her face has nothing of the vexed or sorrowing expression that is often so deeply stamped by a long experience of life. It indicates a strong mind, great sensibility, and the benevolence that, I believe, always proceeds from it if the mental constitution be a sound one, as it eminently is in Miss Baillie's case. She has a pleasing figure— what we call lady-like—that is, delicate, erect, and graceful; not the large-boned, muscular frame of most English women. She wears her own grey hair; a general fashion by-the-way here, which I wish we elderly ladies of America may have the courage and the taste to imitate; and she wears the prettiest of brown silk gowns and bonnets fitting the beau ideal of an old lady; an ideal she might inspire if it has no pre-existence. You would, of course, expect her to be, as she is, free from pedantry and all modes of affectation; but I think you would be surprised to find yourself forgetting, in a domestic and confiding feeling, that you were talking with the woman whose name is best established among the female writers of her country; in short, forgetting everything but that you were in the society of a most charming private gentlewoman. She might (would that all female writers could!) take for her device a flower that closes itself against the noontide sun, and unfolds in the evening shadows*.

* In the United States, Mrs. Barbauld would perhaps divide the suffrages with Miss Baillie; but in England, as

We lunched with Miss Baillie. Mr. Tytler the historian and his sister were present. Lord Woodhouselee, the intimate friend of Scott, was their father. Joanna Baillie appears to us, from Scott's letters to her, to have been his favourite friend; and the conversation among so many personally familiar with him naturally turned upon him, and many a pleasant anecdote was told, many a thrilling word quoted.

It was pleasant to hear these friends of Scott and Mackenzie talk of them as familiarly as we speak of W., B., and other household friends. They all agree in describing Mackenzie as a jovial, hearty sort of person, without any indication in his manners and conversation of the exquisite sentiment he infused into his writings. One of the party remembered his coming home one day in great glee from a cockfight, and his wife saying to him, "Oh, Harry, Harry, you put all your feelings on paper!"

I was glad to hear Miss Baillie, who is an intimate friend of Lady Byron, speak of her with tender reverence, and of her conjugal infelicity as not at all the result of any quality or deficiency on her part, but inevitable†. Strange this is not the universal impression, after Byron's own declaration to Moore that "there never was a better or even a brighter, a kinder, or a more amiable and agreeable being than Lady B."

After lunch we walked over to a villa occupied by Miss Baillie's nephew, the only son of Dr. Baillie. It commands a view almost as beautiful and as English as that from Richmond Hill; a view extending far—far over wide valleys and gently-swelling hills, all standing thick with corn. Returning, we went to a point on Hampstead Hill overlooking the pretty "vale of 'ealth," as our coachman calls it, and which has been to us the vale of hospitality and most homelike welcome. This elevation, Miss B. told me, was equal to that of the ball on the dome of St. Paul's. We could just discern the dome penetrating far into the canopy of smoke that overhangs all London. Miss B. says Scott delighted in this view. It is melancholy, portentous, better suited, I should think, to the genius of Byron. I have seen sublime sights in my life, a midnight thunder-storm at Niagara, and a " gallant breeze" on the sea-shore, but I never saw so spirit-stirring a spectacle as this immense city with its indefinite boundaries and its dull light. Here are nearly two millions

far as my limited observation extended, she is not rated so high, or so generally read as here. She has experienced the great disadvantage of being considered the organ of a sect. Do not the " Address to the Deity," and the " Evening's Meditation," rank with the best English poetry? And are not her essays, that on " Prejudice," and that on the " Inconsistency of Human Expectations," unsurpassed?

† I should not have presumed, by a public mention of Lady Byron, to have penetrated the intrenchments of feminine delicacy and reserve which she has with such dignity maintained, but for the desire, as far as in my humble sphere I might do it, to correct the impression so prevailing among the readers of Moore's biography in this country, that Lady B. is one of those most unlovely of women, who, finding it very easy to preserve a perpendicular line, have no sufferance for the deviations of others, no aptitude, no flexibility. How different this image from the tender, compassionate, loveable reality!—the devoted mother, the trusted friend, the benefactress of poor children.

c

of human beings, with their projects, pursuits, hopes and despairs, their strifes, friendships, and rivalries, their loves and hates, their joys and anguish, some steeped to the lips in poverty, others encumbered with riches, some treading on the confines of heaven, others in the abysses of sin, and all sealed with the seal of immortality.

THE dinner-hour in London, my dear C., is from six to eight. I think we have received no invitation later than for half-past seven. You know the London—the English world, is divided into castes, and our letters have obtained access for us to families that never come together here in social life. We have dined with the suburban gentry, people who, enjoying an income of as many pounds as our country gentleman has dollars, give you a family-dinner of two or three dishes with some simple dessert. For such a dinner one of our country ladies would be apt to make an apology ; the mortifying truth is, that hospitality does not run so much into eating and drinking here, as with us. Everything is of the best quality and served in the best manner, but there is no over-loading. Without exaggeration, I believe that the viands for a rich merchant's dinner-party in New York would suffice for any half-dozen tables I have seen here ; and I am not sure that the supper-table at S.'s ball, just before I left New York, would not have supplied the evening parties of a London season. The young men there drank more Champagne than I have seen in London. May we not hope that in three or four seasons we may adopt these refinements of civilisation ! No, not adopt these precisely. The modes of one country are not transferable, without modification, to another. A people who dine at three or four o'clock need some more substantial refection at ten than a cup of black tea ; but they do not need a lord-mayor's feast, than which nothing can be more essentially vulgar.

I told you, my dear C., that I was going to dine at L—— house. I went, and I honestly confess to you that, when I drove up the approach to this great lord's magnificent mansion, I felt the foolish trepidation I remember to have suffered when, just having emerged from our sequestered country home, I first went to a dinner-party in town. I was alone. I dreaded conventional forms of which I might be ignorant, and still more the insolent observation to which, as a stranger and an American, I might be exposed. But these foolish fears were dissipated by the recollection of the agreeable half-hour I had already passed with Lord L., when I had quite forgotten that he had a lordship tacked to his name, or that he was anything but a plain, highly informed gentleman*. I felt, too, that an unpretending woman is always safe in her simplicity ; and when I alighted and was received by half-a-dozen servants in white

* I have heard that an Englishman, on being asked what struck him most in Americans, replied, "their d—d free and easy manners." There was some truth with much coarseness in this. An American, bred in the best society in his own land, does not feel any more than he acknowledges superiority of rank in another. The distinctions of rank are as vague and imperceptible to him as the imaginary lines are to the puzzled child in his first studies on the globe.

and crimson liveries, and announced through magnificent apartments, I felt no more embarrassment than, as a passably modest woman, I should have done in entering alone a gentleman's house in New York. Lady L. has an air of birth and breeding, and still much beauty, not merely "the remains" of beauty, for so we always speak of a woman past forty. Lady L. was courteous, not condescending, the least acceptable grace of those who stand on a higher level than their associates, since it betrays the consciousness of elevation. There were several persons in the drawing-room to whom I had before been introduced, and I soon forgot that I was a stranger. The modes of English life are identically our own, and there was nothing to remind me I was not at home, save more superb apartments, a larger train of servants and in livery, a dinner-service all of plate, and those most covetable luxuries, first-rate pictures and sculpture. I perceived nothing of the studied stillness we have heard alleged of English society. Everything was natural and easy. Lord L. laughed as heartily as T. does, and M. talked to me across the table.

My dinner the next day was far more trying in its circumstances than that at L—— house. Accident had prevented my seeing the lady who invited me. I unwarily accepted the invitation ; for till you have passed the threshold of acquaintance, it is very awkward to plunge into a dinner-party. My invitations had usually been at seven. I had carelessly forgotten the hour named in Mrs. ——'s note, and we concluded it was safest to take the average hour. The distance was three miles from Half-Moon-street, longer than I supposed ; our dawdling coachman drove slower than usual ; and all the while I was tormenting myself with the fear I might be too late, and that Mrs. —— was thinking what a bore it was to be compelled to civility to a blundering stranger. To put the last drop in my brimming cup of vexation, the coachman made a mistake, and had twice to drive round a large square ; and when I finally arrived, I was ushered into an empty room— "Portentous!" thought I. The gentleman of the house entered, and, disconcerted at my awkward position, and humanely hoping to help me out of it, he said, stammering, "There is some mistake!" "Heavens, yes!" I groaned inwardly. "Our invitation," he continued, "mentioned six as our dinner-hour. We waited till seven, and it is now past," (past! it was nearly eight)—"you can do as you please about going in!" I looked to the window—the carriage was gone ; my ear caught the last faint sound of its receding wheels. There was no escape. A hen, the most timid of breathing things, is courageous when there is no alternative but "to do or die," and so was I. I begged ten thousand pardons, assured Mr. —— that the dinner was a perfectly unimportant circumstance to me ; that I would not lose the only opportunity I might have of seeing Mrs. ——, &c. So, with a dim smile, he gave me his arm, and I entered the dining-room. There were ten or twelve people present. There was an awful silence, an obvious suspension of the whole ceremony of dinner awaiting my decision. My courage was expended ; I felt it ebbing, when H., who was sitting next the lady of the house, came to my relief, both hands extended, as if to save a drowning creature. He is, as I have told you before, the very embodiment of the kindly social principle. He stopped my apologies by assuming that I was the injured party, and dealt his blows to our host and hostess on the right and left. He declared that Mrs. —— wrote a hand no one could decipher. He never, in a long acquaintance, had made out a note of hers, and he was sure I had not been able to tell whether I was invited at six or eight! He would know "how —— had received me." He was certain "he had made some blunder, it was so like him!" I answered, with strict truth, that Mr. —— "had made me feel comfortable in a most uncomfortable position." To my dismay, and in spite of my protestations, Mrs. —— insisted on re-beginning at the Alpha of the dinner; the guests had reached the Omega. The soup was brought back. H. averred that it was most fortunate for him; he had been kept talking, and had not eaten half a dinner; so he started fresh with me, and went *bonâ fide* through, covering me with his aegis as I ran my gauntlet through the courses. The age of chivalry is *not* past. Match this deed of courtesy, if you can, from the lives of the preux chevaliers, taken from their sunrising to their sunsetting. This dinner, like many other things in life, was bitter in its experience and sweet in its remembrance.

Our pleasantest dinner, I think, was at K.'s; he who gave us the "ticket for six" to his breakfast. I knew him before coming here as the friend of many of our friends, and the author of very charming published poetry. At dinner I sat next Procter. He is so well known to you as "Barry Cornwall," that you have perhaps forgotten that is merely his *nom-de-guerre*. He was one of the intimate friends of Charles Lamb, and spoke of him in just the way that we, who look upon him with something of the tenderness that we do upon the departed members of our own household, would like to hear him spoken of. Procter made inquiries about the diffusion of English literature in America, and showed a modest surprise at hearing how well he was known among us.

My DEAR C—, I may say that we have scaled the ladder of evening entertainments here, going from a six-o'clock family tea up to a magnificent concert at L—— house; and the tea at this home-like hour was at Carlyle's. He is living in the suburbs of London, near the Thames; my impression is, in rather an humble way; but when your eye is filled with a grand and beautiful temple, you do not take the dimensions of surrounding objects; and if any man can be independent of them, you might expect Carlyle to be. His head would throw a phrenologist into ecstacies. It looks like the "forge of thought" it is; and his eyes have a preternatural brilliancy. He reminded me of what Lockhart said to me, speaking of the size of Webster's head, that he "had brains enough to fill half-a-dozen hats." Carlyle has as strong a Scotch accent as Mr. Combe. His manner is simple, natural, and kindly. His conversation has the picturesqueness of his writings, and flows as naturally, and as free from Germanism, as his own mountain streams are from any infusion of German soil. He gave us an interesting account

of his first acquaintance with E——n. He was living with his wife in a most secluded part of Scotland. They had no neighbours, no communication with the world, excepting once a week or fortnight, when he went some miles to a post-office in the hope of a letter or some other intimation that the world was going on. One day a stranger came to them—a young American—and "he seemed to them an angel." They spoke of him as if they had never lost their first impression of his celestial nature. Carlyle had met Mr. Webster, and expressed a humorous surprise that a man from over the sea should talk English, and be as familiar as the natives with the English constitution and laws,

" With all that priest or jurist saith,
Of modes of law, or modes of faith."

He said Webster's eyes were like dull furnaces, that only wanted blowing on to lighten them up. And, by the way, it is quite interesting to perceive that our great countryman has made a sensation here, where it is all but as difficult to make one as to make a mark on the ocean. They have given him the sobriquet of "the Great Western," and they seem particularly struck with his appearance. A gentleman said to me, "His eyes open, and open, and open, and you think they will never stop opening;" and a painter was heard to exclaim, on seeing him, "What a head! what eyes! what a mouth! and, my God! what colouring!"

We had a very amusing evening at Mr. Hallam's, whom (thanks to F., as thanks to her for all my best privileges in London) I have had the great pleasure of seeing two or three times. But this kind of seeing is so brief and imperfect, that it amounts to little more than seeing the pictures of these great people. Mr. Hallam has a very pleasing countenance, and a most good-humoured and playful manner. I quite forgot he was the sage of the "Middle Ages." He reminded me of ——; but his simplicity is more genuine; not at all that of the great man trying to play child. You quite forget, in the freedom and ease of the social man, that he is ever the hero in armour. We met Sidney Smith at his house, the best-known of all the wits of the civilised world. The company was small; he was i' the vein, which is like a singer being in voice, and we saw him, I believe, to advantage. His wit was not, as I expected, a succession of brilliant explosions, but a sparkling stream of humour, very like —— when he is at home, and i' the vein too; and, like him also, he seemed to enjoy his own fun, and to have fattened on it*.

He expressed unqualified admiration of Dickens, and said that 10,000 of each number of Nicholas Nickleby were sold. There was a young man present, who, being flushed with some recent literary success, ventured to throw himself into the arena against this old lion-king; and, to a lover of such sport, it would have been pleasant to see how he crackled him up, flesh, bones, and all.

THE concert at L—— house was in a superb gallery of sculpture, with a carved and gilded

---

* I have had the grace here, after transcribing and re-transcribing them, to suppress some fresh bon-mots of Sidney Smith's on recent works of popular authors being spoken of. Grace it is, knowing how much more acceptable to readers are bon-mots than descriptions.

ceiling, and other appropriate and splendid accompaniments. I am told that it is one of the choicest collection of antiques in the kingdom ; but I had no opportunity of judging or enjoying, for the marble divinities were hidden by the glittering mortals. When K. and I entered, the apartments were filled with some hundreds of people of the first station and fashion in the land, luxuriously dressed, and sparkling with diamonds,—a sea of faces, as strange as their diamonds to me. It was an overpowering kind of solitude. Lady L. had politely directed me to a favourable position, and I/ slunk into the first vacant place I could find : where I was beginning to feel quite comfortable in my obscurity, when K. said to me, with something of the feeling of Columbus' men when they first cried "Land ! "—" There is Mr. —— and Mr. —— ! " These gentlemen soon after made their way to us, and dissipated our forlornness. In the course of the evening we met many agreeable persons to whom we had been before introduced, and several of the most noted lions of the London menagerie were pointed out to us,—Bulwer, Taylor, and Talfourd. Lady Seymour was there,—a superb beauty certainly, and well entitled to the elective crown she is to wear, of Queen of Love and Beauty. I was introduced to Mrs. Norton, who is herself a most queenly-looking creature, a Semiramis, a Sappho, or an Amazon (the Greek ideal Amazon, remember, uniting masculine force with feminine delicacy, or anything that expresses the perfection of intellectual and physical beauty). There is another of these Sheridan sisters celebrated for her personal charms. I had read but a few mornings before, as I mentioned to you, that miserable death-bed letter from their penniless grandfather, and I was somewhat struck with the shifting scenes of life when I saw these women occupying the most brilliant position of the most brilliant circle in London. But what are gold and lands to the rich inheritance of Sheridan's genius and Miss Linley's beauty !

It is indeed a royal entertainment to give one's guests such singing as Grisi's, Garcia's, Lablache's, and Rubini's, and can, I suppose, only be given by those who have " royal revenues*. "

WE passed an evening at Miss C.'s ; she is truly what the English call a " nice person ; " as modest in her demeanour as one of our village girls who has a good organ of veneration (rare enough among our young people), and this is saying something for the richest heiress in England. I was first struck here, and only here, with the subdued tone we hear so much of in English society. When we first entered Miss C.'s immense drawing-room, there were a few dowagers scattered up and down, appearing as few and far between as settlers on a prairie, and apparently

finding intercommunication quite as difficult. And though the numbers soon multiplied, till the gentlemen came *genial* from the dinner-table, we were as solemn and as still as a New-England conference-meeting before the minister comes in. This, I think, was rather the effect of accident than fashion, the young lady's quiet and reserved manner having the subduing influence of a whisper. Society here is quieter than ours, certainly. This is perhaps the result of the different materials of which it is compounded. Our New-York evening parties, you know, are made up of about seventy-five parts boys and girls, the other twenty-five being their papas and mammas, and other ripe men and women. The spirits of a mass of young people, even if they be essentially well-bred, will explode in sound ; thence the general din of voices and shouts of laughter at our parties.

I have rarely seen at an evening party here anything beyond a cup of black tea and a bit of cake, dry as " the remainder biscuit after a voyage." Occasionally we have ices, (in alarmingly small quantity !) and lemonade, or something of that sort. At L—— house there was a refreshment-table spread for three or four hundred people, much like Miss D.'s at her New-York soirées, which, you may remember, was considered quite a sumptuary phenomenon. I am thus particular to reiterate to you, dear C., that the English have got so far in civilisation as not to deem eating and drinking necessary to the enjoyment of society. We are a transition people, and I hope we shall not lag far behind them.

I have met many persons here whom to meet was like seeing the originals of familiar pictures. Jane Porter, Mrs. Opie, Mrs. Austen, Lockhart, Milman, Morier, Sir Francis Chantrey, &c†. I owed Mrs. Opie a grudge for having made me, in my youth, cry my eyes out over her stories ; but her fair, cheerful face forced me to forget it. She long ago forswore the world and its vanities, and adopted the Quaker faith and costume : but I fancied that her elaborate simplicity, and the fashionable little train to her pretty satin gown, indicated how much easier it is to adopt a theory than to change one's habits. Mrs. Austen stands high here for personal character, as well as for the very inferior but undisputed property of literary accomplishments. Her translations are so excellent that they class her with good original writers. If her manners were not strikingly conventional, she would constantly remind me of —— ; she has the same Madame Roland order of architecture and outline, but she wants her charm of naturalness and attractive sweetness ; so it may not seem to Mrs. A.'s sisters and fond

---

* I think one of our parties must strike an Englishman like a nursery-ball. Even in this immense assembly at L. house I saw few young people, none extremely young ; but I must confess the *tout ensemble* struck me as very superior in physical condition and beauty to a similar assembly with us. Our *girl*, with her delicate features and nymph-like figure, is far more lovely in her first freshness than the English ; but the English woman, in her ripeness and full development, far surpasses ours. She is superb from twenty to forty-five.

† Some of my readers may be surprised to miss from the list of these eminent persons the names of the two female writers most read in the United States, Miss Martineau and Mrs. Jameson. Miss Martineau was on the Continent when I was in London, and speaking of Mrs. Jameson in this public way would seem to me much like putting the picture of an intimate and dear friend into an exhibition-room. Besides, her rare gifts, her attainments, and the almost unequalled richness and charm of her conversation, are well known in this country. But with all these a woman may be, *after all*, but a kind of monster ; how far they are transcended by the virtues and attractions of her domestic life, it was our happiness to know from seeing her daily in her English home.

friends. A company attitude is rarely anybody's best.

There is a most pleasing frankness and social charm in Sir Francis Chantrey's manner. I called him repeatedly *Mr.* Chantrey, and begged him to pardon me on the ground of not being " to the manner born." He laughed good-naturedly, and said something of having been longer accustomed to the plebeian designation. I heard from Mr. R. a much stronger illustration than this of this celebrated artist's good sense and good feeling too. Chantrey was breakfasting with Mr. R., when, pointing to some carving in wood, he asked R. if he remembered that, some twenty years before, he employed a young man to do that work for him. R. had but an indistinct recollection. " I was that young man," resumed Chantrey, " and very glad to get the five shillings a day you paid me !" Mr. B. told a pendant to this pretty story. Mr. B. was discussing with Sir Francis the propriety of gilding something, I forget what. B. was sure it could be done, Chantrey as sure it could not ; and " I should know," he said, " for I was once apprentice to a carver and gilder." Perhaps, after all, it is not so crowning a grace in Sir Francis Chantrey to refer to the obscure morning of his brilliant day, as it is a disgrace to the paltry world that it should be so considered.

I have seen Owen of Lanark—a curiosity rather from the sensation he at one time produced in our country, than from anything very extraordinary in the man. He is pushing his theories with unabated zeal. He wasted an hour in trying to convince me that he could make the world over and " set all to rights," if he were permitted to substitute two or three truths for two or three prevailing errors ; and on the same morning a philanthropical phrenologist endeavoured to show me how, if his theory were established, the world would soon become healthy, wealthy, and wise. Both believe the good work is going on—happy men ! So it has always been ; there must be some philosopher's stone, some short-hand process, rather than the slow way of education and religious discipline which, to us, Providence seems to have ordained.

You will perhaps like to know, my dear C., more definitely than you can get them from these few anecdotes of my month in London, what impressions I have received here ; and I will give them fairly to you, premising that I am fully aware how imperfect they are, and how false some of them may be. Travellers should be forgiven their monstrous errors when we find there are so few on whose sound judgments we can rely, of the character of their own people and the institutions of their own country.

In the first place, I have been struck with the *identity* of the English and the New England character—the strong family likeness. The oak-tree may be our emblem modified, but never changed by circumstances. Cultivation may give it a more graceful form and polish, and brighten its leaves, or it may shoot up more rapidly and vigorously in a new soil ; but it is always the oak, with its strength, inflexibility, and " nodosities."

With my strong American feelings, and my love of home so excited that my nerves were all on the outside, I was a good deal shocked to find how very little interest was felt about America in the circles I chanced to be in. The truth is, we are so far off, we have so little *apparent* influence on the political machinery of Europe, such slight relations with the literary world, and none with that of art and fashion, that except to the philosopher, the man of science, and the manufacturing and labouring classes, America is yet an undiscovered country, as distant and as dim as—Heaven. It is not, perhaps, to be wondered at. There are new and exciting events every day at their own doors, and there are accumulations of interests in Europe to occupy a lifetime, and there are few anywhere who can abide Johnson's test when he says that " whatever withdraws us from the power of our senses, whatever makes the past, the *distant*, or the future predominate over the present, advances us in the dignity of thinking beings." Inquiries are often put to me about my country, and I laugh at my own eagerness to impart knowledge and exalt their ideas of us, when I perceive my hearers listening with the forced interest of a courteous person to a teller of dreams.

One evening, in a circle of eminent people, the question was started, " what country came next in their affections to England !" I listened, in my greenness, expecting to hear one and all say " America ;" no, not one feeble voice uttered the name. Mrs. ——, with her hot love of art, naturally answered, " Italy is *first* to us all." " Oh, no," replied two or three voices ; " England first, and next—Germany." " England first," said Mrs. A., " Germany next, and I think my third country is—Malta !" I thought of my own land, planted from the English stock, where the productions of these very speakers are most widely circulated, and, if destined to live, must have their longest life ; the land where the most thorough and hopeful experiment of the capacity of the human race for knowledge, virtue, happiness, and self-government is now making ; the land of promise and protection to the poor and disheartened of every country ; and it seemed to me that it should have superseded in their affections countries comparatively foreign to them.

I have seen instances of ignorance of us in quarters where you would scarcely expect it : for example, a very cultivated man, a bishop, asked K. if there were a theatre in America ! and a person of equal dignity inquired " if the Society of Friends was not the prevailing religious sect in Boston !" A literary man of some distinction asked me if the Edinburgh and Quarterly Reviews were read in America ; and one of the cultivated women of England said to me, in a soothing tone, on my expressing admiration of English trees, " Oh, you will have such in time, when your forests are cut down, and they have room for their limbs to spread." I smiled and was silent ; but if I saw in vision our graceful drooping, elm-embowering roods of ground, and, as I looked at the stiff, upright English elm, had something of the pharisaical " holier than thou" flit over my mind, I may be forgiven.

I was walking one day with some young English-women, when a short, sallow, broad man, to whom Nature had been niggardly, to say the least of it, passed us. " I think," said I, " that is a countryman of mine ; I have seen him in New-York."

"I took him for an American," said one of my companions, with perfect nonchalance. "Pray tell me why." "He looks so like the pictures in Mrs. Trollope's book!" It is true, this was a secluded young person in a provincial town, but I felt mortified that in one fair young mind Mrs. Trollope's vulgar caricatures should stand as the type of my countrymen.

I have heard persons repeatedly expressing a desire to visit America—for what! "To see a prairie"—"to see Niagara"—"to witness the manner of the help to their employers; it must be so very comical!" but, above all, "to eat canvass-back ducks." The canvass-backs are in the vision of America what St. Peter's is in the view of Rome. But patience, my dear C. In the first place, it matters little what such thinkers think of us; and then things are mending. The steamers have already cancelled half the distance between the two continents. The two worlds are daily weaving more closely their interests and their friendships. I have been delighted with the high admiration expressed here in all quarters of Dr. Channing, and, above all, to find that his pure religion has, with its angel's wings, surmounted the walls of sectarianism. I have heard him spoken of with enthusiasm by prelates as much distinguished for their religious zeal as for their station. Prescott's History is spoken of in terms of unqualified praise. I have known but one exception. A reviewer, a hypercritic, "dyed in the wool," sat next me at Mrs. ——'s dinner. He said Mr. Prescott must not hope to pass the English custom-house unless he wrote purer English, and he adduced several words which I have forgotten. I ventured to say that new words sprung out of new combinations of circumstances;* that, for example, the French revolution had created many words. "Yes," he replied, "and American words may do for America; but America is, in relation to England, a province. England must give the law to readers and writers of English." After some other flippant criticisms, he ended with saying, that the History of Ferdinand and Isabella was one of the best extant, and that Mr. Prescott had exhausted the subject.

He said, what was quite true before the habits of colonial deference had passed away, but is no longer, "that an American book has no reputation in America till it is stamped with English authority, and then it goes off edition after edition." He uttered sundry other impertinences; but, as he seemed good-natured and unconscious that they were so, I set them down to the account of individual ignorance and prejudice, not to nationality, which has too often to answer for private sins.

Society, as I have before told you, has the same general features here as with us. The women have the same time-wasting mode of making morning visits, which is even more consuming than with us, inasmuch as the distances are

greater. What would Mrs. —— do in London, who thought it reason enough for removing from New-York to the country, that she had to spend one morning of every week in driving about town to leave visiting-cards? One would think that the proposition which circulates as undeniable truth, that time is the most valuable of possessions, would prevent this lavish expenditure. But it is not a truth. Nothing is less valuable to nine-tenths of mere society people, or less valued by them, than time. The only thing they earnestly try to do is to get rid of it.

I have seen nothing here to change my opinion that there is something in the Anglo-Saxon race essentially adverse to the spirit and grace of society. I have seen more invention, spirit, and ease in one soirée in a German family at New-York, than I have ever seen here, or should see in a season in purely American society. An Englishman has an uncomfortable consciousness of the presence and observation of others; an immense love of approbation, with either a shyness or a defiance of opinion.

Thoroughly well-bred people are essentially the same everywhere. You will find much more conventional breeding here than with us, and, of course, the general level of manners is higher and the surface more uniform.

"Society is smoothed to that excess,
That manners differ hardly more than dress."

They are more quiet, and I should say there was less individuality; but from a corresponding remark having been made by English travellers among us, I take it the impression results from the very slight revelations of character that are made on a transient acquaintance. There is much more variety and richness in conversation here, resulting naturally from more leisure and higher cultivation. But, after all, there seems to me to be a great defect in conversation. The feast of wit and reason it may be, but it is not the flow and mingling of soul. The Frenchman, instructed by his *amour propre*, said truly, " *Tout le monde aime à planter son mot†.*" Conversation seems here to be a great arena, where each speaker is a gladiator who must take his turn, put forth his strength, and give place to his successor. Each one is on the watch to seize his opportunity, show his power, and disappear before his vanity is wounded by an indication that he is in the way. Thus conversation becomes a succession of illuminations and triumphs—or failures. There is no such "*horreur*" as a bore; no such bore as a proser. A bore might be defined to be a person that must be listened to. I remember R. saying that "kings are always bores, and so are royal dukes, for they must not be interrupted as long as they please to talk." The crowning grace of conversation, the listening with pleased eagerness, I have rarely seen. When Dr. C. was told that Coleridge pronounced him the most agreeable American he had ever seen, he replied, "Then it was because he found me a good listener, for I said absolutely nothing!" And yet, as far as we may judge from Coleridge's Table-Talk, he would have been the gainer by a fairer battle than that where

"One side only gives and t'other takes the blows."

---

* I was struck with the different views that are taken of th · same subject in different positions, when afterward, in a conversation with the celebrated Manzoni, he asked me if America, in emancipating herself from political depeudence, had also obtained intellectual freedom ; if, unenslaved by the classic models of England, we venture to modify the language, and to use such new phrases and words as naturally sprung from new circumstances?

† " Every man likes to put in his word."

A feature in society here that must be striking to Americans, is the great number of single women. With us, you know, few women live far beyond their minority unmated, and those few sink into the obscurity of some friendly fireside. But here they have an independent existence, pursuits, and influence, and they are much happier for it : mind, I do not say happier than fortunate wives and good mothers, but than those who, not having drawn a husband in the lottery of life, resign themselves to a merely passive existence. English women, married and single, have more leisure, and far more opportunity for intellectual cultivation, than with us. The objects of art are on every side of them, exciting their minds through their sensations, and filling them with images of beauty. There is, with us, far more necessity, and of course opportunity, for the development of a woman's faculties for domestic life, than here ; but this, I think, is counterbalanced by women's necessary independence of the other sex here. On the whole it seems to me there is not a more loveable or lovely woman than the American matron, steadfast in her conjugal duties, devoted to the progress of her children and the happiness of her household, nor a more powerful creature than the Englishwoman in the full strength and development of her character.

Now, my dear C., a word as to dress for the womankind of your family. I do not comprehend what our English friends, who come among us, mean by their comments on the extravagance of dress in America. I have seen more velvet and costly lace in one hour in Kensington Gardens than I ever saw in New-York ; and it would take all the diamonds in the United States to dress a duchess for an evening at L—— house. You may say that lace and diamonds are transmitted luxuries, heir-looms (a species of inheritance we know little about) ; still you must take into the account the immense excess of their wealth over ours, before you can have a notion of the disparity between us.

The women here up to five-and-forty (and splendid women many of them are up to that age) dress with taste—fitness ; after that, abominably. Women to seventy, and Heaven knows how much longer, leave their necks and arms bare ; not here and there one, "blinded, deluded, and misguided," but whole assemblies of fat women—and, O tempora ! O mores !—and lean. Such parchment necks as I have seen bedizened with diamonds, and arms bared, that seemed only fit to hold the scissors of destiny, or to stir the caldron of Macbeth's witches. —— dresses in azure satins and rose-coloured silks, and bares her arms as if they were as round and dimpled as a cherub's, though they are mere bunches of sinews, that seem only kept together by that nice anatomical contrivance of the wristband, on which Paley expatiates. This post-mortem demonstration is, perhaps, after all, an act of penance for past vanities, or perhaps it is a benevolent admonition to the young and fair, that to this favour they must come at last ! Who knows* ?

The entire absence of what seems to us fitness for the season may in part result from the climate. In June and July, you know, we have all our dark and bright colours, and rich stuffs—everything that can elicit the idea of warmth, laid aside ; here we see everyday velvets and boas, and purple, orange, and cherry silks and satins. Cherry, indeed, is the prevailing colour ; cherry feathers the favourite head-dress. I saw the Duchess of Cambridge the other evening at the opera with a crimson-velvet turban ! Remember, it is July !

We have seen in the gardens plenty of delicate muslins over gay-coloured silks ; this is graceful, but to us it seems inappropriate for an out-of-door dress.

The absence of taste in the middling classes produces results that are almost ludicrous. I am inclined to think taste is an original faculty, and only capable of a certain direction. This might explain the art of dress as it exists among the English, with the close neighbourhood of Paris, and French milliners actually living among them ; and this might solve the mystery of the exquisite taste in gardening in England, and the total absence of it in France.

As you descend in the scale to those who can have only reference to the necessities of life in their dress, the English are far superior to us. Here come in their ideas of neatness, comfort, and durability. The labouring classes are much more suitably dressed than ours. They may have less finery for holidays, and their servants may not be so smartly dressed in the evening as are our domestics, but they are never shabby or uncleanly†. Their clothes are of stouter stuffs, their shoes stronger, and their dress better preserved. We have not, you know, been into the manufacturing districts, nor into the dark lanes and holes of London, where poverty hides itself ; but I do not remember, in five weeks in England, with my eyes pretty wide open, ever to have seen a ragged or dirty dress. Dirt and rags are the only things that come under a rigid sumptuary law in England.

Order is England's, as it is Heaven's, first law. Coming from our head-over-heels land, it is striking and beautiful to see the precise order that prevails here. In the public institutions, in private houses, in the streets and thoroughfares, you enjoy the security and comfort of this Heavenborn principle. It raises your ideas of the capacities of human nature to see such masses of beings as there are in London kept, without any violation of their liberty, within the bounds of order. I am told the police system of London has nearly attained perfection. I should think so from the results. It is said that women may go into the street at any hour of the night without fear or danger ; and I know that Mrs. —— has often left us after ten o'clock, refusing the attendance of our servant as superfluous, to go alone through several streets to the omnibus that takes her to her own home‡.

reference to individual circumstances or appearance. Her own countrywomen do not need these suggestions.

† Would it not be better if our rich employers would persuade their women-servants to wear caps, and leave liveries to countries whose institutions they suit ?

‡ When we had been in London some weeks, one of my party asked me if I had not missed the New-York stacks of bricks and mortar, and if I had observed that we had

* It is to be hoped that Mrs. ——, in her promised essay on the philosophy of dress, will give some hints to our old ladies not to violate the harmonies by wearing auburn hair over wrinkled brows, and some to our young women on the bad taste of uniformity of costume, without

THE system of ranks here, as absolute as the Oriental *caste*, is the feature in English society most striking to an American. For the progress of the human race it was worth coming to the New World to get rid of it. Yes, it was worth all that our portion of the human family sacrificed, encountered, and suffered. This system of castes is the more galling, clogging, and unhealthy, from its perfect unfitness to the present state of freedom and progress in England.

Travellers laugh at our pretensions to equality, and Sir Walter Scott has said, as truly as wittily, that there is no perfect equality except among the Hottentots. But our inequalities are as changing as the surface of the ocean, and this makes all the difference. Each rank is set about here with a thorny, impervious, and almost impassable hedge. We have our walls of separation, certainly ; but they are as easily knocked down or surmounted as our rail-fences.

With us, talents, and education, and refined manners command respect and observance ; and so, I am sorry to say, does fortune : but fortune has more than its proverbial mutability in the United States. The rich man of to-day is the poor man of to-morrow, and so *vice versâ*. This unstableness has its evils, undoubtedly, and so has every modification of human condition ; but better the evil that is accidental than that which is authorised, cherished, and inevitable. That system is most generous, most Christian, which allows a fair start to all ; some must reach the goal before others, as, for the most part, the race is ordained to the swift, and the battle to the strong.

But you would rather have my observations than my speculations ; and as, in my brief survey, I have only seen the outside, it is all I can give you, my dear C. I have no details of the vices of any class. I have heard shocking anecdotes of the corruption prevailing among the high people ; and men and women have been pointed out to me in public places who have been guilty of notorious conjugal infidelities, and the grossest violations of parental duty, without losing caste ; and this I have heard imputed to their belonging to a body that is above public opinion. I do not see how this can be, nor why the opinion of their own body does not bear upon them. Surely there should be virtue enough in such people as the Marquis of Lansdowne and the Duchess of Sutherland to banish from their world the violators of those laws of God and man, on which rest the foundations of social virtue and happiness.

Those who from their birth or their successful talents are assured of their rank, have the best manners. They are perfectly tranquil, safe behind the entrenchments that have stood for ages. They leave it to the aspirants to be the videttes and defenders of the outworks. Those persons I have met of the highest rank have the simplest and most informal manners. I have before told you that Lord L—— and the Bishop of —— reminded me of our friends Judge L—— and Judge W——, our best-mannered country-gentlemen. Their lordships have rather more conven-

---

not once heard a cry of "fire !" In these respects the contrast to our building and burning city is striking. In fifteen months' absence I never heard the cry of fire.

---

tionalism, more practice, but there is no essential difference. Descend a little lower, and a very little lower than those gentry who by birth and association are interwoven with the nobility, and you will see people with education and refinement enough, as you would think, to ensure them the tranquillity that comes of self-respect, manifesting a consciousness of inferiority ; in some it appears in servility, as in Mrs. ——, who, having scrambled on to ——'s shoulders, and got a peep into the lord-and-lady world, and heard the buzz that rises from the precincts of Buckingham Palace, entertained us through a long morning visit with third or fourth hand stories about " poor Lady Flora ; " or in obsequiousness, as in the very pretty wife of ——, whose eyes, cheeks, and voice are changed if she is but spoken to by a titled person, though she remains as impassive as polar ice to the influence of a plebeian presence. Some manifest their impatience of this vassalage of caste in a petulant but impotent resistance, and others show a crushed feeling, not the humility of the flower that has grown in the shade, but the abasement and incapacity ever to rise of that which has been trodden under foot. Even the limbs are stiffened and the gait modified by this consciousnes s that haunts them from the cradle to the grave.

A certain great tailor was here yesterday morning to take R.'s directions. His bad grammar, his obsequiousness, and his more than once favouring us with the information that he had an appointment with the Duke of ——, brought forcibly to my mind the person who holds the corresponding position in S——. I thought of his frank and self-respecting manner, his well-informed mind, his good influence, and the probable destiny of his children. I leave you to jump to my conclusion.

The language of the shopmen here indicates a want of education, and their obsequiousness expresses their consciousness that they are the "things that live by bowing." And, by the way, I see nothing like the rapidity of movement and adroitness in serving that you find in a New-York shop. You may buy a winter's supply at Stewart's while half-a-dozen articles are shown to you here. If you buy, they thank you ; and if you refuse to buy, you hear the prescribed automaton, "Thank you !" I say "prescribed," for you often perceive an under current of insolence. You will believe me that it is not civility to which I object.

As you go farther down from the tradesman to the servant, the marks of caste are still more offensive. Miss —— took me to the cottage of their herdsman. He had married a favourite servant, who had lived, I believe, from childhood in the family. The cottage was surrounded and filled with marks of affection and liberality. Miss —— had told me that the woman belonged to a class now nearly extinct in England. " I verily believe," she said, " she thinks my mother and myself are made of a different clay from her ; " and so her manner indicated, as she stood in a corner of the room, with her arms reverently folded, and courtesying with every reply she made to Miss ——, though nothing could be more kindly gracious than her manner. I thought of that dear old nurse who, though wearing the colour that is a brand among us, and not exceeded in devoted-ness by any feudal vassal of any age, expressed in the noble freedom of her manner that she not only felt herself to be of the same clay, but of the same spirit, with those she served.

I confess I do see something more than "urbanity" in this "homage." I do not wish to be reminded, by a man touching his hat or pulling his forelock every time I speak to him, that there is a gulf between us. This is neither good for him nor me. Have those who pretend to fear the encroachments and growing pride of the inferior classes, never any conscientious fears for their own humility! Do their reflections never suggest to them that pride is the natural concomitant of conscious superiority! But to return to these demonstrations of respect; they are not a sign of real deference. I have seen more real insolence here in five weeks in this class of people than I ever saw at home. At the inns, at the slightest dissatisfaction with the remuneration you offer, you are sure to be told, " Such as is *ladies* always gives more." This is meanness as well as insolence.

As we drove off from Southampton, a porter demanded a larger fee than we paid. H. called after us to be sure and give the fellow no more. The fellow knew his quarry; he mounted on the coach, and kept with us through a long street, demanding and entreating with alternate insolence and abjectness. He got the shilling, and then returning to the homage of his station, " Do you sit quite comfortable, ladies?" he asked, in a sycophantic tone. " Yes." " Thank you." " Would not Miss —— like better this seat?" " No." " Thank you." Again I repeat it, it is not the civility I object to. I wish we had more of it in all stations; but it is the hollow sound, which conveys to me no idea but the inevitable and confessed vassalage of a fellow-being.

I am aware that the sins we are not accustomed to are like those we are not inclined to, in the respect that we condemn them heartily and *en masse.* Few Englishmen can tolerate the manners of our tradespeople, our innkeepers, and the domestics at our public-houses. A little more familiarity with them would make them tolerant of the deficiencies that at first disgust them; and after a while they would learn, as we do, to prize the fidelity and quiet kindness that abound among our servants without the expectation of pecuniary reward; and they would feel that it is salutary to be connected with this large class of our humble fellow-creatures by other than sordid ties.

If I have felt painfully that the men and women of what is called " good society " in America are greatly inferior in high cultivation, in the art of conversation, and in accomplishments, to a corresponding class here, I have felt quite assured that the " million" with us occupy a level they can never reach in England, do what they will with penny magazines and diffusive publications, while each class has its stall into which it is driven by the tyranny of an artificially-constructed society.

While the marks No. 2, No. 3, and so on, are seen cut in, there cannot be the conscious power and freedom, and the self-respect brightening the eye, giving free play to all the faculties, and urging onward and upward, which is the glory

of the United States, and a new phase of human society.

With your confirmed habits, my dear C., you might not envy the English the luxuries and magnificence of their high civilisation; but I am sure you would the precise finish of their skilful agriculture, and the all-pervading comfort of their every-day existence. *If you have money,* there is no human contrivance for comfort that you cannot command here. Let you be where you will, in the country or in town, on land or on water, in your home or on the road, but signify your desires, and they may be gratified. And it is rather pleasant, dear C.—it would be with your eye for order—to be in a country where there are no bad—bad! no imperfect roads, no broken or unsound bridges, no swinging gates, no barn-doors off the hinges, no broken glass, no ragged fences, no negligent husbandry, nothing to signify that truth, omnipresent in America, that there is a great deal more work to do than hands to do it. And so it will be with our uncounted acres of unsubdued land for ages to come. But, courage! we are of English blood, and we shall go forward and subdue our great farm, and make it, in some hundreds of years, like the little garden whence our fathers came. In the mean time we must expect the English travellers who come among us to be annoyed with the absence of the home-comforts which habit has made essential to their well-being, and to be startled, and, it may be, disgusted, with the omission of those signs and shows of respect and deference to which they have been accustomed; but let us not be disturbed if they growl, for " 'tis their nature to," and surely they should be forgiven for it*.

July 8.—To-morrow we leave England, having seen but a drop in the ocean of things worthy to be examined. We mean, next year, to travel over it, to see the country, to visit the institutions of benevolence, the schools, &c. We are now to plunge into a foreign country, with a foreign language and foreign customs. It seems like leaving home a second time. If anything could make us forget that we are travellers, it would be such unstinted kindness as we have received here. You cannot see the English in their homes without reverencing and loving them; nor, I think, can an Anglo-American come to this, his ancestral

---

* It is difficult for an American to appreciate the complete change that takes place in a European's position and relations on coming to this country; if he did, he would forgive the disgusts and uneasiness betrayed even by those who have the most philanthropic theories. He who was born in an atmosphere of elegance and refinement, far above the masses of his fellow-beings; who has seen them eager to obey his slightest signal, to minister to his artificial wants, ready to sit at his feet, to open a way for him, or to sustain him on their shoulders—who is always so far above them as to be in danger of entirely overlooking them, finds suddenly that all artificial props are knocked from under him, and he is brought down to a level with these masses, each individual elbowing his own way, and he obliged to depend on his own merit for all the eminence he attains. M. de Tocqueville is a striking illustration of the conflict between a democratic faith and the habits and tastes engendered by a European education. Perhaps some observation and reflection on this subject would convince parents of the injudiciousness of rearing children in Europe who are to live in America.

home, without a pride in his relationship to it, and an extended sense of the obligations imposed by his derivation from the English stock. A war between the two countries, in the present state of their relations and intercourse, would be fratricidal, and this sentiment I have heard expressed on all sides.

Antwerp, July 12, 1839.

MY DEAR C.—We left the Tower Stairs yesterday at twelve, and were rowed to the steamer Soho, lying out in the Thames, in a miserable little boat, the best we could obtain. We found a natural *American* consolation in remarking the superiority of our Whitehall boats. We nearly incurred that first of all minor miseries (if it be minor), losing our baggage. François, not speaking a word of English, has been of little use to us; and in our greatest need, at our arrivals and departures, he has been worse than useless, as John Bull's nerves are disturbed by a foreign tongue, and the sub-officials are sure to get in a fluster. Mr. P.'s intervention came in most timely to our aid, and the last boat from the shore brought us our baggage safely. What we shall do without this friend, whose ministering kindness has been so steadfast and so effective, I know not; though François said, as soon as he had shaken the London dust from his feet, with a ludicrously self-sufficient air, "A present, madame, le courrier fait tout * !"

The Soho, we were told, is the best steamer that plies between London and Antwerp. It is one hundred and seventy-five feet in length, and twenty-eight in breadth. It has some advantages over our Hudson River steamers,—a steadier motion, the result of more perfect machinery, a salle-à-manger (an eating-room where there are no berths), and two dinners, served two hours apart. So that, with one hundred and twenty passengers, there is no scrambling, and the dinner is served with *English* order, and eaten at leisure. I was disappointed to find, last night, our condition quite as bad as in a similar position at home. There were thirty more passengers than berths, and these luckless thirty were strewn over the saloon floor, after having waited till a late hour for the last loitering men to be driven forth from their paradise, the dinner-table. The servants were incompetent, and the bedding was deficient, and in the morning we had no place for washing, no dressing-room but this cluttered, comfortless apartment. We all felt a malignant pleasure in having these annoyances to fret about in an English dominion. Even they cannot beguile Dame Comfort to sea,—like a sensible woman, she is a stayer-at-home, a lover of the fire-side. The English go in troops and caravans to Germany and Switzerland for the summer, and most of our fellow-passengers seemed to be of these gentry, travelling for pleasure. How different from the miscellaneous crowd of an American steamer! There is here more conventional breeding, not more civility, than with us.

When I went on deck in the morning, we had entered the Scheldt, and poor M., with her eyes half open, was dutifully trying to sketch the shores. They are so low and uniform, that a single horizontal stroke of her pencil would suffice to give you

* " From this time your courier does everything."

at home all the idea we got; and, for a fac-simile of the architecture, you may buy a Dutch town at Werkmeister's toy-shop.

We now, for the first, realise † that we are in a foreign land, and feel our distance from home. In our memory and feeling England blends with our own country.

We entered into the court of the Hôtel St. Antoine through an arched stone gateway, and were, for the first time in our lives, in a paved court, round three sides of which the house, in the common Continental fashion, is built. The mistress of the hotel, in pretty full dress, came out to receive us; and, after hearing our wants, we were conducted through a paved gallery to spacious and well-furnished apartments. Before the hotel is a little square, surrounded with three rows of dwarf elm-trees, and in honour of these, I presume, called La Place Verte (Green Place), for there is nothing else green about it. The ground is incessantly trodden by people crossing it, or seated about on the wooden benches in social squads. All the womenkind wear a high lace cap, dropping low at the ears, short gowns, and very full petticoats in the Dutch fashion, with which we were familiar enough formerly at Albany. A better class wear a black shawl over the head hanging down to their feet—a remnant of the Spanish mantilla. It is curious to see this and other vestiges of Spanish occupation here, such as some very grand old Spanish houses.

We have been driving about the town in a comfortable carriage, six of us besides the coachman, after a fat, sleek Flemish horse, who seemed quite able to trot off double the number, if need were. I wish I could give you a glimpse of these streets thronging with human life, and seemingly happy human life too. The "honest Flemings" have a most contented look. I almost doubt my identity as I hear this din of a foreign tongue in my ear, and the clattering of the wooden shoes on the pavement. However, that "I is I," I feel too surely at this moment, having just mounted the tower of the Cathedral, 613 steps: a cathedral built in 1300, and eighty-three years in the building. The tower is beautifully wrought. Charles V. said of it, it should be kept in a case, and Napoleon compared it to Mechlin lace. If these great people have not the fairy gift of dropping pearls from their lips, their words are gold for the guides that haunt these show-places. We paid two francs for the above jeux d'esprit to a young cicerone, who could speak intelligibly French, Spanish, English, Italian, and Flemish of course, but could not write, and had never heard of America !!

We saw from the gallery of the tower to a distance (on the word of our guide) of eighty miles. The atmosphere was perfectly transparent, undimmed by a particle of smoke from the city; a fact accounted for by the fuel used being exclusively a species of hard coal. It is worth while to mount a pinnacle in a country like this, where there is no eminence to intercept the view. You see the Scheldt, which is about as wide as the

† My English reader must pardon the frequent repetition of this word, and may judge of the worth of its American use by the reply of my friend, to whom I said, "I cannot dispense with this word" "Dispense with it! I could as well dispense with bread and water!"

Hudson at Albany, winding far, far away through a sea of green and waving corn*, and towers, churches, and villages innumerable. The view gave us New-World people a new idea of populousness†. After we descended from the tower, a bit of antiquity was pointed out to us that would have interested your young people more than any view in Belgium. It is an old well, covered with an iron canopy wrought by Quentin Matsys, the "Blacksmith of Antwerp;" who, before blacksmiths were made classic by Scott's "Harry of the Wynd," fell in love with the pretty daughter of a painter, and left his anvil and took to painting to win her, and did win her, and for himself won immortality by at least one masterpiece in the art, as all who have seen his "Misers" at Windsor will testify.

Antwerp is rich in paintings. Many masterpieces of the Flemish painters are here, and, first among the first, "Rubens' Descent from the Cross." Do not think, dear C., that, before I have even crossed the threshold of the temple of art, I give you my opinion about such a painting as of any value. I see that the dead body is put into the most difficult position to be painted, and that the painter has completely overcome the difficulty; that the figures are perfect in their anatomy, and that the flesh is flesh, living flesh ; but I confess the picture did not please me. It seemed to me rather a successful representation of the physical man than the embodiment of the moral sublime which the subject demands. Another picture by Rubens, in the church of St. Jacques, was far more interesting to me. It is, considering the subject, fortunately placed, being the altarpiece of the altar belonging to the family of Rubens ; and you look at it with the feeling that you are in the presence of this greatest of Flemish artists, as the marble slab on which you are treading tells you that his body lies beneath it. The revolutionary French, with their dramatic enthusiasm for art, spared this tomb when they broke open and pillaged every other one in this church. The picture is called A Holy Family. The painter, by introducing his own dearest kindred with the names and attributes of saints, has canonised them without leave of pope or cardinal. His own portrait he called St. George ; his father's, St. Jerome ; his old grandfather's, Time ; and his son naturally enough falls into the category of angels. Martha and Mary Magdalen, two most lovely women, are portraits of his two wives ; one of these is said to be the same head as the famous "Chapeau de Paille"—probably the Magdalen.

For the rest—and what a rest of churches, pictures, carvings, and tombs, that cost us hours of toilsome pleasure, I spare you.

Brussels, Monday, 15.—WE came here twentyfive miles by railroad. The cars we thought as good as those on the "Great Western" in England ; and our fare was a third less, and so was our speed. The country was a dead level. A Flemish painter only could work up its creature-comforts into picturesqueness ; rich it certainly is, and enjoyed it appears. After a bustle and confusion at the depôt that made us feel quite at home, we finally got into an omnibus with twelve persons inside, nearly as many outside, and an enormous quantity of baggage, all drawn with apparent ease by two of these gigantic Flemish horses, looking, like their masters, well content with their lot in life.

Brussels is a royal residence, and gay with palaces and park. The park impresses me as twice as large as St. John's in New York ; it has abundance of trees, a bit of water with a rich fringe of flowers, and statues, in bad taste enough. There are splendid edifices overlooking it, and among them the palace of the Prince of Orange, and King Leopold's. That of the Prince of Orange, which Leopold, with singular delicacy for a king, has refused to occupy or touch, is shown to strangers. We were unlucky in the moment of making our application to see it. "First come, first served," is the democratic rule adopted. Four parties were before us, and as we could not bribe the portress to favour us—to her honour I record it—and had no time to waste in waiting, we came away and left unseen its choice collection of paintings. Our coachman, to console us for our disappointment, urged us to go into the royal coach-house and see a carriage presented to William, which, he gave us his assurance—truly professional—was better worth seeing than anything in Brussels ! A gorgeous thing it was, all gold and crimson outside, white satin and embroidery in ; and with a harness emblazoned with crowns. Beside this, were ten other coaches of various degrees of magnificence.

We next visited the lace manufactory of Monsieur Ducepetiaux. The Brussels lace is, as perhaps you do not know, the most esteemed of this most delicate of fabrics. "The flax from which it is made grows near Halle ; the finest sort costs from 3000 to 4000 francs per pound, and is worth its weight in gold. Everything depends on the tenuity of its fibre‡."

It was fête-day, and we found only a few old women at work ; however, we were shown the whole process very courteously, without any other fee being expected than a small alms to the poor work-women, which, after seeing them, it would be difficult to withhold. I observed women from sixty to seventy at this cobweb-work without spectacles, and was told that the eye was so accustomed to it as not to be injured by it ; a wonderful instance of the power of adaptation in the human frame in its most delicate organ. Girls begin at this work at four years of age, and the overseer told us she employed old women of eighty. They begin at six in the morning and work till six in the evening ; the maximum of wages is one franc ; and, to earn this, a woman must work skilfully and rapidly twelve hours and find herself ! I thought of the king's ten coaches. There are a good many changes to be made before this becomes "the best of all possible worlds !"

I spare you our visit to the Cathedral, &c., but I wish, my dear C., I could show you the most fantastical pulpit ever made—the masterpiece of Ver-Bruggen, with the story of Adam and Eve

---

* Some of our readers may not be aware that this word is not applied in Europe, as with us, alone to Indian corn, but to every kind of grain.

† This was from the dense population of the surrounding country. Antwerp itself contains but about 77,000 inhabitants.

‡ Murray's Hand-Book

carved in wood. I am sure the artist had his own private readings of his work. There seemed to me some precious satire in the symbols he has perched about the pulpit—the monkey! the peacock! and the serpent!

We went into the market-place this morning. It was filled with well-looking peasants, with good teeth and rich nice hair. They were selling flowers, fruit, and vegetables. They addressed us in a very kindly manner, always as "ma chère." We saw excellent butter for ten sous per pound, a good cabbage for two sous, two quarts of beans for four sous.

This market-square, now looking so cheerful with the fruits of man's rural industry, has been stained with the blood of martyrs of liberty. It was here that Counts Egmont and Horn were executed by the order of the ruthless Alva ; and in the Hôtel de Ville, overlooking the square, we saw the hall where his master, Charles V., went through the ceremony of abdication.

We pay here, for a good carriage and two horses, two francs per hour. Some difference, M. remarks, between this and the price we paid in London of one pound twelve shillings per day: but nowhere, I believe, is social life so taxed as in London.

We set off this morning for the field of Waterloo, a distance of twelve miles from Brussels. I sat on the box beside our coachman, a civilised young man. Travelling is a corrector of one's vanities. I heard myself designated in the court to-day as "la dame qui s'assit à côté du cocher" —my only distinction here. I liked my position. My friend was intelligent and talkative, and not only gave me such wayside information as I asked, but the history of his father's courtship and a little love-story of his own, which is just at the most critical point of dramatic progress, and of which, alas! I shall never know the dénouement.

It is the anniversary of the Belgian revolution, and, of course, a fête-day. The streets were thronged. I should imagine the whole number of inhabitants, 100,000, were out of doors ; and as the streets are narrow and have no side-walks, we made slow progress through the crowd—but so much the better. It was pleasant looking in their good, cheerful faces, the children in their holiday suits, and the women in their clean caps and freshest ribands. Green boughs hung over the windows, and the fruit-stalls were decked with flowers. I looked up the lanes on the right and left ; they were a dense mass of human beings, looking well fed and comfortably clad. "Where are your poor people ?" I asked my friend. "They are put o' one side," he replied. Alas! so are they everywhere if in the minority. There was wretchedness enough in those lanes that now appeared so well ; but he assured me I might walk through them without fear, "the police was too strong for them." The suburbs were thronged too ; the straggling little villages along the road full of human life. The women and men were sitting on long benches beside the houses, drinking beer and eating cakes. The pressure of the population would have driven Malthus mad. Everything of womankind, down to the girl of four years old, had a baby in her arms, and young things were strewn over the ground, kicking up their heels, and making all manner of youthful demonstrations of happiness.

If some of our worn, pale mothers, who rock their cradles by the hour in close rooms, would turn their young ones into the sweet open air, they would find it play upon their spirits like the breath of heaven on an Æolian harp. I never before saw the young·human animal as happy as other animals, nor felt how much they were the creatures of mere sensation. "You see how well they look," said my friend, who observed my pleasure in gazing at them ; "they work hard too, all that can work, and eat nothing but potatoes and milk." Simple, wholesome diet, and plenty of fresh air : this tells the whole story of health.

The forest of Soignies, which Byron makes poetically grieve over the "unreturning brave," lies now, at least a good portion of it, as low as they ; and in the place of it are wheat, barley, potatoes, &c., which my utilitarian friend thought far better than unedible trees. The king of the Netherlands made a very pretty present to Wellington, along with his title of "Prince of Waterloo," of 1000 acres of this forest land, which is extremely valuable for its timber. Waterloo itself is a straggling, mean little village, in which, as we were going to the burial-place of thousands of brave men, we did not stop to weep over the grave of the Marquis of Anglesea's leg, which, with its monument, epitaph, and weeping willow, is one of the regular Waterloo lions. At Mont St. Jean, on the edge of the field of battle, we took our guide Martin, a peasant with a most humane physiognomy, indicating him fitter to show a battle-field than to fight on it.

Now do not fear that I am about to commit the folly of describing "the field of Waterloo." I shall merely tell you that we have seen the places whose names are magic words in the memories of those who remember 1815. As we left Mont St. Jean, we came upon an unenclosed country, and at the large farmhouse called Ferme de Mont St. Jean, we first saw a mound, surmounted by the Belgic Lion. This mound is two hundred feet high, and covers the common burying-place of friends and foes. The lion is placed over the very spot where the Prince of Orange was wounded, and is cast from the cannon taken in the field of battle. To those cavillers who see no good reason why, amid ·such a mass of valiant sufferers, a wound of the Prince of Orange should be illustrated, or why the Belgic lion should crown the scene, and who lament that the face of the field has been changed by the elevation of the mound, it has been answered pithily, if not satisfactorily, that it is appropriate, "since it serves at once for a memorial, a trophy, and a tomb *."

Hougoumont remains as it was after the day of the battle. It is an old Flemish château, with farm-offices and a walled garden. The house is shattered, and the walls look as if they had been

* It was interesting to read, on the very spot, Byron's testimony to this as a position for a battle-field. "As a plain," he says, "Waterloo seems marked out for ·the scene of some great action, though this may be mere imagination. I have viewed with attention those of Platæa, Troy, Mantinea, Leuctra, Cheronea, and Marathon ; and the field around Mont St. Jean and Hougoumont appears to want little but a better cause, and that undefinable but impressive halo which the lapse of ages throws around a celebrated spot, to vie in interest with any or all of them, except, perhaps, the last-mentioned."

through the wars. There were twenty-seven Englishmen in the chapel, a structure not more than
thirteen feet square, when it took fire. A wooden
image of our Saviour is suspended over the door;
and our guide averred (and, though a guide, with
a moistened eye) that when the flames reached the
image, they stopped. " C'est vrai," he repeated.
" Aux pieds du bon Dieu ! Un miracle, n'est-ce
pas, madame * !" I almost envied the faith that
believed the miracle, and had the miracle to believe.
The English, in their passion for such relics, had
begun chipping off the foot, and our good Martin
said, shuddering, that if the proper authority had
not interfered, " on aurait mis le bon Dieu tout
en pièces !" The Catholic sentiment is nearly
untranslatable into Protestant English.

The inner wall is written over with the names
of visitors. Byron's was there; but some marauding traveller has broken away the plaster, and
carried it off to Paris. " Do you not think," said
our guide, with an honest indignation, " that a man
must be crazy to do this ?" The simple peasant-
guide knew the worth of Byron's name. This is
fame.

We drove round the rich wheat-field to *La
Haye Sainte*. There is no ground in all rich
Belgium so rich as this battle-field. In the spring
the darkest and thickest corn tells were the dead
were buried ! The German Legion slaughtered
at La Haye Sainte are buried on the opposite side
of the road, where there is a simple monument
over them—

"Set where thou wilt thy foot, thou scarce canst tread
Here on a spot unhallow'd by the dead."

La Belle Alliance, where Wellington and Blucher
met after the battle, was pointed out to us; and
Napoleon's different positions, the very spot where
he stood when he first descried Blucher, and his
heart for the last time swelled with anticipated
triumph. How I wished for Hal to stand with me
where Wellington gave that ringing order, " Up,
guards, and at them !"

We were shown the places where Gordon,
Picton, and others of note fell; and there, where
the masses lay weltering in blood, the unknown,
unhonoured, unrecorded, there was

"Horror breathing from the silent ground."

"It was a piteous sight," said our guide, " to see,
the next day, the men, with clasped hands, begging
for a glass of water. Some had lost one side of
the face with a sabre-cut; others had their bowels
laid open ! They prayed us to put an end to their
miseries, and said, surely God would forgive us."
All the peasants, men, women, and children, that
had not been driven clear away, came in to serve
them; but there was not enough; and they died,
burned with thirst; and their wounds gangrened,
for there were not surgeons for the half of them.
They would crawl down to those pools of water and
wash their wounds; the water was red and clotted
with *blood*. Oh, c'est un grand malheur, que la
guerre, mesdames !" he concluded. Martin would
be an eloquent agent for our friend Ladd's Peace
Society.

BELGIUM is a perfect garden. Between Brussels
and Liege, a distance of sixty miles, we did not see,

* " It is indeed true. At the feet of the good God ! A
miracle, was it not, madam ? "

over all the vast plain, one foot of unused earth.
There are crops of wheat, rye, oats, beans, and
peas, and immense cabbage plantations, with no
inclosures, neither fences nor hedges; no apparent
division of property. You might fancy the land
was under the dominion of an agrarian law, and
that each child of man might take an equal share
from mother earth; but, alas ! when the table is
spread there is many a one left without a cover.

On arriving at the depôt, a league from Liege,
we had a scene of confusion unusual in these countries, that should and do get the benefit of order
from their abounding police-men. A number of
ark-like, two-story omnibuses were drawn up.
Calling out being prohibited, the signal to attract
attention was a hiss, and the hissing of rival conductors was like nothing so much as a flock of
enraged geese. We got involved in a dispute that
menaced us with a fate similar to that adjudged by
Solomon to the contested child. *Monsieur le Courrier* had promised us to the " omnibus Jaune,"
and *Mademoiselle la Courrière* to the " omnibus
Rouge;" the yellow finally carried it, and we were
driven off amid such hisses as Dante might have
imagined a fit Inferno for a bad actor. Poor M.
lost her travelling-cloak in the confusion. I can
tell you nothing of Liege, from my own observation, but that it is a most picturesque old place,
with one part of the town rising precipitously above
the other in the fashion of Quebec; and that we
went to see the interior court of the Palais de Justice,
formerly the archbishop's palace, whose name will
recall to you Quentin Durward. It is surrounded
by a colonnade with short pillars, each carved after
a different model. We walked round the space
within the colonnade, which is filled with stalls
containing such smaller merchandise as you find
around our market-places. The English call Liege
the Birmingham of Belgium. Their staple manufacture is firearms, and Mr. Murray tells us " they
produce a better article, and at a lower price, than
can be made for the same sum in England "—a
feather this in the Belgian cap ! The source of
their prosperity is the abundance of coal in the
neighbourhood. " The mines are worked on the
most scientific principles. Previously to the revolution, Holland was supplied with coal from
Belgium; but the home consumption has since
increased to such an extent, from the numerous
manufactories which have sprung up on all sides,
that the Belgian mines are now inadequate to
supply the demand, and a recent law has been
passed, permitting the importation of coals from
Newcastle †." Wise Hollanders !

THE diligences did not suit our hours, and
François could obtain no carriage to take us to
Aix-la-Chapelle but an enormous lumbering omnibus. Imagine what a travelling-carriage ! Though
the distance is but about twenty-five miles, we
were nine mortal hours passing it; however, it
was through a lovely country, varied with hill and
dale, a refreshing variety after the monotonous
dead-level of our preceding days in Belgium.
On leaving Liege we passed the Meuse and ascended a long hill, and from the summit looked
over a world of gracefully-formed land, all under
the dominion of the husbandman. The fields are

† Murray's Hand-Book.

inclosed by hedges, inferior to the English, but resembling them in the trees that intersperse them. There is very little pasture-land amid this garden-like cultivation. I have seen one flock of sheep to-day of a tall, slender breed ; and very beautiful cows, white with brown spots, that, cow-fancier as you are, would enchant you. They rival your Victoria and her mother the duchess.

We passed villages at short intervals, not bearing the smallest resemblance to a New-England village, for there is nothing that bears the name in Europe so beautiful. I may say this without presumption after having seen the English villages. The village here is usually one long street of small mean houses built contiguously. At almost every house there is something exposed to sell. The tenants are all out of doors,—the "seven ages" of man—and at least half are smoking. We saw girls not more than six years old with their pipes ; and they smoke on to old age, apparently cheerful and healthy. Yet we hold tobacco to be a poison ; perhaps the out-of-door life is the antidote. We have passed pretty villas to-day, and substantial farm-houses with capital barns and offices, all indicating rural plenty.

With the threats of beggars in our guide-book, we have been surprised at our general exemption ; but to-day we have seen enough of them, and a sight it is quite as novel to our New-World eyes as a cathedral or a policeman. They have followed us in troops, and started out from their little lairs planted along the road, blind old men and old crones on crutches. As we begin the ascension of the hills, we hear slender young voices, almost overpowered by the rattling of the wheels on the paved road ; by degrees they multiply and grow louder, and before we reach the summit they overpower every other sound, crying out to the mademoiselles in the coupé, and to the monsieur and madame in the *intérieure*, in a mongrel patois of French and Flemish : "Ah, donnez-moi un petit morceau de *brod*—vous n'en serez pas plus pauvre —da-do—charité pour un pauvre aveugle, madame —da-do * !"

A few leagues before reaching Liege we experienced another equally disagreeable characteristic of the social system of the Old World. We passed the Prussian frontier, and were admonished by the black eagle—a proper insignia for a custom-house, a bird of prey—that our baggage must be inspected. We dreaded the disturbance of our trunks, and looked with suitable detestation on the mustachioed officials that approached us. While they were chaffering with François to settle the question whether they should go up to the baggage or the baggage come down to them, and deciding that the mountain *should* come to Mahomet, an officer of as harmless aspect as Deacon I., with spectacles on nose and a baby in his arms, came to our relief, saying that if Monsieur le Courier would give his *parole d'honneur* (a courier's *parole d'honneur* !) that there was nothing to declare—that is, customable—the examination might be omitted. François pledged his word, and there was no further trouble. This contrasts with the torment we had in England, of having all our baggage overhauled and disarranged, and sent home to us, some light

* " Give us a morsel of bread—*da-do*—you will not be the poorer for it—*da-do* !—charity for a poor blind man !"

articles lost, and delicate ones ruined. That this should happen in civilised England at this time of day is disgraceful. I felt it a mortification, as if the barbarism had been committed by my own kindred.

While our lunch was preparing, we strolled off to a little meadow, where there were some young people loading a cart with hay. We sat down on the grass. The scene was pretty and rural, and so home-like that it brought tears to our eyes ; home-like, except that there was a girl not so big as your Grace—no, not five years old, raking hay and smoking a pipe.

Returning to the inn, we passed the open window of our friend the master of the customs. I thanked him for his forbearance. He appeared gratified, and when we came away he came out of his door with a friend, and they bowed low and repeatedly. Better this wayside courtesy than the bickerings that usually occur on similar occasions.

Aix-la-Chapelle.—This name will at once recall to you Charlemagne, whose capital and burying-place it was. We have just returned from La Chapelle, which so conveniently distinguishes this from the other Aix in Europe. Otho built the present church on the site of Charlemagne's chapel, preserving its original octagonal form, which Charlemagne, intending it for his own tomb, adopted from the holy sepulchre at Jerusalem. We stood under the centre of the dome on a large marble slab, inscribed " Carolo Magno ;" and over our heads hung a massive chandelier, the gift of *Frederic Barbarossa.* How these material things conjured back from the dead these mighty chieftains !

The vault must have been a startling sight when Otho opened it and found the emperor, not in the usual supine posture, but seated on his throne in his imperial robes, with the crown on his fleshless brow, his sceptre in his hand, the good sword *Joyeuse* at his side, the Gospels on his knee, the pilgrim's pouch, which, living, he always wore, still at his girdle, and precious jewels sparkling amid decay and ashes. The sacristan showed us his skull— the palace of the soul !—inclosed in a silver case. His lofty soul has, I trust, now a fitter palace. There are shown also several relics found in his tomb which touch a chord of general sympathy : his hunting-horn, a relic of the true cross, and a locket containing the Virgin's hair, which he wore in death, as he had always worn in life.

This church is said to be the oldest in Germany. The choir, built in 1356, is more modern. Its painted windows are so exquisite in their form, that they affect you like a living beauty.

There is a fête to-day. The "*grandes reliques,*" which are shown once in seven years, are exhibiting, and the town is thronged with the peasantry. They were literally packed on the little *place* before the Cathedral. A priest was in a very high gallery with attendants, displaying the relics. This church is rich in these apocryphal treasures. The priest held up one thing after another, the Virgin's chemise, the swaddling-clothes, &c., against a black surface, and at each holy thing down sunk the mass upon their knees. There were exceptions to this devout action ; travellers who, like us, were staring, and talking, and making discord with the deep responses ; and there were a few persons pushing their way through the crowd, hawking little books in German and French describing the relics ; and selling beads that had been blessed by the priest. If not holy, the relics have an historical interest that makes them well worth seeing. They were presented to Charlemagne by a patriarch of Jerusalem, and by a Persian king [*].

The baths of Aix were enjoyed by the Romans. We went to one in the centre of the town, where a brazen lion spouts out the mineral water, and where there is a very handsome building with a colonnade and refreshment rooms. We would have gladly lingered here for a few days instead of these very few hours ; but, like all our country people, we seem always urged by some demon on—on—on.

Cologne.—Still, my dear C., the same story to tell you of yesterday's journey. The peasants have just begun their mowing and harvesting, and the hay and corn are all as thick as the choicest bits in our choice meadows. There were immense plantations of potatoes, oats, peas, and beans ; no fences, hedges, or barrier of any sort—one vast sea of agricultural wealth.

We are now, as Mr. Murray tells us, " in the largest and wealthiest city on the Rhine [†]," and have more than enough to do if we see the half set forth on the eight well-filled pages of his best of all guide-books. We leave here at four P. M. ; so you see how slight a view we can have even of the outside of things. Our habit of breakfasting at nine abridges our active time, but it gives me a quiet morning hour for my journal. Do you know—I did not—that Cologne received its name from Agrippina, Nero's mother ;—surely the most wretched of women ! She was born here, and sent hither a Roman colony, calling the place *Colonia Agrippina.* A happy accident I should think it, if I were a Colognese, that blotted out her infamous name from my birthplace.

We passed the day most diligently ; and as it is not in human nature not to value that which costs us labour, you must feel very grateful to me if I spare you the description of church after church, relics, and pictures. Such relics, too, as the real bones of St. Ursula and her thirteen thousand virgins ! the bones, *real* too, of the Magi,—the three kings of Cologne (whose vile effigies are blazoned on half the sign-boards on the Continent), and such pictures as Rubens' Crucifixion of St. Peter, which he deemed his best, because his last, probably. The *real* thing that would please you better than all the relics in Belgium, is the establishment of Eau de Cologne, of the actual Jean Maria Farina, whose name and fame have penetrated as far as Napoleon's. No wonder that this dirtiest of all towns should have elicited the perfumer's faculties. When some one said " The Rhine washes Cologne," it was pithily asked,— " What washes the Rhine !"

Another sight here, my dear C., would in earnest have pleased you ; the only one of the kind I have seen on the Continent : troops of little boys and girls with their books and slates. A woman of

distinction, who was born here, tells us that the feudal feeling of clanship is in high preservation. " I never come to Cologne," she says, " without being assailed by some one of the *basse classe*, who obliges me to listen to all the details of a family grievance, as if it were the affair of my own household." This sentiment of feudal dependence will probably melt away before the aforesaid books and slates. So the good goes with the bad. It is a pity we have not a moral flail ; but, as of old, the tares and the wheat are too intricately intermingled for human art to separate them. I promised to spare you the churches of Cologne, but I cannot pass by the cathedral. It would be as bad as the proverbial leaving out Hamlet from the enacting of his own tragedy. The Cologne cathedral is not, and probably never will be, finished. It impressed me anew with a conviction of the immortality of the human mind. What an infinite distance between its conceptions and the matter on which it works ! A work of art rises in vision to the divinely-inspired artist ; what years, what ages are consumed in expressing in the slow stone this conception ! and the stone is transformable, perishable. Can the mind be so !

The name of the architect of the Cathedral of Cologne is unknown. No matter ; here are his thoughts written in stone.

You cannot see the Gothic architecture of Europe without being often reminded of Victor Hugo's idea that architecture was, till superseded by printing, " the great book " wherein man wrote his thoughts in " marble letters and granite pages ;" and, being once possessed with this notion, you cannot look at the beautiful arches and columns, at such stupendous flying buttresses as these of the Cologne Cathedral, and its " forest of purfled pinnacles," without feeling as if you were reading a Milton or a Dante. There are innumerable expressions that you cannot comprehend, but, as your eye ranges over them, you read the rapturous praises of a David, and prophecy and lamentation, and, even in these sacred edifices, the keen satires and unbridled humour of the profane poets. Victor Hugo says that, at one period, whoever was born a poet became an architect ; that all other arts were subservient to architecture, all other artists the servants of the architect, " the great master workman [‡]."

I do not know that the ideas which he has so well elaborated originated in his own mind, nor can I tell whether this wondrous art would have suggested the idea to my mind without his previous aid. We see by the bright illumination of another's mind what the feeble light of our own would never reveal ; but remember we do as certainly see.

The Apostles' Church here is exquisitely beautiful. Mr. Hope said it reminded him of some of the oldest Greek churches in Asia Minor ; and that, when looking at the east end, he almost thought himself at Constantinople ; and, though you may think me bitten by Victor Hugo's theory, I will tell you that its romantic and oriental beauty brought to my mind " The Talisman," in Scott's Tales of the Crusaders.

---

[*] " Formerly 150,000 pilgrims resorted to this fête, and so late as 1832 there were 43,000."

[†] Cologne has 65,000 inhabitants.

[‡] "L'architecte, le poète, le maître totalisait en sa personne la sculpture qui lui ciselait ses façades, la peinture qui lui enluminait ses vitraux, la musique qui mettait sa cloche en branle et soufflait dans ses orgues."—*Victor Hugo.*

My dear C.,

Bonn.—We embarked, for the first time, yesterday, on the Rhine, the "father and king of rivers," as the German poets with fond reverence call it. "The majestic Rhine" it has not yet appeared to us, having but just come opposite to the Siebengebirge, a cluster of mountains where the scenery first takes its romantic character. We were four hours, in a good steamer, getting to Bonn, a distance of about twenty miles. This slow ascent of the river is owing to the force of the current. We were much struck with the social, simple, and kindly manners of our German companions in the steamer. Several well-bred persons addressed us, and asked as many questions as a Yankee would have asked in the same time. Some of them made us smile, such as whether the language in America was not very like that spoken in England! and if New York had more than thirty thousand inhabitants! Before we separated, the girls were on familiar terms with some pretty young ladies going to boarding-school, and half-a-dozen people, at least, had ascertained whence we came and whither we were going. M. was quite charmed with this unreserve. "Like to like," you know!

There was a lady on board who rivetted our attention. Without being handsome, she had the "*air noble,*" that is, perhaps, the best substitute for beauty. Her face was intellectual, and her eyes such as I have never seen except in the head of a certain harpy eagle in the zoological gardens. Lest you should get a false impression from this comparison, I must tell you that these harpy eyes haunted me for days after I saw them reviving, with their human expression and wonderful power, my childish superstition about the transmigration of souls.

"That woman is very ill-bred," said M., "to peer at us so steadily through her eyeglass." "We look at her just as steadily, only without eyeglasses," said L.; and as none think themselves ill-bred, we came to the silent conclusion that the stranger might not be so. There was something in her air, and in a peculiarity, as well as elegance of dress, that indicated she felt well assured of her position.

Bonn.—We brought letters to the celebrated Schlegel, who resides here, and to a certain Madame M. Schlegel sent us a note, saying he was kept in by indisposition, but would be most happy to receive us. Soon after breakfast Madame M. was announced, and proved to be the harpy-eyed lady of the steamer. Her manner struck me as cold, and I felt all the horror of thrusting myself on involuntary hospitality. "She is doing a detestable duty," thought I, "in honouring Mrs. ——'s letter of credit in behalf of strangers from a far country, and of a language that she does not speak." By degrees her manner changed from forced courtesy to voluntary kindness. She marked out occupation for all our time at Bonn, lavished invitations on all our party, and insisted on my going home with her to see what was to be seen at her house, which she said, in a way to excite no expectation, "was better than staying at the inn." I went, and found that she had a superb establishment in the best quarter of the town. We met a pretty young woman on the stairs, whom she introduced to me as her daughter. She had her long sleeves tucked up over her elbow, and a cotton apron on, and reminded me of a thrifty New-England *lady* preparing to make her "Thanksgiving pies." Mademoiselle M. soon after brought in a small waiter, with rich hot chocolate and cakes. I asked Madame M. if the accounts we had received of the domestic education of women in Germany of the condition of her daughter were true. She said yes; they were taught everything that appertained to house affairs. We know they do not find this domestic education incompatible with high refinement and cultivation. Knowledge of house-affairs is a necessity for our young country-women: perhaps some of them would think it less an evil if they could see Mademoiselle M. in her luxurious home expressing, as did Eve, Penelope, and other classic dames, by the dainty work of her own hands, that she was "on hospitable thoughts intent."

When I entered Bonn through an ineffably dirty street, I little dreamed it could contain a house with the lovely view there is from Madame M.'s window, of gardens and cornfields; and much less did I anticipate sitting with that fearful lady of the steamer over cases of antique gems—some as old as remote epochs of Grecian art—while she expounded them to me; so at the mercy of accident are the judgments of tourists. Madame M.'s house is filled with productions of the arts, pictures, busts, &c., which I was obliged to leave all too soon to go with my party to pay our respects to Schlegel; and I went, half wishing, as L. did on a similar occasion, that there were no celebrated people that one must see.

Schlegel is past seventy, with an eye still brilliant, and a fresh colour in his cheek. He attracted our attention to his very beautiful bust of Carrara marble, and repeatedly adverted to the decay of the original since the bust was made, with a sensibility which proved that the pleasures and regrets that accompany the possession of beauty are not limited to women. He makes the most of his relics by wearing a particularly becoming black velvet cap, round which his wavy white locks lie as soft as rays of light. He was courteous and agreeable for the half-hour we passed with him; but I brought away no new impression but that I have given you, that he is a handsome man for threescore and ten.

At three, Madame M. came, according to appointment, to show us the Bonn lions and surroundings. We drove first to the University, which is the old electoral palace. Bonn was comprehended within the Electorate of Cologne. The façade of this palace of the lord elector, which has now become a flourishing seat of learning, is nearly a quarter of a mile in extent. The palaces and cottages of Europe indicate its history.

The University, which has now between eight and nine hundred students, was established by the King of Prussia, and is said to owe its reputation to its distinguished professors; Niebuhr was here, and Schlegel is. We were shown a library of one hundred thousand volumes, a museum of natural history, and a very interesting museum of Roman remains found on the banks of the Rhine, altars, vases, weapons, &c. We were conducted through the botanical garden by Monsieur l'Inspecteur, a celebrated botanist, and one of a large family of brothers devoted to the science. "Une aristocratie botaniste," said Madame M. He showed us a rich collection of American plants, and I stood amid the mosses and ferns, my old friends of the iceglen, feeling very much as if I ought to speak to them, as they did to me !

We drove by a road that reminded me of the drives through the Connecticut River meadows, to Godesberg. There was one pretty object, the like of which we shall never see in our Puritan land— a high and beautifully-carved stone cross. It marked the spot where two cavaliers—brothers— fought for their lady-love, and the unhappy survivor erected this cross, hoping the passers-by would stop to say a prayer for the soul of his brother.

There is a cluster of hotels at Godesberg, and some villas belonging to the Cologne noblesse ; it is a favourite summer retreat. We went to see the ruins of the Castle of Godesberg. They crown an isolated mount, which appears, in the midst of the surrounding level, as if it were artificial ; but it is one of those natural elevations which, being castellated and strongly fortified, make up so much of the romantic story of the middle ages, and, with their ruins, so much of the romantic embellishment of the present day. This Castle of Godesberg has its love story, and a true and tragic one. It was here that the Elector of Cologne who married Agnes of Mansfeldt held out against his Catholic enemies. .His marriage made his conversion to Protestantism somewhat questionable ; and the separation and misery in which the unhappy pair died were probably interpreted into a judgment on these two apostate servants of the Church. It has been one of the purest of summer afternoons, and we had a delicious stroll up to the ruins ; a world of beauty there is within the small compass of that mount. Fancy a hill rising from the bosom of meadows as our Laurel Hill does, but twice as high and twice as steep, with a path winding round it, every foot of cultivable earth covered with grape vines, having shrines chiselled in the rocks, and crucifixes and Madonnas for the devout. Half-way up is a little Gothic church and a cemetery, where the monuments and graves—yes, old graves—were decked with fresh garlands, the lilies and roses that have blown out in this day's sun. Is not this a touching expression of faith and love—faith in God, and enduring love for the departed !

What a picture was the country beneath us ; and what a pretty framework for the picture, the stone arches of the old castle ! The earth was washed clean by the morning showers. Beneath us was an illimitable reach of level land covered with crops. The harvesting and hay-making just begun, but not a blade yet taken off the piled lap of mother earth. At our feet were the peasants' dwellings, little brown cottages, almost hidden in fruit-trees ; beyond, the gay villas of the noblesse ; and still farther, the lively-looking town of Bonn, with its five-towered Cathedral. Still farther, on one side Cologne, on the other the Seven Mountains, with the ruins of Drachenfels ; fine wide roads—those unquestionable marks of an old civilisation—traversing the country in every direction, and as far as your eye could reach, that king of roads, the Rhine.

Madame M. so fully enjoyed the delight she was bestowing, that she proposed to prolong it by an excursion to-morrow, which shall be still richer in romance. She will come at ten with two carriages. We shall take our *déjeûner à la fourchette* here, and then drive to Roland's Castle, then pass to the monastery of Nonnenwerth, where, her son officiating as chaplain, she proposes to make a nun of Miss K., all to end in a dinner, for (I must tell you the disenchanting fact) the monastery is converted into an inn. This is too pleasant a project to be rejected, and if—and if—and if—why we are to go.

While enjoying to-day and talking of to-morrow, we had returned to the inn. Tea was preparing at the order of our charming hostess. Dispersed about the house and piazza were coteries of German ladies, who had come out for the afternoon, and were knitting and gossiping most serenely.

Our repast was very like a home tea for a hungry party of pleasure, with the agreeable addition to our cold roast fowl and Westphalian ham and strawberries, of wine, melons, and Swiss cheese.

MY DEAR C.—To-day has played a common trick with yesterday's project—dispersed it in empty air. Compelled to proceed on our journey, we did not lose the highest pleasure we had counted on—Madame M.'s society. She stayed with us to the last moment, and then when saying farewell, a kind impulse seized her ; she sent her footman back for her cloak, and came with us as far as Andernach, where she has one of her many villas. This was just what L. M. would have done on a similar occasion ; but how many of these incidental opportunities of giving pleasure, these chance-boons in the not-too-happy way of life, are foregone and—irretrievable !

At Bonn the romantic beauty of the Rhine begins. I have often heard our Hudson compared to the Rhine ; they are both rivers, and both have beautiful scenery ; but I see no other resemblance except so far as the Highlands extend, and there only in some of the natural features. Both rivers have a very winding course, and precipitous and rocky shores. But remember, these are shores that bear the vine, and so winding for *forty* miles that you might fancy yourself passing through a series of small lakes. I have seen no spot on the Rhine more beautiful by nature than the Hudson from West Point ; but here is

" A blending of all beauties, streams, and dells,
  Fruits, foliage, crag, wood, corn-field, mountain, vine,
  And chiefless castles breathing stern farewells,
From grey but leafy walls, where ruin greenly dwells."

Read Byron's whole description, in his third canto of Childe Harold, of this " abounding and exulting river," and you will get more of the sensation it is fitted to produce than most persons do from actually seeing it. Its architecture is one of its characteristic beauties ; not only its ruined castles—and you have sometimes at one view three or four of these stern monuments on their craggy eminences—but its pretty brown villages, its remains of Roman towers, its walls and bridges, and its military fortifications and monuments :

" A thousand battles have assail'd its banks,"

D

and have sown them richly with their history. And every castle has its domestic legend of faithful or unfaithful love, of broken hopes or baffled treachery. Story, ballad, and tradition have breathed a soul into every tumbling tower and crumbling wall.

We passed the night at Coblentz. The Romans called it Confluentes, " modernised into Coblentz, from its situation at the confluence of the Moselle and the Rhine. It is the capital of the Rhenish provinces of Prussia, and its population, together with that of Ehrenbreitstein, including the garrison, is about 22,000." Thank our guide Murray for the above well-condensed paragraph containing more information than half-a-dozen pages of my weaving.

The younger members of our party, *including myself*, were enterprising enough to quit our luxurious and most comfortable apartments at the Bellevue at ·five o'clock, to go to the fortress of Ehrenbreitstein ("Honour's broad stone," is it not a noble name !).

ʹ We passed the Rhine on a bridge of boats, and followed a veteran Austrian soldier, who was our valet-de-place, to the fortified summit. It has been from the time of the Romans a celebrated military post. Byron saw and described it after it had been battered and dismantled by the French, and not as it now is, capable of resisting, on the word of Wellington, " all but golden bullets." It only yielded to famine when the French besieged it. The Prussians have made it stronger than ever, at an expense of five millions of dollars ! So the men of toil pay for the engines that keep them mere men of toil.

The works struck me as appallingly strong, but, as I could not comprehend their details, after our guide had told me there were magazines capable of containing a ten years' supply of food for 8000 men, that there were cisterns that would hold a ·three years' supply of water, and, when that was exhausted, the Rhine itself could be drawn on by a well which is pierced through the solid rock ; when I had got all this *available* information, I turned to what much better suited me, the lovely view. Oh, for my magic mirror, to show you how lovely appeared, in this morning light, the scene below us ; the blue Moselle coming down through its vine-covered hills, towns, ruins, villas, cottages, and the Rhine itself, " the charm of this enchanted ground !" I think I like it the better that it is frozen three months in the year. This seems to make it a blood relation of our rivers. You cannot imagine how much the peasant girls in their pretty costumes embellish these surroundings. They do not wear bonnets, but, in their stead, an endless variety of headgear. Some wear a little muslin cap or one of gay-coloured embroidery, and others a sort of silver case that just incloses the long hair, which is·always braided and neatly arranged.

Did you know that the prince of diplomatists and arch-enemy of liberty, Metternich, was born at Coblentz ! We have just been to see a fountain, on which is an inscription commemorative of the French invasion of Russia. It was put there by the French prefect of the department, and a few months after, when the Russians passed through here in pursuit of the scattered army of Napoleon, their commander annexed the following happy sarcasm : " Vu et approuvé par nous, commandant Russe," &c. (Seen and approved by us, the Russian commander.)

Wiesbaden, Poste restante,
July 26.

K. and I came here this morning to purvey for the party, and get lodgings for a month or two. The best hotels were full. We were shown disagreeable rooms at the *Poste*, and though the man assured us he could not keep them for us ten minutes, as all the world was rushing to Wiesbaden, we took our chance, and hazed about the streets, finding nothing that we liked. At last I made inquiry in a book-shop, and a good-natured little woman entering into our wants, ran across the street with us, and in five minutes we had made a bargain with a man whose honest German face is as good security as bond and mortgage. We have a very nice parlour and three comfortable rooms for thirty-five florins a week—about fourteen dollars. We pay a franc each for breakfast, for tea the same, and we have delicious bread, good butter, and fresh eggs; for our dinners, we go, according to the custom here, to the table d'hôte of an hotel. We could not get as good accommodations as these in a country town ·at home for the same money, nor for double the sum at a watering place.

My dear C.,
Sunday evening.—We have been here now more than a week, and, with true travellers' conceit, I am sitting down to give you an account of the place and its doings. Wiesbaden (*Meadow-baths*) is the capital of the duchy of Nassau, about two miles from the Rhine. It is a very old German town, and was resorted to by the Romans. It may be called the ducal residence, as the duke, in natural deference to his fair young wife's preference, now resides here a good portion of the time, and is building a large palace for the duchess.

Wiesbaden has more visitors than any of the numerous German bathing-places. The number amounts to from twelve to fifteen thousand annually ; this concourse is occasioned by the unrivalled reputation of its mineral water. At six this morning we went to the Kochbrunnen (boiling spring). There is a small building erected over it, and a square curb around it, within which you see it boiling vehemently. Its temperature is 150° Fahrenheit. Its taste is often compared to chicken-broth. If chicken-broth, it must have been made after the fashion of Dr. T.'s prescription to his hypochondriac patient, who fancied water-gruel too strong for her digestion—" Eight gallons of water, madam, and the shadow of a starved crow !"

From six to eight the water-drinkers did their duty, drinking faithfully. Some read or lounged in a sunny corridor where a band of musicians were stationed playing gay tunes; but the approved fashion is to saunter while you sip. We were mere lookers-on, and it was ludicrous to see these happy-looking Germans, whom it would seem Heaven had exempted from every evil flesh is heir to, save obesity, come down to the spring with their pretty Bohemian glasses of all colours and shapes, walk back again up the long acacia walks, sipping in good faith, and giving the water credit, no doubt, for doing what, perhaps, might be done without it by their plentiful draughts of the sweet early morning air.

After breakfast I went to the window, and here are my notes of what I saw. " How freshly the windows are set out with flowers! Our opposite neighbour has new-garnished her little shop-window with fresh patterns of calico, and scarfs, fichus, and ribands. Two girls are standing at the next door-step, knitting and gossiping; and at the next window sits the self-same pretty young woman that I saw knitting alone there all last Sunday. It is a happy art that distils content-ment out of a passive condition and dull employ-ment. The street is thronging with fair blooming peasant-girls come into town to pass their Sunday holiday. How very neat they look with their white linen caps and gay ribands, and full, dark-blue petticoats, so full that they hang from top to bottom like a fluted ruffle! The bodice is of the same material, and sets off in pretty contrast the plaited, snow-white shift-sleeve. There are the duke's soldiers mingling among them; their gal-lants, I suppose. Their deportment is cheerful and decorous.

" Here is a group of healthy-looking little girls in holiday suit, their long, thick hair well combed, braided, and prettily coiled, and a little worked worsted sack hanging over one shoulder. The visiters of Wiesbaden—German, Russian, English —are passing to and fro; some taking their Sun-day drive, some on foot. Beneath my window, in a small, triangular garden, is a touching chap-ter in human life; the whole book, indeed, from the beginning almost to the end. There is a table under the trees in the universal German fashion, and wine and Seltzer-water on it; and there, in his arm-chair, sits an old blind man, with his children, and grandchildren, and the blossoms of yet another generation around him. While I write it, the young people are touch-ing their glasses to his, and a little thing has clambered up behind him and is holding a rose to his nose."

IF you recollect that we are now in Protestant Germany, you will be astonished at the laxity of the Sabbath. The German reformers never, I believe, undertook to reform the Continental Sab-bath. They probably understood too well the in-flexible nature of national customs, and how much more difficult it is to remodel them than to recast faith. We are accustomed to talk of " the hor-rors of a Continental Sabbath," and are naturally shocked with an aspect of things so different from our own. But, when I remember the dozing con-gregations I have seen, the domestics stretched half the heavy day in bed, the young people sit-ting by the half-closed blind, stealing longing looks out of the window, while the Bible was lying idle on their laps; and the merry shouts of the children at the going down of the sun, as if an enemy had disappeared,—it does not seem to me that we can say to the poor, ignorant, toil-worn peasant of Europe, " I am holier than thou!"

I left my journal to go to church. At all these Continental resorts there is service in English, and here the duke permits it to be held in his own church. The service was performed by a clergy-man of the Church of England.

At four o'clock we set off for our afternoon walk. The gay shops in the colonnade were all open, but there were few buyers, where buyers most do congregate, at the stalls of the all-coloured, beautiful Bohemian glass, and of the stag-horn *jimcracks* so curiously carved by the peasants; even Monsieur Jügel's bookshop was deserted. The English are for the most part the buyers, and they do not buy on Sunday. We went into the Kur-Saal Garden, which at this hour is alive with people, hundreds sitting at their little tables on the gravelled area between the hall and a pretty artificial lake, smoking, sipping coffee, wine, and Seltzer water, and eating ices. A band of capital musicians were playing. We had some discussion whether we should go into the *Kur-Saal*, and finally, determining to see as much as we womankind can of what characterises the place, we entered. The *Kur-Saal* (cure-hall) belongs to the duke, and its spacious apartments are devoted to banqueting, dancing, and gambling. The grand saloon is a spacious apartment with rows of marble pillars, and behind them niches with statues, alternating with mirrors. It was an odd scene for us of Puritan blood and breed-ing to witness. A circular gambling-table in the midst of the apartment was surrounded with peo-ple five or six deep, some players but more spec-tators. The game was, I believe, roulette. It was most curious to see with what a cool, imper-turbable manner these Germans laid down their gold, and won or lost, as the case might be, on the instant. There were not only old and prac-tised gamblers, but young men, and people appa-rently of all conditions, and among them women, *ladies.* These are a small minority, seldom, as I am told, more than half-a-dozen among a hundred men. I watched their faces; they looked intent and eager; but I did not, with their change of fortune, detect any change of colour or expression. We walked through the smaller rooms, and found in all gambling-tables and players in plenty, and that where there were fewest spectators the pas-sions of the players were more unveiled.

This buying and selling, and vicious amusement, is indeed a profaning of the day on which God has ordained his earth to be a temple of sacred rest from labour, and sordid care, and competitions. When and where will it be so used as to do the work it might achieve—regenerate the world!

We soon emerged into the garden again, and were glad to see a great many more people out-side than in. This garden, or rather ornamented ground, for the greater part of it is merely in grass and trees, extends up the narrowing valley for two miles to the ruins of the old castle of Son-nenberg. We passed the little lake with its fringe of bright flowers, its social squads of ducks and its lordly swans, and many a patch of bright flowers and shrubberies, and rustic benches with tête-à-tête pairs or family groups, and kept along a path by a little brook that seems good-naturedly to run just where it looks prettiest and is most wanted, till we mounted the eminence where the feudal castle guarded the pass between two far-reaching valleys, and where the old keep, chapel, and masses and fragments of wall still standing, ex-tend over a space half as large as our village covers. Fragments of the wall form one side of a range of cottages, serving a better purpose than when they were the bulwark of a half-savage warrior.

Sonnenberg is kept in beautiful order by the duke's command and money. There are plantations of furze about the old walls, narrow labyrinthine walks inclosed with shrubbery and embowered with clematis, and seats wherever rests are wanted. I unluckily disturbed a tête-à-tête to-day, which, if there be truth in "love's speechless messages," will make a deep mark in the memory of two happy-looking young people.

There is a compact village nestled close under the ruins of the castle. Here it was that the feudal dependants of the lord lived, and here the rural population is still penned. These villages are picturesque objects in the landscape, but on a close inspection, they are squalid, dirty, most comfortless places, where the labouring poor are huddled together without that good gift—sweet air, and plenty of it, which seems as much their right as the birds'.

When I see the young ones here playing round a heap of manure that is stacked up before their door, I think how favoured are the children of the poorest poor of our New-England villages; but softly—the hard-pressed German peasant, in his pent-up village, has a look of contentment and cheerfulness that our people have not. If his necessities are greater, his desires are fewer. God is the father of all; and these are his compensations.

We got home to Burg-strasse just as the last hues of twilight were fading from the clouds; and just as K. was taking off her hat, she remembered that after coming down from the castle, she turned aside to gather some flowers, and meanwhile hung her bag, containing sundry articles belonging to herself, and *my* purse, on the railing of a bridge. What was to be done? We hoped that in the dusky twilight it might have escaped observation. K. proposed sending for a donkey and going herself in search of it. I consented, being most virtuously inclined (as those to whom it costs nothing are apt to be) to impress on Miss K. a salutary lesson. The donkey came, and off she set, attended by François, and followed by a deformed donkey-driver with the poking-stick, and everlasting *A-R-R-H*, much to the diversion of the denizens of Burg-strasse, who were all on their door-steps looking on. She was hardly out of my sight before I repented sending her off with these foreign people into the now obscure and deserted walk. I thought there was an evil omen in the donkey-boy's hump-back: and, in short, I lost all feeling for "my ducats" in apprehension for "my daughter;" and when she returned in safety without the bag, I cared not for Herr Leisring's assurance "that it would yet be found—that it was rare anything was lost at Wiesbaden."

THIS morning "my ducats" rose again to their full value in my esteem; and just as I was pondering on all I might have done with them, Leisring's broad, charming face appeared at the door with the announcement, "On l'a trouvée, mademoiselle," (It is found!) and he reiterated, with a just burgher pride, "Rarely is anything lost at

Wiesbaden." The bag, he says, was found by a "writer," and left with the police; and Leisring, the writer, and the police all decline compensation or reward. If this abstemiousness had occurred in our country, we might, perhaps, have thought it peculiar to it.

I WENT last evening with the girls to a ball given every week to such as choose to attend it; I went notwithstanding Mr. ——'s assurance (with a horror not quite fitting an American) that we should meet "Tom, Dick, and Harry there." One of the girls replied that "Tom, Dick, and Harry were such very well-behaved people here, that there was no objection to meeting them;" and so, fortified by the approbation of our English friends Miss —— and Miss ——, who are sufficiently fastidious, we went. The company assembled in the grand saloon of the Kur-Saal at the indefinite hour at which our evening lectures are appointed, "early candle-lighting," and it was rather miscellaneous, some in full, some in half dress. The girls had been told it was customary to dance, when asked, without waiting for the formality of an introduction, and they were only too happy to obtain their favourite exercise by a courteous conformity to the customs of the country. They had partners, and very nice ones, in plenty. I was struck with the solemn justice of one youth, who, dispensing his favour with an equal hand, engaged the three at the same time, one for a quadrille, one for a gallopade, and one for a waltz. We had no acquaintance in the room, no onerous dignity to maintain; the girls had respectful partners, plenty of dancing, and no fagging, as we were at home and in bed by eleven.

IT seems to me that Sir F. Head, in his humorous account of the German dinner, has done some injustice to the German *cuisine*. After you have learned to tread its mazes to the last act of its intricate plot, you may, passing by its various greasy messes, find the substantial solace of roast fowls, hare, and delicious venison, that have been pushed back in the course of precedence by the puddings and sweet sauces. These puddings and sauces are lighter and more wholesome than I have seen elsewhere. Indeed, the drama, after the prologue of the soup, opens with a tempting boiled beef, at which I am sure a "Grosvenor-street cat," if not as pampered as my lord's butler, would *not*, in spite of Sir Francis' assertion, turn up his whisker.

We dine at the Quatre Saisons, the hotel nearest to us, and, as we are told, the best table-d'hôte in the place. There is a one-o'clock, and, in deference to the English, a five-o'clock dinner. The universal German dinner-hour is one. The price at one is a florin—about forty-two cents; at five, a Prussian dollar—about seventy-five cents. This is without wine. We dine usually at one; but we have been at the five-o'clock table, and we see no other difference than the more aristocratic price of that aristocratic hour. Besides the *trifling* advantage of dining at one in reference to health, it leaves the best hours of the day free for out-of-door pleasures. The order and accompaniments of our dinner are agreeable; the tables are set on three sides of a spacious *salon-à-manger*, with a smaller table in the centre of the room, where the landlord (who carves artistically) carves the dinner. His eyes are everywhere. Not a guest escapes his observation, not a waiter omits his duty.

When the clock is close upon the stroke of one, people may be seen from every direction bending their steps towards the hotel. You leave your hats and bonnets in an ante-room. The *Ober-kellner* (head waiter) receives you at the door, and conducts you to your seats. The table is always covered with clean (not very fine) German table-linen, and, of course, supplied with napkins. Pots with choice odorous plants in flower are set at short intervals the whole length of the table; a good band of music is playing in the orchestra. The dinner-service is a coarse white porcelain. As soon as you are seated, little girls come round with baskets of bouquets, which you are offered without solicitation. You may have one, if you will, for a halfpenny, and a sweet smile from the little flower-girl thrown into the bargain. Then come young women with a printed sheet containing a register of the arrivals within the last three days, for which you pay a penny. I observe the new-comers always buy one, liking perhaps, for once in their lives, to see their names in print. The *carte à vin* is then presented, and, if you please, you may select an excellent *Rhine* wine for twenty-five cents a bottle, or you may pay the prices we pay at home for Burgundy and Champagne*. These preliminaries over, the dinner begins, and occupies between one and two hours, never less than an hour and a half. The meats are placed on the table, then taken off, carved, and offered to each guest. You see none of those eager looks or hasty movements that betray the anxieties of our people lest a favourite dish should escape. A German eats as long and as leisurely as he pleases at one thing, sure that all will be offered to him in turn; and they are the most indefatigable of eaters; not a meat, not a vegetable comes on table which they do not partake. A single plate of the cabbage saturated with grease that I have seen a German lady eat would, as our little S. said when she squeezed the chicken to death, have "deaded" one of our dyspeptics " *very* dead ;" and this plate of cabbage is one of thirty varieties. The quiet and order of the table are admirable. The servants are never in a hurry, and never blunder. You know what angry, pathetic, and bewildering calls of " Waiter !" " Waiter !" we hear at our tables. I have never heard the call of " Kellner !" from a German.

I leave the table each day expecting half the people will die of apoplexy before to-morrow, but to-morrow they all come forth with placid faces and fresh appetites ! Is this the result of their leisurely eating ! or their serene, social, and enjoying tempers ! or their lives, exempt from the keen competitions and eager pursuits of ours ! or their living out of doors ! or all of these together ! I leave you to solve a problem that puzzles me.

A German, of whatever condition, bows to his neighbours when he sits down and when he rises from table, and addresses some passing civility to them. We are sometimes amused at the questions that are asked us, such as, " Whether English is

* Not the hotel prices, but about one dollar and fifty cents.

spoken in America !" A gentleman asked me " Whether we came from New York or New Orleans !" as if they were our only cities ; and another said, in good faith, " Of course there is no society except in New York !" Oh, genii locorum of our little inland villages, forgive them !

We are too often reminded how far our country is from this. Yesterday a Russian gentleman said to K., " Qui est le souverain de votre pays, mademoiselle !" " Monsieur Van Buren est le Président des Etats Unis." " Ah, oui. Mais j'ai entendu le nom de Jackson. Il est du bas-peuple, n'est-ce pas !"

" Comment s'appellent les chefs des petits arrondissemens † ‡ !" It might be salutary to such of our people as are over anxious about what figure they make in foreign eyes, to know they make none.

I HAVE been attracted to the window every morning since I have been here by the troops of children passing to the public school, their hands full of books and slates ; the girls dressed in cheaper materials, but much like those of our village-schools, except that their rich German hair is uncovered, and they all, the poorest among them, wear good stockings—so much for the universality of German knitting. Education is compulsory here as in Prussia ; the parent who cannot produce a good reason for the absence of the child pays a fine. I went into the girls' school nearest to us this morning. They looked as intelligent, as early developed, and as bright as our own children.

They went successfully through their exercises in reading, geography, and arithmetic. At an interval in these lessons, the master, who was a grave personage some sixty years old, took from a case a violin and gave them a music lesson, which, if one might judge from the apparent refreshment of their young spirits, was an aliment well suited to them. What is to be the result of this education system in Germany ! Will people, thus taught, be contented to work for potatoes and black bread !

We have been in search of an infant-school, which we were told we should find near the *Poste*. To the *Poste* I could go blindfold ; for how many times have I been there with a fluttering heart and come away with it too heavy, as it seemed to me, ever to flutter again !

We passed the *Poste* and lost our clew, so I resorted to my usual resource, a bookseller, who directed me up a steep, narrow street, and told me to ask for the " *Klein Kinder Schule.*" I went on, confident in my " open sesame ;" but nothing could be more ludicrous than my stupefaction when the good people to whom I uttered my given words, not doubting that one who could speak so glibly could also understand, poured out a volume of German upon me ; up—up we went, half the people in the street, with humane interest, looking after us, till we came to the window of an apartment that opened on to a court where the little urchins were seated. The appearance of visitors

† " Who is the sovereign of your country, miss ?" " Mr. Van Buren is the President of the United States." " Ah, yes. But I have heard the name of Jackson. He sprang from the lower class, did he not ?" " Pray what is the title of the chiefs of the lesser departments ?"

was a signal for the cessation of their studies. There was a general rising and rush to their plays ; but first the little things, from two years old to six, came unbidden, with smiling faces, to shake our hands. It puzzles me as much to know how this quality of social freedom gets into the German nature, as how the African's skin became black ! If a stranger were to go, in like manner, among our school children, and they were forced forward by a rule, they would advance with downcast eyes and murky looks, as if the very demon of bashfulness stiffened their limbs. The infantschool is supported by charitable contributions, and conducted much like our infant-schools. The children stay all day, and the parent pays a kreutzer for the dinner of each—less than a penny. We followed them to their plays, and as I looked at them trundling their little barrows and building pyramids of gravel, and the while devouring black bread, I longed to transport them to those unopened storehouses of abundance which the Father of all has reserved in our untrodden " West" for the starved labourers of Europe.

But they were a merry little company, and, if no other, they have here a harvest of contentment and smiles.

Our letters came to-day ! The delay was owing to the change in our plans. While we were every day going to the *Poste* for them, they were lying quietly at Wildbad. This interruption of communication with those who are bound up in the bundle of life with us is one of the severest trials of a traveller. It was past eleven when we had finished reading them, and then I went to bed with mine under my pillow. I could as easily have gone to sleep if the hearts of those who wrote them had been throbbing there ! " Blessings on him who invented sleep !" says Sancho. " Blessings on him," say I, " who invented that art that makes sleep sweet and awaking happy !"

Our good landlord, Leisring, is, in all exigences, our " point d'appui." He has the broad, truthtelling German face, and a bonhomie quite his own. He is, in an humbler position, a Sir Roger de Coverly ; and his family and numerous dependants seem to have as kind a master as was the good knight. He is a master carpenter, and is just now employed in finishing off the new palace which the Duke of Nassau is building for his duchess, and has twelve subordinates in his service—nine journeymen and three apprentices. To the nine journeymen, he tells me, he has paid, in the last four months, one thousand florins, about eleven dollars a month each, besides feeding them. The apprentices he supports, and gives them a trifle in money. They eat in a back building attached to ours. I asked leave to-day, while they were at dinner, to look in upon them. They had clean linen on their table, and everything appeared comfortable. They are allowed three rolls of brown bread for breakfast, and coffee, beer, or schnapps (a mixture with some sort of spirit), whichever they prefer. They have soup, meat, and vegetables for dinner ; and soup, bread, butter, and cheese for supper. A florin and a half (sixty cents) pays for the meat for their dinner *. The best butter is twenty-four kreut-

zers (eighteen cents) a pound ; the rolls, a kreutzer each. Vegetables are excessively cheap.

There is a law in Germany compelling an apprentice, when the term of his apprenticeship is completed, to travel a year, to work in different towns, and enrich himself with the improvements in his art. In each town there is an inn for these travelling mechanics. After reporting himself to the police, he goes there and then finds employment. You meet these young men on the road with their knapsacks, and they often take off their caps and present them at your carriage-window, modestly asking a halfpence. At first we were quite indignant at seeing such decent-looking people begging. But our hasty misjudgments have been corrected by the information that these poor youths go forth penniless ; that it is not considered a degradation for them to solicit in this way ; and that they are, in fact, sustained by the wayside aid of their countrymen.

We have made another experiment of German society. The girls went with E. to a soirée at the Kur-Saal. This was a *soirée musicale*, that is, a ball beginning with a concert ; a higher entertainment, and more choice in its company than the one I have described to you. The only condition for admission was the payment of a little less than a dollar for the ticket of each person. They all came home charmed with the young duchess, with her very sweet, blond beauty, simple dress, and unassuming and affable manners. They were the more pleased as they contrasted her with another sprig, or, rather, sturdy branch of a royal house : a certain Russian princess, who, though assuredly of a very coarse material, fancies herself of a choicer clay than the people about her. This woman, whom we meet everywhere, in the garden, at the table d'hôte, and at the Kochbrunnen, is quite the noisiest and most vulgar person we encounter. Such a person would naturally be fastidious in her associates ; and her prime favourite, if we may judge from their constant juxtaposition, is a coloured man with woolly hair, some say from New Orleans, others that he is a West Indian. I do not speak of this in any disrespect to him, but as a proof that colour is no disqualification in European society.

Last night, while the fair young duchess was dancing at a brilliant soirée at her palace at Bieberich, a courier arrived with the news of the duke's death of apoplexy while drinking the waters of his bubbles of Kissingen. Rather a startling change from that sound of revelry to the knell of widowhood—from being the " cynosure of all eyes" to be the dowager stepdame of the reigning duke !

Our host tells us the duke was " un bon enfant" (a good fellow), and much beloved, and will be much regretted. No one can doubt that a sober, well-intentioned man of forty-five, who is to be succeeded by a boy of twenty, is a great loss to his people. Where power has, as here, no constitutional restrictions, the people are at the mercy of the personal character of the sovereign.

---

* The game is all taken in the duke's preserves, and is
of course, his property. Old venison is four kreutzers a pound ; young, from twelve to sixteen ; a hare without the skin, twenty-four kreutzers (eighteen cents.)

THE good people of Wiesbaden seem to take the death of their political father very coolly. I see no demonstrations of mourning except that the bells are rung an hour daily, and that the music has ceased at our dinners and in the garden, and that the public amusements are stopped : a proceeding not likely to endear the duke's memory to the innkeepers and their host of dependants, who are all in despair lest their guests should take their departure. The influx of the money-spending English is a great source of profit to the duchy of Nassau, so that nothing can be more impolitic than this prohibition, which extends to Schwalbach, Schlangenbad, &c.

WE have now been here more than a month, and I may venture to speak to you of what has been a constant subject of admiration to us all, the manners of the Germans. The English race, root and branch, are, what with their natural shyness, their conventional reserves, and their radical uncourteousness, cold and repelling. The politeness of the French is conventional. It seems in part the result of their sense of personal grace, and in part of a selfish calculation of making the most of what costs nothing ; and partly, no doubt, it is the spontaneous effect of a vivacious nature. There is a deep-seated humanity in the courtesy of the Germans. They always seem to be feeling a gentle pressure from the cord that interlaces them with their species. They do not wait, as Schiller says, till you " freely invite " to " friendlily stretch out a hand," but the hand is instinctively stretched out and the kind deed ready to follow it.

This suavity is not limited to any rank or condition. It extends all the way down from the prince to the poorest peasant. Some of our party driving out in a hackney-coach yesterday, met some German ladies in a coach with four horses, postilions, footmen in livery, and other marks of rank and wealth. What would Americans have done in a similar position ! Probably looked away and seemed unconscious. And English ladies would have done the same, or, as I have seen them in Hyde Park, have leaned back in their carriages, and stared with an air of mingled indifference and insolence through their eye-glasses, as if their inferiors in condition could bear to be stared at. The German ladies bowed most courteously to the humble strangers in the hackney-coach.

Yesterday, at the table d'hôte, I observed a perpendicular old gentleman, who looked as if he had been born before any profane dreams of levelling down the steeps of aristocracy had entered the mind of man, and whose servant, in rich livery, bow to the persons opposite to him as he took his seat, as stiff as himself, was in waiting behind him, bow to the persons opposite to him as he took his seat, and to those on his right hand and his left. Soon after our landlord came to speak to him, and familiarly and quite acceptably, as it appeared, laid his hand on the nobleman's shoulder while addressing him.

Soon after we came here, a gentleman with whom we passed a few hours in a Rhine steamer met us at the table-d'hôte. " Had I not," he said, " the pleasure of coming from Bonn to Cologne with you ! I see one of your party is absent.

She is, I hope, well," &c. To appreciate as they deserve these wayside courtesies, you should see the relentless English we come in contact with, who, like ghosts, *never* " speak till they are spoken to."

A few days since, as we were issuing from our lodgings, a very gentlemanly German stopped us, begging our pardons, and saying " English, I believe !" and then added, that as we appeared to be strangers in quest of lodgings, as he had just been, he would take the liberty to give us the addresses of two or three that had been recommended to him. This was truly a Samaritan—a *German* kindness. The hotel-keepers, that important class to travellers, often blend with the accurate performance of the duties of " mine host" the kindness of a friend. Their civility, freedom, and gentlemanliness remind me of my friend Cozzens and others, the best specimens of their fraternity at home. The landlord often sits at the table with his guests, and, with his own country people, converses on terms of apparent equality*.

The same self-respect blends with the civility of the shopkeeper. He is very happy to serve and suit you ; but if he cannot, he is ready to direct you elsewhere. Shopmen have repeatedly, unasked, sent a person to guide us through the intricate Continental streets to another shop.

The domestics are prompt, faithful, and cheerful in their services. There is freedom, but no presumption in their manners, and nothing of that unhappy uncertainty as to their exact position, so uncomfortable in our people. In all these subordinate classes you see nothing of the cringing servility that marks them in England, and to which they are exposed by their direct dependence on their employers.

Our English friend, Miss ——, who has been repeatedly in Germany, and is a good observer, acquiesces in the truth of my observations, and says this general freedom of deportment comes from people of all ranks freely mingling together. If so, this surely is a healthy influence, a natural and beneficent effect from an obedience to that Divine precept, " Honour all men." Woe to those who set the brethren of one family off into *castes*, and build up walls between them so that they cannot freely grasp hands and exchange smiles !

I HAVE just been to the *Poste* to see our English friends off. Their departure is a sad epoch to us, for they have been our solace and delight. A curious scene is the " Poste" in a Continental town. Here (and ordinarily, I believe) it has a quadrangular court, inclosed on three sides by an hotel and its offices, including that for letters, and having on the fourth side a passage through a stone arch to the street. Here the public coaches arrive, and hence take their departure ; and here the travellers and their luggage are taken up and discharged. I will describe the scene to you precisely as I just saw it. Besides the diligence for Schwalbach, in which our friends were going, and towards which the luggage of various pas-

* This opinion may appear to have been formed on a very slight acquaintance with the country. It was afterward amply confirmed in Germany and Switzerland, where the manners are essentially the same.

sengers was converging, while that which exceeded
the authorised weight was passing through the
post-office window out of the hands of the weigh-
master*, there were private carriages arriving
and departing. Some of these were elegant, and
the horses curveting and prancing right royally,
so that I fancied they must be carrying German
princes, or *Englishmen*, who are princes all over
Europe.

My friend's postilion, with his yellow and black
Nassau livery, his official band round his arm, his
leather boots cut to a peak in front and extending
some inches above his knee, his immense yellow
tassel bobbing over his shoulder, was blowing his
note of preparation from the trumpet he carries
at his side. Fat Germans stood at the windows
of the different stories of the hotel, smoking and
talking to women as fat as they. There were
other Germans, mustachioed and imperturbable,
coolly awaiting the moment of departure, meandering about among the carriages and barrows,
with their pipes dangling from one side of their
mouths, and their incessant " Ja," " Ja wohl"
(Yes—yes, indeed), dropping from the other.
Our friend's female fellow passengers, in caps
without bonnets, had ensconced themselves in a
little nook, where they were knitting as if they
were neither part nor parcel of this stirring
world.

But what a contrast to this quietude, the
English traveller ! You may know him by the
quantity and variety of his luggage, by every
ingenious contrivance for comfort (alas ! comfort
implies fixture), impregnable English trunks,
travelling-bags, dressing-cases, cased provisions
for all the possible wants that civilisation ge-
nerates, and all in travelling armour. There is
no flexibility about an Englishman, no adaptation
to circumstances and exigences. He must stand
forth, wherever he goes, the impersonation of his
island-home. I said his luggage betrayed him ;
I am sure his face and demeanour do. His
muscles are in a state of tension, his nerves seem
to be on the outside of his coat, his eyebrows are
in motion ; he looks, as my friend says she felt
when she first came to such a place as this, " as
if all the people about her were *rats ;*" his voice
is quick and harsh, and his words none of the
sweetest, so that you do not wonder the Continental people have fastened on him the descriptive
sobriquet of " Monsieur God-d—n."

An interesting little episode to me in this
bustling scene was Miss W., the very essence of
refinement and *English gentlewomanliness*, running hither and yon, settling with porters, garçons,
and maîtres de poste, while her Yorkshire maid
was watching with dismay the rough handling of
her lady's precious parcels, and Miss St. L.
looking as if she did not care if they were all lost,
if she could but save her friend from these rough
duties, to which she is compelled by being the
only one of the party who speaks German.

MY DEAR C.—We have been waiting for fine

* The allowed weight of baggage in Germany as well
as in France is small, thirty pounds, I think. And for
the excess of this you pay at so high a rate, that the transportation of one's luggage often costs more than that of
one's self.

weather, that being an indispensable element in a
party of pleasure, for an excursion down the
Rhine, and this morning we set off, the girls and
myself, without any attendant of mankind ; an
elegant superfluity, as we are beginning to think.

While François was getting our *billets,* we,
eager to secure the best places in the diligence,
jostled past the Germans, who stood quietly
awaiting the conductor's summons ; and when,
ten minutes after, our fellow-passengers were
getting in, offering to one another precedence, the
conductor came to us and said, " Ah, ladies, you
are placed ; I had allotted better seats for you."
Was not this an appropriate punishment for our
selfish and truly national hurrying ! I could give
you many instances of similar offences committed
by ourselves and other travellers among these
" live-and-let-live" people. There is a steam navigation company on the Rhine, who have three
boats ascending and descending daily ; this enables
you to pay your passage to a certain place, and
avail yourself of each boat or all, as suits your
convenience. You are at liberty, at any point
you please, to quit the steamer, ramble for two
or three hours on the shore, and then proceed on
your expedition. We are descending the river
rapidly ; the current runs at the rate of six miles
an hour.

The big Russian princess, who is a sort of
" man of the sea" to us, is flourishing up and
down the deck with two of her suite, one on each
side, as if to guard her from contact with the
plebeian world. Every look and motion says " I
do *not* love the people." The royal brood may
wince, but they must submit to the democratic
tendencies of the age. These steamers and rail-
cars are undermining their elevations. I have
not, as you know, my dear C., any vulgar hostility
to those who are the heirs of the usurpations of
elder times—" the accident of an accident"—but
when I see a person radically vulgar like this
woman, queening it among those who are her
superiors in everything but this accidental greatness, my Puritan blood and republican breeding
get the better of my humanity.

We are passing the château of Johannisberg—
a castle of Prince Metternich, an immense white
edifice, which, as we see it, looks much like a
Saratoga hotel. It is on a gently-sloping hill,
covered with vines which confessedly produce the
best Rhine wine. " The extent of the vineyard
is," Murray says, " fifty-five acres. Its produce
in good years amounts to about forty butts, and
has been valued at 80,000 florins." This vineyard
was formerly attached to the abbey of St. John ;
and a genial time, no doubt, the merry monks had
of it. Would they not have regarded the modern
tabooing of wine as the *ne plus ultra* of heresy !
But, poor fellows ! their abbey and their wine
were long ago secularised, and have fallen into
the hands of military and political spoilers. Napoleon made an imperial gift of these vineyards
to Marshal Kellerman, and in 1816 they again
changed hands, being presented to Metternich by
the Emperor of Austria. I have drunk wine
bearing the name of Johannisberg in New-York,
but I have been told by a person who had tasted
it at Metternich's table, that it is only to be
found unadulterated there. Murray informs us
that they permit the grape to pass the point of

seeming perfection before they gather it, believing that the wine gains in body by this, and that so precious are the grapes that those which have fallen are picked up by a fork made for the purpose.

We met a countryman to-day who has been travelling through France and Italy with his sister, "without any language," he says, "but that spoken on the rock of Plymouth," which, true to his English blood, he pronounces, with infinite satisfaction, to be the best and all-sufficient. He is a fair specimen of that class of Anglo-American travellers who find quite enough particulars, in which every country is inferior to their own, to fill up the field of their observation. He has just crossed the deck to say to me, "I have let them know what a *tall* place America is; I have told them that an American steamer will carry 2000 people and 1000 bales of cotton, and go down the river *and up* twice as fast as a Rhine steamer." He has *not* told them that a Rhine steamer is far superior in its arrangement and refinement to ours. These little patriotic vanities are pleasant solaces when one is three thousand miles from home—but truth is better.

Braubach.—WE arrived here at half-past three, having passed about 50 miles of the most enchanting scenery on the Rhine. Imagine, my dear C., a little strip of level land, not very many yards wide, between the river and precipitous rocks; a village with its weather-stained houses in this pent-up space; an old château with its walls and towers, and at the summit of the rocks and hanging over them, for the rocks actually project from the perpendicular, the stern old castle of Marksburg; and you have our present position. Murray says this castle is the only one of the strongholds of the middle ages that has been preserved unaltered, the beau ideal of an old castle; and this is why we have come to see it. I am sitting at the window of the château, now the *Gasthaus zur Phillipsburg.* Under my window is a garden with grapes, interspersed with fruit-trees and flowers, and inclosed by a white paling, and finishing at each end with the old towers of the castle-wall. Along the narrow road between the garden and the river there are peasant-girls going homeward with baskets of fresh-mown grass on their heads, followed by peasants in their dark blouses, with their sickles swung over their shoulders. Little boats are gliding to and fro, guided, and, as their ringing voices tell you, enjoyed by children. But here is mine host to tell us the *esels* are ready—the four asses we have ordered to take us to Marksburg.

OF all "riding privileges," that on a donkey is the least. You are set on to something half-cushion, half-saddle, that neither has itself nor imparts rest. Though there is a semicircular rampart erected, to guard you from the accident of "high-vaulting ambition," it seems inevitable that you must fall on one side or the other. There is a shingle strapped to the saddle for the right foot, and a stirrup for the left; fortunate are you if you can extricate your feet from both. A merry procession we had of it, however, up the winding road to Marksburg. The Braubach

donkeys have not had much custom of late, I fancy, for we ran a race, fairly distancing our donkey-drivers, who seemed much amused with our way of proceeding. The fellow who was spokesman demanded, as I thought, an exorbitant price, and I appealed to one of his comrades, who decided that half he asked was quite enough. I mention this with pleasure, because it is the only thing of the sort we have had to complain of since we came into Germany. The fellow was a stranger and an alien from this worthy household, I am sure; he had a most *un*-German expression.

The castle has been, till recently, a state-prison, and is now occupied by invalid soldiers. We were led through dark passages and up a winding stone staircase to the apartment where prisoners were put to the rack; and we were shown another gloomy den, where there were two uprights and a transverse beam, and beneath them a trap-door; if not satisfied with so much of the story as these objects intimate, you may descend and search for the bones which you will certainly find there! In another apartment are some mediocre paintings on the wall, done with only a gleam of light by a poor fellow who had thus happily beguiled weary years of imprisonment. On the whole, the castle was not so interesting, not nearly so striking, as I expected. Nothing is left to indicate the rude luxury of its lordly masters; its aspect is merely that of an ill-contrived prison.

WHEN we got back to the inn, an old man, who seemed an *habitué,* asked us, in very good French (which Germans of the inferior orders never speak), to walk into the garden. Such a pretty garden, with its towers, its fragment of the old castle-wall, its bowers and wreaths of grapes, and such grapes! oh, you would go mad if you could see them, remembering your seasons of hope and despair over your few frostbitten vines. The old man picked some plums, and served them to us with sylvan grace on a grape-leaf. We fell into conversation. He told me the history of his life; it was common enough, but there was a gentleness and sensibility in his voice and expression very uncommon. He came from Alsace, and was travelling in this vicinity with his wife and only surviving child, a girl, "trying to forget home;" for he had lost at short intervals his three sons, when his daughter was asked in marriage by a young man of Braubach. The parents gave their consent, and, wisely resolving to have but one home among them, he bought this old château, and converted it into the *Hôtel zur Phillipsburg;* and here he and his wife have reposed under the spreading shadow of their posterity. "I am not rich," he said, "but I have enough. I thought myself happy; my life was gliding in the midst of my family and my vines; but man, with whom nothing lasts, should not call himself happy. Seven months ago my wife died"—the old man's eyes filled—"it was a sudden and a hard blow; we must bow before the stroke of the good God! My daughter has four children. I am their instructor. In my youth I was at college, and, afterward being engaged in commerce, I travelled: so I can teach them French, Dutch, and Italian. Certainly I am not a severe master; but they love me, and love can do more than fear. The youngest is sometimes too much for me. He is a superb boy, madam ! When I say, ' Julius, come to your lessons !' he answers, 'Oh, it is too fine weather to study ; see how the sun shines, grandfather, and the boys are all at play ;' and away he goes." You may think me as garrulous as the old man to repeat all this to you, since I cannot send with it this lovely scene in twilight, harmonising so well with the twilight of his closing life.

I inquired into the condition of the poor in this neighbourhood. He says their poverty is extreme. They live on potatoes and *some* black bread ; on Sunday they have for a family, half a pound of meat. A woman with three or four children to support has a florin a month allowed her. Begging is prohibited, but they must subsist on charity. Every hotel has a poor's box, of which the magistrate keeps the key, and comes each month to take out and distribute the travellers' alms*. He says that, whenever a poor woman of the village lies in, she is supplied for fifteen days from their plentiful table. God bless their basket and their store !

WE left Braubach this morning. The old grandfather and that *youngest* grandchild, "a superb boy" truly, came to the shore with us, and we exchanged cordial good wishes at parting.

As we pushed off in our little boat and looked up to the precipitous shore, it seemed, even while we gazed on them, incredible that the vines should be reached for cultivation there, where they hung like a rich drapery. The peasants, women as well as men, scale the precipices to dress their vines, and every particle of manure is carried up on their shoulders.

In the steepest places the vines are put in baskets as the only means of retaining the soil about them. For the most part the vineyards are a series of terraces or steps (we have counted from twenty to thirty) covering the face of the hill. Each terrace is supported by a wall from five to ten feet high. Murray tells us the Rhineland vinedresser is not rich, but generally the possessor of the vineyard he cultivates. What a beautiful gift of Providence is the vine to the patient, contented tiller of ground that would produce nothing but this ! and this "makes glad the heart of man."

The steamer carried us past village after village most beautiful as seen in passing ; but again, my dear C., I warn you not to let this, the greenest word in memory, call before you wide streets, shaded courtyards, ample space, and all rural luxuries. A village here is a mass of wretched dwellings stuck against mouldering walls, where human existence, in point of comfort, is nearly on a level with the brutes ; in fact, the same roof often shelters all the *live-stock*, from the master to his ass. The streets are scarcely wide enough for a carriage to pass, and the lanes are but a flea's leap across—a measurement that naturally occurs here. But mark the compensating blessing ! the denizens of these dreary places, steeped to the very lips in poverty, are a smiling, kindly people.

WE landed at St. Goar's, in the midst of the most enchanting scenery of the Rhine, and in showery weather giving us the most favourable

* I have repeatedly observed these boxes affixed to the wall, and have been told that a German rarely passes them without a donation.

possible light. Nature, like "ladies and fine Holland," owes much of its effect to the right disposition of light and shadow. The mountains inclose this little village. The Mouse and the Cat, the beautiful ruins of two castles, are at either extremity of the view. The "Cat" is well stationed to watch its prey, but, contrary to all precedent, the "Mouse" is said always to have been the strongest when they were held by their lords, rivals, and enemies. The immense Castle of Rheinfels, halfway up the steep behind St. Goar, looks, as L. says, like a great bull-dog that might have kept all its subordinates civil. Rheinfels, as early as the fourteenth century, was the strongest hold on the Rhine. It was built by a Count Deither, who, secure in his power, levied tribute (the exclusive privilege of governments at present, and they, as Murray happily says, call it *laying duties*) with such unsparing cupidity, that the free cities of Germany confederated against him, and not only dismantled his castle, but the other "robbers' nests" on the Rhine.

The girls carried my carpet-bag up to the inn, which being rather weighty with my journal, one of them expressed the pious wish it "might not be so heavy in the reading as the carrying." On our way we went into a most grotesque little Catholic church, where an image of the good hermit who gave his name to the village is preserved. He looks like an honest German, and, though his head had been crowned with a fresh garland of roses last Sunday, and plenty of cherubs were hovering round him, I fancied he would have liked better a pipe in his mouth and a table before him, and the cherubs converted into garçons, to serve him with Rhine wine and Seltzer-water.

We took a boy from the steps of "The Lily" to cross the river with us, and guide us up the Schweitzer Thal (the Swiss Valley). We followed the pathway of a little brook resembling some of our mountain haunts. *Die Kats* hung over our heads half-way up a steep, which Johann (our guide) told us was higher than the Lurleiberg. It may be, but there is nothing on the Rhine so grand as this pile of rocks, which look with scorn on the perishable castles built by man's hands. It is in the whirlpool in their deep shadow that Undine, the loveliest of water-nymphs, holds her court. No wonder it requires, as says the faith of the peasants of St. Goar, the miraculous power of their canonised hermit to deliver the ensnared from her enchantments.

We walked a mile up the valley, and loitered at little nooks, so walled in by the hills that we looked up to the sky as from the bottom of a well. To us it appeared clear and blue as a sapphire ; but we were sprinkled with rain so sparkling that L. said the sun was melting, and coming down in drops ! I amused myself with finding out as much of my little guide's history as could be unlocked with the talismanic words "father," "mother," "brother," helped out with dumb show ; and I found out that he had one sister that was shorter than he, and one brother much taller, who was a soldier, and so would Johann be. Against this resolution I expostulated vehemently (as a friend of William Ladd, and a member of the Peace Society, should do), but Johann laughed at me ; and I doubt not, as soon as he has inches and years enough, he will buckle on his sword.

When we got back to St. Goar the shower came on in earnest, and we took refuge at a jolly miller's—a fit impersonation of that classic character. In an interval of his work he was sitting over his bottle and cracking his jokes. We invited him to go to America. "No," he said, holding up his Rhenish and chuckling over it, "I should not get this there ; and, besides, all the millers that go there die !" He is right to cherish a life so joyous.

The steamer came up at a snail's pace. We had the pleasure of finding on board one of our fellow-passengers in the Saint James. He had been purifying in the bubbles of Schlangenbad, which produce such miraculous effects on the skin that Sir Francis Head avers he heard a Frenchman say, "Monsieur, dans ces bains on devient absolument amoureux de soi-même !" (One falls in love with one's self in these baths.") Our friend was a witness to its recreative virtue.

MY DEAR C.—I will not even name to you the beautiful pictures past which we floated. Everything is here ready for the painter's hand. Oberwesel, with its Roman tower, its turreted walls and Gothic edifices ; the old Castle of Schonberg, Anglicè *Beautiful Hill,* where there are seven petrified maidens, who were converted into these rocks for their stony-heartedness—fit retribution. Villages, vineyards, and ruins appeared and disappeared as the mist, playing its fantastic tricks, veiled and unveiled them. As we drew near to Bingen, the sun shone out, throwing his most beautifying horizontal beams on Rheinstein and other famed points of the landscape, while masses of black clouds, driven on by the gusty wind, threw their deep shadows now here, now there, as if (we flies on the wheel fancied) to enchant the senses of travellers for the picturesque.

After much discussion with a friendly Englishman (an old-stager in these parts) as to the comparative advantage of landing at Bingen or Rüdesheim, we followed his advice and went on shore at the former place, where we found a cheerful welcome in the face of mine host of the Weisse Rosse, but no room in his house. This man is quite my beau ideal of a German innkeeper, and, but that it would take too much space, I should like to tell you the pains he took to get us rooms in another inn, and how, after he did get them, we reconsidered our decision and determined to pass the night at Rüdesheim ; and how, when we came to him with our tongues faltering with some mere pretext for being off, he just good-humouredly brushed aside the flimsy veil, saying, "Never mind, you choose to go, and that is enough ;" and proceeded to select boatmen for us, and to make them promise to take us down to Rheinstein and back again to Rüdesheim at the lowest and a very moderate rate. Would not the world go on swimmingly if all strangers errant were dealt by as mine host of the Weisse Rosse dealt by us ?

How would you like, dear C., to see us, your nearest and dearest relations, boating on the Rhine with men whose German even K. found it hard to comprehend ! There would be no reason for anxiety ; they took us in good faith in half an hour to Rheinstein—or rather the current took us. The Castle of Rheinstein has been restored by Prince Frederic of Prussia, and refurnished, and is now supposed to represent the castles as they were when there was wassail in the hall and love in the bower. The castle itself is the most beautiful on the Rhine. It is planted on a projecting rock, half-way to the summit of a steep, and set off by a dark, rich woodland. It is built of stone taken from the bed of rock that forms its foundation, and you can scarce tell where nature finishes and art begins. In truth, the art is so perfect that you forget it. Nature seems to have put forth her creative power, and to have spoken the word that called from its mother rock this its indescribably beautiful and graceful offspring.

We wound up a path of easy ascent, passed over a drawbridge and under a portcullis, when the warder appeared. He was a sober-suited youth, with a rueful countenance ; love-lorn, the girls said, pointing to his hump-back and a braid of hair round his neck. He bowed without relaxing a muscle, and led us through a walled court where there were green grass and potted plants, and, perched over our heads, in niches of the rock, eagles, who, it would appear but for the bars of iron before them, had selected these eyries of their own free will. Our warder proceeded through a passage with a pretty mosaic pavement to the knights' hall, which is hung with weapons of the middle ages, disposed in regular figures. The ceiling is painted with knights' devices ; and complete suits of armour, helmets, and richly-embossed shields, hang against the wall.

We were repeatedly assured that the furniture was, in truth, of the middle ages, and had been collected by the prince at infinite pains ; and looking at it in good faith as we proceeded, everything pleased us. There is a centre-table with an effigy in stone of Charlemagne, a most fantastical old clock, carved Gothic chairs, oak tables ; in the dining-room an infinite variety of silver drinking-cups, utensils of silver and of ivory richly carved, and very small diamond-shaped mirrors, *all* cracked ;—by-the-way, an incidental proof of their antiquity. The princess' rooms, en suite, are very prettily got up ; her sleeping-room has an oaken bedstead of the fourteenth century, with a high, carved foot-board like a rampart, and curtains of mixed silk and woollen. In the writing-room are beautiful cabinets of ivory inlaid, and wood in marquetrie—that is, flowers represented by inlaying different coloured woods.

In the working-room was a little wheel, which made me reflect with envy on the handiwork of our grandames, so much more vivacious than our stitching. You will probably, without a more prolonged description, my dear C., come to my conclusion, that Rheinstein bears much the same resemblance to a castle of the middle ages that a cottage orné does to a veritable rustic home. I imagined the rough old knights coming from their halls of savage power and rude luxury to laugh at all this *jimcrackery.*

The prince and princess make a holiday visit here every summer, and keep up this fanciful retrocession by wearing the costume of past ages. The warder maintained his unrelenting gravity to the last. "Man pleased him not, nor woman either," or I am sure my laughing companions would have won a smile.

We found going up the river quite a different

affair from coming down. Our oarsmen raised a ragged sail. The wind was flawy, and we were scared ; so they, at our cowardly entreaties, took it down, and then, rowing the boat to the shore, one of the men got out, and fastening one end of a rope to our mast and the other round his body, he began toilsomely towing us up the stream. Our hearts were too soft for this, so we disembarked too, and walked two miles to "The Angel" at Rüdesheim ; an angel indeed to us after this long day of—pleasure.

Friday, Rüdesheim.—THIS morning we set off on an excursion to the Niederwald, "The Echo," "The Temple," "The Enchanted Cave," and the Rossel. Now, let your fancy surround you with the atmosphere of our cool, bright September days, and present the images of your friends, mounted on asses, winding up steep paths among these rich Rüdesheim vineyards, which produce some of the finest wines on the Rhine. See our four *Eselmeisters* slowly gossiping on after us, and our .path crossed, ever and anon, with peasant women emerging from the vineyards with baskets on their heads, piled with grape-cuttings, and weeds to feed the asses, pigs, or—children ! See us passing through the beech and oaken wood of the Niederwald, and coming out upon the "Temple" to look down on the ruins of the Castle of Brömser, amid a world of beauty, and think upon its old Jephtha lord who, when a captive among the Saracens, vowed, if he returned, to devote his only daughter Gisela to the church—of poor Gisela, who had devoted herself to a human divinity, and, finding her crusading father inexorable, threw herself from the tower of the castle into the river. With the clear eye of peasant faith, you may see now, of a dark and gusty night, the pale form of this modern Sappho, and you may hear her wailings somewhere about Hatto's Tower.

Next see us emerging from our woodland path, and taken possession of by a *very* stout woodland nymph, who has the showing of the Bezauberte Höhle (Enchanted Cave) ; but, no ; you shall not see that with our eyes, but read Sir Francis Head's description of it, which proves that, if he has any right to designate himself as "the old man," time has not done its sad work in abating the fervours of his imagination. He has made a prodigious bubble of this cave. His "subterranean passage" was, to our disenchanted vision, but a walled way on upper earth ; and where he looked through fissures of the rock, we had but the prose of windows, whose shutters were slammed open by our Dulcinean wood-nymph. But never mind ! long may he live to verify the fantastical figure in the vignette to the Frankfort edition of his charming work, to walk over the world blowing bubbles so filled with the breath of genius and benevolence that they diffuse sweet odours wherever they float.

See us now standing at the Rossel, looking with the feeling of parting lovers at the queenly Rheinstein sitting on her throne of Nature's masonry—at a long reach of the river up and down—at the lovely Nahe ; not merely at its graceful entrance into the Rhine, but far, far away as it comes serenely gliding along its deep-sunken channel from its mountain-home—at Drusus' bridge, with its misty light of another age and people—at the massy ruin of Ehrenfels under our feet—at the Mouse Tower of old Bishop Hatto on its pretty island—at vineyards without number—at hills sloping to hills, at the green ravines between them, and the roads that traverse them—at villages, towers, and churches ; and, finally, at our little hamlet of Rüdesheim, which, with its 3500 people, is so compact that it appeared as if I might span it with my arms. And remember that into all this rich landscape, history, story, ballad, and tradition have breathed the breath of life. Do you wonder that we turned away with the feeling that we should never again see anything so beautiful ? Thank Heaven, to a scene like this "there can be no farewell !"

We were delighted on getting down to "The Angel" to see the "Victoria" puffing up the Rhine ; for, to confess the truth, now that the feast of our eyes and imaginations was over, we began to feel the cravings of our grosser natures. There is no surer sharpener of the appetite than a long mountain-ride in a cool morning. The Niederwald, the Höhle, the Rossel, all were forgotten in the vision of the pleasantest of all repasts—a dinner on the deck of a Rhine steamer. It was just on the stroke of one when we reached the Victoria. The table was laid, and the company was gathering with a certain look of pleased expectation, and a low murmur of sound much resembling that I have heard from your barnyard family when you were shelling out corn to them. The animal nature is strongest at least once in the twenty-four hours ! The Russian princess was the first person we encountered. "Monsieur Tonson come again." "We'll not have a seat near her," I whispered to the girls, as, with some difficulty, we doubled the end of the table which her enormous royal person occupied. "No ; farthest from her is best," said K. ; so we proceeded to the other extremity of the table, where we were met by the head waiter. "Places for four, if you please," said I. He bowed civilly, was "very sorry, but there was no room." "Surely you can make room !" "Impossible, madam !" A moment's reflection convinced me that a German would not risk the comfort of one guest by crowding in another, so I said, "Well, give us a table to ourselves." "I cannot ; it is impossible !" "What !" exclaimed the girls, "does he say we cannot have places ! Do order a lunch, then ; I am starved :" "And so am I ;" "And I." My next demand showed how narrowed were our prospects. "Then," said I, "I'll ask for nothing more if you will give me some bread and butter, and a bottle of wine !" "Afterward, afterward, madam," he replied, his German patience showing some symptoms of diminution ; "afterward lunch, dinner, or what you please : but now it is impossible." Like the starving Ugolino when he heard the key of the Tower of Famine turned on him,

"Io guardái
Nel viso a' mie' figliuoli senza far motto."

But soon touched by their misery and urged by my own, I once more intercepted the inexorable youth, and mustering all my eloquence, I told him he had no courtesy for ladies, no "sentiment ;" that he would have to answer for the deaths of those three blooming young women, &c. &c. He smiled, and I thought relented ; but the smile was followed with a definite shake of the head, and away he went to perform well duties divided between half-a-dozen half-bred waiters in our country. Nothing remained for us but to submit. In a Hudson River steamer (we remembered regretfully our national despatch) the "afterward" would have been time enough ; at most, an affair of half an hour's waiting, but the perspective of a German's meandering through his "meridian" was endless. Besides, we were to land at Bieberich in two or three hours, so, "ladies most deject," we sat ourselves down in the only vacant place we could find, close to the head of the table. The people, for the most part, had taken their seats ; here and there a chair awaited some loiterer, but one dropped in after another, and my last faint hope that, after all, the waiter would distribute us among them, faded away. There was some delay, and even those seated with the sweet security of dinner began to lose something of their characteristic serenity. There was a low growl from two English gentlemen near us, and the Germans beside us began mumbling their rolls. "Ah," thought I, "if ye who have been, as is your wont, feeding every half-hour since you were out of bed, sitting lazily at your little tables here, could feel ' the thorny point of our distress,' you surely would give us that bread ! "

The soup came, and as each took his plate, from the top to the bottom of the table, the shadows vanished from their faces as I have seen them pass from a field of corn as a cloud was passing off the sun. " I should have been quite content," said M., meekly, " with a plate of soup on our laps." " Yes," said L. in a faltering voice, " I should be quite satisfied with soup and a bit of bread." But away went the soup, no one heeding us but a fat German whose back was towards us, and who, comprehending our dilemma, felt nothing but the ludicrousness of it. He turned when he had swallowed his soup, and smiled significantly.

Next came the fat, tender bouilli, with its three satellites, potatoes à la maître d'hôtel, cucumbers, and a fat compound called "gravy." " I always relish the bouilli," said K., faintly. Bouilli, potatoes, and cucumbers were eaten in turn ; a German has no sins of omission to answer for at table.

Then appeared the entremets, the croquets, sausages, tongue, the queenly cauliflower floating in butter, rouleaux of cabbage, macaroni, preparations of beans and sorrel, and other messes that have baffled all our investigation and guessing.

Now, fully to comprehend the prolongation of our misery, you must remember the German custom of eating each article of food presented, each separately, and lounging through a change of twenty plates as if eating dinner comprehended the whole duty and pleasure of life. " If they would only give us a bit of tongue ! " said K., " or a croquet," said M., " or just one sausage," said L. But tongue, croquet, and sausage vanished within the all-devouring jaws, and again the emptied dishes were swept off, and on came salmon, tench, pike, and trout (served cold and with bits of ice), and the delicious puddings. Now came my trial. The puddings, so light, so wholesome, with their sweet innocent fruit-sauces, are always my poste restante at a German dinner.

But " what was I to Hecuba, or Hecuba to me ! " the pudding, in its turn, was all eaten, and our fat friend, wiping his mouth after the last morsel, turned round and laughed,—yes, actually laughed ; and we, being at that point of nervousness when you must either cry or laugh, laughed too—rather hysterically.

Are you tired ! I have described but the prefatory manœuvring of the light troops. Now came the procession of joints, mutton, veal, and venison, interspersed with salads, stewed fruit, calves'-foot jelly, and blancmanges. " Surely they might spare us one form of jelly," said M. ; " Or a blanc-mange," said K. : but no ; meat, jelly, and all were eaten, and again our stout friend looked round, with less animation this time, for he was beginning to resemble a pampered old house-dog who is too full to bark. The dessert appeared : apricots, cherries, mulberries, pears, and a variety of confectionary. The conductor appeared, too, with the billets. " Surely," I said, " that is not Bieberich ! " " Pardon, madam, we are within a quarter of an hour of Bieberich." " It is a gone case ! " I sighed out to the girls ; and, in truth, we arrived before the Duke of Nassau's heavy palace just as the company, with the most provoking flush of entire satisfaction, were turning away from the table. We had learned to appreciate the virtue of those Lazaruses who, witnessing the feasting of the Dives, go hungry every day.

I have given you an exact inventory of the dinner, " setting down naught in malice " or in misery ; and when you are told that it costs but one florin (forty-two cents), that it is served with nice table-linen, large napkins, and silver forks, you must conclude that provisions are cheap, and that the traveller—if he can "catch the turbot " —is a happy man in Germany *.

When we got into the diligence at Bieberich, there were two neat peasant-women beside us. We saw the Russian princess, whose carriage had disappointed her, waddling about, attended by her suite, in quest of a passage to Wiesbaden. One of the gentlemen said to her, " The sun is hot ; it will be tiresome waiting," and counselled her highness to take a seat in the diligence. " It is quite shocking," she said, " to go in this way." " But there is no other, madam." So she yielded to necessity, and put her royal foot on the step, when, looking up, she shrunk back, exclaiming, " Comment ! il y a des paysannes " (How is this ! there are peasants here ! ") I am sure we should not have been more dismayed if we had been shoved in with the asses that carried us in the morning. We drove off ; and when I compared this woman, with her vacant, gross face, her supercilious demeanour, and her Brussels-lace mantilla, to our peasant companions, with their clean, substantial, well-preserved dresses, their healthful, contented, and serene faces, and their kindly manners, all telling a story of industry, economy, and contentment, I looked proudly, thankfully back to my country of no princesses ! Arrogance and superciliousness exist there, no doubt, but they have no birthright for their exercise.

* The Englishman goes from here to London in two days, and there must pay at an hotel, for the single item in his dinner of a lobster-sauce to his salmon, seventy-five cents ! No wonder he " puts up " with Germany.

I THINK it is Madame de Staël who, in speaking of travelling as a "triste plaisir," dwells much upon that sad part of it, "hurrying to arrive where none expect you." This was not now our case. We were going "home to Wiesbaden," and there sparkling eyes, welcoming voices, and loving hearts awaited us. And, don't be shocked at the unsentimentality of my mentioning the circumstance, we arrived in time for the five-o'clock dinner at the *Quatre Saisons,* after having passed three days that will be for ever bright in memory's calendar, and having paid for all our varied pleasures but about seven dollars each. Had we not them "at a bargain!"

FRANKFORT.

MY DEAR C.,

August 30.—The spell is broken and we have left Wiesbaden. We arrived here last evening, after a drive of four hours through a tame country, varied here and there by a brown village, a church or little chapel, and the old watch-towers near the town, marking the limits of its territory, which does not exceed ten English square miles. I had supposed this was a free city, and I was surprised to meet at the gate we entered, soldiers in the Austrian uniform. We should think it an odd sort of freedom that was protected by the forces of a foreign prince*. The annual fair is just beginning, and the town is crowded, though these fairs are no longer what they were before the general diffusion of commerce and manufactures; the introduction of railroads will soon put an end to them.

We drove to six hotels before we could find a place to lay our heads in: this is certainly a *very* "triste plaisir" that we travellers have now and then.

Having secured a roof to shelter us, we sallied forth for a walk. We went up the principal street, the Zeil, where the buildings are magnificent, looked in at the shop-windows, examined the bronze images at the fountain, and then, as if by instinct, turning at the right places and proceeding just as far as was necessary, we reached the Maine, which is not much wider than the Housatonic in our meadows. Returning, we went into the public gardens, which occupy the place of the old ramparts. This green and flowery belt girdling the town is a pretty illustration of turning the sword into the pruning-hook. The redeemed ground is laid out with economy of space and much taste. We passed through copses, groves, and parterres, and came out upon a growth of firs encircling a bronze bust of a benefactor who had contributed to this adornment. As I looked at the children and various other happy groups we passed, I wished there were some arithmetic that could calculate the amount of happiness produced by a man who originated a public garden, and set it off against the results of the lives of those great conquerors whose effigies and trophies cumber the earth!

* I was afterward informed that there was an alarming effervescence among the students in 1833, which induced the Frankforters to call in the aid of Austria and Prussia, who have kindly since watched over the "tranquillity" of the city—a kind of vigilance in which they excel.

Our first impression of Frankfort is very agreeable. It has not the picturesque aspect of the other Continental towns, but it is clean, with broad streets and modern houses, and appears lively and prosperous, as if one might live and breathe and get a living in it. M., true to her general preference of cleanliness and comfort to the picturesque, declares it is the only place she has seen, since she left England, she could be tempted to live in; while L., as true to her peculiar tastes, prefers the oldest, wretchedest German village, provided there is a ruined castle brooding over it, and plenty of fragments of towers, peasants in costume, &c.

"NECESSITY is the mother of Invention." I believe she is the mother of half our faculties; and so will you, dear C., when I tell you, you who would not trust me to buy a go-cart, that I have selected and bought to-day our travelling carriage. Mr. K. tells me I have good reason to be satisfied with my bargain, though I did not take François' advice, who said to me, as we were entering the coach-warehouse, "No matter if you are very well pleased, always shake your head and say 'Il ne vaut rien'" ("It is good for nothing"): this is a fair specimen of courier diplomacy.

WE took tea this evening with Madame ——. She has a gem of a country-house, half-a-mile from town, resembling the cottage of a Boston gentleman. The grounds are laid out and cultivated with the elaborateness of an English suburban villa. Madame —— received us at the gate, and conducted us to seats beside a green painted table surrounded with flower-beds and under the shadow of fine old chestnuts. She told us her husband was induced by these chestnuts to buy the lot for a playground for his grandchildren. Then, in case of a shower, they must have a shelter, and he built a tea-room, and the shelter expanded to its present comfort and elegance; a pleasant illustration of the growth of a project. Madame —— gave us our choice of taking our tea in the garden, the balcony, or the drawing-room. The Germans seem to me to go into their houses as the pigeons do, only for shelter and sleep. Their gardens are, in fact, their drawing-rooms.

After tea, Madame —— took us a drive. We crossed the Maine on a stone bridge to Sachsenhausen, a suburb of the town, and drove to an eminence, where we had a good view of the town, the river, and very extensive vegetable gardens. We then drove quite round the town, outside the public gardens. The environs are gay with summer-houses and gardens, now brilliant with dahlias and asters. Very cheerful and uniform they looked, as if each one had a fair portion; not one a feast and another a fast, the too general condition of life in the Old World. On our return we passed the new library, with the inscription, "Studiis, libertati, reddita civitas" ("The city returned to studies and freedom"); and we were beginning to feel as if we were surrounded by a home atmosphere, when we plunged into the Jews' quarter, so dark, narrow, and intricate that it reminded me of Fagin's haunts. The old town is very curious. The old houses have grated windows and massive doors, and are many stories high, each story projecting over that below it. The fronts of those which are of stone are curiously carved or painted in compartments. All this, indeed, looked " the ancient, imperial, free city ! "

We finished the day in Madame ——'s box at the theatre, literally the day, for it was yet twilight when we got home. The theatre is by law closed at nine o'clock precisely. This very rational hour obviates a serious objection to the amusement*.

We were fortunate in seeing one of the great dramatic performers of Germany, Emile Devrient. The play was one of the Princess Amelia's ; a tale of domestic sorrow, as I ascertained by my interpreters. There was no scenic effect, no dramatic contrivance to aid it. The scene was not once shifted during the play. Devrient seemed to me, as far as I could judge merely from his action, expression, and voice, to deserve the applauses showered on him. The playing was all natural, and the voices of the women marvellously sweet. Have I never yet remarked to you the sweet, low tone of the German woman's voice? From the cultivated actress to your chambermaid, it is a musical pleasure to hear them speak. Is it an atmospheric effect, or the breath of a placid temper ! The latter, I thought, when, a moment since, my inkstand was overset, and the girl summoned to repair the mischief held up her hands, smiled, and uttered, in a lute-like tone, 'a prolonged g—u—t ! (good !)

WE dined to-day at Mr. Köck's. He is an eminent banker here, and, from his extensive English connexions, is in some sort compelled to be a general receiver of the Continental tourists. We do not bank with him, and therefore have not this claim, such as it is, upon his hospitality ; but, for all that, it has been most liberally extended to us. A family whose hospitality is not exhausted in such a thoroughfare as Frankfort, must have an inexhaustible fountain of humanity. Hospitality in an isolated country residence is the mere gratification of the appetite of a social being ; here it is virtue. Our dinner-table was arranged in a manner quite novel to me. In the centre of the table there was a china vase with a magnificent pyramid of flowers, and the whole table was covered with fruits, flowers, wine, and confectionary.

" Fruit of all kinds, in coat
Rough or smooth rind, or bearded husk or shell."

If you think the confectionary was not quite à la Paradise, remember Milton makes Eve to " temper dulcet creams" " from sweet kernels pressed." Considering her unfortunate love of delicacies, her skill, and the climate, nothing is more probable than that in the " fit vessels" which Milton mentions she converted her " dulcet creams" into ice. However that may be, Madame K.'s table looked

* The theatre at Frankfort was near our hotel, and it used to amuse me to see the people going to it with much the air of quietness and sobriety that you will see an assembly collecting for a lyceum lecture in a New-England village. Ladies go without any male attendant, and in their ordinary dress. The price of a box ticket is fifty cents. The orchestra is said to be one of the best in Germany. Does not all this indicate a high degree of civilisation?

like a sylvan feast. We had the most delicious atmosphere of fruits and flowers, instead of being stupified with the fumes of meat. There was no bustle of changing dishes, no thrusting in of servants' arms. The meat was carved and brought from an adjoining room. We had one of the very largest pineapples I ever saw, raised in Yorkshire * !

Kronthal.—OUR decision is made, and, instead of being on our way to Italy, here we are, close under the Taunus Hills, trying the virtue of a gas-bath, recently discovered. E. says you cannot turn up a stone with your foot in Germany without finding mineral water under it. The bathing-places are innumerable. The water here is very like in its taste to the Hamilton spring at Saratoga. The gas is conveyed in India-rubber pipes into a bathing-tub, in which you sit down dressed, and are shut in, except your head. The perceptible effect is a genial warmth and a slight moisture. We hear marvellous stories of its cures. It makes the deaf hear and the dumb speak ; and, in short, does what all other baths do, if you believe their believing champions. One rare advantage that we have here is a physician of excellent sense, and of a most kind and winning disposition ; another is, that we see the manners of the people of the country, without the slightest approach to foreign fashions or intermixture of foreign society. It is a two hours' drive to Frankfort, over a perfectly level plain. The Frankfort gentry come out every day with their children and servants, and seem to find quite pleasure enough in sitting down at a table before the door, and working worsted, knitting, smoking, drinking wine and Seltzer water, sipping coffee, and eating Mademoiselle Zimmerman's cakes, which are none of the most delicious. Her *very* frugal table must be rather a contrast to those of their luxurious homes ; but I never see a wry face, or hear a discontented word from them. Of a fine day the area before the door is covered with coteries of people, who have no amusement in common, none but such as I have mentioned ; these suffice. They interchange smiles and bows as often as they cross one another's path, and thus flow down the stream of life without ever ruffling a feather.

The Germans never stray beyond the gravelled walks around the house. Such quietude would kill us, so we appease our love and habit of movement with a daily donkey-ride among the Taunus Hills, or a walk through the lovely woodland paths. The famous castles of Kronberg (Crown-hill), Königstein (King's-stone), and Falkenstein are within a reasonable walk. Königstein has been an immense fortress, and its story is interwoven with the annals of the country. We visited the ruins yesterday. The girls wandered away, and left me with an Englishwoman, who, while I was admiring these irregular, romantic hills, and the sea-like plain that extends eastward from their base, without any visible bound, was telling me a marvellous tale, and an " o'er-true one," as she believed. Some other time I will give you the particulars ; I have now only space for the catastrophe. Two

* This mode of serving a dinner was, as I have said, quite novel to me ; but I am told that within the last few months it has become common in New York. So easily do we adopt foreign fashions !

American lovers, whether married or not no one knew, came to Königstein, mounted the loftiest part of the ruin, and, clasped in one another's arms, as the peasant-boy who saw them averred, threw themselves down. " It was from that old tower," said my companion ; " you see how tottering it looks : they say the view is better there ; but it is considered so unsafe that it is forbidden to mount it." I started up, not doubting that my girls, with the instinct that young people seem to have to get into places of peril, had gone there. I fancied them tumbling down after their sensible compatriots. I screamed to them, and was answered distinctly—by a well-mannered echo ! However, I soon found, by a little ragged boy, that they were loitering unharmed about the old tower, and I got them down before they had time to add to the American illustrations of Königstein.

To-day we have been to Falkenstein. It is one of the highest summits of the Taunus, near those loftiest pinnacles, the Fellberg and Alt König. There is a pretty story of a knight having won a daughter of Falkenstein by making a carriage-road in a single night up to the castle-wall ; the most sensible miracle I ever heard being required of a lover. The elf who lent him spades and pickaxes, and worked with him, demanded in payment the fee simple of some wild woodland hereabout. I like this story better than that in Schiller's ballad of the " Lord of Falkenstein." One does not like to mar such a scene as this with the spectre of a treacherous and cruel lover, or to remember, amid this rural peace and beauty, that there are sweet deceived young mothers whose spirits brood over the graves of the children they in madness murdered. And who that has seen Retzsch's exquisite sketch of the peasant-girl of Falkenstein can forget it ! We were there just before sunset. The little stone-built village lay in the deep shadow of the woodland steep which is crowned by the castle. It was a fête-day, and the villagers in their pretty costumes looked so happy and yet so poor, that they almost made me believe in the old adage, " No coin, no care." While the girls sat down to sketch, I escaped from a volunteer companion whose voice was as tiresome as a March wind, and getting into an embowered path, passed the prettiest little Gothic church I have seen since we were in the Isle of Wight. Here in the green earth, as the legend rudely scrawled above them tells you, " ruhen in Gott " (" rest in God") the generations that have passed from the village. Faith, hope, and memory linger about these graves. There are roses and heart's-ease rooted in the ground, and wooden crosses, images of saints, and freshly-platted garlands of flowers over the graves. What more could the richest mausoleum express ! I mounted through a fragrant copsewood to the castle—part rock and part masonry. The tower is standing, and waving from its top is some rich shrubbery, like a plume in a warrior's cap. Falkenstein village, close under the castle, looked like a brood of chickens huddled under its mother's wing. Kronberg and its towers were in shadow ; but the vast plain beyond was bathed in light, and the Maine and the Rhine were sparkling in the distance. All around me was a scene of savage Nature in her stern strength, all beyond of her motherly plentiful production. I

counted eighteen villages ; a familiar eye would probably have seen twice as many more. They are not easily distinguished from the earth, with which their colour blends harmoniously.

" Life is too short," we said, as we forced ourselves away just as the last ray of the sun was kissing the aforesaid green plume of the castle. We did not get home till it was quite dark, but we were as safe and unmolested as if we had been on our own hill-sides.

You will, I know, dear C., think there is " something too much" of these old castles and Taunus scenery ; but consider how they fill up our present existence. But I will be forbearing, and abridge a long, pleasant day's work we have had in going to Eppestein, a village in a *crack* of the Taunus, one of the narrowest, most secluded, wildest abodes that ever man sought refuge in ; for surely it must have been as a hiding-place it was first inhabited.

Some knight must have fled with a few faithful followers, and wedged them in here among the rocks and mountains. The lords have passed away, and the vassals are now peasants. We were invited into the habitation of one of them by a cheerful dame, whose " *jüngste* " (a blooming lassie) she introduced to *my youngest*. I am not willing to lose an opportunity of seeing the inside of a cottage ; hers was all that is habitable of the old castle, and is the neatest and most comfortable peasant's dwelling I have seen. The lord's kitchen was converted into the peasant's salon, where there was a good stove, antique chairs, a bureau, pictures, and a crucifix. In the kitchen I saw a very well filled dresser. The good woman was eager to hear of America ; some of her neighbours had gone there. " They had but money enough to carry them to the ship, and had since sent help to their friends." Strange, it seemed, that there should be a relation between this sequestered valley and our New World, and that our abundance should be setting back upon these poor people. " Ours is a fine country for the young," said I. " Yes," said an old woman from the corner, " but an old tree don't bear transplanting ! "

I should like you to have seen us taking our repast at the mill *Gasthaus*, seated on the pebbly plat in *settles* made of birchen sticks, served by a cheerful hostess, who sat knitting in the intervals of supplying our wants, and supplying them with ne-plus-ultra bread and butter, tender boiled beef, honey, Seltzer water, and wine : four hungry women for sixty cents. The mill-wheel kept its pleasant din the while, and another din there was that amused us from a handsome youth, who occupied a table near us, and who was telling the hostess, with frequent glances at us, of a visit he had paid to London. As he spoke in French, I presume it was more for our edification than that of our hostess. After a very picturesque account of the shocking disparity between the amount of food and the amount of the bill at an English inn, he concluded, " Ah, le triste sejour, que Londres ! On prie le bon Dieu tout le Dimanche—ça n'amuse pas* ! "

I can believe that England would be to a Ger-

---

* " Oh, what a dismal place London is ! They pray all day long on Sunday—not very amusing that ! "

man traveller with stinted means one continued fast and penance.

WE saw to-day fifty peasants gathered under a chestnut tree, and an auction going on ; but as we saw no wares, we were at a loss what to make of it, till we were told the duke's chestnuts were selling. Chestnuts are an article of food here. This neighbourhood abounds in thriving nurseries, which are a main source of revenue to the peasants. There is one on the hill-side, opposite my window. It covers thirty acres, and is divided into small proprieties, and owned by the peasants of Kronberg, to whom it brings an annual revenue of 10,000 florins (4000 dollars) : a shower of gold on these children of toil and hardship.

A labourer in haying and harvesting, the busiest season of the year, is paid one florin twelve kreutzers a day (fifty cents), and finds himself, and works earlier and later than our people. If he works for several days consecutively for one employer, he is allowed a trifle more as *trinkgeld*. A female domestic, in a family where only one servant is kept, is fed and paid twenty florins a year (eight dollars ! !) ; and for this pitiful sum she gives effective, patient, and *cheerful* labour. An accomplished cook can earn twenty-four dollars !

The perfect blending of self-respect with deference, of freedom with courtesy, in the manners of the subordinate classes in Germany, puzzles me. They are, as you perceive by the rate of wages, quite as dependent on their employers as in England, but I have never seen an instance of cringing servility or insolence. The servants are indefatigable in their attendance, grateful for a small gratuity, and always meet your social overtures frankly and cheerfully. A seamstress sewed for us for two or three weeks, a quiet, modest, and respectful girl ; when she parted from us, she kissed us all, including R.,—not our hands, but fairly on the cheek ; a demonstration to which, as she was young and very pretty, neither he nor you would object.

I bought some trunks at Frankfort of a man, who, when we had closed our traffic, asked me to go up stairs and look at his rooms, and the picture of his wife ; and when he saw my pleasure in his very clean, well-furnished home, he said it was all their own earning ; that they had not much, but they had contented minds, and " that made a little go a great way." When he brought home the trunks, he brought his two little boys to see us. I could tell you fifty similar anecdotes, which all go to prove that the bond of brotherhood is sound and strong among them.

The family ties seem to be very strictly maintained. Children are kept much longer in subordination to their parents, and dependence on them, than we have any notion of. The period of minority may be almost said to extend through the parents' life. A very clever German woman lamented to me the effect of an English education upon the habits of her son. And, by the way, she considered his reluctance to submit to the restraints of his father's house, and his notion of complete independence and escape from the thraldom of his minority, to have been perfected by a year's travel in America. After telling me that he had refused to occupy a suite of apartments in his father's house, because he could not submit to be asked,

" Where were you yesterday ? " " Where do you go to-morrow ? " she concluded with, " But I have nothing to complain of—he is a very good young man, but he is no longer a German. We should have foreseen this when we sent him to England. We cannot expect if we plant cabbages they will come up potatoes."

The strict union of families seems to me to be promoted by the general cultivation of music. I say *seems* to me, my dear C. ; for, conscious of my very limited opportunities of observation, I give you my impressions with unaffected diffidence. Almost every member of a family is in some sort a musical performer, and thus is domesticated the most social and exciting of the arts. You would be astonished at the musical cultivation in families where there is no other accomplishment.

There is one of the rights of women secured to them here which I have been assured has an important effect on general prosperity and individual happiness. The German wife has an inextinguishable right to half the joint property of herself and her husband. He cannot deprive her of it by will, nor can it be applied to debts of his contracting. " This it is," said a gentleman to me, " that makes our wives so intelligent in the management of their concerns, so industrious and economical." I don't know how this may be ; but it seems to me to be but common justice that a wife should be an equal partner in a concern of which she bears so heavy a part of the burden. Would not the introduction of such a law have a beneficent effect on the labouring classes in the United States ? How many women would be stimulated to ingenuity and productive labour, if the results of their industry were secured to them ! How many women are first wronged and then disheartened by having an inheritance consumed by a husband's vices, or dispersed by his wild speculations ! How many, well qualified for respectable branches of business, are deterred from attempting them by the impossibility of securing to themselves and their children the proceeds ! How many poor women among the lowest class of labourers have you and I both known, whose daily earnings have been *lawfully* taken from them by their brutal husbands ! This is a pretty serious evil, as in that class at least (you will allow me to say) the destructive vices are pretty much monopolised by your sex.

It is one of our distinctions, thank God, in the New World, that we do not quietly rest in any error ; so I have faith that in good time this matter will be set right.

It is impossible to witness the system of general instruction in Germany, without asking if the rulers are not making an experiment dangerous to the maintenance of their absolutism. Debarred as the lower orders are from all political action, it may be some time before they use the " sharp-edged tools" put into their hands ; and when they once begin to read, to reflect, and to compare, they will hardly go on quietly wearing a master's uniform, doing his work, and eating black bread and potatoes, as if this were their full and fair share.

When you look at the highly-educated classes, at the diffusion of knowledge among them, and consider the activity, boldness, and freedom of the German mind, you are confounded at the apparent serenity and quietude. But is it not the serenity

E

of the mighty ocean, that wants but the moving of the wind to rise in resistless waves!—the quietude of the powder-magazine, inert only till the spark touches it!

We are not in a way to hear political topics agitated. They make no part of general conversation. But I have met with some touching expressions of feelings that I imagine are much diffused under this placid surface of society. One of our German friends spoke to me with deep emotion of her aunt, who is just embarking for the United States. "She is leaving us all," she said; "her children and grandchildren, brothers, nephews, nieces, all the friends of a lifetime—and such a happy home, to go and live with one son in the backwoods of America."

"Is that son so much a favourite!" I asked.

"Oh, no; but he and his brother have suffered for their political opinions. They were imprisoned eight years; one of them died. *He* was a favourite—and so good, so beloved by everybody! My aunt says she cannot breathe the air of Germany. She must have the free air of America!"

There is a captain in the Austrian army at Kronthal for his health, a man about fifty, with a most melancholy expression of countenance. Ever since he knew we were Americans he has manifested an interest in us. He has asked many questions about the country, and let fall on various occasions, in an under tone, his respect for our free institutions. His extreme despondency affected me, and I took an opportunity to endeavour to inspire him with hope in the efficacy of the waters. I repeated to him every instance I had heard of benefit in cases similar to his. At each he shook his head mournfully, and then explained why the "amen stuck in the throat." "It is not my disease," he said; "that may be cured, but it is my incurable position. What am I but a mere tool in the hands of the men of power, employed to watch every generous movement, and support the wrong against the right!" It wants but that this feeling should be a little more general, and the oppressor's rod will be broken.

I leave this country with an interest, respect, and attachment that I did not expect to feel for any country after leaving England. I rather think the heart grows by travelling! I feel richer for the delightful recollections I carry with me of the urbanity of the Germans. Never can I forget the "Guten Tag," "Guten Abend," and "Gute Nacht," ("good-day," "good-evening," and "good-night,") murmured by the soft voices of the peasants from under their drooping loads as we passed them in our walks. Addison says that the general salutations of his type of all benignity. Sir Roger de Coverley, came from the "overflowings of humanity,"—so surely did these. On the whole, the Germans seem to me the most rational people I have seen. We never "are," but always "to be blessed." They enjoy the present, and, with the truest economy of human life, make the most of the materials of contentment that God has given them. Is not this better than vague, illimitable desires, and ever changing pursuits *!

* I cannot be understood to say, or suspected of intimating, that Germany impressed me as happier than our country of general activity, progress, and equalised prosperity. No, every American must feel, wherever he

---

Basle, Switzerland, Sept. 23.

WE have been seven days on the way from Frankfort to this place, a distance of 225 miles. We have posted—a most comfortable mode of travelling in Germany. The postilions are civil, the horses strong and well broken, and changed every six miles. There is no *fast* driving—that would be perfectly *un*-German—but far more to my liking; it is cautious, safe, and uniform. Driving rapidly through a new and beautiful country seems to me in the same good taste as walking with a quick step through a gallery of pictures. Our posting expenses have been at the rate of twelve dollars for thirty-six miles; this, for seven persons, is lower than our ordinary stage-coach fare at home. And how superior the accommodation! You can travel just as far, and stop when, and as long as you please. We have often wished we could turn W.'s corner and drive up to your door, and hear the shouts of the children at what would seem to them a very grotesque appearance. The leaders, attached with rope-traces, are so far from the wheel-horses, that our equipage must be about thirty feet in length. The postilion sits on the near-wheel horse, and guides the leaders with rope reins. He and his horses are all stout, heavy-moulded, and reliable. He wears a short blue coat, turned up behind with red tips. His trumpet is suspended by a cord, from which two huge tassels of bright-coloured worsteds hang bobbing down his back. His breeches are of yellow buckskin, and his boots are cut up to a point in front some inches above the knee, and the whole pleasure of his profession seems to be to keep up an eternal cracking of his whip, which, I found to my surprise, after two or three days' annoyance, we minded no more than his horses did †.

The roads are excellent; quite as good, it seems to me, as the English roads, that is to say, *perfect.* We travelled one hundred and eighty miles without passing an elevation of more than fifteen or twenty feet at the utmost. It is like a road through a meadow, raised some ten or twelve feet above the adjacent ground. This is probably from the accumulation of stones and dirt brought on from year to year to repair it. This level road is called (for some distance) *Berg-strasse* (mountain-road) because it runs parallel to a range of hills which bound your view on the east of the Rhine. R. insisted they had been swung back like a gate for the traveller to pass; and so it appears. They start forth at once from the low ground, without any preparatory slope or an intervening hill, and there they stand as if they had just stepped out of your way. They are covered to their summits with corn and vines, and castle-crowned, of course. It would be as strange to see a man in Berkshire

goes from home, that his is the happiest country for the general interests of humanity—*the favoured land*; but let us remember there are some compensations to other countries—and thank God for it—and imbibe, if we can, their spirit of contentment and enjoyment.

† Posting here, and generally on the Continent, is monopolised by the government. With our preconceived notions of individual rights, we were startled, on arriving at a post-station where there was a deficiency of horses, to hear the postmaster order an impressment of peasants' horses. What would our friends, *Colonel* W. or *Major* D., the gentlemen-yeomen of S., say to such a procedure? We should have a revolution.

standing out of door without his hat, as a hill here without its o'ertopping castle. On our right stretches a vast sandy plain, with the Rhine gliding through it, and bounded, at some sixty miles' distance, by the Vosges—French mountains. You might fancy a painter had laid out the road, so pretty are the views of the villages, so fortunately does the spire of a cathedral come in here and a village church there. The road is often on the outskirts of orchards, and bordered by an avenue of fruit-trees that extend from town to town. At almost every post we observed a new costume. It seemed like the shifting scenes of the theatre. Here we pass peasants and peasant-boys driving their carts, with three-cornered hats such as our old ministers wore. Six miles farther, there were fifty peasant-girls seated on the ground, picking hops from the vine, with immense tortoise-shell combs in their hair. A few miles farther on we saw them scattered over a hay-field, with hats wide enough for umbrellas ; and the next change was a little high-crowned hat with a narrow brim. Here were girls driving a cart drawn by cows, with enormous black bows on the top of their heads, and a few miles further, old women *shovelling out manure*, with red velvet caps bordered with black lace. The prettiest costumes we saw, and they would have done honour to a Parisian *improvisatore des modes* (there are such people, I believe), were on a fête-day at Freyberg. Beside all the varieties I have mentioned, we had, in their holiday freshness, skullcaps of black and coloured velvet, prettily embroidered with silver and gold, and long braids of hair hanging behind and tied with ribands that touched the ground—bodices of velvet with slashed sleeves. Some wore simply a bosom-piece worked with beads, and others had bright-coloured handkerchiefs tied round their throats, and their skirts bound with bright-coloured ribands. Contrast this in your imagination with the working-dresses of our working people. Why, it is the difference between tropical birds and a flock of tame *she*-pigeons !

As we made Southing, we noticed some productions that we had not seen before. Tobacco-fields have abounded. In approaching Freyberg we saw pretty fair patches of Indian corn ; and to-day, trailing down the terraces, our own honest, broad-faced pumpkin has greeted us. The grapes are obviously nearer the vintage. I bought a magnificent bunch yesterday, and, holding it up as I came in so as to display its broad shoulders, said, " I gave but seven kreutz' for this !" " Ah, ça commence !" exclaimed François, his eyes gleaming with his Italian reminiscences.

There are vineyards of wide-spread fame on this route. We drank a delicious red wine at " The Fortune " at Offenburg, kept by Pfählers, called Affenthaler. Our landlord told us he made 50,000 bottles a year, and had had orders from New York. I wish he may have more, and everything else that may minister to his prosperity ; and so I am sure all must wish who have enjoyed, as we did, the comforts and luxuries of " The Fortune."

The first bad bread we have eaten in Europe— a villanous composition with carraway seeds—was at Bruchsal. One would think *good* bread would be one of the first products of any society one advance beyond the savage state ; but we know

that our country is not yet old enough to have perfected the art of making it. Perhaps the reason of the difference is, that with us, except in the large towns, it depends on individual skill, knowledge, *virtue*, and is exposed to various family mischances, whereas in Europe it is uniformly made in bakeries. Heaven speed the time when we shall have no more sour bread, hot bread, heavy bread, bread made with " milk risings," and with no risings at all ! " distressful bread" truly !

We have passed through some very interesting towns on this route, and done travellers' duty in seeing their lions : Darmstadt, not at all interesting, by-the-way, though the residence of the Duke of Hesse Darmstadt. It is filled with gigantic houses, from which the giant proprietors seem to have run away ; a more empty-looking town you never beheld. Heidelberg, with its magnificent old castle, its picturesque sites, and the scenery on the Neckar around it, is worth coming all this way to see.

At Carlsruhe there is the palace of the Grandduke of Baden, and old, extensive, and beautifully-adorned pleasure-grounds, to which the public have free access.

Baden-Baden is, as you know, the most famous watering-place in Germany. As its waters have no longer much reputation, it must owe its chief attraction to the beauty of the scenery. In its natural features it resembles the northern towns in our own Berkshire ; but, with all my home prepossessions, I must confess that it is more beautiful even than Williamstown ; more beautiful, I mean, in its natural aspect. As to what man has built, from the cottage to the cathedral, the difference between the Old and New World is—unmeasurable. In the material, form, and colour of our buildings, we have done, for the most part, all we could do to deform the fair face of our nature. All that we can say for them is, that they are either of so perishable a material, or so slightly put together, that they cannot last long ; and when they are to be replaced, we may hope that the inventive genius of our people, guided by the rules of art, will devise an architecture for us suited to our condition, and embodying the element of beauty. I say " suited to our condition ;" for it is very plain that where property is so diffused as to make individual possession and comfort all but universal, and where society is broken into small multitudinous sects, we have no occasion for the stately palaces, the ducal residences, the cathedrals and splendid churches of Europe ; nor shall we have the beautiful *comfortless* cottage niched in an old tower, or made of the fragments of a castle-wall, so enchanting to the eye in the picture-scenes here. After all, dear C., when I get home, and have nothing to see but our scrawny farm-houses, excrescences, wens as they are on the fair earth, it will be rather a comfort to think they are occupied by those that *own* them ; that under those unsightly, *unthatched*, shingled roofs are independent, clean, and abundant homes, and a *progressive* people. Still, with patriotism, common sense, and, I may add, but a common gratitude to Providence for our home-condition, *on the whole*, I cannot but sigh as I look back upon the delight we had yesterday in seeing surely the most exquisitely beautiful of all cathedrals, the Cathedral of Freyberg, and in joining in the vesper service there in the twilight of the preceding evening : yes, joining, for surely dull must be the spirit that does not allow free course to its devotional instincts in such a place and at such an hour, while people of all conditions are kneeling together. You do not ask or think by what name their religion is called. You feel that the wants of their natures are the wants of your own, and your worship is spontaneous, which it is not *always* in our pharisaical pews, amid a finely-dressed congregation, and while listening to a sermon written for the élite of the élite. Dear C., let us see things as they are ; depend on it, the old faith, with all its corruptions and absurdities, is, in a few of its *usages*, nearer to the Christian source than the new.

We went to the Cathedral again and again, walked round it, and to different points of view, and mounted up a vine-covered hill, and sat down under a crucifix, whence for an hour we gazed on it, and finally looked our last after leaving Freyberg, when the last rays of the sun were upon it, and it was set off by a background of the Black Forest. Our sensations were like those you get from reading an exquisite old poem.

To come to the prose of the matter, the Cathedral was begun some eight hundred years ago, and is the only large Gothic church in Germany which is completed. The tower is finished with a spire ; and though of so ponderous a material as stone, so light in its effect as to give you the idea (it did give it to L.) of an arrow shooting from the bow. I can go on and give you dimensions, colour, and form ; but, after all, there is nothing for you but to come and see *.

Berne, Sept. 25.

MY DEAR C.—MY last letter was from Basle, a town containing twenty-one thousand inhabitants, and our first resting-place in Switzerland. It is at the head of the navigation of the Rhine, and the current is here so rapid and the ascent so difficult, that, as we looked out from the windows of our hotel, *Drei Könige,* whose walls it washes, we should have thought it impossible but for witnessing the fact. We walked out on the terraces over the ramparts, overlooking on one side the Rhine, and on the other beautiful surroundings, bounded by the Jura, the Vosges, and the Black Forest.

We went to the Minster ; not to admire it, for it is a huge clumsy edifice of the eleventh century ; its antiquity desecrated with that Protest-

ant innovation—pews. But we were attracted by a bust of Erasmus, and a monument to him. He and other distinguished reformers were buried here. It did not strike me quite agreeably to see the memorials of these men in a church whose faith they had dissolved, and whose worship they had subjugated. This is too much like converting a conquered enemy's holiest possessions into trophies.

Basle is Holbein's birthplace ; and we saw there a collection of his pictures and sketches—a few of the originals of his most celebrated pictures. It is always interesting to go to the birthplace of a man of genius. However far his fame has extended, there his heart has rested ; that has been the scene of his affections, and, of course, of the happiest hours of his life.

At Basle posting ended, and we took a voiturier†. Shortly after leaving Basle we passed a spot memorable in Swiss history, where a battle was fought in 1444 between the Swiss and French. The Swiss fought with invincible courage, and killed tenfold their number. It was the unblenching valour displayed on this occasion, that led a French monarch to select the Swiss for his bodyguard, and, of course, from this epoch, from this battle-ground, dates the employment of Swiss as mercenaries. This is a foul blot on their escutcheon, but they have done what could be done to diminish it, by serving with a fidelity that has passed into a proverb.

On leaving Bienne we mounted a hill, whence we saw the Lake of Bienne and the lovely island where Rousseau lived ; and it was while we were on this hill that a cry went from mouth to mouth of, "The Alps ! the Alps ! the Alps !" Our hearts and—yes, I will tell you the whole truth— our eyes were full ; for how, but by knowing how we felt, can you estimate the sensations they are fitted to produce ? We have heard of the Alps all our lives. We have read descriptions of them in manuscript and print, in prose and poetry ; we knew their measurement ; we have seen sketches, and paintings, and models of them ; and yet, I think, if we had looked into the planet Jupiter, we could scarcely have felt a stronger emotion of surprise. In truth, up, up, where they hung and shone, they seemed to belong to heaven rather

---

* My readers will thank me, I am sure, for condensing into a few pages my journal of our route from Frankfort to Basle. It was full of variety and beauty in the external world, but there was little incident and no character ; and it requires a skilful artist to make his landscape attractive without figures. We became ourselves tired of the repetition of descriptions of villages and castles ; and, finally, we amused ourselves with making the following summary of epithets. For castles :—" beautiful, brooding, baronial, crowning, elevated, lofty, high, grand, magnificent, superb, sublime, lordly, mounted, mouldering, murky, perched, springing up, suspended, overlooking, watching, protecting, guardian, smiling, frowning, threatening, lowering, hovering, hung, towering, decayed, dilapidated, crumbling, ruinous, picturesque, lovely, light, airy, massy, heavy." Villages :—" Pitched, perched, planted, embosomed, lapped, cradled, nested, sheltered, hidden, concealed, cribbed, ensconced, peeping, terraced." We had the modesty to call them *synonymes.*

† An individual undertakes with one set of horses to conduct you for one or two days, or all over Europe, if you please. They travel from twenty-five to forty miles a day, starting and stopping at an hour agreed on, and resting two hours in the middle of the day. Your postilion is seldom the owner of the horses, but always a reliable person, and we found him uniformly civil: his civility is indeed secured by his wages in some measure depending on the satisfaction he gives. You pay fifteen francs a day for each horse (this includes return fare) ; five francs a day, if he serves you well, to your postilion ; and five francs a day for each horse whenever you wish to lie by. In Italy, perhaps elsewhere, it is very common for the voiturier to provide for you at the inns. In this case you make a contract with him as to the kind and mode of your supplies, and the price to be paid. On the first of two occasions when we tried this we were perfectly well served ; but on a second, being not so well served, we preferred travelling less trammelled, and not quite so much in the fashion of a bale of goods. On the whole, when the roads are good, and the days not at the shortest, to *elderly people* voiturier travelling is a very agreeable mode. We would not recommend it to the impatient or the young, who like to put a girdle " round the earth in forty minutes."

than earth; and yet, such is the mystery of the spirit's kindred with the effulgent beauty of God's works, that they seemed

> " A part
> Of me and of my soul, as I of them."

François ordered the postilion to stop, and for a minute not a sound broke the delicious spell. The day, fortunately, was favourable. The whole range of the Bernese Alps was before us, unclouded, undimmed by a breath of vapour. There they were, like glittering wedges cleaving the blue atmosphere. I had no anticipation of the exquisite effect of the light on these aërial palaces, of a whiteness as glittering and dazzling as the garments of the angels, and the contrast of the *black* shadows, and here and there golden and rose-coloured hues. I have no notion of attempting to describe them; but you shall not reproach me, as we, so soon as we recovered our voices, reproached all our travelled friends with, " Why did not they tell us?" " How cruel, how stupid to let any one live and die without coming to see the Alps!" This morning was an epoch in our lives.

I LEFT them lunching at Aarberg, and walked on alone. I heard with a miser's feeling every minute in this beautiful country. All my life I have been longing to come to Switzerland, and now so rapid must be our passage through it, it seems as if, like the rainbow, it would fade away while I am looking at it. The softer, the comparatively *very* tame parts of it, remind me of our own home surroundings, which we have always deemed and which are so romantically lovely. This resemblance, and the little domestic scenes I passed while straying on alone, gave me a home feeling. Once I sat down on a bridge to look at some peasant women who were dressing flax on a grassy bank sloping to the water's edge, while their children were dabbling in the brook. A little girl, of her own kind will, left her playmates, came straying on to the bridge, and sat down by me, looking up in my face with a sweet, trustful expression, as if she had grown at my side. I perceived one of the flax-dressers suspend her hetchelling to watch our by-play, and, toil-worn, weather-beaten as she was, it was easy to see, in her pleased attention, that she was the mother of the fair, dimpled, bright-eyed little creature beside me. She was a picture in her pretty Bernese costume. I asked her question upon question about her black lace fly-cap, her braids, and chains, and bodice; and she replied, and, though our words were in an unknown tongue, we had no need of an interpreter. She had got her arm around my neck; and as I took her dimpled hand in mine, I was tempted to cross it with silver, but I checked the impulse in time, not to substitute for the kindly feeling that for the moment had knit the little stranger to me, a sordid emotion. It would have been a disturbance of Nature's sympathies and affinities. There should be other intercourse than mere giving and taking between the rich and the poor; it would be well for both parties.

Berne.—I stood in the balcony of Professor V.'s house this morning, while his son pointed out the different summits of the Bernese Alps and gave me their names. It seemed something like being introduced to so many illustrious heroes; and so they are; for there they have stood battling it with the elements since their foundations were laid, inspiring in each generation, as it came and passed, awe and delight. You can hardly imagine a position within the bounds of a town so lovely as that of Professor V.'s house. It has a terraced garden in the rear extending to the Aar more than a hundred feet below it, a stream with a *Swiss* voice. Then think of having these Alps for your daily companions — of the dawn and the sunset upon them! Professor V.'s wife is the sister of our friend Doctor Follen. They assembled their family (very charming young people) and some of their friends to see us. I hardly enjoyed this scene, for, whether I looked out of the window or in, I could only think of our beloved friend, and of what it had cost him to break the ties that bound him to his glorious country and to such kindred. Those who achieve liberty in their homes can hardly estimate the love of freedom, the devotion to human rights, that drives such a man as Charles Follen into voluntary and perpetual exile !

We pride ourselves on the asylum our country offers to the champions of liberty who have become the victims of the Old World's oppressors. This they owe to our fathers. Is not our welcome too often a cold and stinted one? Do we not often regard them with distrust, rather than supply to them, as far as may be, the lost charities of home?

Geneva, Sept. 28.

MY DEAR C.—This place, so long a city of refuge to the victims of a persecuting creed, has a peculiar interest to all lovers of religious liberty. As religious freedom is a natural spur to intellect, Geneva has long been, and is yet, a focus of great names, which have extended indefinitely the intellectual dominions of this little canton; so little, that Voltaire said,—" When I shake out my wig, I powder the whole republic !"

There is nothing very attractive in the aspect of the town. There is the usual opposition found in the Continental towns, of the romantic to the useful, in the contrast between the picturesque, inconvenient old structures, and the modern, light, commodious buildings. Lake Leman you and all the civilised world have by heart through Byron's poetry and Rousseau's eloquent descriptions; and what a world of tiresome journal-reading, " skimble-skamble stuff," you are saved thereby ! We are at an hotel on the Rhone, just where it issues from the lake; " the arrowy Rhone" it truly is here. The water is of an indigo blue colour, a peculiarity which Sir Humphry Davy imputes to the presence of iodine.

We went to the Cathedral this morning, attracted by its association with Calvin's name. It was here this great man preached when he was exercising almost unlimited sway over the consciences and lives of the Genevese, and here he promulged those doctrines that are still the rule

---

* I have omitted our journey from Berne to Geneva, as we retraced this route in 1840, and then passed some most delightful weeks in Switzerland, which came into a subsequent portion of my letters.

of faith to the strictest sects of the religious world. There are various opinions as to the soundness of his doctrines; but no one can question the mental energy of a man, a private individual, and a stranger, who, by the mere force of his fulminations, governed, and with the severest rein, the dress, the dinners, and the amusements of this community.

We found a large congregation listening intently to a preacher, who set before them the duties resulting from the superior light their fathers had enjoyed. He made use of one very discreet tactic. During the sermon he made three pauses of about two minutes each, which not only gave him time to draw his breath and arrange his thoughts, but provided a safety-valve, by which the coughs and other impertinent sounds so annoying were let off, and on we glided in silent attention. The benediction that closed the service was a pleasing variation from the common formula. "Allez en paix, *souvenez-vous des pauvres*, et que la paix de Dieu reste avec vous *!*" You can hardly imagine, my dear C., what a refreshment a good sermon is to those who are deprived, Sunday after Sunday, of their accustomed religious services. The sermon was apparently extempore, and delivered with an unction that delighted us. On coming out, we learned we had heard M. Cockerel of Paris, a celebrated evangelical preacher.

Towards evening, K. and I drove out to M. Sismondi's. He resides at Chesne. We drove away from the lake on a level road, past pleasant villas, and in face of Mont Blanc; thickly veiled his face was though, and, as we are told, he does not show it, on an average, more than sixty times a year. After a pleasant drive of a mile and a half, we reached M. Sismondi's house, a low, cottage-like building, with a pretty hedge before it, and ground enough about it to give it an air of seclusion and refinement. On the opposite side of the road, and withdrawn from it, is a Gothic church, shaded by fine old trees; and before it is the Salève, and Mont Blanc for a back-ground. I envied those who could sit down on the stone benches in the broad vestibule of the church, with these glorious high altars before them. It pleased me to find Sismondi's home in a position so harmonising with the elevation and tranquillity of his philosophic mind. As we drove up the serpentine approach to his door, I felt a little trepidation, lest I might not find a friend in my long and intimate correspondent—a natural dread of the presence of a celebrated man; but I had no sooner seen his benignant face, and heard the earnest tones of his kind welcome, than I felt how foolish, how pitiful was such a dread; and that I might as well have feared going into the sunshine, or into the presence of any other agent, however powerful, that is the source of general health and happiness. To our surprise, we found we were expected. Confalonieri is in Geneva, and, expecting to intercept us, has delayed for some days his return to Paris.

After an hour we came away perfectly satisfied. Not a look, a word, or tone of voice had reminded us that we were meeting for the first time. We seemed naturally, and with the glow of personal

intercourse, to be carrying on the thread of an acquaintance that we had been all our lives weaving. I can say nothing truer, nor to you more expressive, than that the atmosphere of home seemed to enfold us. You would like to know how M. Sismondi looks. I can tell you that he is short, stout, and rather thick; that he has a dark complexion, plenty of black hair, and brilliant hazel eyes; and then you will have just about as adequate a notion of his soul-lit face as you would have of the beauty of Monument Mountain, the Housatonic, and our meadows, if you had never seen the sun shine upon them or the shadows playing over them. I sometimes think it matters not what the original structure is, when the character is written on it, and the golden light of the soul shines over it. It is a very common opinion, but is it not an erroneous one, that you cannot form a correct opinion of an author from his works? Nine-tenths (ninety-nine hundredths!) of authors, so called, are mere collectors—*rifacitori*—ingenious makers of patchwork. An original writer writes with earnestness and sincerity. As Titian is said to have ground up flesh to produce his true colouring, so their works are a portion of their spirits; the book is, in fact, the man.

WE dined at Chesne to-day. Madame S. insisted we should all come, saying, in her kindest manner, "It is but sitting a little closer;" and turning to Confalonieri, "We do not give entertainments; but it is better than Spielberg, my dear count." We found everything as we would wish to find it in the house of a liberal friend. Married people without children have always seemed to me much like mutes, but here I do not miss them—affections that flow full and free will make their own channels. Sismondi rarely dines out, and "has not," Madame S. says, "in his life drunk a half-glass of wine beyond what was good for him;" and surely he has his reward in a clear head, and unshaken hand. He is sixty-seven. Madame S. expressed her regret that he was so near the allotted term of life, while "he had yet so much to do." "I wish," she added, playfully, "that I were nineteen, and my husband twenty-one." Sismondi replied, that he should not care to live his life over again; "it had been so happy, he should not dare to trust the chances." We in our rash love would have exclaimed, "O king, live for ever!" forgetting that he will live for ever without "the chances."

I inquired after a pair of lovers who had suffered from a forbidden attachment, and whose marriage had been effected by Sismondi's intervention. A letter had just been received from the wife expressing in the strongest terms her happiness. Madame S. said "it was indeed a satisfaction to have made one human being happy." "One, and it may be more," added Sismondi; "for there is already one child, and there may be many more." Is it not a sign of a healthy moral condition when a man of sixty-seven takes it for granted that existence is happiness?

You should have heard the clatter of our young people as we drove away. "Who would think M. Sismondi was a celebrated savant!" exclaimed L.; "I should never think of his being a great author, or anything but the best and kindest of men." "Did you observe," said M., whose Ame-

---

* "Go in peace, remember the poor, and may the peace of God dwell with you."

rican feeling is always at welding heat, "how perfectly well informed he is about America, even to the smallest details?" K. declared that, though she had ridiculed the idea of falling in love at first sight, she had already plunged so deep into an affection for Sismondi that she began to think such a catastrophe possible. And then came other characteristic remarks; L. maintaining that "Madame S. could not be an Englishwoman, she was so gentle and lovely!" and M. saying she was like the best specimens of American women—like E. F. and S.; and we finally laid aside all our national biases *pour et contre*, and finished by agreeing that she is

"That kind of creature we could most desire
To honour, serve, and love."

K. AND I walked out this morning to breakfast with the Sismondis. It was scarcely nine when we sat down to the table. He breakfasted on curds and cream, and on these delicate articles Madame S. says he expends all his *gourmandise*. Nine is not late now (October 6), and he had already written three letters and several graceful stanzas for some lady's album. It is by these well-ordered habits of diligence that he accomplishes such an immensity of work. And with all this labour his mind is as free, as much at ease as if he had nothing in the world to do but make his social home the cheerful place it is. He spoke in terms of high commendation of Prescott's Ferdinand and Isabella, but he thought Mr. P. had painted his heroine-queen *en beau*, and he went on to express his detestation of her bigotry, and his horror of its tremendous effects. We women contended for her conjugal and maternal character. "And what," he asked, "had she done for her children but educate a madwoman?" Madame S. reminded him of Catharine of Aragon. "But she," he said, "was not Isabella's daughter." We all smiled, and I said, that I was glad to find him at fault in a point of history. "Ah!" he replied, "history for me is divided into two parts: that which I have written and forgotten, and that which I have not written and have not yet learned."

M. Sismondi was to bring us to town in his carriage, and, before setting off, there was a good-humoured conjugal discussion who, of a swarm of strangers, all, of course, with letters to the Sismondis, were to be invited there in the evening. Madame S. objected to Lady So-and-so; "she would talk 'tittery tattery;'" and to Madame —, who "would come expecting a grand soirée." Sismondi pleaded for all, and finally came away to make his visits to these people with much the feeling that a bountiful man has in going among the poor with a purse full of money, which he feels coerced to withhold by the reigning theories of political economy. And *apropos* of political economy, Sismondi remarked this morning that the English political economists had quite overlooked the most striking circumstance in the condition of the Continental peasantry, that is, that they are either the absolute proprietors of the land they cultivate, or they are metayers, that is, they cultivate it on shares. The lease is sometimes for three hundred years. You see at once this gives a stability and dignity to their condition which the English tenant has not; and the pride

and pleasure of family transmission, and thus an extension of their being.

I asked if the working classes here were making progress. He said "No; on the contrary, there was less development of mind than fifty years ago, for then there existed a law, now annulled, forbidding a master-workman to employ more than two journeymen. Now the tendency of things is to make great capitalists, and to reduce the mass of men to mere 'mechanicals.' As to progress with the peasantry, that was quite out of the question." What a strange and death-like condition this seems to us! When I think of the new, the singularly happy condition of our people among the working classes of the world, I am vexed at their solemn, anxious faces. If they have all outward prosperity, they have not that cheerfulness of the countenance which the wise man says betokeneth the prosperity of the heart. There is something wrong in this—some contravention of Providence.

I MET M. de Candolle last evening at a soirée at Sismondi's. Besides having the greatest name in Europe as a botanist, he is a most agreeable person. He and Sismondi talked across me most courteously of our country, and with a minuteness of information that showed what an interesting field it is to the philosopher and the man of science. De Candolle spoke respectfully of our botanists, Grey, Nuttall, and Elliott, and dwelt on the superior richness of our country, for the botanist, to Europe. "America is for me and not for Sismondi," he said; "for you have no history." He does not imagine how much we make of our little!

There were some dozen people present, and we took our tea round the tea-table, which was spread with biscuits, cake, sweetmeats, and fruit, quite in the rural fashion of New-England. The English, we are told, laugh at this mode of hospitality, and desecrate Lake Leman with the homely title of "*Tea-water Lake*." When will the English learn to look with a philosophic eye on customs that differ from their own?

There was a gentleman present who enacted the part of the fly on the wheel, making a prodigious buzzing. He seemed particularly disturbed with the idea of women intermeddling in politics, but graciously concluded by conceding "they might know what they would on the subject provided they did not talk about it." "On the contrary," said De Candolle, "they may talk as much as they please provided they know nothing." So, pardon the vulgar proverb, the fool put us into the frying-pan, and the wise man pushed us into the fire!

De Candolle adverted to the curious subject of relative happiness. He said you might know the moment of passing from a Protestant to a Catholic canton by the extreme wretchedness of the people; and yet they were far more gay than their Protestant neighbours *. This he imputed in part to their throwing off the burden of their sins every Sunday, and in part to their having no anxious dreams of improving their condition; to their

---

* At the Reformation, the religion of each canton was decided by vote; in some cases by a majority of only one or two voices. The dissenters acquiesced or removed: "Dieu bénisse la plus grande voix," was their motto; their version of "*Vox populi, vox Dei.*"

being, in short, in that respect, in the condition of the brutes that are grazing in the fields. M. De Candolle is right ; it is those " who *have* a prospect " that strain every nerve to press forward. It is the foreseeing, the providing, the *calculating*, that shadows over the countenances of an ever-onward people with anxiety. With so much good we must take the evil patiently *.

Sunday evening.—WE have just returned from taking tea with the Sismondis. Madame S. spoke of the Genevese woman as the most exemplary she has ever known : this, mind ye, is the opinion of an Englishwoman. They are reproached, she says, with being *raide* and pedantic in their virtues, but she maintains that " it is exactness, not pedantry." She attributes much of the merit of their strict performance of their moral duties to the pastors of Geneva. Every young person, on attaining the age of fifteen, enters on a course of religious instruction from the pastor, which excludes other studies and all amusements. All ranks are comprised in this sacred study and noviciate. The neophyte is examined at the end of the year, and, if found wanting, the instruction is extended through another year. When admitted to the communion, she appears dressed in white, veiled, and attended by her friends, and a discourse is preached touching the duties and dangers of her future life. All this must make a deep impression on the mind at its most susceptible period. Madame S. says she has often been astonished at the nice discrimination of her domestics on moral subjects ; and when she asked, " Where did you learn this ? " they replied, " Ah, madam, we learned a great deal during our year of instruction ! "

There is another old institution in Geneva to which she imputes much virtue. This is the *Société des Dimanches* (the " Sunday Society "). When a girl attains the age of five years, she is made a member of a *Société des Dimanches*, consisting of the children of her mother's friends. They meet every Sunday afternoon, attended only by a nurse or governess, who does not prescribe their amusements, and only interferes in case of necessity. The first girl of the community who marries gives her name to the society, and as soon as there is a married woman among them, young men are admitted, on application, by the vote of the sisterhood. Their meetings continue through life. Madame S. says this association supplies to the lonely the attachments and aids of a family circle ; that if a girl falls into misfortune, she is

succoured by her companions ; if her father's fortunes are ruined, there is no apparent change in her condition. This institution is confined to the native Genevese ; of course Madame S. is excluded, and her favourable opinion is the result of her observation of its effects, and not of an esprit de corps. Sismondi is a member of three societies, De Candolle of every one in the place. It was delightful to see the pleased interest with which Sismondi listened to his wife's eulogium of his countrywomen. He drew his chair nearer and nearer, and when she ended he put his arm around her, and said with that simplicity which in him is such a grace, " Je te remercie, mon cœur."

Sismondi said the chief glory of Geneva resulted from its having been the asylum of the oppressed from all parts of Europe. " I can never think without emotion," he continued, " of the band of French Protestants who came here for refuge." His voice was choked ; after a moment he added, " When they reached the summit of the Jura and saw the lake and city before them, they all, with one accord, fell on their knees and sang a psalm ! " His tears again interrupted him, and he apologised for them, saying, " Ce sont les choses qui me meuvent le plus ; je ne peux jamais en parler †." You have an infallible test of the heart when you know what does most move it. In this uncontrollable emotion Sismondi betrayed the unbounded love of freedom and the deep love of his fellow-creatures that breathe in all his works.

SISMONDI was to take K. and me up to-day on his way to Malagny, where we were engaged to dine at Mrs. Marcet's. He came rather late, and somewhat flurried ; one of his horses, a faithful servant stricken in years, had fallen on the way. He lamented him as your Willie would have lamented old Larry. " I must make up my mind to it now," he said ; " he must be shot, I would shoot my wife if she were in such a condition ! "

We got another carriage, and were at Mrs. Marcet's quite in time. This lady, as I am sure your grown-up and growing-up girls will be glad to know (if there is any gratitude in them), is living in affluence, and with great elegance, at one of the most beautiful villas on the lake. Don't let them imagine she has found the philosopher's stone in her scientific researches. She inherited her fortune, and has set them the example of studying for the love of it, and has reaped, distributed, and enjoyed a rich harvest.

WE went last evening to our friends at Chesne to meet a *sewing society* for the poor—just such as we have in our own villages. We found the historian of the Italian Republics, and the writer of other and more books than many people ever read, arranging the chairs and tables with madame, and Henri and Françoise, their servants, whom they treat more like friends than servants. Presently, Madame Martin, the wife of the pastor, entered with a pile of garments cut out and ready for her coadjutors. Their goings-on were much like ours on similar occasions, except that the husbands were allowed admittance, and a quiet

---

* The working man of the Old World has nothing to do, *can* do nothing, but provide for the cravings of nature. What does our working man? Strain every nerve to *educate* a son, and give to all his children " school privileges." Instead of tilling another's land, he improves *his own* farm, or strives to be able to buy a better. Instead of a blind submission to a transmitted faith and an imposed priest, he examines the grounds of his religion and selects its minister ; and in place of an inevitable obedience to absolute rulers and oppressive laws, he chooses his governors, and the legislators that are to make and modify the laws he is to obey. It is obvious what different places in the scale of humanity are occupied by these two classes of *working* men, and why the happiness of the citizens of the United States should not be the happiness of the *peasant*, but should be more elevated, more extended, and more *serious*.

† These are the sort of things that most move me ; I cannot speak of them." Though Sismondi speaks English perfectly well, French is his language, and, when off his guard, he falls into it.

game of whist in the corner, provided they play for a few sous, and give the winnings to the society. M. Martin is a man of superior intellect and most delightful countenance ; I thought so, at least, while he was asking me questions with great interest about my country. The girls had promised to join the sewers, but instead, they were reapers. I turned, and saw them all gathered round M. Sismondi in the corner, L. at his feet, and he reciting Italian verses to them !

WE drank tea last evening with Madame B., a pretty little Genevese, who lives during the summer at a most lovely place on the lake. We walked down to the shore by the twilight, and saw at a short distance a beautiful chaloupe (a yacht) with, as it appeared, a single sailor on board. Madame B. shouted to him, and directly he came in a row-boat to the shore, and proved to be her brother, a youth who, while getting a mercantile education at Liverpool, conceived such a passion for water-pleasures, that his father has given him this chaloupe ;. and every day, after coming from the counting-house in town, he puts on his red flannel shirt and tarpaulin, and enacts the sailor on the lake. He rowed us to the chaloupe. It was a warm and lovely evening, and there we floated in a state of quiet enjoyment, not a sail passing us, or a sound disturbing our tranquillity. What a contrast this lake to what it would be with us ! It is the largest lake in Switzerland, between forty and fifty miles long and six broad, with Geneva, a free town of 30,000 inhabitants, at one end of it, and many populous towns on its shores, and on the great thoroughfare to Italy. Some of the land about it is extremely valuable, selling at one thousand pounds sterling an acre, and producing 8000 bottles of wine ; and finally, Geneva is so mercantile a place in its character, and so thriving, that, as some wag has said, " If you see a man jumping out of a third story window, you may safely jump after him ; you will be sure of making ten per cent. by it."

With all these incitements to activity, there is hardly a sail moving on the lake, and only one little steamer, that plies daily between Geneva and Vevay. No wonder De Tocqueville says he was prepared for everything in America but its general stir.

We had a family party at tea, the father and uncle of our hostess. They have all summer residences within one inclosure ; on one " campagne," as they call a country place here. Our new acquaintances have the sterling currency of our best people at home : intelligence, good sense, and naturalness. The family ties are drawn closer here than with us, where the young birds are driven forth from the parent-nest as soon as fledged.

You would not thank me, perhaps, for saying nothing of Ferney, though I can have nothing new to say of a place that every traveller visits. We made an hour's drive of it to the village of Ferney, a place which grew up under Voltaire's fostering hand during his twenty years' residence here. The church is standing which he erected for *others* to worship in. The pious revolutionists have removed the stone on which he inscribed " *Deo erexit Voltaire.*" The château and grounds

are in good preservation. The show-rooms, Voltaire's bed-room, and an adjoining salon are, with good taste, kept by the proprietor as Voltaire left them,—that is, as far as the virtuoso-spoilers will permit them to be. The bed-curtains have been torn off shred by shred, till only fragments remain. The apartment struck me as one of the saddest monuments of human vanity. There were everywhere traits of that littleness of mind which, in spite of Voltaire's infinite genius and his love of freedom—his utter hatred of bigotry and tyranny ecclesiastical and political—degraded him, justly diminished his influence with most people and destroyed it with the best. None but moral power has an indestructible agency.

There is a picture in the salon—a wretched daub—said to have been painted by his direction, at any rate it was hung up under his eye. He is represented as being led to the throne of Apollo by Henry the Fourth, with the Henriade in his hand, while Fame blows her trumpet, and a host of allegorical winged figures stand ready with smoking censers in their hands to usher him into the temple of Memory. Beneath his feet lie his detractors undergoing every species of torment.

In his bedroom is another apotheosis, a " fantasie," called " Le Tombeau de Voltaire." The four quarters of the globe, represented by emblematical figures, are approaching to do homage, while Ignorance, with bat's wings and bandaged eyes, is advancing to drive them away. America is represented by Franklin in a fur cap, moccasins, and a blanket !—The dear old sage, the very antagonist principle of savage life ! Opposite the fireplace is a huge erection, that looks more like a German stove than anything else, with an urn on the top of it, in which Voltaire's heart was to have been placed. It is thus inscribed : " Mes manes sont consolés puisque mon cœur est au milieu de vous ;" and underneath, " Son esprit est partout, et son cœur est ici." The empire of his mind has contracted to a small space ; and as to his heart—but God forgive us for our narrow judgments !

By the side of a portrait of Catherine II. of Russia, worked in worsted by herself for Voltaire, there is a picture of a very sweet-looking young woman, his laundress, and another of a Savoyard peasant-boy whom he adopted ; this looked well. On one side of the fire-place is a portrait of Madame de Châtelet, tremendously rouged ; and on the other, of Mademoiselle St. Denis. Among some indifferently-engraved heads hanging up, I noticed Racine, Corneille, Milton, Newton, Washington, and Franklin, If, as I have fancied, the pictures a man selects for his bed-room afford some indication of his character, these are good witnesses for Voltaire. The furniture was ordinary, and nothing superfluous.

We walked over the grounds, and were shown the " petite forêt " (a long avenue through a wood), down which he daily drove in great state with six horses and gilded harness. We passed through his " *Berceau*," a walk between elm-trees closely planted and trained to meet overhead, where, it is said, he composed as he walked.

On one side the boundary of his estate is marked by a high embankment, which, we were told, he had made to shut out the view of the château from a man with whom he had had a controversy at law. Was it in his own heart that he found the gall to write his satires on human nature ! He was, they say, the terror of all the little boys in the neighbourhood ; and yet there are local tales of his generosity and benevolence ; an ocean of them could scarcely wash out this stain.

We went to see an old man living in a lodge on the estate, who was the son of Voltaire's gardener, and who had the honour of carrying his note-book for him during his walks the last four years of his life. He drives a good trade, showing "antiquities," as he calls some old rubbish, relics of his saint—canes, wig, &c. The only thing worthy of note was a book of seals, which Voltaire was in the habit of taking from the letters of his correspondents, and preserving in this way for reference, so that he might know who were the writers of subsequent letters, and take them or not, as suited him, from the post-office. To many of them he had affixed after the name a word of comment, as "J. J. Rousseau—un Bouillon !" The prevailing one is "Fou !" The old man gave us an absurd narrative of the beginning of Voltaire's and Gibbon's acquaintance. I do not know what foundation in truth it has, but there is some wit in it. Voltaire had been offended by a sarcasm of Gibbon's on his person ; and when he first visited Ferney, its master shut himself up in his room, desiring his niece to be polite to his visiter. But his visiter persevering in staying, he wrote him the following note : "Don Quichotte prenait les auberges pour des châteaux, mais vous prenez mon château pour une auberge." *

"Eh bien, madame," said François, as we returned to the carriage, "vous avez vu le château du plus grand poète du monde." Oh, shades of Shakspeare, Milton, Dante, that even a courier should thus style Voltaire !—but this is fame.

WE have been to Coppet, about seven miles from Geneva, and all the way a most enchanting drive on the borders of the lake. The château is occupied by the Baroness de Staël, the widow of Madame de Staël's only son—a childless widow. Madame Sismondi told me she saw the poor woman's only child die in her arms. So there is no present, no future to this abode of genius and filial love. The château has a park attached to it, and is a large edifice, with an air of wealth and comfort. The family burying-place is surrounded with so thick a plantation of trees that you can see nothing from without, and all ingress is forbidden to strangers. I like this. The places of our dead should be kept for those who come with soft tread and tearful eyes. I felt a nervous shuddering in looking at this burial-place. There was in Madame de Staël something so opposed to death— a life that "worked up to spirit" what in others is inert, that it seemed as if she herself were struggling to escape from this silence and inactivity. I have heard Madame de Staël spoken of here among her old neighbours and friends as one of the most amiable of women, full of all sorts of gentle humanities ; and yet —— tells me that spending a day at Coppet was in Madame de Staël's lifetime one of the heaviest things imaginable. The Duchess de Broglie and her brother were silent and indifferent. The son was overshadowed by his mother's

* "Don Quixotte took inns for castles ; you have taken my castle for an inn."

genius, and —— thinks the Duchess de Broglie might have been saddened by the violence her mother's life did to her very strict religious ideas. It was not till very near the close of her life that the daughter awoke to a sense of happiness, and then she was a completely altered woman.

Madame de Staël's experience is against the theory of the transmission of genius by the mother. Her son, by De Rocca, now living in Paris, is said to be an excessively ridiculous person, silly and affected ; and, what is worse, rich and avaricious. The world have been much amused with a story of his having jumped out of a window from mere fright. Is it not strange that a son of Madame de Staël and De Rocca, a man of known valour, should have neither intellect nor bravery !

WE have one association with the waters of "clear and placid Leman," not very poetic, though poetic it should be, since so true a poet as Dickens has taken to weaving the warp and woof of working life in "fancy's loom." Directly under the window of our saloon, at a few feet from the shore, and communicating with it by a bridge, there is a wash-house, where at least fifty washerwomen wash every day, and all day from dawn till dark. You know we look upon Monday as the day Job cursed, because it is devoted to this hardest of household labour. But here these poor women are at it week in and week out, rubbing the clothes on an inclined board, beating them, and then stretching out of the window to rinse them in the rushing water. What a holiday is our women's "washing-day" compared to this ! It was well for them they had excited our sympathy, for my laundress has just brought home my clothes with a deficit of a night-dress ; and, on my asking for it, she replied, "Ah, madame, c'est noyé !" (it is drowned ;) an accident which, she tells me, often occurs.

AFTER waiting as long for fair weather † as we discreetly could, we left Geneva yesterday on an excursion to Chamouny ; and though the sun shone out on our starting, we arrived after nightfall at St. Martin's in a pouring rain. This morning, when I rose at six, it was still cloudy, but not raining, and I could see (if I half broke my neck to look straight up rocky ramparts) here and there a pinnacle of the Alps. The peasants were passing in carts and on foot to their labour, very, very poor, but decently clad in substantial stuffs, and, almost without exception, with umbrellas—a rare, and but a holiday luxury with our working people at home !

I went down to a stone-bridge a few yards from our inn, where we are told that in clear weather there is one of the most beautiful views in Switzerland. Even as I saw it, with Mont Blanc hidden and half the sublime mountains that inclose the valley veiled in mist, there was as much beauty as I could take in. I will not attempt to describe it,

† The clouds, or, as they say, the "le chapeau de Mont Blanc," were never fairly off his head while we were at Geneva, for three weeks. We had, however, little rain, and the weather was uniform and of a delicious temperature, the mercury scarcely varying day or night from 64°.

M. Sismondi told me that in winter it sometimes falls as low as 20° below zero, Fahrenheit ; and he had known it in one day fall forty degrees. This approaches our climate of magnificent extremes.

for I could only use terms I have used before, and you would get no new idea ; while to us it seemed as if we stood on the vestibule of another world. While I remained on the bridge in a sort of rapturous trance, I stopped a peasant with the question with which I importune every passer-by, " Shall we see Mont Blanc to-day ?" " Ah ! I do not know—it is possible—cependant le tems est un peu fâcheux." He saw I was *sorrier* than the weather, and lingered to point out to me some promising signs, and we fell into a little talk, in the course of which he found out that I came from New-York, at which he made a vehement exclamation, and added that he had a brother in my country. " In what part of it ?" I asked, " for it is somewhat bigger than Switzerland."

" In Buenos Ayres ! and if Madame would have the goodness to take a letter to him !"

" With all my heart," I said, " but that New York was much farther from Buenos Ayres than St. Martin's from Paris." " Ah ! but it was on the same side of the great sea ;" and he seemed so sure Heaven had sent " madame " an express to take the letter, that I gave him my word I would do my best to get it to his brother ; upon which he was posting off to Sallenches, three or four miles, to obtain a sheet of paper on which to write it. I offered him one, so he came with me to the inn, and I heard him telling our postilion what a capital opportunity he had found to send a letter to his brother ! His letter will put in requisition the best writer of the parish, to get it ready before our return from Chamouny. Poor peasant of St. Martin's ! But there are homesick times, my dear C., when I could envy him his ignorance of distances.

We left St. Martin's at nine in two *chars à bancs*, a little low carriage which, with squeezing, will contain three people, sitting sideways to the horses, who trot at a pretty good pace over the steep and stony hills. The drive to Chamouny is perfectly Swiss in its character ; stern and wild, lonely, and yet most beautiful. The poor peasants, toiling in these sullen solitudes, strike you at one moment as the most helpless and neglected children of earth, and at the next you look at them with a sort of reverence and admiration. You see young creatures just on the threshold of life, and old women just dropping out of it, who all day long are following their cows, their few sheep, and sometimes a single goat, around these rocky precipices, on the verge of *eternal* snow, menaced by avalanches, slides, and torrents, with their knitting in their hands, dauntless and as fearless as if they were in our quiet pastures beside our still waters. " The heavens shall be rent as a scroll, the mountains shall tremble, the earth shall pass away "—the spirit of man remaineth !

You are constantly reminded of man's perils and wants. Here you pass a mute little stream that a few hours' rain swells to a frightful torrent ; and there the bed of a lake that last year was a mirror of beauty, and now is a mass of naked stones and dirt ; everywhere are crucifixes to remind you that where danger is present, religion is felt to be a necessity. The sunshine and shadows that flit over the gleaming needles and walls of rock fill every minute with the sensations of events. Nature speaks here to the soul, as history, poetry, tragedy do elsewhere.

As you approach Chamouny, the interval between the mountains becomes narrower and narrower ; and when you enter what is properly the " valley," and see a little cluster of houses and a sprinkling of cottages over the almost inaccessible hill-sides, you wonder where are bestowed the 3000 people who, our guide-book tells us, dwell here.

It is not quite a hundred years since Chamouny has been visited except by those who came to supply the physical and religious wants of the poor people. Campus Munitus, Champ-muni, or fortified field, perhaps from its mountain boundaries, was the origin of its present name. Now more than three thousand visiters come here in one season ; three thousand happy creatures they must be, at least once in their lives. We could easily believe that the snowy peaks we see belong to Mont Blanc ; but the good people are too loyal to their sovereign to let us enjoy this delusion. " Oh, non, non, ce n'est pas Mont Blanc—c'est bien dommage, mais Mont Blanc est voilé *."

We were posting off to the source of the Averron, but some English explorers have just returned, and, in conjunction with our weary bones aching from the jolting cars, have persuaded us the sight is not worth the pains it costs. So here we are, sitting in the balcony, looking up at the clouds that invest Mont Blanc, and at the bright pinnacles that shoot out from the mist which floats over them and then settles down like a dark belt, cutting them off from earth. Truly, they do appear less of earth than of heaven, and I do not think we should be surprised to see cherubim and seraphim floating over them.

THE evening has been chilly, and drove us in early to share, in common with all the guests of this *Hôtel de Londres*, a small mercy of a fire in the *salon à manger*. There are here, besides us, a few other stragglers on the skirts of the season : two noisy English lads, willing to enjoy and impart such fare as they find ; a good-humoured Frenchman, ready to throw the little information he possesses into currency ; some Germans, civil and satisfied ; and a stately English pair sitting in the corner, the lady with her feet stretched out to the fire, in an attitude to express her right to take her ease, and that she is part of no chance company, nor they of her. We crossed the Channel with these people, and have encountered them repeatedly since, and, for our own convenience, we have bestowed on them the sobriquet of Lord and Lady Soho—the name of our steamer. My lady must belong to the family of the man who could not save a drowning fellow-creature till he was introduced ; though I hardly think that even in such extremity she would *ask* for an introduction. Her husband is less a caricature of the infirmity of his nation. He has twice bowed to us, and once he recommended to R., in the exigency of sour bread and bad butter (which, by-the-way, we have here), roast potatoes. This, I think, was in return for a slight favour I once did him ; for the English are as scrupulous in paying these small, social debts, as they are abstemious in courtesy.

WE were at the window repeatedly during the night ; but, though many pinnacles appeared, like guardsmen bold and good, clouds and darkness were

* " No, that is not Mont Blanc ; it is indeed a pity, but Mont Blanc is hidden."

about Mont Blanc. We were early astir to make our arrangements for the ascension of the Mont-anvert. The whole business of furnishing guides, mules, &c., is placed by the government in the hands of a "*guide en chef;*" whose corps consists of forty men *. We had each a mule and a guide, and paid six francs each; a very moderate price for the service.

E., not being strong enough to ride, was carried in a porte-chaise, by six bearers. Our long procession, as we left the court of the inn, appeared, as my guide, Jacques Simon, said, "like pilgrims going to the shrine of Our Lady." These guides are a peculiar people. They are banded together, and Jacques assures me they have no quarrels; as a proof that they feel their mutual dependence, they maintain a common fund to aid the widows and orphans of their companions. They keep much good company, as men of science, and other educated men and women, come from the ends of the earth to be led by them through these magnificent works of nature. These wise people have, for the moment at least, something like a feeling of good fellowship with their peasant-guides; they are, if I may judge by our own sensations, a little nearer heaven, in the spirit as well as in the body, than they ever were before; and thus that happens which should always happen, the electric fire of humanity is transmitted from the highest to the lowest in the scale.

Simon has been a guide since he was sixteen; he is now fifty-two, and, of course, as familiar with these mountain-paths as you are with that to your door-step. He was talkative and eloquent, for he has learned to interpret the voice of Nature, and to discern her spirit in these her most sublime manifestations†. He described, with a touching grace, the Alpine life of vicissitude, excitement, and hardship. "Our people work hard for a few potatoes," he said; "and a misfortune comes," (a "malheur," meaning an *avalanche* or a *slide*,) "tears up their soil, and overwhelms their cottages." A son of the celebrated Balmat, the first man who ever went to the summit of Mont Blanc, has gone to New York to seek his fortune. Simon has had thoughts of following him. This seemed to me a hard case of the "utile contre le beau;" and forgive me, dear C., if I felt, while winding up the Montanvert, that I would not have exchanged a birthright under its shadow for the fee-simple of the Astor House. I was in L.'s vein, who, on some one asking yesterday, "What is the use of ascending Mont Blanc?" she replied, "I hate *use.*"

And, by the way, Simon has made this formidable ascension three times, but never will again; as each time, he says, has added ten years to his life. This will give you some notion of the undertaking; and yet, last year, a spirited Frenchwoman achieved it, a Mademoiselle d'Angeville, attended only by these mountain-bred people. They were full of anecdotes of her cheerful courage and perseverance, and awarded her the palm over all the pilgrims they had conducted to

* The price is regulated by a fixed tariff.
† Afterward, in seeing more of Switzerland, I became thoroughly convinced that Nature is not her own interpreter to man. I have never seen people that seemed to me merer animals than the Swiss peasants amid their sublimest scenery.

this glorious temple. A feather this in the cap of our womankind!

After crossing the milky Arve, and passing through the wood of firs that skirts the valley, we began winding up the wall-like side of the Montanvert by a zig-zag path, which at every few yards made such sharp turns that I wondered how the lumbering body of my mule got round them. I shuddered when I saw my companions hanging above and below me, and thought that a single misstep of our beasts might send us sheer down thousands of feet. But I was reassured by hearing the merry voices of the girls ringing out like festive bells; and, besides, there is little danger; your mule is, as Simon said, "expressly made for mountain-paths;" your guide is always at your bridle; and if your head is getting giddy, you have only to "look aloft," an old recipe for steadying the nerves. There may be more peril in the descent. Once I proposed dismounting, but Simon, though he admitted there was danger to women of weak nerves, assured me there was no risk to a lady of "such good courage;" so, you see, it is never too late to get a good name, if you cast yourself on the sagacity of—*strangers!*

We were two hours and a half reaching the house of refreshment on the brink of the Mer de Glace. This is a mass of ice which fills up a chasm between the mountains. The guides assured us it was a mile and a half in breadth, and that its extent, as far as your eye could see it, was six miles. This seems quite incredible; but the objects are all on so much larger a scale than you are accustomed to, that their actual measurement amazes you. The nearest pinnacle, the Aiguille du Dru, is five thousand feet higher than the Montanvert; it did not appear to me more than half its actual height. Imagine a river, with mountains for shores, running up into pinnacles, descriptively named aiguilles (needles), and that river arrested and frozen at a moment when it was lashed into sea-like waves, and you have an idea, my dear C., of the features of this place, but none of the sensations its wonderful expression produces.

I cannot tell why, but, till we were actually on the Mer de Glace, I had no adequate idea of the inequalities of its surface. The surface, discoloured by the falling of the dirt from the adjacent heights, appears like a snow-drift that has outlasted the winter. The *crevasses* (crevices) in the ice are three or four feet wide at the surface, and narrow as they descend; and, as you look into them, the ice appears of a greenish hue, transparent, and very beautiful. These crevices have been measured to a depth of three hundred and fifty feet. Our guide gave us an Alpine staff, shod with an iron point, as a necessary safeguard on the Mer de Glace, and attended us most assiduously, taking good care not to underrate his services by diminishing the risks and difficulties. To me there appeared none of any magnitude; and I believe that with Hal, or any other expert boy, I might have crossed it.

We returned to the pavilion to refresh ourselves and our guides. Jaques Simon had dropped a hint, in ascending, of the "bon verre de vin," which expressed to the guide his employer's satisfaction; and when I heard their merry voices as I passed the room where they were regaling themselves, I involuntarily looked in to tell them how pleased I was to see them so cheerful. Their faces changed—they probably thought I had come to express some distrust of their discretion ; but the smiles re-appeared, and they bowed, and bowed, and were " bien obligé, bien obligé."

There are pretty specimens of agate and carnelian found in this vicinity, for sale at the pavilion. I have a souvenir of the Montanvert of twofold value : some seeds of the Alpine rose, which Simon begged me to accept as a " petit cadeau."

WE returned to St. Martin's in a drizzling rain. I was surprised to see a little patch of ripe pumpkins on this high land. I asked a peasant-woman what use they made of them. " They were very good food," she said, " for pigs and poor people ; not for great folk." A vision of our " thanksgiving pumpkin pies " passed before me, and I felt something between a tear and a smile as I thought what good food we made them for our " great folk."

Just before arriving at our inn in the twilight, a poor woman was crossing the road leading a goat with one hand and holding a pail on her head with the other. Our postilion trotted against her, knocked her down, jerked her pail on one side the road, and away scampered the goat on the other. We all called to him, in one breath, to stop ; but he did not heed us. Presently we encountered a priest. The postilion took off his cap, slackened his horses, and proceeded with reverent slowness till we were quite past the sacred person. Rather a striking illustration of " letter-and-spirit " religion, was it not ?

We were hardly housed before our hostess appeared with a large china bowl heaped with peaches and grapes, and, just peeping out at the summit of the pile, my peasant friend's letter. She presented it to me, saying, " Baptiste has left these for you. He is a good and honest lad, and I hope you will not forget his letter." Most assuredly I will not ; but, alas for its chances ! You can hardly imagine, my dear C., how pleasant such an accidental interchange of kindness is to travellers cut off from their habitual social duties and relations. A traveller's progress need not be so barren of humanities as it is, if the art of " improving opportunities " (bless the good old Puritan phrase !) were better understood, or, rather, more faithfully studied. It is easy giving your halfpence to the beggar—giving it can scarcely be called ; it is neither blessed to the giver nor to the receiver—it is a debt surlily paid to a clamorous creditor, and received without gratitude. But a kind look, a tone of sympathy, even if the words be not understood, finds a direct way to the human heart. If a certain friend of ours were to turn traveller, his track would be marked by light in the eyes and smiles on the lips, as the sun's progress is by the reflection of its beams.

MY DEAR C.

Geneva, October 17.—We have had a severe disappointment in being compelled to give up crossing the Simplon. That route was completely broken up by a severe storm some weeks since, and all the other most striking routes are more or less impaired, so that it is not deemed advisable for us, with our invalid, to attempt any other than Mont Cenis, which is always practicable and safe. We leave Geneva to-day, and we are looking and feeling very dismal. We have enjoyed here the benefits of a free government and a well-ordered and healthful society, and we have received much hospitality. This we may find elsewhere ; but never will the happiness of a welcome to such a home as that of our friends at Chesne be repeated to us. Well, we have had it, and we take with us their assured affection ; and our young people, though they will no more hear those dear voices calling them their " American children," have their faith in man confirmed—this is a certain and indestructible good. They have seen a man who has passed through a period of European history which has tried men's principles as with fire, without dimming his fine gold. They have seen that it is possible to live a lifetime with the " world's people," to enjoy success and receive homage, and yet retain the modesty, freshness, tenderness, and enthusiasm of youth ; and, better than all, a benevolence God-like, for it falleth on the just and the unjust.

<hr />

JOURNEY TO LANSLEBOURG.

Sunday Evening, October 20.

HERE we are, my dear C., at the foot of Mont Cenis, at the Hôtel Royal, reading and writing by an excellent wood fire, the first we have had or needed. This inn was built by the order of Napoleon, and K. and I have slept in the room he occupied, more soundly than he did, I fancy.

Our first day's drive to Annecy was through a pretty country of hill and dale. The leaves were falling in showers, almost the only autumnal sign. The ground, highly cultivated, was looking as green as ours does on the first of September, and much as our Berkshire may a hundred years hence. I wonder if that lapse of time will bring us the convenience we find here, of extra horses at the foot of every long hill, ready to be attached to the traveller's carriage.

Annecy is a little place, rendered interesting by its thrift—a singular quality in a Savoy town—and by its old châteaux and sanctuaries, that have a name in history, religious and civil. I went out alone, while the day was dawning, to the sanctuary where the bones of St. François de Sales and La Mère Chantal are permitted to lie side by side. " A tender friendship," says the pious Catholic, " subsisted between these saints." Protestant scandal does not allow this platonic character to the sentiment that united them ; but let religious pity keep close the veil which hides the history of feelings that a forced condition converted into crime. I like to enter a Catholic church in the grey of the morning, while the lights on the altar are struggling through the misty dawn, while the real people that glide in and drop down before the images and pictures are as shadowy as the pictures themselves ; and the poor, old, haggard creatures come tottering in to say in the holy place, as it would seem, their last prayer ; and the busy peasant, with her basket on her arm and her child at her side, drops in to begin her day of toil with an act of worship. I saw in that dim sanctuary a scene that would make too long a story for a letter, dear C. When I entered, two persons (my dramatis personæ) were kneeling before an altar, over which hung a painting representing the frail saint (if, indeed, the Mère Chantal were frail) as triumphantly trampling on temptation in the old form of the serpent.

We stopped for a while at Aix to see baths famous in the time of the Romans, and which are still in good preservation. The water resembles that of the hot springs of Virginia ; its temperature is 110° of Fahrenheit. Till we reached Chambery-Savoy appeared fertile ; and the hills in the approach to this town, its capital ; are covered with vineyards, and very beautiful, but the town itself, or so much of it as we saw, is horrid ; its narrow dirty streets filled with beggars, soldiers, and priests. You may resolve the three classes into one. The beggar frankly begs, the priest begs, pleading the sanction of divine authority, and the soldier takes without the pains of begging.

A priest in the court of our Chambery inn beset François for money to say masses for his dead : " Mes morts," replied our courier philosopher, " Mes morts sont tous en paradis*;" " and if they were not," he added, " what could such men as they do for them ?" Alas for his catholic faith in our heretical company !

The road from Chambery is continually ascending, with Alps on each side, little towns pitched in among the rocks, and habitations sprinkled over the rough and sharp hill-sides, where it seems hard work for a few goats to find subsistence. I have seen many a patch of rye, that I could cover with my shawl, niched in among the rocks, and the people look truly like the offspring of this hard, niggard soil. They are of low stature and shrunken, and their skin like a shrivelled parchment. They reminded us of the Esquimaux, and the pointed cap and shaggy garment are not dissimilar to the dress of the savage. Half of them have goîtres, some so large as to be truly hideous " wallets of flesh." But far more revolting even than these poor wretches with their huge excrescences, are the Cretins ; an abounding species of idiot who infest us, clamorously begging with a sort of brutish chattering, compared to which, the begging children's monotone chant, " Monsieur, donnez—moi—un peu—la charité—s'il vous plait," is music. The Savoyard is far down in the scale below the German peasant ; he will rise as soon as the pressure is removed ; these people are crushed irrecoverably. Various causes are assigned for their prevailing physical and mental diseases : unwholesome water, malaria, and inadequate and bad food sufficiently explain them. The children, to my astonishment, looked fat and healthy. It takes time to overpower the vigour of nature, and counteract the blessed effect of life in the open air. The people in the towns appear more healthy and in more comfortable condition than in the open country. I remarked among them some young women stout and comely enough, with a becoming kind of cap, with broad, stiffly-starched bands, which are so brought together and set off

behind that they resemble white wings. They wear a black riband around the throat (probably adopted to hide the goître) fastened by a large broach, at which hangs a cross. The bottoms of their skirts are ornamented with a narrow-coloured stripe, some with one, some with half-a-dozen. François tells us that a red stripe indicates a dowry of a hundred francs ; but, as this is but courier information, I do not give it to you for verity.

You know it is my habit to walk whenever I can, and to talk with the people by the way-side ; and as the roads have been heavy ever since we left Geneva, and our voiturier is a " merciful man" to his beast, I have had this indulgence for many a mile. The Savoyards speak French well, though they use a patois among themselves. I stopped yesterday to talk to some women who were washing around a fountain on their knees. One of them said, in reply to my inquiry, " It was hard enough !" " But," said I, " you should have cushions to kneel on." " Ah, oui, madame, mais les pauvres ne sont pas les riches† :" there was a world of meaning in this truism.

I joined a peasant-girl in the twilight, last evening, who, after spending her whole day in tending her cow at an hour's walk from her house, was carrying home her five bottles of milk, the product of the cow. What would our peasant-girls think of such a life ! Their leisurely, lady-like afternoons and unmeasured abundance pass in vision before me as I ask the question.

My dear C., how often do I mentally thank God for the condition of our working people ! My poor way-side friend told me she lived on barley, milk, and potatoes ; that she never ate meat ; " how could she, when she had no money to buy it !" But our host at Modane, who is a round, full-fed, jolly widower, gives a different version of the poor's condition, which, from his sunny position, he looks down upon quite cheerily. " They have salted meat for winter," he says, " occasionally a bottle of wine, and plenty of brandy. They can work at night by oil made from nuts and flaxseed ; they have a portion of wood from the commune, and they economise by living in the winter in the stable !" This is the common discrepancy between the rich man's account of the poor and the poor man's own story.

François says, " What think you the charitable send them for medicine when they are ill ? why, bread ; and they get well and live to a hundred or even a hundred and twenty years !" Perhaps some of our feasting Dives, victims of turtle-soup, pâtés de foie gras, and—calomel, might envy these poor wretches, who find in a wheaten loaf " Nature's sweet restorative." " Life is a tesselated pavement, here a bit of black stone and there a bit of white ;" it is not all black even to the Savoyard mountaineer.

Even in Savoy the " schoolmaster is abroad." While some of our party were lunching at St. Michel, K. and I walked on. Our first poste-restante was on the pedestal of a crucifix. While we sat there, a pretty young mother came out of a house opposite with her child. I called the little tottler to me, and the mother followed. What a nice letter of introduction is a child ! We entered into conversation. She told me all the

---

children in St. Michel went to school; that they had two schools for the poor—one supported by the commune, and another where each child paid three francs per month. The little ten-months-old thing gave me her hand at parting, and the mother said, "Au revoir, madame." "*Au revoir!*" where may that be?

There was an inscription on the cross under which we were sitting, purporting that a certain bishop granted an indulgence of forty days to whoever should say a paternoster, an ave, and perform an act of contrition before that crucifix. I asked a good-humoured peasant-girl whom we joined (the road is thronging with peasants of all ages), "what was meant by the act of contrition." She said it was a prayer of confession and humiliation, beginning, "Oh, mon Dieu, je me repens, &c., and that the "indulgence" was forty days' deduction from the time for which the soul prayed for was sentenced to purgatory. "This," thought I, "is an easy *act*, and the bishop barters the indulgence at a bargain!" But the pharisaic feeling was but momentary, my dear C., and I was ashamed when I thought how many weary creatures had paused there and laid down their burdens, while, with a simple faith, they performed their act of worship and humiliation, and of love for the departed. When shall we learn to reverence the spirit and disregard the form?

We have had mists and rain ever since we left Chambery, but the picturesqueness of our journey has been rather heightened by this state of the atmosphere. Mist, you know, sometimes gives a character of sublimity to the molehills which we *call* mountains at home; you may then imagine what its effect must be here, where you look up to mountains folding over mountains, from valleys that you can almost span, and see the rocky ramparts lost in the clouds; or, perhaps, as the mist drops down and their snowy pinnacles catch a passing sunbeam, glittering in mid heaven. The cascades which pour over the precipices feed with a thousand rivulets the Arc, the beautiful stream that rushes along the valley.

Susa, Piedmont, October 21.

WE have crossed the Alps, my dear C., and are in Italy, but not quite so easily as I write it. The weather is as much a matter of speculation to those who are about to make a pass of the Alps as if they were going to sea. This morning at three I was looking out from my window, and found it perfectly clear. My old familiar friends were shining down on the valley of Lanslebourg, Orion on his throne, and Jupiter glittering over one of the mountain-pinnacles. "Now," thought I, "we are sure of a fine day." But when François came round to our doors with his customary reveille, "Gate oope," (François always speaks *English* in the hearing of the natives!) the sky was overcast. We were early astir, which, though "both healthful and good husbandry," is only the virtue of necessity with us.

We took from Lanslebourg five mules to drag up our carriage. Each mule, of course, had his muleteer. The voiturier followed with his horses: and François, whose devious motions often remind me of Wamba's, was at the side of the carriage, before, or behind, wherever he found the best listeners. The "point culminant" of this pass is

six thousand seven hundred and eighty feet above the level of the sea, but only two thousand feet above the valley of Lanslebourg. This was the least difficult pass into Italy before Napoleon came to make a broad and easy way over these frightful barriers. Charlemagne led an army over Mont Cenis in the ninth century[*]; and this was, I believe, always the route by which the Frederics and their successors brought their German barbarians down upon the plains of Italy. The Chevalier Fabroni was the engineer of this road, and was seven years in bringing it to its present perfection. The road is carried up the face of the mountain by easy zig-zags. Again and again we turned and dragged on our weary way, and yet we seemed no farther from Lanslebourg, which was always directly under us; but we saw by our joyous "compagnon de voyage," the Arc, diminishing to a thread, that we were making progress. There are twenty-three houses of refuge (ricoveri) at intervals along this pass. Near some of them the traveller is, at particular seasons, in danger from avalanches, and at all are men and means of succour, kept by the government. The girls and I walked up the greater part of the way, not following the road, but taking the sharp cross-cuts. I had some talk with our chief muleteer, a clever man. Our conversation naturally turned on Napoleon, "small in stature and great in mind," he said; "but a bloody man, that cared not how many he sacrificed to his ambition. He made a beautiful road, not for our good, but to get his cannon into Italy. Cependant," he concluded, "ceux qui l'aiment et ceux qui ne l'aiment pas confessent qu'il n'y a plus de têtes comme celle-là!" ("After all, those who like him and those who like him not, must own that there is no head left equal to his.")

As we ascended we got a sprinkling, and, at the turns, the mist was driving at a rate to be no faint remembrancer of the gust from behind the sheet of water at Niagara. I went into a ricovero to dry my feet. The good dame told me they are often so buried in snow in winter, that she does not step her foot out of doors from fall to spring. There was a baby in the cradle. Here they are born, and live, and may die, for her husband has been *cantonnier* here for fourteen years. He receives the highest pay—thirty sous a day, and his house and firewood; not nearly so much as you pay a man-servant who has his food from your table and food as good as yours, and whose life, compared with these poor people's, is a perfect holiday. Our prudent voiturier dismissed the mules before passing the Savoy barrier, to avoid the tariff of five francs on each animal attached to a carriage; a tax which goes towards maintaining the road. We then gave the *bonne main* to the muleteers; a liberal one, I fancy, from the abundance of their bows, and their cordial "bons voyages!"

Our guide-book had promised us "a tolerable inn," and a regale of trout from the lake; but, unluckily, we went into the kitchen while a fire was kindling in the salon, and the floor, strewn with egg-shells, bones, and vegetable refuse, cured our appetites, albeit we are not over-nice travellers. These mountain-trout have been from

* The *Hospice* on Mont Cenis, till very recently a monastery, was instituted by Charlemagne.

time immemorial a source of revenue, and their only one, to the monks of the Hospice. The Bishop of Susa has lately put forth the lion's claim, [and the poor fathers have been driven away. After passing the plain of Mont Cenis, in which this lake lies, we began descending a broad, smooth road, in many parts cut through the solid rock. Wherever it is necessary to have an artificial support, it is made by a massy wall of masonry. The cascades, which would dash athwart the road, are conveyed underneath by aqueducts, and are let out on the lower side through two openings, doors, windows, mouths, or whatever you please to call them. These waterfalls are the children of the scene, full of life and beauty; we needed their cheerful voices, for the mist became clouds, and we actually seemed rolling along on them. We saw nothing, and, after a little while, these small sweet voices, with every other sound, were overpowered by the rushing of a cataract below us. We were awed and silent. At this moment, two strong, wild-looking wretches burst out upon us. Whether they came from above or below we could not tell. They thrust their hands into the carriage, vehemently demanding charity, and looking very much as if they had a good will to take what we had no will to give. Bacicia cracked his whip at them; this had no effect: he addressed it to his horses, and this had; for they brought us within a very few minutes in sight of a *ricovero*, and our pursuers withdrew. François and the voiturier insist they meant mischief, and, since we have escaped the danger, we are quite willing to believe in it. After going down, down, down, the mist became less dense, the trees began to appear, then the outlines of the hills, and, when we reached Molaret, a group of little dwellings on the hill-side, we were in a clear atmosphere, and the beautiful plains of Italy lay outspread beneath us, in a golden, glowing light. What a contrast to the stern, wild scene from which we had emerged, was their abundance, habitancy, warmth, and smiling loveliness! François sprang over the carriage-wheel, clapping his hands and shouting, "Voilà mon pays!" There were tears in all our eyes as well as in his, for strong emotion, of whatever kind, brings them; and who could for the first time look Italy in the face without emotion—beautiful, beautiful Italy!

Susa appeared quite near enough for us to have jumped down into its cheerful streets; but we had still ten miles of this most gently-descending road down a mountain of most ungentle steepness. Think of going down for twenty-five consecutive miles! but we are down, and are looking up at the mountain-walls which God has set around this fairest of lands. Susa is a cheerful little town in the midst of vine-covered and broken hills, which appear like the advanced guard of the Alps. Villages and solitary dwellings are terraced (K. says burrowed) on the steep acclivities, and are so nearly of the colour of the rocks and soil that they are scarcely distinguishable from them; and positions seem to have been selected for the churches and monasteries of such difficult access, as to give the climbing to them the virtue of a penance. And, finally, there is a back-ground of what we are beginning to think an indispensable component part of a finished landscape, summits

white with *eternal* snows. On one side of our inn is a piazza.*, on the other a river. We have already been out to see an old Roman arch; our path has been crossed by a procession of priests; we have been beset by beggars; and we have come in to give our orders to a cameriero †; in short, we are in Italy.

Turin, 23.—WE arrived here last evening, and entered the town by a magnificent avenue. Turin is a very cheerful town, with some 80,000 inhabitants; a gay capital rather, for it is the capital of Piedmont, and was anciently of Liguria. You see how, on the very threshold of Italy, we instinctively turn from what *is* to what *was*. Turin is said to have grown one-fifth in the last ten years. This singular circumstance in Italian history is, I believe, owing to the fostering care and presence of Charles Albert, the reigning monarch, styled everywhere in Piedmont " the munificent," but better known to us as the treacherous Prince of Carignani. We are at the Hôtel de l'Europe, Piazza Castello; and as it is the best inn and best position in the town, you may like to know precisely our condition in it. We occupy a suite of apartments on the second story. Our drawing-room has sofa-bedsteads, and is converted into a bed-room at night; and for these rooms, with a large ante-room, we pay twenty-four francs a-day.

They have silk hangings, partition walls at least four feet thick, double doors, floors inlaid of different-coloured woods, and painted ceilings hung with paintings and exquisite drawings of broken columns and old friezes, and are so richly furnished that they almost put my eyes out, after our wretched Savoy inns. I am sitting by a window open on to a balcony that overlooks the piazza, and I will describe it to you as it is at this moment. The piazza is as large as St. John's Park; opposite to us is the king's palace, with an inclosure; on our right, the *Palazzo Madama*, or queen's palace; on our left, the opening into the fine street by which we entered the town, and a row of lofty houses, with an arcade to the lower story. Our hotel forms one of a similar range on this side.

Carriages and carts are crossing and recrossing, and a *few* busy people seem to be driving forward with some object before them; but these are exceptions. Here is a little company of Savoyard musicians—I know them by their costume ‡,— a woman, with a guitar, singing national airs, accompanied by a man with a harp, and a boy with a violin. A ring of soldiers gathers round them; loungers drop in on all sides; priests and peasants, plenty of priests. There may be three or four hundred persons in the ring. There comes the royal carriage through the palace-gate;

---

* Piazza is any open public space in a town surrounded with buildings. I know no English word that answers to it. "Square" it is not, for it is of every conceivable form and "without form," but never "void."

† In many Italian inns the services of the chambermaid are performed by men; but the general deference to English customs is doing away, on the travelled routes, with this annoyance.

‡ There is a striking variety in the appearance and costume of the people of Turin. Sardinia, Savoy, and Genoa are included in the King of Piedmont's dominions.

the ring breaks; a line is formed, and all hats are off. A juggler enters upon the scene, and again the circle forms. There goes a procession of nuns, with their superior at their head, holding aloft a black cross. Near the Palazzo Madama stand a knot of Piedmontese peasants; old women, with wrinkles ploughed in deep furrows, and white caps wired up into a sort of tower, and loaded with an unmeasurable quantity of gay-coloured ribands and artificial flowers; there are two very pretty young peasant-girls beside them, with a sort of gipsy hat, with low crowns and immense brims, and a bunch of flowers on one side.

Here are some mendicant friars, with long beards, bare heads, grey cloaks tied with hempen cords, and sandals on their otherwise bare feet. The king appears on horseback, with officers attendant, and servants in scarlet livery, and again the ring breaks and all hats are doffed.

Now, my dear C., this may be very tiresome to you, since I cannot make it vivid to your mental, as it is to my bodily eye; but to me it seems as if the world had indeed turned into a stage, and the men and women into players, and actors of some poetic dream of my youth. And as I have set down just what I have seen, and nothing that I have not seen, since I sat at this window, as it is not a festa-day, and not more than ten o'clock A. M., it may be curious to you to compare life here with life in our working-day world.

WE have just returned from a drive. Turin pleases us. The streets are as regular as those of Philadelphia; but here the resemblance ends, as these streets sometimes terminate in a long and superb avenue, and sometimes the perspective finishes with a church or a palace. The houses are regular, too, but twice as high as ours (don't count feet and inches against me), and built of a light stone. First we went to a new bridge over the Doria, a single arch, and reckoned the most beautiful bridge of its kind in the world. While the bridge was constructing, its stability was doubted, and there were clamorous predictions that when the scaffolding was removed it would fall. When it was finished, the architect placed himself under the centre of the arch and ordered the supports to be taken away—cross or crown—crown it proved! We then went to the Church of the Consolata to see a famous silver statue of the Virgin, made to commemorate her saving Turin from the cholera! Most wretched beggars followed us to the church-door; and when I contrasted its silver shrine and gorgeous ornaments with their squalid poverty, I remembered the apostolic charity, "Silver and gold *have I none*, but such as I have give *I thee!*"

We drove through the new quarter of the town, where there are fine fresh rows of houses, and a most natural home-odour of brick and mortar. In short, we have been to see bridges, statues, churches, a botanic garden, a museum of most rare Egyptian antiquities, a Pharaoh (huge enough to have eaten up the Israelites), an effigy which Champollion pronounced to be contemporary with Abraham!—And we have been to the Palazzo Madama, where strangers are admitted, without fee, to a gallery of very fine paintings; as it is the first we have seen, please give me due credit for not

talking very learnedly of Carlo Dolcis, Guidos, Murillos, &c.

But we have seen something here that will probably interest you more than all the pictures in Italy, Silvio Pellico. He lives near Turin, as librarian to a certain marchesa. We wrote him a note, and asked the privilege of paying our respects to him, on the ground of being able to give him news of his friends, and our dear friends, the exiles, who were his companions at Spielberg. He came immediately to us. He is of low stature, and slightly made: a sort of etching of a man, with delicate and symmetrical features, just enough body to gravitate and keep the spirit from its natural upward flight—a more shadowy Dr. Channing! His manners have a sweetness, gentleness, and low tone, that correspond well with his spiritual appearance. He was gratified with our good tidings of his friends, and much interested with our account of his godchild, Maroncelli's little Silvia. His parents have died within a year or two.—"Dieu m'a fait la grace," he said, "de les revoir en sortant de la prison. Dieu fait tout pour notre mieux; c'est cette conviction qui m'a soutenu et qui me soutient encore*." In reply to his saying that he lived a life of retirement, and had few acquaintances in Turin, we told him that he had friends all over the world. "That proves," he said, "that there are everywhere 'belles ames.'" His looks, his manner, his voice, and every word he spoke, were in harmony with his book, certainly one of the most remarkable productions of our day.

I have been very sorry to hear some of his countrymen speak distrustfully of Pellico, and express an opinion—a reluctant one—that he had sunken into willing subjection to political despotism and priestly craft. It is even said that he has joined the order of Jesuits. I do not believe this, nor have I heard any evidence adduced in support of it that tends to invalidate the proof of the incorruptibility of Pellico's soul contained in *Le Mie Prigioni*. He is a saint that *cannot* fall from grace. There seems to me nothing in his present unqualified submission incompatible with his former history and professions. His phase of the Christian character has always been that of sufferance. He is the gentle Melancthon, not the bold and valiant Luther; the loving John, not the fearless Paul.

FRANÇOIS is a Piedmontese, and has now returned to his country for the first time after pursuing successfully his courier career for six years. He went last evening to see his family, and carried them a handful of Geneva trinkets; and this morning, after a whole night's vigil and revel with them, he brought his father and mother to see us; she a buxom stepdame, wearing a cap covered with red ribands and artificial flowers, and earrings, and a string of gold beads as big as Lima beans. Good gold, François assures us they are, and that these ornaments are the most esteemed signs of the peasant's wealth, and are transmitted from generation to generation. Happy should be

* "God granted me the mercy of seeing my parents when I came out of prison. God orders all for our best good. It is this conviction which has hitherto supported, and still sustains me."

the condition of the peasant in the rich, spacious plains around us !

Turin is at the foot of the Alps, watered by the Po and the Doria, and enriched with corn, the vine, and the mulberry. The Muscat grape grows here in the greatest perfection and abundance. It is most delicious, and so is the Asti wine made from it, which, we are told, is too delicate for transportation. We find always in a rich agricultural country, as we have found here, excellent bread and butter. They make bread in a form which they call grisane,—a sort of bread-canes or fagots. Bundles of them are placed at the head and foot of the table. The dwellers in the poor cold valley of Lanslebourg bring all their wheaten bread from Chambery, not less than eighty miles, and we paid for our fare accordingly.

We passed our first night, after leaving Turin, at Cigliano, a considerable place on a great route. To give you an idea of what an Italian inn is,— which English travel has not yet remodelled,—I will set down our breakfast-service : tumblers for tea-cups, a tureen and ladle for boiled milk, and a pudding-dish for a slop-bowl !

We lunched at Verceil the second day—a place that I remember figures on the scene in Sismondi's Italian Republics, and which occupies half a page in our guide-book, setting forth churches, chapels, and pictures to be seen, and how Marius gained a victory under its walls, and how Nero built a temple here. To us it appeared a most disagreeable place; and, if I built anything, it would be an altar with an ex voto, representing our carriage driving out of it. We went to the market-place, which was filled with ugly old women, sitting behind stacks—Alps of apricots, pears, grapes, pomegranates, and most splendid peaches, but neither soft nor flavorous. I have eaten but one peach since I came to Europe that would be thought above par in New York or Philadelphia ! The market-place in Verceil was filled with idle men, who collected about us, and stared so unmercifully at the girls that they clung to me, and I felt, for the first time in my life, rather duennaish, and glad enough to get back to the hotel. Accustomed as we have been to the quiet ways of going on in Germany and Switzerland, where we felt as much freedom as in our own country, it is very annoying to be cut off at once from the free use and enjoyment of our faculties. Young women cannot walk out here without a male attendant, or a woman pretty well stricken in years.

Bacicia, who ordinarily is no dawdler, dawdled at the Verceil inn till we were out of patience. His delay was explained when we found the bridge which crosses the Sesia, a mile from the town, was impassable for the carriage; there was a ferry-boat, but our way was obstructed by great numbers of carts and carriages, which had precedence of us. Bacicia knew it was market-day, and had foreseen this exigency, and calculated that we should be driven back to Verceil by the lateness of the hour, and thus he should gain twenty francs, and a day's rest for his horses. François' imagination conjured up robbers pouring in with the fast-coming night from Turin, Milan, and Genoa; but our Yankee wit was not to be outwitted by our tricky voiturier, nor our resolution vanquished

by a courier's staple alarms, so we seated ourselves on the bridge, and watched the progress of the miserable little boat, which occupied twenty-five minutes in loading, crossing, unloading, reloading, and recrossing. It had five passages to make before our turn came. We tried in vain to buy a precedence, which the poor market-people would gladly have sold us, but the superintending gendarmes forbade this traffic. In the mean time, up drove a coach with post-horses, and went before us all. "Ah," said François, who was walking up and down in a brigand fever, " les gouvernemens sont tous des voleurs !" The sun was just sinking as we got into our carriage, and we had yet fifteen miles to travel; but the moon rose upon us, and, though François once persuaded us to stop and look at some bedrooms in a filthy inn, we came on to Navarro, our appointed sleeping-place, cheerfully and safely. The truth is, there is very little danger of meeting "gentlemen of the road" at the present time on the great routes of Italy. The governments are vigilant, and their licensed robbers are too strong for volunteer companies. Poor François' fears were genuine and inherited. His mother actually died of the consequences of fright, from an attack of highwaymen a few days before his birth.

We crossed the Ticino, ten miles from Navarro, on a massive granite-bridge, and there entered the Lombardo-Venetian kingdom, and at the little town of Buffalero our carriage was taken possession of by Austrian soldiers, ready to do the courteous honours of welcome which their imperial master appoints to strangers. As we were not Quixotic enough to attempt to reform the code of national morals, we directed François to pay the customary fee to save our imperials from a ransacking, and to get the necessary certificate that they were filled with honest gowns, skirts, &c. What a disgrace to civilised Europe are these annoying delays and petty robberies * ! Thank Heaven, we have passed our lives exempt from them, as we are often reminded by François' exclamation, " Que votre pays est heureux ; ah, c'est le pays de la jolie liberté !" (" Yours is a happy country ; the country of liberty !")

The country between Turin and Milan is fertile beyond description. You have often heard, my dear C., of the rich plains of Lombardy, watered by rivers and intersected with canals ; but you can hardly imagine the perfection of its husbandry. The corn is now six—eight inches high, and the ground as green as ours in June, and we have reached, remember, the twenty-sixth of October ! The road is bordered with mulberry-trees. The country is too level for picturesque beauty, and it has not the highest charm of agricultural life. There are no signs of rural cheerfulness ; no look of habitancy. The cultivators live in compact, dirty little villages. The very few country-houses

* The Italians suffer more from police regulations than strangers. A Milanese lady, whose husband has a large patrimonial estate in Piedmont, told me they had given up going to it, on account of the indignities she was obliged to suffer at Buffalero, the frontier, where a room and female officers are appointed to undress and search Italian ladies. The travel in our country would be somewhat diminished if we had such regulations on the frontiers of Pennsylvania and New York, or Massachusetts.

are surrounded with high walls, with their lower windows grated; even the barn-windows have this jail-like provision. What a state of morals and government does this suggest! what a contrast to rural life in England! what comparisons to the condition of things in our little village of S., where a certain friend of ours fastens her outer door with a carving-knive, leaving all her plate unlocked in a pantry hard by, and only puts in a second knife when she hears that a thief has been marauding some fifty miles off. "Oh, pays heureux!" François may well exclaim, and we repeat.

Milan, 27.—THANKS to all our friends, dear C., for the half-bushel of letters we have received here after a month's fasting, and five days less than a month old: François brought us from the Post-office forty francs' worth—forty! forty thousand. We may shrink from other expenses, but letters are an indispensable luxury—at this distance from you all, a necessary of life. What a pleasant evening's reading we had, here a tear dropping, and there a laugh bursting forth. Home-voices rung in our ears, home-faces smiled; we were at S. and L.; and I think I shall never forget the shock and confusion in our ideas when the door opened for an inquiry about the "*lampa di notte*." We were disenchanted; the hills and valleys of Berkshire vanished, and here we were at the Hôtel de Ville, in a lofty apartment, with painted ceilings, pictures of Vesuvius, and a plaster-stove surmounted with a statue!

Yes, dear C., we are in Milan, once the illustrious capital of Cisalpine Gaul, and still more illustrious as the metropolis of Lombardy and queen of the northern Italian republics in the glorious days of their successful struggles against the Frederics and the Henrys of Germany; and as we think, with our democratic principles, yet more glorious for the resistance of the people to the nobles[*]. Images of ecclesiastical pomp and power, of military occupancy, and processions; of the exit and return of the Caroccio—the Lombard Ark of the Covenant—of art, industry, and riches, throng upon us. But, as you know, dear C., it is nothing so far gone and impersonal as its history, that makes Milan the sacred shrine it is in our pilgrimage. Here is the memory of our friends. This was the scene of their high aspirations and their keen disappointments, perhaps of their keenest suffering. Here they sowed in tears what I trust those who come after them will reap in joy[†].

---

[*] The rising of the people of Milan in the eleventh century upon the nobles, and the deadly war they made upon them in their fortified castles within the walls of the city, till they drove them forth, in order to revenge the insult done to one of their body, whom a noble struck with his cane in mid-day in the open street, is an evidence of the spirit of equal rights hardly surpassed in our democratic age.

[†] The persons here alluded to are the Italian gentlemen concerned in the affair of 1821, at the head of whom stood the distinguished Milanese, Count Confalioneri, styled by Sir James Mackintosh, "Italy's noblest son." These gentlemen, after *seventeen years'* imprisonment and the horrors of Spielberg (which have been partially exposed by Pellico, Maroncelli, and Andreanli), were exiled to America, where circumstances threw them into intimate intercourse with my family. I could wish that those who ignorantly think lightly and speak disparagingly of "Italians" could know these men, who have resisted and

We have been disappointed to find that most of the persons to whom our letters are addressed are still at their villas. We have sent them, however, notwithstanding we hear that an American gentleman who brought a letter from one of our exile-friends was ordered by the police to leave Milan within twelve hours. A caravan consisting of one invalid gentleman and five obscure womankind can scarcely awaken the jealousy even of an Austrian police.

THE friends of our friends have come in from their country residences to honour the letters addressed to them, and have received us with unmeasured cordiality. It is cold, Novemberish, and raining, as it has been for the last ten days; but, in spite of it, we have had a very agreeable drive about the city with the brothers C—a. The streets are labyrinthian, and are just now looking dull and dingy enough. The gay people have not yet returned from their summer retreats; and of the 140,000 inhabitants of Milan we see only bourgeois, soldiers, priests, and women in veils (instead of bonnets) pattering to mass. The streets are paved with small round stones, with a double wheel-track of granite brought from the shores of Maggiore and Como, the blocks so nicely joined that the wheels roll as smoothly and almost as rapidly as over rails, and they are so granulated that there is no danger of the horse slipping. The houses are large; you might turn half-a-dozen of ours into one of them; and the palaces magnificent, as you may imagine from our mistaking La Casa Saporetti for La Scala, which we had been forewarned was the largest opera-house in Europe.

We drove to the Arch of Peace, the fit termination for his Simplon road, and adornment of his Cisalpine republic, projected by Napoleon, but not finished till within the last few months. The work was begun in 1807, and the first artists were employed on statues and bas-reliefs intended to illustrate the most brilliant events of Napoleon's life. When the work was finished, his power and life had ended; and art, too often the passive slave of tyrants, was compelled to sacrifice truth and beauty, to desecrate its own work, by cutting off Napoleon's head (that noble head made to be eternised in marble), and substituting in its place the imbecile head and mean features of the Emperor Francis. And poor Josephine, who had no tendencies to such an apotheosis, is transformed into the cold Goddess of Wisdom, and wears Minerva's casque. Illustrations of Napoleon's victories, and the great political eras of his life, are made sometimes, by the mere substitution of names, to stand for epochs in Austrian history, with what verisimilitude you may imagine. Where this species of travesty was impossible, new blocks of marble have been substituted, which may be detected by the difference of shade. The struc-

---

overcome seventeen years of trials and temptations, such as human nature has rarely been subjected to. We honour our fathers for the few years of difficulty through which they struggled; and can we refuse our homage to these men, who sacrificed everything, and *for ever*, that man holds most dear, to the sacred cause of freedom and truth? And, let me ask, what should we in reason infer of the nation whence they came? Surely, that there are many ready "to go and do likewise."

ture is seventy-five feet in height and seventy-three feet in breadth. The columns, which are extremely beautiful, are thirty-eight and a half feet high. The arch is surmounted by a figure of Victory with four horses attached to a car in full career. The details are elaborate and highly finished, and the whole gave me some idea of what Italy must have been in the days of the Romans, when their monuments were fresh and unimpaired, and of the dazzling whiteness of this.

In entering the city from the Simplon road through this arch, you come upon a very noble place (*Piazza d'Armi*), where the soldiers are exercised. We crossed this to an amphitheatre built by Napoleon, and first opened for a fête after the peace of Tilsit. It was designed for feats of arms and equestrian exercises. It is of an elliptical form, and surrounded by tiers of seats, where 30,000 people may be seated—they are now grass-grown!

We next visited the Brera, formerly a college of the Jesuits, but now secularised and liberalised by a consecration to the arts and sciences. We did not take any portion of our brief time to walk through the library and look at the *outsides* of the 100,000 volumes there. Once up the staircase where, on the landing-places, are the statues of Parini, Monti, and Beccaria, we spent all our time in the gallery enjoying its priceless pictures. I first sought out Guercino's " Sending away Hagar," and, once found, it is difficult to leave it. The colouring and composition are, as they should always be, made subservient to the moral effect—the outer reveals the inner man. In Abraham, the Jewish patriarch, the head of the chosen people, you see the patriot triumphing over the father and lover ; Hagar, with her face steeped in tears, is the loving girl urging the claim of true and tender passion against what seems to her an incredible sentence ; Sara is the very personification of " legal rights ;" and the poor little boy, burying his face in his mother's gown, is the ruined favourite.

We were shown in an obscure apartment a superb bronze statue of Napoleon by Canova ; a grand work, but strangely failing in resemblance. Till within two years, the Austrians have kept it hidden in a cellar—*buried alive.* One cannot but smile at their terror at Napoleon's mere effigy.

As we were passing through one of the rooms, C. C—a pointed to the bust of the Emperor Francis with an inscription, in which he is called " our father." "*Our father!*" he repeated; " Gaëtano's and mine !" His emphasis recalled their reasons for a filial sentiment, C. having been imprisoned by the " good Francis" three years, and his brother seventeen ! While we were driving, the gentlemen pointed out to us the cannon, kept always loaded, guarded, and pointed against the town —against the homes of its citizens !

We saw in the refectory of the old monastery of S. Maria delle Grazie one of the world's wonders, Leonardo da Vinci's " Last Supper," painted on the wall, and now in parts so faded as to be nearly obliterated. Time and the elements have not been its worst enemies. The wall was whitewashed, and a door cut through it by a decree of the chapter, that the monks might have their dinner served hot from the adjoining kitchen. To complete the desecration, the door was cut through the figure of our Saviour. Would it not be a Dantesque punishment for these brutish epicures to be condemned to a purgatorio where they should for ever enact " Wall and Moonshine," and eat only cold dinners !

Leonardo, like other people who have too many irons in the fire (for he was painter, sculptor, architect, and author), let some of them grow cold ; he was so long about this picture that the Prior of the convent reproached him bitterly, and he took his revenge by making Judas' head a fac-simile of the Prior's. Vasari has recorded Leonardo's reply to the Prior's complaint, which strikes us as rather bold, considering the relative position of the parties. " O se forse nol troverò, io vi porro quello di questo padre Priore che ora me si molesta, che maravigliosamente gli se confarà " (" Or if, perchance, I do not find it (the face of Judas), I will put in that of the Father Prior who is tormenting me ; it will suit wonderfully well !"[*]) The engravings of this picture give you a better idea of most of the heads than the original now does, and of the movement of the disciples when that declaration struck on their hearts : " Behold, the hand of him that betrayeth me is with me on the table !" but no copy that I have seen has approached this face of Jesus, so holy, calm, and beautiful ; it is " God manifest in the flesh ;" you are ready to exclaim with Peter, " Though I die with thee, yet will I never betray thee !" And yet it is said the painter left it unfinished, alleging that he could never express his conceptions of the character of Jesus!

BY way of a *divertimento nazionale,* we have just had two men in our drawing-room exhibiting a crucifix which their grandfather cut out of wood fifty years ago ; he must have been, I fancy, fifty years cutting it. There are 2000 figures on it, and an infinity of ornamental details illustrating the history of Christ. " You don't believe a word of that story of the crucifixion !" said François aside to me. This is an unbelieving Catholic's notion of a Protestant's faith. When the men, to exalt our ideas of the privilege we were enjoying, said we were the first to whom the thing had been shown, François whispered, " They have been showing it these five years ; the Italians are all liars !" Belief or unbelief in God and man go together.

MADAME S. has been to see us. She is a fragile-looking little creature, and, though now a grandmother, as shy as a timid girl of thirteen. There is a tender solemnity in her voice and manner that constantly reminded me of Spielberg and of C—a, though she spoke little of him, and when she did, turned away her face to hide an emotion perceptible enough in the pressure of her delicate little hand, which is not very much bigger or stronger than a canary's claw. I wish those who confound all Italian women in one condemnation could know as we know the character of this good wife, devoted mother, and martyr-sister.

* The painter may inflict a severer punishment by putting on a head, than the executioner by taking one off. Who can ever forget the " man of sin," (Pope Urban VIII.,) whom Guido's Archangel Michael is transfixing with his spear?

We went last evening, escorted by J. C—a, to La Scala. It is built, as are the other nine theatres of Milan, on the ruins of a church.

Gendarmes, tall, muscular young men, were stationed at the entrance of the house, at the foot of the stairs, on the landing-places, and in the lobbies, looking, with their swords and high-furred caps, rather frightful to us, who have a sort of hydrophobic dread of an Austrian police. J. C—a took us up four flights of stairs, to "l'ordre cinquième," that we might have a coup-d'œil of the whole theatre. This fifth row bears no resemblance to our galleries or to those of the English theatres. The box we entered was one of several called "loges de société." They are fitted up as saloons for clubs of gentlemen, with carpets, tables, and sofas, and are well lighted. The effect of the theatre from this height is, or would be, magnificent when they have an "illuminazione a giorni" (a daylight illumination). Ordinarily the blaze of light is reserved for the stage; the audience is in comparative obscurity; and, consequently, though La Scala is perhaps twice as large as the opera-house in London, its effect is by no means so brilliant as that where the light is diffused and reflected by richly-dressed people. Here we could only imperfectly discern, now a matron's cap, and then a young lady's *coiffure*, as they peeped from behind the silk curtains of their boxes. The six rows of boxes are curtained with light silk bordered with crimson. The front box is the emperor's. It occupies both the second and third rows, is as large as a small drawing-room, is royally fitted up with damask hangings, and has a gilded crown suspended over it. The theatre is the great rendezvous of Milanese society. The ladies receive in their boxes instead of at home, and being constructed with reference to this custom, they are deep and narrow. Not more than two persons can occupy a front seat. Between the seats in the pit and the front boxes there is a wide space left for the gentlemen to promenade.

The music is a secondary object, holding the same place it does in a drawing-room. A favourite air or a favourite performer arrests attention for a few moments; but, as far as I have observed, even the musical Italian is not exempt from the common infirmity of preferring the sound of his own voice to another's, though *his* be not attuned to heavenly harmony.

There was the abashing effrontery in staring, which, when occurring in the street, I have imputed to it being rather a phenomenon to see *young* ladies walking about as our girls do. But the gaze of men lounging before our box, and sometimes planting their eye-glasses and reconnoitring for the space of two or three minutes, compared with the respect with which our women at home are treated, indicates rather strongly their relative position in the two countries.

After having heard Grisi, Persiani, Rubini, Lablache, &c., the singing here was no great affair. The Italians can no longer afford to pay their best singers. The presence of art and the result of study are striking in the stage-management. The opera, with all its accessories, is the *study* of this nation, as "financial systems" are the study of England and the United States.

During the ballet, which, by the way, is interjected between the acts of the opera, much to the disturbance of its effect, there was a corps of between forty and fifty dancing-girls on the stage at the same moment, not perceptibly varying in height. These children are trained for the ballet at a school supported by the government—for the ballet, *and for what besides?* This should be a fearful question to those who must answer it. It would, I should hope, cure our people's mad enthusiasm for opera-dancers to witness the exhibition of these poor young things. I felt *sorry* for our dear girls, and mortified for myself that we were present at such obscenity. I cannot call it by a more compromising name.

There were 500 persons on the stage at one time, among them 200 soldiers belonging to the Austrian army. The emperor pays a large sum annually to support the opera at La Scala, considering it an efficient instrument for tranquillising the political pulse of Italy. No wonder that sirens must be employed to sing lullabies to those who have a master's cannon pointed at their homes. Among other proofs which the emperor has that the love of freedom (that divine and inextinguishable essence) is at work in the hearts of the Milanese, is the fact that no Italian lady receives an Austrian officer in her box with impunity. It matters not what rank he holds; if she receives him, she is put into Coventry by her countrymen. Is there not hope of a people who, while their chains are clanking, dare thus openly to disdain their masters* ?

The two counts, the brothers C—i, have just been to see us, and expressed their eagerness to honour Confalonieri's letter. The elder C. is Podesta of the city, an office that has fallen from its original potentiality to a mere mayoralty; but still, as its gift is a proof of Austrian favour, its incumbent will probably be discreetly shy of the friends of the exiles. But, apart from this policy, we have little reason to expect hospitality. The Italians have no fellowship with the English, and into that category we fall. The habits and modes of society in the two countries are so different that there can be but little pleasure in their social intercourse. The English gentleman in England invites his Italian acquaintance to his home; he comes here, and is offered the entrée of the Italian's *loge*. He is offended and cold, and there their intercourse ends. After the gentlemen left us, R.

* It is true, we see no rational prospect of freedom for Italy; overshadowed as it is by Austrian despotism, and overpowered by the presence of her immense military force, and, what is still worse, broken into small and hostile states without one federative principle or feeling. But we *cannot* despair of a people who, like the Milanese, show that they have inherited the spirit of their fathers; a spirit so heroically expressed in the twelfth century, when Frederic had separated their allies from them, ravaged their territory, exhausted their treasure, and killed off their bravest soldiers. "We are feeble, forsaken, and crushed," they said; "be it so: it does not belong to us to vanquish fortune, but to our country we devote our remaining possessions, the strength still left in our arms, and the blood yet boiling in our veins. They were given to us to resist despotism, and, before submitting, we will wait, not till the hope of conquering is lost—that it has long been—but till no means of resistance remain!"— *Histoire des Républiques Italiennes*. Is there a nobler declaration of a love of freedom on record than this?

asked K., who had been talking with C——i, "how she liked him." "Very much: he is not only aware that rice does not grow in New England, and that the Ohio does not empty into the Atlantic, but he seems as familiar with the topography of our country as if he had lived there." The count is a man of the world, and understands the most delicate mode of flattery.

Nov. 4.—This is the greatest of all Milan's fête-days—the fête of San Carlo Borromeo. The ceremonies were in the Duomo, and the Podesta obtained us places in a "correto," one of the little galleries sometimes used, I believe, for the display of relics : and, to crown all, we had the advantage of Count C.'s escort.

The Duomo, which, you know, is the great Cathedral of Milan, and esteemed the second church in Italy, strikes a Protestant stranger at this time as a temple consecrated to St. Charles as its divinity. Illustrations of his life, for the most part indifferently painted, are hanging between its hundred and sixty marble columns. Directly under the dome, in the crypt, there is a chapel, where the saint's mortal remains, decorated with rich jewels, are preserved in a crystal sarcophagus overlaid with silver, without (as I am told) having undergone any very frightful change. I did not look within. I do not like to see the image of God mummied. The altar of this little chapel, in which silver lamps are always burning, is of solid silver. The walls are hung with tapestry of crimson and gold, woven in Milan, which cost thirteen pounds sterling the braccio (less than three-quarters of a yard). Eight bas-reliefs in pure silver, depicting the most striking events in the saint's life, cover panels of the wall ; and at each angle is a statue of pure silver. One of the bas-reliefs represents the saint distributing to the poor twenty thousand pounds, the avails of an estate which he sold to relieve them in a time of extraordinary distress. Query, how would he approve the wealth in mortmain in his chapel ! I have been thus particular, my dear C., to show you how the generous gratitude of the pious has been wasted and perverted by priestly ignorance and superstition. This chapel is no just memorial of St. Charles. His records are scattered over the Milanese territory in wise and merciful institutions ; so you may turn your denunciation of Catholic abuses into the wholesome channel of veneration for Christian virtues in Catholic form. St. Charles deserves everything short of the divine honours rendered to him. He was made archbishop and cardinal in his twenty-third year. He lived with the simplicity of Fenelon, subsisting on vegetables, sleeping on a straw bed, and dispensing in private with the attendance of servants. He visited the obscurest villages of his diocese, and penetrated even into the recesses of the Alps. He reformed the monastic establishments and instituted parochial schools. He was the *originator of Sunday-schools.* We saw a large collection of boys and girls in the Duomo, taught by priests and laymen, and learned this school was instituted by St. Charles. We saw the peasants flocking to their parish church on Sunday, and were told they were going to the instruction provided by St. Charles ! He founded schools, colleges, hospitals, and a lazaretto. In every town in which

he resided, he left a memorial of his enlightened generosity—a college, an hospital, or a fountain. There are ten hospitals and five colleges of his founding, and fountains without number. He poured out gifts of gold like water, and, better than this, he submitted his expenditure to a rigid scrutiny. After hearing all this, you would not stint the homage rendered to him, though you might wish to modify its form.

I must confess that, to a Protestant Puritan, disdaining forms and symbols, and disabused of the mysteries of the Church, the ceremonies appear like a theatrical pageant. On the high altar there were statues in massive silver of St. Charles and of St. Ambrose, the patron-saint of Milan, and, filling the interval between them, busts with mitred heads, also of silver. The treasure of the church was arranged against a crimson hanging, much as dishes are arranged on a dresser. On one side sat the archbishop on a throne with a golden mitre, and in magnificent robes.

Within the choir opposite to us sat the civic representatives of the city, the Podesta at their head, before a table covered with a rich cloth, on which were emblazoned the armorial bearings of Milan in her happier—her free days ! The choir was filled with bishops, priests, and canons. Directly beneath us stood, with fixed bayonets, and helmet-like caps, a line of *gardes-feu.* The nave was nearly filled with people of all conditions ; and what a multitude there might be without a crowd, you may imagine from the Cathedral being 449 Paris feet in length, and 275 in breadth.

If it were possible for me to describe the ceremonies, it would be most tiresome to you. There was chanting and music, good and bad, as lively as a merry dance and as solemn as a dirge. There was a consecration of the host and burning of incense, and a kneeling of the vast multitude. There was much mummery of the priests. The archbishop was disrobed ; and as he laid aside each consecrated article of his apparel, he kissed it. A kneeling priest presented him a golden ewer, and he washed his hands. There was a procession of priests, and homage rendered by the civic representatives, and a bestowal of peace by the archbishop, transmitted by the priests in a manner which the girls likened to the elegant diversion of our childhood, "Hold fast what I give you." The whole concluded with a discourse on the merits of St. Charles, in the midst of which we came away, with the feeling that we had been witnessing a sort of melo-drama. But I rather think this feeling was quite as far from Christian as the ceremonies we contemned. Time and use have consecrated them to the pious Catholic. To him, each observation of this to us empty and inexpressive show embodies some pious thought or holy memory. And, encumbered as the Catholic faith is, and perverted as it assuredly is from the original simplicity of the Gospel, it has, *we know,* its living saints, and many a worshipper, I trust, who, in spite of all these clouds and darkness, worships in spirit and in truth.

Count C——i came again to-day to lionise us, and we went forth in spite of the rain, for we have not time to wait till the waters "abate from the face of the earth." Will you not like, my dear C., to hear something of the charitable institutions of

Milan, and to know that this work of Christian love is well done here!

We drove first to the institution for female orphans. This was founded in the fifteenth century by one of the Borromeo family, a cousin of St. Charles. The building is spacious, built, as I believe all the large habitations are here, around a court, and with broad porticoes on the four sides, where the girls can have plenty of free exercise when the bad weather keeps them from their garden. Their garden is even now, on the heels of winter, beautiful; the grapes still in leaf, roses in bloom, and the foliage not more faded than ours is towards the last of September. The establishment is well endowed. The girls are received from the age of seven to ten, and retained till they are eighteen. They are instructed in reading, writing, ciphering, composition, and in female handicraft. They excel in embroidery. We saw most delicate work in progress for royal trousseaux. When the girls leave the institution, if they are not so fortunate as to get husbands at once—not a rare occurrence, the matron told us—they are placed as domestics or in shops. We saw them in their long work-room, with the picture of the Virgin Mary at one end of it (that holiest image of love to a Catholic eye), ranged on each side of the table, with their work-baskets, cushions, and the implements of their art in the neatest order; some were making garments, the most accomplished embroidering, and the youngest at plain sewing or knitting. There is a little pulpit half-way up the room, from which one of the girls reads prayers daily, and occasionally a book of devotion. Secular books are not permitted.

The dormitories are spacious apartments, lofty and *well ventilated*, and as tidily arranged as our neighbours the Shaking Quakers, and with rather more to feed the imagination. Besides each single bed, spread with a pure white Marseilles cover, there hangs the picture of a saint, sometimes a crucifix, and always a rosary; and about the walls are pictures of those good old men and pious women that constitute the world of the pious Catholic; and for each compagnia (or class) there is an altar, with all proper appurtenances thereunto belonging, where prayers are said night and morning.

We went into the chapel, the kitchen, and the distilling-room, where several girls were busily employed; and finally into the dining-room, just as the bell was ringing for dinner. The girls came trooping in in ordinary files—beautiful girls they were —and each, as she passed, saluted us with a graceful bow and a sweet smile. I wish teaching could give such manners, and our stiff-jointed girls could be taught them! The table was neatly spread, with a napkin at each plate. The soup was excellent, as I proved by taking a spoon from one of the little things and tasting it, at which she looked up so pleased that you would certainly have kissed the blooming round cheek she willingly turned to me—and so did I. Besides the soup there was a small portion of meat, potatoes, excellent bread, and *white and red wine*. Their supper consists of bread, salad, and fruit. On the whole, I came to the conclusion that the Orphan's Providence in Milan is better than father and mother.

Our conductress, who looked very like a respect-able New England countrywoman, gave me a bouquet at parting; and as we got into the carriage, our most elegant of cavaliers took off his hat and bowed to her with as deferential a courtesy as if she had been a royal princess.

Our next visit was to an infant-school of one hundred and fifty children, under six years of age, of which Count C—i is director. This is one of seven infant-schools in Milan, all supported by private charities. The children, boys and girls, were dressed alike in blouses of a stout cotton plaid. They were eating a good soup when we entered, all except one little transgressor, who stood in a corner of the room, condemned to expiate some sin in this purgatory. He attracted C.'s compassions, and his superb figure bending over him was a picture. The little penitent was, of course, soon transferred to a hungry boy's paradise—the dinner-table. After chanting an after-dinner grace, they tramped into an adjoining room, where they went through a drill for our edification, showing themselves as well instructed as the young savans of similar institutions in our New-England Athens.

They finished with a catechism somewhat differing from ours. "Where is Paradise?" asked their teacher. "In the invisible heaven." "Why invisible?" To which, while I was expecting in response some metaphysical enigma, the boy replied, "Perchè se vedo nò" ("Because it is not seen.") "What did you become by baptism" asked the teacher. "A Christian." "Are you! all Christians?" They replied in chorus, "Noi siamo tutti Cristiani, per la grazia di Dio!" ("We are all Christians by the grace of God.") Poor little fellows! May they learn by experience what the glorious possession is, signified by the name which alone the rite of baptism can give!

We awoke this morning to a bright day, the first unclouded one we have had for *weeks*—and this is " bella Italia!" The girls were enchanted, as girls may be, with sallying forth in their new bonnets and fair-weather dresses. C.'s carriage was at our hotel at an early hour (for this was to be a busy day), and off we drove to the hospital, an institution founded in 1456 by Francesco Sforza, fourth Duke of Milan. He gave his palace, a curious antique it is now, however, forming but a small portion of the pile of buildings. Successive donations have enriched the institution, till its income amounts to two hundred and fifty thousand dollars. There is provision for two thousand two hundred and forty persons, and during the past summer the hospital has been full.

Supported by this foundation, but without the town, there is an insane hospital, a lying-in hospital, and a foundling hospital, where there are now nine thousand children! And, besides this, charities are distributed to individuals throughout the Milanese territory, in cases where it is considered inexpedient to remove them to the hospital.

There is a fine bathing establishment. Some baths are appropriated exclusively to patients afflicted with a fever peculiar to Lombardy, resembling leprosy, for which the warm bath is the only known remedy. There are plenty of diseases, I fancy, prevailing among the poor in Italy, for which the warm bath and plenty of soap would be a cure.

After going through the repositories for clothes, the galleries and courts for exercise, the laboratory, the kitchen (where immense quantities of wholesome food were in preparation), I said to C—i, " The peasants must be very glad to have a good reason for coming here." " On the contrary," he said, " they are unwilling to leave their homes, and never come till forced by misery." Truly He who " set the solitary in families " knew the elements of the affections He had given and for which He was providing.

We passed through some of the apartments where were great congregations of the sick, each surrounded with suffering, and yet in what was to him complete solitude. No wonder man everywhere clings to the wretchedest home where he can feel a mother's hand, meet the eye of a wife or sister, hear the voices of his children, and see some mute objects that touch the springs of memory and hope !

I suppose this is much like other hospitals. I never was in one before, and the scene haunts me —those haggard faces of vacancy, or of weakness and misery. A few were reading religious books ; one man was confessing to his priest, and a convalescent was receiving instruction from a layman, one of a society of men and women who devote themselves to the ignorant poor. A screen was drawn around one bed, to hide the unconscious tenant from whom the world was for ever hidden.

In the " Archivia " we were shown Sforza's original deed of gift, with his autograph, and, what pleased me much more, a deed of gift from my favourite St. Charles, with *his* autograph. This slight record of our superficial observation of the charitable institutions of Milan will convince you that Italy is not merely the mass of vice, beggary, and impotence it is so often represented, but that there are yet left more than the ten righteous to save the cities.

On leaving the hospital a change came "o'er the spirit of our dream." C—i said the day was made to see the view from the spire of the Duomo ; so we went there, and wound up the almost interminable but convenient staircase to the lower roof.

This cathedral is of white marble, that is, originally white ; but as it was begun in the fourteenth century, a great part is discoloured, nearly blackened. It, however, contrasts well with the glittering whiteness of that portion finished in the time of Napoleon. It is a history in stone, going far back into the dim ages. I am always on the verge of a description of these bewitching cathedrals, in spite of my resolution against it. But I *can* give none, and therefore merely tell you that the edifice is supported by fifty-two marble columns ; that three of its sides are covered with bas-reliefs, with single figures and groups of figures ; that there are more than 3000 statues on it ; that there are 100 spires running up into points called needles, each surmounted with a statue ; and in the centre, and rising above all, a marble gilt statue of the Virgin crowned Queen of Heaven. You have no conception of the prodigality of its adornments till you are on the roof, and pass from marble terrace to terrace, up one

flight of marble stairs and another, and another, and through labyrinths of galleries, and groups of statues, of old monks, pilgrims, saints, cherubs, and children ; every angle, every little niche filled with them ; and see, far above you, those hundred figures on their airy pinnacles, appearing as if they were native to the element they are in, and might move upon it. You may, perhaps, have some idea of the extent of this intricate maze of art and beauty when I tell you that persons have wandered about here for hours, lost, and unable to find a clew to the place where they entered.

If Gibbon, who was not addicted to pious reflections, exclaimed after his elaborate description of St. Sophia, " How dull is the artifice, how small the labour, compared with the formation of the vilest insect that creeps upon the surface of the temple ! " what, think you, must have been our sensations when, having passed every obstruction to our sight, we raised our eyes from this gorgeous edifice to a temple not built with man's hands—to God's most beautiful work on earth, to the Alps, bounding one-third of a horizon of magnificent extent, every point defined, every outline marked on the clear atmosphere—to Monte Rosa, sitting a Queen of Beauty on her high throne, shining like the angel in the Apocalypse, whom the rapt apostle saw standing in the sun. We were in danger of forgetting our humanity, but our sight was overpowered, our field of vision contracted to the rich plains of Lombardy, then to the city under us, to the *piazza del Duomo*, and to those detestable loaded and primed Austrian cannon, and we became quite conscious that this was *not* the best of all possible worlds !

After winding up the staircase within the central and loftiest spire, we reached a point from which our first resting-place seemed hardly removed from the ground. We came down to the marble wilderness again, and wandered for an hour over it. Once C—i paused, and, placing his hand on a balustrade, said, " Do you like tragedies ! " Young people always do, and ours looking like the eager listeners they were, he proceeded :—" Two years ago there was a Milanese passionately attached to a young married woman of our city, whose husband became jealous and fearful to the lovers. In their mad passion and despair, they agreed to meet here and throw themselves off. Both were true to the appointment ; but when the woman saw before her the terrible death to which she had consented, her nerves were not strong enough, and she tried to escape from her lover. His resolve, however, was unshaken ; for an hour he pursued, she flying through these galleries, over the terraces, running up these long staircases and gliding down, now hiding, now darting out again ; but finally he caught her, dragged her here, and, while she was shrieking, clasped her in his arms, and leaped from this balustrade—look down, and you may imagine the horrors of the death." We looked down at the jutting points that interrupted the descent to the pavement, and all turned away silent and shuddering.

We found Madame T. at our hotel, full of cordiality, animation, and kindness. She had come in from her villa at Desio to keep her appointment with us. She first took us to her townhouse, which has recently undergone a remodelling and refurnishing, and a most luxurious establishment it is. The perfection of Parisian taste, the masterly workmanship of England, and the beautiful art of her own country, have all been made subservient to wealth almost unlimited. It seemed to me like the realisation of an Arabian tale. I have seen luxurious furniture elsewhere, but nothing,—not even at Windsor Castle,—so beautiful as Madame T.'s painted ceilings, her mosaic floors, and a window painted by Palaggio, in the exquisite colours which modern art has revived, illustrating Ivanhoe. How Scott has chained the arts to his triumphal car! There was a screen, too, exquisitely painted by the same artist. We went through the whole suite of apartments, dining-room, coffee-room, drawing-room, music-room, billiard-room, &c., Madame T. pointing out the details to us with the undisguised naïve pleasure of a child. " Je vous assure," she said, " que lorsque les rideaux en velours et satin blanc, avec les derrière-rideaux en tulle brodé, sont montés, ç'a fait un bel effet*." An English or American woman would have affected some little reserve; the frankness of the Italian lady was better. When we expressed our admiration, Madame T. said, " This is all very well, but you must see the Countess S.'s house. It is far superior to mine†."

Madame T. accompanied us to the studii of Hayez and Palaggio, the two most celebrated painters of Northern Italy. An Italian studio is always interesting, enriched as it is with the models, drawings, &c. &c., that are the studies of the artist. Palaggio is an architect and antiquary, as well as painter, and spends whatever he acquires (which is no trifle) upon some treasure or curiosity of art, so that his rooms looked more like a museum than a studio. I might bore you with a description of some things that we saw here, but that my mind was too pre-occupied to observe Palaggio's paintings, or even to heed his friend Madame T.'s enthusiastic praises of them. In coming here, she had pointed out to us Confalonieri's house, the suite of apartments occupied by his angelic countess, and the cupola through which he attempted to escape when he was seized by the Austrian police. All this produced too vivid an impression of our friend's sufferings to

* "I assure you that when the curtains of velvet and white satin, with the under-curtains of embroidered tulle, are up, the effect is beautiful."

† We were afterwards shown the Countess S.'s apartments. The furniture was most luxurious, and there were beautiful sculpture and painting, but the house was not in as good taste as Madame T.'s, nor more magnificent. I was attracted by a striking, fierce-looking portrait, and asked an Italian gentleman with us if that was the countess's husband. "Oh, no," he replied, " she has not lived with her husband for some years. This is the picture of an opera-singer, a favourite of the countess—she has no children, I believe," he added, appealing to our cicerone. "I beg your pardon," replied the man coolly, "she has one, not quite a year old." I afterward learned this woman had a notoriety that rivalled Catherine's of Russia; and yet that, whenever these superb rooms were thrown open, they were filled with the noblest society in Milan. "Mais que voulez-vous ? " said a Milanese gentleman to a young English lady who had declined the countess's invitation. " C'est est une femme charmante—parfaitement bien élevée!" Backwoods barbarisms are better than this !

allow any pleasant sensations immediately to succeed it. You will be glad to hear that Count C—i has been the faithful steward of Confalonieri, as Madame T. expressed it, " La vraie Providence." R. and the girls passed the evening in the Podesta's loge at the opera.

This morning we set off on an excursion planned for us by our kind friends, and came first, attended by G—a, to Monza, some eight or nine miles from Milan. This city, you know, is often named in the history of the Italian Republics. It has now an imperial palace, where the viceroy occasionally lives, where he has a noble park, which, however, does not suffice for his royal hunts, and so there are additions to it ; parings cut off from the grounds of the neighbouring gentlemen called " cacia riservata," which they must by no means intrude on. What thorns must these encroachments be to the impatient spirit of the Italians!

We went over the grounds ; they are richly varied with artificial water, waterfalls, a grotto, &c. But the chief object of attraction at Monza is the famed iron crown of Lombardy. I felt, I confess, a keen desire to see it ; for whatever doubts the sceptic may throw over the transmission of the veritable nails of the cross from St. Helena to Queen Theolinda, which form the circlet of the iron crown, it was, beyond a doubt, once placed on the brow of Charlemagne and of Napoleon‡. It is kept in the Cathedral of Monza, a rare old edifice with much barbaric ornament, and containing among its treasure some curious relics of Theolinda, the favourite Queen of Lombardy. We scarcely " improved the privilege " of seeing these things, and looked only at a ponderous fan with which her majesty must rather have heated than cooled herself ; at a very indifferent dressing-comb with a richly-jewelled handle, and at the sapphire cup, wrought from a single stone, in which her majesty pledged her second husband !

It was evident that our friends had made great efforts to obtain for us a sight of the real crown, and that very solemn observances were necessary to showing it, which we were quite incapable of appreciating. Several priests entered and put on their sacred robes. One knelt, while others placed a ladder against the wall to ascend to the shrine where, above the high altar, this crown is kept inclosed. Three locks were turned with golden keys. The kneeling priest flourished his silver censer ; sending up a cloud of incense, and half veiled by it, a huge cross, resplendent with jewels, was brought down, and the sacred crown forming its centre was revealed to our profane eyes. The nails are made into a ring of iron, inclosed by a circlet of pure gold, studded with priceless jewels. In the arms of the cross, which is of wood covered with gold, are set, at short spaces apart, small

‡ Lady Morgan concludes a most minute description of the pomp that attended the conveying the iron crown from Monza to Milan, for Napoleon's coronation, thus:— " Last came a carriage with the master of ceremonies, bearing the crown on a velvet cushion. Twenty-five of Buonaparte's old guard surrounded the honoured vehicle. The crown was received in Milan with a salvo of artillery and the ringing of bells, and at the portal of the cathedral by the Cardinal-Archbishop of Milan, who bore it through the church, and deposited it on the altar. The guards watched round it during the night."

glass cases containing precious relics, the sponge and reed of the crucifixion, bits of the true cross, &c. The cross was restored to its position with a repetition of the ceremonies, the prayers, and the incense ; and, finally, the principal official took off his robes one by one, and kissed each as he reverently folded it. I was glad when it was all over ; for these religious ceremonies, where I am for ever vibrating between the humility of conscious ignorance and the pride of a superior liberty, are always painful to me.

That grand old barbaric monarch, Frederic Barbarossa, by turns the scourge and victim of the church, lies here. We were obliged to pass without examination his sarcophagus and monument, and the curious frescoes of this cathedral, for we wanted time on our way to Desio to stop at the monument to the Countess Confalonieri. She is buried in the grounds of her brother, our friend Count C. C—i. The spot is inclosed, and a marble monument is over it, with the following beautiful inscription written by Manzoni :

" Teresa, nata da Gasparo Casati e da Maria Origoni il XVIII. Settembre, MDCCLXXXVII., maritata a Frederico Confalonieri il XIV. Ottobre, MDCCCVI. Ornò modestamente la prospera sorte di lui, l'afflitta soccorse con l'opera, e partecipò con l'animo, quanto ad opera e ad animo umano è conceduto. Consunta, ma non vinta dal cordoglio, morì, sperando nel Signore dei desolati, il XXVI. Settembre, MDCCCXXX.

" Gabrio, Angelo, Camillo Casati alla sorella amantissima ed amatissima, eressero ed a se preparano questo monumento, per riposare tutti un giorno accanto alle ossa care e venerate. Vale intanto, anima forte e soave ! Noi, porgendo tuttavia preci, ed offerendo sagrificii, per te, confidiamo che, accolta nell' eterna luce, discerni ora i misteri di misericordia nascosti quaggiù nei rigori di Dio." *

The whole reading world is now familiar with the character of Theresa Confalonieri ; with the particulars of the heroic conjugal devotion of this victim to Austrian despotism, and martyr to conjugal affection. Let your children, for the sake of their charities, my dear C., remember that this character was formed in the bosom of the Catholic church, and sustained in a country where they will be often told the women are *all* of a piece with the Countess S. That the organisation of society here, as far as women are concerned, is bad enough, I doubt not ; but let us not believe that to be universal which is only general.

Madame T.'s villa is near the little town of Desio. After arriving at Desio we had an hour of rich twilight before dinner to see her grounds, which have given us new ideas of an Italian villa, and would lead us to think it is not so much a

* " Theresa, born of Jasper Casati and of Maria Origoni on the 18th of September, 1787, was married to Frederic Confalonieri on the 14th of October, 1806. She adorned his prosperity, and, in as far as sympathy and benefaction are permitted to a human being, her soul shared his adversity, and her deeds softened it. Consumed, but not overcome by sorrow, she died on the 20th of September, 1830, trusting in the God of the desolate.

" Gabrio, Angelo, and Camillo Casati have erected this monument to their most loving and beloved sister, and prepared it for themselves, that they may one day repose beside her dear and venerated remains. Farewell, meanwhile, brave and gentle spirit ! We, continually offering up prayers and sacrifices for thee, trust that thou, received into eternal life, canst now penetrate the mysteries of mercy which here below are hidden in the chastenings of God."

want of taste for rural life as a want of means to carry out their ideas of art and beauty, that drives the Italian gentry from their country-places. Madame T. lacks nothing to produce the result she wills. Her conservatories, extending many hundred feet on each side her mansion, indicate princely wealth. They are filled with exotic fruits and flowers ; one with pines in great perfection and positive abundance—some five or six thousand well-grown plants of the Camellia japonica intimate the magnificent scale of things here.

On one side of the estate there is an old abbey which serves the purpose of stables and other offices, and which, last year, must have looked rather ruinous and *Italianish ;* this has been recently ingeniously masked under the direction of the artist Palaggio, and now appears to be fragments of an aqueduct and an old abbey church with a tower, from which you have a view over half the rich plains of Lombardy, of an amphitheatre of Alps, of Como in the distance, and—I could fill my sheet with names that would make your heart beat *if you had been here.* Within the edifice there is a theatre and a salle d'armes, which is to be also a museum, and is already well begun with a collection of antiques.

There are noble avenues of old trees that might make an Englishman look up and around him. Through one of these we went to a pretty toy of a labyrinth, where one might get " a little lost." We were soon extricated by our lady, who held the clew, and who led us around the winding, bosky margin of a lake so extensive that I did not dream nature had not set it there and filled its generous basin, till Madame T. told me it was fed by a stream of water brought from Lake Como ; and this stream flows through the grounds ; now leaping over a precipice, and now dancing over a rocky channel, and singing on its way as if it chose its own pleasant path. There are many artificial elevations ; we passed over one half as high as our Laurel Hill, with full-grown trees upon it ; and between this and another is a wild dell with a cascade, an aërial bridge, and tangled shrubbery : a cabinet picture of some passages in Switzerland ; and on my saying this, Madame T. replied, she called it her " Suisse." At one end of the lake, near a fisherman's hut, is a monument to Tasso, half hidden with bays. There was a fishing-boat near the hut, and so I took it for a *true story ;* but, on Madame T. throwing open the door, we entered an apartment fitted up with musical instruments, which she modestly called her sewing-room. How fit it is for that sedative employment you may judge : there is a lovely statue in the middle of the room ; the walls and ceiling are covered with illustrations of Tasso in fresco, and from each window is a different and most enchanting view.

" What a happy woman you must be ! " said I to our charming hostess, " to be the mistress of this most lovely place ! " (a foolish remark enough, by-the-by ;) her face changed, her eyes filled with tears, and after alluding to repeated afflictions from the severance of domestic ties by death, and to the sufferings of her friends for their political opinions, she concluded, " You know something of the human heart—judge for me, can I be happy ! " Alas ! alas ! what contrasts are there between the exterior and interior of life !

The deepening twilight drove us in, and Madame T., who, to the refinements of her elegant hospitality, adds the higher grace of frank, unceremonious kindness, conducted us herself to our apartments, where we truly were lost in six immense rooms, each as large as half an American house, and a pretty fair-sized one too. We drew as nearly together as we could, and made a settlement in these vast solitudes, which, I confess, look rather dreary, with our prejudices in favour of carpets, snugness, comfort, and such un-Italian, unartistic ideas !

There was a family party at dinner. Madame T.'s nieces and grand-nieces are staying with her. The children were at table. " Our Italian custom," Madame T. says, and a wholesome one it is. The dinner was served in the fashion of Madame K.'s at Frankfort ; fruit, flowers, and sweetmeats only placed on the table, and being but little more than a family dinner, would, I think, rather have startled those people who fancy Italians all live on maccaroni and eau sucrée. The cookery was in the best French style. The French, I believe, give the law to the kitchens as well as the toilets of the civilised world. We had a delicacy much esteemed here—the Piedmontese truffle. . It was served as a salad, is white, very good, and very costly. The gentleman who sat on my right, (the curate of the village, a person certainly not falling within the condemnation of the gourmand who says a man is a fool who does not love truffles) told me, in the intervals of swallowing at least half a pound of them, that they cost between seven and fourteen francs the ounce ! Besides all the fruits in season, and delicious *home-grown* pines, we had a fruit called *nespoli*, much liked here, which, to my taste, resembled the frozen and thawed apple I have picked up under our apple-trees in a sunny March day; and, will you believe it, villanous as it was, it had a smack of home and childish and rustic things, that in this far land, in the midst of all these luxuries, brought tears to my eyes. There was another strange foreign fruit, very pretty, and passably good, resembling the seed-vessel of some flower, and called *chichingie.* The evening was filled up with Chinese billiards for the girls, and common billiards for the gentlemen, and a diverting lesson in Milanese from the count to the girls, who are highly amused with the cracking sound of this spurious Italian. My evening was spent in talking with Madame T. and with the curate of the Catholic religion in America. He was much surprised at the idea of its gaining ground there, and much delighted too ; and he proposed to an octogenarian brother of Monsieur T. a pilgrimage to the valley of the Mississippi, about which, I suspect, I gave him his most definite notion by telling him that no truffles grew there !

Madame T., who uses her privilege of sex in talking freely (and eloquently, too) on forbidden subjects, roused old our sympathies by her particulars of the petty and irritating annoyances to which the Austrian surveillance subjects them.

My dear C., it is worth the trouble of a pilgrimage to the Old World to learn to feel—to *realise* our political blessings and our political exemptions. And what do those renegadoes deserve—I cannot call them by a gentler name—who, enjoying the *order* of despotism in travelling through Europe,

come home and extol the Austrian government, and sigh for those countries where there is no danger that freedom may run into the madness of " Lynch-law ? " What is every tyrannical decree of absolutism but a Lynch-law ! I have met an Englishman who was not ashamed to prefer the *quiet* of Austrian dominion to a government that involved the tumult of an English election ! Would these people be cured, think ye, by a year's solitary reflection in the dungeons of Spielberg ! But " good night ;" I am too tired for political or any other speculation—remember, we began the day at Monza.

Milan, November 11.

MY DEAR C.—We have returned from our three days' excursion, and as I hear the rain pattering on the pavement, and look up through our dingy window, it seems but a brilliant dream. We waked at Desio to such a morning as might have inspired Guido's conception of his Aurora, and, after a breakfast which our bountiful hostess enriched with every barbarism, English and American, she had ever heard of, including *tea*, whose odorous breath for the first time, I fancy, incensed that old Italian mansion, we set off in two carriages for Como. I was much amused and somewhat instructed by questions which Madame T. and the count put to me relative to American courtships and marriages. The count had just come from the marriage of a niece who had seen her husband but once or twice, and never but in the presence of her family. Italian marriages in high life were all, he confessed, mere marriages of *convenance*, arranged by the parents ;¡so that, as Byron has said, " marrying for the parents, they love for themselves."

I asked if their young women were always passive under these contracts made by their guardians —no ; the reluctance was sometimes too strong to be mastered, and it was not uncommon for them to draw back, even at the altar. " But was it possible," he asked, " that our young people were allowed perfectly unshackled intercourse after the engagement, without the eye of the mother or any guardian whatever ! " And then, at my plain story of our modes of proceeding, there were such " Mon Dieus ! " and " Dio Mios ! " But, finally, they ended with an honest and hearty admiration of that system where freedom and confidence ensured safety, and afforded the best chance and security for affection. Young unmarried women in Milan, C—i said, were as much secluded as in Turkey. " They go from their houses to the theatre, and in the summer to their villas. They are as incapable as children of taking care of themselves ; you might as well send the Duomo flying through the air, as five Italian ladies to travel ! " " Do you know," he asked me, " how you would instantly be known in the streets of any Italian city to be English ● ! " " No." " Because you *precede* your young ladies ; an Italian lady always keeps her protegées under her eye." Is not this a key to our relative position !

We came all too soon to Como, now a poor little town on the lake-side, with some vestiges of its

* Americans are for the most part merged in the English on the Continent. One of our party said to an Italian, "But we are not English." "Ah—no; but English Americans—all the same."

former magnificence in towers and walls, a rich old cathedral, antique columns, &c. The approach to it is picturesque. The ruins of a fine old feudal castle, standing on an almost inaccessible pinnacle, overhang it ; but there is little left to remind you that it was once the rival of Milan.

Madame T. had arranged our excursion, and here, to our great regret, she was obliged to leave us. But we are becoming philosophic ; we turned from our vanishing pleasures to the lake basking in sunshine, to the picturesque little boats floating about on it, and to a certain most attractive one with a pretty centre-table and scarlet cushions, which our cavaliers were deftly arranging ; and in a few minutes more we were in it, and, rowed by four stout oarsmen, passed the gate-like entrance to the lake, guarded by statues, and fairly entered on our miniature voyage. The air (November 9th!) was as soft as in one of our mellowest June evenings, and the foliage had a summer freshness. We have seen and felt nothing before like this Oriental beauty, luxury, and warmth. The vines are fresh ; myrtles, olive, and fig-trees are intermingled with them ; the narrow margin of the lake is studded with villas ; the high hills that rise precipitously over it are terraced ; and summer-houses, statues, and temples, all give it the appearance of festive ground, where Summer, Queen of Love and Beauty, holds perpetual revels. The Alps bound the horizon on the north. There " winter and rough weather" have their reign ; and as I looked at their stern outline and unrelenting " eternal" snows, they appeared to me the fitting emblem of Austrian despotism brooding over this land of beauty !

We passed Queen Caroline's villa. These surroundings, you may remember, were the scene of some of the scandal that came out on her most scandalous trial ; and we passed a lovely residence of Pasta's, where this woman, who held the music-loving world in thraldom, is living in happy seclusion on " country contentments," an example of filial and maternal devotion. A beautiful villa belonging to Count Porro was pointed out to us ; and as I looked on its lovely position and rich adornments, I felt what these noble Italian exiles risked and lost in their holy cause—but not lost ! Every self-sacrificing effort in this cause is written in the book of life !

We saw the *Pliniana*, where the little rivulet Pliny described nearly 2000 years ago ebbs and flows as it did then*. It gives one strange sensations to see one unchanged thing where the world has undergone such mutations.

For a while, my dear C., we felt as if we could spend our lives in floating over this lovely lake—do not be shocked—you at home can afford for once to be forgotten. But, by degrees, our mortality got uppermost, the "meal above the malt," our voices one by one died away ; our superb cavalier looked a little qualmish ; G.'s gentle current ebbed ; L. laid her head on the table and fell asleep, and by the time we arrived at Bellagio, twenty miles from Como, the shores were wrapped

---

* Pliny stands in the light of a patron-saint of Como. He provided a fund for the support of freed children here. He instituted a public school with an able teacher, contributed munificently to its support, and resigned a legacy in favour of the inhabitants. His statue, with an inscription, is still here.

in a dusky veil, and we were very glad to exchange our boating-pleasure for a most comfortable inn.

WE went to bed at Bellagio, feeling that it would be little short of presumption to expect a third fine day, and heroically resolving to be " equal to either fortune," clouds or sunshine. I confess I crept to the window in the morning with dread ; but there I saw Venus at her morning watch over the lake, the sky a spotless blue, and the lake as still and lovely as a sleeping child. I was malicious enough to reply to K.'s drowsy interrogatory, " Raining again !" But the morning was too fine to be belied. We were all soon assembled in a little *rosary* surrounding the inn ; for so you might call a court filled to the very water's edge with rose-bushes in full bud and flower. We met our cavaliers profaning the perfumed air with cigars, which, however, they gallantly discarded, and attended us to the Villa Serbelloni, which covers a hill overhanging Bellagio. It is the property of a gentleman in the Austrian service who serving (according to the universal Austrian policy) far from his own country, leaves the delight of embellishing and enjoying it to a relative. This gentleman is now making a carriage-road around the place, and up a steep acclivity, where, at no trifling expense of course, it is supported on arches of solid mason-work. The whole hill is converted into a highly-embellished garden, filled with roses, laurestines, magnolias, bays, laurels, myrtles, and every species of flowering shrub, growing luxuriantly in the open air. The aloe, which will not bear our September frosts, grows unscathed here ; and, as a proof of the invariable softness of the climate, C—i pointed out an olive-tree to me three or four hundred years old. This mildness is the result of the formation of the shores of the lake, for within a few miles the winters are severe.

We wandered up and down and around the château, coming out here and there on the most exquisite views. Once our pleasures were diversified, not interrupted, by shrieks from L. I hastened forward and found her flying from a posse of cock-turkeys that her crimson shawl had enraged. C. was leaning on his cane and shouting with laughter at her girlish terror at these " bêtes féroces," and rather, as I thought, confederate with them.

Serbelloni is on a promontory that divides the lake into two branches, and thence you have a view of both ; of Tremezzina on one side and Ravenna on the other. And, dear C., it was in the morning light, with the rose-coloured hues on the Alps, and villages, villas, and gardens, looking bright in the early day ; morn's " russet mantle " close drawn here, and there the lake laughing in the sunshine, and no sound but a waterfall on the opposite shore, or the chiming bells of a distant church. It was a scene of pure enchantment for us children of the cold, sterile North ! and you will comprehend its effect, and forgive R. into the bargain, if I tell you that, when I first met him on coming back into the "rosary," he exclaimed, his feeble frame thrilling with a sense of renovation and delicious beauty, " I will never go back to America—*I cannot !*" Nature is, indeed, here a tender restoring nurse !

After breakfast we left Bellagio (for ever, alas!) and walked through an avenue of sycamores to the Villa Melzi. Melzi was president of the Cisalpine republic; but when Napoleon made the republic a kingdom, and assumed its crown, he made Melzi Duke of Lodi. The place has now fallen into the hands of the duke's son, a lad of eighteen. The house fronts the lake. There is a look of nature about the grounds, and soft and quiet beauty; but, as they lie nearly on the level of the lake, they are inferior in picturesque charm to Serbelloni. Art always comes in in Italy to help Nature, to perfect her, or to make you forget her. We met Beatrice, and Dante, and other statues grouped and single, and on the conservatory were busts of Josephine and Madame Letitia among many others, expressing Melzi's homage to his master. There is a chapel at a short distance from the house, with a beautiful altar-piece sculptured, I think, by Marchesi; and monuments to different members of the Melzi family, that either express some domestic story or are allegorical— I could not make out which. Of all things, I should like an ancestral chapel, with the good deeds of my progenitors told in painting and stone!

I will not make you follow me through the suite of apartments, beautiful as they are; but, just to get a notion of the refinement of Italian taste, pause in the dining-room, where two little enchanting marble boys are standing on a side-table, the one with a sad, injured countenance, holding an empty bird's nest, from which the other, a little imp of mischief and fun, has rifled the eggs *.

There are six groups of children, painted on different compartments of the wall, all having some allusion to dinner viands. In one, a little rascal is holding wide open the mouth of a fish as if to swallow a younger boy, who, to the infinite diversion of his merry comrades, is running away, scared out of his wits. In the next, one boy is sustaining another on his shoulders, that he may steal the fruit from a basket on the head of a third; and in the next, a murderous little tribe are shooting their arrows at a dove tied to a tree— and so on to the end.

There is a capital picture of Napoleon, with an expression of keen hopes, unaccomplished projects, and unrealised ambitions.

From Melzi we crossed the lake to Tremezzina, called, from the extreme softness of the air through the winter, Baiæ. The count assured us, as far as climate was concerned, we might as well remain here as go to Naples. We landed at the Villa Sommariva, the crack show-place of all the "petits paradis" of Lake Como. We ascended to the mansion by several flights of marble steps, with odorous vines and shrubs in flower clustering round the balustrades, and a fountain at every landing-place, and entered a magnificent vestibule, in the centre of which stands a Mars and Venus, in form, costume, and expression, such as you would expect to find the aborigines of this land— types of valour and love.

The chef-d'œuvre of the villa is in this apartment, one of Thorwaldsen's most celebrated works: a frieze in bas-reliefs representing the triumph of Alexander, but designed with con-

* I afterwards saw this trait of Nature as an antique bas-relief; I think at the Doria Villa at Rome.

summate art to bear an obvious allusion to the most striking events of Napoleon's life. The work was begun by Napoleon's order; but, before it was finished, he could neither be flattered by its refined adulation, nor reward it. Count Sommariva purchased it, and it subsequently passed, with the villa, into the hands of a man, by the name of Richad, who had been quietly gaining money while Napoleon was winning and losing empires. Richad is dead, and his only son has lately died intestate, leaving this superb place, where art has, as usual, been chained to fortune, to some far-off cousins, poor and plebeian, who hardly know a bust from a block of marble.

Here, in another apartment, is "the Palamedes," considered one of Canova's masterpieces. They told us an anecdote of this that will please you. When Canova had nearly completed this statue, it fell, and the artist just escaped being crushed by it. The statue was badly mutilated, and Canova at once wrote to Sommariva that he should make him another in its stead. Sommariva replied, that he would have this statue and no other, and that he should value it all the more for being connected with so interesting a circumstance as the providential preservation of the great artist; so, good surgery being done upon it, here it stands, a monument of the integrity of the great artist, and the delicacy and generosity of his employer. Remember, these are traits of Italian character, and that such incidental instances of virtue are proofs they are not quite the degraded people prejudice and ignorance represent them. There are other beautiful works of Canova here: his Cupid and Psyche, an exquisite personification of grace and love, as innocent as if it had been modelled in paradise before bad thoughts were put into Eve's head. I noticed a pretty clock, designed by Thorwaldsen: two lovers sleeping with clasped hands, while time is passing unheeded. There is an Andromeda, an antique, charming—but I am not giving you an inventory— the house is filled with works of art. Among the paintings, and the gem of them all, is the portrait of a beautiful woman, by Leonardo da Vinci— some human beauty, like Laura and Beatrice, that the poetry of love idealised.

I have been more particular than usual, my dear C., in my account of the Italian villas; for I think it will rather surprise you, as it did me, after the chilling accounts we have read of the neglected grounds and ruined palaces of the poverty-stricken Italians, to find that some of them are enjoying all the luxuries of life in the midst of gardens to which nature, climate, art, and wealth have given the last touch of perfection.

We were hardly in our boat again when the clouds spread like an unfurling sail over us, and a wind called Breva came down from Como, curling the lake into yeasty waves. We were all shivering, and the boatmen sagaciously proposed we should warm ourselves with a walk; so we got out into the footpath that skirts all the margin of the lake. It is paved, and about two feet wide, and kept in admirable order by the communes of the different villages, between which it is the only land communication, and the only land outlet to the world beyond Lake Como. The formation of the ground does not permit a carriage-road; but how picturesque is this footpath, skirting along villas and gardens, under arches and over stone bridges, and with vineyards hanging over your heads! Some of us, unwilling to leave it, walked all the way to Como, eight miles; a pedestrian feat in the eyes of our Italian friends.

Those of us in the boat crossed the lake again to pass once more close under Pasta's villa; but the cloudy twilight was so dreary, and so rapidly deepening, that we had little hope of getting even a glimpse of the *genius loci*. But, just as we were gliding under her terrace, her daughter appeared on it, followed by another lady. "*E Pasta! è Pasta!*" exclaimed our bateliers, in suppressed voices, thrilling with enthusiasm, that none but Italians in their condition would have felt in such a presence. They suspended their oars, and we stood on tiptoe, and heard a few accents of that voice that has thrilled millions. It was in the harsh, crackling Milanese, however, so that our excitement was a pure homage to genius.

WE passed the night at Como, and took our last look of its lovely lake this morning. Last looks are always sad ones. In travelling you have many a love at first sight—with Nature. You grow into sudden acquaintance with material things. They are your friends—for lack of others, dear C.

The road from Como to Milan is such as you would expect princes to make for their own chariot-wheels. The Austrian government, sparing as it is in all other improvements for the public good, is at immense expense to maintain the roads in this absolute perfection. After four or five weeks of continued and drenching rain, there is not as much mud as an ordinary summer shower would make on one of our best "turnpikes!" In many places the road is raised ten and twelve feet above the level of the surrounding ground. There is a footpath on each side, protected by granite blocks like our milestones, which occur at intervals of twelve or fifteen feet. Each block costs seven francs. The lands here are possessed by great proprietors, and those which are suited to the culture of the mulberry produce large profits. Some mulberry lands are valued at a thousand livres the perche. A perche is one thousand eight hundred square braccia, and a braccia is twenty-two and a half English inches. An Austrian livre, or zwanziger, is nearly equivalent to a Yankee shilling (seventeen and a half cents). The ordinary price of a perche is four hundred zwanzigers. The peasants are paid by shares of the products. We asked C—i, from whom we were receiving this information, how the landlord could be sure of the tenant's fair dealing. He said the landlord's right to send him adrift was enough to secure that. A threat to do this is always effectual. All his little world of associations and traditions bind him to the soil on which he was born. Knowledge opens no vistas for him into other and richer lands. He never hears the feeblest echo of the "march of improvement." He is rooted.to the soil, and so far from a wish to emigrate, no prospect of advancement will induce him to migrate from one village to another; ejection is a sentence of death. The Comasques are peculiar in their customs. Each valley has its trade. An ingenious man goes off

to Milan and sets up his workshop. He receives apprentices only from his own valley. As soon as he acquires a little property, he returns to his native place—invariably returns. Wherever you see an Italian, in London, or Paris, or New York, hawking little images about the streets, you may be sure he comes from the shores of Lake Como, and that he will follow his guiding-star back there. They return with enough to make them passing rich in these poor districts. You meet men in these secluded places speaking half-a-dozen languages.

Each commune is obliged to maintain a physician, a surgeon, and a midwife.

St. Charles made great efforts to elevate the character of the people, and C—i imputes the superior morality of the Milanese to other Italians to this philanthropic saint. In his zealous reforms of the priesthood he went to the source of Catholic morality. It has become a law of the commune to maintain the schools he instituted; but the people are too poor and too ignorant to profit as they should by them. Without a theoretical notion of the effects of freedom and property, they feel that there is no advantage in learning the use of tools while they are bound hand and foot.

I told you they were maintained by shares of the products. The extremely low rate of wages, when they receive them, will show you how small their share is. A labouring man is paid sixteen Milanese sous (seventeen to a franc) per day, a woman ten, and a child seven. With this they find themselves. Think of our labourers with their dollar a day—their meat three times per diem—their tea, and sugar, and butter, and what not! while the Milanese peasant lives on coarse bread and thin broth, and only eats meat on his patron saint's day, at a wedding, or at Christmas; and this is the gift of his landlord. One who eats rice every day is opulent, and he who eats *meat* every day is the aristocrat of the village. The improvement in manufactures is putting it into the power of a few among them to wear woollens in winter. But, thank Heaven, their soft airs wrap them about as with a blanket; and the cheerfulness which their delicious climate, and perhaps the simplicity of their food, inspire, is like the fresh and fruitful young boughs of their olives springing from a decayed and sapless stem.

It is possible the peasant may derive a certain kind of pleasure from knowing that, politically, he is on a level with his lord. The government is, in one sense, to them a perfect democracy—a dead level of nothingness. Our proud and noble friend had the same liability to Austrian conscription as the meanest peasant on his estate, and his vote (they do vote in municipal affairs) counts no more than his who eats broth and black bread. The spirit of the Milanese gentleman is not broken down by ages of oppression. Very few among them court the favour of the Austrian government, or will accept a share in it. Like the most intelligent and conscientious of our slave-holders (and with far better reason), they submit to the evil only because they hold it to be irremediable. But is any moral evil irremediable to those who will adopt the axiom of the noble old blind man of Ancona, "Nothing is impossible to those who fear not death!"

C—i believes the government of the Lombardo-

Venetian kingdom to be the best in Italy. He was cautious in his expressions, and went no farther than to say, in relation to the newspapers allowed ("*privilegiati*") in Milan, "We only know so much as the government chooses we shall know. Our opinions are our own while we keep them to ourselves; but he who should express liberal ones would incur the risk of a ' chambre obscure.' "

With our defective opportunities of personal observation, you may imagine the conversation of a man so intelligent and highly informed as C—i, and who, from being the lord of a long-transmitted inheritance, has much practical acquaintance with the organisation and peculiarities of Italian life, was a pleasure to us; and our drive seemed to have been a very short one when we entered the gate of Milan, and C—i ordered his coachman to drive on to the Corso. The day was dingy; and, though there were a few brilliant coaches, and handsome ladies in them, C—i warned us not to imagine we had any adequate impression of this drive, which is second in display only to that of Hyde Park. We noticed the viceroy's gilded coach with six horses drawn up, while he and his family were enjoying the luxury of a walk.

ANOTHER day in Milan has been busily passed in visiting the Ambrosian library, where we saw, among many celebrated pictures, an exquisite one designed by Leonardo da Vinci, and finished by his pupil Luini. It is called a Madonna, but is, in fact, a prophetic portrait of M. W., the same full, rich eye with all a mother's rapture in it; the same capacity of sympathy with joy or sorrow expressed in the flexible lips; as unlike as possible to the gentle, not to say tame Madonnas that throng the galleries indicating merely placid maternal satisfaction.

We saw papyrus with writing 2000 years old, and notes to a book in Petrarch's autograph, and various other things that it is well to see, but very tiresome to hear about. The *Casino de' Negosiante* was shown us by way of giving us a glimpse of Italian modes of society. It is a large house with a series of apartments: a ball, drawing-room, &c. &c., where gentlemen and ladies meet together on stated evenings to amuse themselves. All classes have these casinos. They save the bother of invitations and intrusion on the order of families, and much of the expense of private entertainment.

We went in the evening, by his appointment, to Manzoni's. The Italian seems to indemnify himself for not roving over the world by walling in a little world of his own, which he calls a house. We were shown through a suite of empty apartments to the drawing-room, where we found Manzoni, his mother, wife, and children, and all the shows and appliances of comfortable domestic life. Manzoni is a little past fifty, with an intellectual and rather handsome face, and a striking expression of goodness. His manner is gentlemanly and modest, not shy, as we have been told. Indeed, his reputation for shyness and fondness for seclusion induced us to decline a very kind invitation to pass a day at his country place. We thought it but common humanity not to take advantage of his readiness to honour Confalonieri's

draft in our behalf on his hospitality—now I regret an irretrievable opportunity lost.

He was cordial in his manners, and frank and fluent in his conversation. He and his mother (the daughter of Beccaria), a superb-looking old lady, expressed an intelligent interest in our country, and poured out their expressions of gratitude for what they were pleased to term our kindness to their exiles, as if we had cherished their own lost children. I put in a disclaimer, saying, you know how truly, that we considered it a most happy chance that had made us intimately acquainted with men who were an honour to their species. Manzoni said this was all very well in relation to Confalonieri; he came to us with his renown; but as to the rest, we must have been ignorant of everything about them but their sufferings. "G.," he said, "has found a country with you; and he deserves it, for he is an angel upon earth*." When I responded earnestly, he replied with a significant laugh, "Now that you know what our *mauvais sujets* are, you can imagine what our honest men must be!"

Manzoni had not heard of the American translation of the Promessi Sposi, and he seemed gratified that his fame was extending over the New World. Would that it could go fairly forth without the shackles of a translation! He told us some interesting anecdotes of Beccaria. He said he was so indolent that he never wrote without being in some sort forced upon it; that his celebrated essay on criminal law was procured by the energetic management of a friend who invited him to his house, and locked him up, declaring he should not come out till he had written down his inestimable thoughts on that subject. Beccaria good-naturedly acquiesced, and the work was actually finished in his friendly prison.

"And much reason," Madame Manzoni (the elder) said, "my father had to rejoice in it, for he often received letters of most grateful acknowledgment from individuals who had profited by the humane doctrines of his book."

OUR friends have continued their kindness to the last moment—the whole family, C., Count C—i, and dear Madame T. She urged us to renounce our journey to Venice, and spend a week at her villa. This was almost irresistible; but leaving out Venice in seeing Italy is like losing bishop or castle in a game of chess. So our bills are paid, our post-horses ordered, and we are going, feeling as if we had lived a little life here; for we have made acquaintance, and ripened them into friendships; we have gone out and returned; we have eaten, and drunk, and made merry, and must now go forth again, unknowing and unknown. There is no such lengthener of human life as travelling.

Brescia.—A BRIGHT attractive-looking town, with thirty thousand inhabitants, clean streets,

* I trust I shall not appear to have been betrayed into publishing the above by a petty vanity. The little kindness we have had the opportunity of extending to the exiled Italians we count good fortune, not merit. It has been requited a hundred fold by the privilege of their intimate acquaintance. But I would, as far as in my humble way I can, remove the narrow belief that there is no hospitality, no gratitude, among their countrymen.

and fine old edifices, built from the ruins of ancient temples, and a rich surrounding country, covered with villas, vines, and mulberries, and watered by three rivers, which are just now fearfully illustrating the old proverb, "Good servants, but bad masters." Italy has been anything but a land of the sun to us. This morning the clouds dispersed, for the first time since we were on Lake Como, and François assures us that the priests, who "know all about these matters," pronounce the rain "une chose finie." "La Sainte Vierge" has been gracious, and to-morrow she is to be unveiled and exhibited to her worshippers. In the mean time, half the country is submerged; the fearful Po has burst through its embankments and overwhelmed several villages. It is a pity "La Sainte Vierge" has been so slow in her compassions.

We have just been to see the "scavi," or Roman remains, which, within the last twenty years, have been discovered and disinterred here. In 1820, the top of a pillar was seen. This led to excavations, which ended in bringing to upper earth a temple of Hercules, a curia, very beautiful mosaic pavements, richly-sculptured altars, a multitude of busts, shattered friezes, and broken pillars, and a bronze statue of Victory of the best period of Grecian art. Victory! I doubt it; she has an expression of such Divine sweetness, as if she might weep at the fantastic tricks and cruel games men have played and called them *victories*. This is the first time we have seen any striking remains of Roman magnificence and art, on the very spot where they stood in the eye of those whose souls were breathed into their forms; and the *first* time is an epoch in one's life!

Verona.—WE left Brescia this morning at seven; a morning *comme il y en a peu* now-a-days. When I opened my blind at six, Venus hung over our jessamine-embowered balcony, as brilliant as when she kept her watch at Bellagio. We have been driving on the *Via Emilia*—a pretty old road, and kept in excellent repair. Our first halt was at Desenzano, on the shores of the Lago di Garda, the ancient Benacus. The lake is nearly inclosed by Alps, and the climate is so softened by its mountain-wall, that the most delicate southern fruits are ripened on its shores. The fish of this lake was sung by epicure-poets of old, and are quite as much relished by the moderns. Catullus, who was born at Verona, had his favourite villa here, on the peninsula of Sermione. Its beautiful position was pointed out to us. The lake preserves the stormy character Virgil gave it in his time. Not a breath stirred the leaves as we walked along the shore, and yet the blue waves came with their white crests dancing towards us, and gave K. rather too spirited a salutation. Always excepting Como, this Lago di Garda, with its surroundings, is the most beautiful sheet of water I have ever seen*. For an hour we drove in view of the lake, and during the whole drive we have had beautiful objects under our eyes: a château with its long lawn and avenues, a shrine, a crucifix, an old wall, a bridge,

* I had not then been to Bevay and Montreux, nor seen the lake of Luzerne; but each has its peculiar charm, that is not lessened by comparing it to another.

and the Alps bounding our horizon. The sterile Alps, our guide-book calls them, but what is there on earth so rich in beauty, so suggestive to the imagination! This is the richest part of Lombardy, covered with mulberries and vines, and thronging with, as it appears to us, a healthy population, full fed from the cradle to the grave. The children are stout and rosy, with masses of bright curling hair. The women are tall and well-developed, and the old people so old that one would think they must themselves have forgotten they were ever young—the last thing they do forget. But they are never "rocked in the cradle of reposing age"—never cease from their labours. We see even the very old women, with their grey heads bare or covered with a fanciful straw hat, driving asses and leading cows on the highway. Whenever our carriage stops there are plenty of beggars around us, but they are for the most part sick or maimed. Comparing the peasantry of Savoy with that here, this climate would seem to be bed and board to them.

The first object that struck our eyes on entering Verona was a very curious old bridge over the Adige, and from that moment till we reached our inn, we kept up a choral exclamation at the piazzas, the famous old palaces, the immense houses, half as high as the Alps, and at the heavy stone balconies.

Verona, a powerful city in the time of the Romans, and so distinguished in the middle ages when the bold lords of the Scala family ruled its destinies, has now dwindled down to a population of 50,000. To me it bears a charmed name, as recalling the time when, a child of seven years, I sat down on the carpet by the "old book-case" to read "The Two Gentlemen of Verona," the only one of Shakspeare's plays now to me unreadable. But Juliet is, to every English-blooded traveller, the *genius loci* of Verona; Juliet, that sweetest impersonation of the universal passion whose mortality Shakspeare has converted into immortality, and fixed her shrine here. We set off in a half-hour after our arrival, with a dirty, snuffing old valet-de-place (I have an antipathy to the best of the genus), to see the *locales* of the "sweet saint." The palace of the Capulets, *so called*, is a gloomy, dark old rack-rent edifice, now a hostelrie! We were conducted through an arched way into a court lumbered with carts loaded with wine-casks. The "balcony" was half-way to heaven, where poor Juliet needed, in truth, a "falconer's voice" to be heard by her lover. The garden, we were told, was beyond the court; but we saw no "orchard-wall, high and hard to climb," that "Love's light" wings alone might pass, and we were eager to get away before imagination should lose for ever the power of recalling the orange groves and myrtle bowers, the passionate girl in the balcony, the lover in the garden, and the moon "tipping with silver all those fruit-tree tops."

We drove half a mile beyond the gate to the old Franciscan monastery, where tradition has placed the tomb of the Capulets; and here, in a dreary garden, we were shown the spot where the tomb *was*. And alas for the disenchantments that yet awaited us! A servitora unlocked something very like a barn-door, and admitted us into something very like a barn, where she showed us an open stone sarcophagus of Verona marble, which, she assured us, contained Juliet's body when it was removed from the garden to this place for *safe keeping.* There was a stone pillow for her head, and a socket for a candle, which it is, to this day, the custom of the Veronese to place lighted in the coffin. There were two holes drilled for ventilation, probably to admit air enough to support the flame.

In the heart of the city, inclosed by an iron railing of most delicate workmanship, are the tombs of the Scala family. When all records are lost but Shakspeare's, which will undoubtedly outlive all others, these may be shown for the tombs of the Capulets. There are monuments curiously sculptured, with marble sarcophagi and effigies. Three are elaborate, and these run up into pinnacles and are surmounted with statues, an equestrian one overshadowing the rest. "This," our cicerone said, "was of the greatest lord of Verona." It should then be of Cane della Scala *.

There is an amphitheatre here built of blocks of stone without cement, and as early as Trajan's time, which is in admirable preservation. Napoleon repaired it in excellent taste, so that it now appears quite perfect. It can accommodate 25,000 persons. I have not half finished the sight-seeing of this crowded afternoon, but I spare you.

K. and I returned from a truant stroll in the morning in time to swallow our breakfasts, and to remonstrate against an overcharge in our bill: a hateful task that falls to my share, and often makes me regret the days when I went on *like a lady,* quietly paying prices, and scarcely knowing them. But we have, in truth, little to complain of. The inn-charges are seldom extravagant; and as to impositions strictly, I think we rarely meet with them. Good policy has arranged these matters on these great high-roads. We poorer Americans must pay the rates which luxurious English travellers, who "lard this lean earth," have introduced.

Padua.—We have now travelled nearly across the Lombardo-Venetian kingdom. The posting, which all over the Continent is a government monopoly, is well arranged, but much dearer than in Germany. The German postilion is the least civilised of Germans, but the Italian is still lower in the scale of humanity. His horses, too, are inferior in size and muscle, but they seem to have a portion of the spirit of their masters, and travel more fleetly than the heavy German horse.

Though we are on the verge of winter, the characteristics of the country are manifest. Roses are yet blooming. At the post-stations women throng to our coach-windows with waiters filled with grapes, pears, apples, and nespoli. The people are all out of doors, women spinning by the roadside, combing their hair, and performing

other offices that we at all seasons reserve for indoors. We stopped at Vicenza, which is now a town of some 30,000 inhabitants, long enough to see some of the best productions of Palladio, one of the celebrated architects of Italy, who lived in the sixteenth century, and was born here. All Northern Italy is embellished by his designs and works. I am no critic in these matters, but a too lavish profusion of ornament seems to me to characterise them. The work esteemed his masterpiece is at Vicenza. It is called the Olympic Theatre, and was built precisely on the model of the ancient Greek theatre, that the Vicenzans might get a precise idea of the mode of Grecian dramatic exhibitions. The scenery is a fixture, representing the entrance of a Greek town and the openings into seven different streets, where you see houses, temples, and triumphal arches. The stage is not much larger than a generous dining-table. Then there are Corinthian columns and rows of statues extending all around the theatre. There are fourteen ranges of seats for the spectators; and with all this lavishment of genius, art, and money, there have been but two exhibitions here, one for the emperor, and one for his viceroy. You will agree with me that Palladio might have spent his time, and the Vicenzans their money, better than on this, after all, mere toy. The private houses here are most richly ornamented with architectural embellishments. Palladio was one of the few prophets honoured in his own country.

The inhabitants of Padua have dwindled down to 55,000 : about three times the number of the students it once gathered within the walls of that venerable university where Galileo lectured. The exterior wall of the university is covered with busts in bas-reliefs, escutcheons, and various sculpture, illustrating the men who have been distinguished here.

Petrarch, you know, was born at Arqua in this neighbourhood, and was a canon in the church here, where, if one may judge by the zeal with which every memorial of him is cherished, his love-sonnets were not considered uncanonical. There is a picture of the Madonna at the Cathedral presented by him. There was a curtain over it; our servitora said, "If the ladies commanded, it should be uncovered." We were so disgusted with this contrivance to exact a fee, this covering up a picture from its worshippers to uncover it to the gaze of heretics for a paltry hire, that we declined the offer†. We saw in the sacristy a bust of Petrarch, and a portrait painted by his contemporary Ciambellini.

We have a strange feeling in this old world, dear C., as if the dead of all past ages were rising to life on every side of us. We saw in the hall of justice here—a noble hall 300 feet long, and adorned with frescoes by Giotto—a bust of Titus Livius, which was disinterred in the environs of

---

* "The first of the Lombard princes, he protected the arts and sciences; his court, the asylum of all the exiled Ghibelines, drew together the first poets, painters, and sculptors of Italy. There are still at Verona glorious monuments of the protection he extended to architecture. But war was his favourite passion, &c."—*Histoire des Républiques Italiennes.*

† We were not long in learning to smile at our own pharisaical Quixotism, and to discard it. The best pictures in the Italian churches are veiled, that they may be "ne'er seen but wondered at" by the devout, and ne'er seen but paid for by the stranger, be he heretic or orthodox. And certainly it is just the possessor should derive an income from such a capital; and the sight of the picture is worth ten times the trifling sum it costs.

this his native city. The Roman remains and memorials in Lombardy are comparatively few; and it is not to the days of Roman dominion that the mind recurs, but to the period of Italian independence. You perceive in these rich plains of Lombardy the source in nature of the individual life, vigour, and power of the free Italian cities, in these warm plains completely irrigated, and producing without measure corn, wine, and the mulberry-tree, those surest natural sources of wealth. And you perceive still, in the noble physiognomy of the people, the intellectual character that made Italy the seat of art, literature, commerce, and manufactures, while civilisation had scarcely dawned on the rest of Europe. With what feelings must idle, shackled, impotent Italy look back on those days when her looms were sending their gorgeous fabrics wherever there was money to pay for them; when her envoys could truly declare in Eastern courts that they saw nothing there more luxurious than they had seen in the palaces of their native princes; the days when their historians, their poets, and their painters were creating works for all posterity! These were the days when Milan and Brescia, Verona, Vicenza, and Padua, and all the rest of their glorious company, were republics; when freedom was so dearly prized that it was an axiom that "blessed were those that died for liberty and their country;" when an insolent imperial letter was torn from a herald's hands and trampled under foot; when a beautiful matron, in a famishing town, with her infant in her arms, who had subsisted for days on boiled leather, offered the nourishment in her breast to a fainting soldier, that he might up and "do or die;" when Milan, with her houses razed to the ground, and her inhabitants driven forth, again rose and successfully resisted imperial aggression. And now Austrian soldiers keep the gates of these cities, and say who shall enter and who depart. No wonder that the Italian's heart burns within him, that the noblest spirits are torpid with despair languish in prison, or are driven into exile.

Venice, November 18.—THERE are three posts (about seven miles each) from Padua to Venice. The usual boundaries of land and water are so changed by the overflowings of the rivers, that I fear we are getting no very accurate notions of the face of the country in its ordinary condition. You are conscious you are approaching a city that gathered to itself the riches of the world, and whose market converted marshy lands into gardens, vineyards, and golden fields. There are, what we have not seen elsewhere, pleasant-looking, isolated cottages, with thatched and conical roofs, and an infinity of villages, churches, chapels, and magnificent villas, whose grounds appear like drawing-rooms pretty well filled with poetic gentlemen and ladies, dressed and undressed artistically. In sober truth, there are many more statues out of doors here than you see people with us in the finest weather. The houses are magnificent, many built after the designs of Palladio, and, like everything of his, prodigally ornamented; they are surrounded with high walls, with arched stone entrances and iron gates, with statues at the gates, and statues on the walls with short intervals.

The roses are still in bloom, though the trees are nearly stripped of their leaves. Last night, for the first time, we had a slight frost. At Fusina, a miserable little town, infested with beggars, postilions, *douaniers*, and loungers, screaming, and racketing, and racking us, we left our carriage and embarked in a gondola. Yes, dear C., a gondola—which, all our heroic-poetic associations to the contrary notwithstanding, is the most funereal-looking affair you ever saw afloat. They are without exception covered by a black awning, first imposed by a sumptuary law of the republic, and maintained, probably, by the sumptuary laws of poverty.

Venice is five miles from Fusina, and seen from thence appears like a city that has floated from its moorings, and, while distance lends its "enchantment to the view," still like a queen "throned on her hundred isles," or, rather—as its proud representative, who refused his oath of adhesion to Henry VII., said—as if it were "a fifth essence, belonging neither to the Church nor the emperor, the sea nor the land!" Nature, too, lent us her enchantments; the sun setting, as we crossed the Lagoon, coloured the Rhætian Alps with rose and purple hues, which the waves that played around our gondola reflected, while the pale moon hung over the Adriatic. I cannot describe to you the sensation of approaching such fallen greatness as that of Venice. It is as if a "buried majesty" appeared to you from the dead. We passed in silence the magnificent Piazza St. Marco, and were landed at the steps of the Hôtel Reale, formerly the *Palazzo Bernardo*.

WE went in the twilight last evening, my dear C., to the Piazza, passed the ducal palace and the Bridge of Sighs, to get the feeling that we are actually in Venice; and in this piazza, surrounded as you are by magnificent and unimpaired objects, it is not difficult to realise Venice's past wealth and splendour; it is only difficult to believe that it is *past*. There is the Church of St. Mark, uniting Oriental magnificence with Moorish architecture and Christian emblems; its façade embellished with ecclesiastical history written in mosaic* ; and over its principal arched entrance the four horses of Lysippus, the seeming insignia of victory, so often have they tramped over the world attached to the victor's car. These mute images put the greatness and the littleness of the world and its players into striking antithesis. They were the emblems of Corinth's glory, of Rome's, of Constantinople's, of Venice's, and of Napoleon's. Their kingdoms, their glory, and their generations have passed away, and here these four brazen horses stand unscathed! Three sides of the piazza are surrounded with very handsome edifices; with

* At least that little episode in the history of the church is depicted here which relates to the transfer of St. Mark's body from Alexandria to Venice. The first scene represented is the pious fraud enacted by the Christians, when they hid the body of their saint in a basket under piles of pork, from which the Mussulmans are represented as recoiling. The story ends with the last Judgment. St. Mark's Gospel, *said* to be written by his own hand, is among the treasures of the church. "The Venetians chose St. Mark," says M. Sismondi, "patron of their state; his lion figured in their arms, and his name in their language whenever they designated with peculiar affection their country or government."

arcades gay with shops and cafés *. On the fourth is a space open to the sea, called the Piazzetta (small piazza). On one side of this is the very beautiful façade of the ducal palace ; a mixture, I believe, of Gothic and Moorish architecture, but so unlike anything European that we have seen, and so like architectural pictures of the East, that we seemed at once to have passed into the Asiatic world. Near the water stand two granite columns, one surmounted by the lion of St. Mark, the other by the statue of a saint. Both these columns were brought from the East, and are trophies of the conquests of the Republic in the eleventh century. Opposite the ducal palace is another palace of beautiful architecture, and beside it the campanile, the same on which Galileo stood to make his observations. " This is Venice !" we said, as, after gazing for a half-hour on this unimpaired magnificence, we turned to go to our hotel ; but our illusion vanished when we looked off upon the water, and saw but here and there a little boat, where there were once

" Argosies bound
From Tripolis, from Mexico, and England,—
From Lisbon, Barbary, and India !"

I went before breakfast this morning to St. Mark's, and as I paused for a moment at the door to look up at the figure of the saint, on a ground of blue and gold, two persons, sinners I am sure, drew my eyes and thoughts from him. They were young men, who appeared as if they had that moment landed from some piratical expedition. The one was looking about him with a careless curiosity ; there was a wild, savage desolation about the other I never can forget : his face was bronzed, and his tangled locks stood out as if they were of iron. I met his quick, glancing eye, but I am sure he did not see me, nor anything in the world around him ; the gorgeous ceiling, the Oriental marbles, the costly altars, pictures, bronzes, were to him as if they were not ; and on he strode as if he were on a sea-beach, straight through the kneeling congregation, not pausing till he reached the steps before the high altar, when he threw himself prostrate on them, and seemed as if he would have buried his face in the marble. The people were passing up and down, jostling him, treading on him ; he moved no more than if he had been struck dead there. It seemed to me that I could hear the cry from his soul, " God be merciful to me a sinner !" and not till the mass was over, when he rose with an expression somewhat softened and calmed, taking his companion, who had been listlessly staring about, by the arm, and hastened away, could I see anything but him ; and when I did look around upon this most gorgeous of Christian temples, enriched as it is with the spoils of Candia, Cyprus, and the Morea, it seemed poor indeed compared with the worth of this sinning, suffering, and penitent spirit; for so I am certain it was.

Few churches are so enriched with historical associations as St. Mark's. It was here that the subjection of imperial to papal power was consummated by the dramatic exhibition of the humiliation of Frederic Barbarossa to Pope Alexander,

* Over these cafés and shops the nobles once had luxurious casinos, where they indulged in every species of pleasure.

when the emperor prostrated himself before his holiness, and suffered him to plant his foot upon his neck †. The history of this church from the time it was a chapel—a mere appendage to the ducal palace—would be a history of Venice ‡.

WE have been over the ducal palace, up the " Giant's Stairs," and the golden-roofed staircase, and through the immense halls whose ceilings and walls are embellished by Tintoretto, Paul Veronese, and Titian, with, to me—I am profane, or perhaps most ignorant, to say so—uninteresting pictures. The portraits of the doges, which hang below the cornice, encircling one apartment, are not so. They are all there excepting one, and on the tablet where that should be is painted a black veil, with an inscription to signify that this was assigned to Marino Faliero ! Poor old man ! Byron has painted his picture there ; and those who see it beneath the black veil scarcely look at the 120 others. The doges have passed away, and you meet here only tourists, to whom the ciceroni are explaining, in a semi-barbarous dialect, the painted histories of their reigns and triumphs.

We went out of the palace on to the " Bridge of Sighs," and to the prisons of the Inquisition ; for, as you know, there is

" A palace and a prison on each hand."

We went into the dungeons on a level with the sea ; those below its level were destroyed for ever by the French revolutionists, who, in their days of madness, did this among many other righteous deeds.

The curiosities of prisons are horrors, and I shall not detail to you those that were shown us §, but leave them all for the cell where we saw the in-

† This most abject circumstance in Frederic's humiliation is, I suspect, an interpolation of the papal legendaries. M. Sismondi, the most reliable of historians, merely says, " He (the emperor) threw aside his cloak, prostrated himself before Alexander, and kissed his feet." The foot upon the neck was, however, too picturesque a circumstance to be lost, and so a Venetian painter has given it perpetuity in a splendid picture which hangs in the ducal palace.

‡ It was here that one of the finest scenes in the great drama of the crusades was enacted, when the heroic Henry Dandolo, blind, and ninety-four years old, addressed the crowds of Venetians and crusaders, royal, noble, and plebeian, who were assembled in St. Mark's. " Lords," he said, " you are of the first gentry in the world, and banded together for the noblest cause men ever undertook. I am a feeble old man who need repose ; but ill fitted as is my body for the service, I perceive there is none who can so well lead and govern you as I who am your lord. If you will suffer that I take the cross to watch over and teach you, and that my son remain to guard the land, I will go forth to live and die with you, and with the pilgrims." And when this was heard, " Yes," they cried all with one voice, " and we pray God, also, to permit that you come forth with us and do it." This, with many more particulars, may be found in the touching language of the old chronicler in M. Sismondi's Italian Republics.

§ These hideous prisons are not more than six or seven feet square, with mud floors, and a grating, a few inches in length and breadth, which opens into a gallery, into which the only ray of light that ever came was from the torch of the turnkey, when, once a day, he brought the prisoner his food. The French, when they came to Venice, found a man in one of these cells who had been there for fourteen years. They set him free, and carried him in procession through the grand piazza. The poor wretch was struck blind, and died in two or three days.

G 2

scription which Lord Byron copied, and which you may recollect in the notes to his Childe Harold. Our cicerone, who was of a calibre very superior to most of his craft, read the lines with Italian taste and grace, and told us that Lord Byron had taken the pains to retrace and deepen them, "Yes, *with his own hand* *."

20th.—WE have been all the morning in our goudola. We first rowed through the grand canal, which is bordered for two miles by churches and palaces; affecting memorials of the rise, dominion, perfection, decay, desertion, and death of "Venice;" a death so recent that the freshness and beauty of life have not quite passed away†. A few of these palaces are still in the possession and occupancy of their noble families, but wherever you see one in its original splendour (and most splendid they are) you see the *collar-mark* upon it, "*Provinsie di Venesie*," indicating that it is appropriated to the officers and purposes of the Austrian government. For the most part they are dilapidated ‡, with broken glass, parchment panes, and indications that they are degraded to base uses.

As we passed the Foscari palace we saw a Venetian washing, patched calico gowns and all manner of trumpery drying over the massive and sculptured stone balconies of that princely home, to behold which once more an exiled son of the house risked and lost his life. Nearly opposite this palace is that which Byron occupied: its location may have suggested the tragedy of "The Two Foscari." And what painful and pleasant remembrances did his residence suggest to us as we passed under its balcony, and thought of Moore's groping his way through the dark hall after Byron, while he called out, "Keep clear of the dog! take care, or that monkey will fly at you!" and his droll exclamation as they stood together on the moonlit balcony, "*Don't* be poetical, Tom!" and, alas! of the mock-tragic drama enacted here by his Fornarina, and of other episodes in his life that he must have wished to blot out, and of which those who admire and pity him must wish his biographer had spared the record. Byron's is the greatest and best known of English names in Italy.

Some of the Venetian palaces still contain treasures of art. In the *Palazzo Barbarigo*, where Titian long lived, and where he died, there is a gallery called "*Scuola di Tiziano*." Here we saw a Magdalen, the last he ever painted, and the *first*, I think, ever painted. It belongs to the highest class of that intellectual painting which reveals the secrets of the soul. You see a woman who has been forgiven much because she loved much; a voluptuary by nature and a saint by grace; and you feel assured, from the depth and *calmness* of her feelings,

that she will sin no more. The old woman who showed us the gallery, and who, in her progress, had poured out the usual quantity of a cicerone's superbas! and magnificas! said, "Other pictures have their prices; this is priceless!" We have seen other pictures by Titian in Venice which seem to me to come into the same category, truly to be "priceless," the Assumption (called his masterpiece) where the loveliest cherubs, alias winged *Italian* children, are floating in a wreath of clouds around her; or the Sacrifice of Isaac, on the ceiling of the sacristy in Santa Maria della Salute. The beautiful boy is bending over the pile, awaiting the stroke, with an expression of most dutiful obedience, and something more; there is a trustfulness, as if he felt his father could not do him wrong. The angel appears with a blended expression of Divine authority and human sympathy, and you *feel* the command which he eagerly utters, and which the awe-struck patriarch has turned to receive, "Lay not thine hand upon the lad §!" This picture is a lyric poem; but for the epics of the "Venetian school," with their architecture and landscape, their complication of action and variety of character—their groups of men, women, and children, Jews, infidels, and brutes, it requires more artistic education and far more time than we have to comprehend and enjoy them.

The Rialto ‖ is a stone bridge over the grand canal, and in its material of stone and mortar precisely what it was when merchants there "most did congregate." But the princely merchants, who unlocked and locked at pleasure the golden gates of the East, have disappeared, and in their places are people walking up and down between the rows of mean shops, hawking, in the loudest and most dissonant tones, tortone (a famous species of candy), cakes, *fish*, and like fancy articles. An old Jew sleeping in the shadow of the bridge, over whom we stumbled as we got out of our gondola, for a moment recalled my poetic associations with the Rialto; but to retain them undisturbed one should not see it. The bridge is a high arch, and the street on each side of it is of course continued over it between the mean one-story shops which are built on it. The bridge has two other broad passages between the shabby rear of the shops and its balustrades, and thus encumbered and defaced is the aspect it presents as you approach it on the canal.

WE visited the Arsenal as a memorial rather than an actual existence. Its silent forges and empty magazines only serve to impress you with the vast commerce and power of the fallen republic. It occupies an island three miles in circumference, and has the aspect of an independent fortress. The winged lion, brought from the Piræus of Athens, still guards its entrance, but you know too surely that his teeth and claws are

---

* I was sorry afterward to hear this man agreeing with a hard-favoured wretch in calling Silvio Pellico a "menteur," and maintaining that he had never been in "*the leads*," which by the way, they spoke of as "*beaux* prisons."

† "The foundation of Venice preceded by seven centuries the emancipation of the Lombard cities, and its fall was three centuries after the subjection of Florence." Truly it had a long life of power and glory.

‡ We were told they would be taken down, and small tenantable houses built from their materials, but for an order of the Austrian government forbidding it—why, I know not, unless they wish to preserve them as a trophy.

§ After seeing Titian's masterpieces, one enjoys the old story of Charles the Fifth's reproof of his nobles' scorn of his plebeian favourite. "I can create with a breath a hundred dukes, counts, and barons, but, alas! I cannot make one Titian!"

‖ I do not understand why the name Rialto is used merely to designate the bridge. "It was in 809," says M. Sismondi, "that the Venetians made choice of the little *island of the Rialto*, near which they assembled their fleet, with their collected wealth on board, and built the city of Venice, the capital of their republic."

gone by his watchdogs in Austrian uniform *.
We passed along a portico lined with every species
of workshop relating to ship-building—all silent
now—and, crossing through a spacious dockyard
where there were a score or two of galley-slaves
in long, clanking chains, working under the surveillance of other slaves in a different uniform and
without chains, called *gendarmes*, we entered the
model-room. There, among a vast variety of
curious things, we saw an exact miniature of the
galley in which the doges were accustomed to
perform the ceremony of their espousals with the
Adriatic. It is of a most graceful form, its
exterior gilded and embossed with devices illustrative of the history of Venice. The canopy is
of crimson velvet ; Venice, "a proud ladye," sits
in the prow, with Peace at her feet and the scale
of Justice in her right hand. In the stern is the
throne of the doge, and at its back an opening
through which he threw the wedding-ring to his
sea-bride. Opposite the throne sits Time, with
his admonitory scythe and hour-glass. When this
was rigged, with four stalwart Venetians at each
crimsoned and gilded oar, it must have been a
pretty show !

We were shown an immense hall filled with
trophies, banners, and weapons of all their conquered enemies, Christians and Turks, and halls
filled with Venetian armour ; and, among other
curiosities, a *very entertaining* collection of the
Inquisition's instruments of torture ; some among
them ingenious and perfect enough to have been
forged in the lower regions. Ah, cruelty has
ever gone hand in hand with power, my dear C.

THE perfect repose, the indolent luxury, of a
gondola has not been exaggerated. I cannot
convey to you a notion of the delight of its soft
cushions and gliding motion after two hours of
such tedious sight-seeing as we had at the arsenal ;
it puts you into that delicious state between waking and sleeping, between the consciousness of
fatigue and cares, and the unconsciousness of
oblivion.

We were rowed out to an island in the sea, San
Lazzaro, to see the Armenian convent and college,
whose foundations were laid long ago by an Armenian who bought the island, and instituted a school
here for his countrymen. The pupils receive a
learned education for various professions. The
college has a printing-press, and prints books in
forty or fifty different languages†. A large reve-

nue is realised from their sale. We were conducted about the institution by a very intelligent
and courteous Armenian priest, and we encountered some fine old Eastern people with long, sil-
vered beards. The young men were extremely
handsome. As you go east and south the beauty
of the human race improves ; there is a richer
colouring and more spirit, more of the sun's light
in the eyes.

Our conductor showed us the room in which
Byron received his lessons "when his lordship
took the *whim*," he said, "to study Armenian, and
to swim across to us from the Lido !"

As we were rowing homeward, a Venetian gentleman who accompanied us pointed out the *Canali
degli Orfani*, where bodies are thrown which any
one wishes quietly to dispose of. "Fishing here,"
he said, "is forbidden, lest it should lead to unpleasant discoveries !"

OUR hotel was so full on the first day of our
arrival in Venice that we could only get dismal
apartments in the rear, where we felt as if more
than the ducal palace had a prison attached to it.
But the following morning we were transferred to
a superb suite of apartments in front, looking out
upon the sea, which have to us a charm from
having been occupied by the Countess Confalonieri
when she was suing for her husband's pardon, with
long-deferred and finally baffled hope, to the Austrian court. I am alone, the family being all at
the opera, and I have just been standing in the
balcony looking at the moon, which is pouring a
flood of light through this clear atmosphere down
upon the sea. In her effulgence Orion is but
dimly visible. I can look up to the familiar
objects in the heavens and almost forget my distance from you ; but the painful sense returns as
I bring my eyes to earth, for oh ! how different is
this earth from ours ! There is the splendid
Church of San Georgio with her tall campanili,
and Santa Maria della Salute with her cupolas ;
and here are gondolas gliding out of the little canal
into the Giudecca, and others gliding in and out
among the vessels that lie at anchor in the harbour. On my right is the ducal palace and prison ;
I cannot *see* the Bridge of Sighs, but it is almost
within my touch, so near that I feel the atmosphere that surrounds it, and am glad to be cheered
by the lively voices of a merry troop that are
passing on to the Piazzetta, and, as that sound dies
away, to hear the delicious voice of a cavalier in
a gondola, who is singing for his own pleasure—
and certainly for mine.

WE hear so much of the gondola in Venice that
we almost forget there is "solid earth for tread of
feet," though for the most part artificial. After
passing the greater part of five delicious days in
a gondola, I went this morning, the beginning of,
alas ! our last day in Venice, to the Rialto on foot,
that I might see something of the terra-firma of
this singular town. There is nothing, I believe,
in the world like the streets of Venice ; streets
they can scarcely be called, nor lanes, nor alleys,
for they have not the peculiarities of either. They
are lined by such lofty houses, that, excepting at
noonday, a ray of the sun never reaches them ; no
wheel turns in them, no horse's hoof treads over
them. They are intersected by the canals, and

---

* These gentry refused entrance to our courier ; service
being a disqualifier for such privilege here, as colour is in
our *enlightened* country. We trust these shadows will,
ere long, pass quite off the civilised world.

† Lady Morgan fancied if there were a free press in the
world it must be "the *ocean-press* of San Lazzaro ; " and
she relates, in her best manner, her conversation with the
librarian, who asserted *it was a free press*. She asked if
he would print a book for her that required a "very free
press." "Certainly," he replied ; "any book that her
ladyship might write." "What, if she should speak ill of
the Emperor of Austria ?" Certainly not." "Might she
have a hit at his holiness ?" This was worse still. Unwilling, she says, to lose her game, she started the grand
seignior. "The grand seignior was a powerful neighbour."
"In a word, it was evident," she concludes, "that the
press of San Lazzaro was just as free as the Continental
presses of Europe, where one might print freely under the
inspection of two or three censors !"

filled with petty shops that in nowise recall the time when Venice was the mart and channel of the productions of the East.

The manners of the tradespeople are civil, but not obsequious or obtrusive. They have the general Italian habit of asking one price, and offering to take the half of it, "for the pleasure of serving madam," or "to make a beginning," or for some other ready and most reasonable reason * ! We bought on the Rialto some trifling specimens of the exquisitely fine gold-chain work done here, a pendant for the Brussels lace manufacture. These gold chains, some fabrics of beads, and some rather curious but inferior glass manufactures (all that remain of the unrivalled Venetian glass-works), are now the only products peculiar to Venice.

WE have merely seen the outside of things here. Our only acquaintance, a Venetian exquisite, who seems not to suspect there is any but an outside to life, could give no very enlightening answers to our many questions. In reply to an inquiry about the education of women, he shrugged his shoulders, and said, " ça commence !" So I suppose they are about as well instructed as they were in Byron's time here, when, as you may remember, a conversation turning upon Washington, a *learned* lady asked " if he were not the man killed in a duel by Burke."

I asked our acquaintance, when we were passing the mad-house, which looked very like a prison, " if the patients were well taken care of." " Assez bien " (" Well enough "), he replied, stroking his moustache. " Luck *is* a lord." We had our fortune at Milan ; we must take the turn of the wheel here †.

Ferrara, Nov. 24.

MY DEAR C.—WE are seldom annoyed in Italy with any apparent dissatisfaction in the people we employ. The servants at the inns, coachmen, valets de place, &c., &c., are all paid by fees. They have a pride or self-respect which prevents their murmuring when they are not content ‡. There is a monstrous disproportion between the wages of people and the fees ; for instance, a labourer working out of doors all day gets ten sous, and your waiter, who gives you, perhaps, two or three hours of very light work, expects two francs from each person, which, from a party of six, amounts to two dollars and thirty cents per day. We made a deduction from this at the Hôtel Reale, and our garçon, who sported his Venetian gold chain, was " *très mécontent.*"

* It is to be earnestly desired that our tradesmen should not yield to the temptation of this habit, which most certainly leads to a depravation of mercantile morality.

† I perhaps owe an apology for publishing the above meagre notices of Venice. Where there is most to be said it is very difficult to say a little well. We spent five beautiful days in going in our gondola from sight to sight, in visiting churches and palaces. Our dawns and twilights were passed at St. Mark's, within two minutes' walk of our hotel. Of course, we accumulated immense lists of things which are mere lists, and have been well expanded by a hundred tourists who have preceded us.

‡ This remark does not apply to Southern Italy. All such delicacy has vanished long before you reach Naples, where " poor Oliver *asks for more*," till it would become ludicrous if it were not most pitiable.

So was not our gondolier friend, Andrea Donaio. He has attended us all day, the best of gondoliers, the most sagacious and prompt of cicerones. As we came away, he stood at the foot of the stone staircase, hat in hand, in his close-fitted, scarlet-corded dress, his fine black hair waving off his bronzed temples ; his sound white teeth shown off by a kindly smile. I told him how glad we should be to see him some bright day in New-York, and his " Grazie, signore," and " Buon viaggio, excellenza !" were the last words we heard as we got into our gondola to pass for the last time before the prisons, the Bridge of Sighs, the ducal palace, the piazza, and all its magnificent accompaniments, into the Giudecca.

Andrea's wishes were vain. We have had a dismal journey hither. As we left Venice, the rain came on again, and has continued ; the rivers are still rising, and menacing the country with destruction. You can hardly imagine anything more frightful than the aspect of the valley of the Po 'at this moment. The course of the river is through a flat country. Deposits of slime and gravel from year to year have so raised its bed, that, to prevent it from submerging the adjacent land, dykes have been erected, and as the level of the river has risen, the dykes have been raised higher and higher, till now the river, at its ordinary level, is in some places thirty feet higher than the land on the other side of the embankment. Whenever the river rises three feet above its usual level, great alarm is felt, and guards are placed with proper instruments ready to repair the slightest breach in the dyke. As we passed along the road on the top of the embankment, the brimming, muddy river was rushing furiously on one side of us ; and on the other, many feet below us, lay villages and farm-houses, those on the lowest ground half under water, and all appearing as if they might at any moment be swallowed up. At intervals of a few yards along the road there were tents of matting, saturated with a forty days' rain, and under each two watchmen, peasants, stretched on the wet ground, their enemy on the one side, and their menaced homes on the other, with an anxiety and despair in their faces that expressed how hopelessly they opposed themselves to the unbridled elements.

Poor fellows, their case is a hard one ! The winter-grain is so soaked that it is certain it must all be rotted. In our thinly-peopled land, where the failure of one year's crops is but a disappointment, you can hardly imagine the effect of such a disaster where the fullest supplies are in fearful disproportion to the consumption. The streets of Ferrara to-day are crowded with people whose homes are under water ; 1500 are provided for —being drowned ! It is said that the King of Piedmont and the Duke of Tuscany, fearing the consequences of the despair of their people, have already made liberal appropriations for their relief. I hope they may have been instigated by a better motive than fear. The virtue called forth by physical evil is its only satisfactory solution §.

§ The f llowing anecdote, which I afterward heard from Mr. W. at Florence, may appear to others, as it did to me, an illustration of the above remark. While we were looking at the superb Strozzi palace, Mr. W. said, " The head of this house, the marquis, was on his country estates during the distress on the Po last autumn. Seeing

We were to cross the Po at the barrier of the pope's dominions, and here, at their very portal, we had a charming illustration of the imbecility of the papal government, the most imbecile in Italy. The ferry appertains to his holiness. There was no boat on our side of the river ; and though the postilions, gendarmes, and loungers, shouted at the very top of their voices, no answer was returned ; at last we despatched a row-boat, and after an hour we saw a sluggish machine destined for our transport, and moving as though it moved not. It was drawn by a rope attached to horses on the shore a mile and a half up the river, and then dropped down the current to us. After infinite difficulty, with pushing, pulling, and hoisting, and the din of twenty Italians who were all helping and all helpless, our heavy carriage was got on board the boat, and we were landed safely on the other side, and were charged by his holiness's servants for these admirable facilities six dollars.

Ferrara is a *clean*, fine old city, with immense, unoccupied houses, and wide, grass-grown streets, looking little like the seat of the independent and proud house of Este. Its chief interest to us results from its being the home of our friend Foresti, whose character does it more honour than all this princely house from beginning to end. Byron, you remember, says of Italy, "their life is not our life—their moral is not our moral." This is but in part true. There is a moral that is universal ; and wherever man exists, in savage or in civilised life, he renders an instinctive homage to such an uncompromising pursuit of justice and love of freedom as Foresti has manifested in persecution, in prison, in bonds, and under sentence of death. I believe that if, at this moment, his youth, country, and high position could be restored to him, *with* his experience of sixteen years of chains and most dreary imprisonment, he would again sacrifice all, and suffer all over again in the same cause—such is the *unorushable* material of his noble character.

Well, here we are, in the midst of his family and friends. One of them, a man of letters, Signor B., called immediately after breakfast, and attended us, first, to the casino, where 300 persons, the gentry of Ferrara, who are its proprietors, meet every evening ; and, unless there is a ball, or they are otherwise particularly well amused, adjourn to an adjoining theatre ; truly, "their life is not our life." We next went to St. Anne's Hospital, once a monastery, and now converted to the really Christian purpose of sheltering the sick and insane. The insane are under the care of a distinguished man of science, and, what is more to

the purpose, a genuine philanthropist. We have been told to-day many anecdotes of him, from which we infer that his organ of benevolence, like our honoured friend Woodward's, has a particular development for the management of mad people*. The "minister to the mind diseased," in our Puritan land, takes his patients to church ; the Italian professor conducts them to the theatre—the universal panacea in Italy ; K. says, " the *conforto* and *ristoro* of old and young, rich and poor." The different modes of proceeding are nationally characteristic ; both prove that excitement, properly administered, is healthful, and not hurtful, to the insane patient.

We were shown the cell of the hospital in which Tasso was imprisoned. Our old custode had a loyal feeling for the house of Este, and would fain have us believe that, dismal as the place appeared to us, it was quite a pleasant residence in Tasso's time, with one look-out upon a street and another upon a garden ! There was as much common sense as genius in Byron shutting himself up in this cell to write his "Lament of Tasso." He was sure to find the actual *local* of suffering innocence and kindred genius a heated furnace for his imagination.

The old man told us some particulars of Lord Byron's visit, and showed us his name written by himself in deep-cut characters. "Under Lord Byron's name," he said, " was that of his *Segretario*, Samuel Rogers." We all smiled, recurring at once to Mr. Rogers, as we had recently seen him, with his own poetic reputation, surrounded by the respect that waits on age, heightened into homage by his personal character ; and K. expostulated, and tried to enlighten the old man's ignorance—but in vain. Byron's is the only English name that has risen, or ever will rise, above his horizon, and " the *Segretario*" must remain a dim reflected light.

B. escorted us to his house, where we were kindly received by the signora, and admitted to the studio of her son, who has just received a prize at Florence for miniature painting. They showed us some exquisite pictures of his execution, upon which I said, " You are a fortunate mother to have a son of such genius." " Ah !" she replied, " but he is so good—so good !" This does indeed make the fortunate mother. In this country of art, my dear C., the painter's studio is a sort of museum. Young B.'s occupied several apartments containing pretty casts, and the walls were covered with sketches, studies of anatomy, engravings, and paintings.

B., the father, gave us various works of his own writing : a work on botany, tragedies, and translations from Byron†. He is an enlightened man, and a first-rate hater of priests and kings. In-

---

some persons on the roof of a house in instant danger of being swept off, he offered a large sum to some boatmen if they would go to the rescue. The peril was too great, and they refused. He doubled his offer—they still refused —they had wives and families, they said. ' Would they go if he would go with them ?' ' Yes, they would do anything the *Padroni* would do.' The marquis wrote a few lines to a friend and embarked with them. At tremendous hazard they succeeded in their enterprise. By some mistake the note, which was only to have been opened in case the marquis did not return, was read, and was found to contain instructions that, in case his companions should be lost, their families should be provided for from his estate. When I was at Florence this same marquis was spending his time driving four-in-hand, and philandering fine ladies. Truly, calamities have their uses.

* He uses the same enlightened means, substituting truth, gentleness, and persuasion, for manœuvring, sternness, and authority. We saw some of the incurables quietly basking in the sunshine in a pleasant garden.

† Signor B. said, "If men write in Italy, it is to get a name, or for the love of it—there is no pecuniary compensation. Divided as we are into thirteen states, there is no protection for literary property." If most authors are to be believed, this should not lessen the number of books. They write merely to enlighten or improve their public ! Scott is one of the few authors who has had the honesty to avow that getting money was a distinct motive for writing.

defatigable as all are who have the hard fortune to take our caravan in train, he accompanied us to the green square, where there has been recently placed a colossal statue of Ariosto on a beautifully-sculptured white marble pillar, with this comprehensive inscription : " A Ludovico Ariosto la Patria." *Multum in parvo!* is there not ! The Jesuits made a furious opposition to the erection of the statue, being no lovers of Ariosto, or favourers of any homage to secular eminence. They wished to put the statue of his holiness on the pillar, and wrote to Rome for a decree to that effect ; but before the answer came, the wits of Ferrara had outwitted them. By dint of working 'night and day the statue had been placed on its lofty pedestal ; and buried under it is a history of the controversy, and, as B—i said, " *mille belles choses*" of the Jesuits, which, when time shall have knocked down the column, will serve to enlighten posterity as to the history and true character of the bigots. In the mean time, the poet stands, as he did in life, high above his fellows.

As a natural sequence we visited a house which Ariosto built, and where he lived and died. The room in which he wrote has a fine bust of him on one side, and on the other the following inscription : " Ludovico Ariosto in questa camera scrisse, e questa casa da lui abitata edificò ; laquale 289 anni dopo la morte del divino poeta fù da Girolamo Cicognara podestà co' denari del commune comprà e ristaurata perchè alla venerazione delle genti se mantenesse *. Next to the possession of greatness is the sentiment that reverences it, and this you find everywhere in Italy. The door of Tasso's prison and that to Ariosto's room have been well chipped for relics.

B. conducted us to the cemetery, an old monastic establishment, wrested from the priests after, as he said, a "*guerre à mort*," and converted to the good purpose of burying the dead instead of the living. The long perspective of the cloisters is beautiful. Many of the monks' cells are converted into family vaults, and decorated with monuments, frescoes, and bas-reliefs. One large apartment is appropriated to " the illustrious men of Ferrara."

WE had a *scene* in the twilight, which I can best describe to you, my dear C., by copying K.'s account of it from her journal. She says, " What was my astonishment, when I came into the drawing-room, to find Uncle R. in a corner of the room, his face covered with his hands, Aunt L. leaning on the mantelpiece also in tears ; Aunt K. holding the hand of a lady in black who, with vehement gestures, was pouring out a rapid succession of broken sentences, and L. and M. looking on in most solemn silence. Aunt K. seized me and said, ' This is Foresti's sister. Tell her how much he is beloved and respected in New-York—tell her we try to make him feel he has a home among us.' As well as I could, I played my part of interpreter, and Teresa, in a voice interrupted by many sighs and tears, tried to

express her gratitude, but exclaimed every few minutes in a paroxysm of anguish, stretching out her arms, ' Io non so più parlare ; non so più far altro che piangere e pregar la mia Madonna !' Taking up her black gown, she said, ' Questo è un abito di voto ; l'ho messo quando era in prigione il mio Felice, per farlo liberare ; dal momento delle sue disgrazie sono caduta ammalata. Stave per morire ; i medici credettero che non potessi guarire. Sono solamente tre anni che sto un po' meglio ; ho perso tutti i capelli, ne aveva molti. Non ho voluto mandare il mio ritratto al fratello perchè sono tanto combiata tanto brutta che non mi riconoscerebbe. Non posso dormire. Prego, prego sempre la mia Madonna che mi guarisca di quest' orribile veglia e che mi faccia abbracciare una volta il mio Felice prima di morire. Non è che la speranza di vederlo che mi tiene in vita† !' This is a gathering up of the fragments of her discourse ; but I cannot give an idea of her sorrow-worn countenance, her impassioned tears, and expressive gestures, which gave the most powerful effect to every word she uttered, and left a deep and sad impression on our minds. Just Heaven ! what must be the import to Francis, ' *the father of his people*,' of that sentence, ' With what measure ye mete it shall be measured to you again !' " Yes, truly, those who have turned the sweet streams of domestic love into such bitter, bitter waters— the Francises and Metternichs— will have a fearful account to render.

My dear C., we have so many exiles among us, we so glorify ourselves with the idea that our free country is their asylum, that I fear we are sometimes deficient in that keen sympathy which we should feel in their personal misfortunes, if we realised the sundered ties and languishing affections of the broken hearts in their violated homes. Professor B. and some other friends of Foresti passed the evening with us, partly at the theatre and partly at home. In spite of the wear and tear of twenty years' separation, their attachment to him is unimpaired. Among them was an old curate, who said that, " but for his age, he would go to America to see Foresti." Professor B. is a highly-cultivated man, with that great advantage to a new acquaintance, a beautiful countenance and charming manners, and, withal, he is a hearty liberal. He told us some facts which may give you an idea of the shackles and discomforts the government imposes here, and of the inextinguishable spirit of these noble Italians. There is an association of the literary and scientific men of the different states of Italy recently formed, which is to have an annual meeting. It is favoured by the King of Piedmont and the Grand-duke of Tuscany ; but the pope, who stops every crevice at which light may enter, has issued

* " Ludovico Ariosto wrote in this room ; and this house, built and inhabited by him, was 289 years afterward bought and restored by Girolamo Cicognara with the commune's money, that it might be preserved for the veneration of mankind."

† " I no longer know how to talk. I can only weep and pray to Our Lady !" Taking up her black gown, she said, " I put on this mourning when my brother went to prison, with a vow to wear it till he was freed. From the moment of his misfortune I fell sick. I have been near to death. The physicians believed it was impossible to cure me. For the last three years only have I been a little better. I have lost all my hair. I once had a great deal. I would not send my portrait to my brother ; I am so changed, he would not know me. I cannot sleep ; I pray and pray to Our Lady to cure me of this horrible wakefulness, and that she will permit me to embrace my brother once before I die. The hope of seeing him is all that keeps me alive !"

a bull, declaring that if a subject of his shall be present at one of these meetings, he shall be held a traitor, and suffer accordingly.

A physician is not permitted to make a professional visit beyond the walls of the city without going first to the police to declare where he is going, and the name and disease of his patient! Professor B. said, "In 1831, when we all believed the favourable moment had arrived for asserting our liberty, I, who had belonged to no secret society, nor had had anything to do with promoting the excitement, declared my sympathy with the liberals, and was delegated by them to warn the apostolic legate that he was about to be deprived of all power, moral and physical, but that his person would be untouched. He courteously expressed his obligations to me; but when, at the end of our twenty-six days of *happiness*, he was re-established, I found that my name was placed at the head of the black-list. I was deprived of all the public trusts I held, and I have been ever since so closely watched that I am but a prisoner. I cannot cross the frontier within ten miles of Ferrara, nor even go to Rome without a special permission from the secretary of state, which can only be procured by stating that I am going on professional business, and shall be in such and such houses, see such and such people, and be absent such a number of days." This is the condition of the best subjects of a government of which the head is also the head of the greatest body of Christians in the world. Oh! my countrymen, thank God for your religious and civil freedom, and cherish it!

Bologna.—We had nothing notable during our dreary, cloudy drive to Bologna, but a rencounter with the beggars at our last post-station. As usual, beggars of all ages, from first to second childhood, flocked around our carriage. We had given away all our sous, and we had recourse to our lunch-basket. I arranged the bread and chicken, and L. dispensed. "Oh! give me a bit," she said, "for this boy with heavenly eyes!" "Here it is: now give this to that blind old woman." "Oh! I must give this to that little Tot who is stretching up her arm to me; what a perfect cherub she would be if her face was washed!—keep off, you snatcher!" to a lean, tall half-idiot who was intercepting the cherub's slice. "Now, L., this must go to that sick, shivering old man!" "Oh! wait, see this poor, pale girl." "Now for the old woman!" but the bit went to a trembling boy who looked like a leper, with a withered arm; and when my old woman was at last supplied, there was an evil-eyed hag and four boys who jostled the first-comers away, and two of them, after devouring, like hungry dogs, what we gave them, followed us half a mile, calling "ca-ri-ta!" Beside the dramatis personæ I have described, and who were actually *en scène*, we saw, as we drove off, others, lame and blind, coming from their more distant stations towards us.

You must attribute some portion of the barrenness of my travelling journal, my dear C., to the bad weather that, almost without exception, has attended us in our passages from place to place since we entered Italy. The advanced season, too, is against us. All rural occupation is suspended; the vintage is past, the corn is hus-

banded, and the country has now (November 26) as bare an aspect as it ever has in Italy. Bologna, as you first see it, lying under the shadow of the Apennines, with its antique spires and leaning towers, is a most picturesque town; but all is picturesque in Italy, down to the laden ass and the beggar. From the villas and villages that surround the town, you may imagine how rich and smiling the suburbs must be in any but this desolate season. As we drove through the streets we were struck with the long lines of arcades and columns that front all the edifices, and which afford a perfect protection to the foot-passenger. They were designed, I think, by the luxurious citizens, when the sumptuary laws of the republic forbade the use of covered carriages. There is an arcade of 640 arches, extending from the town to a church of the Madonna, on a hill three miles from the city. Truly the church has kept itself free of sumptuary laws.

The Piazzo del Gigante, to which I have just *walked* in a pouring rain, is one of the most characteristic and grandest monuments of the Italian republics that we have yet seen in Italy. With the fountain of Neptune, the masterpiece of John of Bologna, in the centre, it is surrounded by churches, superb old palaces, towers, and other buildings with the most curious Gothic fronts.

The "Academy of the Fine Arts" here contains one of the best galleries of pictures in the world. They are the masterpieces of the first masters, and what masters they were! I feel now more than ever what nonsense it is to write about these pictures, since, with all I have read about them, I find I had no conception of their power—none worth having of their divine beauty. I make it a rule, in these galleries, not to go bewildering myself about from room to room, but to confine my attention to the best pictures; and I have adhered to my rule to-day, hardly glancing even at the pictures of the three Caracci, all natives of Bologna.

There is a painted tragedy here by Guido that would break your heart: "The murder of the Innocents." The trustfulness of the lovely children, who feel themselves safe in the close embrace of the mother, contrasted with her terror and anguish, is most touching. But the most affecting figure is a mother with her hands clasped and her two dead children at her feet. It is all over with her; she has nothing farther to hope or fear, and the resignation of the saint is struggling with the despair of the parent. You want to throw yourself at her feet and weep with her.

The martyrdom of St. Agnes by Domenichino, with its glorious golden light, is a picture that even dear J., with all her horror of representations of physical suffering, could not turn away from; there is such sweet peace on the face of the young woman. Art could not better illustrate that true and beautiful declaration of the prophet, "The work of righteousness shall be peace, and the effect of righteousness, quietness and assurance for ever." The executioner grasps her bright, wavy hair, with one hand, while with hot pincers in the other he is burning out the flesh of her throat and bosom. The judge looks gloatingly on, and cherubs are floating over the *naissant* saint, one holding the crown of martyrdom, 'and another a pen to record her triumphs. I pass over *Guido's* "*Madonna del Pieta,*" the "*Rosario,*" and even that embodiment of perfect grace and beauty, "Raphael's "St. Cecilia" (their names thrill those who have seen them!) for Guido's "Crucifixion," which, like the very scene, fills you with solemnity and awe. There are but four figures, and they are as large as life; that of Jesus expresses "It is finished!" Mary is not, as in most of her pictures, to the gross violation of truth, represented young, but in the unimpaired ripeness of womanhood. She has the same face, dress, and attitude as in the Pieta, but there she divides your attention with the admirable portraits of the four adoring saints; there Scripture truth and simplicity are sacrificed to a fable or an imagination of the church; here you see the real Mary—the bereft mother—and the unfathomable depths of her sorrow show the prophecy accomplished: "the sword *has* pierced her soul." John, standing on the other side of the cross, is the personification of gentleness and tenderness worthy that highest trust of his master, "Woman, behold thy son!" The only imperfection that struck me in the picture is a want of a right expression in Mary Magdalene. She is a beautiful, sorrowing young girl, kneeling at the foot of the cross, and pressing her brow against it, but she is not the forgiven penitent. Surely the reformers forgot that nine tenths of mankind receive their strongest impressions through their senses, when they excluded such glorious presentments of Divine truth from their churches. I should have but a poor opinion of him whose devotion was not warmed by Guido's Crucifixion.

A masterly head of an old man arrested my attention. I examined my catalogue, and found it was painted by Guercino in a single night, and was called "the head of the Eternal Father!" The attempt is as futile as profane to represent Him whom "no man can see, and live."

While enjoying these sublime works of art as a new revelation, we were hurried away to see something else that must be seen now or never. The *Campo Santo*, being the most beautiful thing of its kind in Italy, we could not overlook; accordingly we drove there. This was formerly a chartreuse —an immense monastic establishment; once the dreary habitation of the living, who suffered in its magnificent solitude, now the beautiful abode of the dead, who cannot enjoy it. Such are the perversions of human things! The cemetery at Ferrara dwindled to insignificance compared with this. I can give you no idea of the immense perspective of its cloisters, all lined with tablets, and monuments, and fresco paintings, or of the almost infinite series of cells, converted into family tombs by the exclusives of Bologna. These open from the cloisters, and are so arranged as to produce a most picturesque architectural effect. "The million" are laid in four large, open courts in classes, one for men, one for women, one for boys, and another for girls. There seemed to me in this a cold neglect of the law of family love, that governs all mankind. There are some splendid public monuments, and a pantheon is building for the illustrious of Bologna, and in the mean time there is a large apartment filled with their busts. I noticed a very fine one of a woman who was pro-

fessor of Greek in the University of Bologna within the present century[*].

Immense as the establishment is, large additions are making. "You mean to have room for all Bologna," I said to our conductor. "Oui, madame, tout le monde entre et personne en sort. C'est pourquoi qu'il faut toujours bâtir." ("All come in and none go out. So we have to keep on building.")

IT has been our great pleasure to meet Miss —— here. You can hardly imagine the delight, after being exclusively among foreign people, of meeting a high-bred Englishwoman who is *not* foreign to us. She sang for us, and truly, as Mrs. —— said of her, she does not sing like an angel, but "like a choir of angels." Music is the key that unlocks her soul, and brings its rich revelations to her face. She looks, while singing, like an inspired sibyl. We went to the opera with her, where we saw, for the first time, a *decent* ballet. The house is very pretty. There are balconies projecting from the *loges*, which show off the audience, and give the house a lively aspect unusual in the Italian theatres.

Nov. 28.—A wretched morning, and the rain pouring, my dear C.; but our letters are at Florence, and there must we be—so ho! for the Apennines.

Fillagare.—As we drove out of Bologna I had a melancholy sense of the ludicrous insufficiency of two rainy days in a place where we might have been employed for six months in studying the almost unimpaired records of its days of power and magnificence. In spite of the pouring rain, we enjoyed the environs of Bologna. They are richly embellished.

At our second post we took a third pair of horses, and at the first ascent a yoke of oxen in addition, and then began a slow drag up the Apennines, which we continued till six this evening, with the exception of a race down the hills as fearless and careless as the driving in our own country. This is a new experience; for, till now, the caution of our postilions has gone even a little beyond my cowardly notions of prudence.

The Apennines are a congregation of hills; those we have passed to-day are much higher, but not unlike, in their formation, the hills between Berkshire and Hampshire, though, judging from their productions, very unlike in their climate. Here are fine fields of well-started winter-grain, and occasional plantations of grapes flung from tree to tree. Once the misty atmosphere cleared, and we got a peep at the Adriatic and the Mediterranean. We have been all day thinking of you. It is "Thanksgiving Day;" and our position in a

---

[*] It is said that Italy has produced more learned women than any part of Europe, and that Bologna has longest continued to respect and reward the literary acquisitions of women. It was a lady of Bologna who, in the fifteenth century, was so zealous a champion of her sex as to employ her wit and learning to prove the world has been all this while in error, and that it was Adam who tempted Eve. It is curious that the most illustrious examples of learned women should spring up in a country where they are condemned, *en masse*, to ignorance; where a conventual education prescribes religion as their only duty, and their instincts cherish love as their only happiness.

huge, lonely inn in the midst of the Apennines, with a salon over a stable, is a sorry contrast to your sweet savours and social pleasures round the hearth of our childhood! We have entered Tuscany, and I fancy I can see the spirit of this most fortunate land of Italy in our buxom, frank, good-humoured hostess and her beautiful progeny, with their black eyes and golden skins. We have been talking with the eldest, Candida and Clementina, and petting the youngest, Giulio and Angiolino! "a pretty Italianizing of Tom and Sam," K. says. I like, of all things, to stop at these inns which are not the regular stopping-places. The people are social and frank, and you get some insight into the national modes of getting on. You will find no teacups and no tea (but that first of necessaries you always have with you), and you have a droll medley for your table-service ; and, instead of a dandy waiter with his meagre French, and his "Subito, signora," and his action *never* suited to the word, you have all the family to serve you, with their amusing individualities, and all eager and indefatigable.

WE left our shelter at Fillagare at nine this morning. We are often wondering at the complaints we have heard of the impositions in Italy. We had excellent bread and delicious butter from the cascina (the duke's dairy) with fresh eggs in the morning, generous un-Italian fires in two rooms, and a pair of chickens for to-day's lunch, all for one dollar each ; and being an inn where travellers seldom stop, they had the temptation to pluck well the goose that is rarely caught.

I walked on in advance of the carriage this morning, and a heavy, impenetrable mist came scudding over the hills in one direction, and far, far away in another the light streamed down in a silvery shower, in which the whole faith of the land would have enveloped a descending Divinity. I was amid scenery so wild and solitary that it recalled my earliest ideas of Italy got from Mrs. Radcliffe's romances, when I was suddenly awakened from a reverie to an uncomfortable consciousness of my isolation and helplessness by the apparition of a savage-looking wretch clothed in sheep-skins. He, however, betook himself to the reliable occupation of tending his sheep. Soon after an ass-rider overtook me, and I tried to keep pace with his beast, thinking that he was a safe-guard who possessed even so much property as an ass, but the brute ambled away from me ; and while I paused, hesitating whether to proceed or turn towards the carriage, I perceived a ragged, wild-looking man in an adjoining field, who eyed me for an instant, and then came rapidly towards me. I hesitated no longer, but turned and walked quickly down the hill, seeing, as I looked askance at my pursuer, that he gained on me. "Oh," thought I, "what a fool I was, when François told me yesterday this was no country for a lady to walk alone in, to try it a second time!" Like the Irishman, I thought all the world might hear the singing in my ears, when, to my unspeakable relief, our great machine, with its attelage of six horses, appeared in sight. How brave I felt as I again turned and eyed my enemy, who immediately retreated, giving me thus some colour of reason to believe that I had been on the verge of an incident very rare of late years! It is surprising to me, with the temptations of booty which the rich English travellers offer, the urgency of the people's wants, and the favourable positions occurring on the great thoroughfares, that robberies are not frequent in Italy.

The wind blew furiously to-day on the summits of the Apennines. These gusts of wind, as M. read to us from our guide-book (at the moment it seemed to be swelling to a hurricane), formerly carried away carriages, travellers, and all ; but now all danger of such a catastrophe is obviated by stone walls erected for protection by the "paternal grand-duke."

At our fourth post the wildness and sterility disappeared, and we came down upon declivities with large tracts of rich pasturage, where herds of cattle and flocks of sheep were grazing, and a little lower down appeared plantations of vines and olives. As we approached this most beautiful city of Florence, the hills, even at this sear season, appeared like terraced gardens; and as we came down the last long descent, with the valley of the Arno at our feet, and fair Florence with its spires and domes before us, we seemed to have passed into another world. The olive-tree resembles our ordinary sized willow in its shape and in the hue of its foliage. Some person has happily said that "it looks as if it grew in moonlight ;" an idea exquisitely transfused into poetry by Kenyon in his address to his "sphered vestal!"

> "Or adding yet a paler pensiveness
> To the pale olive-tree."

The olive lives to such an age that the peasant believes the oldest were planted in the time of our Saviour. The bearing-limbs are continually renewed by trimming, but the main stems are apparently sapless, and so decayed and hollow that you wonder how the juices can be kept in circulation. And yet they are in full bearing in the most sterile places, where, as our friend K—n said too poetically in prose, "they pump oil from the rocks."

We are settled for a week at the Scheiderff hotel on the Arno, formerly one of the palaces of the Medici. This, I fancy, is the season when most English are to be found in Florence. It seems like an English colony. The coaches in the streets are English, with English ladies and English liveries. The shops are thronged with English, and the galleries filled with them*.

Sienna, December 8.

MY DEAR C.—We arrived here last evening just at the moment of the only Italian sunset we have seen to be compared with our brilliant sunsets. The golden and crimson rays reminded me of home, but how different from anything at home the Gothic structures and towers that reflected them! Our drive yesterday was through as lovely a country as can be imagined; broken into steep, high hills, whose declivities of every form are enriched by the highest cultivation, which shows, even now, what a garden Tuscany is ; that here "Nature makes her happy home with man."

* I have omitted my first delightful impressions of Florence. We returned to it at a pleasanter season, when my records were more particular and may prove more interesting. At any rate, I shall avoid the tediousness of repetition.

There seems to be a fitness and harmony between the ground and its tillers. We have seen nowhere so handsome and attractive a peasantry. They have bright cheeks and bright eyes, and the most graceful cheerfulness. The animals, too, seem the fit offspring of this their bountiful mother-earth. The oxen are mouse-coloured, large, fat, and beautifully formed.

When we arrived at the inn, we found that all the apartments *au premier* were held in reserve for an expected " milord Anglais " (all the English on the Continent are " my lords "); so we are obliged to put up with a little saloon without a fire, and to hover round a smoky chimney in R.'s bedroom*.

As we have been looking forward to a pleasant Sunday here, you must forgive my grumbling. We fully realise the happiness of travelling in a large party when we assemble, a little Christian congregation, *for our mass*. That being over this morning, we sallied forth to the Cathedral, old and grand, rich without and within. It has a rare mosaic pavement of black and white marble, representing Scripture history, and events and characters of the Catholic Church, in a masterly style, by a mere outlining. It bears a very curious resemblance to Retzsch's etchings. There are frescoes in the sacristy, designed by Raphael, in which there are three portraits of himself; if not *en peintre* idealised, he must have had an outer fitting his inner man. In the same sacristy are twenty-five volumes of church music, illustrated by Benedictine monks in the fifteenth century, in colours as vivid as the rainbow, and with the most elaborate finish. For the rest (I adopt a great authority) " vide Guide-book," which guide-book sent us off in search of the Fonte-Blanda, to which Dante, by a simple mention, has given an " immortal youth." So up we mounted and down we strode

* I once asked an English friend, who, I thought, was sufficiently a philosopher to endure and perhaps to solve the question, " how it happens that the English are so much disliked on the Continent." " How can it be otherwise," he replied, " when they occupy the best apartments, ride in the best carriages, use the best horses, and, in short, forestal the natives in everything?" And when to this potentiality are added the Englishman's shyness and pride, his island inaptitude at adaptation, his exclusiveness, from principle, taste, and habit, and the consciousness of indisputable superiority that he manifests in all parts of the world, thus everywhere running afoul of other people's self-loves, national pride, and, I may add, just self-estimation, it is very explicable why he is the subject of general dislike. It is a pity he should thus lose the benefit of his wide-spread benefactions. It is the Englishman who keeps alive and astir the needy population of these old cities. It is he who builds the hotels, who sets the wheels in motion on the roads, who makes a beaten path to the temples of old art, however secluded, and to the everlasting temples of nature, however difficult of access. But this all goes for nothing so long as he maintains his national demeanour, and (as an Italian gentleman said to a friend of mine) " comes down into Italy as if he were at the head of a victorious army !" The American travellers being as yet but a handful in comparison with the English, and speaking the same language, are merged in them. If not English, why then, they say, " you are English Americans." But the moment they become fully aware that you belong to a separate and independent nation, they open their hearts, and pour out a flood of griefs against the English. As we are a young nation, we should be flexible, and avoid the foibles of the parent stock.

through a street that no carriage could pass; and at the foot of it, and at the gate of the city, we found the fountain. Sienna is celebrated for the purity and abundance of its water. Here it flows through several pipes and by grotesque mouths into an immense basin, which is covered with a stone-vaulted roof of three arches; and, hanging over this, on the verge of a perpendicular hill, is a large church dedicated to St. Catherine. It is a most picturesque place; but what is *not* picturesque in Italy ? The old hags I saw skinning lambs, as we again mounted the steep hill, were subjects for Michael Angelo. If these old women had been born in New-England, they would as soon have flayed themselves as flayed lambs in the street of a Sunday. So much for conventional virtue ! It was festa-day in Sienna, and these secular employments were a curious episode enough in the general " idlesse " and gaiety of the streets. It was St. Catherine's festa, too, being her natal day, and we were passing by a little chapel, built on the site of the very house in which she was born; so we pushed aside the curtain to the door, and turned into it, expecting to find it crowded; but she whom the painters more effectually than the church have canonised, has met with the common fate, and has little honour in her own country— or her own chapel. There were some twenty children kneeling about the door, who suspended their prayers to stare at us; and the young priests who were going in and out, I inferred from the direction of their eyes, thought less of the saint than of the blooming young heretics who were with me.

Radicofane.—WE were up betimes this morning, and before seven drove from the little piazza, with its antique column surmounted with the nursing mother of Romulus and Remus, and her human cubs. We were but a few miles from Sienna when I discovered that I had left my shawl and mantilla at the head of my bed, where I had placed them to raise my scant pillow. I sent back a line from the next post, but, I take it, there is little hope in Italy of retrieving such a loss. If the master of the hotel chances to be honest, the *cameriera* will be too quick for him†.

As we have proceeded on our journey to-day, the country has become sterile and beggars multiply. We have been followed up and down hill by a tail of little beggars clothed in a mass of *ragged* patches; yet their beauty, with a certain grace and refinement in their expressions, went to my heart. They are not beggars " by theirs or their parents' fault ;" and when their little hands were stretched out for " *carita*," I longed to take them and lead them to my free unoccupied country; and they were quite as kindly

† I have transferred the above from my journal, and am willing to bear the shame of it, if, by recording the issue, I may save others from such sweeping and unfair judgments. My property was sent after me to Rome by vetturino, with a very civil note from our host of the Aquila Nera. The man who brought it merely required a receipt for it, and persisted in refusing a reward for his service. This would have been a rare instance of disinterested civility in America, and singular in England; but still Americans and English go on vituperating Italian cupidity !

disposed to us, promising us for our few halfpence the protection of all the saints, the company of "Maria Santissima," and, to crown all, access to Paradise!

K. asked a boy of twelve years, who wore a cotton jacket and trousers (December 9, two thousand four hundred and seventy feet above the Mediterranean), and *manifestly* no under-clothes, " if he knew where America was !" "No ; nor England, nor Rome, nor Florence !" Another still older, had heard of Rome, but he had been four years to school ! " His mother was dead, and there was no one to pay for him, and give him bread any longer; and," he concluded, " there is no work—ah, signorina, questo paese è molto povero—molto miserabile."

Poor and miserable indeed ! It consists of a range of volcanic hills without soil, excepting here and there enough to sustain pasturage for a few sheep. We are on one of the highest, dreariest summits, and are now, just as the evening is closing, sitting in the huge balcony of our barrack-like inn. I will sketch the scene before us for you. · No ; we are not quite at the summit, for that is crowned with a ruined fortress, and cowering under its walls is a wretched village, between which and our inn the road passes. Before our door is an old stone fountain with the armorial bearings of some forgotten family. From the fountain there is a straight steep path to the village above. Ascending this path are asses with immense bundles of fire-wood on each side (a family's winter supply probably), consisting of mere twigs and withs. There are priests too (the only people here, François says, who do not work and do eat), with their gowns and three-cornered hats, dawdling up the path. And there, driving their scanty flock to the fold, goes a shepherd and shepherdess, and their little girl, looking lean and wearied, their windowed raggedness half hidden with dark red mantles (here the shepherd's costume), which hang to the ground behind. Round the fountain are gathered ass-drivers drinking with their asses, and beside them is an old hag, who having just espied us, has pressed her fingers on the sightless eyeballs of a child beside her, and then wildly stretching her arms towards us, is crying, " Carita !"

In the street under us is a smart English travelling-carriage waiting for a change of horses. The courier is sauntering round it, and my lady's maid is in the rumble : a gentleman is standing beside the open door, a very pretty young woman is in the carriage with three pet-dogs. The little ragged escort that followed us up the hill have surrounded the carriage, reinforced by some half-dozen blind and maimed old creatures whom the sound of wheels has brought down from the village. The lady is caressing her pets, feeding them with raisins and biscuits as well as I can see ; she gives no heed to the beggars' clatter—yes, she is tired of it—she asks the gentleman to get in, and they coolly close the windows. I do not know what my poor little beggarly friends think, but this turning aside from human necessities to pamper brutes seems to me one of those " fantastic tricks at which the angels weep."

My dear C., you may say " something too much of this ;" but beggary here, remember, makes up a good portion of the history of the country, or,

rather, a running commentary on the neglect and abuses of its governments*.

Viterbo.—WE left that wild place up in the clouds this morning with only just light enough to see our winding way. We again entered the papal territory at the end of our first post, and we find increasing wretchedness, and our own wretched condition in bad roads, puny horses, ragged harness, and incompetent postilions, all betokening his holiness' dominion. We passed to-day through Bolsena, now a miserable little town, but once an ancient Etruscan capital, whence the Romans are said to have removed 2000 statues. " The world *is* a stage," and the scenes, with but a little longer interval of time, as shifting as the scenes of a theatre.

I wish you could have seen us, dear C., an hour ago, escorted about by two little fellows, ragged and beautiful, who would fain have persuaded us to go to the church of Santa Rosa to see the saint's body, which is exhibited in her own church. But though our conductors reiterated in most persuasive tones, " è una bella Santa—Santa Rosa," we persisted in leaving the vilely dirty streets of Viterbo for the suburbs, where we had a delightful stroll to a chapel of St. Francis, which we entered just as a procession of Franciscans went in to their vesper-service. Our little guides dropped on their knees and joined in the service ; and so did we in our hearts. How skilfully the Catholics have made many of the offices of their religion to harmonise with the wants and spontaneous feelings of man ! A vesper service is the very poetry of worship.

ON our return, our cicerone, without warning us, knocked at the door of a house, into which we were admitted by an old crone, who, on the boys saying something to her in a low-toned patois, conducted us through a suite of apartments, and passed us over to the " *Padrone.*" He led us out into a garden, and told us this had been Madame Letitia's, and was still in the possession of the Bonaparte family. I fancied this was a mere invention to filch us of a few pauls ; so I was grudgingly offering the fee, when the gentleman, with a very dignified bow and a " grazie," declined it, and turned away to pluck us bouquets of roses and geraniums. It was now my turn to say " grazie," and to feel as if I had been guilty of a meanness quite equal to that which, with a true traveller's prejudice, I had gratuitously imputed to the Italian gentleman.

It is difficult for us to imagine that this little town, which now contains about 13,000 inhabitants (not so many as some of our western towns accumulate in three or four years' growth), has been standing ever since the time of the Etruscans, was a celebrated place in their day, and has since often been a papal residence ; but these Old World towns have, as an Irishman might say, a growth two ways.

WE left Viterbo at seven this morning, little thinking of what dread moment to one human

* No one born and bred in Europe can well imagine how striking the want and beggary of the Old World is to an American eye. I must be forgiven for a tedious recurrence to it—I could not otherwise fairly give my impressions.

being was the instant of our departure. We started with six horses, and, according to the laws of posting in the pope's dominions, with a postilion to each span of horses. They were all young men, one a boy of thirteen, and all impetuous and noisy, beyond what you can well conceive, never having heard the clamour of Italian postboys. There were two carriages ready to start at the inn-door. François, anxious to have the advantage of precedence on the road, urged our postilions, who needed no urging, and we set off at a gallop down the steep street of Viterbo, and into the market-place crowded with people. I shuddered as I saw them jumping on one side and the other to avoid us. I called to François to check our speed; he did not hear me; and on we dashed, turned a corner, and a moment after we felt a slight jolt of the carriage as if it were passing over something, and a momentary check of the horses, and heard cries and exclamations, and again the postilions' clamour burst forth, and the horses were put to their speed. I thrust my head out of the window, and saw the girls in the rumble as pale as death; K. bent forward and said, " We have run over a woman. I called to François and the postilions to stop; they did not hear me; say nothing in the carriage; it will do no good to stop now." The postilions were still urging their horses, we were actually racing up-hill, the scene of the tragedy was already far behind, and fearing, as K. did, to shock her uncle by communicating the disaster, I submitted to the apparent barbarity of galloping away, unheeding the misery we had inflicted. A half-hour afterward a courier who passed us on horseback called out, " è morta ! " (" she is dead ! ") It has been a gloomy day to us.

Nothing could exceed the dismay and dread in the faces of the young postilions when we stopped at the post-house, except the boy, who, being the son of the postmaster, was sure of acquittal, and bore with perfect unconcern all the blame which his comrades heaped upon him, imputing the disaster to his unskilfulness in not turning aside his horses. François confirmed their statement, and K., at their earnest supplication, wrote as mitigatory a statement for them as the case admitted, to be presented to the police of Viterbo. François tells us now that she will be recalled to Viterbo as a witness, and congratulates himself on his superior wariness in not putting his name to the testimonial. " Miss K.," he says, coolly, " did not think." " No, François; but if she had, she could not have refused to do justice to those men because she exposed herself to inconvenience." " Ah, madam, one must take care for one's self first * ! "

* We went through the usual transitions, being first incensed at the postilions, and then, when we felt the misery of exchanging the free gallop over hill and dale for a prison in Viterbo, itself a prison, with the curses of all the town, and the horror of having sent a fellow-creature "unanointed, unannealed," to purgatory, we pitied them. François afterward recognised one of them at Rome, who told him he had got off with a few weeks' imprisonment. "Was the woman young ?" asked François. "So-so." "Had she a husband ?" "Yes." "Did you not fear he would stab you ?" "At first, yes; but he was a sensible fellow—he thanked me, and offered to treat me to a dinner !"

OUR last posts were through the dreary wastes that encompass Rome. The Campagna is not, as I had ignorantly believed, a level, but presents an undulating surface, without morasses or stagnant water, or anything that indicates unwholesomeness except its utter desertion. The grass looks rich and rank, as if it sprung from a virgin soil, and its tints are glowing, even at this season. There are scattered here and there large flocks of sheep, with lean, haggard, and half-clothed shepherds, and shepherd's dogs; and there are herds of oxen of a very large and fine species, and with horns as beautiful as antlers. But, with these exceptions, there is no life. From the summits of the hills, and there are considerable hills, the eye stretches over a wide reach of country, extending for miles in every direction, and here and there an old barrack-like dwelling, a crumbling tower, a shrine or a crucifix; but no cheerful habitations, no curling smoke, no domestic sounds, nothing that indicates human life and " country contentments." It is one vast desolation; a fit surrounding for the tomb of nations. As we caught the view of St. Peter's, and the domes and spires of the three hundred and sixty churches of Rome, it seemed as if life were still beating at the heart of the body doomed to die first at the extremities.

You may expect to know my sensations on first seeing Rome. I cannot tell them, my dear C. I do not myself know what they were. I forgot myself.

Two miles from Rome we passed the Tiber, on the Ponte Molle, the place where Constantine saw the vision of the cross ! and, after passing this, the aspect of the country changes, and immediately around the walls of Rome there is a belt of villas and gardens, a little discordant with what has preceded, like gaily-dressed people in a funeral train. The city, as we entered it at the Piazza del Popolo†, has the gay aspect of a modern capital, with its fountain, statues, churches, and uniform modern edifices; but there are certain antiques, like the Egyptian obelisk, covered with hieroglyphics, which resemble heirlooms in the house of young people who have just set up housekeeping. We had plenty of time for observation, while François was trying to soften the officials. But their hearts were too hard for his rhetoric, and so we drove to the Dogana through the Corso, the principal street in Rome, long and narrow, looking, I fancy, as we proceeded at a foot-pace, with a soldier on each side, like captured contrabandists. The Corso was full of gay equipages, filled with English people, and lined, for the most part, with mean shops, with mean, every-day commodities; such shops and such " goods " as you would see in the " Main-street " of Hudson, or in any other second-rate town. We had no feeling of Rome till we arrived at the custom-house, and saw there some witnesses for the old city, in a portico with superb antique Corinthian pillars. After a little fussy ceremony, a mere make-believe peep into our baggage, and the payment of a few pauls for this gentle treatment, we were released, and are at this moment

† This place is said to derive its name, not from the people—they do not figure in these parts—but from an ancient grove of poplars.

in comfortable apartments in the Hôtel de Russie. *We are in Rome!* We were beginning to think the deep-blue sky of Italy a traveller's story, but here it is. The evening is delicious; there is

"An ampler ether, a diviner air."

Our apartments open on a terraced garden, and we have been walking in it amid orange and lemon trees bent with fruit, and roses and flowering shrubs in bloom. Some of these, planted in vases, stand on fragments of antique sculptured pillars. I observed one on a colossal foot, chiselled, perhaps, by a Greek artist. At every turn there are statues, antiques too, patched as our grandmothers patched china—Greeks with modern Roman throats, toes and fingers pieced on *ad libitum*, and even a trunk with legs, arms, and head supplied. How the organ of veneration must thrive in Rome !

W. CAME to us immediately on our arrival. Could anything be more fortunate than our meeting him here where the girls most need the brother !—friend he will be to them, and we all need the refreshment of his society and the comfort of his co-operation. K——n is here too for the winter ; so we have suddenly come into possession of an independent fortune ! W. has engaged our lodgings near Monte Cavallo, looking out on a green hill, the Viminal, with a garden adjoining in English occupancy, and, of course, in high cultivation, and, what is better than all the rest, with the sun shining on us from its rising to its setting. We pay twenty-three louis, one hundred and one dollars, a month for our rooms ; all other expenses are a separate affair. This low price, as we are assured it is, is in consequence of our being far from the English (fashionable) quarter. But, as we have no acquaintances, that does not signify; and the acquaintances we wish to make, and daily visit, the Colosseum, the Forum, &c., are very near to us. The tribute which pilgrims from all parts of the world pay to these ruins is now the chief support of Rome. There are here every year from ten to twenty thousand strangers, many residents for the winters, and English people noted for the liberality of their expenditure.

We have been to the Colosseum, not farther from us than your neighbour S——y is from you— not a quarter of a mile. Where it stands, apart from modern Rome, the ground is grass-grown and broken into foot-paths. You have seen a hundred pictures of it, read at least a hundred descriptions, and you know its dimensions*, and yet, my dear C., you cannot imagine its impression. I do not mean the impression of its unbroken circle ; of its gradation of Doric, Ionic, and Corinthian orders; of the soft colour of its stone with its ages of weather-staining ; of the shrubs waving like banners from its lofty heights; of the slender vines that penetrate its crevices, and hang out their flexile curtains ; of its beds of glowing flowers, or of the mossy matting of its ruined stairs †. Now all this is form and colouring, which here, as elsewhere, holds discourse with the senses. But it

* Its circumference is 1641 feet; its height, 157. The length of the arena is 285 feet, and its breadth 182.

† A book has been written on the botany of the Colosseum, in which 260 species of plants are noted.

is while standing under the shadow of this mighty ruin that you first fully realise that you are in Rome—ancient Rome; that you are treading the ground Cæsar, Cicero, and Brutus trod, and seeing what they saw ; that this is the scene of the magnificent crimes and great deeds that fill the blackest and brightest pages in the Old World's story. Under your foot is a remnant of the massive pavement on which the triumphal procession trod ; before you is the *Via Sacra*, the Roman Forum, the broken temples of the gods, the Palatine Hill, the ruins of the Cæsars' palaces, the arches of Constantine and Titus, and the Flavian amphitheatre, the Niagara of ruins !

"The heart runs o'er
With silent worship of the great of old;
The dead but sceptred sovereigns, who still rule
Our spirits from their urns."

This is no poetic exaggeration. I am inclined to think Byron is the only person who can describe sensations which people of far more common mould than his feel here.

The Colosseum was built chiefly by the Jewish captives after the destruction of Jerusalem, and was dedicated by Titus with the slaughter of 5000 wild beasts. It was devoted to gladiatorial contests, to the fight of captive men with captive beasts and with one another; subsequently it was the great arena where Christians furnished forth the dramatic show of being torn limb from limb for the entertainment of their fellow-men and women ‡. The gladiatorial games were celebrated here for the last time in the fifth century Telemachus, a Christian who in vain had remonstrated against them, threw himself between the combatants, and was immediately killed by the enraged spectators. In consequence of this, the Emperor Honorius abolished the games, and the martyr became a saint.

The structure remained entire until the eleventh century, when by a Roman noble it was converted into a fortress esteemed nearly impregnable. In 1332 it was the scene of a bullfight. At the end of the fourteenth century it was converted into an hospital. In the fifteenth a portion of its marble was burned into lime. In the sixteenth century it became the quarry from which the nobles of Rome constructed their palaces, and partisans of all parties their fortifications. In the seventeenth, Sixtus V. attempted to establish a woollen manufactory here ! After all these vicissitudes, the papal authority was at last interposed to save this magnificent relic of antiquity by Christian consecration. Benedict XIV. in the middle of the last century sanctified it, and erected a cross in the centre of the arena.

Considerable reparations have been made from time to time, and are still making. The original elevation is preserved entire but in one small segment of the circle, and there it appears stupendous. Its five rows of seats are in part still manifest. The seats of the first and second rows were cushioned, and the senators and those of

‡ Those who take disheartening views of the progress of man should solace themselves with looking back in the world's history. What would now be thought of the autocrats of Austria and Russia (not men noted for hearts over-soft) if they were to furnish for their subjects the shows that amused the polished Romans ? Has not Christianity done something for us?

consular rank occupied them. They ascended in position as they descended in rank, till they came to the poor women who were above and below all!

When I thought of the purpose to which this theatre was devoted, I felt my impression of its sublimity abated by my consciousness of the degradation of humanity. My imagination called back from the dead the hundred thousand people who filled this vast circuit. I saw the Roman ladies looking down on the poor captives of the forest, and the human sacrifice; and I wondered if, when they met in their passage through the vomitories, they talked of the last new fashion, and tenderly inquired of the young mother " if her baby had yet cut a tooth!" That monster, "*custom*" does so harden the heart!

WE have been to St. Peter's, and are *not* disappointed. The great works of nature and art always surpass my expectations. We walked in silence up and down the nave, made the circuit of the wall, stood under the glorious dome, and contented ourselves with the effect of its atmosphere without studying the details. The most beautiful object in approaching St. Peter's is certainly not itself; the dome is lost in this view, and the façade has neither grandeur nor harmony. Nor the colonnades with their row of statues, but the beautiful fountains, the very types of life, grace, and youth, where everything else is fixed and heavy.

Sunday.—WE have been out of the Porta del Popolo to-day to attend service in the English chapel. It is greatly to the honour of the pope that he permits the public worship of heretics here in the very heart of his dominion. This is better than the burning of the convent in our land of liberty of conscience and universal toleration! There was a congregation of from six to seven hundred people, without any notable attraction in the officiating clergyman. It is cheering to see the English, wherever they most congregate, maintaining the observances of their religion. We found at Wiesbaden, Frankfort, Geneva, and here at Rome, a regular English service on Sunday; not a nominal thing, for the English, with very few exceptions, scrupulously attend it*.

I HAD been walking about St. Peter's to-day till I felt the exaltation which the grandeur, the vast riches, and endless wonders of that glorious church produce, when I was suddenly attracted by the changing group around the bronze statue of St. Peter. This, formerly a statue of Jupiter, has been made by papal consecration the presiding divinity of the Christian temple. It is a

* We rarely saw English people travelling on Sunday; and as it involves no discredit, and to abstain from it often imposes disappointment and discomfort, this indicates the steadfastness of their religious principles. Captain Basil Hall's "Patchwork," just published, contains an interesting history of the steady efforts of the English at Rome, which resulted in the establishment of "a Protestant cemetery, a Church of England service, and a charitable fund dispensed at a Reformed altar to the subjects of the sovereign pontiff." God save the nation that binds to its altars its domestic ties and its charities!

sitting figure, elevated a few feet from the floor, with a circlet round the head (now a glory), the left hand raised, and the right pressing a key to the breast. The rigid face has a cold, inflexible expression, most unsuited to the impulsive disciple. It looks like the idol it is; and rather singularly in keeping with this expression is the right foot protruding from the drapery, condescendingly presented to the kiss of the faithful.

I have often heard of the kissing of St. Peter's toe; but, till I saw grown-up men and women actually press their lips to this worn bronze toe, then rub their foreheads against it (a phrenological manifestation!), and finally kneel before the image, I had never fairly conceived of this idolatry; and, yet, should we call it so! Who shall analyse the feeling in which love and reverence blend! a nicer art than to separate the ray of light; who shall judge and condemn the impulses of devotion in an ignorant mind! I will not, but rather describe the scene I saw before this image to-day. Among the throng who came and went were two peasant-women, both in costume. Each had a child in her arms, one a boy about two years old, the other a girl somewhat younger. They were ragged, but I am accustomed to seeing these little, lost cherubs in rags; and happily, in preparation for a visit to the grand Basilica, they had undergone the rare ceremony of a washing; and their brilliant eyes shone out from the unsullied golden ground of the Roman complexion—but golden or yellow hardly describes their peculiar tint of skin—Victor Hugo has done it well in poetry :—

"Il semble qu'il est doré du rayon du soleil."

About this glowing complexion hung the richest curling hair of a glossy golden brown. The mother of the boy, after kissing the toe herself, put his lips to it. He submitted to the ceremony somewhat reluctantly, faintly touching it with his lips, and giving his nose a brush across it.

As he raised his head, he saw the little girl whose mother was waiting for her turn, and half springing from his mother's arms, he kissed the child's round cheek of warm flesh and blood, and uttered a joyous chuckle at its contrast with the bronze toe that resounded through arch and aisle. It was a pretty triumph of nature; a living picture in this land of pictures †!

December 30.—A MOST beautiful morning, my dear C. The sun has just risen above the Viminal Hill. I perceive a slight hoarfrost on the garden opposite to us. The leaves on the tall orange-tree by our window look slightly chilled; and the poor women who are passing with their shawls close drawn over their heads shrink from the enemy as ours would if the mercury were ten degrees below zero. This is the first frost we have felt in Rome.

We devoted yesterday morning to Crawford's and Thorwaldsen's studii. They present a striking contrast to the toils, privations, and difficulties of

† I observed the decent-looking people among the faithful discreetly wiped the toe before kissing it; and Mr. G. told us that when his holiness does it this reverence, his attendants first spring forward and give it an effective rub with their cambric handkerchiefs.

the young and struggling genius, with the comfort, riches, and glory that wait on him who has won the day. Crawford is at this moment laid up, dangerously ill from overwork, and Thorwaldsen is making a visit in his native country which is little short of a triumphal progress. Sculptors, from the weight of their material, are compelled to work on the ground floor. Crawford's studio occupies three obscure, small, and sunless apartments, so cold and damp that they strike a chill through you. Here he has a few things finished, and several spirited and beautiful models that are to be done into marble if he has orders for them. The sculptor labours under a disadvantage from the costliness of his material; if he be poor, he cannot put his design into marble till it is in part paid for. Our countrymen, not being practised in these matters, have not sufficiently considered this, and orders have been sometimes given with generous intentions, but with the mercantile idea of payment on delivery of the goods, which could not be executed for want of money to buy the block of marble. It is the English custom to pay half the price of the work on giving the order. Among Crawford's designs is a very noble statue of Franklin. It is meant to illustrate his discoveries in electricity; he is looking up to the clouds with a calm assurance of conscious power. What an embellishment would this be for one of the Philadelphia squares! Another design, which seemed to me to belong to the romantic school, is the rain of snakes described in the Apocalypse. The curse is falling on a family. The group inevitably reminds you of the Laocoon, and in one respect it seemed to me superior; the parental instinct here triumphs over physical anguish. Crawford's last and most finished work is an Orpheus, which, as far as discovery has yet gone, has no prototype among the ancient sculptures. He has presented the rare husband at the moment of entering hell. Cerberus is lulled, and his heads are fallen in sleep; the lyre is closely pressed under Orpheus's left arm, and his right hand shades his eyes, as if to concentrate the light on entering the dark region. The figure will, I believe, bear anatomical criticism; it has the effect, at any rate, to an unscientific eye, of anatomical success. It is light, graceful, and spirited; a most expressive embodying of poetic thought. There is the beauty of perfect symmetry in the face, with a shade of earnestness which, though unusual in classical models, does not at all impair its classical serenity. The young man is said to possess the courage and perseverance that are bone and muscle to genius; if this be true, he is sure of success, and this cold, cheerless studio will, at some future time, be one of the Meccas of our countrymen*.

We had some discussion last evening with our English friend K—n on the character of American

* On our return to Rome from Naples we had the pleasure of personal acquaintance with Mr. Crawford, and of confirming our prepossessions in his favour by actual observation. The tide had even then turned in his favour. He had recovered his health and become known to many of his countrymen. While this book is going through the press we hear that a sum of 2500 dollars has been made up in Boston for his Orpheus. We hope that New York will not lag behind, but will extend her hand to her own son while there is yet some faith and generosity in doing so. When he becomes better known, there will be no merit in sending him orders.

intellect, which ended in his confessing his surprise at what we are achieving. "I find," he said, "established here and at Florence, three American artists (Greenough, Powers, and Crawford). We have but three—Gibson, Wyatt, and M'Donald: and you have Mr. Wilde at Florence, who has set himself down there to write the life of Dante, and is investigating his subject with the acuteness of a thorough-bred lawyer; and here is Green, your consul, who, with frail health, has determined to devote twenty years to a history of Italy! I told a friend the other day that we must put to whip and spur, or we should be distanced." It is something new to hear our country admired for anything but cutting down forests and building up towns in a day, or making railroads and canals; but, surely the same power that in one stage of our progress overcomes physical difficulties, will in another achieve intellectual conquests.

The extensive stables of the Barberini palace have been converted into a studio for Thorwaldsen, and they are filled with the most exquisite forms which invention, memory, imagination, and love can take. The collection of sculptures that bears his name gives you some idea of the variety and beauty of his works. That which impressed me most, and brought tears to my eyes, which I ignorantly supposed marble could not, is a colossal statue of Christ. His arms are extended, and he seems on the point of saying, "Come unto me, all ye that are weary and heavy laden, and I will give you rest." There is a most affecting blending of benignity and power in his expression; you feel that "God has anointed him above his fellows," and that "he will save to the uttermost those that come unto him." The head of our Saviour in Leonardo da Vinci's Last Supper is the only one that approaches this in force of expression. Christ is attended by his disciples, six on either side. The statues were done for a church in Copenhagen.

There is another admirable set of figures, designed, I believe, for the pediment of the same church. These are necessarily so arranged as to make on each side a descending line from the centre figure. This is done with consummate art; each figure seems, without design or choice, to have fallen into the attitude expressive of the feeling of the moment. John the Baptist preaching is the middle figure; next stands a scoffer, his head thrown back. An old man bends over his staff in devout attention; a young shepherd is rivetted to the spot, while two boys are playing with his dog; a child is leaning on his mother's shoulder; and another mother is sitting on the ground, with her infant in her arms. Besides sending these great productions to his native country, Thorwaldsen has founded a museum in Copenhagen, and enriched it with copies of his works; and thus he will send pilgrims trooping from all parts of the world to his far, cold land. No wonder the Danes love him, and follow his footsteps, loading him with gifts and honours.

My Dear C.—This is the festa of St. Peter; of course a great day in Rome. As we have been so long negligent of the privilege we may any day enjoy, of seeing the pope, we went this morning to high mass at St. Peter's, where he was to be present. He has the merit of having risen from the lowest grade of men, and is said, besides having considerable learning, to be an amiable, inoffensive old man. You know the great democratic principle of the admission of all to all employments has ever been fundamental in the Catholic church.

A Catholic ceremony is, to the eye of a Protestant, more or less a dramatic show, with a rich theatrical wardrobe and dull actors. What, I wonder, would an humble student of the Gospels, who had never heard of the Catholic church, think on coming into St. Peter's, and walking up the nave under its vaulted and golden ceiling, with its incrustations of precious marbles, its sculptured columns, its magnificent arches, statues, mosaic pictures, and monuments; its gilded bronze baldachino (made of the spoils of the Pantheon), its hundred lamps burning round St. Peter's tomb, with his image presiding—and let it be his festa, with the pope in the triple crown, gorgeously arrayed, surrounded by his cardinals in crimson and embroidered satin, attended by his Swiss guard in their fantastic uniform, and by his *guarda nobile;* what if there were such an uninformed person as I have imagined among these multifarious spectators from all quarters of the world, what would he think on being told that this was a Christian temple, and these the disciples and ministers of the meek and lowly Jesus, who taught that God only accepted such as worshipped Him in spirit and in truth!

The ceremonies we saw to-day (and which certainly would not contribute to this supposed person's farther enlightenment) I shall not describe to you. The pope, who is an ugly old man with a big nose and a stupid expression, had an elevated seat behind the tribune, where his priestly attendants seemed chiefly occupied in the care of his embroidered vestment which flowed many a yard on the ground when he stood, was borne by them when he moved, and nicely folded and replaced in his lap when he again sat down. The cardinals, as a class of men, are very noble in their appearance. With the exception of two or three middle-aged men, they are old, and have the badge of age, their thin and white locks fringing their crimson scullcaps. They too had train-bearers from an inferior order of priests. One part of the ceremony was solemn and thrilling, as a devotional sentiment expressed simultaneously by a mass of men must always be. At the elevation of the Host all the Catholics present bared their heads and fell on their knees, the swords of the soldiers ringing on the pavement. The music was delicious. After the chantings were finished, and his holiness had blessed the assembly, he was placed on a chair covered with red velvet, the triple and jewelled crown was put on his head, the chair was placed on poles also covered with red velvet, and borne on the shoulders of twelve priests. On each side was carried a huge fan of peacock's feathers; and thus suited and attended, he made a progress down the nave and into a side-chapel. He shut his eyes, drooped his head, and appeared to me like a sanctimonious old woman; but, to show how just such passing judgments are, I was afterward told the poor old man said he habitually closed his eyes to escape the giddiness occasioned by his position.

As we stood in the vestibule awaiting our carriage, cardinal after cardinal drove off; and as I saw each heavy coach with fat black horses, gilded and tasselled harness, and its complement of three footmen in embroidered liveries, dash through au ignorant, wretched multitude, nearly running over the blind and lame, those words of doom occurred to me:—" Woe be to the shepherds of Israel that feed themselves! should not the shepherds feed the flocks!" " The diseased have ye not strengthened, neither have ye healed that which was sick, neither have ye bound up that which was broken, neither have ye brought again that which was driven away, neither have ye sought that which was lost." But let us not forget, my dear C., that from the herd of priests and monks issued such men as Wickliffe and Luther, and that in their body, and having died or to die in their faith, are such men as San Carlo, Fenelon, and our own C.*

Tired of waiting, K. and I left the rest and walked home. Passing a half-open door, we heard a murmuring of tiny voices, and, looking in, we saw in a dark, damp, cold den, lighted only through this half-open door, a dame's infant-school†. The teacher, a hard-featured subject, was knitting away for life, and teaching these little things, two, three, and four years old, their prayers in *Latin,* which they repeated with the appointed crossings and genuflexions! Most of them were ragged and dirty, but beautiful enough for Guido's angels. I thought of the well-lighted, warmed, and spacious school-rooms in my own country, and of the light poured into the young mind there‡!

WE have been looking at frescoes to-day; and if I should run into rant, my dear C., about them, do not think it is to impose on you New World people who never have seen them, but that it is the effect of novelty and surprise added to their intrinsic beauty. You are probably aware, as the name implies, that they are put on the wall while the plaster is fresh; of course they must be executed with great rapidity. The ceiling and the walls of the private houses in Italy are embellished in this way; and though often done without much expenditure of art or money, they are so very pretty that I rather dread seeing again our blank ceilings. Fresco-painting is to us a new revelation of the power of the art; and such a fresco as Raphael's Sibyls, his School of Athens, or Domenichino's Life and Death of St. Cecilia, in a certain

---

* And here, too, for the sake of our charities, I quote M. Sismondi, who is no lover of priests, and assuredly no favourer of the Roman Catholic religion. He says, " The pontifical government counts among its servants more men distinguished for talents, and fewer for their vices or want of probity, than any government of Europe!" Query —Does he not mean of Continental Europe?

† The powerful writer of the address to the working classes in Italy, in the "Apostolato Popolare," says, in speaking of the defective teaching to the few of that class in Italy who are taught:—"Even religious books are given to them in a dead language which they do not understand. The books which the rulers cause to be distributed in the elementary schools teach them to be servile, poor-spirited, and selfish; and after the Austrian catechism—the common model—' That subjects should deport themselves towards their sovereigns as *slaves* towards their *masters,*' and that the power of the sovereign ' extends to their property as well as to their person.'"

‡ What a curiosity to an Italian teacher would a list of our school-books be! What an inestimable treasure to Italian pupils a single one—Miss Robbins's Popular Lessons, for example!

little chapel here, seem to me as superior to an easel-painting as an epic is to a lyric poem. Unfortunately, there are but few of these masterpieces in good preservation. They suffer more than oil-paintings from damp and neglect. The Romans had this art in great perfection. I have seen in a gallery of Titus's baths, in an apartment of Augustus's palace, and in the tomb of Augustus's freedmen, all now far under ground, frescoes, medallions, flowers, birds, divinities, &c., traced with accuracy and grace, and the colours still vivid. The Nozze Aldobrandini, now hanging in the library of the Vatican, is one of the most beautiful of the old frescoes. It is a representation of a Greek wedding, is supposed to be a Greek painting, and was found in the baths of Titus. Guido's Aurora, one of the most exquisite poetic conceptions ever manifested to the eye of man, is still as fresh as if it were just dyed in the rainbow, on the ceiling of an apartment in the Ruspigliosi palace.

Raphael's Sibyls is also a masterpiece, and it has an advantage over the Aurora in bearing the impress of the true religion. It seems to me the most fortunate subject a painter ever chose. It is painted in an obscure little church (*Santa Maria della Pace*); so uncalculating is genius! The place to be covered was an arch in the nave, the most awkward possible, it would seem, for the disposition of the figures. But difficulties were only spurs to the genius of Raphael; and so perfect are the grace and nature of this picture, that it would never occur to you he had not place and space at will. As this, after seeing the galleries of Florence and Rome, is my favourite picture, suffer me to describe it to you, my dear C.

The four sibyls, the lay prophetesses who are supposed to have intimated to the Old World the revelations they had received of the coming of our Saviour, are the subjects of the picture. The time chosen is the moment of the angels' communication to the inspired women. The first is a beautiful young creature in the freshest ripeness of womanhood. Her record-book is in her lap, and her glowing face, turned towards the angel, conveys the annunciation, " Glory to God in the highest, and on earth peace and good-will to man!" The face of the cherub, who is looking at her intently, with his chin resting on his closed hand, indicates the joy there is in heaven at these tidings to man.

The next sibyl is writing down the revelation as her heavenly messenger reveals it. Her face is in profile. It has something more than mere joy; a comprehension of the obstacles to be met and the moral revolutions to be made. There is eagerness in the angel's face, and an almost Divine energy in the young woman's. The art that could give such force to such delicate lines is amazing. The face is the most spiritual, and I think the most beautiful, I ever saw. Her whole soul is so intent on the record she is making, that it seems as if her pen would cut through the tablet.

The next figure reminds you of classical models, of something pre-existent in art, which nothing else in the picture does. It is very lovely, and expresses perfect awe and reverence, as if her inward eye beheld the " King of all living things."

The fourth is a dark old woman, who comprehends the coming struggles with the powers of darkness,

the martyrdoms, the seed to be sown in tears, and, seeing the end, is unflinching and unfearing.

What must Raphael have thought and felt before he painted this picture! He is the Shakspeare of painters, and with almost as full a measure of inspiration. The picture is a poem, such as I hope may be found in the libraries of heaven, if the soul read there without the intervention of letters.

Domenichino's Evangelists are in the four angles of the dome of St. Andrea della Valle. They are reckoned his best frescoes, and he is reckoned second only to Raphael. The freedom and vigour of the figures, and the freshness and harmony of the colouring, are striking. St. Mark's muscular arm actually stands out from the picture. There is a lion (his symbol) at his feet, with lovely children playing on his back, at whom he looks round so gently that he reminded me of the humane lion of Bottom's Pyramus and Thisbe.

St. John, an angel who holds his inkstand, and two little boys at his feet twined in one another's arms, are all personifications of love; commentaries on that Divine admonition, " Little children, love one another!"

These frescoes are the transfer and perpetuation of actual existence. They have but the one fault of Donatello's statue—" they do not breathe."

After looking at these pictures till our necks were stiff, we went to San Carlo to see the Cardinal Virtues, also by Domenichino. But we had hardly got in when a young priest ordered us out, because there was to be an exposition of the sacrament, and the presence of Protestant ladies must not profane the ceremony. We had just come from witnessing, unmolested, the same service in the Sistine Chapel, in the august presence of the pope, and so we told him. But the young priest was inexorable; exorcise us he would; and so, casting a pitiful look at the Lady Charity, who sat impotent among the Cardinal Virtues, we were swept out. This is the first discourtesy of the sort we have met with here. Narducci, our landlord, was so scandalised when we told him of it, that, after many exclamations of " Is it possible! this—a Roma!" he went to the priest and brought an apology, and a very civil invitation to come again to the church. It is the studied policy of the Roman people, from the pope down, to conciliate the English; and such is the precedence given them at the religious ceremonies, and so great their number in comparison with that of the Italians, that you might imagine they were spectacles got up for their edification*.

January 1.

My DEAR C.—You must know by this time that our friend K—n is *not* one of those visiters at Rome whom M. Sismondi justly reproaches with regarding it merely as " a museum where pictures, statues, monuments of antiquity, and all the various productions of the fine arts, are exhibited to their curiosity, to whom the 160,000 or 180,000 inhabitants who live within the walls of Rome appear merely an accessory." K—n sent us a note this morning, informing us

---

* There is another reason, as I have been told by a pious Catholic, why so few of his faith are seen at the ceremonies at St. Peter's. They are considered by them as rather spectacles than for religious edification.

that there would be an immense concourse of the Roman people in costume at the Piazza Navona, and our carriage being soon announced by our coachman sending us up two splendid bouquets—new-year's favours *—we set off to see the show. The Piazza Navona is the largest market-place in Rome. It was so completely filled with the people, and their products and wares, that it was with some difficulty we made our way among them. At last we got a station in the centre of the piazza near a fountain, where four river-gods, seated on rocks from which the water issues, are sustaining an obelisk. There was a fair going on. Very few of the people were in costume, unless, alas ! the general badge of Southern Italy, rags, may be so termed. The graceful white head-dress which you see in the pictures of the Roman peasantry is uncommon now. The women wear in its place a cotton handkerchief tied under the chin, which, being of a bright colour, has rather a pretty effect. Some of them wear cheap English cottons, but the general dress at this season is a stout woollen plaid, almost perdurable †. The men wear hats with high sugar-loaf crowns ; the shape of the brims it would be difficult to tell, for I think I have never seen a whole one. Their breeches are unstrapped at the knee, and their legs sometimes bare, but usually covered with what may, by a stretch of courtesy, be called a stocking. Every man who can command such a luxury once in his life (it is kept on as long as it retains a semblance of the original garment) wears a cloak, and as gracefully as if he were a troubadour. They really look like princes in disguise, so lofty, independent, and majestical is their bearing. Mr. Gibson, the English artist, in speaking to me of the striking grace of the Roman people, imputed it, in part, to the affability with which they are treated by their superiors, which saves them from the shyness and constraint whose " natural language " (to borrow the phrenological term) is awkwardness. We alighted to see better what was going on. Mariano cautioned us to leave in the carriage whatever might be purloined, as the place was full of " Lombardi," and explaining his meaning by the synonyme *Ladri* (thieves). A curious memorial this of the old wars with the Lombards. We made our way amid grain, vegetables, poultry, honey, eggs, coarse wares, wretched toys, and a most clamorous crowd, and were followed by ragged boys screaming " Vuole un facchino ! " (" Do you wish a porter ! ") and were glad to get back to the carriage with some paltry toys, the best we could find, for Mariano's children. I have never seen the children look so happy as to-day ; not one but had some trifling toy.

Lady D. finds the Roman people much deteriorated during her twenty years' acquaintance with them, incivility and surliness in the place of

their former graciousness and " captivating sweetness of manners." This may possibly be, in part, owing to the influx of English, whose national manners are not calculated to call forth " captivating sweetness " in return. It is certain the people here do not manifest the light-heartedness and careless buoyancy we have seen elsewhere in Italy ; but may there not be the faint dawn of a better day in their thoughtfulness, even though it be sullen and sad !

It is said that the Romish religion is nowhere less respected than at Rome ; that the women are still under its dominion ; but that among the men there is a pervading infidelity, and, of course, a discontent with the government, that will urge them to join in any hopeful movement against it. How can it be otherwise when the government, instead of affording them aid and protection, only puts forth its power and ingenuity to tax and harass them ! " Rome," says M. Sismondi, " pretending to have eternity at its disposal, takes little care of the future of this world."

The streets are thronged with idle men. A portion of them are the labourers on the campagna, who, to avoid the malaria, come into the city whenever unemployed ; and as festas, including Sundays, occur twice or thrice a week, this is nearly half the time. On my remarking this concourse of idlers to Mr. G., he said, " Perhaps you are not aware that many who appear mere idlers are *facchini* (porters) who are waiting for employment." I can only say I always see them " *waiting*," never employed ; and in Rome, where there is no commerce and no manufactures, what employment can there be for this herd of facchini ! Not absolutely no manufactures, for there are many thousand sculptors, workers in mosaic, makers of conchiliglias, and other like *jim-crackeries* for milords Anglais ; but remember, these are all articles of superfluity for which there is no regular and certain demand. The interchange of productions between the different states of Italy is discouraged and shackled in every way by their rulers, so that the beautiful Roman mosaic has no market at Florence, nor the pietra-dura, the manufacture par excellence of Florence, at Rome.

There is no comfort in buying anything here ; no article has a fixed value or price. The seller asks the highest price he has any hope of obtaining from ignorance and credulity, and the buyer " beats down " till his time or his patience is exhausted. I have been taken in more than once by supposing that " *fixed prices* " in great letters announced, as it would with us, the inflexible rule of the dealer. On one occasion I was looking at an article, when K. whispered to me that the price was extravagant—I should offer less. I pointed to the " fixed prices," and shook my head, and after paying the price demanded, I had the mortification, before leaving the shop, to see another purchaser come in, and, after a little trafficking, buy the article at half the price I had given. Frequently, after solemn asseverations that the thing has been offered to us at its ultimate price, we have been followed out of the shop and on to the pavement with proffers of reduction, and finally it has been sent home to us at our own price. And to this degree of debasement is a people brought who are born in one of the richest

---

* This was not an uncommon kindness in our coachman : often, on returning to our carriage from some sight-seeing, we found a knot of jonquils, or violets, or a paper of delicious smoking chestnuts. " The happiness of life is made up of minute fractions, of little (*not*) soon forgotten charities." The humblest, like our good Mariano, may throw in their mite.

† These stuffs are, for the most part, manufactured at an establishment belonging to the government. They cost seventy-five cents per yard, a yard and a quarter in width. They are sometimes home-made.

climates of the world, and loaded with God's good gifts !

But do not imagine, my dear C., that this debasement is universal. It obtrudes itself upon the notice of strangers because those who traffic with them are most exposed to temptation.

An American gentleman who has resided in Italy for many years, told W. that, leaving out of the account conjugal fidelity, he had never found in any part of the world better faith or more virtue than in Italy. This testimony does not prove all it asserts, but certainly it intimates that there is some good faith and much virtue. Our consul is married to an Italian lady, an exceedingly pretty and attractive person, who, in our exacting New-England, might be held up as a pattern-wife.

Signor N., from whom we hire our rooms, occupies an apartment next to us, and we are on the friendliest terms. We have found him honourable and liberal in his dealings, and most kind in his attentions. His wife is a highly-accomplished artist, one of a large family, all qualified by the education which a widowed mother, by dint of energy and struggling, obtained for them, to secure an independent existence. They now cherish that mother with filial devotion. And, to come down to the humblest life, our coachman, who spends all the daylight of every day in our service, is invariably faithful and patient, and moderate in his demands. Now, my dear C., if the only Romans we chance to know would be valuable members of society anywhere, is it not a hint to us to take the denunciations of travellers with some allowance, and, at any rate, that we may safely enlarge our charities ! A little more on this head, and I have done. I will repeat to you, without the slightest deviation, a story I have just heard from an English gentleman. A friend of his, an artist, who was residing in Rome with his wife, lost one or two children. In their first anguish they were advised by their Italian nurse to change the scene : and with that instinct of nature which always turns to the birthplace as the universal panacea, she begged them to go to her native village, fifty miles from Rome. They had scarcely reached there when the cholera broke out, and they were put in quarantine. They had expected to remain but a few days, and had little money with them, and there was no possibility of communicating with their friends. Rather a dilemma to be thrown in among the priests and Levites of this world ! There was no borrowing ; for, save some few dollars laid up in the village for the payment of taxes, it was as moneyless as one of our Western settlements. They lived by barter. The English strangers were obliged to remain four months. All their wants were supplied. The people trusted them indefinitely. Quantities of grain were brought to them, which they exchanged for smaller commodities. They made acquaintance with a gentleman in the neighbourhood who lived a secluded but *luxurious* life upon two hundred dollars a year ! He had a good library, was highly cultivated, particularly well informed in regard to everything in England, and furthermore one of the excellent of the earth. All this, dear C., among the dishonest, lying, murdering, treacherous Italians ! There is some superfluous reviling in this world !

Is it a fancy of mine, think you, dear C., or is it remarkable that most of the best-preserved monuments here are associated with good names that shine out among the great ones of old Rome ! The Colosseum bears the family name of Vespasian, and is the record of the magnificence and triumphs of his son. The Arch of Titus, the conqueror of the Jews—the man who, when master of the world, sighed over every day unmarked with a good deed as lost—still spans, almost entire, the *Sacra Via ;* Drusus, Constantine, and Septimius Severus, whose arches are remaining, are, if not at the extreme right, somewhere about the *juste milieu* of ancient names ; and the lofty column of Trajan, "best of the good," still bears the record of his deeds. The unimpaired column of Antoninus Pius is the memorial of a man whose name designated his eminent goodness. Almost every day we drive under the still perfect arch of the gentle Nerva's Forum, while the palaces of the Cæsars, extended and embellished by such beastly wretches as Nero, Caligula, and Domitian, are a shapeless mass of ruins !

If I had your powers of description in this way, dear C., or Cruikshank's of illustration, I would give you a letter worth having on the beggars of Rome. The Italian has sentiment in his nature, and the beggar expresses it in the form of his petition. His "Non m' abbandonate," and "Carita, signora, per l'amor di questa imagine* !" kindle your imagination if not your heart. How I should like to show you the fellow who sits, like a monarch on his throne, on the stairs of the *Piazza di Spagna,* and whose smile, disclosing teeth strong enough to grind all the grist in Rome, and his hearty salutation, "Buon giorno, signor," are well worth the *baioc'* he asks much more as a right than a favour. He is an old receiver of customs, and is well known to have a full treasury. "How dare you beg of me," asked Mr. G., "when you are already so rich !" "Ah, signor, I have my donkey to feed." "You are well able to feed your donkey." "But I have my nine children, signor." There is no answer to be made to a fellow who confesses to such luxury ! Then there is the poor moiety of a man whose trunk (torso !) trussed on to a circular bit of wood slightly concave, comes daily down our street of St. Vitale at a jocund pace ; and the two old crones at *Santa Maria Maggiore* who hobble towards you with a sort of pas-de-deux, and seem as well content that one should get your baioc' as the other, "equal to either fortune." They are probably partners in the trade. And there is the handsome youth by the French Academy, who has been dying with a "sagne di bocca" (spitting of blood) for the last fifteen years without any apparent diminution of the vital current ! And the little troop of mountain-peasants, whose hunting-ground is somewhere about the American consul's, with their bewitching smiles, sweet voices, and most winning ways ; a genuine lover of happy young faces ought to pay them for a sight of theirs. Even beggary is picturesque here.

* " Do not abandon me !" and "Charity, lady, for the love of this image !" This last supplication is made near a shrine of the pitiful-looking Virgin, where the beggar has what in our trafficking country would be called " a good stand for business."

WE went this morning to the church of St. Agostino to see Raphael's Isaiah, one of his most famous frescoes ; the church was so dark, we could not perceive its excellence. But we did see what to you, a student of human nature, would be far more interesting. This church has a statue of the Madonna and child, which has peculiar virtue. Some poor girl having, in an ecstacy of devotion, seen the Holy Mother open and shut her eyes upon her, miracles have ever since been wrought for the faithful who kneel before this image. I am not sure whether it be of wood or stone ; but whichever it be, the foot is so worn away with kissing that it has been shodden with silver. The altar on which it is placed was (at midday) brilliantly lighted with candles, and a semicircle of lamps hung before it. The mother is sitting ; the child stands on her knee on one foot in a pert attitude. Both images wear glittering crowns. The mother's throat is covered with strings of pearls. She has a complete breastplate of jewels ; her arms are laden with bracelets, and her fingers with rings ; and, to make her look completely like the queen of strolling players, her hand is filled with artificial flowers. Kneeling before this image in *earnest* devotion (I saw many tears, but not a wandering eye) were a multitude of men and women, for the most part ragged and filthy beyond description, all of whom, as they came in or went out, kissed the silver-shod toe— some again and again fondly, as a mother kisses her child !

But the most extraordinary thing of all is the garniture of a pillar on the Virgin's right. It is literally covered with every species of small weapon : daggers, pistols, and knives, &c. These have been dedicated to the Holy Mother by two classes of persons : by those who have been rescued from the murderer, and by the murderer who has escaped the penalty of his crime. The sanctuary privilege is still in force at Rome. A gendarme dare not follow an offender into a church ; he may remain there till he is driven by starvation to surrender, but no one is permitted to supply his necessities. The police of Rome is wretched. The laws are ill administered. Atrocious offences escape justice ; and small ones, if they be against the church, are rigidly punished. I believe reports of crime here are much exaggerated. We have been repeatedly told that our street, which is retired, and has few habitations, is dangerous after nightfall ; but our friends come and go every evening without molestation, and W. seldom leaves us before eleven. The truth is, the couriers, who daily meet and gossip on the *Piazza di Spagna*, choose to give a bad name to all lodgings remote from that neighbourhood ; and they amuse their idle hours with weaving little tragic romances, taking care to make them "deep "—like a certain young friend of ours, who, in her maiden tragedy, burned all her dramatis personæ alive on the stage.

Mr. G. and W. had an animated discussion here this evening, W. insisting that it is the common testimony of mankind that the Romans are addicted to assassination, and Mr. G. maintaining that they do not strike often, and never but with good cause ; that there being no public justice to right them, they are compelled, like savages, to take the matter into their own hands. He said that, notwithstanding all the reports about robberies, during a twelve years' acquaintance with Rome he had known but one ! and that, when the Romans rob, they do not stab ; they have no cold-blooded cruelty.

Love, which runs into disease only among the higher classes in other countries, plays its daily tragedies here among the humblest. It is the natural offspring of idleness. With these hot-blooded, impetuous Italians jealousy is almost sure to spring up with it ; it is, par excellence, the passion of social life in Italy. There was a beautiful young woman hired by a foreign artist to sit for him ; this is one of the most productive of the passive industries of Rome. Her husband forbade her going to the painter's ; she replied that he did nothing for her, and she must earn what she could. Yesterday he followed her to the artist's studio, and asked to see the picture of his wife. The artist readily admitted him, whereupon he plunged a knife into his wife's bosom ; she fled, and he stabbed her a second time. To-day she died. Public opinion is in the husband's favour, and it is said he will only pay the penalty of a few days' imprisonment.

But what morals can be expected of a people who have the worst examples of bad faith from those who should be their models as well as protectors ! K—n told me a story of some brigands who had become formidable on the road between here and Naples some years since. As the ceremonies of the Holy Week approached, the outlaws felt an irresistible desire to " walk the Seven Basilicæ ; " which means, I take it, confessing and doing penance in these supremely holy sanctuaries, an observance very dear to all good Catholics[*]. Their chief entered into a treaty with the pope for permission to come and go unmolested, and the holy father, loath to repress so pious a wish, granted it. Their rendezvous in Rome was known, and the pope sent his emissaries to persuade them to relinquish their unholy trade. The conference was proceeding amicably when the pope's lambs turned into wolves, alias gendarmes, and the betrayed brigands were seized and bound. " Ah, for shame ! " I exclaimed, at the conclusion of the story ; " this is as bad as our treatment of the Indians." " And ours of the East Indians ! " responded K—n ; " all great nations have their peccadilloes ! " When will nations hold themselves bound by the strict rule that governs an upright individual ! When they are in deed as well as in name Christian nations —and not till then.

The tombs are among the most interesting monuments about Rome. They annihilate time, and level all national and individual differences by speaking to you of ties that are universal, and of experience common to all. Here, where parents and children have wept, you feel the strain of a common humanity ; and the only difference between you and those who have lived and suffered

[*] " Boniface in 1300, the year of the jubilee, proclaimed 'une indulgence plénière' for such as, having confessed, should visit for fifteen consecutive days the churches of St. Peter and St. Paul. Villani reports that during the year there were 200,000 strangers at Rome."—*Sismondi.* His holiness, Boniface, understood the art of indirect taxation.

ages before you is, that wherein you are most blessed they were most wretched. The angel of life did not keep his watch over the burial-places of their dead. If, perchance, a ray of hope penetrated the clouds and darkness that wrapped the tomb, it came from their own natures, and was wavering and uncertain, most unlike that steadfast and inextinguishable light which shines in upon the Christian's soul. And this, I take it, was in part the reason why the ancients built their splendid mausoleums, such as the tomb of Adrian and that of Cecilia Metella, and those on the Appian Way, which, even in ruin, appear like the vestiges of fortresses and palaces. The *past* was all to them. Pride and love sought to perpetuate the memorial of an ended existence. Memory fondly lingered where hope had not yet come. We have been to the tomb of the Scipios. It is not more than fifty years since the tomb of the Scipios was opened, and now an exact copy of its most beautiful sarcophagus embellishes a cemetery in our New World*. Above the entrance to a vineyard is the inscription, " *Sepolcro degli Scipioni.*" The barred door was opened to us by a woman, who, provided with wax tapers, conducted us down a flight of steps and into the interior of the vault by a narrow winding way, through the burial-place of one of the most illustrious families of Rome, and where we were treading they came in sad procession to lay their dead. We saw on the walls of these corridors the names, and exact copies of the original inscriptions, which have been carried off to the Vatican. The niches where the sarcophagi, busts, and other funereal ornaments were placed are empty. Some of these we have seen in the Vatican.

We have been to the Columbarium, which contains the remains of the freedmen of Augustus. They are called Columbarium from the resemblance of the small compartments where the urns were placed to pigeon-holes. We knocked, as all *antiquity*-hunters must do at Rome, whether they are in quest of a palace or a tomb, a bath or a temple, at a huge, strong, wooden gate resembling an immense barn-door, and were admitted into a vineyard, where we were at once in the midst of sacred relics. Broken, antique, sepulchral inscriptions are inserted in the wall, some made in vanity no doubt, and some in love ; I noticed one of a father, *filiæ dulcissimæ.* Fragments of columns, bits of bas-reliefs, and terra-cotta urns were strewn over the ground. We descended a dozen steps into the Columbarium, a small apartment with a vaulted ceiling delicately painted in fresco. The bones, resolved by fire to small fragments and ashes, are in terra-cotta vessels with covers, more like our garden-pots than like urns. These are placed in the pigeon-holes. Thus reduced, men and women may be packed away in a very small compass ; 8000 are said to have been bestowed here. There are some small marble sarcophagi embellished with bas-reliefs. Octavia's tomb is unknown ; and here is an inscription on her dressing-maid, and another on her worker in silver.

But one of the most interesting sepulchral monuments that I have seen is that of some honest bakers, close to the walls of Rome. A very noble arch with Ionic pillars has lately been uncovered

* That to Spurzheim at Mount Auburn.

there. When Totila, with his barbarians, had possession of the city, they pulled down the walls. Belisarius, who was lying at Ostia, returned as soon as Totila retired, and, hastily reconstructing the wall, made use of whatever would help to shorten his labour. In this way the tomb of Caius Cestus came to make a part of the wall, and thus this superb arch, and the baker's tomb just in its shadow, were covered up ; the tomb is of marble, and in the sides of the walls are openings to represent ovens. The frieze is sculptured with bas-reliefs representing the baker's art, kneading, moulding, weighing the loaves, and piling them in baskets ; bread and baskets are of the identical form used by the Roman bakers of the present day. In a house hard by, whither they have been removed from the tomb, are the statues of the baker and his wife, worthy elderly people, lying side by side on a stone tablet. After going about, day after day, to see the ruins of temples to imaginary divinities, triumphal arches, palaces, circuses, and amphitheatres, memorials of the pride and luxury of individuals and the misery of "the million," it was refreshing, dear C., to find in this baker's pretty tomb a proof that the humbler virtues and domestic arts were sometimes honoured.

' *Sunday.*

MY DEAR C.—We went to the Church of St. Cecilia to-day to see the profession of a nun. Signora N. accompanied us, and expressed as sound opinions on conventual life as if, instead of a good Catholic living under the dropping of monasteries, she had been bred in Boston. A carpet was spread in the nave, with a double row of chairs set around it, and the inclosure was guarded by a small detachment from the pope's Swiss guards. By Signor N.'s interest, we obtained a place on these extra-exclusive seats. We waited two mortal hours. The cardinal who was to come here to bury the living, was engaged in burying the dead. The mother, with the nurse and young bride of heaven, sat near us, and ——, who, if she had before appeared to me as a mere fashionable inanity floating over the surface of life, now made me feel that there was a certain dignity in an existence that comprehended the affections of a wife and mother.

The circle of chairs was filled, and a large audience, chiefly English, gathered round ; finally in came the cardinal and the officiating priests, who robed him in embroidered satin and point lace, which they took from a trunk previously brought. When he was completely equipped, with his jewelled mitre on his head, a chant announced the bride's approach ; and she entered the church with a friend at her side, and a train attendant. She appeared about nineteen, and with that peculiar expression of repressed exultation that you may have seen on a silly young girl whose head was *exaltée* with the éclat of a wedding. She was dressed in a load of finery, to make more striking her renunciation of the pomps and vanities of the world. Her head was tricked off with all-coloured false jewels, feathers, gold chains, and artificial flowers. Her profuse black hair, her only personal wealth, hung in ringlets over her face, neck, and shoulders, and falling over the back of her head she had a gauze veil embroidered with silver. The folds of her embroidered satin gown were sustained by an ultra fashionable hump (*tournure*, par *courtoisie*), and her train was held up by two children three or four years old, bedizened in blue and pink satin, spangles, silver fringe, and tawdry artificial flowers, who, as I inferred from feather wings sewed to their backs, personated angels !

The poor thing knelt before the cardinal and made her vow of renunciation. She then sat as inexpressive as a wax figure, while he addressed to her a sing-song exhortation, in which he held up before her a long line of female saints who had endured *unendurable* inflictions and mortifications. When this precious homily, recited and received without a sign of emotion, was over, she was led out by the cardinal, and we again saw her, but very imperfectly, through a grated door in a side chapel ; there she was disrobed, her hair cut off, and, in the nun's habit and veil, she lay under a pall while the service for the dead was chanted over her. It is not long since this whole ceremony was performed in the nave of the church ; and the present decent innovation of withdrawing behind the scenes is a faint sign that there is life and progress even here. It was, after all, though I have spoken of it flippantly, a touching sight to see a young creature self-immolated through the force of most unnatural circumstances ; but I do not wonder that in a country where the alternative is, for the most part, between vice and vacuity, a woman should choose to give a religious colour to the latter.

Female school-education here is in the hands of the nuns. You may imagine how well fitted to prepare girls to be wives and mothers, and effective members of society, these poor wretches must be, who know the world only through their sighs and unavailing regrets.

THE bells are ringing, and so they are in Rome at every hour of the twenty-four. There are certain convent-bells that ring every fifteen minutes, and others that ring through the hour. When I am suddenly awaked in the night by the ringing of the bells, with the deep-sunken impressions of years, I fancy myself in my room in W. street, and an Albany steamer announcing its arrival. What a deadly home-sickness comes over me as I awake to the reality, and contrast the indications of the bells of the two countries, pretty fairly illustrative of their different condition ! The steamer's bell announces the arrival of the politician, busy with the project of making a new governor and dislodging an old one, or framing new laws and abolishing the old ; of the philanthropist, who has come to examine prisons, establish a peace society, disseminate Bibles, or help on the extermination of slavery ; of an author, about to publish some new theory in religion, or politics, or social life, which is to reform the morals and mend the manners of mankind ; of the inventor of a new machine which is to improve the fortunes of the human race and make his own ; of a host of merchants to buy and to sell. While the bells are ringing they are all on shore ; no passports, no *Dogana* ! And what say the midnight bells of Rome ? Why, that the poor monks and nuns must out of their beds and troop to prayers ! In the severer orders he summons

is repeated three and four times during the night—this, dear C., is the productive labour of Rome !

I ASKED an Italian gentleman who was mending the fire at Miss M.'s, in the hopeless endeavour to send the smoke up the chimney, if the chimneys in Rome were not apt to smoke. "They *all* smoke," he replied ; "and how can it be otherwise ! the houses have been built hundreds of years, and the chimneys recently put in." They are an English luxury ; and seem contrived, as an English writer says, rather " to ventilate than to warm." The Italians consider fires injurious to health *. There is ice in the street now, and a blazing fire of half-a dozen good-sized sticks is essential to our comfort, while our delicate little landlady is warmed with a few coals in an earthen pot (called a *marito*) with an upright handle, a most inconvenient affair. The immense marble-floored apartments of the palaces are warmed only by a brasier with a few coals. Once I have seen, at some villa, a blazing fire ; at the Borghese, probably, for Prince Borghese is married to an Englishwoman. The shrivelled, shivering old women sitting out of doors with a *marito* at their feet are forlorn objects.

You would be surprised at the articles of food exposed for sale here, such as cock's combs, the claws of poultry, blood, and the entrails of animals. I smile when I recall the time when our village butcher refused to make a charge for a " calf's head and feet," and that even now it is considered a bold innovation to *sell* liver. Meat is sold here in bits as small as we distribute about the table ; indeed, the poorer classes scarce taste meat at all. Polenta (hasty-pudding) is here, as in other parts of Italy, a prime article of food †. The bread they eat is of a good quality, and often made quite luxurious by a spreading of *lard*. They have delicate preparations of milk, resembling our curds, but much nicer, called *ricotta* and *giuncata*. These are thought to be inimitably prepared by the peasants of the neighbouring mountains ; we thought them so the other day when they came to us from a kind friend in pretty baskets covered with fresh leaves.

Vegetables are very cheap, and the very poor almost live on the coarser kinds. I have seen old women in the streets devouring the stumps of cabbages. Soup is their luxury ; *soup* by courtesy, but really the thinnest of broths. Wine holds the place to them that tea does to our working people. Our servant was looking very surly, and on inquiry we learned it was because we had not provided wine for her breakfast ! Chesnuts are bread here ; they are cheap, abundant, and very delicious, much larger than ours, sweet and marrowy, and approaching the lusciousness of fruit. Their sweet odours as they are roasting perfume the streets, which sadly need perfuming. You will hardly be able to estimate the poverty of the Roman people by the indications of the

---

* Our medical gentleman at Naples was so fearful of the feverish influence of the fire, that when he passed through the drawing-room to his patient's apartment, he crept round by the wall.

† We ordered it now and then for a reminiscence of home, but it was made disagreeable to our taste by the admixture of oil.

food on which they live, without knowing the extreme cheapness of good provisions. W. tells me that he can get a dinner at a restaurant for twenty-five cents, consisting of soup, three or four kinds of meat, a variety of vegetables, a pudding, and a dessert of fruits and nuts.

I WISH our grumbling housewives, who fancy there is no plague with servants but " it lights on their shoulders," could hear the statements of grievances I hear here, and such as I often heard in England. The men-servants here are more capable than the women, but they are utterly unreliable ; not having the "fear of God before their eyes," there is no dependance to be placed either on their word or their honesty. The women are uninstructed, and miserable gossips and dawdlers ; but being still under the dominion of their religion, you have a hold on their consciences. François avers there is not a woman in Italy who knows how to cook ; but François holds to the old-school opinion of women's capacities. My hearsay information is of little worth, but I have none other to give. We have employed but two women-servants ; the one faithless and efficient, the other inefficient and true—passably so. There is nothing peculiar to any country in this experience.

The whole tendency of service here is to corruption. Service, for the most part, is paid by fees which are irregular and uncertain. Many servants of cardinals and princes are not paid by their employers, but subsist on fees ; they are, in fact, birds of prey. For example, a gentleman residing here in an official station told me that twice every year, on the first of January and on the first of July, the servants of the princes and cardinals whom he visits come to demand a fee from him, and he must pay it. The day after his first official interview with the pope, a servant's bill, amounting to sixteen dollars, was sent to him. When the noted banker Torlonia gives a ball, his servants levy their tribute—black mail—the next day on the guests. To show you in what estimation this same gentleman Torlonia is held in Rome, it is a common report that his servants give his balls !

MY DEAR C.—You may almost doubt my being in Rome, since I have not yet said one word of the Vatican, where the history and religion of the Old World are recorded by the hand of art. The truth is, that from the moment of my visit to Winchester Cathedral, I have felt, as I fancy those do who go to another world, that the sensations resulting from a new state and new manifestations are incommunicable. I cannot convey to you what I have enjoyed, and am enjoying, from painting, sculpture, and architecture ; and when I involuntarily shudder at the idea of leaving all these magnificent and lovely forms, I doubt the wisdom of our New World people coming here to acquire hankerings which cannot be appeased at home. I would advise no American to come to Italy who has not strong domestic affections and close domestic ties, or some absorbing and worthy pursuit at home. Without these strong bonds to his country, he may feel, when he returns there, as one does who attempts to read a treatise on

political economy after being lost in the interest of a captivating romance.

You would fully comprehend this danger if you had passed but this day with me. First we went to the Orti Farnesiana (the Farnese Gardens), where we were first shown the remains of Augustus' bath *, for so a large reservoir of Tiburtine stone is called, into which flows a stream of the "acqua felice," copious enough to drown half-a-dozen emperors. Then we were led down broken steps into the baths of Livia, where, now buried in the bowels of the earth, are apartments suited to imperial luxury. The ceiling (shown by wax tapers) is vaulted, and painted with a border of the richest colour, encircling medallions of miniature animals, loves, and fauns. The statues have been removed from the niches. These are unquestionable remains of imperial luxury, and our pleasure was not disturbed with doubts, as it sometimes is, when we are told, before a broken stack of bricks half hidden with thorns and ivy, " This is the palace of the Cæsars !" When we emerged into daylight, our guide led us up a flight of steps, and, pointing to a shapeless mass of bricks, said, " These are the remains of Romulus' house !" Our friend, who used to admire the "moral effect" of General ———'s swearing, would call this bold lying the "moral courage" of a Roman guide. But the view from the little platform where we stood was no fiction. Before us was an amphitheatre of mountains melting into the atmosphere, their snowy edges like glittering clouds ; the dome of St. Peter's enfolded in ether ; domes, towers, churches, ruins on every side ; beyond them the campagna, a land-sea, with its soft, green, wavy surface, and the Mediterranean in the distance, gleaming like steel in the sun. No scenery that I have ever seen is more beautiful, none can be more expressive, than that in and about Rome. From the garden we drove quite to the other extremity of Rome, and mounted a hill to visit the Church of St. Onofrio, where Tasso was buried. It was in the convent adjoining this church that he lodged when he came to Rome to receive the poet's crown. There is a tablet with an inscription on the wall over the sacred spot where his remains were laid. But a more touching memorial of him is an oak-tree in the adjoining garden. It is the largest oak in Rome, and is called Tasso's, from the circumstance of his having been carried at his own desire to sit under its shadow the day before he died. What a scene for a dying poet ! the entire city of Rome with its thrilling memories under his eye, and the mountains inclosing the campagna, that, if they appeared as they appeared to-day, so shadowy and ethereal, must have spoken to his soul of that world on whose threshold he stood.

Come away with us now, dear C., to the Vatican, whose galleries the pope graciously opens to the public at twelve o'clock on the Monday and Thursday of every week, and permits them to remain open till three, when his guards appear, and drive the lingering spectators, like a flock of sheep, from room to room, till they are fairly out of the palace. The Vatican, as you well know, is the pontifical palace. It is an irregular mass of buildings, " a company of palaces," appended to St. Peter's, built from time to time, according to

* These attractive names are given and changed " à discrétion," by the antiquaries and guides of Rome.

the ability or whim of successive pontiffs, without reference, in its external, to architectural harmony or beauty of any kind. Mrs. Stark gives 70,000 feet as the circumference of these edifices. At twelve o'clock the Piazza of St. Peter's is thronged with English equipages, and visitors from all parts of the civilised world. They enter the colonnade that leads to St. Peter's, turn and ascend a side staircase, mount to a spacious open court (to which privileged carriages may drive by making the circuit of St. Peter's), and then enter the palace, where, scattered through the immense galleries and numberless apartments of the Museum, the multitudinous congregation that pressed through the portals appear but as a few wanderers.

My dear C., I shall not attempt to enumerate or describe to you the treasures of these marble halls. You know that the creative genius of nations which had passed away when Rome was founded, has contributed to fill them ; that here are monuments of Egyptian and Etruscan art ; that here is embodied the "graceful mythology" of Greece ; that here, in enduring marble, are her philosophers, poets, priestesses, and nymphs ; and that here is our real world of old Rome in her rulers and heroes ; and, chiselled while the eye of the artist was on their living heads, are the busts of Julius Cæsar, Cicero, Augustus, Titus, Trajan, and—but a list of them would fill a book instead of a letter *.

Besides the men of past ages, you have their history, their occupations, their religious offices, their games written in marble. These are gradations of adornment, as if to accustom your eye to increase of light. The walls at the entrance of the first hall are covered with sepulchral inscriptions ; as you proceed, these are interspersed with fragments of friezes and cornices. Along the sides of the walls are placed sarcophagi, baths, altars, fountains, urns, vases, and capitals. You proceed on through lengthening galleries with side-halls, and apartments with pictured ceilings, and mosaic pavements, and marble columns, to a small octagonal court, in the midst of which is a fountain sparkling in the bright, unobstructed sun-beams. Around this court is a portico containing the most precious remains of art, baths in which emperors have bathed, and sarcophagi sculptured for their mouldering bodies†. Inclosed in the four angles of this portico are masterpieces : the Apollo, the Laocoon, the Antinous, and, last, Canova's great works, Perseus and the Pugilists‡.

From this portico you pass to the hall of animals, where, I confess, I can never linger, though it is filled with works admirable for their art ; but serpents, fish, reptiles, even stags and dogs, have little chance when pitted against gods and men. There is one most enchanting little apartment that we can never pass by, called the *Stanza delle Maschere* (Chamber of the Masks), from the masks represented in its mosaic pavement. Among several masterpieces, it has an exquisite faun in *rosso antico*, found in Hadrian's villa, with the faun's insignia, the basket, the goat, and the grapes hanging round his joyous face. There is another we always enter too, if we can tear ourselves from the Apollo in time, in which stands, on an exquisite mosaic pavement§, a porphyry tazza, or vase, forty-two feet in circumference.

But, my dear C., I must hurry on through apartments filled with busts, candelabra, and every form of magnificent vase of marble, alabaster, and jasper ; through "the hall of geographical maps," a quarter of a mile in length, on whose walls are painted in fresco maps of all the pope's dominions and ground-plans of his cities, to the halls of tapestry, worked after Raphael's cartoons. But not even here can a lover of Raphael linger, for on and above are his Madonna di Fuligno, his Transfiguration, and his *Camere*. These camere or chambers are four large unfurnished (unfurnished !) rooms painted in fresco, walls and ceiling, by Raphael, or by his best pupils, from his designs‖. Each picture occupies one side of a room. After glancing at the rest, I always find myself standing before "the School of Athens." This was a subject of Raphael's own selection. He was unshackled by dictum of pope or cardinal, and freely followed out the suggestions of his inspired genius ; and you have the result in the most dramatic combination of character, circumstance, and expression¶.

<hr/>

Thorwaldsen's, have been admitted into the Vatican ; and I hope my presumption may be forgiven if I express a doubt whether Canova's will retain their enviable position, after the partiality of his contemporaries has passed away. The author of "Rome in the Nineteenth Century" says, that Canova's "Perseus looks more like an actor representing Perseus than like Perseus himself." A similar criticism might be extended to his other works ; they have not the free, untouched nature of the antiques.

§ This is the most beautiful pavement (except the unparalleled fragment of Pompeii) we saw in Italy. It was found fifty miles from Rome, and, encircling a colossal head of Medusa, represents the combat of the Centaurs and Lapithæ.

‖ The ceiling of one apartment is an exception. The rooms were given into Raphael's hands with orders to efface the paintings already there. He refused to touch one ceiling, which had been done by his master, Perugino ; and this remains a memorial of his affections, more precious even than the memorials of his genius that surround it.

¶ I shall do my readers a favour by transcribing the description of this picture from "Rome in the Nineteenth Century :"—"On the steps of a Grecian portico stand Aristotle and Plato engaged in argument, and each holding a volume in his hand. Their disciples are ranged around, attentively listening to them. Beneath is Diogenes, an inimitable figure, listlessly extended on the steps. On the left, at the top, is Socrates earnestly talking to young Alcibiades, who listens in a lounging sort of attitude, as if half subdued by the wisdom, half willing to turn away from it, yet still resolved to give the reins to pleasure, and run the career of gay enjoyment. I know

<hr/>

* The bust of Julius Cæsar is said by the antiquaries to be a faithful portrait. The face is so deeply furrowed that you can hardly believe it to be that of a man not more than fifty-six (his age at the time of his death). The face is a record of inflexible resolution, invincible purpose, and unintermitting anxieties. The mouth is rather like Washington's. There is a bust of Augustus Cæsar, said to have been made when he was a boy of eight or nine, and said to be the most beautiful bust in the world. It is faultless in its symmetry ; and if he were the crafty and selfish monarch history represents him, he must sadly have perverted his nature.

† Some of the sarcophagi are among the most beautiful works of art, such as that famous one in the Capitol on which the battle of the Amazons is sculptured. That with the story of Clytemnestra, and many others which I examined, would seem to us subjects most unsuited to sepulchral embellishment.

‡ No works of modern artists, excepting Canova's and

It would seem like profanity to leave the Vatican without mentioning the Transfiguration and the Communion of St. Jerome, by Domenichino. They are called the two great masterpieces of the world. Raphael's was the last picture on which he worked, was not quite finished when he died, and was borne before his body in his funeral procession. Domenichino received but twelve guineas for his from ignorant monks, who suffered it afterward to be thrown into a garret. But here it now stands, for the admiration of the world, and to dispute the palm with Raphael's favourite work. Between these pictures we always finish our day at the Vatican, and are only driven from them by the unwelcome cry of the guards, " Si chiude !," the signal for closing the gates of Paradise upon us.

We make our exit through the arcades, or *Loggie di Raffaelle*. These arcades are attached to three stories of the palace, running along one side, and are more like what we call a piazza than anything else. They are all painted by Raphael. In one series he begins, as some preachers do in their maiden-sermon, at the creation of the world, and comes down to the crucifixion. They repay the study of days, but we have not yet contrived to save a half-hour for them ; and you will not wonder at this, my dear C., if you remember how much the Vatican contains to be examined besides the galleries through which you may well think I have taken but a bat's flight ; its immense library, and the Paolini and *Sistine* Chapels, both painted by Michael Angelo—the Sistine with his masterpiece, the Last Judgment *.

My dear C., we began this morning with looking at the antiquities of old Rome ; then followed a memorial of the middle ages at Tasso's tomb, and in the museum of the Vatican we have been looking back, through ages and ages, far into the shadowy past. Do you wonder at the common testimony of travellers that you live a month in every day at Rome ! and what a month it is !

I WALKED an hour this morning with R. up and down the colonnade of St. Peter's. There had been a ceremony in the Sistine Chapel, and the *guarda nobile*, in their rich uniforms, as they came slowly winding down the magnificent marble staircase in deep shadow, and the Swiss guards in

not, however, why the young Grecian was not made more handsome. The old man beside him, with a cap on, listening to Socrates, is inimitable. Another, looking over the shoulder of Pythagoras, who is writing his works, is, if possible, still finer. The figure in deep, abstracted thought, leaning on his elbow, with a pen in his hand, is Zoroaster holding a globe ; Archimedes is stooping to trace a geometrical figure with compasses on a slate on the ground ; and the whole group that surrounds him are beyond all praise. In the corner, on the right, the figure with a black cap is the portrait of Raphael himself, and that beside him of Pietro Perugino." It is strange that the writer of this description, a woman, should have omitted to notice the figure of Aspasia, whose intellectual beauty is so shaded with sadness. She reminded me of Hamlet, in his soliloquy of " To be, or not to be." She seems revolving in her mind a mystery—the capacities of her nature and the degradation of her sex.

* The author of " Rome in the Nineteenth Century" asserts, on the authority of a " very accurate " Italian, "that you cannot see the Vatican Museum without walking a mile and three quarters !"

their motley, at the end of the colonnade, their arms gleaming in the fitful sunbeams, and the light glancing over Charlemagne and his voluminous drapery, made a picture for us as we pursued our damp and otherwise gloomy walk.

We finished the morning in the Vatican Library, where we had a pleasure quite peculiar to it, I believe, of walking through the largest library in the world without seeing a book ! not the largest in the number of books, for, though it is enriched by the accumulations of ages and the bequests of monarchs, the number, including MSS., does not exceed 100,000 volumes—but largest in space ! The principal hall is 1200 feet long, and into this you enter by one of 200 feet which, in my ignorance, I took for the whole, and dawdled through it, looking at its rich vases and frescoed walls, which are adorned with portraits of all the great promoters of learning from *Adam* down. The books and MSS. are locked in wooden cases, of which I presume his holiness keeps the key more tenaciously than he does that he holds in St. Peter's right, as he had far rather open the gates of Paradise to the dead than the Paradise of knowledge to the living. The pictures on the library walls representing the munificent popes graciously receiving from their authors literary productions and discoveries in science, seemed rather a severe comment on the present pontiff's exclusion of letters and *veto* of literary associations !

The custode unlocked many of the cases to exhibit their treasures. Among them are a quantity of quaint old pictures of the earliest period of the revival of the arts. It is curious to see how the patronage of the Church has prevented the exercise of the painter's invention. Here are the same crucifixions, martyrdoms, and Holy Families that you see now freshly painted in Camucini's studio.

We saw relics of the early Christians' crucifixes and lamps that were found in the catacombs. A strange passage the mind makes, dear C., from this pontifical palace to St. Peter and his friends lighting these lamps in the caverns of the dead for their proscribed worship.

A curious relic of another kind was shown us ; the hair of a woman found in a tomb on the Appian Way. There they are—a little mouldy—the very tresses that some 2000 years ago adorned the head of a Roman lady, probably the only unchanged mortal remains of all the masses of men and women that lived in ancient Rome !

MY DEAR C.—The museum of the Capitol, its sculpture, paintings, and relics of antiquity, would be quite enough to draw the travelling world to Rome, if everything else here were swallowed up. Volumes have been written upon it, but I shall wisely abstain from writing even one letter, and only tell you what exquisite pleasure I have had from visiting again and again the Dying Gladiator which is in this collection. The artists appear to me often to have sacrificed expression to serenity—to a sort of superhuman, divine tranquillity ; but the brow and lip of the dying gladiator express the deepest, saddest emotion. Perhaps it owes something of its effect to Byron's admirable interpretation. But it seems to me that if he had never written, and this statue had never received its suggestive appellation, one could not look at it without seeing a man of refined nature death-stricken without hope, and whose most dejected thoughts are on some distant object of tenderest love. It was for Byron's gifted vision to see in these objects "his young barbarians at play."

There are masterpieces in the hall of paintings in the Capitol. The picture that kept me standing before it half an hour when I was sick with weariness, is Guido's St. Sebastian. The martyrdom of this poor saint is a favourite subject with the painters, and you see him in all the galleries stuck full of arrows. Mere physical suffering is a vulgar means of producing effect. Guido exhibits the physical sensation to show the triumph of the soul ; it is the deep shadow that brings out the light. The young martyr is a beautiful boy of fourteen, innocent as a baby and fresh as a Hebe. His hands are tied together above his head to a tree ; they have not only an unresisting expression, but one of voluntary submission ; one arrow is sticking in his side, another in his arm-pit. The calm, sweet resignation of his face expresses, " Though he slay me, yet will I trust in him."

Among the curiosities of the Capitol (we always look in faith, dear C. ; it is a great help at Rome) is the bronze wolf, with her foster-sons mentioned by Cicero, and said to have been struck in the prophetic storm on the night before Cæsar's death—the first *rostral column*, as appears by its inscription—and the *Fasti Consulares*, or lists of the consuls (nearly entire), with the date of their election and the term of their service engraved upon stone tablets.

THE generosity of the proprietors of the Roman palaces, in throwing them open to the occupation of visiters, is worthy of all praise. *Occupation* it may be called, as from morning to night they are traversed by these new hordes of Northern invaders. The ground story of a Roman palace is given up to menial offices and shops ; the picture-gallery occupies the second, or the greater part of it. A range of spacious rooms and halls is filled from floor to ceiling with pictures. There is little furniture ; curtains, perhaps, of faded damask, and chairs and tables centuries old. I have never seen, excepting in the S—— Palace, any look of habitancy. There we found warm rooms, and a table spread with books, drawings, and the delicate needlework of a lady who had been driven from the room by our entrance. Within the last few days, rumour says that the obstinacy of this lady in insisting on having the choice of her own rooms has led to a conjugal quarrel, and ended in her leaving her husband's bed and board, and taking lodgings in another palace. I could fill a letter with a mere list of the pictures of one of these galleries. They are vast storehouses of art, more or less valuable ; but not one of them but contains some works of the first painters who have ever lived. Almost every day we have a new one to visit. Estimate our industry, if you can, and thank me for imitating Byron's sensible example, and, instead of dragging you round with us, writing " Vide Guide-book ;" and if that guide-book should chance to be Madame Stark's, you will admire her laconic opinions of pictures thus expressed after the insertion of the name, !—!!—!!!!

Of all countries, the southern part of Italy would appear the most delicious for rural enjoyments. The villas about Rome are abandoned from dread of the malaria. Their possessors go to them in winter only, and then for short periods. The Romans, with their resources of soil and climate, might make paradises of their villas, if they studied and obeyed nature, instead of torturing her with trimming their trees into every fantastical form, imprisoning their avenues with hedges that look as much as possible like solid green walls, and laying out their garden-grounds, like those of Albani, with coloured stones or flowers in arabesque patterns ! But why, you may ask me, with the everlasting inconsistency of human expectations, look for *everything* here ! I am not sure I should not steal away from the faultless beauty and perfection of adornment of an English nobleman's park, garden, and conservatories, to wander over the old Mattei Villa on the Cœlian Hill, ruined and abandoned as it is, with its ragged berceaus, its untrimmed rose-hedges, its broken-nosed statues, and its vineyard, as it now is, brown and sear ; for from its high-swelling grounds you have an unbroken view of the mountains that half girdle Rome. You turn you eyes from *Soracte* to *Tivoli*, to the *Sabine Mount*, to *Albano ;* they bear names to conjure with ; and it seems as if Nature delighted in showing them in a light she has for nothing else. They are invested with a silvery mist ; you would call it ethereal, for there is nothing dimming or shadowy about it ; but I fear ethereal mist is nonsense. It is a sheathed light, a brighter moonlight. The outlines blend with the atmosphere. Before you is the wide, desolate campagna, with its sepulchral grass, and the long lines of broken aqueducts, Cecilia Metella's tomb, the huge ruins of Caracalla's baths, St. John Lateran's statues standing boldly up against the sky, the walls of Rome, with their gates, towers, turrets, and voices of history ; and the whole city of Rome beneath you, with its living crowds, and its dead congregations, its St. Peter's, and its desolate places where the " tent-roofed pine " and the slender cypress stand as mourners for the dead.

At the Villa Albani, whose treasures of art any monarch in Europe might envy, we found something much rarer in the dwelling of a Roman prince than chefs-d'œuvre of painting or sculpture ; carpeted rooms with a comfortable enjoyed aspect, fire in the chimney, and English books and fresh journals on the tables. Irving's Alhambra was among them. Our cicerone told us the padrone read English : a sign of intellectual life. You will not think me quite a savage, dear C., though the lovers of art might, if I tell you what most interested me at the Villa Albani. I had been looking at the admirable group of Dædalus and Icarus ; and as I turned from it my eye fell on some toys thrown by a tired child into a magnificent old vase. I forgot the gods, nymphs, and heroes about me ; my thoughts flew home to you, my dear C. ; to your " young barbarians at play," and I hung brooding over the little tin coach and battered doll till I was summoned away.

The Borghese Villa is on the Pincian Hill, just under the walls of Rome, and is, indeed, princely in its extent and decorations. Prince Borghese is noted for his liberality, and as, alas ! few Roman princes now are, for his immense wealth.

The author of " Rome in the Nineteenth Century" happily says that "Julius Cæsar only *be-queathed* his gardens to the Roman people, the Borghese princes *give* theirs." Their gates and doors are always open, and the visitor enters them when and how he pleases. R. and E. often vary their drives by going through those beautiful grounds, where the fountains are gushing, the grass is always green; where the hedges and long avenues of trees are always verdant, and the birds always singing; and where you may lose yourself in the sweet fancy of a perpetual summer if you will not foolishly look about for bird-cages, and observe that the trees are cypress and ilex (a species of oak that never changes), and the hedges of laurels. Certainly there was no illusion in the roses we saw blooming there in profusion on the 29th of December. How far below zero stood your mercury on that day, dear C.!

I passed four hours on Friday in walking through the glades and avenues of the Dorian Villa with Lady D., and came to the conclusion that four hours could scarcely be more delightfully passed than with an agreeable companion there. It is on the western side of the Tiber. Its present mistress is a beautiful young Englishwoman of the Talbot family; but there is no English mark upon her villa; and perhaps it is good taste to keep up what is national and characteristic. Nothing can be better than the noble pines that embellish these grounds, and which, wherever you see them, appear in striking harmony with the spirit of the scenery of Rome. The pine of Italy is unlike any that we have, and that of Rome seems to me richer and broader than I have seen elsewhere. It has a straight and lofty trunk, and a broad horizontal top of foliage that seems to have been growing deeper and deeper ever since it or the world stood. The affluence of fountains at this villa is, too, a characteristic beauty. The same stream that supplies the Paulina, the Niagara of Roman fountains, is conducted across the Doria Villa.

It is peculiar to Rome that, stay here as long as you will, if you have a month, a day, an hour, ten minutes to spare, you may fill it with some object of deep interest. We had a half-hour on our hands after leaving the Dorian Villa, and Lady D., who selects her objects with the skill that can only be acquired by a long familiarity with everything in and about Rome, drove to the Paulina Fountain, to the beautiful view on the Janiculum, and to St. Pietro in Montorio, where, in a court adjoining the church, is a small circular temple designed by Michael Angelo, with columns of Oriental granite, erected on the very spot where St. Peter was crucified. So says tradition, and so believe the faithful.

MY DEAR C.—You can hardly imagine anything more sombre than a drive in the evening through the wretchedly-lighted streets of Rome. Teeming as they are with human life in the daytime, by eight o'clock you see only here and there a dim form shrinking away from your coach-wheels, or an indistinct figure stealing along in the deepest shade where all is shadow. There is the gloom of night among the tombs, without the consciousness that "the weary are at rest, and the wicked have ceased from troubling." If you go to visit a friend lodged in a palace, you will have the happiness to find the staircase lighted, and a porter ready to

admit you; but a Roman *house* is like a closed prison. We went last evening to see our countrywoman, Mrs. L. After François had rapped repeatedly, we heard a child's voice uttering the never-failing inquiry, "Chi è" ("Who is it?"), to which François responded "Amici" ("Friends"). After a long pause and impatient shouts from François, seconded by Mariano, of "Aprite!" "Aprite!" ("Open the door!"), "Ecco!" said the little voice, and "Bravo!" cried François; and the parley was ended by the child opening the door and conducting us up a long staircase by the light of a brazen antique lamp in her hand, rather taller, it seemed to me, than she was.

The lower classes of the people are *en scène* in the streets; and the stranger, who has no opportunity of seeing the better condition of Italian life, has here his best opportunities for observation; and I assure you, my dear C., these streets are a curious and affecting spectacle to one accustomed to the bustling achieving industry of New York, or to the quiet diligence and innocent leisure of our village life. The first thing that meets my eye as I come into the drawing-room in the morning is the drilling of soldiers before our window. This is the great instruction and business of Rome!

As we drove over to the Vatican to-day, I was fancying how our little B., with her quick sympathies, would endure the aspect of this throng of people, who, in the affecting language of F. B.'s slave, "have no prospect:" how she would by turns laugh and cry; but I fear the tears would carry the day—try it, dear B. Take this seat beside me. The streets, with an unclouded sun for weeks, are muddy and slimy; they are so narrow and the houses are so high, that at this season they have no chance to dry. That heap of indescribable filth is permitted, as you perceive by the word "immondezza" on the wall—this, like many corners of the streets, is a place of common deposit. We have turned into the *Via Serpenti*, and here you may see the average condition of life in Rome. In the English quarter it is better, in other quarters much worse. The windows of the lower stories are grated, not glazed. Most of the workshops have no windows; the light is admitted through the open door, and most cheerless and comfortless they are in these damp, sunless streets, when the weather is as cold as our ordinary March. But, alas! there are few people in these workshops, and little to be done in them *! You are shuddering, B. You fear we shall trample down some of the people in this crowd; there is no danger; the coachmen are accustomed to driving through full streets, and the people know so well how to take care of themselves that they never move aside till the horses' hoofs are close upon them. Do you observe the sullen, brooding aspect of those men who are sauntering up and down in the sun, neither talking, observing, nor observed! or the man leaning against that ruined arch wrapped in his tattered cloak with a remnant of a hat!

* Where there is an impoverished population like that of Rome, there is, of course, little employment for domestic artisans, the hatter, the shoemaker, &c. The visiters at Rome provide for their personal wants before they go there. Woe be unto you if you chance to need a new hat, a pair of shoes, or gloves in the city of the Cæsars! you can get them, but of a wretched quality and at a dear rate.

What a majestic, free, and graceful air he has ! he looks like a ruined rebel-chieftain brooding over fresh mischief. But I see the men on the piazza, playing at ball, quoits, and mora, have caught your eye—or are you looking at the women in that door-step who are clamouring and gesticulating at such a rate ! Do you think they have detected a thief or discovered a murderer ! no, it is but their ordinary manner. They are more cheerful than the men, because they are even more ignorant ; they think less, and they have some employment ; sewing and knitting are unfailing to women. You are wasting your pity on those babies ; for though they are left to the tending of these pale, lean little children not more than four or five years old, and though (as I am told) those swaddling-clothes in which they are wrapped like mummies are not opened more than *once a-week*, yet they are quiet and contented.

In five weeks that we have now been here, and every day, and all day, in the street amid this baby population I have never heard but one crying ; is not this a fact in favour of the virtue of the open air ! This seems to me their only advantage. These beginnings of human life, so hailed and cherished with us as the blossoms of future-sustaining fruit, are here but a burden. I have never once seen a child caressed in Rome, even by its mother ! Do you ask why there are so many soldiers, idle as the idlest, mingling with the crowd !—dogs watching the flock, my dear, but ill-trained, ill-fed, and inoperative ; the pope's government has not energy enough to maintain a vigorous police. Those are Capuchins ; you will meet them in every street in Rome, with their butternut-coloured, hooded gowns, fastened with cords around their waists, their long beards, and their feet shodden only with an incrustation of dirt ; and this is a procession of Dominicans—noble-looking men, are they not ! these vehicles have stopped to let them pass, and we must stop too. What huge animals are the oxen attached to these vehicles ! and observe the half-circular pent-house of skins by which the driver shelters himself from the wind—not a bad contrivance. Ah, the beggars are taking advantage of our pause to come out upon us from the sunny steps of that magnificent church, where they always congregate. Listen to them ; mark the words of their petition, for ever repeated and often true, and thank God, dear B., that you never heard it in your own country. " Ho fame ! " " Muoio della fame ! " " Non m'abbandonate ! " (" I am hungry ! " " I am dying with hunger ! " " Do not abandon me ! ")

See, as we pass the bridge of St. Angelo, and the filthy street that debouches into the Piazza di San Pietro, able-bodied men lolling on those wooden benches, and women in rags, with faces and forms that might personate Sabine matrons. See the blind and old stretching their hands for charity, and the cardinal's gilded coach dashing on before us. But we are at the Vatican—shall we go in, and in that beautiful marble world forget this world of flesh and blood—of sensation and suffering * !

* There is enough inexplicable misery in the world ; the want and suffering of the Roman people are not so. There is in M. Sismondi's " Etudes sur l'Economie Politique," a very instructive essay on the Campagna of Rome, in

I HAVE never yet met a stranger in Italy who did not profess to *love* Rome. Here he lingers, and here he returns ; here, though he be of the dullest mould, he will be waked to a new existence ; and after a little while will find himself getting the feeling of a lover for the desolate places of the old city. I have been disappointed in the ruins ; not in their effect, but in their condition. Excepting the Colosseum, the Pantheon, the Temple of Vesta, and a few others, they are such mere ruins, so changed in form, and stripped of their original embellishments, that they only serve to kindle the enthusiast or puzzle the antiquary†.

which he shows, after laborious investigation and accurate personal observation, that the condition of the land, and the misery resulting from it, are owing to a violation of those laws of Providence which, if strictly observed, would secure food and raiment to every member of the human family. He does not look at the Campagna through the veil in which poets and picturesque tourists invest it ; but he sees and exposes the abuses which have reduced it to its present desolateness, and cursed it with malaria. It is impossible to compress M. Sismondi's facts into our narrow limits ; but it is easy to see that malaria, and every other mischief, must result from the present mode of cultivation. An extent of territory, raying in some directions twenty, in others fifty miles from Rome, is in the hands of about eighty proprietors, whose only object is to get the greatest possible amount of revenue for themselves, with the least possible cost of labour. As, in its present vicious mode of cultivation, grazing produces greater returns to the proprietor than tillage, no portion of the land is ploughed more than once in ten years. There is one man over all, called *Mercante di Campagna ;* he has superintendants under him, who, like the overseers of the slaves of the South, traverse the fields on horseback, seeing that others work. The actual labourers are brought, *not from Rome,* but from the mountains—some even from the kingdom of Naples. They come with their families, sometimes in companies of five hundred. They encamp on the Campagna, and sleep on the ground, or creep at night into the catacombs, the old towers, or the tombs. They are fed in the cheapest possible manner. Is it strange that, at the most moderate computation, at least a tenth of their number perish every season, though the season be short—the sowers being from one district, the reapers from another, and so on ? The principle by which human life is multiplied, and sustenance, comfort, and progress secured to it, is totally neglected, viz., the giving to the labourer a fair share of the product of his labour, and connecting him by residence on, and interest in, the soil he cultivates. Compare the condition of the foreign and stinted labourer on the Campagna, with that of the hopeful young proprietor on our most unwholesome new lands : no wonder that in the one case the malaria is conquered, and that in the other it goes on conquering and to conquer, till Rome must become its own inevitable tomb.

† Our servant was quite *un-Italian* in his tastes, and often amused himself with our zeal. " You like broken stones," he said ; " I like news" (meaning new things). " I would not give Astor house for all the ruins in Rome." This he said when we had kept his dinner waiting, having spent the day in wandering through the broken arches of the palace of the Cæsars, and visiting Sallust's garden. The massive foundations only of the house of this doubtful and luxurious Roman are traceable. The form of the circus adjoining his garden is discernible, and at its extremity is the fragment of the wall of a temple, and a few of the niches in which beautiful statues were found. One of the obelisks that adorn the modern city was found here. But though these adornments have long ago disappeared, we felt, as we walked through the rustling canes, with broken buttresses matted with dangling ivy hanging over our heads, the presence of the great men who had walked and talked here, and, perhaps, sometimes not more wisely

But there are objects in Rome that indescribably surpass your expectations, which indeed, I honestly confess, scarcely entered into mine ; among these are the *scenery of Rome* and its surroundings, the obelisks, and pillars, and the fountains which almost realise your fancies of Oriental adornment. As to art in Rome, antique and modern, as you may imagine even from my very inadequate expression of our pleasure, it creates for us of the New World a new life.

I have as yet said nothing to you of the churches of Rome, simply because so much has already been said, and for another, not quite as satisfactory reason, that so much remains to say which I have no power to communicate. There is little beauty in their exterior, and that little is impaired by their being hedged in by other buildings. The effect of the exterior of an old Gothic village church in England, with its harmonious accompaniments, is better than that of any church in Rome ; but, compared with the interior of these churches, any Protestant church that I have seen, even Winchester Cathedral, is like a disfurnished house. The Romish churches have fallen heirs to the accumulated art and wealth of the Old World. The columns that embellished the temples of the gods now support the roofs of the Christian temple. The jasper and porphyry that adorned their palaces, and the sarcophagi in which their emperors and heroes were embalmed, are now consecrated to the altars of the saints. The vases for their lustral water are now the *bénitiers* from which the pious Catholic crosses himself.

These churches have been enriched, too, with the spoils of the Eastern world, with the gifts of emperors and queens from St. Helena's days to ours, and with the offerings of rich penitents who hoped at the last to drive a good bargain by purchasing the treasures of the other world with those they could no longer enjoy in this. Infinite industry has been employed on them, and art has given them its divinest works—such works as Raphael's Sibyls, Guido's Archangel Michael, and Domenichino's Frescoes *.

How I have sometimes wished for some of you at home who have worshipped all your lives in a Puritan "*meeting-house,*" to walk up the nave of Santa Maria Maggiore with me (a church very near us), between its double row of most magnificent Ionic pillars, which once adorned a temple of Juno, and passing by chapels and altars laden with vessels of silver and gold, where candles are for ever burning before the pictures of saints and

than we ! When you measure the extent of private possession in old Rome, the gardens, circuses, and all the appliances of individual luxury within the walls of the city, you wonder where the million were lodged—truly, they were herded together as

    " Woollen vassals, things created
To buy and sell with groats, to show bare heads
    In congregations.''

It was reserved for a later period of the world, and a then undiscovered country, to put within the power of those " rank-scented" vassals a name, a political existence, and a home with all its sweet charities.

  * These are but a few examples of the many masterpieces remaining in the churches for which they were originally designed ;—some have been removed—they either hung where they could be but imperfectly seen, or they were exposed to premature decay from the dampness of their position.

martyrdoms, sit down with me on the steps of the Borghese Chapel, the richest in the world ! It has cost millions, and it is but a side apartment of the church, a rich pendant to a chain. There is a beautiful pavement, the walls are incrusted with Oriental marbles, the ceiling is painted with frescoes ; there are columns of porphyry and lapis lazuli, rich carvings, pictures in mosaic, and splendid monuments ; not a square inch is left unembellished. And yet, dear C., I think your eye would turn from all this gorgeousness to the squalid, lean beggar, kneeling on the step beside you.

The Colosseum is now a church, and the Pantheon, once a temple for all the gods, is now consecrated to the one true God †. The statues of the divinities have disappeared from the Pantheon, and the niches they occupied are now filled with tawdrily-dressed altars and the pictures of saints.

There is a little chapel of the Capuchins near the Piazza Barberini with pictures that you would like to see every day in the year. But of all the churches in Rome, and I assure you I have visited the most renowned of the three hundred and sixty-five, not one among them—I hesitate as I except St. Peter's—has given me more delightful sensations than Santa Maria degli Angeli. It is built after a design of Michael Angelo on the ruins of Diocletian's baths. The roof is supported by huge granite columns which stood in Diocletian's hall. It is in the form of a Greek cross, and when you enter, the harmony of its perfect proportions affects you as if a strain of music burst from the walls ‡.

If you do not care for art, or if you are tired of pictures and statuary, you may visit the churches for their curiosities. Through one you go down into the Mamertine prisons, one of the few remaining works of the republic, where Catiline's conspirators were imprisoned, Jugurtha was starved to death, and St. Peter miraculously set free ; or you may dive into the subterranean church where Constantine held his councils, or see in old St. Clement's the model of all churches, or at San Pietro in Vincoli the very chain with which St. Peter was bound. In short, my dear C., a thorough examination of the Roman churches would be quite work enough for one lifetime ; do not imagine that I flatter myself I have given you any notion of them in this brief and flippant notice §.

† If architecture is a species of writing, what must we think of the disparity between the genius that produced the Pantheon, and that which designed the façade of St. Peter's? The worship of the gods has long ago passed, and with some of us the worship of the saints ; but there is one altar in the Pantheon at which we all offer our homage: it is a plain tablet over the ashes of Raphael, whose life you feel in Rome more than that of thousands you see, and yet, as this tablet tells you, he died at the age of thirty-seven : what a glorious immortality he achieved in this brief period ! The veneration of the man who never heard the name of Raphael without touching his hat, does not seem exaggerated to one who has been to Rome.

‡ There is no exaggeration in this. I suppose that the ingenious theorist who resolved music into mathematics could give a satisfactory explanation of my simple fact.

§ I am aware it requires an art which I do not possess to make this subject interesting, and therefore I have condensed pages into a few paragraphs. I *walked* these splendid edifices daily with the enthusiasm, if not the devotion of a pilgrim. The limits of my book are drawing to a

Velletri, February 13.

WE have left Rome, my dear C., and left it, after a sojourn of but two months, with the fond feeling of lovers. Nowhere do you get such an attachment to material objects;—the living are dead here, but the dead are living. I looked mournfully round for the last time on our sunny rooms, and out upon our pleasant garden, with its ripening oranges, ever-blooming roses, and singing birds. We have the pleasant sadness, too, of leaving friends at Rome [*]. N., our landlord, was unfeignedly sorry to part with us; madame wept; and dear little Enrico could not speak " because the signore were going away!" I would find a better reason for my tears, as we drove on to the Appian Way, than the fear that we were looking for the last time upon the tortuous old walls of Rome—on the towers, domes, columns, and all the grey city, surrounded with an atmosphere that the mind's eye fills with "millions of spirits."

You cannot imagine, dear C., for we have nothing bearing the most distant resemblance to it, the solemn solitude of the drive across the Campagna from Rome to the Alban hills, a distance of twelve miles. There are remains of tombs and broken lines of aqueducts (most beautiful ruins they make) on each side ; but scarcely the note of a bird or the sound of an animal to break the eloquent silence. Could this have been a solitary drive in Cicero's time! he alludes to the danger of robbery in going from Rome to Albano in broad daylight.

As we began the ascent of the Alban Mount, the aspect of the country changed. The declivities of the hills are covered with ilexes and olives. Instead of going into the hotel, K., L., and myself took a guide, and went off a mile and a half through a *galleria*, or imbowered walk, to the Alban Lake— a crater lake, deep sunk within high surrounding hills, which K—n, with his usual aptness, compared to a teaspoonful of tea left in the bottom of a teacup. At the end of the *galleria* we came upon a village, terminated by an ugly summer-palace of the pope. The peasants, whose dwellings are nested in the nooks and angles of an old fortress, were all in the street ; the old women, with their distaffs and spindles, walking and spinning, and looking as fit to spin an evil destiny as Michael Angelo's Fates, though, like the young girls, they were dressed in short gowns of a brilliant red, and head-gear of the same colour. Men and children were sitting in the doorways pursuing the pleasures of the chase—*heads* their hunting-ground ! Young children were teaching younger ones in leading-strings to walk[†], and there was the usual quota of

blind, lame, and sick beggars. You will scarcely believe me, but it is true that, in a progress of a hundred miles through New-England villages, I have not seen so much beauty as I saw this morning. The peasants of Tivoli, of Frascati, and of Albano are beautiful ; and I could scarcely turn my eye from these last to look to the Alban Mount towering up into the clouds, where our guide pointed out a monastery standing on the site of the temple of the Latian Jove. That has passed away ; but the *Via Triumphalis,* by which the Roman generals approached it for their ovations, and the Roman emperors for their sacrifices, still exists. There are moments in this Old World, and this on the secluded Alban Lake was one of them, when the

> " Strong barriers round thy dark domain,
> Thou unrelenting Past ! "

disappear, and the long-gone generations rise before you in all their pomp and sacred offices.

But we were soon recalled to actual life by our cicerone, who, like all his countrymen in sunshine, with plenty of *antichiti* to show, and a good fee in view, was in a high state of excitement. Fancy one of our common labourers striking his breast, casting up his eyes, and exclaiming, " Dio mio— bella giornata—bellissima giornata, excellenza ! ah ! dà piacere anchè la vita [‡] !" And then he poured out such compliments on the girls, calling them " Belle ! belle ! belle assai !" for which pleasing improvisation K. insists he charged two pauls extra, and that the next lady he conducts will find herself perfectly angelic.

In our way we passed the ruins of Domitian's villa and the place where was the *Emissario,* an outlet for the lake cut through the mountains in obedience to an oracle [§].

We found R. and E. sitting out on a terrace that overlooked a lovely garden. Here they had taken their lunch and remained for two hours. Is not this a blessed country for invalids !

THREE miles from Albano we overtook our inamorato, who had jogged ahead on a donkey, to have the privilege of escorting us to the Lake of Nemi, called by the ancients *Speculum Dianæ.*

> " Mirror of Dian ! aptly named by those
> Who dwelt near Nemi's wooded wave."

We saw nothing but a solitary beggar, and some cows grazing where Diana had a temple and Egeria her favourite haunt, and where goddesses and nymphs might, indeed, love to dwell ! I am now sitting at Velletri, looking from a very pleasant window at the sun, as he drops his urn into the Mediterranean, which has appeared in the distance for the last hour, like a sheet of molten gold.

TORRE TREPONTI.

AFTER winding down the Alban Hills this morning, we soon came on to the Pontine marshes, formerly so fatal, and now pestilential, during the

---

close, and I am obliged to omit our excursion to Tivoli and Frascati, which occupied the last days of our first visit to Rome. The memory of my delightful visit to Frascati, and the remains of Cicero's Tusculum Villa, his " eyes of Italy," blends with the better memory of the English friend to whose zealous kindness I owed this pleasure.

[*] I should be ungrateful not to specify among these friends our consul, Mr. Greene, who so honourably represents his country at Rome. Though withheld by assiduous devotion to literary pursuits from general and useless attentions to his countrymen, his kindness, when needed, is prompt, unmeasured, and effective.

[†] This mode of learning to walk, a nursery tale with us, is universal in Italy.

[‡] " My God—your excellency ! what a beautiful, most beautiful day ! Life alone is a pleasure !"

[§] " This great work," Eustace says, " was done in the year of Rome 356, to prevent the sudden and mischievous swells of the lake, which had then recently occasioned considerable alarm."

hot months. They are twenty-four miles in length, and from six to twelve in breadth. The draining of them was carried on by the Cæsars, by the popes, and by the Medici, and to its present state by Pius VI., who rebuilt the former Appian Way, and made it what it now is, one of the best roads in Europe.

This is supposed to be the place spoken of by St. Paul as Appii Forum, and this, say the authorities, was Horace's second resting-place on his journey to Brundusium. I trust they found the elements as kind as we do. Our carriage is drawn up on the turf while our horses are taking their meridian; and as the inn is a secularised old convent, most uninviting, we prefer remaining out of doors. R. is taking his siesta in the carriage, E. is at her worsted-work, K. reading aloud the " Morals of a Soldier" from a book given her by a ci-devant Italian militaire, and L. is hazing about with an ivy wreath on her bonnet, and the fresh flowers tucked on one side which our handsome *cameriero* put on our breakfast table as a signal of the *primavera*. The wide, green level land on each side of us is broken only by canals and stagnant water, and covered with herds of buffaloes and beeves, flocks of sheep and droves of horses; a long, level horizon bounds the view on the Mediterranean side, and on the east, beyond the morass, are steep and rugged mountains. Two or three miserable villages are visible on their acclivities. At Sezza there stood once a temple to Saturn one hundred and thirty feet high. Before and behind, as far as we can see, stretches the road, completely embowered and looking like a beautiful avenue. Beside the inn there is another dwelling for human beings, a thing made of sticks and straw. I walked past it and looked in; ragged wretches, blighted with want and malaria, were playing cards; like lean and sallow creatures are sauntering up and down before our carriage, staring at us; gendarmes are standing at the inn door, and two *healthy*-looking little boys are sitting on the step devouring a crust of bread—Oh, youth and nature, how potent are ye!

Terracina.—WE are again on the seashore; the waves are breaking as softly under my window as the ripple of a lake. The fishing-boats are drawn up on the shore, and the nets are drying. So a seashore might have appeared in the patriarchal stage of society; and here was an important town of the Volsci, an independent nation! and here, on the very spot where the little boats seem sleeping in the moonlight, were once the ships of an important naval station! On the land-side of our inn is a most curious pile of stone of Nature's masonry, and a little back from the summit are some regular stone arches, the remains of a palace of Theodoric *or* a temple of Hercules. We clambered up a street almost perpendicular, to see the Cathedral built on the ruins of a temple of Apollo, but we were frightened by the ragged ruffianly-looking wretches in the piazza; and, without seeing the consecrated pillars, we came down again, *au galop*.

* We are happily so constituted that the minor miseries of life are forgotten as soon as past, and, therefore, never but at the moment, and by the susceptible traveller, can the misery inflicted by the fleas in Italy be estimated. Ours was at its acme at Terracina, where, during a

Mola di Gaeta.

MY DEAR C.—Would that I could surround you with the odorous, balmy atmosphere of this most delicious place, and transport you to its orange-bowers! but since that cannot be, pray, the next time you pass my bookcase, take down a certain yellow-covered book, "Kenyon's Poems," and read the few last lines of "Moonlight," and you will find the poet doing for you what I cannot. This morning, six miles on this side Terracina, at a huge gate between two stone towers, we passed from the Roman States into the Neapolitan territory. You have had something too much of this, or I would describe to you the mob of beggars that surrounded us at Fondi. We needed to have been "Principesse," as they called us, to have afforded relief to such numbers. Just in proportion as we advance south the poverty increases. Shoes are becoming a rare luxury, and, as François says, " he is accounted a rich man who wears them." In their place they wear leather soles fastened on with cords that are wound around their legs. The working people wear a cotton shirt and drawers extending a little below the knee—the shirt is a *winter* garment. We have seen children to-day with nothing on but thin, short, ragged cotton drawers!

A mile and a half before we reached Mola we passed the very spot where, as it is believed, Cicero was killed, and within a vineyard a few yards from the road is a cenotaph erected to his memory†. It is three stories high and circular, and incloses a column of the height of the edifice. The stones and bricks are bare and mouldering. The marbles that incrusted them have given place to a mantling of ivy, roses, and laurustinus, whose rich breath incenses the dearest name of all Roman antiquity.

Our inn has the loveliest position I have seen in Italy. It is in the midst of a large garden, or, rather, of orange and lemon groves. For the first time in our lives we have seen to-day these tropical fruit-trees in perfection, as spreading (not as

wretched night, I never closed my eyes. We kept for some days a list of the killed; of fugitives, of course, no account could be made. On one day they amounted to twenty-five; on the next, to thirty; and, finally, the amount ran up to a hundred, when we desisted! If it be remembered that even one of these most subtile little beasts of the field can make his victim perfectly wretched, it cannot be wondered at if sometimes, amid the softest airs of Italy, some of our party longed for the cold winds and *killing* frosts of their own country. Lest a delicate reader should be shocked at the introduction of this topic into a lady's journal, I must be allowed to say that it is a very common one among the most refined of the suffering travellers in Italy; that I have heard it discussed for half an evening in a society of lords and ladies, where, on one side, lavender was recommended as a sovereign antidote, and on the other it was maintained that the essential oils only occasioned the little wretches to faint, or *feign* fainting! "Fleas" make a distinct article in the guide-books, and fleas are the subject of the fine arts. In one of the galleries of Rome there is a picture of a pretty young woman with a basin of water, most intently engaged in finding victims for her *noyade*.

† It is better to look at these places, and, I think, even to hear of them, without recurring to the doubts in which the uncertainty of tradition necessarily invests them. Let the antiquaries dispute, and the learned doubt, we, the unlearned, will enjoy the pleasure of believing.

I

high) as an apple-tree, and bending under the weight of their fruit. The gardens are in the recess of a crescent bay, and fill with their terraces the interval between the last slopes of bare, rugged mountains and the sea. These slopes are covered with vines and olives, and through some openings in our orange-bowers we get glimpses of a narrow, grey village pent in between us and the hill-side. Our inn and garden, formerly the villa of an Italian prince, are supposed to cover the site of Cicero's *Formian Villa*, and upon the strength of that supposition bears the attractive name of *La Villa di Cicerone*. We have been down to the shore, and seen the foundations of edifices, and subterranean arches and columns, that indicate Roman magnificence. We wandered about till the twilight deepened upon us, with nothing to remind us that we were not in Paradise, till, on retracing our way to the inn, we heard a *yell* after us of " Signore ! signore ! qualche cosa per il giardiniere ! " (" Ladies ! ladies ! give something to the gardener ! ") and, turning, we perceived a tall, swarthy fellow, in Neapolitan *undress*, pursuing us for his tax on the sweet air we had breathed.

I have never enjoyed anything so perfect of its kind as the quiet Sunday we have been passing at Mola di Gaeta. We left it just at evening, and drove from our orange-bowers into the very narrow street of the village, so charming seen through our garden vistas. It being Sunday, the people were, of course, in their festa-dresses— such as had them—and they were like a swarm of bees in that narrow street ; standing, leaning, lying, sitting, it seemed next to impossible that our carriage should find a passage through them ; and such a mingled shout of begging and salutation assailed us, some hands stretched out for " Carita, per l'amor di Dio ! " and others to give us the graceful Italian greeting. At the end of the street a troop of masqueraders gathered about us, playing their antics, to the infinite diversion— of the boys and girls, I would have said ; but *all* were merry as merriest childhood.

My dear C., let us be thankful for the system of compensation that makes their delicious sunshine not only meat, drink, and clothing to these children of the South, but a fountain of ever-springing cheerfulness !

The scene has changed. We are at St. Agata, at a dirty inn. Our philosopher, François, laughs at our fallen mercury, and says, " So it always is in life. You had the good at Mola, you must expect the bad at St. Agata ! " Unworthy wretches that we are ! The Padrone has just sent us up a letter from W., announcing that he and K—n have engaged delightful lodgings for us at Naples, where we hope to be to-morrow.

Naples, February 17.

MY DEAR C.—After a pleasant drive through a long stretch of vineyards and olive-orchards, we arrived at the gate of Naples at four o'clock P.M. W. (our good angel) met us at the Dogana, where we had the torment of a long detention.

We drove down the long street of the Toledo ; such swarming of human life I never saw, nor heard such clamour ; it was as if all the Bedlamites on earth had been let loose upon it. Broad-

way is a quiet solitude in comparison* ! However, we forgot its turmoil and every other vexation when we entered our spacious drawing-room at 28, St. Lucia, and sat down by the window to gaze upon the *Bay of Naples*, directly under us, without any apparent interposing object, for we overlook the street between us and the water. The crescent-like curve from us to the base of Vesuvius brings the mountain in front of us. The light smoke curling up from the crater caught the beams of the just-risen full moon, while the mountain itself and Monte Somma were a dark mass of shadow. We sat watching the little white houses at Portici becoming distinct as one after another caught the moonbeams, and the tiny boats which, with their spread sails, shot across the path of quivering beams, and then again vanished in shadow. Yes, we sat as if spell-bound till we were roused by a familiar voice asking, " Is there anything better than this ! " " Nothing," we replied with one voice ; but " deeds speak louder than words." We turned away from the most beautiful harmonies of nature to exchange greetings with our dear friend K—n, to whose actual presence they were, after all, but " mere moonshine."

We are rich at Naples : W. makes one of our family ; K—n is at the Crocella, almost within shaking-hands' distance ; an English lady, our acquaintance, who is not one of those who " isolent leur cœur en cultivant leur esprit," has lodgings over us ; our chargé, Mr. Throop, is showering kindness on us ; and, finally, our consul, Mr. Hammet, a man of sterling qualities, with twenty years' experience here, is bestowing upon us essential favours, the advantage of his society being that we esteem above all the rest.

We met here letters of introduction obtained by C—i from exiles at Paris to distinguished Neapolitans. They are shy of us, and, as we are told, compelled to be so by the dastardly system of espionage and persecution maintained by the king. General Pepe, the commander of the Italian detachment of Napoleon's Russian army, has been several times to see us. His fine countenance has a most melancholy expression : no wonder ; he told me that of the two regiments he led into Russia, the finest fellows in the Neapolitan service, all, save thirty-four, perished in one night.

---

* I extract from the journal of one of my companions a description of the scene at the Dogana, too characteristic of Naples to be omitted :—" We were stopped at the custom-house, and W. came running out to meet us. How delightful to be *welcomed* to this strange place ! Our carriage was instantly surrounded by beggars, who have increased in numbers and importunity at every step of our way since we entered the Neapolitan dominion. The sentinels, pointing their bayonets at them, gruffly cried, ' Indietro ! ' (' Back ! ') Uncle R. and W. poked them with their canes, and a young officer, who just then came up, flourished his sword over their heads, and made them recede for a moment ; but they closed round again instantly, like water that had been disturbed by a pebble. Such tatters I never saw. It was difficult to divine what kept them together. There were maimed, halt, blind, and mutes ; some real, some feigned, and all as vexing as moschetoes in a walk in the woods in summer." It may well be imagined what a hardening process we had gone through in our progress southward, when a young person neither selfish nor stony-hearted could thus describe such a spectacle.

He lives in perfect retirement, but it is said that in any emergency the king will be glad to employ him*.

One of our daily pleasures is a walk in the *Villa Reale*, a public promenade-garden between the Chiaia—the great street of Naples—and the bay. The garden is about a mile in length, well planted with trees and flowering shrubs, and abounding in fountains—the very spirit and voice of this land of the South. The brightest flowers are the English children who take their daily recreation in the garden; beautiful scions they are of a noble stock. They show themselves exotics here, with their fair skins, ruddy cheeks, blue eyes, and long flaxen curls. No carriages or beggars are permitted within the garden. We now and then see a pretty costume diversifying the uniform fashion of the upper classes of all countries; for instance, we saw to-day a Neapolitan nurse in a rich, dark blue skirt with a broad gold border round the bottom, a bright scarlet jacket with gold bands round the wrist, and a gold comb in her hair, a sort of human paroquet. The garden is embellished with statues, casts of our friends in Rome, the Apollo, Antinous, and certain not strikingly modest groups, whose exposure in these public grounds shows a remarkable *consistency* in the king, who, in a fit of sudden, or, as K—n terms it, Turkish prudery, has put all the Venuses in his museum under lock and key. The unrivalled charm of the Villa Reale is the view of the bay. The very name of the "*Bay of Naples*" sets all your ideas of beauty in a ferment, and so let it; they will create no image approaching in loveliness to the all-surpassing reality. Yet, in the very face of its blue waters and delicious atmosphere—of Capri, lying like a crouching lion at its mouth—of its other amethyst islands—of Vesuvius, with its fresh fringing of yesterday's snow—our countryman, Mr ——, maintained to me that it was not to be compared to the Bay of New York. "I have at one time," he said, "counted fifty merchant-ships there, and what is there here but fishing-smacks!" Truly, what is there!

The Studii, or Royal Museum of Naples, has, after the Vatican, the richest collection of statuary in the world. Unfortunately, the rooms are dark and noisy; one of the thoroughfares of noisy Naples passing by it. It may be a mere fancy, but these serene statues, with their solemn associations, seem to me to require an atmosphere of tomb-like silence. Noise is discord, and a Neapolitan street is a congregation of discords. Herculaneum, Pompeii, Capua, and all these surroundings, have yielded up their treasures to fill this museum. Among them is an Aristides, the finest statue in the world—in Canova's judgment. The figure is enveloped in a mantle. There is a conscious mental force, and a beautiful simplicity, in its quiet, erect attitude, and an expression of tranquil, intellectual dignity in the head and face, fitting the godlike character of "The Just." Strange as it may seem, there is a Venus in the collection (happily not locked up, *pour faire péni-*

tence), who appears to me to express as much moral strength as the Aristides. This is the "*Venus Victrix*." She stands with her head inclining towards Cupid, with a gentle reproof in her air, and a purity in her expression, as if she were, indeed, o'er all the frailties of her sex victorious. One of the prettiest groups is "Cupid sporting with a Dolphin." Cupid, with a most lovely laughing face and curly hair, has his round arms wreathed about the neck of a dolphin, whose tail coiling around his body, has thrust his legs into the air. There is in this group an expression of life and frolic inconceivable to one who has not seen in the antiques how art subdues matter, converting marble into the image of God's creations. If this exquisite whim of art, instead of being housed in a sunless room, stood, as it was designed to stand, in the midst of a fountain, in the odorous atmosphere of an orange grove, with lights and shadows playing over it, its effect would be magical.

Not one of the masterpieces here, but a curiosity, certainly, is an Ephesian Diana, a most elaborate piece of workmanship. The head and hands are of black marble, highly finished; the body is inclosed, mummy-like, in an alabaster case, upon which are carved heads of animals and other ornaments. This image, as W. suggested, explains the opposition of the artificers of Ephesus to the faith which was to put an end to their profitable labour. We found ourselves, day after day, leaving halls filled with busts, statues, and groups, to stand before a mutilated thing—the mere fragment of a statue. The arms are gone, and the lower part of the body, the back and top of the head are shaved off; nothing remains perfect but the face and neck. It is called a Psyche, and is truly the type of the soul. It is the perfection of spiritual beauty and grace. There is something in the hang of the head, and a touch of sadness in the expression, that reminded K. of the angel in Retzsch's game of chess; but the face appeared to me far more powerful and comprehensive.

If I had to answer all the libels of the scoffers at my sex, or to defend the "rights of women," I would appeal to this Psyche, to Raphael's Sibyls, to Dante's Beatrice, and to Shakspeare's Portia, Isabella, and Desdemona, to show what the inspired teachers of the world have believed of our faculties and virtues.

The bronzes in one apartment of the museum are said to be the finest in the world. They were anterior to sculpture in marble. Among them is a life-like bust of Seneca, with sharp features, sunken cheeks, straight, matted locks, and his neck eagerly stretched forward as if on the point of speaking; and there are exquisite Mercuries, Fauns, and Amazons. One among a long suite of rooms is devoted to paintings, and one alone contains some of the best treasures of art; a Magdalen by Guercino, which is only less powerful than Titian's, and less tender than Guido's. There is a masterpiece of Domenichino's: a boy four or five years old in a blue kirtle is standing with his hands folded in prayer. The "man of sin" is crouching at his feet; and though the child does not see him, he betrays a consciousness of the presence of evil, and a feeling of weakness and danger. Behind him stands a beautiful young

---

* This opinion was verified. Before we left Naples the alarm of a rupture with England occurred, and General Pepe was placed at the head of the army.

angel in all the repose of security, pointing to a glory above, and interposing his shielding wing between the devil and the boy.

THE Carnival of Naples is inferior in gaiety and excess to that of Rome ; but it is said to be only second to that. It is generally remarked that its interest is dying away from year to year. Those who think its amusements were only suited to an age when men could neither read nor write, impute this to the "march of mind," which does march, though much in snail fashion, even here. Others maintain that all thinking people feel so deeply the oppression and misery of their condition that they have little heart for amusements of any kind. Such as it is, and so much (or rather so little) as ladies could see of it, we have seen, and childish sport enough you will think it.

During the carnival, the *corso*, which is a course of carriages through the Toledo, the main street of Naples, occurs twice every week. We joined in it to-day ; Mr. T. took a portion of our party in his carriage, and the rest followed in our own. Mr. T.'s carriage was furnished with baskets of sugar-plums and bouquets of flowers, as his station here compels him to be in some sort a participator of the frolic. We soon entered the Toledo, and took a place in the line of coaches. The street was a dense mass of human beings, with just space enough for the ascending and descending lines of carriages ; and the windows and balconies of the houses to the fifth and sixth stories were crowded. Guards on horseback, looking like equestrian statues, were stationed at short intervals, and made conspicuous by the red flag which they held. The king and royal family were out. His majesty, with some twenty gentlemen, was in an ornamented car drawn by six horses. The king wore no badge of distinction; they were all dressed in gay dominos and velvet caps with white plumes, and all wore masks. The ladies of the court were in a similar car, and dressed in a like fashion. Both cars were furnished with sacks containing bushels of sugar-plums made of lime with a thin coating of sugar. These are scooped up and showered around. The great contest is, who shall throw most, and most dexterously. Bouquets of flowers are thrown about; our girls had their laps filled with them. Of course an acquaintance, a quaint masker, or a pretty woman is the favourite aim. When the royal cars meet, they stop, the carriages of both lines halt behind them, and a general *guerre à mort* ensues. You are not absolutely killed, but "kilt" grievously. The missiles are as large as very large gooseberries. The face is protected by a mask of wire. Our defenceless hands were sadly bruised ; mine are yet black and blue. Some carriages were protected by cloth curtains, but in general they merrily took as well as gave. Showers fell from the balconies, and the poor wretches in the streets scrambled for them. In bygone times the royal cars dispensed veritable sugar-plums ; but even this grace has ceased. The novelty amused us for two or three hours, but I think we should all rather play hunt-the-slipper at home than go again to the Corso*.

* We were, however, a few days after involuntary partakers, or, rather, victims of this sport. We had forgotten the carnival, and having spent the morning at the Studii,

THE Carnival concludes with a masked ball at San Carlo, the largest theatre in Italy. It begins at 12 o'clock on Sunday night. I was over-persuaded to go by our kind friend Mr. T., and K—n's suggestion that " it is best to see things, that you may substitute an idea for a word." But as you, dear C., can have only the words, I shall make them as few as possible. The theatre was brilliantly lighted, and viewed from the depth of the stage was a splendid spectacle. The tallest grenadiers in the king's service were planted like beacons about the house. The royal family were in their box, and the king came down and mingled with the crowd. He is a tall, stout, burly, yeoman-like-looking man. I observed, as he stopped for a few moments near our box, that he excited little attention, and was as much jostled and pushed as his subjects. The dancing was confined to the harlequins, and was a mere romp. There were few maskers, and these few supported no characters, and merely walked up and down, uttering common-places in feigned voices. There was an excessively pretty young woman in the box next to us, who attracted general attention, and it was to join the starers at her that the king had stopped near us. She was the sister of a lady whose beauty had captivated a brother of the king. The lady's husband was assassinated a few days before the carnival, and the royal lover went off the next day to Florence—*for his health !*

Save the little excitement occasioned by our pretty neighbour's presence, and the impertinences addressed to her by the maskers, the ball was a heavy affair. The carnival has had its day. Men can remain children a great while, but not for ever.

MR. THROOP procured us invitations to the court-ball†, and last evening we went. The mere forms of society are much alike all over the civilised world. The ball (with rather more space to move in, for there were fifteen or twenty rooms of the palace open) was conducted much like one of our balls. Nothing struck me about the Neapolitan women but the vacuity of their faces, and the abundance and brilliancy of their diamonds. The Italian princes retain their diamonds, as they do their pictures, when every other sign of wealth is gone. The queen, who looks like a quiet body, designed by nature to nurse babies and keep the house tidy, sat with the court-ladies at one end of the dancing-room, and rose once to make a progress through the apartments. The royal family supped by themselves. Several tables were spread for the guests. Besides the knick-knacks of our evening entertainments, there were fish, oysters, and game, and on each table an entire wild-boar, stuck with silver arrows‡. The ladies gathered

were walking home through the Toledo, when all at once we perceived the guards taking their stations previously to the corso beginning. The balconies were filling. We were the only *ladies* in the street, and, consequently, rather conspicuous, and mercilessly were we pelted as we ran our gauntlet homeward.

† This was not one of the balls of the *Accademia Reale*, which are given weekly by a company, of whom the king is one, and to which foreigners are liberally admitted upon the application of their representative.

‡ Of course it was merely a stuffed boar's skin. A boar-

hungrily about the tables, and ate like good trencher-women.

We retired after supper to an adjoining room, and sat down in a most liberty-equality style near a coterie of ladies, who put up their eye-glasses and stared at us, but without any other uncivil demonstration.

We soon perceived they were the ladies of the court, and they no doubt forgave us on the flattering ground of our being North American savages.

Nothing can exceed the fertility of the soil about Naples. The crops on the best ground are each season as follows : pears and apples, grapes, two harvests of Indian corn and one of wheat, and at the end of the season a crop of turnips or some other vegetable. But what avails it to the multitudinous swarms who go hungry every day ! A man who can get work earns only, by the hardest labour in summer, sixteen cents a-day, and he pays a tax of three dollars for every bushel of salt he consumes*. He is forbidden to use the salt water that washes the shore. All articles of necessary consumption are inordinately taxed. There is a tax of 25 per cent. on the income of real estate†.

We hear much of the indolence of the lazzaroni of Naples ; they are idle ; but Mr. Hammet, who is a sagacious observer, says they are not indo- lent ; he has never known one of them to refuse work when offered to him, and they will work for the smallest sum. We complain of their extreme abjectness, of their invariably besetting us, after being paid the price agreed on, " for a little more." " Ah," he says, " they are so very poor." If the man had half a soul, the " King of the Laz- zaroni" would be most wretched ; but his people are only his to provide for his pleasures and feed his avarice. Avarice is his ruling passion ‡. During the cholera an impost of half a million of ducats was laid to alleviate the extreme distress of the poor. Fifty thousand only went to relieve their necessities, and the remainder to the king's coffers.

Whenever the provinces require expenditures for repairs or improvements, they raise money by laying a tax ; but the money so raised cannot be laid out till a certain officer of the government makes a report as to the appropriation. If three years pass without a report being made, the money escheats to the king. Repeatedly the tax has been laid, the money collected, and the report never

hunt in the royal preserves, near Naples, is a favourite royal amusement, and is attended by ladies. On one bright morning, while we were there, the queen killed, with her own fair hand, seventeen boars—a feminine syl- van sport !

* The price of salt is very low, some few cents a bushel.

† As if each potentate were not sufficiently ingenious in laying taxes, one plays into the hand of another. Meat is of course proscribed during Lent, but his holiness grants a dispensation on the payment of three carlini *to the king.*

‡ The alarm of a war with England occurred while we were at Naples. The English deserted the town immedi- ately, and the people suffered much loss, and the usual confusion and anxiety incident to such a report. It was afterward said the king got up the alarm that he might speculate in the stocks ! This might be truth or satire, it does not matter much which.

made. The avarice of a private individual is a folly, in a king it is a crime §.

We had heard a very pretty story of the king braving the cholera, and remaining with his family at Naples that he might share the common danger and calm the panic. The truth is, that he re- mained at Caserta, a royal residence at a distance from the danger, and that once, when he drove into the city, and was passing through the Mercata, the despairing people gathered about him and threw their black bread into his carriage. He threw it out again, and bade them flock to the churches and pray God to pardon them for the crimes for which he had sent this scourge upon them ! Does it seem to you, dear C., that our world of free people and responsible governors can be the same in which this selfish wretch lives, a king, and permitted to transmit his power to his like !

He has been educated by priests, and is now in the hands of the Jesuits. His tutor has published the course of instruction by which he trained his royal and docile pupil. The king is there set forth as the shepherd, and the people as his sheep, over whom he has absolute power to lead them whither he will, to give life or inflict death.

As neither the people nor the soldiers have any attachment to the government, there might be some hope of a better future if it were not backed by the power of Austria. The disaffection of the soldiery is so notorious that even the king himself is aware of it. He had at one time a fancy to give the troops a new uniform. " Dress them as you will," said his father, " at their first opportunity they will run away from you !"

There is a deep and general depravation here, doubtless, but the spirit of manhood is not extinct. A few days since a Calabrian soldier was struck by his superior officer. He complained to his colonel, who treated the grievance as a bagatelle. The next day, on the parade, the soldier shot the officer, and then walked quietly away. He was, of course, seized, and the next morning executed. To the last he was unfaltering, and said coolly that he had only done what should have been done for him !

Neither is humanity extinct here ; and, as you rejoice in the knowledge of a good deed as a gem- fancier does in the discovery of an antique, or a picture-buyer in the acquisition of a Raphael, I will tell you a story Mr. T. told us of a gentle- man whose benevolent countenance he pointed out at the court-ball. The person in question is the king's master of ceremonies, nobly born, for a lineal ancestor of his received a sword from Fran- cis the First at the battle of Pavia. The descend- ant has done something better than giving or receiving swords. During the cholera he took under his protection eighty recent orphans. He built an asylum for them which cost thirty thou-

§ The system of espionage is so much more severe in the provinces than at Naples, that the country gentlemen flock to the city for protection. We knew intimately one of these—a most amiable and accomplished young man— whose whole family had suffered political persecution. Some had lost their lives, some were maimed, and some had died of broken hearts. While we look with detesta- tion on the vices of a government that thus afflicts its subjects, we must not forget the virtue that thus resists.

sand dollars. He has ever since defrayed its expenses and superintended it daily. His income does not exceed nine thousand ducats per annum *.

March 10.—We went yesterday, my dear C., to Pompeii. We drove past fields in which there were masses of ashes and lava of last year's eruption. It appears now strange that Pompeii should so long have remained buried. The surface of the ground yet unopened indicates what is beneath: it resembles a burying-ground, except that the tumuli are higher and more irregular. You ignorantly wonder that the people of the villages at the base of Vesuvius do not live in constant terror: experience has taught them better. The stream of lava rolls slowly, like honey on an inclined plane, and you may be near enough to touch it with a cane and retreat before it reaches you †. After a drive of twelve miles we reached Pompeii, and alighting, entered the *Strada dei Sepolcri*,—Street of Tombs. This fitting entrance brings you immediately into sympathy with the people who lived here; for their dead, those they loved, wept, and honoured, are as near to you as the dead of yesterday! This street of tombs was outside the gates of the city ‡; the tombs are raised several feet above the general level, and crowned with monuments beautifully sculptured, and in some cases nearly entire. The interior of the wall surrounding the tomb is coarsely wrought in bas-relief. The streets are narrow, and paved with large flat stones which bear the traces of wheels, but the pavement is unbroken and far better than that in the older parts of New-York. There are raised side-walks; a luxury you do not find in the modern Italian cities.

Now, my dear C., I feel it to be quite in vain to attempt to convey to you sensations indefinable,

* I have adverted to the controversy with England which occurred during our sojourn at Naples. The king fancied he could extricate himself from the difficulty by requiring his minister to falsify the word he had pledged to an English company. He refused to do this. The king threatened, he persisted, and was consequently deprived of his office, and ordered to retire to a strong house in one of the provinces, infected with malaria. He was poor; his daughters (his only children), in the deepest affliction, said they would throw themselves at the king's feet, and entreat his pardon. " Then you will do it at the peril of my everlasting displeasure," said the father. " I have only done my duty; shall I ask pardon for that? No, my children. Leave me my integrity; it is all that remains to me." A gendarme present told him he was indiscreet to say these things in his presence. He replied, " You will do me a favour if you repeat them to his majesty." I asked a Neapolitan friend if this affair was spoken of. " Yes," he said, " but each man looks before he speaks to see who is within hearing!"

† When there is an eruption the people go on with their usual occupations till they see the stream coming their way; then they pack up their valuables—a small burden —and trudge off to Naples. If their houses are buried, they return, when the lava cools, to build new ones, and cultivate a soil inexhaustibly fertile.

‡ The Romans, except in the case of eminent individuals, forbade interments within the walls of their cities. The author of " Rome in the Nineteenth Century " justly remarks that the Roman custom of burying on either side of the highway explains the common inscription, " *Siste, Viator !* " (" Stop, Traveller ! ") so appropriate for them, and so absurd as used in village churchyards, where no traveller ever passes.

unutterably strange, and yet thrilling us with a fresh and undreamed-of pleasure; I know not why, unless it be from a sort of triumph over time; for here the past *is* given back, and the dead are yielded up! We passed thresholds where the words " *Salve* " and " *Have* " saluted us almost audibly. We ranged through rooms where people 1800 years ago went to bed at night and rose again in the morning; we sat down in porticoes where they once sat talking of what Cæsar was doing in the provinces and Cicero was saying in the Forum. We looked on the architectural designs and figures still in vivid colours on the walls, and fancied how the possessor of the Actæon torn by the dogs of Diana triumphed in having a picture more beautiful than any of her neighbours, and how her rival might have exulted over her in the " Cupid and Dolphin sporting " on the now vacant pedestal of her fountain. We entered the boudoir where the gold bracelet weighing a pound was discovered; and as we looked at the two doves, wrought in its mosaic pavement, hovering over a jewel casket, while one of them draws out a necklace, we fancied the happy artist showing his successful work to his employer. We saw the baby-heir of the house creeping over the marble floor to the masterpiece of all mosaics, while his nurse pointed out Alexander and his helmeted Greeks, and Darius and his turbaned Persians! We fancied the errand-boy reading the name, still legible, of the oil-merchant, and turning in to purchase oil from the jars sunken in the counter, and yet perfect. We saw the jovial wine-drinker setting down his drinking-cup on the marble slab that still bears its mark. We sat down on a semicircular stone-bench on the side-walk, and heard the old man tell his gossips how well he fought at Jerusalem under their good Titus, and the nurse promise the listening boy he should go up to Rome and see the wild beasts fight in the new Flavian amphitheatre. We imagined the luxurious Pompeian, after his bath, sitting on the bronze bench over a brazier in the still perfect bathing-room, and looking up with Roman pride at the effigies of the captive barbarian kings supporting the shelves on which stood the pots of precious ointments. We fancied the Pompeian Rogers dispensing the hospitality of " the house of the Faun," which, from the treasures found there, seems, like that of our host in London, to have been a museum of art and beauty; and as we walked over its mosaic pavements made of precious marbles obtained from elder ruins, and passed walls built of the lava of previous eruptions, we heard the antiquary of Pompeii explaining former pioggie §, and the moralist prosing, as we were, on the mutations of human affairs! We stood in the tragic theatre, and saw the audience stirred by allusions to localities and celestial phenomena which no roof hid from them. We heard the cries of the workmen in the Forum when the eruption burst forth, and they let fall their tools, and left the walls but half rebuilt, and the columns but half restored that had been overthrown by an earthquake sixteen years before. We heard the sounds of labour in the narrow lanes, and, emerging into a broad street, imagined what must have been the sensations of those who filled it when, looking through its long

§ The Italians thus designate an eruption.

vista, they saw the flames bursting from Vesuvius, and turning back, beheld them glaring on the snow-capped mountains opposite. And, finally, my dear C., after going over the ruined temples of Isis and Hercules, we returned to our own actual life—all that was left of it unexhausted—and, sitting down on the steps of the temple of Venus, we ate buns, and drank our Capri, and jocosely sympathised with one of our friends, who affected to fear that he should outstay his Naples dinner and his favourite omelette soufflée, and laughed at an unhappy English pair whom we had repeatedly encountered, the man swearing it was "all a d—d bore, these old rattletrap places," and his consort, with Madame Starke open in her hands, learning where she was to give one, and where two notes of admiration !

My DEAR C.—We went early this morning to the Studii, and by way of an appropriate sequence to yesterday, we proceeded directly to the apartments containing the personal ornaments, domestic utensils, &c., of the Pompeians*. There are four rooms, containing more than four thousand vases and other vessels of terra-cotta. They are embellished with classical subjects, and their workmanship marks successive eras of art. The value set on them you may imagine from two among them being estimated at ten thousand ducats each ! In another apartment is a collection of precious gems, sapphires, amethysts, carnelians, &c., cut into fine cameos. What think you of a cup (in which some Pompeian Cleopatra may have melted her pearls and swallowed them) as large round as the top of a pint-bowl, made of alabaster, with a rim of sardonyx, having on one side a group in bas-relief of seven figures, representing, with wonderful expression, an apotheosis, and on the other an exquisite Medusa's head ! There are a great variety of personal ornaments, necklaces, bracelets, rings, pins, &c., from which our fashionable jewellery of late years has been copied. We saw the necklace and bracelets that Diomed's wife wore for one thousand eight hundred years ! Yesterday we went into her wine-cellar, where she was found with her purse in her hand, and where the wine-jars are still standing† !

There is an immense quantity of bronze armour, some of it beautifully embossed, and so heavy that it would seem to require a giant's strength to sustain it. One helmet was found on a soldier who stood it out bravely at his post ; he was discovered at a gate of his city, still on guard, when the ashes were removed !

There is an endless variety of bronze lamps, some very beautiful, and small stoves ; one, that seemed to me a nice contrivance, had a fireplace in the middle, pipes running round it, and cylinders at each corner. There is every article a housewife could desire to furnish her kitchen ; kettles, saucepans, colanders, tunnels, dippers, steelyards, with bronze busts for weights ! and in short, dear C., there is everything to identify the wants, usages, and comforts of the ancients with

* With these are intermingled the treasures found in Herculaneum.

† The poor lady is supposed to have sought refuge in the cellar. Very few skeletons have been found at Pompeii, from which it appears that most of the inhabitants had time to escape.

our own — surgical instruments, keys, garden tools. We observed a writing-case *precisely* in the fashion of a compact little affair K. is now using, and which she bought at a bazaar in London.

The drinking-cups are various and beautiful. There are seventy alike of silver, small and fluted, which were taken from a table outspread for a dinner that was never eaten ; and perhaps it was for this very dinner that some meat which we saw in a stewpan was in preparation.

There are wheat, rice, oats, honey, figs, prunes, and almonds, all unchanged to the eye, except darkened in colour ; and there is dough all ready for the oven, and a cake just taken out of it marked into slices, and looking precisely like a "composition cake" prepared for one of our rural tea-tables—I did not taste it !—and I saw a little cake made in the form of a ring, and set aside—perhaps—to cool for some pet child at school. Strange thoughts all these objects called up of human projects and pursuits, and of human blindness.

You will be pleased to know that your profession at Naples, though not *sans reproche*, have a benevolent association for the gratuitous prosecution of the causes of the poor. This society meets every Sunday morning, and goes in a body to church to say prayers. On every Thursday morning four of their number are in waiting to receive applications. Our friend L—a, who is one of them, says it does not amount to much, not from the fault of the lawyers, but from the reluctance of the clients, who have no confidence that the right can prevail without the customary accessory of bribes. A bribe to the judge is about as much a matter of course as a fee to the lawyer !

L—a took us yesterday to see the civil courts held in the Vicaria, a palace formerly occupied by the sovereigns of Naples. The lower story and subterranean apartments are devoted to prisons, and are in a horrible condition. The upper story is another kind of prison ; there the archives of the state are kept, and among them precious historical records, jealously locked up. Foreigners are occasionally permitted a few hours' research among them, and a few favoured Neapolitans have been admitted for a very short time.

In going up the wet stone staircase we passed a half-famished-looking woman sitting asleep, with one child at her breast, in vain seeking food there, and another lean pallid thing nestled close to her. Would not such a spectacle in the precincts of your courts have brought down a shower of alms ? these people clattered past them as regardless as if these human things were a part of the stone they sat upon. This is "custom." God has not given the Neapolitans hearts harder than ours up in Berkshire. We went through several crowded ante-rooms filled with lawyers, clients, and idlers, hawkers of stationery, and beggars. One long hall was lined on both sides with desks occupied by scriveners, who, amid such clamour as I am sure you never heard, were going on as undisturbed as if they had been in your quiet office. We made our way through three rooms where courts were in session, and where the business was conducted quietly and decently, much, as it seemed to me, in form like the business of our legal tribunals, except in one particular. There is one officer called the *procuratore*, whose business it is to expound the law and apply its principles to the cause in question. Accustomed as I have always been to regard our judges as uncorrupted and incorruptible, I felt a sort of shuddering in looking at these men, whose vices are diseases of the heart that must carry disease and death into every part of the body of the state. There are *four thousand* lawyers in Naples, including clerks and scriveners, and it would seem that they, and all their dependents and followers, were within the walls of this old palace. These masses looked busy and intelligent, and much more respectable than the populace in the street—as if it had been sifted indeed, and this was the grain, that the chaff. The lawyers are marked by the government, as it is well known that they best understand the rights of the people. Authors are marked men too; and with good reason, if they reflect and feel as well as write *.

I am tempted here, my dear C., to copy a passage from ——'s journal, which lies open before me, relating to a persecuted author, whose poems the girls have been reading with our Neapolitan friend L. It will at least serve to show you how groundless were your fears that our young people, in the enchantment of these countries, would lose their sense of the advantages of their own.

" L. considers Count Leopardi the finest poet since Alfieri, and certainly there is great power in some of the things we read ; and, oh ! it gives us such a feeling, such a ' realising sense' of the mental suffering endured here by men who have one spark left of that love of freedom which seems to be God's universal gift, who have their eyes open to what is passing round them, and aspirations after better things.

" And as we read with L., and see how excited he becomes, how, from the very innermost depths of his soul, he responds to the bitter invectives and keen sarcasms of the poet, we too kindle into a glow of indignation, and feel ourselves animated by the spirit of uncompromising resistance ; and

* There is a young Neapolitan who obtained permission to print a history of the kingdom of Naples. He went on smoothly till he came to the seventh century, when the invasion of the Saracens gave rise to some patriotic expressions — the publication was stopped, and his MSS. seized. Nothing daunted, he began again ; and now, as fast as he completes a certain portion, he sends it out of the country to be printed. There is an institution here called *L'Albergo de' Poveri* (Asylum for the Poor), which has large funds, but so fraudulently managed, that the inmates are little benefited by them (the sum allotted to each person is thirty-nine ducats a year, and not more than the half of this is spent upon him). The young historian resolved to expose these abuses, and he wrote a clever poem, in which he caricatured several persons concerned in them. This was printed here with a foreign superscription. He was seized and imprisoned. He confessed the authorship, but maintained there was no law forbidding his *writing* what he would; and as to the printing, the printer must answer for that. He was steadfast and prevailed, but he is a *marked man*. One poor fellow, for a much lighter offence, was sent to a madhouse, plunged into the *bagno di sopresa*, chained, and confined with the "furiously mad." He excited such sympathy, and called forth such powerful intercession, that he was finally released, and is now in Paris.

when we lay aside the book, we thank Heaven more than ever, that our lot is cast in a land where we can think, speak, and act as the spirit moveth us ; and America rises before us in a halo of light, brightening and brightening. As Dante says on his first seeing Paradise,

> ' E disubito parve giorno à giorno
> Essere aggiunto come quel che puote,
> Avesse 'l ciel d'un altro sole adorno.' "

For a quiet person, who does not care to run after sights, I can imagine nothing more delightful than to sit at the window as I do now, and look out on the bay and the golden clouds floating over Vesuvius and Somma, and at Vesuvius itself bathed in purple light. But the chief pleasure of a residence in Naples, after visiting the Studii, driving up the *Strada Nuova*, a superb terrace-road overlooking the bay—after walking through the royal pleasure-grounds at Capo di Monte, through the *Boschi*, a green Posilippo with " ver-d'rous walls," and looking at the king's *seven hundred* peacocks dragging their green, their white, and their azure blue plumes over the green turf—and after ranging through the terra-cotta, coral, and lava shops—the chief pleasure at Naples is from the excursions about its rich environs.

The girls have ascended Vesuvius, and will give you their report. We have of course visited the tomb of Virgil, hardly to be called an excursion, for it is just at the end of the city, over the entrance to Posilippo. The fact of its being the tomb of Virgil is disputed. Eustace argues earnestly for the *real presence ;* but Eustace is an easy believer. It is, however, a position the poet might have chosen if he looked fondly back to earth. It is in a vineyard, amid grotesque forms of tufa, which give a picturesque effect to the ilex, ivy, and laurel that hang caressingly about the tomb, as if they had voluntarily grown there. There are various openings, affording glimpses of Vesuvius, of the glorious bay, and its lovely shores. The tomb itself is an ordinary columbarium, with niches enough for all the Latin poets who have come down to us.

We have just returned from Pozzuoli, the ancient Puteoli. After driving to the end of the gay Chiaia, we entered the grotto of Posilippo, which is a tunnel cut through a tufa hill, and is 2316 English feet in length, twenty-two in breadth, and where loftiest, eighty-seven feet in height. It has a few dim lamps, whose insufficient light is inadequately supplied by the few rays of outer day that penetrate the arched entrances at each extremity. The passage is wild and impressive. The imprisoned and heightened sound reverberating from the walls is like nothing earthly. The smiths who are working by fitful fires in a deep cavity at one entrance, seem stationed at the threshold of Pluto's realm. An almost impalpable powder, from ground which no drop of rain ever touches, darkens and thickens the atmosphere ; a carriage drives past you with noise enough for a train of railroad cars ; then a Neapolitan car, with a little demon of a horse with only a patch of skin here and there, and *no* flesh, dashes along, its nine or ten wild, ragged passengers *stuck* on, chaffering, yelling, and laughing, and all vanishing as soon as past, seeming mere shadows in a shadow land. Suddenly a bright gleam of lamplight illumines the figure of a bareheaded, grey old woman, driving an ass with panniers, or falls on a strapping, bare-legged girl following another loaded with piles of wood. They but appear and vanish in darkness. There are shrines niched in the wall, where a lamp burns before an image or a crucifix ; and in the very heart of the passage is a chapel to the Virgin scooped in the rock. I have seen this illuminated ; and when its lights are glaring on two or three kneeling worshippers, and on a haggard beggar pointing to the image of the Holy Mother, and stretching his hand to you, it produces a startling effect.

It is remarkable that the date of this work is unknown. It is mentioned by Pliny and Strabo, and is supposed to have been done by the Cumæana, to connect Neapolis with Puteoli. After emerging from the grotto this morning—and what a delicious transit it is to the open sky and earth !— we turned off our road towards Agnano, a pretty secluded crater-lake, devoted to the king's aquatic birds. Such numbers were emerging from it, that it seemed a fountain of life, and as if its waters were at every moment becoming incorporate in feathers and wings—poor things, they had a doomed look !

We left our carriage on the lake-shore to walk up a steep hill to Astroni, where we were admitted within a stone-wall of four or five miles in circumference, which encloses the king's preserves. It was here the queen did that delicate bit of lady-like work—killed her seventeen boars of a fine morning ! From the hill where we stood, we looked down five or six hundred feet into what was once the crater of a volcano, and is now a spacious plain, overgrown by trees and walled round by steep precipices. There is no tradition of the volcano, and no other record of it than that which the earth bears on her bosom. To an American eye these preserves suggest the idea of uncleared land, upon which the settler is beginning his work ; the sound of the woodman's axe comes up musically from this deep solitude. L. and I wandered about the eminences among the superb ilexes, gathering the white heath, and catching glimpses of the bay, the queenly Nisida, and the great St. Angelo.

We returned to the high road, and proceeded along the margin of the Bay of Baia to Pozzuoli. This, once a great maritime town of Southern Italy, is now a miserable, beggarly place, containing about 9000 inhabitants, chiefly fishermen, and, as it would appear from the troops that besiege you, beggars, ciceroni, and vendors of " antichi," as you are assured the little lamps and bronze images are which are thrust into your carriage by stout clamorous fellows, who meet you a mile out of the town, and keep pace with your horses. Ah ! there is a horrid tariff on all out-of-door pleasures in Italy. Your compact made with your cicerone, your condition improves, the venders drop off in despair, and the beggars subside, it being a part of his duty to drive them off, which he often does amusingly enough, by reiterating the only English word he knows, and which beggars and all soon learn in the good English society they keep : " d—n ! d—n ! d—n ! "

If you can forget the living people at Pozzuoli, you may enjoy fine remains of the dead. There are columns of travertine of a temple of Jupiter Serapis thirty-five feet high. They bear a curious record of the passage of time and the work of the elements ; for six feet from the base they are entire and smooth, and thus far they have been buried in the sand ; above that they are nearly perforated, made to resemble a sponge, by pholas, creatures that live only in salt water—so that the sea has at one time advanced upon the temple, nearly covered it for ages, and again receded. It is surrounded by baths. The sick who came to bathe in the mineral water brought their propitiatory offerings to the god and to the priest. The ring to which the victims were attached is still riveted in the stone ; the pavement below the altar is nearly perfect ; and all around are strewn steps, capitals, and fragments of bas-reliefs.

At a short distance from the temple we found workmen employed excavating an amphitheatre, which will approach the Coliseum in extent, and is found in a good state of preservation. We went through an opened corridor where the masonry was as perfect as if it were done yesterday.

But by far the most interesting sight at Pozzuoli is the *Via Campagna*, a part of the ancient Via Appia, leading hence to Gaeta. It is for two miles a street of tombs. The road (its pavement still in perfect preservation) is a deep cut between high rugged banks in which the tombs were imbedded, two and three tiers one above the other. Those that are opened are made in the form of the columbarium. There was an altar opposite the entrance, and around the sides a double row of niches (pigeon-holes) to contain the urns. Their ashes are now dispersed to the winds, and Nature, as if to veil the sanctuaries she had so long hidden in her bosom, has dropped over the opening a matted drapery of wild creeping plants. Nothing can well be imagined more solemn and more touching than the silence and solitude of this street of tombs. The throngs of the city that daily sent hither its funeral train are themselves a part of the mighty congregation of the dead, and oblivion has effaced their records.

" The wheel has come full circle."

March 20.—THIS morning the sun rose clear for the first time in many days. Our own ungenial spring has followed us ; and what with clouds without, and illness and pressing anxiety within, we have had some heavy hours. But this has been a day of compensations.

We determined at breakfast on an excursion to Misenum, and on going down-stairs to our carriage we met our friend L——s, who said he should pass the day at Astrone, but if " we had asked him he should have gone with us !" whereupon we eagerly offered him the best or the worst seat of the coach. He took that on the box, the " best or worst," according to one's fancy. As we drove round the Villa Reale, strapping men, who in our country would be wrestling with Nature and subduing it, besieged us, entreating us to buy little bunches of violets. L——s, who, I observe, seizes eagerly upon every pretext to evade the money-saving, modern non-giving doctrines, bought his hands full and threw them into the carriage.

The Chiaia had a true Neapolitan aspect. Equipages were in waiting at the doors of the English " appartemens meublés," for the luxurious strangers who were yet loitering over their ten-o'clock breakfasts. English gentlemen were galloping up and down the trottoir. Every Neapolitan living thing had come out and was basking in the sun ; and for contrasts they were striking enough, dear C. Under the curtained windows of these English princes, and between their doors and their carriages, lay asleep, and sleeping away the sense of hunger, men in the heyday of life, one pillowed on the body of another ; closely packed in with them were women, in masses of rags and patches, looking heads—a regular branch of industry here*— and there were squads of stout ragged children playing games, and knots of women and herds of sailors talking and gesticulating more vehemently than we should if a revolution were on the point of exploding. They are an *outside* people. The passions that lie deep in our souls, and that are only called forth by the voice of their master, and to effect a purpose, are continually breaking out here. But theirs is but heat lightning ; ours rives the oak.

At Pozzuoli we were, as usual, besieged by a little army of ciceroni. I had previously promised my patronage to a bright lad who had begged me to ask for Michael Angelo. I did so ; and a stout, ragged, ruffian-looking wretch started forth, exclaiming, " Ecco ! ecco ! Sono *Michael Angelo !*" The ruse only brought down upon him the laugh of his comrades, and we drove off with a certain Andrea, a nice fellow, whom L—s, a fancier of human faces, had at once selected from his tribe. We turned off near the ruins of the ancient mole (supposed to have been built by the Cumæans, and repaired by the Roman emperors) to which Caligula attached his bridge of boats. Here we left our carriage at the Lucrine Lake, and went off by a footpath to the Lake of Avernus, the Tartarus which Virgil describes in the sixth book of the Æneid. It is like all the crater-lakes we have seen, deep sunk amid barren and precipitous hills. On the shore of this lake are the ruins of a temple which has been assigned to Pluto ; a pretty fair guess ; for who but an infernal deity should have his temple on Tartarus ! We turned from the lake to the grotto of the Cumæan Sibyl, the long-sought and honoured oracle to whom Domenichino has given such divine grace ; sacrificing, as it seems to me, inspiration, to youth, beauty, and harmony. We know not what art has done for us till we find it peopling these dreary solitudes with such exquisite forms. The grotto is a low, vaulted passage (a miniature of Posilippo), piercing the hill, and coming out on the other side. We discreetly declined groping through it, contenting ourselves with a bouquet of ivy-leaves and violets plucked about its entrance.

We returned to the carriage, and drove round the Bay of Baia, a most secure shelter for shipping. It was here that Pompey, Crassus, and Pompeius dined on board a galley, when Pompey had not the courage to do the treacherous act he would have permitted his servant to do for him†.

Here was the scene of Nero's parricide ; here lay the elder Pliny when the eruption that destroyed Pompeii burst forth ; and here his nephew wrote that letter which has made us all as familiar with the circumstances that urged his uncle into the scene of danger, with the curiosity of the philosopher and the benevolence of the friend, as if both uncle and nephew were our contemporaries, and we had received the letter by yesterday's post ! We went up into the little village of Bauli, on the ruins of Lucullus' villa, where Tiberius expired, and where the people are now nested in little holes, crannies, and angles of old walls. We descended to the foundations of a celebrated reservoir which the Romans constructed to supply their fleet with fresh water when their fleet lay in the Bay of Baiæ, of which forty-eight piers are still entire, to show how this magnificent people could provide for an exigency ! We went to the *Mare Morto*, a little inlet of the sea, the Stygian Lake of Virgil, and over his Elysian Fields ; and wherever we went, we turned a new leaf in the views of this land of loveliness. We stood on the sites and amid the ruins of temples, palaces, and villas ; for here they *are*, to borrow again Dewey's most descriptive expression, " kneaded into the soil." ‖

As we paused on the shore near the ruins of two magnificent temples, I looked across to Pozzuoli ‡, and thought of the moment when St. Paul first set his foot on Roman ground there. Who could then have prophesied that the words of this tent-maker should be a law to the conscience, when men standing where we stood should smile doubtfully at being told, " Here was Nero's palace, there was Cicero's villa, and there Lucullus' ; and there, on Nisida, lived Brutus with Portia, Cato's daughter, the ' well-reputed woman,' so fathered and so husbanded !" and should guess whether this ruin was a temple to Venus, or Hercules, or no temple at all ! or this other to Mercury and Diana ! Imagination should reconstruct these temples, rebuild these villas, repeople this Roman world, and refill it with its luxury and pomp, to estimate the faith of the brave apostle, who, in the midst of it all, " counted all things but loss for the excellency of the knowledge of Christ Jesus our Lord !"

But to return to ourselves, dear C. Our carriage was, as usual, followed by a train—not of loathsome beggars this time, but of young, Moorish-looking girls, who held up saucers with bits of precious marbles from the ruins, which, as they truly said, were " molto bello ! molto graziozo !"§ Their leader, a joyous creature, addressed a sort of badinage flattery to me, telling me I too was " graziosa e bella !" and when I shook my head, she shouted merrily, and said I should be, " if I bought her marbles !" The train swelled as we proceeded, and among them was a young mute, who had her spindle and distaff, and spun as she walked. She seemed about seventeen, with a most graceful, fragile figure, and with a shade of pro-

---

* Some of my readers may be shocked by the grossness of such particulars ; but without them they could not get a just notion of the abject condition of this much-wronged people.

† " Why," asked his freedman, " do you not cut the cables, and make yourself master of the world ? " " Why," he replied, " did you not do it for me without asking me ? "

‡ The ancient Puteoli.

§ There are still striking memorials of the Saracen invasion of Southern Italy in the features and colouring of many of the people.

phetic sadness over features so beautiful that they reminded me of Raphael's saints.

We had left our carriage and gone up through a defile to get a view of the queen's oyster-eating lodge ; and when we returned, our merry troop, clamouring and laughing, met us half-way. Would that I could describe the scene to you, my dear C.! but I can only give you the materials, and you must make out the picture for yourself. On one side were the ruins of temples, on the other the monstrous foundations of mouldering villas; before us the bay, and Vesuvius with its blue wreath of smoke, and the Apennines brilliant in their caps of snow, and Capri far off in the bay, so soft and dreamy that it seemed melting away while we were gazing at it; and clouds were driving over us, with fitful sunbeams glancing through them. Our merry followers were joined by an old woman, with a bright red handkerchief tied over her grisly locks. She was the living image of Raphael's Cumæan Sibyl; the same wrinkled brow, and channelled cheeks, and unquenched energy burning in her eye; the resemblance was perfect, even to the two protruding teeth*. She was sitting on the fragment of a marble column, holding above her head a tambarine, on which she was playing one of the wild airs to which they dance the tarantella, and accompanying it with her cracked voice. To this music the gleeful bare-legged girl I have described to you, having seized a strapping companion, was dancing a tarantella around L—s, who, though far enough from a Bacchus or Faun, has in his fine English face much of the joyousness of these genial and jovial worthies. My merry girl danced and shouted like a frantic Bacchante. I never saw a mouth so expressive of glee, nor an eye whose brightness was so near the wildness of insanity; there were children with tangled locks of motley brown and gold, and eyes like precious stones, leaping and clapping their hands, and joining in the old woman's chorus; and my pretty mute was among them, with a chastened mirth and most eloquent silence. Apart stood four girls, as grave and fixed as Caryatides, with immense piles of brush on their heads, which they had just brought down from the hills; and we pilgrims from the cold North were looking on. L—s, who had begun by regarding our followers as troublesome sellers of " cose molle curiose," had by degrees given himself up to the spirit of the scene. The floodgates of poetry, and of sympathy with these wild children of the South, were opened; and over his soul-lit face there was an indescribable shade of melancholy, as if by magic he were beholding the elder and classic time, and that were an actual perception which before had been imperfectly transmitted by poetry, painting, and sculpture. He threw a shower of silver among the happy creatures, and we drove off.

I have in vain tried to put this scene on paper for you. I have seen nothing in Italy so characteristic and enchanting; and when L—s came to us in the evening, I found I had not exaggerated, nor even fully estimated his enjoyment.

We have been with our English friends to Pæstum ; and, though it rained torrents through one

of our three days of absence, we had quite pleasure enough to repay us for crossing the ocean. What think you, then, of the scale in which these three days are but a make-weight!

Nothing was ever better suited than the approach to Pæstum over a wide, wild, and most desolate plain, with no living thing visible, excepting, at far intervals, a shepherd, in the primeval dress of skins, tending a flock of gaunt, ragged sheep—a herd of buffaloes, looking, as R. says, as if made of the refuse of all other animals, or a solitary wretch on an ass, who appears, like the snail, to carry his house and household goods with him. The approach is suited to the ruins, my dear C., because there is nothing to divert your attention for one moment from them. There they stand, between the mountains and the sea, in a wide blank page, scarcely ruins, but monuments of the art, wealth, and faith of a nation long effaced from the earth—temples erected to an unknown God by an unknown people.

I could condense pages of description and speculation from tourists more learned than I; but, after all, they settle nothing; we are still left to wonder and conjecture, as the Emperor Augustus did when he came from Rome to Pæstum, nearly 2000 years ago, to gaze as ignorantly (and as admiringly, I trust) as we now do.

The cork models have given you an accurate idea of the form of these edifices ; but you must see them in this affecting solitude with God's temples, the mountains, behind them, the sea sweeping before them, and the long grass waving from their crevices, to feel them—to class the sensations they produce with those excited by the most magnificent works of nature, Niagara and the Alps.

We stood before them, we walked through them and around them, and then returned to the little Trattoria, the only shelter here, to comfort ourselves beside the blazing fagots with hot soup and mezzo caldo, and laugh at the eating and clattering parties—English, German, and Italian—who seemed pouring down with the rain upon Pæstum, and whose vehement demands our poor little host tried in vain to supply. Among them was an honest German, who seemed to have come for nothing but the " Pæstum roses" which the elder poets celebrate, and which he expected to find as immortal as their poetry. We left him still tramping over the wet grass in fruitless search of them†.

April 10.—To-morrow, my dear C., we leave Naples, and take the first homeward step as joyful as the Israelites when they turned towards the Holy City. You may well have got the impression from my letters that the beggars are the only company we keep here, and, in truth, the beggars and the street denizens (here lazzaroni, at Rome facchini, and idlers everywhere) are the only inhabitants of the country of whom we have much knowledge. There are so few elements in their

---

* Such old women are not uncommon in Italy. I have seen half a score, at least, of living fac-similes of Michael Angelo's Parchæ.

† Aware that my book is outlasting the patience of my readers, I have omitted, excepting the few paragraphs above, my Journal of our excursion to Pæstum. My descriptions of the beauty of some portions of the route would give but an imperfect idea to those who have not seen it ; and those who have, need not to be reminded how much there is to be enjoyed.

condition, that " he who runs may read them."
All, theoretically, acknowledge that they have
" organs, dimensions, senses, affections, passions;"
bodies with human wants, souls with an immortal
destiny ; and yet, while we tourists give volumes
to ruins and pictures, the Lazzaroni are slurred
over with a line or a sneer. We forget the
wrongs which have brought them to their present
abjectness and keep them in it, and quiet our
sympathies by reiterating that " the Lazzaroni
are the most cheerful people in the world !" and
so they are (except, perhaps, our slaves !) far
more cheerful, as a friend of ours says, " than
they have any right to be ;" happier than you
and I, dear C., if happiness be indicated by a
careless brow and merry shouts ; but is not the
happiness of a reflecting being shaded by serious-
ness, looking, as he must, before and after ! and
is not the cheerfulness of these people the most
hopeless thing about them, proving, as it does,
an unconsciousness that marks the lowest point
of human degradation !—no, not the *lowest* point
—I would rather be one of the Lazzaroni than
the *king of the Lazzaroni*. Is it not strange,
dear C., that people should leave well-ordered
countries to come here to *live ?* There are many
strangers, for the most part, English, who, seduced
by the attractions of the climate and the loveliness of the adjacent country, remain here year
after year. Life is rather too short, too full of
import, to be consumed in mere passive enjoyment* !

Terni, April 24.

WE have left Rome†, my dear C., and with
feelings too much like parting with a friend for
ever to say anything about them. We took good
advice, and, instead of returning to Florence by
the dreary way we came, we are on the Perugia
route, which is filled with beauty, and is beginning
to realise my early and most romantic dreams of

* My last walk in Naples was too characteristic of the
place to be left untranscribed from my notes. I had
hardly gone ten paces, when a decrepit old hag hobbled
on her staff towards me, crying with her cracked voice,
" Eccellen ! " and I gave her a few grani from my side-
pocket. Her feeble blessing me into " Paradiso " had
scarce died upon my ear, when I felt a hand thrust into
this same pocket, and, turning, caught a youngster in the
act of exploring it. I forgot that he was Italian, and I of
another tongue. I forgot, too, that I kept nothing in this
pocket but halfpence for the beggars; and, feeling as if I had
been robbed of all I was worth in the world, I poured out
my indignation in a volley of sound English, every word
as good as a blow. The lad smiled at my impotent wrath,
drew back a step, and pointed to a tall companion to indicate that he was the offender ; and then stretching out his
hand, said, in the true sotto-voce tone, " Ah, eccelen !
date mi qualche cosa." As I passed the Duke of Bordeaux'
palace, a poor woman was sitting on the pavement, leaning her head against the wall, with a half-famished child
asleep in her arms. She said nothing, but her looks should
have persuaded something better than halfpence from my
pocket. It did not; my heart was as hard as the Levite's;
and I walked rapidly on to escape *three* masses of dirty
rags with human heads, hands, and feet, that were coming towards me, crying, " Excellen, per l'amor di Dio! "
" Excellen, moro di fam !" The distance from my lodging
to the shop was not one-sixth of a mile.

† We passed the Holy Week at Rome. My readers are
already familiar with its splendid ceremonies, and as I
cannot give fresh interest to them, I have discreetly
omitted them.

Italian scenery. We scarcely know what spring
is ; our change of season is like the Russian bath,
the plunge from the snowdrift to hot water. Here
the muses and the graces seem to have taken the
thing into their own hands, and all nature is embodied poetry and grace.

After winding around hills covered with home-
looking houses, and peering down into the deep
pathway which the Nar has made for itself
through their ravines, we arrived here at twelve
o'clock this morning, and have spent the afternoon in visiting the Falls. " If you have seen
Niagara and Terni," said François, " you may
die content." But Terni hardly deserves this
companionship. The cascade, as perhaps you
know, is artificial, the waters that overspread the
country above it having been drawn off by the
Romans into the Velino, a small stream, and sent
over the rocks into the Nar. It does not owe its
charm to the amount of water, but to its height,
its most graceful form, and, above all, to its accessories ; to the varied slopes and cone-like mountains ; to the lovely view out into a gardened
world ; and to its memories : Cicero came here
from Rome to argue a cause about this very wa-
tercourse. We saw the fall at every point of
view, from the summit to the base : it was late in
the afternoon, and we had the advantage of deep
shadows below and bright lights above, and the
iris playing over it, *not* like

" Love watching Madness with unalterable mien—"

but more like Love fondly hovering around Beauty.
In truth, Byron's whole description is an extra-
vaganza ; his " infernal surge" is so soft and
sprayey, that you can scarce tell whether it move
up or down ; it might be formed of the glittering
wings of angels ascending and descending. Byron
should have seen Niagara, and he *could* have described it.

We came from the fall by a lovely winding
footpath through tall chesnut-trees bursting into
fresh verdure, and shrubs, and white feathery
heath, and sweet violets, and cherry columbines,
and through the orange-bowers of a certain Count
Graziani. Ah ! my dear C., this *is* spring. And
the girls who met us with asses whereon we were
to ascend the hill to Papigna, were as beautiful
as Raphael would have painted wood-nymphs.
Terni owes a portion of its fame to this atmosphere of exceeding beauty.

Foligno.—THE day has been warm, and towards
noon we crossed La Somma, a high peak of the
Apennines. We had a yoke of oxen attached to
our four horses, to drag us up this three mile
ascent. K. and I walked the greater part of the
way, and amused ourselves talking with the train
of beggars that we accumulated, not " stropi and
ciechi " (lame and blind), but stout dames and
pretty children. The oxen pulled sturdily (the
vetturino taking care to let them do all the work),
till, when we were within a few yards of the summit, one of them suddenly stopped and staggered.
Their master detached them, when the poor beast
gave a convulsive leap, and fell dead. His owner
broke out into the most violent expressions of
despair, beating his breast, clasping his hands,
plucking off his hat, and throwing himself on the
ground. Do not laugh at me, for truly he re-

minded me of Lear's anguish over the dead body of Cordelia. There could in no case be more demonstration of grief. Our beggarly retinue forgot themselves, and gathered round him, expressing their sympathy most vehemently ; while he continued touching gently the animal's horns, and crying out "O Gigio mio !" "O Dio mio !" "che faccio io !" drawing open one eyelid, and then the other, and exclaiming, "è morto ! è morto ! O Dio mio !"

This was all unaffected. The oxen were probably the only means of living the poor man possessed—his sole dependence for bread for himself and his family ; but he showed all he felt ; they are a demonstrative people. Do you remember a story Mr. Hoffman tells of one of our backwoodsmen, who, having left his wife and children alone in their log habitation to go into the forest, found them all, on coming back, lying murdered before his door, killed by Indians ! He made no movement, no gesticulation, but said quietly, "Well, now, if this is not too ridiculous * !"

La Magione.—After crawling to-day at a snail's pace up the immense hill on which the old Etruscan city, Perugia, stands, we were induced to retrace our way, by the report of the recent opening of a tomb in which some of the heroes of this brave old eyrie have slept for more than two thousand years.

After descending the hill in a little post-carriage, and crossing a field, we descended a ladder, and a doubly-locked door being opened to us, we entered the tomb of a noble Etruscan family. Opposite our entrance hung suspended a bronze Divinity "in little." There are nine small vaulted chambers, built of square blocks of tufa, with a well-cut Medusa's head in the centre of each ceiling, and about it dolphins and dragons, I think ; but our survey was so hasty that I do not vouch for its accuracy. One apartment only is left as it was found ; from the rest the monuments and ornaments have been removed. In this are several sarcophagi of travertine as white as marble, and as perfect in all respects as when they came from the sculptor's hands. There was a half-recumbent figure on each, supposed to be the effigy of the person whose remains were within the sarcophagus ; a curious portrait-gallery to be opened to exhibition after 2500 years, is it not ! Everything is as fresh and uninjured as when the Etruscan mourners laid their dead here. Why, the tomb of the Scipios is a *parvenu* to this !

We had only time for a strange, bewildering sensation, none to go into a palace hard by to examine some very precious bronzes found in the tomb, and removed there for safe keeping, and which, we were told, as travellers usually are on like occasions, were better worth seeing than all the rest.

We are this evening at an inn in a straggling village half-way up a steep hill, where, I fancy, no travelling-carriage ever stopped before. Any rooms, with an invalid, are better than none ; and

* It is possible that this man was neither a brute nor a clod, but that a year afterward he exhibited the signs of premature old age. Different races have different manifestations.

our vetturino threatened us with the probability of sleeping in our carriage if we proceeded to the regular stopping-place : so here we are, in the midst of an Italian rustic family, all serving us, all curious, clamorous, and good-humoured. Teacups have been borrowed from a luxurious neighbour ; a messenger was sent a mile and a half to bring milk for us ; and our thoughtful vetturino provided butter at Perugia. So you see how extremes meet. An isolated Western *settler*, in a like exigency, would have had recourse to like expedients. But I wonder if ever but in this land, where grace and beauty are native to the soil, there was so pretty a rustic lass as is at this moment, with the help of two strapping dames, arranging our beds. I can scarce write for looking at her ; and, from that elective affinity which I believe we all feel, she returns my glance, and a smile into the bargain. She is not an Italian beauty ; there is no brilliancy of colouring ; but such perfect symmetry, and such a trustful, appealing, touching expression. She skims over the floor as a bird over the surface of the water ; I never saw motion so light and full of grace—it would make the fortune of an actress of pastoral comedy. I must ask her name, and something of her history.

Her name is Clotilde Poggione ; and for her story she has none, she says. Her father is dead —every one's father dies sooner or later ; her mother is very poor, but neither is that any distinction here, and she earns her bread with these good people of the inn. "You have never been to America !" "No," she replied with infinite simplicity, "nor to Perugia." "She would like to go to Perugia," said her friend, archly. "Ah ! you have a lover there, Clotilde," said I. "No, no ; I will be a nun." I looked at her gay-coloured woollen scarf becomingly drawn over her bosom and confined at her slender waist, and shook my head, and, taking hold of her string of corals, asked her if it were not a love-token ; she smiled and blushed, and her companion, laughing outright, said, " It is, it is ! and she has a love-letter in her pocket." Clotilde at first denied the charge, but a moment after she frankly gave it to me, laying her hand on my shoulder affectionately, and whispering that I might read it if I would. "Yes," she answered to my inquiries, " he is handsome, and very good, but I shall never marry him ; he is a *professore*." She said all this with a sweet simplicity that reminded me of the poor maiden of Burns' lines to a daisy. She left the letter with me. It was written by an educated man, and had the due proportions of love and jealousy. I asked her friend, " Would the ' professor ' marry her !" " Oh no ! Clotilde has no dowry, and his father will not let him take a wife without a dowry :" poor thing ! It needs no prophetic eye to foresee her destiny, and, living in a Catholic country, she will probably end the love-tale in a convent.

Clotilde hung about us last night, attracted by her sympathy with the young *Forestiere*, till I was obliged to send her away. I gave her a word of advice which I am sure, from her eager, grateful expression, she means to follow. She was at my door again this morning at five o'clock with a bunch of sweet flowers. Here I have pressed one for a memorial of her ; may it not outlast the innocence and loveliness of this " bonnie gem," Clotilde Poggione * !

AFTER leaving Magione we wound around the declivities of beautiful hills, and soon came in sight of Thrasymene, the very image of peace, as it lies deeply imbedded among these hills. Even our vetturino felt that this was a sight worth seeing, and he voluntarily halted for us to alight. We walked down to the water's edge, and I recalled the days when, in our " noon-time," at the old school-house, I used to creep under my pine desk to read the story of Hannibal, and devoutly hope that he might always be victorious. Do not all children sympathise with the boy who swore eternal hatred to the Romans, and kept his oath so filially ? I do still. I plucked some grass, and baptised it in the consecrated lake. The road led us round the margin of the lake to the little town of Passignano, which is on a promontory jutting into the lake, and where a mountain rises so precipitously as to make it an important and dangerous military pass. This is the pass into which the " crafty " Hannibal is supposed to have decoyed Flaminius ; but why not the " stupid" Flaminius, to lead his men into a trap between a rugged mountain and an unfordable lake ? Because probably the Romans told the story.

I have little interest in battle scenes ; but this, though two hundred and seventeen years before our Christian era, was vivid to me. The very form of the ground recalled the actual state of mind, the deliberations and decisions of this most inexorable hater of Rome, who to the pride of a military conqueror added the keen pleasure of success in a personal cause. Hannibal needed not much superstition to have believed, when he looked from the sunny heights where he stood down upon the level plain where his enemy was inclosed in a fog, that his tutelar divinity had spread the snare for them. This alluvial plain is now thick set with olives and grain. Yesterday we passed the bright city from which he turned aside, not daring to attempt it, and probably with a feeling preluding his final discomfiture. Perugia still sits queen-like on the throne Nature erected for her, but " who now so poor to do her reverence ! "

We passed over the little rivulet Sanguinetto†, which, with the small town above it, took its name from the bloody work of this battle. We too have

* One of my young companions prophesied that this incident at Magione would furnish a story for some Souvenir of 1842. It was a tempting bit of raw material for my humble craft ; but I preferred preserving the unadorned fact to engrafting upon it apocryphal additions for the sated appetites of Souvenir readers

‡ The following slight stanzas were written by a friend on this " bloody rivulet." I am not sure that they are among his published poetry, and therefore quote them without his name :—

" We win where least we care to strive,
    And where the most we strive we miss.
Old Hannibal, if now alive,
    Might sadly testify to this.

" He miss'd the Rome for which he came,
    And what he never had in petto,
Won for the little brook a name,
    Its mournful name of Sanguinetto."

our " Bloody Brook ;" and so, I suppose, have all nations had since Cain first began the work of killing.

WE passed last night at Arezzo, a *nice* town— an epithet that in our sense, the old English sense, must be charily bestowed in Italy‡. But everything appears nice to us, in the strictest and in the most generous sense of the word, since our return into Tuscany. We were here before in the dreariest month of the year ; we had not yet seen the abounding, abject misery of Southern Italy, and certainly we were not struck with the flourishing condition of Tuscany ; now it seems all thrift, abundance, and cheerfulness—a cheerfulness to be coveted and enjoyed. This is the glad season of the year, and this the gladdest of all lands, teeming, as it is, with the richest productions of nature, and now gay with blossoming trees and budding vines. The Tuscan mode of training the vine is very beautiful ; trees are planted from ten to fifteen feet apart, in rows or encircling a field. The limbs are cut off a few feet from the main stem, and so managed as to resemble the framework of a basket ; around this the vine is led, with a pendant from each limb. Sometimes they are festooned from tree to tree, and are often led in several parallel straight lines. The blending of grace with neatness and accuracy in the Tuscan cultivation, seems to me to indicate a rural population superior to any we have yet seen in Italy§.

‡ Our people are at first confounded by the modern English use of this word, by the " nice countenance," " nice ruin," &c.

§ Those of my readers who chance to be ignorant on the subject will thank me for translating for them a few extracts from M. Sismondi's accurate account of the Tuscan peasant, instead of giving them the superficial observations of my own very limited opportunities. M. Sismondi, in his article " Sur le bonheur des Cultivateurs Toscans," endeavours to show that they are the happiest of all the people on earth who have only their own hands to depend on. The Metayer system prevails in Tuscany. The landlord furnishes the land, house, and implements of husbandry. The peasant cultivates the soil, and renders to the landlord half the product. " The Tuscan *Métayer*," says M. Sismondi, " receives from the hands of Nature his whole subsistence. He has little want of money, for he has scarcely any payment to make. He hardly knows the existence of taxes, as they are paid by the proprietor ; and as he has nothing to quarrel about with the government, he is in general attached to it ; neither has he any interest to settle with the church. Tithes having been long abolished, his contributions are voluntary." " In fine, the Metayer, in his relations with his proprietor, considers himself as a partner in the community of interests ; he has nothing to discuss with him. Usage has fixed his rights and obligations ; his contract may, it is true, be broken any year by his misconduct ; experience has taught the proprietor that he loses and never gains by discarding a peasant, for none will give him more than half the product. Thus the Metayer lives upon the land as if it were his inheritance, loving it devotedly, labouring to improve it, trusting in the future— believing that the fields he works upon will be cultivated by his children and grandchildren. And, in fact, they live on the same land from generation to generation. They understand it with a precision that the feeling of property alone can give." " The terraces, elevated one above the other, are often not more than four feet wide ; the individual character of each is known to the *Métayer*; this is dry, that is cold and damp ; here the soil is deep, there it is merely the incrustation of a rock ; wheat thrives best here, barley there ; here it would be lost labour to

Had you, my dear C., passed this afternoon with us, I should have but to write *Florence*, and

" This brightest star of star-bright Italy "

would rise before you

" Amid her Tuscan fields and hills,"

with the Arno winding through her loveliest of valleys, and the Apennines in the background

plant Indian corn, even beans or peas; a little farther flax flourishes wonderfully, and the border of this brook is capital for hemp. Thus you learn with surprise from the Metayer that, in a space of ten acres, the soil, the aspect, and ' the lay of the land ' present to him a greater variety than a rich farmer knows to exist in his farm of five or six hundred acres."

After enumerating some grievances in the existing laws which cause litigations, vexations, and disappointments among the proprietors, M. Sismondi says : " The gentleness and benevolence of the Tuscan character are often spoken of : but the cause is not sufficiently remarked, which is, that all cause of quarrel is removed from the cultivators, who constitute three-quarters of the population."

M. Sismondi, having an estate in Tuscany, and residing there a portion of his time, gives from actual observation, and *con amore*, a picture of the peasant's life as admirable for its exactness as it is attractive for its beauty.

" When you leave the great roads and climb up the hills of the valley of Nievole, you meet at every step little paths, which, winding among the vines and olives, are never traced by a wheel, and are only passable for mountain horses with their loads. Along these paths, at every hundred steps, you find, upon some flowery hill-side, a little house, which presents the sweet image of industry fully rewarded—of man's love of the land—of abundance and peace. The house built substantially, with good walls, has always one story, often two, above the ground floor. Usually there are on the ground floor a kitchen, a stable for two-horned cattle, and the store-room, which takes its name *tinaia* from the large vats in which the wine is fermented without putting it to press. It is here, also, that the Metayer locks up his casks, oil, and grain. He has ordinarily a shed leaning against the house, where he can repair his utensils and prepare the provender for his animals, sheltered from the weather. On the first and second stories there are often two, three, and even four bedchambers. The windows are without glass; they have only shutters; but we must remember there is no ice in winter. The most spacious and airy of these rooms are devoted, during the months of May and June, to the growth of the silkworm. Large chests for clothes and linen, and some wooden chairs, are the principal furniture of the chambers. A bride always brings her nut-wood bureau. The beds have neither curtain nor valance ; but on each, besides a good straw bed, made of the elastic husk of the Indian corn, there are two mattresses of wool, or, with the very poorest of tow, a good quilt, sheets of strong hempen cloth, and over the best bed a spread of raw silk, which is displayed on fête-days. There is no chimney except in the kitchen. There is always in one room a large wooden dining-table, with benches ; a kneading-trough, in which provisions are also kept ; a sufficient assortment of earthen jars, dishes, and plates; one or two brass lamps, steelyards, and at least two copper vessels in which to fetch and keep water.

" All the linen and working-dresses of the family are home-made. These dresses, the men's as well as the women's, are of a kind of stuff they call *mezza lana* (linsey-woolsey ?) if thick, *mola* if thin. The warp is a coarse thread of flax or tow; the filling is of wool or cotton. It is dyed by the same women who weave it. One can hardly imagine the quantity of linen or *mezza lana* which the women, by assiduous labour, accumulate ; how many sheets are in the common dépôt, how many chemises, vests, pantaloons, skirts, and gowns. To give an idea of it, we add a part of an inventory of the family best known

guarding her with its fortress-heights, and pouring oil and wine into her storehouses from the sunny hills that slope down to her feet. But you have not seen it, and neither the word nor all the descriptive accompaniments I may tack to it will give you so much pleasure as to know we are thus far on our homeward track, and that we found our faithful friend Mr. H. on the steps of the Hôtel de York, where, though the town is full of strangers, he has secured agreeable apartments for us, from which we have a look-out on the Duomo, its Campanile, Baptistery, and gay piazza.

FLORENCE, as all the world knows, my dear C., is almost unrivalled in the beauty of its position and surroundings : it is most curious, as the best-preserved monument of the middle ages ; but, apart from all this, it has interest to an American, a claim on the sympathy of the citizens of a free and working country, that belongs to no other part of Italy. Florence derived the glory and power of its brilliant day from its industry and freedom ; not the freedom of a few lawless nobles, but the freedom of its working classes [*], who, in 1260, formed themselves into twelve companies of " arts and trades " (the seven major arts having their consuls, captains, and ensigns), and got so completely the upper hand of the nobles, that a title rendered a man ineligible to office.

There is a curious memorial of the exercise of popular power existing in the architecture of the city. More than 200 towers, which originally were the fortresses of the nobility, and which were, by an ordinance of the people, reduced from the height of 180 feet to 80 feet, are now incorporated into other buildings [†], and constitute a part of that massive architecture which makes Florence strike a stranger as " a city of nobles of individual force, where the power of the public was sometimes feeble, but where each man was master and lord in his own house." These towns were wretchedly lighted, and the nobles resorted to an expedient

to us ; a family neither among the poorest nor richest, but living happily on the half of the product of less than ten acres of land.

" Inventory of the bridal clothes (*trousseau*) of Jane, &c. &c. : 28 chemises, 3 gowns of coloured silk, 4 gowns of coarse coloured silk, 7 gowns of cotton cloth, 2 winter working gowns (mezza lana), 2 summer working gowns and skirts, 3 white skirts, 5 calico aprons, 1 black silk apron, 1 black merino apron, 9 coloured working aprons, 4 white handkerchiefs, 8 coloured handkerchiefs, 2 worked veils and 1 tulle veil, 3 towels, 14 pairs of stockings, 2 hats, 1 felt and 1 fine straw,—2 gold cameos, 2 pairs gold earrings, 1 chaplet with two Roman piastres, 1 coral necklace with a gold cross."

We should be proud to see our farmers' daughters with an outfit as substantial and suitable as this.

[*] The Florentines began rightly. Villani, writing late in the thirteenth century of their forefathers, after telling us that the finest of their grand-dames thought themselves dressed enough in a narrow gown of coarse scarlet cloth, &c., adds, " with all this external coarseness they had loyal minds; they were faithful to one another and to their country. In their poor and rustic lives they did the most virtuous deeds, and contributed far more to the honour of their families and their country than those who live more luxuriously."

[†] " The material." says M. Sismondi, " which these private fortifications furnished was employed for the common defence. A portion of the city-wall, and the palace of the Podesta, now a prison, were built with it."

suited to their delicious climate. Near the towers they built *Loggie* arcades, which served them for offices, market-places, and *drawing-rooms.* Some of them still remain. The unimpaired Loggia dei Lanzi is embellished with groups of statues in bronze, and, with its Greek arches and columns, is a beautiful specimen of architecture. The Pitti Palace, the residence of the grand-duke, and fit for an imperial palace, was built by a merchant, as were many of these immense structures, which may stand, for aught that I can see, as long as the solid foundations of nature. They are built of immense blocks of stone, without cement, and without architectural ornament; but to me their simplicity and strength are more effective than any decoration. They have a curious appendage, large iron or brass rings, in which they placed wax lights for illuminations, and to which they suspended the standards of the rival factions. They built compactly, to save the expense of an extended wall. The oldest streets are too narrow to allow a carriage to pass : across some of them you might grasp hands from palace to palace. I am sadly disappointed in the Arno. It embellishes the city, certainly; but it is turbid, and, like all the Italian streams I have seen, with the exception of one or two rivulets, it appears as if it had been stirred up with French chalk.

WE have just returned from Santa Croce, and are overpowered with the heat. I do not wonder at the proverb that no one can die in Florence in the winter, and no one can live here in summer. But for Santa Croce : it is our third visit to the "centre of pilgrimage—the Mecca of Italy." So, indeed, may that sacred place be justly called where are the monuments of such prophets as Dante, Galileo, and Michael Angelo. The monuments are immense piles of marble ; not one of them ·impresses me with its excellence as a work of art. But art would be but secondary here. *After* Westminster Abbey—after the place hallowed by the great spirits of our own language, there is no monumental effect like that of Santa Croce. It is a sad thought that we have for the last time walked up and down its long line of columns, on the marble pavement trodden by generations long gone, before the monuments of Machiavel, Michael Angelo, Dante, Galileo, and Alfieri !

Santa Croce was begun in 1294, and is still unfinished, as are all the façades of the Florence churches. This is to save the heavy tax imposed by the pope on the completion of a church, and in part, probably, from the richness of the plan exceeding the ability for its execution. The Piazza of Santa Croce has historical associations that make it quite worthy of the church. " The richest Florentine citizens " (bourgeois), says M. Sismondi, " having excited one another to arms, assembled in the Piazza of Santa Croce before a church ; and there, where now are the tombs of the great men of Florence, the republic of the dead, was first formed the popular state of Florence."

We went quite to the other extreme from this theatre of popular associations, in going from Santa Croce to San Lorenzo, where are the splendid memorials of the Medici, the final subverters of the liberty of Florence. The Cappella de' Principi was designed by Michael Angelo, and its embellishments in great part executed by him. There are on two monuments figures in attitudes that it would be difficult for a posture-master to maintain ; they are called Day and Night, and Aurora and Twilight. Dr. Bell sees in the Aurora " a spring of thought," " an awakening principle ;" marble is a hard material for an allegorical refinement ! The celebrated statue of the Duke of Urbino, called *Pensiero,* from its wonderful expression of deep thought, is in this chapel. I cannot but think that this and other masterpieces of Michael Angelo throw a dazzling effulgence over his inferior works ; and that in these statues on the Medicean monuments and ·n his Mosé he has half taken the step from the sublime to the ridiculous ; but this is as dangerous as to talk democracy in an Austrian saloon !

The gorgeous though yet unfinished *Cappella de' Medici* is also at San Lorenzo. It is dedicated to the monuments of the grand-dukes of Tuscany, and all that can be done to glorify these mighty " accidents" by walls incrusted with the costliest marbles, and the most exquisite work in pietra dura, is done : but what is it all, in effect, to the name of " Galileo " on his tomb, or the inscription on Dante's, " Onorate l' altissimo Poeta !"

We have seen Mr. Greenough's statue of Washington. It is a seated colossal figure ; the arms and breast are bare ; one hand is extended in the act of resigning the sword, and the other raised, as if appealing to Heaven. I have heard objections to the double action ; but why, since they are related, and produce a unity of impression ! The drapery, too, is criticised, and will, no doubt, be condemned by many of our people, who are intolerant of any degree of nudity. But what was Mr. Greenough to do ! As he says, a French artist made a cast of Washington, while he was living, in military costume, and nobody liked it. Canova put him into a Roman toga, and Chantrey into a cloak, such as neither Roman nor American ever wore. Nothing remained for him but to present him artistically, and certainly the drapery is arranged with expression and grace. The head is noble, expressing, almost to the point of sublimity, wisdom and firmness, with as near an approach to benignity as Washington's face will bear without a sacrifice of verisimilitude ; good, not quite benignant. The subjects of the bas-relief embellishments are happily chosen. Aurora is on one side —a fitting type of our young country—and on the other is the infant Hercules strangling the serpent : a subject suggested, I presume, by Dr. Franklin's medal, and sarcastically indicating our struggle with the mother country. Mr. Greenough, even with his previous reputation, may be satisfied with this work, and our country proud of it. It is something to say for our progress in art that, in forty years from Washington's death, the best statue of him is by his own countryman.

I HAVE been walking about Florence with Mr. W., who naturally first showed me some memorials of his hero. Mr. W. was, as you know, a few years since in our congress—what a change from the arena of Washington to ferreting out the life of Dante from the Tuscan archives ! Mr. W. is among the few fortunate men who, from a false position, has by his own wit found out, and by his own energy achieved, his true one. We went first to a tablet inserted in the pavement of the Piazzi di Duomo, which informs you that there Dante was accustomed to sit ; and there he contemplated this church, which, before 1300, as Mr. W. has discovered by a registered vote in favour of Arnolfo, its architect, was pronounced " the most beautiful edifice in Tuscany." When shall we have such inscriptions to mark the haunts of Washington and Franklin ! Might not the memory of these men be made more operative by appeals through the senses to the active popular mind of our country !

We next visited the house Dante lived in before his banishment, and then proceeded to Beatrice's (she had a local habitation), in a street parallel to that in which Dante lived, and so near to his that her lover might have *signalised* her, in the seaman's sense.

We went, too, to Michael Angelo's house, where a suite of apartments are preserved as he left them by the present possessor, one of the house of Buonarotti. We were rather surprised to find what snug and comfortable apartments were enjoyed by the artist, who has so associated himself in our minds with the vast and extravagant. There are a few characteristic sketches of his on the walls, shadowings of great thoughts ; some humble relics, such as his slippers, and, what pleased me more than all, a rosary, and shrine with its crucifix, before which he may have received the inspiration he infused into his works.

We finished the morning in the gardens of the Pitti Palace. Magnificent they are in extent, variety of surface, and embellishment. The entrance is free to all. They are not more lovely now, excepting that the country which you see from them has the fresh aspect of spring, than they were when we were here on the first of December. The fountains were then playing in a warm atmosphere ; the statues looked perfectly comfortable out of doors ; and there were such walls of laurel and laurustinus in blossom, with a variety of other evergreens, that it seemed as if a charmed circle were drawn around it, which " winter and rough weather" could not pass. The sun was then an enjoyment, and the shade to-day a positive one, and there we sat a long time listening to Mr. W.'s romantic stories of the stormy days of Florence, and to his tribute to the character of the reigning duke, Leopold, of whom we were very willing to believe all good while we were luxuriating in his grounds. He is one of the few sovereigns who have the enjoyments of sovereignty without its penalties. His territory is so small that he is not of sufficient consequence to be molested or to be dictated to by his royal brothers ; so he gets on very quietly, is kind and indulgent to his people, and hospitable to strangers, even though branded as liberals. It is not long since he received a letter (written at the suggestion of Russia) from his brother of Austria, containing a list of Poles who had sought refuge in Florence, whence Leopold was advised to expel them. You are aware that advice means command in the Austrian vocabulary. The list was headed " Dangerous men." Leopold received it in council. He cast his eye over it ; put his own

name at the head of these *dangerous men*, and returned it without any farther notice to his minister ! Very *nice*, was it not, for a man who has Austrian blood in his veins* !

WE drove yesterday to the great silk-manufactory at the Villa Donato, where steam is introduced for many of the processes ; but there is nothing going on at present but weaving, which is done in the old-fashioned loom. The girls were particularly enchanted with four iron Doric columns supporting a steam-engine, looking, as they said, like an Italian temple. The Italian atmosphere seemed to them to have subdued the principal antagonist to all poetry. The Villa Donato is a beautiful one, and its present appropriation reminds you forcibly of the time when the merchants of Florence were its princes.

WE have been to Fiesole, the old Etruscan city to which Florence was once but a suburb. It was built, like all the Etruscan cities, on an immense height, about as conveniently placed as a city would be half-way up Saddle Mountain. Those of us who could walk, walked up the steepest ascent, and R. and E. were drawn by oxen in a sort of sledge of the most inartificial kind. When they rather revolted at this mode of climbing, they were soothed with the assurance that the grandduke himself had no better. We pedestrians stopped at a farm-house, where we were charmed with rural thrift, cheerfulness, and kindness. The womankind were all engaged, from old age to childhood, either in weaving, spinning, knitting, or braiding straw. There was no misery, no begging. K. gave an old woman, who fetched her a glass of water with eager kindness, a half-paul, at which the old crone pressed K.'s hand in both hers, and said earnestly, " Dio vi lo rimerite." The glass of water was the boon that deserved the " God reward ye !"

On the almost inaccessible summit we found a church, a seminary, and a monastery, but no remains of the Roman Fæsulæ, excepting some columns of an ancient temple, and a grand bit of Cyclopean wall, made of massive stones seven or eight feet in length, laid together without cement. What a comment on the history of man, in his social relations and liabilities, this little fragment of a wall !

But the thing to go to Fiesole for is the view of Florence ; truly a queen of beauty in the lap of hills covered to their summits with vines, and olives, and lovely villas. Such a scene of abundance, grace, and beauty, of nature and art in loving harmony, I never beheld. No wonder the device of Florence was a rose in a field of lilies.

We leave Florence to-morrow, my dear C., and I have said nothing to you of what now *is Florence;* its unrivalled galleries of pictures ; that of the Palazzo Vecchio, *The* Gallery, and that of the Pitti Palace, which is confessedly the finest single collection in the world ! It is in itself a world ; and when I am there looking at those glorious pictures

* The grand duke's liberality attracts strangers to Florence, and it is natural they should linger there in the midst of a happy and beautiful people, surrounded by a country that is a paradise, and admitted, without fees or vexations of any sort, to the daily enjoyment of its magnificent drives, gardens, and *galleries.*

K

that remain in unfading beauty while generation after generation comes hither to see them, I feel fully what was so well said by the old man, who for seventy years had shown a famous picture in the Escurial, "We are the shadows, they are the realities!"

I do not now wonder at the love of art which astonished me on first coming to the Old World. With us it is comparatively nothing; in Europe it makes up the occupation of the idle portion of the world; and so much does the appetite grow by what it feeds on, that I begin to feel the danger (the existence of which I have but just learned) of forgetting the actual in the painted world. But do not be alarmed, my dear C.; though the eyes of some of us were half blinded with tears as we looked at our favourite pictures for the last time to-day, we cannot yet say with the dying Medici, before whom his priest was setting the joy of the heavenly mansions, "Caro amico, son contento col Palazzo Pitti!" ("My dear friend, I am perfectly content with the Pitti Palace!") and we shall once more to-morrow set our faces joyfully towards our earthly heaven—your and our home.

Our route from Florence to Genoa was a scene of enchantment; and, finally, when we embarked at Genoa and left the Italian shore, we felt much as I fancy Adam and Eve did when the gates of Paradise were closed upon them.

We passed through the southern provinces of France to Switzerland, a country as full of excitement, in a different way, as Italy—perhaps the only country that one can pass into from Italy without ennui. My book is already too long to break new ground, and I finish it with the earnest wish that my readers may have the happiness of seeing for themselves scenes which I have feebly presented.

THE END.

LONDON: BRADBURY AND EVANS, PRINTERS, WHITEFRIARS.